Contemporary Theories in COUNSELING AND PSYCHOTHERAPY

Contemporary Theories in

COUNSELING AND PSYCHOTHERAPY

Edward Neukrug, Editor

Bassim Hamadeh, CEO and Publisher
Amy Smith, Senior Project Editor
Abbey Hastings, Associate Production Editor
Emely Villavicencio, Senior Graphic Designer
Stephanie Kohl, Licensing Coordinator
Jaye Pratt, Interior Designer
Natalie Piccotti, Director of Marketing
Kassie Graves, Vice President of Editorial
Jamie Giganti, Director of Academic Publishing

Printed in the United States of America.

Brief Contents

Detailed Contents

Preface

I am excited about this first edition of *Contemporary Theories in Counseling and Psychotherapy* because it is one of the first, and perhaps only, books to tackle some of the more current and popular theories used today by clinicians. Although those in training programs are typically taught the classic theories, they are rarely taught the many commonly used theories widely practiced by clinicians today. Thus, a thorough review of the following theories is highlighted in the text:

- Contemporary Psychodynamic Therapy (CTP)
- Contemporary Person-Centered Counseling (CPCC)
- Cognitive-Behavioral Therapy (CBT)
- Integrative Postmodern Therapy (IPMT)
- Dialectical Behavior Therapy (DBT)
- Acceptance and Commitment Therapy (ACT)
- Motivational Interviewing (MI)
- Positive Counseling
- Neurocounseling
- Complementary, Alternative, and Integrative Modalities (CAM)

Each chapter contains learning outcomes, a brief history of the theory, the theory's view of human nature, key concepts associated with the theory, common techniques of the theory, the counseling process, social and cultural issues related to the theory, efficacy of the theory, key words and names, and a case study based on a member of the Miller family. A description of the Millers can be found in Appendix I, and prior to reading the case study at the end of each chapter, it is important that you read about the family.

In today's psychotherapeutic environment there are some counselors and therapists who follow a classical purist approach, often practicing one of the following theories: psychoanalytic, Jungian, Adlerian, person-centered, existential, gestalt, behavioral, cognitive-behavioral, rational emotive behavior therapy, reality therapy, narrative, solution-focused, or relational-cultural. In fact, in my companion text, *Counseling Theory and Practice*, all of these theories are examined in detail. Most counselors and therapists today, however, do not practice a purist approach and have adopted an integrative approach to some of these theories or use one of the more recent popular approaches. These are the approaches that are focused upon in this text. The following offers very brief descriptions of these ten approaches.

CHAPTER 1: CONTEMPORARY PSYCHODYNAMIC THERAPY (CPT)

Today, many counselors and therapists practice an integrative approach to psychodynamic therapy. Leaving the determinism of Freud behind, they adhere to many of the general concepts of psychoanalysis, such as focusing on the unconscious, early attachments with primary caregivers, and working with resistance, transference, and countertransference. They acknowledge, however, the influence of the environment and developmental changes on a person and see the individual as much more adaptable than did Freud. Also, they view the relationship between the therapist and the client as much more open and fluid than the aloof therapeutic relationship found in psychoanalysis. This chapter provides an overview of how contemporary psychodynamic therapy may be practiced by some today.

CHAPTER 2: CONTEMPORARY PERSON-CENTERED COUNSELING (CPCC)

This approach embraces many of the concepts from classic person-centered counseling and classic existential therapy but integrates and expands on them. For instance, although classic techniques such as acceptance, empathy, and authenticity are used, this approach pulls in a number of other techniques not generally found in classic person-centered or existential theory, including the use of clarifying, tentative, preferred goals, and solution-oriented questions; affirmation and encouragement; using "now" language; the empty chair technique; identifying choices and goal setting; offering advice; and saying what you think.

CHAPTER 3: COGNITIVE BEHAVIOR THERAPY (CBT)

Although in some ways a classic approach, this chapter was included in the text because it continues to be one of the most popular approaches used today. Here we describe the origins of the theory and offer an explanation of the underlying key concepts, such as core beliefs, intermediate beliefs, cognitive distortions, and automatic thoughts. A wide range of cognitive and behavioral techniques are also included in this chapter, and as with all the chapters, a case study exemplifies how the theory is applied.

CHAPTER 4: INTEGRATIVE POSTMODERN THERAPY (IPMT)

Today, many counselors use narrative therapy, solution-focused brief therapy, or an adaptation of relational cultural therapy, and these approaches are thoroughly covered in the companion book, *Counseling Theory and Practice*. Many counselors, however, also integrate key concepts and major techniques from these postmodern approaches into their own unique approach.

The integrative approach described in this chapter explains the key concepts of postmodernism; post-structuralism; social constructionism; analyzing power; non-pathologizing; thin to thick descriptions; mutually enhancing, empathic, empowering relationships; and re-authoring. Major techniques aligned with these key concepts and borrowed from these three approaches are examined.

CHAPTER 5: DIALECTICAL BEHAVIOR THERAPY (DBT)

One of the more popular approaches used today, and rarely taught in undergraduate or graduate training programs, is dialectical behavior therapy (DBT). An approach that initially focused almost exclusively on those with borderline personality disorder, it has expanded to treat individuals with many related disorders. It focuses on helping clients regulate their emotions through psychoeducation and a variety of behavioral and Eastern techniques (e.g., mindfulness). It uses individual therapy and intense group-skills involvement while also encouraging phone coaching when needed.

CHAPTER 6: ACCEPTANCE AND COMMITMENT THERAPY (ACT)

Based on relational frame theory (RFT), which shows how the development of language and prisms from which we see the world are built, this approach suggests that we often have a tendency to develop psychological inflexibility. RFT suggests that our way of seeing the world has been developed over years, and to change it we need to accept ourselves and develop new prisms or frames. Thus, the goal of this approach is to use a variety of techniques to develop psychological flexibility, which is the ability of an individual to live in the present moment, accept one's current state of being, and act in accordance with his or her chosen values. A number of techniques to develop psychological flexibility are described in the chapter.

CHAPTER 7: MOTIVATIONAL INTERVIEWING (MI)

Motivational interviewing (MI) began as an approach that was used mostly with people with addictive disorders but has expanded as a stand-alone or complementary approach to counseling in the treatment of many mental health problems. Based on a number of existential-humanistic, postmodern, and cognitive behavioral ideas, some of its key concepts include the MI Spirit (compassion, collaboration, acceptance, and evocation), understanding ambivalence, encouraging change talk, avoiding confrontation, and FRAMES (Feedback, Responsibility, Advice, Menu of options, Empathy, and Self-efficacy). Techniques that are grounded in developing the therapeutic alliance while gently encouraging the client to change are discussed.

CHAPTER 8: POSITIVE COUNSELING

This approach is based on identifying strengths and positive qualities, logical positivism, anti-determinism, intentionality, and the build-what's-strong approach. It can be used as a stand-alone approach to clients, especially those who are not struggling with severe pathology; however, it can also be used in a complementary fashion to almost any theoretical approach to counseling. Explanations of how this can be done are described in this chapter. Some of its major techniques include assessing well-being, identifying things done well, increasing one's positivity ratio, mindfulness, strength-based exercises, gratitude exercises, hope and optimism exercises, and other positive psychotherapy interventions.

CHAPTER 9: NEUROCOUNSELING

Neurocounseling is an emerging theory that examines how the brain responds to toxins and stress as well as positive interventions that can boost brain function. Based on a wellness, strength-based, developmental, and structural biological approach to counseling, neurocounseling assumes that certain techniques can increase neuroplasticity, which is the ability of the brain to expand old neural networks and build new ones. Some of the major techniques and approaches that seem to facilitate this process include neuroeducation, assessing lifestyle, biofeedback and self-regulation skills (diaphragmatic breathing, mindfulness, and technological approaches to biofeedback), neurofeedback, and neuroscience-informed therapies, such as prolonged exposure therapy (PE) and eye-movement desensitization and reprocessing (EMDR).

CHAPTER 10: COMPLEMENTARY, ALTERNATIVE, AND INTEGRATIVE MODALITIES (CAM)

CAM is one of the newest additions to counseling and psychotherapy but is based on some of the oldest traditions known. These approaches are often grounded in Eastern techniques and theories that are sometimes thousands of years old and can be used in a complementary, alternative, or integrative fashion. Some of the techniques we briefly examine include natural products of herbs (aka, botanicals), vitamins and minerals, and probiotics; the mind-body practices of yoga, chiropractic and osteopathic manipulation, meditation and mindfulness, acupuncture, relaxation techniques, tai chi and qigong, hypnotherapy, and other mind-body practices; and other complementary health approaches, such as ayurvedic medicine, traditional Chinese medicine, homeopathy, and naturopathy. Examples of how some of these practices can be integrated within a session or used to complement sessions are provided.

HOW TO USE THIS BOOK

If you are an instructor, you might want to combine chapters from this book with chapters from its companion book *Counseling Theory and Practice*. Choose the theories that you believe are most relevant for your classes and Cognella Academic Publishing will be glad to create a book that specifically meets your needs. A case study regarding a member of the Miller family is described at the end of each chapter in both books and questions regarding the case study are provided. In *Counseling Theory and Practice* there are videos showing how each theory is conducted. In this book, the first four chapters have videos that demonstrate the theory.

If you are a student, you will find interesting vignettes, experiential exercises, and case studies throughout each chapter. I encourage you to read the chapters and the case studies carefully and answer the questions at the end of each case study. Also, actively respond to the experiential activities—they tend to be interesting and fun and should help you learn the theory. As you read the different theories, reflect on which theories you seem most affiliated with, and then consider what your view of human nature is and how it is similar, or different, from the various theories in your book. If interested, a survey that assesses which of the classic theories (found in *Counseling Theory and Practice*) most closely matches your view of human nature can be taken at my website, www.odu.edu/~eneukrug. Click on "Survey of your theoretical orientation" and then "Click here to take the survey." On this same web page you will also find a site called "Great Therapists of the Twentieth Century," which offers caricatures of seventeen famous therapists talking about their theories.

ACKNOWLEDGMENTS

Many people contributed to the development of this book. First, I would like to thank the various authors who spent much time writing the chapters. Their names are listed in each chapter and short bios can be found near the end of the book. In addition, I would like to offer thanks to Dr. Rosanne Nunnery of Cappella University who spent much time reviewing and offering feedback for the chapter on dialectical behavior therapy. Similarly, Dr. Traci Richards, from Old Dominion University and an LPC in private practice, reviewed the chapter on acceptance and commitment therapy and provided vital feedback ways of strengthening it. Thanks also to Joshua Abraham who helped us work on the neurocounseling chapter. Finally, thanks to the following graduate students in counseling, from Old Dominion University, who assisted with the ancillaries of the text: Ashley Casey, Nessalyn Dearce, Alexandra Johnston, and Olivia M. Lewis.

From Cognella Academic Publishing, a variety of people worked hard to ensure publication of this book, including Abbey Hastings, production editor; Emely Villavicencio, cover designer; Henry Fuentes, copy editor; and Amy Smith, senior project editor. As always, a special thanks to Kassie Graves, Vice President, Editorial of Cognella, who I so admire and who facilitates me doing my best work.

1

Contemporary Psychodynamic Therapy

Ed Neukrug and Kevin C. Snow

LEARNING OUTCOMES

- To provide a brief overview of the antecedents of contemporary psychodynamic therapy (CPT) including psychoanalysis, Jungian therapy, Adlerian therapy, neo-Freudians, object-relations theorists, attachment therapies, and relational and intersubjectivity approaches.
- To examine the view of human nature of CPT, which is less deterministic and more optimistic and holistic than its predecessors; focuses on psychosocial and developmental factors in personality formation; believes that the unconscious affects thoughts, feelings, and behaviors; stresses the occurrence of recurring themes in life; focuses on how the past impacts affect, emotions, and behaviors; and suggests individuals use defenses to protect from underlying distress.
- To understand key concepts of the conscious and unconscious minds, drives and instincts, defense mechanisms, transference and countertransference, early attachments and patterns of relating, and lifespan influences.
- To explore commonly used techniques of conducting a thorough assessment, creating a trusting atmosphere, using questions, free association, analysis of resistance, dream analysis, analysis of transference, exploring countertransference, and other techniques.
- To describe the counseling process of CPT.

- To examine social and cultural applicability of CPT.
- To review the efficacy of CPT.
- To offer a case study that demonstrates the CPT process.

BRIEF HISTORY OF CONTEMPORARY PSYCHODYNAMIC THERAPY

> One of the greatest misconceptions regarding psychodynamic therapy is that it has remained unchanged since Freud introduced it at the turn of the century … (Novotney, 2017a, p. 40)

Sigmund Freud's theory of **psychoanalysis** revolutionized the manner in which counseling was provided, and his ideas changed mental health treatment and influenced how individuals were conceptualized. Freud (1961-a, -b) believed that instincts (e.g., sex and aggression), housed by the **id**, drive behavior. As the young child grows, the id is mediated by the **ego**, which deals with reality, and later monitored by the **superego**, which places brakes on the id through guilt. Within the first five or six years of life, child-rearing practices of caregivers impact the development of each child's id-ego-superego structure as they pass through the oral, then anal, and lastly phallic stages of development. Based on each child's unique structure, **defense mechanisms** (e.g., repression, intellectualization, projection, denial) are developed to protect the ego from anxiety that is the result of unacceptable thoughts and feelings that originate from the id and superego. Freud believed that much of how this all operates occurs unconsciously, thus awareness of why we behave the way we do is limited. To understand one's unique personality structure takes years and is limited, since one is working with unconscious desires and patterning that took place early in one's life, often prior to language attainment and not accessible through memory.

Contemporaries of Freud questioned some of his ideas. For instance, both **Carl Jung** and **Alfred Adler** did not view sexual and aggressive drives as primary drives (Neukrug, 2018). Jung's **analytical therapy** believed there was a **conscious**, **personal unconscious**, and **collective unconscious** (Neukrug, 2018; Gabrinetti, 2015) and saw our egos being formed fairly early in life, mostly through one's interactions with caregivers. Egos reflect each person's **psychological type**; that is, whether one's personality lends itself more to introversion or extraversion, intuition or sensations, and thinking or feeling. Information received and experiences

Want to Meet Sigmund Freud?

Want to hear a brief biography about Freud from the man himself and find other tidbits of information about him? Go to https://silver.odu.edu/psyadm/ to see a caricature of Freud talking about himself and his theory. Click on the psychodynamic door and then go into Freud's office.

lived that do not align with one's psychological type (way of viewing the world), and abusive behaviors, are repressed in the personal unconscious. Meanwhile, **archetypes**, which are blueprints that all humans have for acting in certain ways (e.g., mother, father, god, hero, warrior, and other archetypes), are housed in the collective unconscious. Archetypes can interact with one's repressed material in the personal unconscious to develop certain unconscious **complexes**. Jung felt that through therapy, however, one can come to understand the psychological type a person is, the archetypes that impact the person, and the person's repressed material. Through such understanding, he suggested, one can become whole as the individual embraces parts of oneself that he or she is not.

Adler's **individual psychology** believed in one true drive: **striving for perfection** or **superiority** (Neukrug, 2018; Watts, 2015). We all, said Adler, want to be competent and obtain mastery over what we do. When not impeded by **feelings of inferiority**, an individual can master his or her natural abilities and talents in positive ways for oneself and for one's community. However, if hindered by feelings of inferiority, usually from early in life, one develops behaviors that lead to a striving for superiority. Such behaviors tend to be narcissistic and focused on personal gain. Adler believed that one's **style of life** is reflective of the direction one is moving toward and can be understood through unconscious and conscious behaviors, though the line between the conscious and unconscious is much more fluid compared with Freud's theory. Adler proposed that individuals can understand their feelings of inferiority that drive them toward superiority. Through such knowledge, he suggested, the individual can move toward wholeness, completeness, and positive ways of living in the world. Adler's theory was much less deterministic and more positive and holistic compared with what had come before him.

Although Jung and Adler are sometimes included in what are called the **neo-Freudian** school of thought, three of the most well-known neo-Freudians were **Karen Horney**, **Erich Fromm**, and **Erik Erikson** (Bishop, 2015a; Wilson, 2015). Being particularly popular between the 1930s through the 1960s, the neo-Freudians repudiated the idea that instincts played a major role in development and that one's psychological self is largely set at an early age. Sometimes called **socio-psychoanalysis**, these theorists had a much more positive view of human nature and believed that neurosis is partly a function of societal and cultural issues and that development occurred over the lifespan. For instance, Horney eschewed Freud's notion of sexual and aggressive instincts being primary in the development of personality and instead believed that social factors played a much greater role. She particularly spoke out against Freud's patriarchal views of development that saw women as inferior than—and envious of—men. Fromm embraced somewhat of an **existential-humanistic perspective** and believed that social variables, particularly economics, impacted a client's sense of self. For instance, he believed that capitalism and industrialization alienated the individual and thought that a socialist-democratic society would be more conducive to individuals finding balance between "having" (e.g., material possessions) and "being" (loving and community) in the world. Erikson developed a lifespan stage theory of development that suggested individuals had certain tasks to accomplish relative to the life stage they are in and that such tasks are greatly influenced by social factors (Erikson Institute, 2019). The neo-Freudians had an existential flavor to their theories as they believed individuals could make more effective choices in their lives that would lead them to increased meaning and more loving relationships. Many of the tools they used, however, were notoriously reminiscent of classical psychoanalysis, such as the examination of early childhood relationships, knowing the unconscious, examining defense, using free association, conducting dream analysis, and using interpretation, though interpretation had much more of a client-centered focus (Wilson, 2015).

During the 1940s, individuals such as **Melanie Klein** and **Ronald Fairburn** developed **object relations theory** that viewed the **need to be in relationships** to be a primary motivator of behavior, and that early relationships, often with our mother, become the template for the manner in which we see the world (Bishop, 2015b; Donaldson, 2015; Wilson, 2015). **Good-enough parenting** can provide an environment that helps children manage their feelings and individuate successfully. From object relations theory many of the **attachment therapies** were born that examined affectional bonds between children and caregivers and how they influence development (Cosentino & Dermer, 2015; Wilson, 2015). These therapies used many of the traditional Freudian techniques, though the major focus tended to be how the client projects early attachments onto the counselor. Soon after development of object relations theory came **self psychology**, developed by **Heinz Kohut** during the 1960s and 1970s. Here, we again see more of an emphasis on the early relationship between parents and children; however, Kohut believed that empathy, not drives, are key to the development of healthy self-esteem.

More recently, we have seen the development of **relational and intersubjectivity approaches** to psychodynamic therapy (Aron & McIntosh, 2015; Giordano, 2015; Starr-Karlin, 2015). These approaches believe that the independent mind, assumed by all the psychodynamic theories that came before, is mostly a myth and instead examine how the interplay of subjective experiences between people, including the therapist and the client, impacts one's understanding of self. These approaches focus on the importance of having a deep personal encounter with clients, one in which the therapist uses empathy and carefully timed self-disclosure in an effort to help the client see how his or her reactions to such self-disclosure mimics early relational patterns in unconscious ways.

Freud, and those who came after him, have developed an elaborate understanding of the individual and have applied it to the therapeutic relationship. Contemporary psychodynamic therapy integrates a number of well-known beliefs and practices from many of these approaches. This chapter will highlight some of the principles and techniques often used by individuals who practice CPT without being steadfast attached to any one approach.

VIEW OF HUMAN NATURE

> Although many psychoanalytic ideas still have their roots in Freud's theories, new psychoanalytic schools have developed with different and sometimes competing ways of thinking. Psychoanalytic theory as a whole is best thought of as a series of intellectual systems or conceptual frameworks which converge at numerous places and share a large number of basic assumptions, but also diverge in important ways. (Spurling, 2009, p. 45)

The therapies just briefly highlighted can all be placed into one school called **psychodynamic therapies**, sometimes called **post-psychoanalytic approaches**, which can be loosely defined as approaches "that postulate[s] that unconscious mental activity affects our conscious thoughts, feelings, and behavior" (Cabaniss et al., 2017, p. 4). Although there continue to be many purists who practice a neo-Freudian, object relations, attachment, or any of a number of post-psychoanalytic approaches, many today take a more integrative approach and are not rigidly attached to any one of these theories (Jacobs, 2017). These individuals, which we will call contemporary psychodynamic therapists, tend to embrace **seven common themes** that drive its view of human nature (Blagys & Hilsenroth, 2000; Shedler, 2010).

1. *A focus on affect and emotions*: Although intellectual insight may be important, in some cases, understanding and being able to identify feelings, particularly repressed feelings, is important if a person is to have clarity about his or her problems in life.
2. *Examining the avoidance of distressing thoughts and emotions*: Avoidance of thoughts and emotions are signs that clients have developed defenses against underlying distress. Understanding how one tries to avoid distressing thoughts and emotions can help a person make sense of the problematic issues behind them.
3. *Identifying and understanding recurrent themes*: Recurring themes and patterns, especially destructive ones, are often indications of early, unfinished business that clients need to examine.
4. *Discussing the past*: It is important to understand how past experiences have impacted present day behavior, and will, unless explored, impact future behavior, sometimes in ways that are distressful to the client.
5. *Focusing on interpersonal issues*: Current relationships help us understand how we have made attachments to people in the past and the patterns that have developed that form our sense of self.
6. *Examining the relationship with the therapist*: As with all relationships, the patterns that arise in the therapeutic relationship reflect the kinds of relationships one has had

in the past. Clients will tend to transfer past patterns onto their therapist, thus an examination of the transference relationship is important.

7. *Understanding and exploring one's fantasy life.* One's fantasy life is alive and well in our dreams, daydreams, desires, and fantasies and are an indication of how we view ourselves and others and can help us identify unfinished business and unfulfilled needs. Thus, exploring one's fantasy life is important in psychodynamic therapy.

CPT therapists have moved away from the Freudian concept that the **id**, and the instincts it embodies, unconsciously motivates behavior and focuses more on how a variety of factors contribute to the development of one's temperament or personality (Wilson, 2015). It proposes that human behavior is a function of how the self is developed via any of a variety of drives; one's interactions with parents, caregivers, and significant others (including therapists); social and cultural influences; and lifespan developmental stages. Although these approaches still tend to view the **psyche** as functioning with conscious and unconscious minds, they tend to be less deterministic than psychoanalysis and believe that change can occur more quickly than those who practice traditional psychoanalysis.

Although these approaches believe that early childhood influences affect personality formation (Bishop, 2015-a, -b; Wilson, 2015), they are more positive about change and less deterministic than traditional psychoanalysis as they do not view the individual as being rigidly locked into ways of behaving that stem from childhood. Finally, these approaches tend to highlight the personality of the therapist to a much greater degree than traditional psychoanalytic therapy. Thus, authenticity and self-disclosure become important tools used by the therapist to help clients understand early patterns and attachments.

One can see that the psychodynamic view of human nature is one that assumes the past is critical to current-day functioning; that one must be able to build a relationship with the client to understand the past; that the self is formed, and can be reformed, through interaction with others over one's lifespan; that external factors, such as cultural influences, can impact the client's developing self; that unconscious factors and defenses need to be explored; and that therapy may take a bit of time to complete (Wilson, 2015). Although the past does not determine the future, it is an indication of how one has developed, and by developing an in-depth understanding of the past, it can help us redirect our future.

KEY CONCEPTS

A number of cross-theoretical concepts are key to understanding CPT today. They include the importance of the **conscious and unconscious minds, drives and instincts, defense mechanisms, transference and countertransference, early attachments and patterns of relating**, and **lifespan influences.**

Conscious and Unconscious Minds

CPT therapists believe that clients are often driven by **unconscious** thoughts, feelings, and fantasies and that an understanding of how the unconscious impacts the individual can help a person become more purposeful and autonomous in his or her life (Wilson, 2015). As opposed to many of the early psychodynamic therapists who believed that the unconscious was a formidable structure that takes years to unravel, CPT therapists believe that the individual has the ability to be aware of a large portion of their unconscious thoughts, feelings, and fantasies within a briefer amount of time. Thus, making large portions of the unconscious **conscious** is one of the goals of CPT and is often achieved in months, not years, of counseling.

Drives and Instincts

> While Freud's early structural model (id, ego, and superego) is still used to introduce people to psychoanalytic concepts, contemporary practice makes virtually no use of it. (Wilson, 2015, p. 230)

Although most contemporary psychodynamic therapists believe that individuals are driven in unconscious ways by drives, sometimes called instincts, they tend to vary regarding the kinds of drives and instincts that most influence the person (Wilson, 2015). Whereas some may take the traditional route that Freud took and believe there is a coexisting **life instinct (Eros)** and **death instinct (Thanatos)**, often simplified into sex and aggression, others believe that the **need for attachment** or the **striving for mastery or superiority** of self are critical drives. Still many, perhaps most, do not identify specific drives but listen to each client's understanding of self to help determine what drives the individual person.

Although most CPT therapists believe that drives are largely unconscious, they also believe that they are accessible and knowable. Thus, through therapy, they can help an individual come to know what drives are pressing on them and how they affect them in unconscious ways. When unconscious drives become conscious through therapy, the individual can make mindful choices about how to approach these drives so they are no longer victims of them.

Defense Mechanisms

The purpose of defenses is to avoid unacceptable thoughts, feelings, and fantasies that might result in anxiety or other symptoms and to help the person live in the world in a manner they believe to be acceptable (Freud, 1936/1966; Wilson, 2015; see Box 1.1). However, what may be unacceptable thoughts, feelings, and fantasies to one person, may be harmless to another person. For instance, the conservative religious person may have developed defense mechanisms to prevent the individual from experiencing what would be considered unacceptable sexual urges (e.g., same-sex attractions, sexual feelings outside of marriage, and so forth). Similarly, the individual who was physically abused as a child may develop defenses to avoid memories of the abuse; however, the abuse may continue to impact his or her behaviors in life, such as the adult woman who avoids loving interactions with men because her repressed memories of the abuse unconsciously suggest to her, "Stay away from all men."

Unfortunately, defenses can have the effect of preventing wholeness and impede the person from having awareness of aspects of oneself. The purpose of CPT is to deconstruct one's defense mechanisms, understand how they came to be, bring the unthinkable into consciousness, and help the client move toward a more whole and congruent life where the he or she is no longer dictated by the past (Wilson, 2015). Although the classic defense mechanisms are listed in Box 1.1, CPT therapists believe that humans have an infinite number of ways to avoid unacceptable thoughts, feelings, and fantasies. Can you come up with ways that you, or others, avoid difficult thoughts, feelings, and fantasies?

BOX 1.1 DEFENSE MECHANISMS

Asceticism: The repudiation of needs in an effort to deny urges and desires.
Example: The anorexic is not only denying himself or herself food, but also his or her sexual impulses.
Compensation: The replacement of a perceived weak behavior by a perceived strong behavior.
Example: A man becomes a bodybuilder because he feels inadequate as a conversationalist with women.
Denial: Not admitting that something has occurred.
Example: The parent who refuses to admit that his or her child was molested.
Displacement: Redirecting an unacceptable impulse to a more acceptable object or person.
Examples: An individual who has sexual urges toward a sibling becomes involved with computer sex. Or, murderous feelings toward one's parent become enraged feelings toward a political figure (e.g., the president).
Dissociation: The removal of oneself from feelings to delay experiencing those feelings.
Example: A rape victim dissociates during the violent act to separate self from the fear and rage within.
Humor: Using comic relief to defer feelings.
Example: After hearing that she needs a mastectomy for advanced breast cancer, the woman says to her friend, "Well, at least I won't be viewed as a sex object any longer!"
Idealization: Overstating and overestimating the value of an object or a person to deny negative feelings toward that person.

Example: A husband who is often criticized by his wife states, "My wife—she is the best person ever—she's bright, gorgeous, kind, and just perfect!"
Identification: Associating with certain individuals or groups to affiliate with specific values and deflect underlying feelings.
Example: An individual becomes caught up with the "Virgin Vow Ministries," which professes the importance of remaining a virgin until marriage.
Intellectualization: Concentrating on the intellectual components of a situation to distance oneself from the anxiety-provoking emotions associated with the situation.
Example: A person who has just been diagnosed with a virulent form of cancer wants to know all about the science of the disease.
Introjection: Identifying with an idea so completely that you accept it with little question.
Example: The religious zealot who never questions her parents' or church's views on religion. This has the result of not having to fear certain of life's ambiguities or uncertainties (e.g., death).
Projection: Attributing unacceptable qualities in others that the individual actually has.
Example: An individual calling a coworker "judgmental and bossy," when the individual actually acts in that manner and has urges to tell others how to act.
Rationalization: The cognitive distorting of events to make them more acceptable with the implications being that there are good reasons for some unacceptable actions.
Example: A parishioner says, "Our minister didn't harm anyone; he just had an affair—so what if she was married? The way he was treated after his wife died, you can understand why he would have an affair with someone who was putting herself out there."
Reaction formation: The replacing or conversion of an unacceptable impulse into an acceptable one.
Example: An individual who has strong attractions to the same sex becomes virulently anti-gay and protests same-sex marriage.
Regression: Reverting to behavior from an earlier stage of development.
Examples: A 10-year-old suddenly starts to wet his bed after he discovers his parents are getting divorced. Or, after losing his job, a 50-year-old becomes overly dependent on his wife.
Repression: Pushing out of consciousness threatening or painful thoughts.
Example: The individual who does not allow herself to remember being molested.
Somatization: Converting strong feelings or impulses into physical symptoms.
Example: An individual's fear of his sexuality is converted into hypochondriacal symptoms.
Splitting: Viewing people or objects as "all bad" or "all good."
Example: "Guns are horrible killing machines," or "My coworker is evil—she is just out for herself."

Sublimation: The channeling or refocusing of unacceptable impulses into socially accepted forms of behavior.
Example: A person struggling with extreme anger becomes a butcher or boxer, or a person's sexual energy is channeled into creative and artistic endeavors.
Suppression: The act of pushing conscious thoughts into the preconscious because they are too anxiety-evoking.
Example: The "good wife" who has thoughts of having an affair with a neighbor's husband pushes those thoughts out of consciousness.
Undoing: Performing a ritualistic or magical gesture to undo a behavior for which one is feeling guilty.
Examples: Following a woman's passionate lovemaking, she always has to clean the house. Or, after spanking his children, a father takes them out for ice cream.

Transference and Countertranference

> The patients, too, gradually learnt to realize that in these transferences on to the figure of the physician it was a question of a compulsion and an illusion which melted away with the conclusion of the analysis. (Freud & Breuer, 1895/1974, p. 392)

Early on, Freud realized that individuals were making what he called **false connections** between themselves and their analyst (Freud & Breuer, 1895/1974). False connections occurred when clients projected, or transferred, the reactions of their parents, or major caregivers, onto the therapist, and subsequently believed that the therapist had the qualities of their parents or major caregivers. Transference leads to the individual responding to others from old memories, and not from current reality. Since clients generally know little about their therapist, believing that he or she has certain qualities is a fantasy and leads to Freud's notion of false connections. Early analysts, however, believed that false connections did not just occur with therapists, but with all people a person would encounter. Thus, our lives are ultimately a fiction, as we believe others have qualities that they do not have as we project our early relationships onto them. And the people to whom we are projecting, are projecting onto us. Thus, the relationships we believe are "real" are mostly a fiction created out of a series of false projections onto one another. CPT therapists also believe in this important concept, though how it is perceived, and the magnitude of its impact, will vary based on the individual CPT therapist (Wilson, 2015). Understanding these projections can help a therapist unravel a client's early experiences and is a major focus of CPT.

Like clients, therapists too can have transferences onto others, and if the therapist has not examined how early experiences have impacted his or her relationships with others, the therapeutic process can wreak havoc on clients. Thus, it is critical that therapists have attended their own therapy so that an overabundance of countertransference can be avoided. Countertransference can take many forms (e.g., feeling attracted to a client, believing the client has qualities that he or she does not have, making false assumptions about clients), but in any form it can be a hindrance to the relationship as it prevents the client from actively understanding self and focusing on his or her own transferences. When the therapist believes he or she is all knowing but is actually incapacitated due to countertransference, and the client listens attentively to what the "expert" says, the client can actually be harmed by the therapist's false understanding. Understanding self, and not harming clients, is a critical reason why therapists must attend their own therapy in an effort to limit their countertransference. This is why Freud (1937) said, "Every analyst should periodically—at intervals of five years or so—submit himself to analysis once more, without feeling ashamed of taking this step." (p. 249; Figure 1.1)

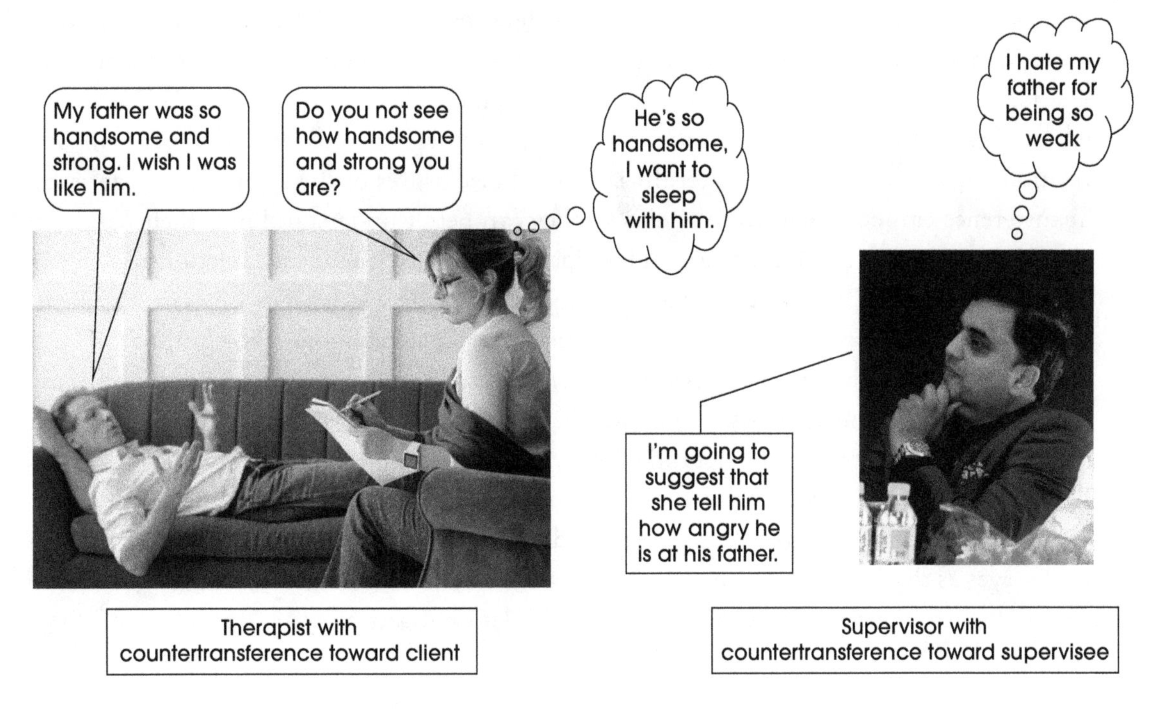

Figure 1.1 Countertransference Gone Awry

Early Attachments and Patterns of Relating

CPT therapists view the **Self** as developing from internalized images of significant, early relationships in people's lives (e.g., parents; Wilson, 2015). The remnants of those images impact how individuals relate to—and attach with—others and to themselves. However, in contrast with the static early psychoanalytic theories, CPT suggests that these early patterns can change as individuals relate and interact with others. Whereas the early psychodynamic models subscribed to the **myth of the independent mind**, which means that the mind is formed early and its structure and function determined early (Stolorow & Atwood,1992; Stolorow, 2013), these models believe that personality and the patterns of understanding and relating to others develop throughout one's lifespan as each person's Self interacts with others.

> Freud views mind as fundamentally monadic; something inherent, wired in, pre-structured, is pushing from within. Mind for Freud emerges in the form of endogenous pressures. Relational-model theories view mind as fundamentally dyadic and *interactive*; above all else, mind seeks contact, engagement with other minds. Psychic organization and structures are built from the patterns which shape those interactions. (Mitchell, 1988, pp. 3–4)

Although early patterns of relationship are clearly powerful and do impact unconscious processes, these approaches do not see them as all powerful, and CPT therapists believe that through interactions with others, particularly therapists, one can understand old patterns and develop new interactional modes with people (Giordano, 2015; Starr-Karlin, 2015). Therapists who embrace this perspective give attention and voice to transference within the therapeutic relationship and may also use carefully timed self-disclosures of their countertransference. Transference can be explained to clients so they can better understand how their past relationships perpetuate and mimic current relationships (e.g., the therapeutic relationship). Some CPT therapists will also use their countertransference to initiate discussion with the client about why he or she is responding to the counselor in a particular way. For instance, if I am conscious that I am having feelings toward a client that mimic feelings I had with one of my parents, I can engage in a discussion with my client about how and why he or she draws that out of me. Thus, the client can understand how certain personality styles (e.g., the client "acting" like my parent) may attract certain responses from some people (e.g., response to the client as if he or she is my parent). Indeed, it is this deep sharing that stems from the unconscious that serves as the staging area for recognizing and integrating disowned parts of self, denied emotional experiencing, and counterproductive relational patterns.

Lifespan Influences

CPT therapists do not believe that **individuals** are determined by their early experiences, such as those from parents and/or other caretakers. They do, however, acknowledge the importance of such early experiences, and they view other experiences as also critical to the development of the person. Some of these other factors include **birth order**, **psychosocial influences**, and **cross-cultural influences**.

Birth Order

Alfred Adler was one of the first psychodynamic theorists to suggest that family placement had an important impact on the development of the person (Adler, 2006). Today's CPT therapists would also acknowledge the importance of placement in the family as critical to the development of Self. For instance, with first-born children parents are generally anxious about being good parents, are very concerned with how the child is growing and learning, are extremely focused on the needs of the child, and place more demands on this child compared with later-born children. Is it surprising that this child is often a high achiever and perfectionist? In a similar vein, second-born children experience not being the "first love" and often attempt to catch up or dethrone the first-born. And, as you might expect, the middle child often feels "squeezed" and ends up being the "mediator" or "negotiator" of the family. In fact, a person who becomes proficient in understanding birth order can regularly pick out where in the family a client is positioned. However, birth order alone is not the only factor that impacts the developing personality within the family. Leman (2015) suggests nine other factors that can mediate the development of the child, including physical, mental, emotional differences; relationship between parents; birth order of parents; blending of families; judgmental parents; sex of the child; sibling deaths; adoptions; and spacing.

Psychosocial Influences

Current CPT therapists acknowledge the influences that social forces can play on the developing psyche over the lifespan. One model, often cited, is Erik Erikson's **eight stages of lifespan development** (Erikson, 1963, 1968, 1980, 1982). Erikson suggested that as individuals pass through eight stages, they are faced with a *task*, sometimes called a *crisis*. Portrayed as a pair of opposing forces, Erikson described the first opposing task in each stage as *syntonic*, or of positive emotional quality, and the second task as *dystonic*, or of negative emotional quality. He suggested that individuals needed to experience both the syntonic and dystonic qualities. In the end, however, one has to find a balance between the two, with individuals leaning toward the syntonic quality. For instance, trust is a critical factor in all people's lives, as we must generally trust others if we are to get along with one another. However, a certain amount of mistrust is also important. If you're walking down a dark street and see an ominous figure, you should react with a fair amount of mistrust. More generally, Erikson believed that too much trust would lead to what he called *sensory distortion*, while too much mistrust would lead to *withdrawal* (see Table 1.1). Similarly, too much autonomy would lead to *impulsivity*, while too much shame and doubt would lead to *compulsion*, and so forth. Clearly, the role of significant others in the early stages had much influence over the individual's ability to find the correct balance between the syntonic and dystonic qualities. What really sets Erikson's theory apart from the earlier psychodynamic theories is the idea that with education and awareness of these stages, others (e.g., parents) can change the way they are parenting and adopt a more positive parenting style and individuals can examine their own stage development and make changes as needed.

TABLE 1.1 ERIKSON'S EIGHTS STAGES OF DEVELOPMENT

STAGE	NAME OF STAGE (AGES)	VIRTUE OF STAGE	DESCRIPTION OF STAGE
1	Trust vs. Mistrust (birth–1)	Hope	In this stage, the infant is building a sense of trust or mistrust, which can be facilitated by significant others' ability to provide a sense of psychological safety to the infant.
2	Autonomy vs. Shame and Doubt (1–2)	Will	Here, the toddler explores the environment and is beginning to gain control over his or her body. Significant others can either promote or inhibit the child's newfound abilities and facilitate the development of autonomy or shame and doubt.
3	Initiative vs. Guilt (3–5)	Purpose	As physical and intellectual growth continues and exploration of the environment increases, a sense of initiative or guilt can be developed by significant others who are either encouraging or discouraging of the child's physical and intellectual curiosity.
4	Industry vs. Inferiority (6–11)	Competence	An increased sense of what the child is good at, especially relative to his or her peers, can either be reinforced or negated by significant others (e.g., parents, teachers, peers), leading to feeling worthwhile or discouraged by others, leading to feeling inferior.
5	Identity vs. Role Confusion (adolescence)	Fidelity	Positive role models and experiences can lead to increased understanding of temperament, values, interests, and abilities that define one's sense of self. Negative role models and limited experiences will lead to role confusion.
6	Intimacy vs. Isolation (early adulthood)	Love	A good sense of self and self-understanding leads to the ability to form intimate relationships highlighted by mutually supporting relationships that encourage individuality with interdependency. Otherwise, the young adult feels isolated.

STAGE	NAME OF STAGE (AGES)	VIRTUE OF STAGE	DESCRIPTION OF STAGE
7	Generativity vs. Stagnation (middle adulthood)	Caring	Healthy development in this stage is highlighted by concern for others and for future generations. This individual is able to maintain a productive and responsible lifestyle and can find meaning through work, volunteerism, parenting, and/or community activities. Otherwise, the adult feels stagnant.
8	Ego Integrity vs. Despair (later life)	Wisdom	The older adult who examines his or her life either feels a sense of fulfillment or despair. Successfully mastering the developmental tasks from the preceding stages will lead to a sense of integrity for the individual.

Cross-Cultural Influences

Whereas traditional psychodynamic approaches paid little attention to cross-cultural influences and differences, this is not the case with CPT. Today's CPT therapists will explore a number of cultural factors and how they impact the client and the therapeutic relationship, including: **therapist bias, understanding indigenous narratives, examining client language**, and **understanding the influences of social oppression** (Tummala-Narra, 2015).

Therapist Bias: CPT therapists will examine their own biases and how it impacts the counseling relationship. Unconscious bias can lead to misdiagnosis, misinterpretation of client issues, misunderstanding of client problems, and result in clients prematurely dropping out of therapy.

Understanding Indigenous Narratives: Every culture has narratives that drive behaviors. Such narratives can be conscious or unconscious, and dictate the kinds of actions people take in their lives. Borrowed from narrative therapy, CPT therapists want to understand a client's cultural narratives and see how they have impacted the client, bring those narratives to consciousness, and help the client make decisions regarding whether a particular narrative is a positive influence in the client's life.

Examining Client Language: Closely related to the client's narratives is the language a client uses in therapy. The CTP therapist carefully listens to clients to understand how language reflects certain narratives and whether the language used is a positive influence on the client. It is also important to remember that certain language may be perceived by a client as positive, but considered negatively by some in society (e.g., language used by a client who is embracing the Black Lives Matter movement may be viewed negatively by some in society). Ultimately, it is the goal of the CPT therapist to help clients become more conscious of the roots of the language they use and to make thoughtful, client-driven decisions about the kind of language they will use in the future. This does not negate the importance of someone who chooses to speak out in support of Black Lives Matter; however, it does speak to the importance of making intentional conscious decisions about what and how to say things.

Understanding the Influences of Social Oppression: Whereas traditional psychodynamic therapy viewed oppression as secondary to other important developmental influences, the CPT therapist believes oppressive factors in society are critical in the development of narratives and language usage. Such factors as sexism, discrimination, racism, classism, ageism, ableism, and other isms can greatly influence how the individual views the world and are examined in the therapeutic context. It is hoped that as clients gain increased consciousness of the impact of these forces, they can make thoughtful, intentional choices about how to respond to oppressive forces in the future. Consciousness can also lead to advocacy work by the client, and the therapist, that can address and possibly reduce social oppression.

TECHNIQUES

CPT uses a variety of techniques to help the therapist understand the client and to assist the client in the development of insight and awareness. Many of the techniques used are similar to those found in traditional psychoanalysis, yet are used in a manner that lessens interpretation, focuses more on collaboration than directiveness, and are more client-centered (Gabbard, 2017). Some of the more popular techniques used by CPT therapists include **conducting a thorough assessment, creating a trusting atmosphere, the use of questions, free association, analysis of resistance, dream analysis, analysis of transference, exploring countertransference,** and **other techniques** (Cabaniss et al., 2017).

Conducting a Thorough Assessment

When the client initially enters therapy, the CPT therapist should assess for several areas in the client's life including family background, history of trauma, biological and health issues, substance abuse, developmental factors, external stressors, cross-cultural factors, and ego strength. These can all help in making an accurate **DSM-5 diagnosis** that can be used for treatment planning (Cabaniss et al., 2017; Gabbard, 2017). The following briefly describes each of these areas:

Family background: This includes early memories, parenting styles of early caregivers, placement in the family, significant events in the family, feelings of inferiority, abuse, and so forth. Often, a structured interview is used to gather detailed information from the client.

History of trauma: Trauma can be a major contributor to several mental health concerns and should be assessed early in counseling. A questionnaire can be used to assess for a wide range of traumatic experiences to which a person may have been exposed, including war, accidents, disasters, illnesses, unwanted sexual contact, crimes, witnessing death, and more (Schnurr et al. 1999).

Biological and health issues: A wide range of health issues can cause, or contribute to, mental illness and can be assessed by a referral to a family practitioner for an overall health screening.

Substance abuse issues: Substance abuse can be a cause, or a symptom, of other issues and should be assessed early in the relationship. A screening instrument such as the Substance Abuse Subtle Screening Inventory (SASSI), which is 94% accurate in assessing for drug and alcohol abuse, can be used and only takes a short time to administer (SASSI Institute, 2018).

Developmental factors: Knowing that psychosocial factors can positively or negatively impact a person's development over the lifespan, the CPT therapist will do a careful analysis of life stages and how they have impacted the individual. Such models as Erikson's (1982) eight stages can be used to focus the developmental discussion (see Table 1.1).

External stressors: Situational factors in a person's life, such as the death of a loved one, job loss, natural and person-made disasters, and more will impact a person's level of functioning and should be assessed for during the interview.

Cross-cultural factors: Cultural factors can negatively influence a person's development through racism, discrimination, and bias. Using an assessment model, such as the RESPECTFUL model, examines a wide range of factors including religion, economic, sexual identify, psychological development, ethnic/racial identity, chronological/developmental challenges, trauma, family background, unique physical characteristics, and location and language differences (Lewis et al., 2001).

Ego strength: Ego strength has to do with the ability of the individual to deal with the internal and external stressors of life, especially when one is being negatively impacted by unpleasant conditions. Cabaniss et al. (2017) identifies a number of variables that one might look at when assessing for ego strength (see Box 1.2).

BOX 1.2 ASSESSING FOR EGO STRENGTH

1. *Reality testing*: Being able to deal effectively with what is real.
2. *Judgment*: Being able to make good judgments, even in difficult times.
3. *Relationships with others*: The ability to form and sustain healthy relationships.
4. *Sensory stimulus regulation*: Being able to lessen the "noise" in one's life in order to live fully and wholly.
5. *Affect/anxiety tolerance*: Being able to tolerate uncomfortable times when there is moderate affect and/or anxiety.
6. *Impulse control*: Being able to control urges and feelings that could result in negative behaviors.

7. *Capacity to play*: Having the ability to relax and chill out, even in difficult times.
8. *Self-awareness/psychological mindedness*: Having insight and being able to understand the part that one plays in relationships.
9. *Self-esteem regulation/accurate self-appraisal*: Being able to accurately assess oneself when difficult situations arise and make adjustments to Self as needed.
10. *Cognitive functions*: The ability to use one's intelligence, memory, and appropriate thinking in difficult times.
11. *Defenses*: Using defenses in ways that protect the individual and do not lead to neurotic or psychotic behaviors.

Creating a Trusting Atmosphere

Classic psychoanalysts had clients lie on a couch, looking away from the analyst, so that the client would feel comfortable sharing whatever came into his or her mind and to help build a transference relationship, whereby the client would project early relationship patterns onto the analyst (Cabaniss et al., 2017). These analysts would take on an air of **analytic neutrality** in which they would encourage clients to share their deepest thoughts while the analyst responded nonjudgmentally or not at all. The CPT therapist today, however, is much more engaged with the client. Today, the CPT therapist sits across from the client, is **nonjudgmental**, and uses a fair amount of **active listening** and **empathy** to build the relationship (Gabbard, 2017). Creating a trusting relationship allows clients to feel comfortable sharing deep parts of themselves and is also the raw material for developing a transference relationship. Thus, it is assumed that early patterns of relating and attachment will quickly arise within the therapeutic relationship, regardless of whether the therapist has the client lie on a couch or sit across from the therapist.

Use of Questions

As clients gradually feel safer in the therapeutic environment, the CPT therapist will increasingly probe through the use of questions (Jacobs, 2017). Questions need not be confrontational but should be respectfully asked and show the therapist's curiosity about the client's predicament. Some basic questions might be:

Therapist: "So, can you tell me a bit about your childhood?"
Therapist: "What do you think your relationship was like with your … ?"
Therapist: "Why do you think that experience had such a powerful influence on you?"
Therapist: "Who in your life do you think most influenced you?"
Therapist: "You seem to react strongly when talking about that experience. What do you think is going on?"

Mixed with a good share of empathy, questions allow clients to explore situations in their lives at deeper levels than they have in the past.

Free Association

As clients feel increasingly comfortable talking with their CPT therapist, the therapist may suggest that the client practice free association, or the process of freely saying whatever comes to mind, to access parts of themselves that they may be unconsciously hiding from self and others (Gabbard, 2017). This shedding of cognitive restraints allows the client to share whatever comes to mind, regardless of how personal or irreverent the material may be. It enables the client to cut through his or her defenses and resistances "much as cartographers of the mind would create a model of the networks that lead the patient to think, feel, and act in specific ways" (Gabbard, 2017, p. 110). When clients feel fully comfortable sharing the deepest recesses of their minds, their hidden thoughts, guilt, shameful behaviors, and most painful feelings are able to arise and be examined. It is only through this process that the client can begin to examine early memories and patterns of attachment that led to subsequent behaviors, feelings, and thoughts. It is critical that the CPT therapist respond to the client nonjudgmentally when this occurs, for any hint at judgment will cause the client to stop the free association process and become resistant to an in-depth discussion of issues.

Analysis of Resistance

Resistance, or actions that block the therapeutic process (Cabaniss et al., 2017; Gabbard, 2017), comes in many forms and usually occur as clients become close to revealing aspects of themselves of which they are embarrassed, ashamed, or guilty. Whereas free association and creating a trusting atmosphere allows a client to move closer to unconscious memories and the expression or revelation about difficult feelings, thoughts, and behaviors, a juxtaposition is often unconsciously created to prevent such revelations in order to protect the ego from pain. Thus, unconsciously the psyche is saying, "Don't take me there," "Be careful what you reveal," or "There will be negative consequences to you sharing this." Resistance is demonstrated in dozens of ways, with some of the more common responses being coming late to sessions, missing appointments, being argumentative with the therapist, suggesting that the therapist is wrong, not attending to what the therapist says, not responding during the sessions, and shutting down emotionally. CPT therapists, much as traditional analysts, realize that resistance is positive—it indicates the client is close to dealing with something particularly important but repressed. However, push the client too much to talk about his or her resistance, and you might push the client out of therapy. Yet, to not confront clients at all about their resistance is a missed opportunity. Thus, CPT therapists need to find the correct balance between discussing client resistance and ensuring that clients do not feel so pressured to reveal their resistance that they might drop out of therapy. Tentative questions can help with this process:

Therapist: "So, I noticed you've been late for sessions the last couple of times. Any ideas about why that is so?"

Or,

Therapist: "Every time I ask you about your relationship with your father, you seem to talk about something else. Any thoughts on that?"

Dream Analysis

The interpretation of dreams is the royal road to a knowledge of the unconscious activities of the mind. (Freud, 1899/1976, p. 769)

Although most CPT therapists believe in the importance of dreams reflecting aspects of unconscious drives and memories (Cabaniss, 2017), few rigidly hold to Freud's notion that dreams had representative meanings that need to be interpreted to the client by the therapist. Instead, more like the Jungian approach to dreams, CPT therapists view them as holding meaning that the client can uncover, with a bit of encouragement by the therapist.

To access unconscious elements, clients are encouraged to try and remember their dreams. This can occur by simply encouraging a client to have a sleep journal near his or her bed, and when awake, the client reflects on what he or she has dreamt and writes it down. The sleep journal can then be brought to therapy and discussed.

CPT therapists tend not to interpret dreams for clients but do try and help them understand the meaning of their dreams (Gabbard, 2017). And, much as traditional psychoanalysts, CPT therapists believe that dreams may have **manifest** and **latent** meanings. Manifest meanings are the obvious, more conscious meanings of the dreams, while latent meanings are underlying, preconscious meanings—meanings that are repressed in our dreams but can be discovered through analysis.

As clients feel increasingly comfortable in therapy, they begin to make their own connections to their dreams. Thus, when I dream of my father working as a construction worker and sweating profusely, the manifest meaning is that my father had to work hard to make a living for his family. But if I allow my mind to wander, I come up with a latent meaning—my father is me, and I feel pressure to work hard to ensure everyone's safety in my family. And while he seems virile in the dream, his hard work is stressful and there is an underlying belief that he may be harming himself—or I may be harming myself. You can see how dreams can become pretty involved and complex.

After getting to know a client well, a CPT therapist might make a very tentative suggestion about what a dream meant. For instance, the therapist might start a response in any of the following ways:

Therapist: "Well, since knowing you, I see your father as an extension of you and wonder what that hard-working man in the dream says about you?"

Or,

Therapist: "If this was my dream, it would mean ..."

Or,

Therapist: "So, what do you think the meaning behind the meaning is for that dream?"

Analysis of Transference

As noted earlier, a critical issue in CPT therapy is understanding how the transference relationship reflects early attachments and ways of relating that have been developed by the client (Spurling, 2017). As the transference relationship is built, the client begins to project, or transfer, patterns of behavior that were indicative of early relationships, often parents, onto the therapist. The CPT therapist is always looking for such patterns and is hoping to point them out to the client. For instance, if a client tells the therapist that he or she does not care about the client as much as the therapist cares about other clients, the therapist might suggest, "You know, I think this is how you felt growing up. You always felt like you were the sibling who was least loved." Such statements, when said at the appropriate time, can lead to an explosion of insights by the client as he or she realizes that in most relationships, he or she feels like the one who is left out, not loved, or not as important as others in the person's life. Slowly, clients begin to realize that they react to others not as the other person actually is, but how the client perceives the other person to be based on the client's projections. These are critical moments in therapy and can be life changing.

Exploring Countertransference

CPT therapists not only examine the client's transference but also examine countertransference, which, in a sense, can be called the therapist's transference onto the client (Cabaniss et al., 2017; Summers & Barber, 2010). Since countertransference is mostly unconscious, it can cause havoc on the relationship as the therapist responds not to the client, but to his or her own projections onto the client (Freud, 1937). But when therapists are keenly aware of how their feelings are being stirred up by a client, they can examine their countertransference and potentially use it in the therapeutic relationship.

Whereas some CPT therapists will want to be aware of their countertransference to avoid empathic failures, misinterpretation, and sub-par therapy, others will use the information stirred up by the countertransference within the therapeutic relationship (Giordano, 2015; Starr-Karlin, 2015).

This perspective gives attention to the notion that the client is being impacted by the therapist countertransference and such countertransference can elicit important information about the client. Consequently, the dynamic relational process between therapist and client becomes grist for the mill. This perspective uses **empathy** to help the therapist hear the client and to help the client hear himself or herself. In addition, carefully expressed therapist **self-disclosure** concerning how the client impacts the therapist helps the client see his or her role in relationships more clearly. An example of this might look like the following in a session:

Client: "All my life I've felt rejected by my dad, but all I ever wanted was for him to care about me ... to really, and truly love me the way I am. I know he disapproved, but I tried hard to live life the way he wanted me to."

Counselor: "You've worked so hard in your life for his acceptance, but even though you feel you did things according to his "way" it never was good enough. Say more about that."

Client: "Dad always told me to follow my dreams, to not compromise what I wanted and that I was capable of being anything if I worked hard enough for it. That was such an important value to him, and he lived his life reaching for what he wanted, working hard, and achieving it as far as I could see—sometimes at the expense of others, though. So, when I decided to become a teacher, something I dreamed about since elementary school, it hurt me a lot when dad told me teaching was too "soft" of a profession and he said I was a fool that would never make any money in life. I was crushed. What did I do wrong?"

Counselor: "You know ... listening to you share about your relationship with your dad, I'm overwhelmed by how much your experience has been like mine in life. I feel deeply sad right now, as my dad behaved similarly toward me and my chosen profession. My heart really aches for how your dad treated you the way my dad did me."

Client: "Really? I'm somewhat taken aback by this. I actually thought you might tell me something similar to what my dad told me. You remind me of my dad, in a way, how you carry yourself, and you sound a bit like him. I was expecting you to tell me I was wrong too."

Counselor: "You've been responding to me at times as if I was your dad, I suspect, but in reality, I'm not him and I experienced something so much like your own relationship with your dad ... that rejection yet yearning for love and acceptance. What is it like to hear this from me?"

Client: "It really stuns me. I have been treating you like my dad, and I think I've been doing this elsewhere in my life, now that I think of it."

Counselor: "Let's explore this further. Who else in your life reminds you of your dad or do you respond to as if they were him?"

From this expression of empathy and self-disclosure on the counselor's part the client can see connections to how he or she is responding in other relationships and gain insight toward becoming healthier in those relationships. The timing of self-disclosure is critical and must be offered when the client is able to hear such feedback (Giordano, 2015; Starr-Karlin, 2015). Through such disclosures, clients can begin to understand how certain relational patterns are remnants of early relationships and continue to cause dysfunctional ways of relating. In addition to self-disclosing to the client, the therapist encourages the client to self-disclose and share his or her feelings about the therapist. This process is painful, hopeful, and empowering as the client experiences wounds from the past that continue to affect his or her life and subsequently learns how to transcend them.

Other Techniques

In addition to the techniques just discussed, CPT strays from a strict adherence of certain techniques used in traditional psychoanalysis. For instance, Gabbard (2017) suggests a series of secondary techniques, many of which are not traditionally used in psychodynamic therapies, including:

1. *Suggestions*: Sometimes, after exploration of root causes, clients are aware of changes they need to make but are reticent to do so. Making suggestions for change can urge the client on in his or her life.
2. *Confronting dysfunctional or irrational beliefs*: Early patterns of development lead to dysfunctional thinking, behaving, and negative feelings. Directly highlighting certain dysfunctional or irrational beliefs, and developing strategies for changing them, can be helpful in changing these old habits.
3. *Conscious decision making or problem solving*: When clients are about to make poor decisions based on early patterns of development, the CPT therapist can bring to consciousness the reasons why they are making these decisions and help them move toward healthier decision making.
4. *Exposure*: A classic behavioral technique, this can be used when patterns of behaving are such that they are embedded in one's neural network and "talk therapy" just won't work in the change process. Thus, the client is asked to expose himself or herself to a painful situation (e.g., phobia of elevators, PTSD situational exposure) until the anxiety level begins to decrease. Multiple exposures are often needed.

5. *Self-disclosure*: Noted earlier when discussing countertransference, appropriate self-disclosure by the CPT therapist can help clients understand how their behaviors impact others and bring up residue from past relationships that continue to impact current relationships.
6. *Affirmation*: Affirming client past pains and trauma can help clients feel accepted and lead to increased self-disclosure on their part.
7. *Creative techniques*: Often, creative techniques such as painting, working with clay, and working with figurines can bring out unconscious thoughts and feelings that talk therapy would not. Thus, some CPT therapists will use these techniques to explore the unconscious.
8. *Facilitative techniques*: There is a whole range of other techniques that can be used to help bring consciousness to unconscious processes. Some may include psychoeducation, humor, or gestalt techniques such as the empty chair to encourage the discussion of unfinished business, and more.

THE COUNSELING PROCESS

In contrast with the more traditional forms of psychoanalysis, today's psychodynamic therapists sit face-to-face with their clients and therapy only occurs once or twice a week, for anywhere from six months to three or more years (Leichsenring & Leibing, 2003; Novotney, 2017b). The counseling process starts with a thorough assessment of the client along the eight factors noted earlier: family background, history of trauma, biological and health issues, substance abuse, developmental factors, external stressors, cross-cultural factors, and ego strength. This results in a diagnosis that can help with treatment planning. Assessing for these factors helps determine the client's ability to undergo therapy and gives the therapist a sense for how long therapy will take. Those with more ego strength are better at adapting to situations and at examining unconscious factors and will be more attuned to the therapeutic process early on.

After the initial assessment is completed, the therapist sits across from the client, is nonjudgmental, and uses active listening and empathy to build a trusting relationship. Such a relationship allows the client to feel comfortable sharing unconscious aspects of himself or herself and helps to develop a transference relationship. As the client feels increasingly comfortable, the therapist can use questions to probe areas of the client's life more deeply. In addition, the therapist will encourage the client to use free association to shed his or her cognitive restraints and allow unconscious material to become conscious. As the client increasingly comes closer to sharing intimate details of his or her life, he or she may become resistant to the process as fears arise as to how the therapist will respond. These fears are related to early patterns of development with caregivers. At this point, delicately, the therapist can interpret resistance for the client and begin to suggest how patterns in the transference relationship are related to the client's early attachment with others.

As therapy continues, the therapist will increasingly encourage the client to delve deeper into his or her unconscious processes by asking the client to do more free association, to examine the manifest and latent meaning of dreams, and to use other techniques that make unconscious thoughts conscious. In addition, carefully timed self-disclosures by the therapist of his or her reaction to the client's reactions to the therapist are fodder for continued exploration of the transference relationship. As clients dig deeper into self, the therapist might use carefully timed affirmations that acknowledge the client's hard work.

As unconscious processes become conscious, and as patterns of relating become obvious, the client will be encouraged to make intentional efforts to change unhealthy ways of living. Here, conscious decision-making and problem-solving techniques will be used, cognitive behavioral techniques to address specific negative behaviors may be tried, disputation of irrational or dysfunctional thinking may be applied, and suggestions for change will be offered by the therapist.

As patterns change and the client builds a healthier life, the client will begin to consider terminating from therapy. Although there are brief forms of CPT, usually CPT is considered a long-term therapy as compared with most other therapies today, but certainly not as long as traditional psychodynamic approaches. Thus, the termination process will very likely not begin until one year of therapy has occurred and sometimes therapy will last several years.

BOX 1.3 ANGELA WITH A CPT COUNSELOR

Your instructor might have you view Angela with a counselor who uses an integrative approach to counseling, combining a number of psychodynamic approaches in the counselor's work with Angela. After you view the video, consider how effective the counselor was at doing this and reflect on whether you think it would be better if a counselor practiced a "pure" approach (e.g., strictly psychoanalytic, Jungian, Adlerian, object-relations, attachment, relational and intersubjectivity, etc.).

SOCIAL AND CULTURAL ISSUES

Many of the post-psychoanalytic theories, much as their forbearers, have been criticized for being narrow in that their focus reflected the particularities of the culture, time, and place in which they were created. But some, such as Erikson, attempted to develop a universally applied conceptualization of human development and treatment (Ochse & Plug, 1986). For instance, Erikson made early attempts to be inclusive of diverse cultures in his work, including Native Americans with whom he lived among during his life (Karcher & Benne, 2008). His experiences and studies of different cultures most likely helped him apply his identity development ideas across cultures and contribute to the potential universal salience of his ideas (Karcher & Benne, 2008). Some researchers have looked at Erikson's ideas from a cultural standpoint, such as the large quantitative study of 1,859 White and Black individuals in South Africa conducted by Ochse and Plug (1983). These authors found the efficacy of Erikson's theories to be sufficiently reliable in the diverse population of their study but recommended more research be conducted. Another study (Salamone & Salamone, 1993) looked at the utility of Erikson's psychosocial theories within the Hausa indigenous group of Nigeria and, though differences were found, sufficient relevance was located to encourage the researchers of the usefulness of his ideas with this population. Additionally, Howard-Hamilton (2002) listed Erikson's theory as one of four "Africentric theoretical frameworks" useful when working with African American college-age men in counseling (p. 20).

Considering other post-psychoanalytic approaches to psychotherapy, Tummala-Narra (2015) suggests it appears that these adaptive approaches have been shown to have greater utility across diverse cultures as compared with earlier psychoanalytic approaches that seem to deserve much of the cultural criticism they received. This author states "relational psychoanalytic approaches have challenged Western Eurocentric ideals of human development," noting that in recent writings "... the concepts of healthy attachment, separation-individuation, and good-enough mothering have been revisited outside of Western Euro American contexts" (p. 280). Her conclusion is that significant multicultural work is being done in modern post-psychoanalytic scholarship and that "these approaches reflect a call for both active engagement of psychoanalytic theory with cultural competence and the application of psychoanalytic contributions to culturally competent therapeutic practice" (p. 282).

Although CPT clings to many of the concepts of its predecessors (e.g., transference, resistance, an unconscious), it also challenges many ideas that were core to a Western examination of the person. For instance, challenging the "independent mind," by suggesting that individuals co-create reality, is a more inclusive way of understanding individuals. In addition, its increasingly collaborative stance with clients, instead of objectifying them, is more inviting to diverse clients. As CPT moves forward, an examination of its efficacy with a wide range of diverse clients will need to be conducted.

EFFICACY

Like other psychodynamic theories such as psychoanalysis, analytical therapy, or individual psychology (Kernberg, 2006), it can be difficult to measure the effectiveness of CPT due to the nature of its concepts and methods of treatment. Yet, researchers are attempting to examine the effectiveness of these treatments, against no treatment and in some cases against other approaches more commonly studied. For example, Driessen et al. (2013) examined 341 adults randomly assigned to 16 sessions of cognitive behavioral therapy or psychodynamic therapy. They found that nearly one fourth of patients reached remission and that there were no differences in treatment groups rates of remission. In other words, psychodynamic therapy group was as effective as CBT, though longer treatment is probably necessary for most patients with depression. In research that examined 20 studies of changes in brain function, Fonagy and Lemma (2014) note that there was a substantial increase in those brain receptors that are critical for depression and a "normalization of neuronal activity in patients with somatoform disorders" (p. 18) for those who participated in psychodynamic and other therapies.

Shedler (2010) reviewed a number of meta-analyses that examined the efficacy of psychodynamic therapy between 1980 and 2009 and suggested that the benefits are as robust and long-lasting as many other therapies, including cognitive behavioral therapy. He noted that "the 'active ingredients' of therapy are not necessarily those presumed by the theory or treatment model," and "that randomized controlled trials that evaluate a therapy as a 'package' do not provide support for its theoretical premises or the specific interventions that derive from them" (Shedler, 2010, p. 103). Thus, he suggested that many therapeutic approaches often employ effective methods of change (e.g., building the relationship) different than those stated by the theorists. Consequently, all therapies have some effectiveness if done well and it is hard to really know what is working or not working for any particular therapeutic approach (Hilsenroth, 2014; Shedler, 2010; Wampold & Imel, 2015).

Looking more recently at psychodynamic effectiveness, Fonagy (2015) engaged in a meta-analytical review of many studies looking at the effectiveness of a broad range of psychodynamic therapy approaches for the treatment of numerous mental health issues (e.g., depression, anxiety, eating disorders, psychosomatic symptoms, substance dependence). He concluded that many of the studies both supporting and refuting the effectiveness of psychodynamic theories have numerous flaws, but the research clearly demonstrates that psychodynamic approaches "benefit individuals who present with depression, some forms of anxiety, eating disorders, and somatic problems" (Fonagy, 2015, p. 144). He further concluded that psychodynamic approaches have not been shown to be more effective than other treatments, nor were they shown to be less effective, especially when accounting for highly trained, competent clinicians who implement the elements of these therapies that have been shown to be effective.

SUMMARY

This chapter first reviewed some of the predecessors to CPT, starting with Freud's classic theory of psychoanalysis. Over the next 100 years, a number of related theories developed that tended to be less deterministic and more positive and holistic. These included the psychodynamic theories of Jung (analytical therapy) and Adler (individual psychology); the neo-Freudians, such as Horney, Fromm, and Erikson; object relations theories developed by Klein, Fairburn and others; self-psychology as developed by Kohut, and the recent development of relational and intersubjectivity approaches.

All these post-psychoanalytic theories can be loosely placed into what we call the psychodynamic school of therapy. We suggested that those who practice an integrative approach to these theories today can collectively be called contemporary psychodynamic therapies (CPT). These theories suggest that the unconscious affects one's conscious thoughts, feelings, and behaviors, and tend to embrace seven common themes: a focus on affect and emotions, examining the avoidance of distressing thoughts and emotions, identifying and understanding recurrent themes, discussing the past, focusing on interpersonal issues, examining the relationship with the therapist, and understanding and exploring one's fantasy life.

CPT also proposes that human behavior is a function of how the self is developed via the individual's interactions with parents, social and cultural influences, and important individuals in one's life, even psychotherapists. CPT views the psyche as functioning with conscious and unconscious minds, is less deterministic than psychoanalysis, and believes that change can occur relatively quickly as compared with psychoanalysis. CPT brings more of the therapist into the relationship, assumes the past is critical to current day functioning, underscores the importance of building a relationship with the client to understand the past, highlights that the self can be formed and reformed over the lifespan, suggests that unconscious factors and defenses need to be explored, and suggests that external factors, such as cultural influences, can impact the client's developing self.

We emphasized several key concepts in this chapter. For instance, we noted that CPT therapists suggest that drives and instincts may be unconscious, are knowable, and CPT therapists will vary on which drives they view as important for any particular client. We highlighted the importance of defense mechanisms in the avoidance of unacceptable thoughts, feelings, and fantasies and noted that they become harmful if they prevent a person from embracing important parts of themselves. We gave examples of several defense mechanisms and suggested that wholeness is the capacity to understand one's defense mechanisms, deconstruct how they came to be, and construct new and healthier ways of living. We noted that Freud believed that individuals had "false connections" with others because they projected their early experiences with important caregivers onto others and that clients transferred these early experiences onto their therapists. Thus, one of the important processes of CPT was to help clients understand the transference relationship. CPT therapists will sometimes use their countertransference by self-disclosing what they are experiencing from the client in order to help the client understand his or her transference.

Continuing with key concepts, we noted that early psychodynamic models subscribed to the "myth of the independent mind" and that many CPT therapists believe that the mind, instead, is constantly seeking and developing by engaging with other minds. Thus, early forms of attachment are related to how individuals engage with one another, and these attachments become the maps for how we live our lives and are demonstrated through the transference relationship; however, new patterns of relating, such as those developed in the therapeutic relationship, can give rise to healthier ways of living. Finally, we noted that a number of lifespan influences can impact the individual, including birth order, psychosocial influences, and cross-cultural influences, such as therapist bias, understanding indigenous narratives, examining client language, and understanding the influences of social oppression.

In the chapter we underscored several important techniques. First, we spoke of the importance of conducting a thorough assessment, which includes obtaining information about family background, history of trauma, biological and health issues, substance abuse issues, development factors, external stressors, cross-cultural factors, and ego strength. We noted the importance of being engaged with clients, sitting across from clients, and creating a trusting environment through active listening and empathy. We pointed out that CPT therapists will gently probe, using gentle questions. We noted that free association allows clients to access deep, unconscious parts of self and that when a client comes close to reckoning painful unconscious processes, he or she may become resistant and that it was important for clients to recognize how their resistance blocks them from examining deep-seated issues. We pointed out how dreams have manifest and latent meanings and that latent meanings reflect unconscious processes. We noted how transference, and countertransference, can be used to explore early patterns of relating that negatively impact the client. Finally, we briefly highlighted several secondary techniques that can be used in the counseling process, including suggestions, confronting dysfunctional or irrational beliefs, conscious decision making or problem solving, exposure, self-disclosure, affirmation, creative techniques, and facilitative techniques.

As the chapter neared its conclusion, we examined the counseling process. Generally, the therapist starts with a thorough assessment, then works on building a trusting relationship that allows for the sharing of unconscious material. Next, therapists will use techniques to better understand unconscious material and early patterns of relating. Here the therapist will use free association, interpretation of resistance, examining the transference relationship, and the exploration of dreams. Self-disclosure by the therapist might be used to further delve into how the client's projections create the transference relationship and are indicative of early patterns of relating. As clients begin to understand unconscious motivations, patterns, and projections, they become more conscious and whole and can make better choices in their lives.

Although post-psychoanalytic theories, such as CPT, have been criticized for being narrow in that their focus reflects the particularities of the culture, time, and place they were created in, there is clearly some movement to increased inclusiveness in these more modern approaches. Erikson, for one, formulated a developmental model that he believed was universal, and relational approaches examined attachment within varying cultures. In fact, challenging the "independent mind" by suggesting that individuals co-create reality is seen as more inclusive of diverse individuals, as is developing a CTP model that stresses collaboration instead of objectification.

As with psychoanalysis, CPT is a difficult therapy to measure as one is dealing with qualities, such as changes in the unconscious, which are hard to assess. Nevertheless, several studies and metanalyses have shown that CPT, and related therapies, have been shown to be as effective as other types of therapies (e.g., cognitive behavioral therapy) in the treatment of a wide range of disorders. In addition, some recent research on changes in brain function seems to show positive changes in brain receptors for individuals who were depressed and underwent psychodynamic therapy. Although positive outcomes of CPT and related therapies may be a function of other factors, such as the therapist's ability to build a relationship, whatever it is that makes CPT and related therapy work, it does seem to work.

KEY WORDS AND NAMES

Active listening
Adler, Alfred
Analysis of resistance
Analysis of transference
Analytic neutrality
Analytical therapy
Archetypes
Attachment therapies
Birth order
Collective unconscious
Complexes
Conducting a thorough assessment
Conscious
Conscious and unconscious minds
Countertransference
Cross-cultural influences
Death instinct (Thanatos)
Defense mechanisms
Drives and instincts
Early attachments and patterns of relating
Ego
Eight stages of lifespan development
Empathy
Erikson, Erik
Examining client language
Existential-humanistic perspective
Exploring countertransference
Fairburn, Ronald
False connection
Feelings of inferiority
Free association
Freud, Anna
Freud, Sigmund
Horney, Karen
Id
Individual psychology
Kohut, Heinz
Jung, Carl
Klein, Melanie
Latent meaning
Life instinct (Eros)
Lifespan influences
Manifest meaning
Myth of the independent mind
Need for attachment
Need to be in relationships
Nonjudgmental
Object relations theory
Other techniques
Personal unconscious
Post-psychoanalytic approaches
Psyche
Psychoanalysis
Psychodynamic therapies
Psychological type
Psychosocial influences
Relational and intersubjectivity approaches
Resistance
Self psychology
Self-disclosure
Seven common themes
Socio-psychoanalysis
Striving for perfection
Striving for superiority
Style of life
Superego
Superiority
Therapist bias
Transference
Unconscious
Understanding indigenous narratives
Understanding the influences of social oppression

REFERENCES

Adler, A. (2006). Position in family constellation influences life-style. In S. Slavik & J. Carlson (Eds), *Readings in the theory of individual psychology* (pp. 297–306). Routledge.

Aron, L., & McIntosh, M. K. (2015). Relational psychoanalysis. In E. S. Neukrug (Ed.), *The SAGE encyclopedia of theory in counseling and psychotherapy* (Vol. 2, pp. 884–887). SAGE Publications.

Bishop, A. (2015a). Neo-Freudian psychoanalysis. In E. S. Neukrug (Ed.), *The SAGE encyclopedia of theory in counseling and psychotherapy* (Vol. 2, pp. 702–706). SAGE Publications.

Bishop, A. (2015b). Object-relations theory In E. S. Neukrug (Ed.), *The SAGE encyclopedia of theory in counseling and psychotherapy* (Vol. 2, pp. 731–735). SAGE Publications.

Blagys, M. D., & Hilsenroth, M. J. (2000). Distinctive feature of short-term psychodynamic-interpersonal psychotherapy: A review of the comparative psychotherapy process literature. *Clinical Psychology: Science and Practice, 7*(2), 167–188. https://doi.org/10.1093/clipsy.7.2.167

Cabaniss, D. L., Cherry, S., Douglas, C. J., & Schwartz, A. (2017). *Psychodynamic psychotherapy: A clinical manual* (2nd ed.). John Wiley & Sons.

Cosentino, A., & Dermer, S. (2015). Attachment theory and attachment therapies. In E. S. Neukrug (Ed.), *The SAGE encyclopedia of theory in counseling and psychotherapy* (Vol. 1, pp. 70–75). SAGE Publications.

Donaldson, G. (2015). Klein, Melanie. In E. S. Neukrug (Ed.), *The SAGE encyclopedia of theory in counseling and psychotherapy* (Vol. 2, pp. 604–606). SAGE Publications.

Driessen, E., Van, H. L., Don, F. J., Peen, J., Kool, S. Westra, D., … Dekker, J. J. (2013). The efficacy of cognitive-behavioral therapy and psychodynamic therapy in the outpatient treatment of major depression: A randomized clinical trial. *American Journal of Psychiatry, 170*, 1041–1050. https://doi.org/10.1176/appi.ajp.2013.12070899

Erikson, E. H. (1963). *Childhood and society* (2nd ed.). Norton.

Erikson, E. H. (1968). *Identity: Youth and crisis.* Norton.

Erikson, E. H. (1980). *Identity and the life cycle.* Norton.

Erikson, E. H. (1982). *The life cycle completed.* Norton.

Erikson Institute (2019). *Erik H. Erikson—Erikson Institute's namesake.* https://www.erikson.edu/about/history/erik-erikson/

Fonagy, P. (2015). The effectiveness of psychodynamic psychotherapies: An update. *World Psychiatry, 14*, 137–150. https://doi.org/10.1002/wps.20235

Fonagy, P., & Lemma, A. (2012). Psychoanalysis: Does it have a valuable place in modern mental health services? *British Medical Journal, 344*(7845), p. 18–19. https://doi.org/10.1136/bmj.e1188

Freud, S. (1937). Analysis terminable and interminable. In J. Strachey (Ed. & Trans.), *Complete psychological works of Sigmund Freud* (pp. 210–253). Hogarth.

Freud, A. (1966). *The ego and the mechanisms of defense.* International Universities Press. (Original work published 1936)

Freud, S. (1961a). *Beyond the pleasure principle.* (J. Strachey, Trans.). W. W. Norton. (Original work published 1920)

Freud, S. (1961b). *The future of an illusion.* (J. Strachey, Trans.). W. W. Norton. (Original work published 1927)

Freud, S. (1976). *The interpretation of dreams.* (J. Strachey, Trans.). Penguin Books. (Original work published 1899)

Freud, S., & Breuer, J. (1974). *3 studies in hysteria.* (J. Strachey, Trans.). Penguin Books. (Original work published 1895)

Gabbard, G. O. (2017). *Long-term psychodynamic psychotherapy: A basic text* (3rd ed.). American Psychiatric Association.

Gabrinetti, P. A. (2015). Analytical psychology. In E. S. Neukrug (Ed.), *The SAGE encyclopedia of theory in counseling and psychotherapy* (Vol. 1, pp. 43–48). SAGE Publications.

Giordano, F. G. (2015). Interpersonal psychotherapy. In E. S. Neukrug (Ed.), *The SAGE encyclopedia of theory in counseling and psychotherapy* (Vol. 1, pp. 574–577). SAGE Publications.

Hilsenroth, M. (Ed.). (2014). Common factors [Special section]. *Psychotherapy, 51*, 467–524.

Jacobs, M. (2017). *Psychodynamic counselling in action* (5th ed.). SAGE Publications.

Leichsenring, F., & Leibing, E. (2003). The effectiveness of psychodynamic therapy and cognitive behavior therapy in the treatment of personality disorders: A meta-analysis. *American Journal of Psychiatry, 160*(7), 1223–1232. https://doi.org/10.1176/appi.ajp.160.7.1223

Leman, K. (2015). *The birth order book: Why you are the way you are* (rev. ed.). Revell.

Lewis, J. A., Lewis, M. D., Daniels, J. A., & D'Andrea, M. J. (2010). *Community counseling: A multicultural-social justice perspective* (4th ed.). Cengage.

Mitchell, S. A. (1988). *Relational concepts in psychoanalysis: An integration*. Harvard University Press.

Neukrug, E. S. (2018). *Counseling theory and practice* (2nd ed.) Cognella Academic Publishing.

Novotney, A. (2017a). Not your great-grandfather's psychoanalysis: Psychologists have modernized the approach to better serve patients and have conducted more research that validates its success. *Monitor on Psychology, 48*(11), 40.

Novotney, A. (2017b). Psychoanalysis vs. psychodynamic therapy. *Monitor on Psychology, 48*(11), 45.

SASSI Institute. (2018). *Substance use measures*. https://sassi.com/sassi-online/

Schnurr, P. Vielhauer, M., Weathers, F., & Findler, M. (1999). *The Brief Trauma Questionnaire (BTQ)*. https://www.ptsd.va.gov/professional/assessment/documents/BTQ.pdf

Shedler, J. (2010). The efficacy of psychodynamic psychotherapy. *American Psychologist, 63*(2), 98–109. https://doi.org/10.1037/a0018378

Spurling, L. (2017). *An introduction to psychodynamic counselling* (3rd ed.). Palgrave Macmillan.

Star-Karlin, P. S. (2015). Intersubjective-systems theory. In E. S. Neukrug (Ed.), *The SAGE encyclopedia of theory in counseling and psychotherapy* (Vol. 1, pp. 586–589). SAGE Publications.

Stolorow, R. D. (2013). Intersubjective-systems theory: A phenomenological-contextualist psychoanalytic perspective. *Psychoanalytic Dialogues*, 23, 383–389. https://doi.org/10.1080/10481885.2013.810486

Stolorow, R., & Atwood, G. (1992). Contexts of being: *The intersubjective foundations of psychological life*. Psychoanalytic Inquiry Book Series (Vol. 12). Analytic Press.

Summers, R. F., & Barber, J. P. (2010). *Psychodynamic therapy: A guide to evidence-based practice*. Guilford Press.

Tummala-Narra, P. (2015). Cultural competence as a core emphasis of psychoanalytic psychotherapy. *Psychoanalytic Psychology*, 23, 275–292. http://dx.doi.org/10.1037/a0034041

Watts, R. E. (2015). Adlerian therapy. In E. S. Neukrug (Ed.), *The SAGE encyclopedia of theory in counseling and psychotherapy* (Vol. 1, pp. 30–35). SAGE Publications.

Wampold, B. E., & Imel, Z. E. (2015). *The great psychotherapy debate: The evidence for what makes psychotherapy work* (2nd ed.). Routledge.

Wilson, N. (2015). Contemporary psychodynamic-based therapies: Overview. In E. S. Neukrug (Ed.), *The SAGE encyclopedia of theory in counseling and psychotherapy* (Vol. 1, pp. 229–234). SAGE Publications.

CASE STUDY: ANGELA'S EXPERIENCE IN CPT

(Please read about the Millers in Appendix I prior to reading this case study)

Angela always felt like she was a good mother, a good wife, and a good daughter. So, she was a bit thrown when suddenly, her husband Jake, was accusing her of not doing enough to take care of the children. Since the near accident with their kids, Jake had become increasingly vigilante about everyone's safety, especially the kids, and he has been wanting Angela to give up her job and homeschool the children. The couple had grown apart in recent months, everyone seemed stressed, and Angela was feeling depressed.

Angela had dabbled in therapy before, and it was helpful. But she increasingly felt as if she needed something to help her look at herself in deeper ways that would lead to more long-lasting change. She had taken some basic psychology courses in college and had read about Sigmund Freud and wondered whether psychoanalysis was the thing that would finally "cure" her. She began putting out feelers for a psychoanalytic therapist with her friends, many who had been in their own therapy. She soon found that while many of her friends had been in "depth therapy," none had been in pure psychoanalysis. One of her friends, in particular, told her she might want to try her therapist. Her friend told her that although similar to psychoanalysis, her therapist was "more real" than most psychoanalysts. Angela decided to give it a try.

Angela went to Dr. Sophia Drummond's office on a rainy Tuesday morning. She thought how the rain seemed to match her mood. As soon as she arrived, she welcomed the comfortable chairs and couches in the waiting room. A dark-haired woman in a flowing dress soon came out and said, "Angela?" Angela responded, "Yes." "I'm Dr. Sophia Drummond. Why don't you come with me to my office." They entered an office filled with trinkets and modern art, all of which seemed to be saying, "Let's talk." Dr. Drummond informed Angela that the first, and perhaps second session, would be focused on obtaining a range of information and that actual counseling would take place soon after. Dr. Drummond went on to explain the type of therapy she conducted, which she described as a neo-Freudian approach.

During the first couple of sessions Angela took a couple of instruments—one to assess substance and alcohol abuse and one to assess trauma. A full family history was obtained, and Dr. Drummond asked Angela about her earliest memories. She also asked Angela about her cultural background, developmental concerns, and environmental stressors in her life. At the end of the second session, Dr. Drummond looked at Angela and said, "Seems like you were taught, from a very young age, how to be the proper girl and how to take care of others. In addition, it's pretty clear that since a young age, you've been struggling with your identity—who are you as a biracial person, a mother, a wife, and an independent woman. Seems like there have also been forces pushing you in some different directions. On the one hand, you've been taught how to be the caretaker and perfect wife, and on the other hand, there's a part of you that wants to experience more, discover other aspects of yourself, and be free from some restraints that have been internalized. One thing that we might do is to take a look at the parts of you that you have repressed—the somewhat unknown parts of you. We can do this by exploring some of your dreams and maybe even do some creative work with clay right here in the office."

When Angela showed up for her next session, she had a dream she wanted to discuss, but also said she was interested in working with the clay that Dr. Drummond had mentioned. Dr. Drummond said, "Your decision." Angela quickly replied, "Let's do the clay," at which point Dr. Drummond took out some large pieces of clay, put them on a 4-foot-square plastic table, and said, "Why don't you use the clay to show me who you are and what you want your life to be."

Angela worked with the clay for about 10 minutes, at which point she said, "Okay, I'm done for now." "Tell me what this all means," said Dr. Drummond, and Angela noted, "Well, there are two Angela's here. Over there is one Angela holding her children closely and in the other corner is another Angela with her arms stretched out reaching for the stars—free and having nothing to hold her down." "And where is Jake, Angela?" asked Dr. Drummond. "He's not in the picture. He's just harming the kids right now, so I don't want them near him, and when I'm free, I don't see him with me. And, that kind of reminds me of my dream, also." "Go ahead, Angela, tell me about that dream," Dr. Drummond encouraged. "Well, in the dream I'm on a train, by myself. I see some kids sitting across from me crying, and I immediately want to help them, but I restrain myself. Suddenly, the train stops, and as I walk off the train, I realize I'm in a fantasy land—a little like Disneyland. It's beautiful. Everyone is so nice, and everyone tells me, 'You're free, you can do whatever you want.' I start to dance, and suddenly, I feel guilty and start to cry. Someone comes over to me and holds me and I sob. It first feels good, then I tell them—to stay away from me. I can handle this on my own. Then I woke up."

"So interesting," says Dr. Drummond. "Your dream and your clay work say so much about you. I have some thoughts about what they mean, but I'm wondering if you do also?" Angela thinks to herself, and suddenly blurts out, "I think my parents screwed me." "How do you mean?" asks Dr. Drummond. "Well, they made me act like the perfect little girl and also made me the perfect caretaker. So perfect, that I felt like I could never be me and never have any fun." "Yes, and that seems pretty obvious by the clay and the dream," said Dr. Drummond. "I call that the manifest, or obvious meaning. Any other, maybe deeper meanings?" Angela sits still, and says, "That's all I can think of now." Dr. Drummond looks at Angela for a moment, and says, "You know, I was wondering why you couldn't accept the love from that person who held you." "Interesting," replies Angela. "I think I push people away who try to take care of me." "I wonder if your parents were kind of distant and although they would sometimes show they cared for you, you were left feeling like, in the end, they would not be there for you. Instead, you always had to be there for others." As Angela listens, she begins to feel sadness, and begins to sob. Dr. Drummond listens, and tells her, "I'm here for you, Angela."

As Angela and Dr. Drummond continue in counseling, Angela spends a lot of time talking about her early relationships with her parents and her placement in the family. She realizes how stifling it was to be the caretaker of her siblings and to always have to be the "perfect child." She realizes the anger she feels toward her parents for not allowing her to experience other parts of herself. At one point, in therapy, Angela begins to feel anger toward Dr. Drummond. It is then that she begins to miss some appointments. Dr. Drummond confronts Angela and says, "I wonder if you're missing appointments because you're getting closer to some important information." She also tells Angela, "I wonder if your anger at me is your expectation that like your parents, I too will remove my love for you. I think this is the same thing you expect everyone to do—even Jake."

QUESTIONS FOR YOU TO PONDER

1. What are some positive and negative thoughts about starting counseling with a thorough assessment as did Dr. Drummond?
2. Dr. Drummond did not find substance abuse or trauma in Angela's life. If she had, how do you think it might have changed the counseling process?
3. How did Dr. Drummond build the relationship with Angela? What specific skills did she use?
4. Why do you think Dr. Drummond gave Angela the choice of either talking about her dream or doing work with clay?
5. How effectively did Dr. Drummond use questions in her work with Angela?
6. What were the manifest and latent meanings of Angela's dream?
7. How did Angela show resistance? What purpose did this resistance serve?
8. Although Dr. Drummond never says this specifically, she does address the transference relationship. Explain Angela's transference relationship.
9. When Dr. Drummond says to Angela, "I'm here for you," she departs dramatically from traditional psychoanalysts. How does she depart and why do you think she does this?
10. How is Angela's transference relationship indicative of most of her relationships in her life? Speak to how it may be reflected in her relationship with Jake.
11. CPT therapy tends to be somewhat lengthy. How long do you think Angela might be in therapy? Why?
12. In what areas of your life do you believe CPT therapy could be helpful?

Credits

2

Contemporary Person-Centered Counseling (CPCC)

Ed Neukrug and Amber Pope

LEARNING OUTCOMES

- To learn the historical antecedents of contemporary person-centered counseling (CPCC).
- To understand the phenomenological, humanistic, existential, and strength-based view of human nature of CPCC.
- To understand key concepts of CPCC, including the actualizing tendency, the incongruent or non-genuine self, conditions of worth, symptoms as a message to self, unfinished business, phenomenology, meaning making, choice, and universal and repressed needs.
- To review the following techniques of CPCC: honoring and respecting, normalizing not pathologizing, acceptance, empathy, authenticity, the use of questions (clarifying, tentative, and preferred goals and solution-oriented), affirmation and encouragement, using "now" language, the empty chair technique, identifying choices and goal setting, offering advice and saying what you think, and other techniques.
- To describe the counseling process of CPCC.
- To examine social and cultural applicability of CPCC.
- To review the efficacy of CPCC.
- To offer a case study that demonstrates the CPCC process.

BRIEF HISTORY OF CONTEMPORARY PERSON-CENTERED COUNSELING

With its roots in existential-humanistic therapies and philosophies, contemporary person-centered counseling (CPCC) is particularly driven by the ideas of **Carl Rogers's** theory of **person-centered counseling**, but also greatly influenced by **Viktor Frankl's** ideas on **existential-humanistic therapy**, **Fritz Perls's** views on **gestalt therapy**, **Abraham Maslow's** ideas about **humanistic psychology** and **needs**, and concepts drawn from the **strength-based approaches** such as **solution-focused brief therapy (SFBT)** (cf. Bohart, 2012; Grogan, 2013). Let's take a look at how all of these approaches influenced CPCC.

In 2007 Carl Rogers was voted, by therapists, as the most influential psychotherapist of the 20th century (Cook et al., 2009; "The top 10," 2007). There were many reasons for this, but very likely this accolade was mostly due to the popularity of his **core conditions** for counseling, which included **empathy**, **unconditional positive regard**, and **genuineness** (Rogers, 1957a, 1980). These conditions became a mainstay of training programs, and models for how to teach them and train budding counselors and therapists thrived. Rogers's popularity has waxed and waned over the years, but these conditions have remained central to his approach. In more recent years, a number of meta-analyses were conducted that underscored the importance of these conditions to positive client outcomes (Wampold & Imel, 2015). Now seen as critical to the **common factors** found in all therapies and important to positive client outcomes, the core conditions seem to be a large part of what makes therapy work, in part to their importance in establishing the therapeutic relationship. Clearly, depending on the type of therapy one does, other factors are also important, but there is little doubt today that the core conditions contribute to effective therapy.

Person-centered counseling is seen as one of several approaches from the existential-humanistic school (Neukrug, 2018). A mainstay of this school has been the ideas of Viktor Frankl. Confined to concentration camps for a number of years, Frankl developed his existential therapy, called **logotherapy**, from his experiences in the camps and from his work with suicidal and schizophrenic clients. Frankl's ideas were a great shift from the psychodynamic approaches of Sigmund Freud,

Want to Meet Carl Rogers?

Want to hear a brief biography about Carl Rogers from the man himself and find other tidbits of information about him? Go to https://silver.odu.edu/psyadm/ to see a caricature of Rogers talking about himself and his theory. Click on the existential-humanistic door and go into Rogers's office.

Carl Jung, and others, and they quickly took hold as a new, and more optimistic, approach to the "old school" therapies. In particular, he highlighted the importance of gaining consciousness regarding one's ultimate demise (death) and the importance of making intentional choices in life that define one's sense of purpose and meaning. He suggested that meaning can be found by living authentically, giving to the world through creativity and self-expression, and knowing that a person can choose his or her attitude regardless of the situation with which one is faced (Burton, 2012/2019). Frankl believed that the past impacts who one is today but suggested that counseling should be mostly present- and future-focused as the decisions one makes in the present defines who one is (Winston, 2015).

On the heels of the development of existential therapy was gestalt therapy, and many of the core concepts found in the existential approaches are embedded in this approach. (Batthydiny & Costello, 2015; Conyen, 2015; Perls et al., 1951; Polster & Polster, 1973). Developed by Fritz Perls and others, this approach was more active and directive and employed a number of techniques that often gently, but sometimes not so gently, pushed individuals into experiencing their **now of existence**. Such techniques were designed to help clients resolve **unfinished business**, defined as past unmet needs that subtly influences the behaviors of individuals in ways in which they were unaware. CPCC borrows a few important concepts from gestalt therapy, especially its focus on the present, its belief that unmet needs lead to unfinished business, and that unfinished business can lead to a non-genuine or inauthentic existence. Although gestalt therapy developed a number of techniques to help clients resolve unfinished business, **using now language** and the **empty chair technique** are two techniques often used by the CPCC counselor.

During the 1940s, Abraham Maslow, one of the founders of the humanistic psychology movement, embraced the idea that when placed in an environment that facilitated movement through his **needs hierarchy**, individuals would naturally move toward **self-actualization**. Self-actualization occurs when clients reach their natural potential and embrace such qualities as goodness, wholeness, justice, self-sufficiency and autonomy, spontaneity, and more (Maslow, 1943, 1954). This popular positive approach toward human growth challenged the existing deterministic notions of development held by Freud and others, and his model became world renowned. In particular, his idea that lower order needs, such as food, shelter, and safety, had to be met prior to higher order needs became common. Although his basic positive focus continues to be embraced by many, in more recent years some have suggested that need hierarchies might vary as a function of culture (Kenrick et al., 2010). In either case, the basic idea that certain needs must be addressed remains, and CPCC has borrowed these ideas when working with clients. Sometimes, CPCC suggests that advocacy work is also critical, such as times when clients are facing systemic oppression, discrimination, and racism.

In recent years, solution-focused brief therapy (SFBT) has become popular. This strength-based, positive approach to counseling suggests that counseling should be largely present- or future-oriented and focused on solutions, not problems, and that clients can be seen in a relatively short amount of time (Ellerman, 1999; McAuliffe, 2019). Although CPCC counselors do not practice brief counseling as is done in SFBT, their approach is certainly briefer than the classic psychodynamic approaches. In addition, SFBT offers a number of strength-based questions that can help facilitate client growth and movement toward goals. Such questions as "What would you like to see happen by the end of our counseling sessions?" helps a client re-envision his or her future and can be facilitative in setting goals. Thus, CPCC borrows some of these questions in its model.

Many counselors and therapists learn about person-centered counseling, existential therapy, and gestalt therapy within their training programs; however, today there are few practitioners who are solely person-centered, existential, or gestalt. This chapter presents a modern-day version of what it's like, in the real world, to practice the CPCC approach that borrows many ideas from these therapeutic approaches and also incorporates some ideas from SFBT. This modern approach to person-centered counseling is more realistic, integrates ideas that many practitioners who align with basic existential-humanistic ideas might use, and borrows from other therapies that are in line with basic existential-humanistic philosophy. Let's take a look at CPCC.

VIEW OF HUMAN NATURE

> In my experience I have discovered man to have characteristics which seem inherent in his species, and the terms which have at different times seemed to me descriptive of these characteristics are such terms as positive, forward-moving, constructive, realistic, trustworthy. (Rogers, 1957b, p. 200)

CPCC is a **phenomenological, humanistic, existential**, and **strength-based** counseling approach. From a phenomenological perspective, the counselor accepts the world view of the client and also believes, as the quote just cited states, that the individual is **naturally positive, looking toward the future**, and has the capacity to **construct and reconstruct his or her reality** (Crocker & Philippson, 2005; Moreira, 2012; Rogers, 1980). These counselor characteristics allow the client to freely explore his or her experiences and take the session in the direction he or she chooses. This is why, similar to CPCC's forebearer, **client-centered counseling**, the CPCC counselor uses skills to ensure that the session is **nondirective** and **client-centered.**

Steeped in **humanism**, CPCC is an **anti-deterministic** approach that assumes that individuals have an **actualizing tendency**, which means that, under the right conditions, they will realize their natural or innate talents, abilities, temperament, and ways of being (Bazzano, 2017; Rogers, 1951). Much as the flower, when placed in a fertile environment growth is ensured, but placed in a toxic environment the chance of growth is thwarted. A fertile, or nurturing, environment is one in which the CPCC counselor **honors and respects** his or her clients, shows **acceptance** toward them, utilizes **empathic** responses, and **normalizes rather than pathologizes** their symptoms (Winston, 2015).

CPCC counselors believe it is common for **conditions of worth** to be placed on individuals, often at a very young age, and that this results in individuals acting as others want them to be, rather than being themselves (Bohart, 2017; Rogers, 1959). This occurs because the **need to be regarded** by important individuals in one's life is so powerful that people develop ways of living that are **incongruent** with their **true selves** and become someone they think others want them to be rather than being their **genuine selves.** This **false self** experiences anxiety, depression, neurosis, pathology, or other mental health problems due to the incongruence between one's behaviors and inner sense of who one actually is. But if a trusting therapeutic atmosphere is developed in which a person can clearly see who he or she is, that person can recognize how his or her symptoms are a signal of living a life of **incongruence** or **non-genuineness.**

CPCC recognizes that individuals have **universal needs** (e.g., food, shelter, safety, relationship, self-esteem, and self-actualization) and **repressed needs** (e.g., need to be loved by a parent who was abusive) and that **unmet needs** lead to **unfinished business** (Conyen, 2015; Perls et al., 1951; Polster & Polster, 1973). Thus, one of the roles of the counselor is to address the needs of the client. Since the importance of some needs seem to be impacted by cultural background, understanding the significance of any particular need of the client should be explored (Kenrick et al., 2010). For instance, in some cultures a need for autonomy might take precedence over a need for belonging, or vice versa. When attainment of a need is negatively impacted by systemic oppression, discrimination, and racism, the counselor may take on more of an **advocacy role.**

From an existential perspective, CPCC believes that as individuals increasingly become aware of their incongruence, they can make better **choices** in their lives and live an increasingly **congruent** life, which means that a person's thoughts, feelings, and actions are in sync and the person is living a life in line with his or her natural or innate talents, abilities, temperament, and ways of being (Rogers, 1959, 1961; Winston, 2015). Choices are also intimately related to how individuals make meaning in their lives and define their purpose. Thus, better choices result in a better sense of meaning and purpose in life. In addition, as individuals become more congruent, they are better able to see how choices not only impact self, but also impact the world, thus underscoring the importance of making **responsible choices.**

Finally, CPCC is strength-based because it does not assume there is inherent pathology, or that the past determines the future, and it looks at making positive change in the present and in the future. Rather than harping on past problems, it is a **here and now therapy** that will employ preferred goals and solution-oriented questions in an effort to help the client move forward in a positive manner.

KEY CONCEPTS

Many key concepts basic to CPCC are borrowed, but adapted, from the ideas of Rogers, Frankl, Perls, and Maslow. They include the **actualizing tendency, conditions of worth, symptoms as a message to self, unfinished business, phenomenology, meaning making, choice,** and **universal and repressed needs.**

Actualizing Tendency

Each individual is born with natural or innate talents, abilities, temperament, and ways of being. When a person is placed in an environment that exudes warmth, empathy, and acceptance (called **unconditional positive regard** by Rogers), these attributes will show themselves fully and the individual will develop into his or her **true** or **real self** (Ismail & Tekke, 2015); however, when a person is placed in a toxic environment, such as when conditions of worth are placed on the person, the individual will not actualize himself or herself.

Conditions of Worth

Conditions of worth occur when important people in a person's life subliminally, or overtly, place conditions on how the person should think, act, or feel in life (Proctor, 2017; Rogers, 1959). Since all people have a **need to be regarded by others** (Rogers, 1959), when conditions of worth are placed on them by important people in their lives, they will sometimes act in ways that are at odds with their natural or innate talents, abilities, temperament, and ways of being in order to obtain love and approval from their loved ones. This results in the person developing an **incongruent** or **non-genuine self** (see next section). Incongruence results in anxiety, depression, or other mental health problems (see Box 2.1).

BOX 2.1 JAIME AND CONDITIONS OF WORTH

What follows is the story of Jaime, which although fictitious is similar to a number of stories I have heard from individuals over the years. Identify the conditions of worth that impacted Jaime, and consider other conditions of worth that may impact transgender clients or clients whose gender is different than the male/female binary. Although this is a dramatic example, when you read this vignette keep in mind that conditions of worth can occur with any person and sometimes in very subtle ways.

Jaime's biological sex at birth was male; however, since the time she could speak, she identified as a girl. She loved wearing girl's clothes, played mostly with the girls, and stated, "I am a girl, I am not a boy." At first Jaime's parents thought this was cute, but when Jaime was about three or four, they began to believe there was something wrong with her. At that time they made her wear boy's clothes, would become angry at her when she said she was a girl, and told her she would "get in trouble" if she did "girl things." As Jaime grew older, she continued to see herself as a girl; however, she lived out a life as a boy due to her parents' insistence that she do so. Externally, she acted as a boy, but internally she felt that something was wrong. At times she would forget that she self-identified as a girl, but every once in a while she realized that something was off-kilter. In high school, Jaime began to secretly wear girl's clothes, and after high school she would often have relationships with boys in which she would "act like the girl." Eventually, Jaime married a woman. Although she cared for her wife deeply, she continued to feel as if something was not right and was scared of disclosing her feelings to her wife. After a few years of marriage, Jaime entered counseling. Here, she realized that she had always identified as a girl, that pressure from her parents led her to live out a life as a boy, and that she would never be happy in her current way of living in the world. Slowly, Jaime had to reveal her authentic self to her wife, to her friends, and to her family. This was a slow and painful process but eventually Jaime acknowledged her identity as a transgender female and felt free to be who she was.

Incongruent or Non-Genuine Self

Being incongruent or non-genuine occurs after conditions of worth are placed on a person. In these cases, one's need to be regarded by important people is so great that they act in a manner they believe others want them to act, not in a manner congruent with their thoughts, feelings, and behaviors. Conditions of worth are a product of toxic environments, which occur when others act demeaning, critical, faultfinding, judgmental, blaming, condemning, disapproving, and so forth (Rogers, 1959; Worth & Proctor, 2017). A major goal of CPCC counseling is to help individuals understand the conditions of worth that have been placed on them and to move from an inauthentic, incongruent existence to **authenticity, genuineness,** and **congruence** in relationships.

Symptoms as a Message to Self

When individuals are incongruent, they live antithetical to their innate talents, abilities, temperament, and/or ways of being—and are not their true selves (Ismail & Tekke, 2015). Mild forms of incongruency may be experienced as a slight tug, or minor sense of anxiety, and in subtle ways telegraphs to the person that something is not right in the person's life (Rogers, 1957b). Extreme forms of incongruence can lead to major anxiety, major depression, acting out or acting in, or other serious mental health problems. Since almost all people experience some conditions of worth, either from significant others in their childhood or from their current partners and friends, it is usual for most people to experience some amount of anxiety or uncomfortableness as they try to balance their need to be who they are and their desire for love from important individuals in their lives who are asking them to act in a manner that is not natural for them. When conditions of worth are placed on a person in early childhood and the individual continues to live out those conditions despite the fact that the original perpetrator is no longer around, counseling is needed to help the individual understand that he or she is living an incongruent life as a result of these early conditions.

It is very natural to want another person to act in a manner other than the way that person is acting; however, each attempt to change another person is placing conditions of worth on that person. Thus, in all relationships we find some conditions of worth placed on one another. Through counseling, one can understand the conditions of worth being placed on him or her and develop strategies in relationships to lessen such conditions. When the conditions are relatively minor (e.g., "I like westerns and you want me to like romantic comedies"), individuals might feel a sense of annoyance. Here, individuals can learn to express their opinions and conversations can enhance the relationship as both individuals learn to honor the other and come to a mutual decision when differences arise. But when conditions of worth are great (e.g., "You better not act that way or I'll beat you"), longer term counseling may be needed for both individuals to be able to hear each other. Or, in some cases, an individual may decide to leave a relationship to leave such conditions and demands (see Box 2.2).

BOX 2.2 SYMPTOMS AS A MESSAGE TO YOURSELF

We all have had conditions of worth placed on us, and sometimes they result in symptoms that can range from mild discomfort to great amounts of anxiety and depression. In the space provided, identify people in your life that may have placed conditions of worth on you and any symptoms you struggled with as a result. The following is an example. You may want to share some of these with your classmates.

PERSON	CONDITIONS OF WORTH	SYMPTOMS
Mother	Don't ever get angry	Frustration/Non-communication
Father	Don't hug	Rigidity over touch/anxiety when people get close

Unfinished Business

Unfinished business is the product of **unmet needs,** which leaves an individual feeling unresolved (Mann, 2010; Wollants, 2012). Often, such unmet needs are from earlier in life and are the result of conditions of worth having been placed on an individual. For instance, a person who never experienced love from his father lives with this unmet need of wanting to be loved by him. Usually, such unmet needs fall to the background of experience, yet still impacts one's life in subtle, but powerful ways. To compensate for unmet needs, individuals will devise any of an infinite number of **compensatory strategies** to avoid the pain of not having an important need met. For instance, the person who longs for his or her father's love may drink too much, while another may work too much, or a third may blindly attempt to find a substitute father love figure. Compensatory strategies prevent a person from actualizing his or her real self. Thus, one goal in therapy is to bring unfinished business to the foreground and make efforts to heal the wound left by the unmet need. This leads to an increasingly congruent self.

Phenomenology

CPCC counselors take a phenomenological perspective when working with clients, which means they accept the subjective worldview of the client and do not attach extraneous meaning to what the client is saying (Crocker & Philippson, 2005; Moreira, 2012). In other words, they are not interpreting client actions or thoughts, not assuming what the client says means something other than what they are presenting, and do not judge the client's expression of his or her experiences.

Since most people, including counselors, grow up with certain ways of understanding the world and specific belief systems they assume are correct, adopting a phenomenological stance takes practice and means that one has to let go of one's biases and be a neutral vessel for the client's verbal and nonverbal experiences; that is, they must take in what the client is saying without passing judgement and with the assumption that it is the client's experience of his or her truth. Since this is done for every client, whose experience is different from every other client, the counselor must embrace **relativism**, which assumes that individuals have different truths and that each truth is correct for that individual. This means the counselor has the ability to hear **multiple perspectives** from different clients, and even from the same client, as sometimes clients will see different truths within themselves. Being relativistic usually becomes easier as one is older, more educated, and has been around people and partaken in experiences that help them understand how reality shifts from person to person. There are certainly many younger individuals, however, who are relativistic in their views and older ones who are dualistic and see the world as black or white or wrong and right.

Meaning Making

One of the most important things a human being can do is to create meaning or purpose out of their lives (Batthydiny & Costello, 2015; Frankl, 1946/2014; Rubin, 2015). But such purpose can only be fully accomplished if one understands his or her natural or innate talents, abilities, temperament, and ways of being. Since these attributes are often hidden as a result of conditions of worth and the resulting incongruent self that is formed, individuals can only begin to make meaningful choices after they have identified their true selves—see who they actually are. Once this is accomplished, new and more meaningful choices can be made. In addition, individuals who become more congruent begin to see the natural connection between the choices they make for themselves and how such choices impact others, and ultimately, the world. Similar to the concept of karma, poor choices lead to negative consequences while choices from a congruent self lead to positive consequences. Also, positive consequences get passed along and impact many others—perhaps more than one might acknowledge (see Box 2.3).

BOX 2.3 BUTTERFLY EFFECT

In 1972, meteorologist Edward Lorenz gave a talk in which he presented evidence that the flapping of a seagull's wing in Brazil could cause a tornado in Texas (Hilbon, 2000). Somehow, this later became known as the "butterfly effect" and changed to how the wings of a butterfly could affect the weather in the United States. In either case, the point was that the smallest action in a part of the world could affect others in another part of the world. Having consciousness that every action we take will affect those around us, and very likely impact the world in some fashion, is a monumental weight that carries with it a humbling responsibility. It is only by embracing this concept, however, that we can have true peace and harmony in the world. It is only when each of us come to believe in the butterfly effect that we can realize the effects of our actions on others.

Choice

As individuals become increasingly aware of their incongruence, they consider ways in which they can live a more genuine and meaningful life (Rogers, 1961). Thus, they take actions that better match their real selves. This can include a wide variety of changes in their lives, such as embracing a new, more congruent identity (e.g., a person who has hidden his or her sexual orientation, decides to "come out"), asserting oneself in relationships (e.g., a person who always deferred to his or her partner, starts to state his or her preferences), initiating new dialogues with people with whom one is close (e.g., suggesting to a close friend that he or she no longer use toxic language toward others or that they share more meaningful aspects of their lives with each other), becoming involved with causes indicative of social responsibility that match their beliefs (e.g., joining the Sierra Club or advocating for civil rights issues). Carl Rogers noted that as a person becomes increasingly congruent, his or her choices become clearer, as if there were no choice (Winston, 2015). This person is so in tune with his or her real self, clarity about one's choices are self-evident.

UNIVERSAL AND REPRESSED NEEDS

Universal Needs

In the middle of the 20th century, Abraham Maslow (1943, 1954) suggested there was a hierarchy of universal human needs and that individuals have a tendency to seek unmet lower order needs prior to higher order needs (Figure 2.1). Although research over the years suggests that need hierarchies may vary cross-culturally and that other needs may be also be important (e.g., affiliation, parenting, and so forth) (Kenrick et al., 2010), understanding the needs of an individual in determining treatment strategies is critical.

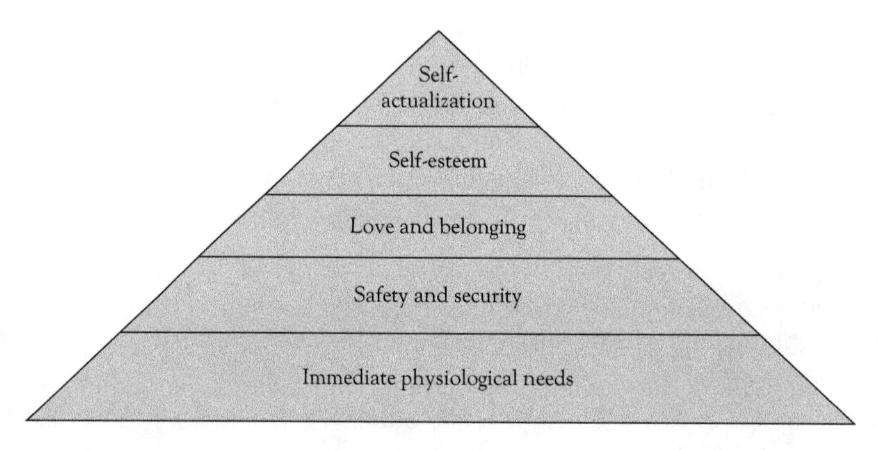

Figure 2.1 Maslow's Hierarchy of Needs

Universal needs can be fluid, in the sense that one may be working on what Maslow considered a higher order need (e.g., high self-esteem, self-actualization) at one point in one's life, then, at a later point, find oneself struggling with what he called lower order needs (physiological and safety needs: shelter, hunger, and so forth). Counselors should determine a client's personal need hierarchy and set goals based on the needs of the individual. A client who does not have shelter may need a referral to a specific social service agency, be taught how to advocate for self, or have the counselor advocate for the client to help gain such shelter. Clients struggling with low self-esteem, on the other hand, most likely need more traditional counseling.

Repressed Needs

Sometimes, important individuals in a person's life will place conditions of worth on an individual that result in that individual repressing a need. In this case, a need is pushed out of awareness, to what some may call the "unconscious" (Yonteff, 1976). For instance, a child who experiences himself or herself as gay, who is told not to be that way, may have his or her need for same-sex companionship repressed in an effort to gain approval from a significant person in the individual's life. Through counseling, the individual can regain the part of self that has been repressed and begin to live a more authentic life.

TECHNIQUES

A number of techniques borrowed from person-centered counseling, existential therapy, gestalt therapy, solution-focused therapy, and other related therapies are used by the CPCC counselor.

These include **honoring and respecting, normalizing not pathologizing, acceptance, empathy, authenticity, the use of questions** (clarifying, tentative, and preferred goals and solution-oriented), **affirmation and encouragement, using "now" language, the empty chair technique, identifying choices and goal setting, offering advice and saying what you think**, and **other techniques.**

Honoring and Respecting

Honoring and respecting clients are ways that counselors demonstrate to their clients that they are valued and appreciated for the unique paths they have taken and will take in life (Gold, 2008; Jansson, 2016; Sung & Dunkle, 2009). Such respect is created by a counselor being friendly, warm, nonjudgmental, and positive (Hough, 2014), and is demonstrated via accepting eye contact, reassuring "uh-huhs," a nodding of the head that says "I'm with you—I understand," other nonverbal or short verbal statements acknowledging that the client is valued, and being a good listener. To understand what it is like to honor and respect a client, consider how you might act if placed in an unfamiliar culture and wanted to show respect for the differences you were about to experience.

Normalizing Not Pathologizing

An offshoot of honoring and respecting a client is the process of normalizing client symptoms rather than pathologizing them (Winston, 2015). Clients will often present with a mixture of symptoms, which can frequently be found in the Diagnostic and Statistical Manual-5 (DSM-5). Instead of automatically going to the DSM-5, the CPCC counselor understands that clients' symptoms are a natural, functional, and rational response to conditions of worth and other life problems clients have faced (Bohart, 2017). This does not deny potential biological and genetic causes of mental illness but adds another dimension to their potential causes. For instance, what may be seen as "resistance" by some counselors is viewed as a needed way the client brings himself or herself into the relationship due to past experiences. Thus, in this context, resistance is understood and even cherished by the counselor. Similarly, the depressed client's sadness is seen as a message to the person about his or her life, not a sign that there is something inherently wrong with the client or that he or she can never get better. Or, the cynical client is seen as a person who has a reason for being skeptical, and that the helper's goal is to understand why the client has this attitude and to respect it. Accepting clients in all of their feelings and attitudes, understanding the context in which clients have lived, and having a desire to help clients are the goals of the counselor.

Acceptance

Acceptance is the ability to allow others to express their points of view and not feel a need to change others. Called **unconditional positive regard** by Rogers (1957a), individuals who are accepting are **nonjudgmental** and **nondogmatic**, open to understanding the views of others, open to feedback, and even open to changing their perception of the world after hearing other perspectives. Such individuals can accept people in their differences, regardless of dissimilar cultural heritage, values, or beliefs. Lack of acceptance, on the other hand, prevents one from listening and usually results in a person trying to change the other. Beginning counselors often must practice being accepting as their own views and biases will creep into the conversation. However, as counselors become more seasoned, they are better able to separate their personal values from the counseling relationship and offer a nonjudgmental atmosphere, which allows clients the freedom to say whatever is on their mind. Acceptance is demonstrated by listening that is not infiltrated by the personal views of the listener. Not surprisingly, research shows a relationship between acceptance and the ability to be a good listener, and as you might expect, acceptance leads to positive client outcomes (Laska et al., 2014).

Empathy

> The state of empathy, or being empathic, is to perceive the internal frame of reference of another with accuracy and with the emotional components and meanings which pertain thereto as if one were the person, but without ever losing the "as if" condition. (Rogers, 1959, pp. 210–211)

Viewed as both a skill and as a quality to embrace, empathy is seen as the most valuable tool a CPCC can use. Empathic individuals have a deep understanding of another person's point of view, and can feel, sense, and taste the flavor of another person's experience (Bayne & Neukrug, 2017). Also, empathic people communicate their understanding of the person's experience to them accurately. Empathy is critical to the counseling relationship as it builds the working alliance and helps to elicit information from the client (Egan & Reese, 2019). Research bears out the importance of being empathic as it has consistently shown empathy to be one of the most powerful factors in producing positive client outcomes, regardless of the theory used (Elliot et al., 2011; Laska et al., 2014; Norcross, 2011). Although adapted for use by most theories today, empathy continues to be most associated with the existential-humanistic theories, particularly classic person-centered counseling, because of the importance these approaches place on taking a phenomenological perspective with clients.

The popularity of Rogers's work during the 20th century, and his emphasis on the use of empathy, led to the development of a number of scales to measure empathy. One particular instrument, the *Carkhuff Scale*, has been widely used over the years (Carkhuff, 2009; Cormier, Nurius, & Osborn, 2013, Neukrug, 2017b; Neukrug, 2019). The Carkhuff Scale ranges from a low of 1.0 to a high of 5.0, with .5 increments. Any response below a 3.0 is considered **subtractive** or non-empathic, responses that are around a Level 3 are often called **basic empathy,** and responses over 3.0 are called **additive** or **advanced empathy** (Figure 2.2).

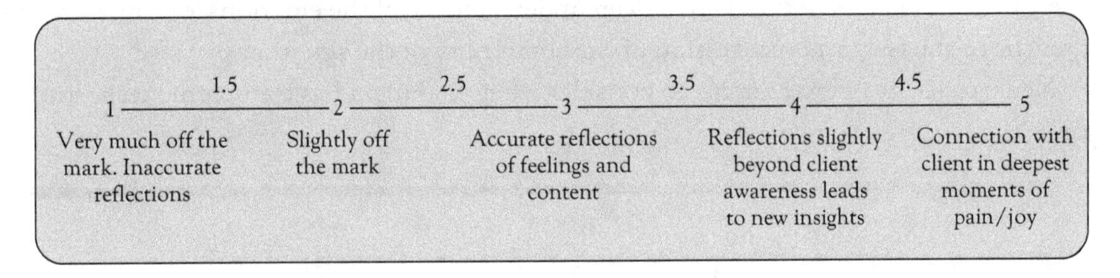

Figure 2.2 The Carkhuff Scale

The Carkhuff Scale defines Level 1 and Level 2 responses as detracting from what the person is saying (e.g., advice giving, reflecting inaccurate feelings or content), with a Level 1 response being way off the mark and a Level 2 only slightly off. On the other hand, a Level 3 response accurately reflects the affect and meaning of what the client has said. Levels 4 and 5 responses reflect feelings and meaning beyond what the person is saying and offer new awareness about a client's feeling or thinking state (Neukrug, 2017). For instance, look at the Level 1, 2, 3, and 4 responses to the following client.

Client: "I don't know what's wrong with me. I'm anxious all the time, have heart palpitations, becoming a recluse, and scared of talking with almost anyone. I'm a mess."

Level 1
Counselor: "Well, you need to get your life in order so you can get through this" (advice giving and being judgmental).

Level 2
Counselor: "Sounds like you're dealing with some stress right now" (does not reflect the intensity of the feeling and is not specific enough about the content).

Level 3
Counselor: "You are really going through a lot right now. You're feeling intense anxiety, and I hear what a struggle it has been to even talk with people." (accurately reflects the feelings and content of the person)

Level 4

Counselor: "It sounds like you're really distressed and increasingly finding yourself isolating from everyone else" (this introduces a new feeling—"isolated"—which the client didn't outwardly state, but is indeed feeling, and brings to awareness something that had been slightly out of consciousness).

Level 5 responses, which are generally made in long-term therapeutic relationships with expert helpers, express to the client a deep understanding of the emotions (e.g., intense pain or joy) he or she feels and recognition of the complexity of the situation.

Neukrug (2019) offers 12 items to consider when making a basic empathic response (see Box 1.1).

BOX 2.4 KEYS TO MAKING BASIC (LEVEL 3) EMPATHIC RESPONSE

1. Reflect back feelings accurately.
2. Reflect back content accurately.
3. If client talks for a lengthy amount of time, reflect back most poignant feelings and content only.
4. Use paraphrasing and similar words as the client.
5. Use language attuned to the client's level of understanding.
6. Do not add new feelings or new content.
7. Do not respond with a question (e.g., "Sounds like you're feeling bad about the situation?").
8. Do not make the response too lengthy (keep it to about one sentence or two short sentences).
9. Do not hypothesize or make guesses about what the client is saying.
10. If the client verbally or nonverbally says your response is "off," assume it is and move on.
11. Do not ask, "Is this correct?" (or something akin to that) at the end of your sentence (but listen to the client's response; you'll know if it's correct).
12. Don't get caught up thinking about the next response—you'll have trouble listening to the client.

The best empathic responses are made when the client can most readily absorb the helper's reflections. For instance, one might sense a deep sadness or anger in a client and reflect these feelings to him or her; however, if the client is not ready to accept these feelings, then the timing is off and the response is considered subtractive. But make the same response when the client can take it in, and to which the client says, "Yes, exactly—that's how I feel," and the helper has provided the client with a new understanding of himself or herself.

CREATIVE AND NOVEL EMPATHIC RESPONSES

Whereas basic empathic responses are straightforward reflections of feelings and content, creative and novel empathic responses are the pizzazz of empathic responses (Bayne & Neukrug, 2017; Neukrug, 2017; Neukrug et al., 2012). These responses offer innovative ways of reflecting feelings and content and sometimes are taken in by the client in different neural pathways than the traditional verbal response. Such responses can have a long-term effect upon individuals. Well-made creative and novel empathic responses are at least a 3.0 on the Carkhuff Scale and will often be higher. Not only do these types of responses give clients new ways of examining their situations, they are often the pre-cursor to developing new goals. Neukrug (2017; Neukrug et al., 2012) has identified 10 ways of making creative and novel empathic responses, including (1) *reflecting nonverbal behaviors*, (2) *reflecting deeper feelings*, (3) *pointing out conflictual feelings or thoughts*, (4) *using visual imagery*, (5) *using analogies*, (6) *using metaphors*, (7) *using targeted self-disclosure*, (8) *reflecting tactile responses*, (9) *using media*, and (10) *using discursive responses*, which is bringing known client historical events into a response. Very brief examples of these can be found in Table 2.1. Keep in mind that to understand these responses in their entirety, the longer context of the client situation needs to be heard.

TABLE 2.1 EXAMPLES OF CREATIVE AND NOVEL EMPATHIC RESPONSES.

	CREATIVE AND NOVEL EMPATHIC RESPONSES
Reflecting Nonverbal Behaviors	*Client:* Client sits across from counselor, wringing his hands and looking all over the room. *Counselor:* "Your hands and general demeanor are telling me you must be feeling pretty anxious."
Reflecting Deeper Feelings	*Client:* "I'm really sad that my daughter won't listen to me." *Counselor:* "I hear your sadness, but it seems like you're pretty angry at her too." [Note: response based on other things client said and client nonverbals.]
Point Out Conflictual Feelings or Thoughts	*Client:* "I've been at this job a long time, and I still love coming to work, but I often think about other things I could be doing." *Counselor:* "So, on one hand, you feel settled in and grounded at your job, on the other hand, you wonder if there is something else for you out there."

(Continued)

TABLE 2.1 (CONTINUED)

	CREATIVE AND NOVEL EMPATHIC RESPONSES
Using Visual Imagery	*Client:* "Everyone relies on me—they all seem to get easily flustered, but they know they can come to me as a sounding board." *Counselor:* "I see you as the wise person, sitting in a special large chair, and people coming to you for advice."
Using Analogies	*Client:* "I keep trying to make changes, but nothing works. I'm really trying hard." *Counselor:* "It's kind of like you're swimming upstream and not making any progress."
Using Metaphors	*Client:* "We care about each other so much and have been together so long, but still argue a lot." *Counselor:* "Sometimes love is a battleground."
Using Targeted Self-Disclosure	*Client:* "My sister is constantly angry and bitter with me. I just can't have a conversation with her—I just get angry back." *Counselor:* "You know, I used to have a similar situation with my brother. That can be rather frustrating."
Reflecting Tactile Responses	*Client:* "They all want so much from me. I just can't handle all of their constant need for help." *Counselor:* "You know, when you talk to me about this, I can feel this weight on my shoulders. I kind of think this is how you must feel."
Using Media	*Client:* "They treat me like I'm the only person of color to have ever done well at this job before. It's so demeaning. I just feel like they're always watching me." *Counselor:* "It reminds me the response some had to the most recent *Little Mermaid* movie. ... Like, people suddenly think its extraordinary for a person of color to play a mermaid."
Discursive Responses	*Client:* "No matter what I say, I feel like it's going to end up in a fight." *Counselor:* "Kind of reminds me of what always happened with your parents. It seems like you're always reliving that picture in your mind."

Authenticity

Carl Rogers noted the importance of being authentic or genuine with clients within the context of the counseling relationship, sometimes through **self-disclosure**. Two main types of self-disclosure include **self-disclosing statements** and **self-involving statements**. Self-disclosing statements involve sharing personal experiences or information with clients, such as when a counselor who has had a similar medical procedure as a client shares that information.

This can help a client feel closer to the counselor and the counselor and client can discuss common issues related to the medical issue. Self-disclosure should occur as a way to solidify the therapeutic alliance, not to help the counselor feel better. Self-involving statements are an aspect of **immediacy**, disclosing feelings or reactions toward clients in the present moment (Yalom, 2002; Sturges, 2012). Thus, if a counselor consistently feels concerned, irritated, upset, or even angry at a client, the counselor would share those feelings through a self-involving statement. This authenticity is similar to the **I-Thou relationship** that many existential therapists talk about (Buber, 1923/1970; Rubin & Lichtanski, 2015; van Deurzen, 2012; Yalom, 2002), which is indicative of a direct, immediate, real, and open relationship with another person. Significantly, Rogers noted it is important to *not* talk about certain feelings in the moment with a client. Rogers, and others, saw the counseling relationship as one which the client initially comes to with little knowledge of his or her inner world, or with lack of trust to share his or her inner world. Over time, as the counselor builds trust by being accepting and showing empathy, the client begins to "peel away the layers of the onion" that have been protecting the client's inner self. Slowly the client shares deeper parts of self. Thus, what the counselor initially experiences is an outer shell of the person, not the inner transparent self. While one can be angry at the outer shell, one is never angry at the inner transparent parts of a person. That is why Rogers suggests that if a counselor feels negatively toward a client, he or she should wait a period of time before expressing those feelings as they very likely will dissipate as the inner shell is revealed. Yalom (2002) suggests that all self-involving statements should pass one test: Is the disclosure for the benefit of the client? But if a counselor continues to feel that way, it would be important to share those feelings as a form of self-involving disclosure—otherwise the relationship would be earmarked as inauthentic.

The Use of Questions

Since CPCC counseling is client-centered, only questions that can maintain the sanctify of a client-centered relationship are used. Thus, "why questions," or questions that are directive ("How about talking to your wife about that?"), are rarely used. Certain questions, however, can assist the counselor in better understanding the client's situations and can gently nudge the client toward new insights. They include clarifying questions, tentative questions, and preferred goals and solution-oriented questions (Neukrug, 2019).

Clarifying Questions

Sometimes, when a counselor thinks he or she may understand a client's situation, but is not sure, a tentative question can be asked. For instance, to a teenager who says he is constantly angry at his parents, the counselor who is unsure about the reason for the anger might say:

> *Counselor:* "I'm wondering if your anger toward your parents is related to the fact that they're always telling you what to do?"

Tentative questions fall nicely on the ears of clients, and are often one step away from being empathic responses. Clearly, if the counselor felt sure about her response, she could have responded empathically: "It sounds like your anger is related to the fact that your parents are always telling you what to do." A tentative question is not confrontational but does help to gently push the session along.

Preferred Goals and Solution-Oriented Questions

Preferred goals and solution-oriented questions help clients look to the future and identify ways in which they would want their lives to look. Although these questions had their origins with solution-focused brief therapy (SFBT), in CPCC counseling they are generally used after clients have spent some time understanding the reasons they have lived a non-genuine or incongruent life and are ready to move toward authenticity in their relationships. The classic solution-oriented question is the miracle question:

> Suppose that one night, while you were asleep, there was a miracle and this problem was solved. How would you know? What would be different? (de Shazer, 1988, p. 5)

Other solution-oriented questions may be:

- How would your life look different if you were not depressed or anxious (or ________)?
- If you were given a magic pill that somehow made everything better, what would your life look like?
- If you could change anything so you would feel better, how would things be different?
- When is the problem not a problem? What are you doing differently at those times?

Some typical preferred goals questions include:

- What would you want to be doing differently if things were getting better for you?
- How will you know when things are getting different and better?
- How would you act differently in the future, if coming here has been worthwhile for you?
- If your life was better in one month, six months, or a year, what would be happening?

Affirmation and Encouragement

Whether called "reinforcement" or a "genuine positive response," affirmations are an important aspect of acknowledging a client's actions and positive move toward change, and if done well and at the correct moment, can be a significant tool for raising a client's self-esteem (Dean, 2015; Lively, 2014: Wong, 2015). Statements such as "Good job," "You are lovable and capable," or "You are a good person" help the client feel supported and worthwhile. Other statements and behaviors, such as saying, "Well done!" "I'm happy for you," and giving caring handshakes, warm hugs, and approving smiles, are other effective ways of communicating affirmation. Affirmations are a natural part of all healthy relationships and are ways that individuals acknowledge positive aspects of others.

Wong (2015) suggests that encouragement is "the expression of affirmation through language or other symbolic representations [e.g., nonverbal gestures] to instill courage, perseverance, confidence, inspiration, or hope in a person(s) within the context of addressing a challenging situation or realizing a potential" (p. 183). Thus, encouragement picks up from affirmation and takes it one step further by helping a client achieve a specific goal. You can see why encouragement can also be vital tool for raising a client's self-esteem. Encouragement includes statements such as "I know you can do it," "Just keep trying," "You've made a great start," and so forth. Within the helping relationship, encouragement is generally focused on being a cheerleader for a client while he or she attempts to reach identified goals.

Using 'Now' Language

Clients can easily move away from their experience by using **there and then language** or by talking "about" something that occurred, and counselors can help to redirect their focus to the present—what some call **here and now language.** Sometimes, in an effort to have clients experience the present, therapists will ask such questions as "What are you experiencing or feeling now?" or "Where are you feeling that in your body?" And, when clients begin to talk about the past, the counselor can redirect the client by asking him or her to bring the past into the present. Therefore, if I were to begin to talk about the death of my mother and how I wish I had been there when she had died, the CPCC counselor could say, "Why don't you have a conversation with your mother now, and tell her how you feel about not being with her when she died?" Oftentimes, when dialoging with another person, the counselor may use the empty chair technique that follows.

Empty Chair Technique

Since much of one's unfinished business has to do with unmet needs or conditions of worth related to important people in a client's life, having an opportunity to talk with an individual associated with this unfinished business can help resolve the issue (Perls et al., 1951). Thus, whether alive or dead, a person can be figuratively brought into a room and a present-centered conversation can occur between the client and the individual. This can sometimes be done via the empty chair technique in which the client will talk to an empty chair as if the person were seated there (Conyne, 2015). Here, clients can imagine the person sitting in the empty chair and can be prompted by such therapist statements as "Tell __________ what you're feeling," "What is it like to talk with __________?," and "What do you need to say to __________?" Let's take a look at the following conversation between a young man and his mom, who has passed away.

Joshua: "Mom, I know my siblings always said you loved me best, but I never felt loved by you."

Joshua: "I wish you had said 'I love you' and showed me your love. I felt like you showed me love in other ways, like cooking and taking care of me, but never felt it from your directly" (Joshua becomes tearful).

Counselor: "Johsua, tell your mother why you're so sad."

Joshua: "Mom, I feel like I missed out on so much from you and that I'm always looking for love from women because I never felt it from you."

You can see how the dialogue can continue, and sometimes, the counselor might ask Joshua how his mother would respond. Sometimes the empty chair techniques can also be done with different parts of oneself. For instance, imagine the person who struggles with introversion, who can have a dialogue with himself or herself—one part playing the introvert and one playing the extrovert. Similarly, Boccone (2016) suggests that bisexual individuals struggling with internalized biphobia can use the technique to address confusion resulting from biphobia and to successfully understand the different parts of one's sexual identity development.

Identifying Choices and Goal Setting

As clients increasingly become more congruent and authentic, they realize that their life of inauthenticity has led them to choices that reinforce their inauthentic way of living. As clients are wanting to become real and embrace their more natural or innate talents, abilities, temperament, and ways of being, new choices will have to be made along with associated goals. Such goals are usually a natural outgrowth of the therapeutic process, though counselors can facilitate the decision-making process by making preferred goals or solution-oriented questions:

- "It seems you're ready to make some changes in your life. Any thoughts on what those might be?"
- "How would you like to move ahead at this point, now that you realize you'd like to live differently?"
- "If you could make any changes in your life, what might they be?"
- "You've identified some important ideals for yourself, how would you like to move forward toward them?"

Ultimately, goal setting in CPCC is a collaborative process in the sense that counselors help clients determine goals through open conversations with them about which goals should be identified and how those goals can be accomplished (Smull, 2007). Although counselors may offer advice, they always do so tentatively and defer to the client based on the client's preferences. Once goals are decided upon and actions to reach the goals are agreed to, it is important for counselors to encourage clients toward their goals and affirm them when they make progress. Counselors should inquire whether goals have been accomplished—and if not, counselors and clients should reconsider the goals. If the goals seem on target, clients can again be encouraged to move forward with them. If not, new goals can be established.

Offering Advice and Saying What You Think

The CPCC counselor does feel comfortable offering advice to the client and telling the client what he or she thinks, though this is done very gently. This is because the counselor has developed a deep understanding of the client and has a good sense of when the client might be involved in behaviors not helpful to the client—that is, does not match the manner in which the client wants to live. For instance, this might be a typical counselor-client dialogue:

> *Client:* "Last night I was so angry at my wife, that I started to yell at her, then decided just to leave and have some beers."
>
> *Counselor:* "Well, first I hear how angry you were, yet I know how much you love her. And, I also know that, as we've talked before, drinking is not something that is good for you or something that you want to do."
>
> *Client:* "Yeah, I was pretty upset at myself for drinking. Actually, upset that I got so angry and not able to work things out amenably. I think my 'old self' just got a hold of me. I'm going to try and get back on track."
>
> *Counselor:* I hear you—you don't want to be that old self anymore, and it's kind of like you had a slip. But, I'm also hearing you want to be someone different; someone who you think is more your image of who you really are."
>
> *Client:* "Yes, that's it exactly."

You can see that in CPCC, offering advice is very indirect. Here, it is just reminding the client that he doesn't want to drink and suggesting that he wants to be someone different. Offering advice and saying what you think can facilitate a client's desire to focus on his or her goals. Counselors should feel free to be authentic, in this manner, but always remember that the main focus of counseling is on empathy and being nondirective.

Other Techniques

CPCC counselors feel free to integrate other techniques into the counseling relationships. These techniques, however, should help the client understand his or her true or real self, stay within the framework of being nondirective and client-focused, come from an existential and humanistic perspective, and, of course, be helpful in assisting the client to reach his or her goals.

THE COUNSELING PROCESS

Although there is no one way that clients go through CPCC, there is a general direction that many will experience. The following represents the general flow of CPCC:

Initial Sessions of Counseling

Clients that first come to a CPCC counselor experience a warm, accepting, and empathic person who is open to hearing about the client's life and emotional concerns. The counselor honors and respects clients and identifies problematic behaviors, although they are normalized, not pathologized. Thus, clients are not viewed as having something inherently wrong with them.

Early in Counseling

This phase of counseling is mostly focused on developing the working alliance. Thus, the counselor will mostly use empathy and be accepting and nonjudgmental with clients. Clarifying and tentative questions will be used to more clearly understand clients' situations. As this stage continues, clients begin to feel more comfortable with the relationship and more at ease with sharing deeper aspects of self. This allows clients to understand the conditions of worth placed on them and their resulting unmet needs and unfinished business.

Middle Phase of Counseling

As the relationship continues, clients becomes increasingly in touch with their incongruence and its sources. At this point, using now language, the empty chair technique, or other techniques can be used to assist clients in illuminating these sources. As clients increasingly understand their incongruence, they will realize that choices were made based on the need to please others and clients begin to want to live a more congruent and authentic life and make choices more in line with their true selves.

Later Phase of Counseling

As clients increasingly identify their true selves, new choices congruent with that self are made. Thus, clients identify goals in line with this new, authentic self. To facilitate this process, preferred goals and solution-oriented questions can be used. As clients continue in counseling and increasingly reach their goals, they will tend to see themselves acting differently. At times, the counselor may give advice or share thoughts about the client's situation, but this is always when the counselor is fairly confident that clients are veering off of their desired path. Offering advice and saying what one thinks should be done infrequently and carefully. At this point, counselors may also integrate other techniques that will help facilitate client understanding of self or attainment of goals, though these techniques should be congruent with a nondirective, client-centered, existential-humanistic, and collaborative approach.

As clients continue in counseling, they will increasingly feel more real and authentic, experience a sense of empowerment, have an easier time asserting their true selves, be more willing to take risks in relationships, be more empathic, and increasingly rely on themselves in making important decisions in life. Eventually, they will feel confident enough to be themselves and rely less on others, including the counselor. At this point, counseling can end. (see Box 2.5)

BOX 2.5 JAKE WITH A CPCC COUNSELOR

Your instructor might have you view Jake with a counselor who uses an integrative approach to counseling, combining some basic person-centered counseling techniques with related existential-humanistic techniques. After you view the video, consider how effective the counselor was at doing this and reflect on whether you believe it would be better if a counselor practiced a "pure" approach (e.g., strictly person-centered, existential, etc.) or an integrative approach.

SOCIAL AND CULTURAL ISSUES

The practice of CPCC, in theory, suggests that it could be applied to most clients. This is because the nature of the CPCC relationship is one in which acceptance of client truth and empathy for the client's experience takes precedence over the counselor's values or social mores. There may be times, however, when such an approach is not helpful. Using common sense, one should probably be wary, or at least careful, when applying a CPCC under the following circumstances:

- *When the client is from a culture that extols external advice, or religious doctrine, and eschews an internal locus of control.* CPCC is contraindicated when clients come from cultures in which religious scripture, moral truths, societal values, advice from others, or parental dictates are more important than the development of an independent self (Al-Thani, 2012).
- *When therapy needs to be brief and focused.* Although not necessarily as lengthy as the psychodynamic approaches, CPCC is not considered brief therapy. Thus, if a client is wanting a brief approach, this may not be the best therapy to use.

- *When being in touch with feelings is frowned upon by the client or within the client's culture.* Being accepting, showing respect, being empathic, and being client-centered lends itself to the expression of feelings. Some individuals, or cultures, frown on the expression of feelings and these individuals would most likely struggle more with this type of an approach than some others that do not focus as much on feelings (Guo & Hanley, 2014).
- *When the presenting problem does not lend itself to the person-centered approach.* Research shows that some problems may be best served by other forms of therapy. For instance, "anxiety disorders, somatoform disorders, bulimia, anger control problems, and general stress" seem to be best treated through cognitive behavioral therapy (Hofman, et al., 2012). Thus, although CPCC may be an adjunct to these therapies, or a therapy to be involved in after the presenting problem has been addressed, CPCC very likely is not the first treatment of choice in these cases. Counselors should know the efficacy of different therapeutic approaches with varying presenting problems and when CPCC would be the therapy of first choice.
- *When the counselor's cognitive complexity is not evolved.* Cognitive complex counselors, such as counselors who think in complex ways and view the world from multiple perspectives, are more likely to be good at expressing empathy and hearing others (Youngvorst & Jones, 2017). Counselors who are dualistic and unable to take on multiple perspectives, however, may lack empathy and unconditional positive regard and have difficulty understating a client's situation.
- *When the cultural competence of the counselor is lacking.* As with cognitive complexity, lack of cultural competence will prevent counselors from being fully engaged with their clients and hinder the ability to show empathy (Shallcross, 2013).

EFFICACY

During the 1940s and 1950s, Rogers obtained a series of grants that would allow he and his staff members at the University of Chicago Counseling Center to become some of the first researchers to examine client change (Kirschenbaum, 1979, 2009). The researchers completed a series of experimental studies, with control groups, that included the use of what was called the **Q-sort technique**. Here, they examined a wide range of outcomes related to what was then called client-centered counseling. In particular, they found that client-centered counseling had success at reducing the gap between how clients actually saw themselves (their **self-concept**) and how they wanted to be (their **ideal concept**). Although criticized as being methodologically weak by some, this research was seen as groundbreaking, as it was the first to use client self-report, along with client tapes and transcripts of sessions, to examine client change. Although CPCC is not the same as person-centered counseling, there are enough parallels that would lead one to assume that the efficacy in one would be similar in the other.

Similar to person-centered counseling, CPCC has a large emphasis on the working alliance, and in recent years this has been shown to be one of the driving forces in positive client outcomes (Hilsenroth, 2014; Wampold, & Budge, 2012; Wampold & Imel, 2015). In fact, the elements that seem to be most important in the working alliance are empathy, acceptance, and genuineness. Research that specifically focuses on the use of empathy has shown it to be the most critical factor for effective client outcomes (Elliot et al., 2011; Laska et al., 2014; Norcross, 2011). The use of empathy may have some limitations, however, and its value may be contingent on: (1) the stage of the counseling relationship (more important in relationship-building stages), (2) the kind of client problem (e.g., depression, low self-esteem), (3) the ability of the clinician to be empathic, (4) the cognitive complexity of the clinician, and (5) the ability of the client to recognize empathy (e.g., a person who is psychotic may not have this capacity). Similarly, research on congruence (authenticity) also shows it to be an important aspect of the therapeutic process (Kolden, et al., 2018).

Person-centered counseling has shown to be as efficacious as other forms of therapy (Elliott, 2013), and with CPCC being an offshoot of pure person-centered counseling, it very likely will fare well in clinical studies. But the efficacy of CPCC is probably limited in certain cases. For instance, as noted under the section on social and cultural issues, CPCC is probably not as efficacious when working with an individual who is less likely to want to express emotions, comes from a collectivist culture that stresses external locus of control, delivered by a counselor with low cognitive complexity, and for individuals looking for brief therapy. It is also recommended that it should not be used when other treatment modalities have clearly shown better efficacy in treating certain problems; however, in that it shares many of the basic tenets of person-centered counseling, it is probably efficacious for a wide range of other problems and as effective as psychodynamic and cognitive behavioral approaches (Jacobs & Reupert, 2014; Sa'ad et al., 2014). Clearly, for issues such as depression, embedded anxiety disorders, relationship concerns, and self-esteem issues, person-centered counseling would often be the treatment of choice.

SUMMARY

CPCC is a phenomenological, humanistic, existential, and strength-based counseling approach. Many of the ideas of CPCC are derived from Carl Rogers's person-centered counseling, Frits Perls's gestalt therapy, the humanistic ideas of Abraham Maslow, and the strength-based approach of solution-focused brief therapy (SFBT).

As a phenomenologically based approach, CPCC counselors accept the subjective worldview of the client and do not attach extraneous meaning to what the client is saying. CPCC is naturally positive, looks toward the future, and assumes that individuals can construct and reconstruct their realities. A client-centered and nondirective approach, it is also anti-deterministic and assumes that people have an actualizing tendency. This means, under the right conditions, that they can actualize their natural or innate talents, abilities, temperament, and ways of being. The counselor who practices this approach honors and respects their clients, shows acceptance toward them, are empathic with them, and normalizes rather than pathologizes their symptoms.

CPCC believes that it is common for conditions of worth to be placed upon people, often at a young age, which results in people acting as others want them to be rather than individuals being their true or real selves. Rogers called this incongruence or non-genuineness. It is also known as an inauthentic way of living. People live incongruently because they have a need to be regarded by important people in their lives and this need takes precedence over their actualizing tendency, and they thus live a life that reflects how others want them to be, rather than who they actually are.

CPCC also believes that individuals have universal needs and repressed needs, and that unmet needs lead to unfinished business that press on a person in ways that are out of consciousness, yet still impacting them in their lives. Thus, it is the role of the counselor to assess these unmet needs and help clients resolve them. When attainment of a need is negatively impacted by systemic oppression, discrimination, and racism the counselor may take on more of an advocacy role.

In CPCC, as clients increasingly realize their incongruence and become more in touch with their real selves, they are better able to make choices that match their innate talents, abilities, temperament, and ways of being. They also realize the importance of making choices that positively impact the world. Rather than harping on past problems, CPCC is a here and now therapy that will employ preferred goals and solution-oriented questions in an effort to help the client move forward in a positive manner as they increasingly make better choices that match their true selves. To highlight the theory and its ideas, a number of key concepts were expounded upon in this chapter, including the actualizing tendency, the incongruent or non-genuine self, conditions of worth, symptoms as a message to self, unfinished business, phenomenology, meaning making, choice, and universal and repressed needs.

Certain techniques are used by CPCC counselors that underscore its phenomenological, humanistic, existential, and strength-based underpinnings. These include honoring and respecting, normalizing not pathologizing, acceptance, empathy, authenticity, the use of questions (clarifying, tentative, and preferred goals and solution-oriented), affirmation and encouragement, using "now" language, the empty chair technique, identifying choices and goal setting, offering advice and saying what you think, and other techniques.

We next talked about a general flow or direction that is seen in CCPC counseling. This includes the initial sessions in which the client experiences a warm, accepting, and empathic counselor who honors and respects the client while normalizing symptoms and not pathologizing. Next, in the early part of counseling, the focus is mostly on developing the working alliance, mostly by using empathy and being nonjudgmental. In the middle phase, the client increasingly gets in touch with his or her incongruence and more active techniques can be used (e.g., using now language, the empty chair technique). As counseling continues into the later phase, the client increasingly identifies his or her true self and new choices congruent with the real self are made. Here, we increasingly see the use of preferred goals and solution-oriented questions. The counselor, at this point, may also feel more at ease in giving advice or saying what he or she thinks. Goals are now identified, in a collaborative manner, and increasingly the client begins to feel more real and live a more authentic existence.

Relative to social and cultural issues, we noted that one should be wary when using CPCC under the following conditions: when the client is from a culture that extols external advice, or religious doctrine, and eschews an internal locus of control; when therapy needs to be brief and focused; when being in touch with feelings is frowned upon by the client or within the client's culture; when the presenting problem does not lend itself to the person-centered approach; when the counselor's cognitive complexity is not evolved; and when the cultural competence of the counselor is lacking.

The chapter went on to note that Rogers did research on person-centered counseling in the 1940s and 1950s using the Q-sort technique, which found that client-centered counseling had success at reducing the gap between how clients actually saw themselves (their self-concept) and how they wanted to be (their ideal concept). We also noted that CPCC has a large emphasis on the working alliance (e.g., the use of empathy, acceptance, and genuineness), and in recent years this has been shown to be one of the driving forces to positive client outcomes. Although empathy may have some limitations, it does seem to be critical to positive client outcomes. We also noted that CPCC, similar to person-centered counseling, will very likely be as efficacious as other forms of therapy and can be used for the treatment of a large range of problems, particularly depression, embedded anxiety disorders, relationship concerns, and self-esteem issues.

KEY WORDS AND NAMES

Acceptance
Actualizing tendency
Additive or advanced empathy
Advocacy role
Affirmation and encouragement
Anti-deterministic
Authenticity
Basic empathy
Choice
Clarifying questions
Client-centered counseling
Compensatory strategies
Conditions of worth
Congruence
Congruent
Construct and reconstruct his or her reality
Core conditions
Creative and novel empathic responses
Empathic
Empathy
Empty chair technique
Existential-humanistic therapy
False or incongruent self
False self
Frankl, Viktor
Genuine selves
Genuineness
Gestalt therapy
Here and now language
Here and now therapy
Honoring and respecting
Humanism
Humanistic
Humanistic psychology
Ideal concept
Identifying choices and goal setting

Immediacy
Incongruence
Incongruent
I-Thou relationship
Logotherapy
Looking toward the future
Maslow, Abraham
Meaning making
Multiple perspectives
Naturally positive
Need to be regarded
Needs
Needs hierarchy
Nondirective
Nondogmatic
Non-genuineness
Nonjudgmental
Normalizing not pathologizing
Now of existence
Offering advice and saying what you think
Other techniques
Perls, Fritz
Person-centered counseling
Phenomenological
Phenomenology
Preferred goals and solution-oriented questions
Q-sort technique
Relativism
Repressed needs
Responsible choices
Rogers, Carl
Self-actualization
Self-concept
Self-disclosure
Self-disclosing statements
Self-involving statements
Solution-focused brief therapy
Strength-based approaches
Subtractive
Symptoms as a message to self
Tentative questions
There and then language
Toxic environments
True or real self
Unconditional positive regard
Unfinished business
Universal needs
Unmet needs
Use of questions
Using now language

REFERENCES

Al-Thani, A. (2012). The person-centered approach and the Islamic view of counseling. *Healthcare Counselling and Psychotherapy Journal, 12*(1), 16–20.

Batthydiny, A., & Costello, S. J. (2015). Viktor Frankl. In E. S. Neukrug (Ed.), *The SAGE encyclopedia of theory in counseling and psychotherapy* (Vol. 1, pp. 321–434). SAGE Publications.

Bazzano, M. (2017). A bid for freedom: The actualizing tendency updated. *Person-centered & Experiential Psychotherapies, 16*(4), 303–315. https://doi.org/10.1080/14779757.2017.1361860

Bayne, H., & Neukrug, E. (2017). Metaphors for empathy: Getting into character. In S. E. Stewart-Spencer & Dean, C. J. (Eds.), *Metaphors and therapy: Enhancing clinical supervision and education.* Independent Therapy.

Bland, A. (2019, December). Beyond SMART goals: A humanistic approach to treatment planning that satisfies managed care requirements. *Society for Humanistic Psychology Newsletter.* https://www.apadivisions.org/division-32/publications/newsletters/humanistic/2016/12/treatment-planning

Boccone, P. J. (2016). Embracing the whole self: Using the empty chair technique to process internalized biphobia during bisexual identity enactment. *Journal of LGBT Issues in Counseling, 10*(3), 150–158, https://doi.org/10.1080/15538605.2016.1199291

Bohart, A. C. (2012). Can you be integrative and a person-centered therapist at the same time?, *Person-Centered & Experiential Psychotherapies, 11*(1), 1–13. https://doi.org/10.1080/14779757.2011.639461

Bohart, A. C. (2017). A client-centered perspective on 'psychopathology.' *Person-Centered & Experiential Psychotherapies, 16*(1), 14–26. https://doi.org/10.1080/14779757.2017.1298051

Buber, M. (1970). *I and thou* (W. Kaufman, Trans.) Charles Scribner's Sons. (Original work published 1923)

Burton, N. (2019, May 24). Man's search for meaning: Meaning as a cure for depression and other ills. *Psychology Today.* https://www.psychologytoday.com/us/blog/hide-and-seek/201205/mans-search-meaning (Original work published 2012)

Conyen, R. K. (2105). Gestalt group psychotherapy. In E. S. Neukrug (Ed.), *The SAGE encyclopedia of theory in counseling and psychotherapy* (Vol. 1, pp. 452–456). SAGE Publications.

Cook, J. M., Biyanova, T., & Coyne, J. C. (2009). Influential psychotherapy figures, authors, and books: An internet survey of over 2,000 psychotherapists. *Psychotherapy: Theory, Research, Practice, Training, 46*(1), 42–51. https://doi.org/10.1037/a0015152

Crocker, S. F., & Philippson, P. (2005). Phenomenology, existentialism, and Eastern thought in gestalt therapy. In A. L. Woldt & S. M. Toman (Eds.), *Gestalt therapy: History, theory, and practice* (pp. 65–80). SAGE Publications.

Dean, L. (2015). Motivational interviewing. In E. Neukrug (Ed.), *The SAGE encyclopedia of theory in counseling and psychotherapy* (Vol. 1, pp. 668–672). SAGE Publications.

Ellerman, C. P. (1999). Pragmatic existential therapy. *Journal of Contemporary Psychotherapy, 29,* 49–64. https://doi.org/10.1023/A:1022957209378

Elliot, R., Bohart, A. C., Watson, J. C., & Greenberg, L. Sl. (2011). Empathy. *Psychotherapy, 48,* 43–49. https://doi.org/10.1037/a0022187

de Shazer, S. (1988). *Clues: Investigating solutions in brief therapy.* W. W. Norton.

Egan, G., & Reese, R. J. (2019). *The skilled helper: A problem management and opportunity-development approach to helping* (11th ed.). Cengage.

Elliott, R. (2013). Research. In M. Cooper, M. O'Hara, P. F. Schmid, & A. C. Bohart. (Eds.), *The handbook of person-centered psychotherapy and counselling* (2nd ed., pp. 428–482). Palgrave Macmillan.

Frankl, V. E. (2014). *Man's search for meaning.* Beacon Press. (Original work published 1946)

Grogran, J. (2013). *Encountering America: Humanistic psychology, sixties culture and the shaping of the modern self.* HarperCollins.

Guo, F., & Hanley, T. (2015). Adapting cognitive behavioral therapy to meet the needs of Chinese clients: Opportunities and challenges. *Psych Journal, 4,* 55–65. https://doi.org/10.1002/pchj.75

Hilbon, R. C. (2000). *Chaos and nonlinear dynamics: An introduction for scientists and engineers* (2nd ed.). Oxford University Press.

Hilsenroth, M. (Ed.). (2014). Common factors [Special section]. *Psychotherapy, 51,* 467–524.

Hofmann, S. G., Asnaani, A., Vonk, I. J., Sawyer, A. T., & Fang, A. (2012). The efficacy of cognitive behavioral therapy: A review of meta-analyses. *Cognitive Therapy and Research, 36*(5), 427–440. https://doi.org/10.1007/s10608-012-9476-1

Hough, M. (2014). *Counselling skills and theory* (4th ed.). Bookpoint.

Ismail, N. A. H., & Tekke, M. (2015). Rediscovering Rogers's self theory and personality. *Journal of Educational, Health and Community Psychology, 4*(3), 28–36.

Jacobs, N., & Reupert, A. (2014). *The effectiveness of supportive counselling, based on Rogerian principles: A systematic review of recent international and Australian research.* Psychotherapy and Counselling Foundation of Australia.

Kenrick, D. T, Griskevicius, V, Neuberg, S. L, & Schaller, M. (2010). Renovating the pyramid of needs: Contemporary extensions built upon ancient foundations. *Perspectives on Psychological Science; 5*(3), 292–314. https://doi.org/10.1177/1745691610369469

Kirschenbaum, H. (1979). *On becoming Carl Rogers*. Delacorte Press.

Kirschenbaum, H. (2009). *The life and work of Carl Rogers* (2nd ed.). American Counseling Association.

Kolden, G. G., Wang, C.-C., Austin, S. B., Chang, Y., & Klein, M. H. (2018). Congruence/genuineness: A meta-analysis. *Psychotherapy, 55*(4), 424–433. https://doi.org/10.1037/pst0000162

Laska, K. M., Gurman, A. S., & Wampold, B. E. (2014). Expanding the lens of evidence-based practice in psychotherapy: A common factors perspective. *Psychotherapy, 51,* 467–481.

Lively, K. J. (2014, March 12). Affirmations: The why, what, and how, and what if? *Psychology Today.* https://www.psychologytoday.com/us/blog/smart-relationships/201403/affirmations-the-why-what-how-and-what-if

Mann, D. (2010). *Gestalt therapy: 100 key points and techniques*. Routledge.

Maslow, A. H. (1943). A theory of human motivation. *Psychological Review, 50*(4), 370–96.

Maslow, A. H. (1954). *Motivation and personality.* Harper and Row.

Moreira, V. (2012). From person-centered to humanistic-phenomenological psychotherapy: The contribution of Merleau-Ponty to Carl Rogers's thought. *Perspectives on Psychological Science; 11*(1), 48–43. https://doi.org/10.1177/1745691610369469

Neukrug, E. (2017, February 2). Creative and novel approaches to empathy. *Counseling Today.* http://ct.counseling.org/2017/02/creative-novel-approaches-empathy/

Neukrug, E. S. (2018). *Counseling theory and practice* (2nd ed.). Cognella Academic Publishing.

Neukrug, E. S. (2019). *Counseling and helping skills: Critical techniques to becoming a counselor.* Cognella Academic Publishing.

Neukrug, E., Bayne, H., Dean-Nganga, L., & Pusateri, C. (2012). Creative and novel approaches to empathy: A neo-Rogerian perspective. *Journal of Mental Health Counseling, 35*(1), 29–42. https://doi.org/10.17744/mehc.35.1.5q375220327000t2

Norcross, J. C. (Ed.). (2011). *Psychotherapy relationships that work: Evidence-based responsiveness.* Oxford University Press.

Perls, F., Hefferline, R., & Goodman, P. (1951). *Gestalt therapy: Excitement and growth in human personality.* Julian Press.

Polster, E., & Polster, M. (1973). *Gestalt therapy integrated: Contours of theory and practice.* Brunner/Mazel.

Proctor, C. (2017). Conditions of worth. In V. Zeigler-Hill & T. K. Shackelford (Eds.), *Encyclopedia of personality and individual differences*. Springer.

Rogers, C. R. (1951). *Client-centered therapy: Its current practice, implications and theory*. Houghton Mifflin.

Rogers, C. R. (1957a). The necessary and sufficient conditions of therapeutic personality change. *Journal of Consulting Psychology, 21*, 95–103. http://dx.doi.org/10.1037/h0045357

Rogers, C. R. (1957b). A note on the "nature of man." *Journal of Counseling Psychology, 4*(3), 199–203.

Rogers, C. R. (1959). A theory of therapy, personality and interpersonal relationships, as developed in the client-centered framework. In S. Koch (Ed.), *Psychology: A study of science*. (pp. 184–256). McGraw Hill.

Rogers, C. R. (1980). *A way of being. Boston*. Houghton Mifflin.

Rubin, S., & Lichtanski, K. L. (2015). Existential therapy. In E. S. Neukrug (Ed.), *The SAGE encyclopedia of theory in counseling and psychotherapy* (Vol. 1, pp. 368–373). SAGE Publications.

Sa'ad, F. M., Yusoof, F., Nen, S., & Subhi, N. (2014). The effectiveness of person-centered therapy and cognitive psychology add-in group counseling on self-concept, depression and resilience of pregnant out-of-wedlock teenagers. *Procedia—Social and Behavioral Sciences*, 114, 927–932. doi:10.1016/j.sbspro.2013.12.809

Shallcross, L. (2013, September 1). Multicultural competence: A continual pursuit. *Counseling Today*, https://ct.counseling.org/2013/09/multicultural-competence-a-continual-pursuit/

Smull, M. W. (2007). Revisiting choice. In J. O'Brien & C. L. O'Brien (Eds.), *A little book about person-centered planning* (pp. 37–49). Inclusion.

Sturges, J. W. (2012). Use of therapist self-disclosure and self-involving statements. *The Behavior Therapist, 35*, 90–93.

The top 10: The most influential therapists of the past quarter-century. (2007, March/April). *Psychotherapy Networker*. https://www.psychotherapynetworker.org/magazine/article/661/the-top-10

van Deurzen, E. (2012). *Existential counseling and psychotherapy in practice* (3rd ed.). SAGE Publications.

Wampold, B. E., & Budge, S. L. (2012). The relationship—and its relationship to the common and specific factors in psychotherapy. The *Counseling Psychologist, 40*, 601–623. https://doi.org/10.1177/0011000011432709

Wampold, B. E., & Imel, Z. E. (2015). *The great psychotherapy debate: The evidence for what makes psychotherapy work* (2nd ed.). Routledge.

Winston, C. N. (2015). Points of convergence and divergence between existential and humanistic psychology: A few observations. *The Humanistic Psychologist, 43*, 40–53. https://doi.org/10.1080/08873267.2014.993067

Wollants, G. (2012). *Gestalt therapy: Therapy of the situation*. SAGE Publications.

Wong, J. Y. (2015). The psychology of encouragement: Theory, research, and applications. *The Counseling Psychologist, 43*(2) 178–216. https://doi.org/10.1177/0011000014545091

Worth, P. & Proctor, C. (2017). Congruence/incongruence. In V. Zeigler-Hill & T. K. Shackelford (Eds.), *Encyclopedia of personality and individual differences*. Springer. http://www.pprc.gg/wp-content/uploads/2017/03/Congruence.Incongruence.pdf

Yalom, I. D. (2002). *The gift of therapy*. HarperCollins.

Yonteff, G. M. (1976). Theory of Gestalt therapy. In C. Hatcher & P. Himelstein (Eds.), *The handbook of Gestalt therapy* (pp. 213–221). Jason Aronson.

Youngvorst, L. J., & Jones, S. M. (2017). The influence of cognitive complexity, empathy, and mindfulness on person-centered message evaluations. *Communication Quarterly, 65*, 549–564. https://doi.org/10.1080/01463373.2017.1301508

CASE STUDY: MARKUS'S EXPERIENCE IN CPCC

(Please read about the Millers in Appendix I prior to reading this case study)

Markus's partner Rob had been gone for five months to the Middle East on a project for his government job. Markus missed Rob terribly and had sought counseling at that time because he was having trouble focusing on finishing his PhD. Counseling was helpful, and Markus had made some progress toward his doctorate, having taken and passed his comps. He was now working on his dissertation. He was, however, increasingly feeling depressed since Rob had returned home, and he wasn't sure why. He had thought that once Rob was home, everything would be fine—in fact, more than fine. Instead, he was experiencing this constant, low level depression. For the most part, he could work his way through it, but he knew this was not a way to live life. Although he liked his last therapist, he was hoping to find someone who was a bit less directive and more comforting—someone he could simply talk to. Then, kind of out of the blue, one of his fellow doc students began telling him that she was depressed and seeing this wonderful counselor, Dr. Bauer. She said he was a great listener and had really thoughtful responses to her situation. Markus decided to give him a chance.

Sitting in the waiting room, Markus was taken by the comfortable furniture and the sounds of the Zen fountain, which seemed to be saying, "Just relax, you're okay." A tall, bearded man then walked out, held out his hand, and said, "Hi Markus, I'm glad you're here, why don't you come in."

Markus followed Dr. Bauer into his office, which had a large leather chair, which was clearly the "therapist chair," a comfortable-looking couch, a comfortable-looking chair, and a smaller chair that seemed a bit out of place. Dr. Bauer looked at Markus and said, "Sit wherever you like." Markus sat in the comfortable chair. Markus was 6 feet tall, yet Dr. Bauer seemed to tower over him as he sat in the chair across from him. Dr. Bauer's height and girth, on one hand, was intimidating, while on the other made him feel safe. Dr. Bauer looked directly at Markus and said, "How can I help you?" Markus reviewed his situation, and then said, "I just don't know why I'm now depressed. Everything is the way I wanted it." He then went on to describe his relationship with Rob, his sister Angela, and his parents.

After hearing from Markus, Dr. Bauer said, "It sounds like you were expecting everything to go well after Rob came home, but, instead, there's this cloud over your head and you're not sure why." "Yes, that's exactly it," said Markus, who began to feel his eyes tear up. "I see how sad you're feeling, and yet, you're not exactly sure why," said Dr. Bauer. Markus sat still for a minute, and then said, "You know, to be honest, a large part of my life I've felt a little down—not like suicidal or anything, just this kind of low level depression—even when I was a kid." Dr. Bauer replied: "So, I guess I'm thinking that you thought your relationship with Rob would make you feel better, but you've found that you're still struggling with this, as you call it, low level depression."

Markus thought silently for a minute about Dr. Bauer's last statement. Although not a question, it seemed as one—as though the therapist was asking him, "Why do you think you feel this way?" The two men sat in silence for what seemed like an eternity to Markus, but it gave Markus time to think about his life. Marc reflected on his childhood, his young adulthood, and his relationship with Rob. He suddenly had a thought, and said, "You know, Dr. Bauer, my whole life I feel like people have taken care of me, that no one ever let me be me." "Tell me more," the therapist said. "Well, my mother was an extreme nurturer and always took care of me. My dad, well, I can tell he wanted me to be more of 'a man,' but never said that—just let mom take over. And then there was Angela, my older sister. I love her so much, but she too was always taking care of me—never really letting me be me. Maybe that was partly because I was younger and adopted—and, well, gay. Well, I think everyone knew I was gay from a young age, though no one said it. And when I came out at 13, no one seemed surprised and no one made a big deal of it. Even my dad—you know, he's an academic and they love being 'liberal.' So, being gay was not a big deal in my family, but I guess I kind of got used to being taken care of. Then, when I got older, I guess I kind of looked for a caretaker in a relationship, and that's when I found Rob. He's so independent and strong, and maybe that balances my introversion and lack of assertiveness. But all of them—they all squashed a part of me, and I think I'm a little over it."

Dr. Bauer let all of what Markus said sink in, and then after what seemed like another long pause, said, "Well, you certainly said a lot there, and it seems like you gave a good summary of a main theme in your life. If I have this right, you're feeling like there's a part of you that has never been acknowledged—a strong, assertive part, and people have always overwhelmed that part of you—or not let you express it. I think I'm also hearing that you sometimes allowed that to happen." "Yes, that's exactly it—on all counts," said Markus.

"So, Markus, I kind of have an image of you with all these people around you, and you have tape around your mouth—like you can't talk. I would guess you have a lot to say to people—to your mom, dad, Angela, and even Rob." Markus thought about it for a moment, and said, "Yeah, I really love them all, but also want them to back off a bit and let me be me.

They've all gotten so used to taking care of me and telling me who I should be and not allowing me to express myself." Dr. Bauer said, simply, "Interesting," before adding, "You know, if I was to take that image of you with the tape on your mouth one step further, I guess I also see that your hands are free and you are not removing the tape." Markus, looking at Dr. Bauer through tears, said, "Yes, I guess I have had a lot to do with continuing this theme in my life. I need to take the tape off."

"Markus, if you were to talk to any one of those important people in your life and tell them how you felt, who would you start with?" Markus thought about it for a few moments, and said, "You know, I think it would be Angela. She probably could best hear me and that would be a good beginning." "Dr. Bauer then said, "want to try here in the office?" "Here—how do you mean?" asked Markus. "Well, you'll notice I've got this extra chair in here," said Dr. Bauer. "Yeah, it seemed out of place," answered Markus. "Well, you can imagine Angela sitting in it, so practice what you would say to her." "Practice right here—right now?" said Markus. "Sure," answered Dr. Bauer. Markus looked at Dr. Bauer for a moment, then replied, "Okay, let's give it a try."

Dr. Bauer set up the chair so it is directly across from Markus, and said, "Imagine Angela is sitting right here, tell her what you need to say to her." Markus looks at the empty chair before replying. "You know, Angela, I love you dearly, but you've been treating me like a little kid forever. Damn, I almost have my PhD, and you talk to me like I'm 10. And, you're always trying to do everything for me. I love that you want to take care of me, but I think we need a new relationship. One that's a bit more equal."

"Great job," said Dr. Bauer. "I'm impressed with how those words just flowed out of you. Do you think you can do that with her in person?" Markus assertively shakes his head "Yes." Markus goes on to say that he wants to talk with Angela and have the conversation.

After a few minutes, Dr. Bauer says, "So, Markus, if your world was exactly like you wanted it to be, what would it look like?" Markus gives it a thought, and says, "You know, I need to have a similar conversation with Rob and my mom. And, I need to talk to my dad—break through his icy exterior and tell him who I am." Dr. Bauer looks at him for a bit, and says, "Sounds like you're realizing that you have some work to do with Angela, your mom, Rob, and your dad." "Yes, I do—and you know what, I think I can do it."

"You've done some great work today, and I am confident you can continue the work outside of the office," said Dr. Bauer. "Maybe, we can finish up today by talking about what you might be able to do between now and the next time we meet. Like, who you might want to talk with. You clearly have some choices about what you want to tackle, and I respect whatever those might be." Markus replies, "Yes, let's talk about what might be best."

For the next few minutes the client and therapist talk more about the important themes that Markus identified during the session, and about how and who he was going to talk with. Dr. Bauer listens and reflects his thoughts. They then set some tentative goals. Dr. Bauer finishes the session by saying, "I see the maturity, strength, and courage you have, Markus, and

I'm rather impressed. I also like that you see the complexity of your relationships, the issues you have in them, the love you feel for the people involved, and the work you want to do on them. Nice job." Markus thanks Dr. Bauer, and the two decide to meet in a week.

QUESTIONS FOR YOU TO PONDER

1. Dr. Bauer begins the session with a fair amount of empathy. How important is it that he does this at the beginning of therapy?
2. At one point, there is a long pause after Markus says something. Do you believe you could sit with such a pause with a client? How is it helpful? Can it hinder the relationship?
3. When Markus is reviewing his life situation he says, "You know, Dr. Bauer, my whole life I feel like people have taken care of me, that no one ever let me be me." Dr. Bauer responds by saying, "Tell me more about that." What do you think about that response? Do you believe that a different response might have been better? If so, what?
4. At one point, Dr. Bauer uses an analogy of Markus with his loved ones around him and Markus with tape on his mouth. Do you believe you can make an advanced and creative empathic response such as this? Do you believe it was useful?
5. Dr. Bauer goes on to expand his analogy by saying that Markus is partly responsible for his situation because he hasn't taken the tape off of his mouth, even though his hands are free. How is this type of response related to "choice," "taking responsibility," and existential theory?
6. Dr. Bauer encourages Markus to use the empty chair technique with Angela. Do you believe this was helpful? Why or why not?
7. Do you think you can use the empty chair technique with clients?
8. When does Dr. Bauer use affirmation and encouragement with Markus? Do you believe these responses were helpful? Why or why not?
9. How does Dr. Bauer incorporate solution-oriented questions? How helpful do you think this technique was with Markus?
10. How, if at all, is Dr. Bauer collaborative with Markus?
11. Overall, do you believe Dr. Bauer was positive, respectful, forward looking, and non-judgmental? How?
12. Talk about something in your life that you believe would be helped in therapy such as this? Why might it be facilitative for your issues?

Credit

Img. 2.1: Source: https://www.youtube.com/watch?v=o0neRQzudzw.

3

Cognitive Behavior Therapy (CBT)

Ed Neukrug

LEARNING OUTCOMES

- Provide a brief history of cognitive behavior therapy (CBT).
- Learn about the rational, active, educative, structured, time sensitive, empirical, anti-deterministic, and, some say, constructionist view of human nature of CBT, and the relationship among genetic predispositions, biological factors, and experiences on the development of core beliefs.
- Learn key concepts of CBT, including the cognitive model (core beliefs, intermediate beliefs, and automatic thoughts and images), cognitive distortions, coping or compensatory strategies, and cognitive conceptualization.
- Identity 10 principles to effective treatment of CBT and review essential techniques of CBT, including building a strong therapeutic alliance, educating the client about the cognitive model, Socratic questioning, identifying and challenging automatic thoughts and images, identifying and challenging cognitive distortions, identifying intermediate beliefs, identifying and challenging core beliefs, and doing homework assignments.
- Review commonly used techniques of CBT, including thought-stopping, imagery-changing, rational–emotional role-play, and behavioral and emotive techniques.
- To describe the counseling process of CBT.

- To examine social and cultural applicability of CBT.
- To review the efficacy of CBT.
- To offer a case study that demonstrates the CBT process.

BRIEF HISTORY OF COGNITIVE BEHAVIOR THERAPY

> Cognitive therapy seeks to alleviate psychological stresses by correcting faulty conceptions and self-signals. By correcting erroneous beliefs we can lower excessive reactions. (Beck, 1976, p. 216)

The cognitive therapy movement began during the 1960s with the development of two parallel theories: **Aaron "Tim" Beck's cognitive therapy** and **Albert Ellis's rational therapy.** Later called **cognitive behavior therapy (CBT)** and **rational emotive behavior therapy (REBT)**, respectively, these two approaches are widely used with clients today. Although both approaches are used extensively, this chapter will focus mostly on cognitive behavior therapy, as its evidence base is larger than that of REBT and its use is wider spread than REBT. There are, however, many similarities between the two, and if you would like to learn more about REBT, I refer you to my book *Counseling Theory and Practice,* which has a chapter on REBT (Neukrug, 2018).

REBT and CBT are considered the **second wave of cognitive behavioral therapies. First-wave cognitive behavioral therapy** focused exlusively on behaviors and included operant conditioning, classical conditioning, and modeling, while **third-wave cognitive behavioral therapy** took a look at how context impacts the person and included such therapies as **dialectical behavior therapy** and **acceptance and commitment therapy**, two theories included in this book. In contrast, second-wave cognitive behavioral therapy focuses on how cognitions can be examined and changed and result in associated changes in behaviors, feelings, and physiological responses. Although originating during the 1960s, it is included in this book on contemporary theories because its popularity has remained high and its approach to individuals has been somewhat adapted over time.

Similar to most psychiatrists of his time, Aaron Beck started as a psychoanalyst but slowly began to question its efficacy and usefulness (Krapp, 2005; Weishaar, 1993, 2015). This skepticism increased after he found many of his clients having streams of private thoughts that commented on their experiences. Others, not aware of their private thoughts, quickly became conscious of them once Beck began to probe with them the possibility that such thoughts were present. Calling them **automatic thoughts**, Beck realized that they "provided running commentary on the person's experience" (Weishaar, 1993, p. 20). Beck concluded that these thoughts were a function of an internal conversation with self, were not associated with interpersonal dialogue, and were not generally discussed in the therapies of the time

(A. Beck, 1991). He came to believe that such thoughts and beliefs affected individuals' feelings, behaviors, and physiological responses.

Over time, Beck's interest in cognitive work grew, and in the 1960s he began to write about his new cognitive approach to psychotherapy. Having struggled with mild depression, in 1961 Beck published the **Beck Depression Scale** and began to write about the connection between depression and thinking. Beck soon completed a large, funded study that compared cognitive therapy with the use of antidepressants in treating moderately depressed clients. Out of this research came the book *Cognitive Therapy of Depression* (Beck et al., 1979), one of the first books to draw attention to cognitive theory and advocated for a relatively short-term approach to counseling. In 1963, Albert Ellis realized that he and Beck were independently developing similar theories and reached out to Beck (Padesky & Beck, 2003). Although Beck and Ellis rarely wrote or researched together, they did share ideas and met professionally. At one point, Beck even consulted Ellis for continued anxiety he had about public speaking. Beck's and Ellis's writings and research were soon to usher in what some called the **cognitive revolution in psychology** of the 1970s (Weishaar, 1993, p. 27).

As Beck's theory evolved, he realized that different disorders presented with specific **cognitive distortions**, or false beliefs about the world, that fueled the disorder (Rice, 2015; Weishaar, 2015). Beck then developed training manuals that clinicians could use to help ameliorate the presenting problem by targeting the cognitive distortion(s) and behaviors associated with specific disorders. To assess clinical effectiveness of his training manuals, Beck developed several measures, including those that assessed depression, hopelessness, anxiety, self-concept, sociotropy–autonomy, and suicide. This process allowed Beck to establish hundreds of studies that showed the effectiveness of CBT with a wide range of disorders. Most of this research was conducted at the University of Pennsylvania and later at the **Beck Institute for Cognitive Behavior Therapy in Philadelphia**, which he cofounded, with his daughter **Judith Beck**, in 1994 (Beck Institute, 2019a).

Beck has published more than 600 articles and written 25 books (Beck Institute, 2019b). An unassuming man, over the years Beck's research and writing have brought him praise and dozens of awards (Weishaar, 2015), and he was listed as the second most influential psychotherapist in recent times, just behind Carl Rogers ("The top 10," 2007).

Want to Meet Aaron Beck and Albert Ellis?

Want to hear more about Beck and Ellis and their theories? Go to https://silver.odu.edu/psyadm/ and click the cognitive behavioral button, then enter the offices of Beck and Ellis and other cognitive behavioral theorists and hear them talk about themselves and their theories.

VIEW OF HUMAN NATURE

Believing there is a **genetic and evolutionary predisposition toward emotional responses** (A. Beck, 1967, 1976, 1999, 2005), Beck suggested that these older, emotional responses can continue into the modern world and be maladaptive, creating excessive anger, anxiety, depression or other negative feelings (Scott & Freeman, 2010). Called the **continuity hypothesis**, Beck found that some people were genetically predisposed to have a heightened sensitivity to these older emotional responses that would lead them to develop a mental disorder when placed under stress. For instance, whereas it might have been helpful to constantly be vigilante for attacks from wild animals, that constant vigilance and associated anxiety, generally, would not be helpful in today's world. He called this **the diathesis–stress model of mental disorders**.

Although some individuals have a tendency toward exhibiting maladaptive emotional responses, others will not express them if they were taught effective skills by parents and others, even if they had a genetic predisposition toward them. And, taking a **rational**, **pragmatic**, and some say **constructionist** perspective, Beck assumes that even those who do exhibit maladaptive responses can change, in a relatively short amount of time, through therapeutic discourse with others, particularly if an individual learns how to modify his or her cognitive processes (J. Beck, 2005; O'Connor, 2015; Rice, 2015). Thus, CBT is an **anti-deterministic, active, educative, structured, time sensitive,** and **empirical approach** to counseling that suggests people can manage and effect changes in their way of living in the world if given the tools to understand their cognitive processes and how they affect feelings, behaviors, and physiological responses (Beck Institute, 2019c).

Beck, and other cognitive therapists, believe that a combination of genetics, biological factors, and experiences combine to produce specific **core beliefs**, some of which may lie dormant and then suddenly appear as the result of stress and other conditions impinging on the person. Core beliefs are embedded, underlying beliefs that provide direction toward the manner in which one lives in the world (A. Beck, 1967, 1991; Scott & Freeman, 2010), with negative core beliefs leading to negative feelings and dysfunctional behaviors, and positive core beliefs leading to healthy ways of living. Beck suggests that most individuals are not aware of their core beliefs. Instead, such beliefs become the underlying mechanism for the creation of **intermediate beliefs**, which set the attitudes, rules and expectations, and assumptions we live by. These attitudes, rules and expectations, and assumptions result in **automatic thoughts** and associated **cognitive distortions**, which, in turn, lead to specific behaviors, feelings, and physiological responses that end up reinforcing core beliefs. And thus, the cycle is continued.

Beck has demonstrated how certain mental disorders are related to specific core beliefs, intermediate beliefs, and automatic thoughts (and associated cognitive distortions). Thus, if a counselor can accurately diagnose a client, that counselor can begin to make an educated guess as to some of the automatic thoughts and associated cognitive distortions, intermediate beliefs, and core beliefs the client might have.

Although CBT is mostly a **present-focused approach**, J. Beck (2011) suggests that examining the past might be helpful when the patient has a strong desire to do so, when avoiding such a discussion could harm the therapeutic alliance, and when an understanding of the past can illuminate why clients think the way they do and thus help them change their rigid thinking. In addition, today's cognitive therapists believe it is important to address all aspects of the individual if change is to occur relatively quickly. Thus, many who practice Beck's approach, or other similar cognitive approaches, will focus on cognitions *and* behaviors when working with clients, thus the recent, more inclusive term cognitive behavior therapy as opposed to the older term, cognitive therapy.

KEY CONCEPTS

Some key concepts that underlie CBT include Beck's **cognitive model**, which comprises **core beliefs, intermediate beliefs, automatic thoughts and images** and related **cognitive distortions, coping or compensatory strategies**, and **cognitive conceptualization.**

The Cognitive Model

The cognitive model comprises three levels of cognition: core beliefs, or the fundamental beliefs that underlie how we think, feel, and behave; intermediate beliefs, which consist of attitudes, rules and expectations, and assumptions that are outgrowth of our core beliefs; and resulting automatic thoughts, which are those thoughts that are readily assessible and result in our behaviors, feelings, and physiological responses, and are the outgrowth of the attitudes, rules and expectations, and assumptions.

Because core beliefs are embedded, deep-seated beliefs about self, cognitive therapists suggest it is generally important to initially focus on the more assessable automatic thoughts (Figure 3.1). For instance, the core belief of "I am unlovable" is much more difficult for a client to initially grasp than an automatic thought of "I'm too nervous to ask that person out." By assessing and diagnosing the client, and by examining the client's automatic thoughts, the therapist can begin to hypothesize about the intermediate beliefs that produce the automatic thoughts and ultimately begin to understand the core beliefs that fuel the intermediate beliefs. The following briefly describes core beliefs, intermediate beliefs, and automatic thoughts.

Core Beliefs

Beck originally distinguished between what he identified as **cognitive schemas** and **core beliefs** (A. Beck, 1967), and defined schemas as cognitive structures and core beliefs as the content that result from the structures. But others, including Judith Beck (1995; Rice, 2015; Nezu & Nezu, 2016), suggest the differences are minimal and often refer simply to them as cognitive beliefs. For simplicity, we will only use the term core beliefs, which is broadly defined as those embedded beliefs that impact our intermediate beliefs, automatic thoughts, and cognitive distortions, all of which lend direction toward the way we interpret events which results in our feelings, behaviors, and physiological responses. All of us have some positive core beliefs that lead toward positive ways of living (e.g., "I am an okay person," "I can control my life to

Figure 3.1 The Development of Core Beliefs, Intermediate Beliefs, and Automatic Thoughts

a certain degree," "I can achieve"), and many of us have some negative core beliefs that negatively color our lives and lead to debilitating, depressing, anger-evoking, anxiety-producing, and dysfunctional ways of living. Three negative core beliefs identified by Beck and supported through research include "I am helpless," "I am worthless," and "I am unlovable" (Osmo et al., 2018). Those who are particularly distressed are largely governed by their negative core beliefs, and many of us, when stressed, can become dominated by negative core beliefs for short periods of time (see Box 3.1).

BOX 3.1 NEGATIVE CORE BELIEFS

When driven by one or more of the following three negative core beliefs, individuals tend to take on one or more of the following attributes associated with that core belief:

Helpless Core Beliefs

"I am incompetent, ineffective, needy, trapped, out of control, a failure, defective, not good enough, a loser, helpless, powerless, weak, vulnerable, a victim, and/or I can't do anything right."

Unlovable Core Beliefs

"I am unlovable, unlikeable, undesirable, unattractive, unwanted, uncared for, different, bad so others won't love me, defective, not good enough to be loved by others, bound to be rejected, bound to be abandoned, and/or bound to be alone ..."

Worthless Core Beliefs

"I am worthless, unacceptable, bad, a waste, immoral dangerous, toxic, evil, and/or I don't deserve to live."

Adapted from: Beck, J. S. (2011). *Cognitive therapy: Basics and beyond* (2nd ed.). Guilford Press. p. 223.

Intermediate Beliefs

Our core beliefs affect the kinds of attitudes, rules and expectations, and assumptions we have in life, which Beck calls our intermediate beliefs. Thus, if one of my major positive core beliefs is that I am capable of working out my problems, then when I face challenges my attitude will be something such as: "I'm okay, because I will make sure things will work out in the end." My rule and expectation might be: "Working hard resolves problems," and the assumption I live by is: "I assume things will work out if I work hard." On the other hand, consider the person who has the following negative core belief: "I am helpless." This person's attitude when something goes wrong is similar to: "Life sucks and there's little I can do about it." His or her rule and expectation is: "I expect that even if I try hard to change things, it will not work out, so why bother?," and the assumption: "There is little I can do to make my lot in life better."

Automatic Thoughts and Images

Automatic thoughts are those fleeting thoughts that cross our mind all day long—some of which we are aware, some of which are slightly out of awareness. When situations arise, individuals respond with automatic thoughts that are product of their attitudes, rules and expectations, and assumptions (intermediate beliefs), which themselves are a product of one's core beliefs.

For instance, in the example just given, if the individual has a core belief that he or she is powerless to change his or her life, and that individual is suddenly faced with the breakup of a relationship, the situation (the breakup) will result in automatic thoughts based on the individual's intermediate beliefs that are, in turn, dictated by the individual's core belief of being powerless. Thus, this person might "automatically" say to himself or herself: "I knew she'd (he'd) break up with me," "This always happens to me," or "I'd ask that person out, but she (he) probably already is involved." Automatic thoughts that are the result of negative core beliefs and resulting intermediate beliefs and are closely associated with **cognitive distortions,** which are inaccurate statements or beliefs about the world that result in problematic behaviors and feelings. If you explore a person's automatic thoughts while he or she is in a period of distress, you will generally find that one or more of the cognitive distortions, listed in Box 3.2, are at play. Interestingly, Albert Ellis came up with a similar list of cognitive distortions in his theory.

BOX 3.2 COGNITIVE DISTORTIONS

1. *All-or-nothing thinking:* Sometimes called *dualistic, black-and-white,* or *dichotomous* thinking, this occurs when individuals see the world in two categories, rather than in a more complex fashion.
   Example: "I am never good at my job." Or, "You are always happy."
2. *Catastrophisizing*: Making assumptions that something will go wrong rather than looking at situations more realistically or scientifically.
   Example: "I shouldn't have said that to my boss, I know I'll get fired." Or, "If I fly, the plane will crash."
3. *Disqualifying or discounting the positive:* Even when a positive event occurs, assuming it means little in the total scheme of things.
   Example: "That award I won at work is meaningless, everybody wins awards."
4. *Emotional reasoning:* Assuming that your feelings are always correct, even when there is evidence to the contrary.
   Example: "My wife and kids may tell me they love me, but I know I'm unlovable because I feel like no one can love me."
5. *Labeling:* Defining oneself in terms of a "label" or "type" instead of seeing oneself in more complex and nuanced ways.
   Example: "I'm just a negative person." Or, "I'm always introverted."
6. *Magnification/minimization*: Magnifying the negative or minimizing the positive about oneself, another, or a situation.
   Example: "I might have done well on that one test, but I know I'm not good in that subject." Or, "That incident at work proves that I am no good at what I do."

7. *Mental filter*: Focusing on one negative aspect of oneself, another, or a situation.
   Example: "I know why people stay away from me: They always see my disability."
8. *Mind reading*: Making assumptions about what other people are thinking without considering other possibilities.
   Example: "She thinks I'm ugly. "
9. *Overgeneralization*: Making large generalizations from a small event.
   Example: "That dinner for my kids was horrible; I'll never be a good parent."
10. *Personalization*: Believing you are the cause for aother person's negative behavior without taking into account other possible explanations.
    Example: "My colleague, James, was in a bad mood today because I didn't get that project to him in time."
11. *"Should" and "must" statements*: Believing that oneself and others should act in a specific manner, and when they don't you believe it is horrible.
    Example: "My grandmother was outrageous today; she never should have acted so boldly in front of the company."
12. *Tunnel vision*: Only seeing the downside or negative aspect of a situation.
    Example: "Her expressing her opinion is uncalled-for. We'll never get friends that way."

Adapted from: Beck, J. (2011). *Cognitive therapy: Basics and beyond* (2nd ed.). Guilford Press. pp. 181–182.

Similar to automatic thoughts are the ongoing images we have that cross our minds throughout our day. For instance, a person who has difficulty finishing a project for work might be saying to himself or herself, "I simply can't do this," or could have an image of his or her boss coming in with a disappointed look. Automatic thoughts and images result in behaviors, feelings, and physiological responses that reinforce core beliefs. Thus, a vicious cycle is developed.

Examining the Relationship Among Core Beliefs, Intermediate Beliefs, Automatic Thoughts and Images, Cognitive Distortions, and Reactions

Figure 3.2 diagrams the relationship between core beliefs, intermediate beliefs, automatic thoughts (and images), and cognitive distortions, and how they affect and are affected by situations in a person's life. The arrows highlight how one's emotional, behavioral, and physiological responses reinforce the original core belief.

As an example, imagine the individual who has the core belief "I am powerless." When a situation occurs, automatic thoughts or images related to one's intermediate beliefs, which, in turn are a product of one's core beliefs, kick in (Figure 3.3). After looking at the automatic thoughts listed in Figure 3.3, refer to Box 3.2 and consider what cognitive distortions may be at play?

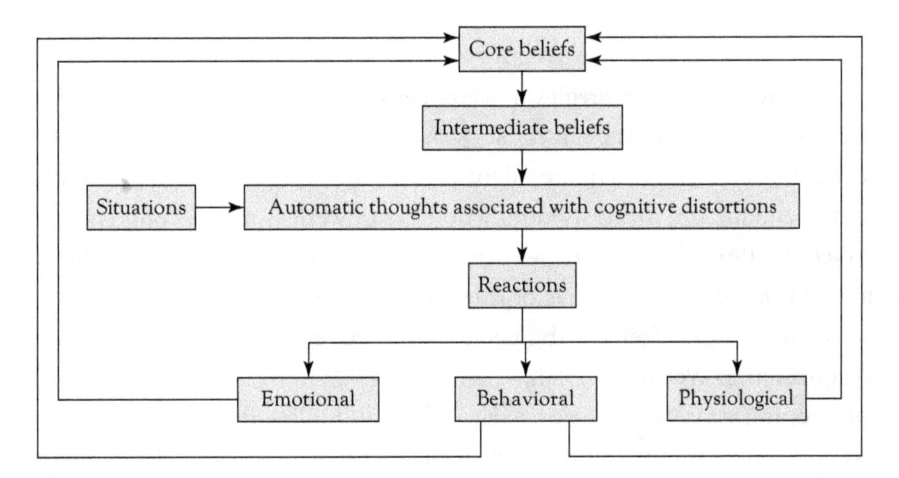

Figure 3.2 Relationships among Core Beliefs, Intermediate Beliefs, and Automatic Thoughts

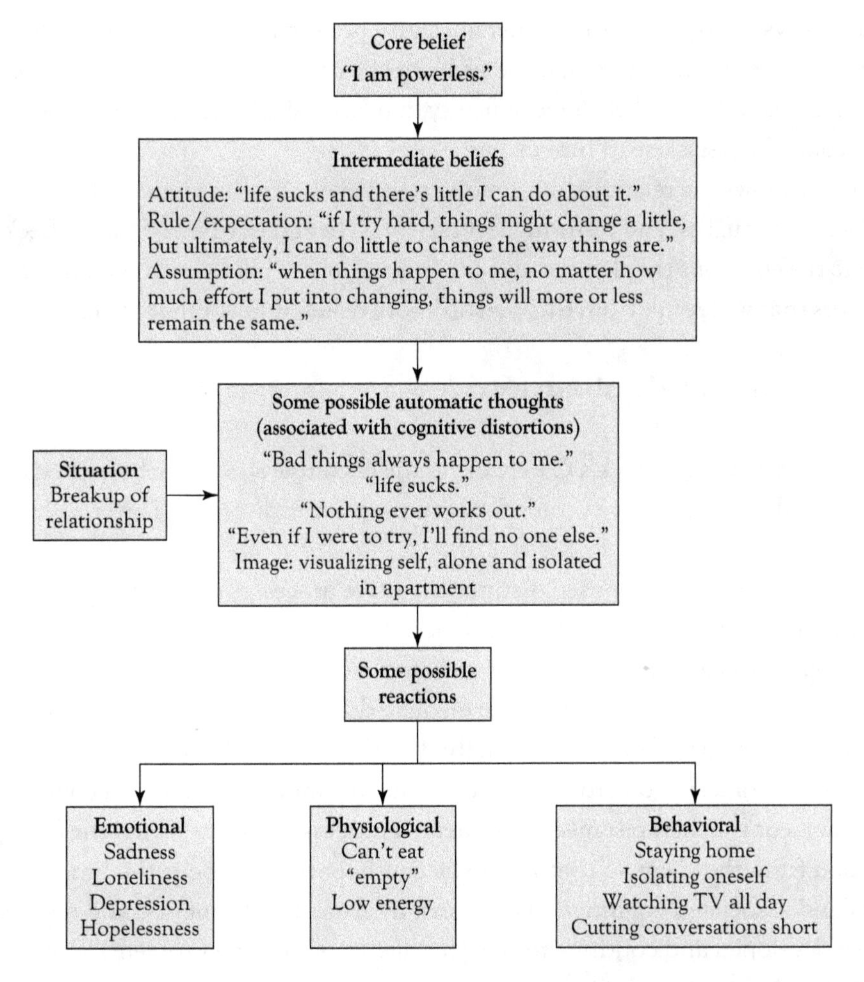

Figure 3.3 Example of the Relationships among Core Beliefs, Intermediate Beliefs, and Automatic Thoughts

Coping or Compensatory Strategies

Individuals will develop **coping strategies** (aka **compensatory strategies**) to steer them away from the pain their negative core beliefs will cause (J. Beck, 2005, 2011). For instance, a person with a core belief that he or she is inadequate might become an overachiever to prevent him or her from feeling inadequate. Or, an individual who feels powerless might compensate by trying to become all-controlling. Such strategies are remarkably similar to Alfred Adler's compensatory behaviors used to avoid feelings of inferiority. Perhaps it's not by chance that Aaron Beck developed these ideas after having been enamored, earlier in his life, by the Adlerian approach to counseling (Weishaar, 1993).

Generally, coping strategies develop early in life, and allow individuals to avoid dealing with the strong negative feelings that result from their negative core beliefs; however, these behaviors do not rid the person of their negative core beliefs, and often, over time, the coping strategies become increasingly maladaptive for individuals. For instance, consider two individuals. The first one is constantly striving to achieve so as to not feel inadequate, and the second is always trying to control others because he or she feels powerless. Over time, the first person might become more stressed as he or she compulsively tries to achieve, while the second person would very likely have difficulty in relationships because he or she is constantly trying to control those close to him or her.

Figure 3.4 shows the relationships among core beliefs, intermediate beliefs, coping strategies, automatic thoughts, and resulting feelings for a client described by Judith Beck (2005). In addition to the emotions the client would experience (lowest boxes), you can imagine the kinds of behaviors that will result from this person's core beliefs and coping strategies. (See Box 3.3)

Cognitive Conceptualization

> A distinctive feature of Beck's CT theory is the cognitive specificity hypothesis, which proposes a distinct cognitive profile for each psychiatric disorder. (Tower, 2011, p. 30)

Beck and others have proposed distinct cognitive processes and behavioral patterns that characterize specific psychological disorders (Beck Institute, 2019c; Beck & Haigh, 2014; J. Beck, 2011). If a counselor can accurately assess a client's disorder, then specific automatic thoughts and associated cognitive distortions, intermediate thoughts, and core beliefs can be inferred. In addition, treatment plans can be matched to the specific disorder and to the cognitive processes that parallel the disorder, increasing the likelihood of success in counseling. Thus, from the moment the therapist meets the client, a process begins in which the therapist elicits information from the client so that he or she can hypothesize about the kinds of automatic thoughts and associated cognitive distortions, intermediate thoughts, and core beliefs that have been developed and continue to fuel the client's presenting problems. Several activities can help in this process, including:

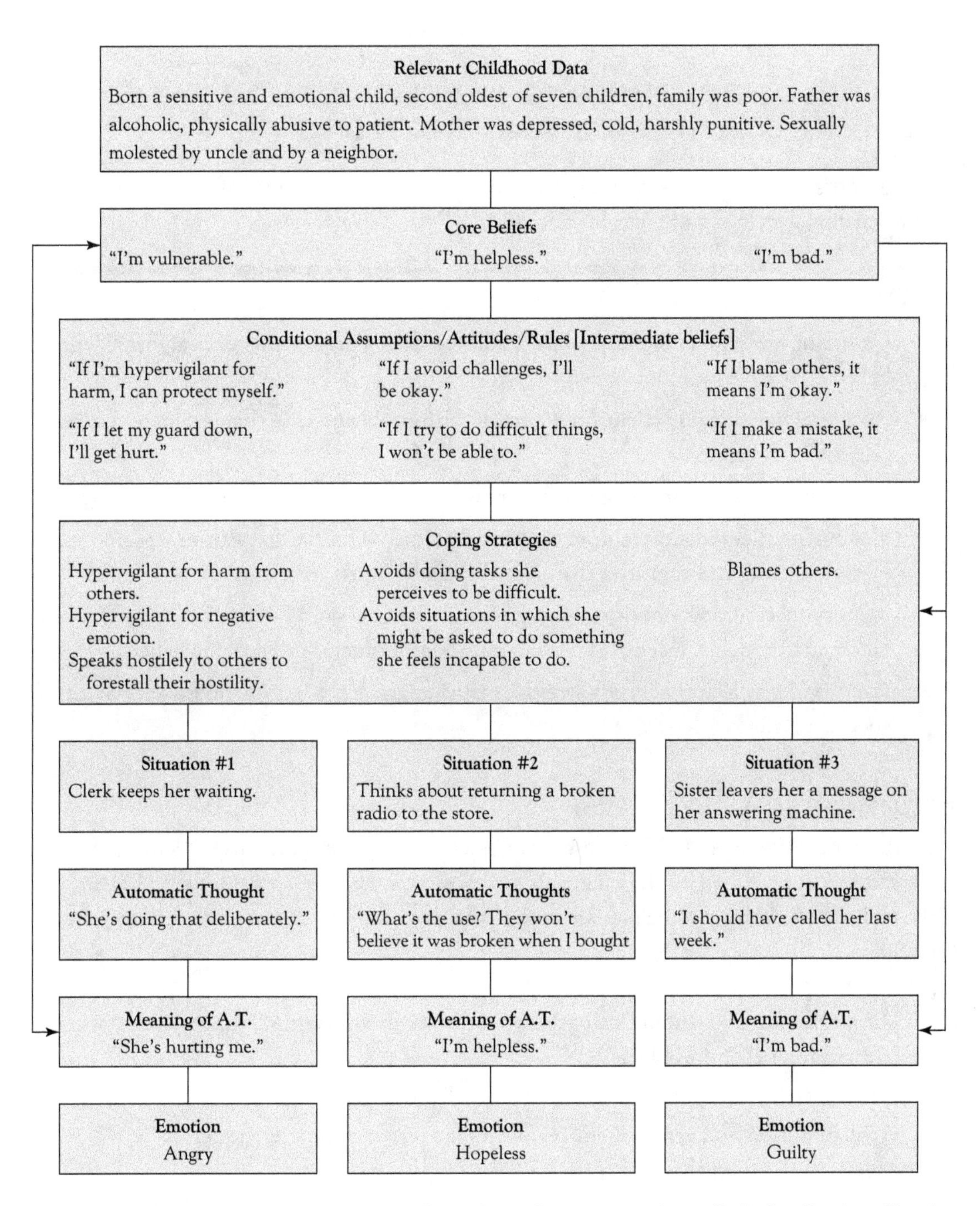

Figure 3.4 Relationships among Core Beliefs, Intermediate Beliefs, Coping Strategies, Automatic Thoughts, Behaviors, and Feelings

BOX 3.3 DECIPHERING YOUR BELIEFS, THOUGHTS, COPING STRATEGIES, AND EMOTIONS

Use Figure 3.4 as a template, and see if you can complete the figure by replacing the information with information from your life.

- Gathering important childhood data (understanding a person's history can help identify beliefs that have been developed).
- Accurately identifying client problems (certain problems lend themselves toward certain kinds of beliefs).
- Determining the client's diagnosis (diagnoses tend to correlate with specific beliefs).
- Having the client identify automatic thoughts and cognitive distortions (specific automatic thoughts and cognitive distortions are associated with underlying beliefs).
- Identifying resulting emotions, physiological responses, and behaviors related to the automatic thoughts (responses tend to cluster as a function of specific beliefs).
- Identifying past and current stressors that might have led to the development of specific beliefs.

TECHNIQUES

More than most therapies, CBT has a host of essential and commonly used techniques that therapists can apply based on the diagnosis and presenting problem of the client. Regardless of the techniques, 10 **basic principles** are core to the therapeutic process, and include (J. Beck, 2011; Dobson, 2012; Rice, 2015):

1. Strategies for CBT should be based on a thorough understanding, or case conceptualization, of client problems.
2. A solid therapeutic alliance is critical for CBT to be effective.
3. Collaboration and active client involvement is important to treatment.
4. Treatment should be goal-oriented and problem-focused.
5. CBT should mostly focus on the present.
6. Therapy teaches clients how to be their own therapist to prevent relapse.
7. CBT should generally be brief and time limited (five to 20 sessions, though some clients may take up to two years).
8. CBT sessions should be structured.

9. CBT should teach clients how to identify their thoughts and beliefs, determine if they are dysfunctional, and respond to them by making positive changes.
10. A wide range of techniques should be used in CBT if one is to change one's thinking, feelings, and behaviors.

Essential Techniques

These techniques, used by many cognitive therapists most of the time, include building **a strong therapeutic alliance, educating the client about the cognitive model, Socratic questioning, identifying and challenging automatic thoughts and images, identifying and challenging cognitive distortions, identifying intermediate beliefs, identifying and challenging core beliefs,** and **doing homework assignments** (J. Beck 2011; Dobson, 2012; Neuman, 2016; Rice, 2015).

Building a Strong Therapeutic Alliance

CBT therapists see a strong therapeutic relationship as critical to effective outcomes in counseling. Several ways to accomplish this include being collaborative; being empathic, caring, and optimistic; and adapting one's therapeutic style to the client's needs.

Collaboration

Being collaborative, or viewing the counselor–client alliance as a team, is key to the therapeutic alliance; however, it is also understood that the therapist has expertise and can help guide the client toward certain ways of thinking and acting. Thus, it is usual for therapists to make suggestions while respecting the client's opinion and feedback. In fact, at the end of each session it is common for the CBT therapist to ask their clients such questions as "How has this session been for you?," "Does what we did today make sense to you?," or "Are the goals we set in sync with where you think we should be going?"

Demonstrate empathy, caring, and optimism

These basic counseling skills are important for most forms of therapy. For the cognitive therapist, who can easily slip into a role of objective scientist, it is particularly important to remember not to view therapy as "clinical process" but as a joint therapeutic venture in which two people are sitting together in an effort to help one of them feel better. Clients who work with detached, objective scientists would be more likely to give up than clients who work with therapists who show deep understanding and caring, and who are hopeful about the future.

Adapt one's therapeutic style

Cognizant of the fact that clients respond differently to varying personality styles, J. Beck suggests that therapists adjust their style based on how the client presents to the therapist. For instance, while some clients find they like a "touch feely" therapist, others might be more comfortable with a therapist who is a bit more directive. It is important to change one's style to help the client feel comfortable within the therapeutic relationship.

Educating the Client About the Cognitive Model

Early on in counseling, therapists educate their clients about the cognitive model, often using graphics such as those found in Figures 3.1 through 3.4 (J. Beck, 2011; Dobson, 2012). Starting with the basics, therapists explain automatic thoughts and images and help clients identify them. Although spending time to help clients understand core beliefs early in the therapy may be futile, focusing on automatic thoughts and images can be eye-opening, as most clients will "get it." After identifying automatic thoughts, clients will work on understanding associated cognitive distortions, intermediate beliefs, and, eventually, core beliefs.

Socratic Questioning

Gently challenging clients to think differently and rationally about their situation to illuminate alternative ways of understanding predicaments is core to the Socratic questioning process. Conducted with a helpful spirit, such questioning is mostly used after the relationship has been established to identify and challenge the client's use of dysfunctional automatic thoughts and cognitive distortions, rigid rules and assumptions, and negative core beliefs. Some examples follow in the next section.

Identifying and Challenging Automatic Thoughts and Images

Since cognitive therapists "work backward" toward helping clients see how their core beliefs affect the very basis of who they are, the first step after building the relationship is to help clients identify their automatic thoughts and images (J. Beck, 2011; Newman, 2016). These thoughts and images are readily accessible, and clients can easily "catch" them and quickly see the connection between their thoughts and their negative feelings and dysfunctional behaviors. For example, the client who has just broken up with his or her lover comes in feeling depressed. After gathering basic information, the counselor might ask the client:

> "Are you aware of anything that you are saying to yourself that may be causing you to feel this badly?"
>
> "Can you imagine what kinds of self-statements, thoughts, or images you are having that could cause you to feel this way?"
>
> "Have you noticed any thoughts or images you have that kind of drift through your mind while you have been feeling this way?"

As clients become more aware of their automatic thoughts and images, therapists can gently challenge their rationality. For example, if a client has an automatic thought such as "I am not as smart as my coworkers," leading to feelings and behaviors that are self-destructive (feeling unmotivated, not working hard), which then results in poor supervisor evaluations, the therapist might ask such questions as:

"Are you really not as smart as your coworkers?"

"What evidence do you have that you're not as smart as your coworkers?"

"My experience has been that people have different strengths. What are your strengths at work?"

"How might this belief stop you from being smarter?"

"What do you think your life would look like if you didn't have these thoughts?"

Identifying and Challenging Cognitive Distortions

Since automatic thoughts are often based on one or more cognitive distortions identified in Box 3.2, after identifying automatic thoughts, therapists will often suggest which cognitive distortions are most likely to be associated with the client's thoughts (J. Beck, 2011; Neuman, 2016). They may sometimes do this by simply handing the client the list of distortions and reviewing it with them. After one or more distortions have been identified, the therapist and client will often engage in a discussion about the irrationality of such distortions and how changing one's automatic thoughts can help to moderate or even eliminate the cognitive distortions and their debilitating results.

Identifying Intermediate Beliefs

Once clients can identify and challenge their automatic thoughts and images and associated cognitive distortions, they can move to the next level of beliefs by examining the attitudes, rules and expectations, and assumptions that drive their thoughts and associated distortions. Often, a worksheet, such as that used in Figure 3.3, can be helpful for the client, as the therapist tests hypotheses with the client about the kinds of attitudes, rules and expectations, and assumptions that tend to run his or her life. Identifying such beliefs moves the client toward the next phase of therapy, which is identifying and challenging core beliefs.

Identifying and Challenging Core Beliefs

Usually, seamless movement occurs from the client's awareness of his or her attitudes, rules and expectations, and assumptions (intermediate beliefs), to an understanding of the core beliefs that created them. Thus, as soon as intermediate beliefs are acknowledged, the therapist points out the logical connection between those beliefs and the client's core beliefs. The next challenge is to confront the core beliefs. Sometimes, this is done by completing a core belief worksheet in which the client identifies a negative core belief, highlights a new positive core belief that he or she can strive toward, and shows evidence that contradicts or reframes the client's old core belief and moves the client toward the new positive core belief. For instance, look in Box 3.4 to see how Juan contradicts his old core belief, "I am ineffective."

BOX 3.4 CORE BELIEF WORKSHEET

Old core belief: "I am ineffective."

"How much do you believe the old core belief right now?" (0–100): 25%

"What's the most you've believed it this week?" (0–100): 55%

"What's the most you did *not* believe it this week?" (0–100): 90%

New belief: "I am pretty good at most things I do and I usually try hard."

"How much do you believe the new belief right now?" (0–100): 75%

Evidence Contradicting Old Belief

Supporting New Belief

Went to daughter's child–parent conference.
Had trouble understanding new project.
Helped kids with homework.
Spent time making children their lunches.
Researched an important paper for work.
Boss praised me three times.
Kids gave me lots of hugs this week.
Wife told me I'm a great father.
Worked hard to fix things around the house.
Took kids and wife bowling.

Reframing Old Belief

Had trouble understanding new project at work. But asked for help from coworkers and believe I am capable of understanding it and doing a good job.
Only put the kids to bed once this week. But had a hard week at work, and wife and kids didn't seem to mind. I can do more next week, and I have other signs that I am a good dad.
Couldn't fix the broken back door. But I realize I'm not perfect at everything and I did a lot of other things around the house this week.

Adapted from: Beck, J. (1995). *Cognitive therapy: Basics and beyond*. Guilford. p. 177.

Homework

An active, ongoing process, homework reinforces new beliefs and facilitates movement toward clients managing their own problems (Rice, 2015). Homework often progresses from catching automatic thoughts and images, to challenging automatic thoughts and images, to challenging intermediate beliefs, and, finally, to challenging core beliefs. Homework is often related to the practice of new behaviors that will reinforce newly identified beliefs. For instance, the individual who has the automatic thought of "I am horrible at talking with people" may have the homework assignment of finding five strangers to talk with during the week in addition to developing new thoughts, such as "I am as good as most when talking with others." There are hundreds of different kinds of homework assignments that can be given, and all of the "commonly used techniques" highlighted in the next section are frequently used in this manner.

Commonly Used Techniques

Some commonly used techniques by many cognitive therapists include **thought-stopping, imagery-changing, rational–emotional role-play,** and **behavioral and emotive techniques.**

Thought-Stopping

Since negative automatic thoughts and images are related to negative feelings and dysfunctional behaviors (Bakker, 2008), it is often suggested that clients find ways to prevent their negative thoughts. One method, thought-stopping, can be accomplished in a variety of ways, such as:

- replacing a negative thought or image with a newly identified positive one,
- yelling to oneself, or out loud, "Stop it!" when a negative thought is identified,
- placing a rubber band on one's wrist and snapping it whenever one has a negative thought,
- actively diverting one's thoughts or images to more pleasant thoughts, and
- participating in a relaxation exercise to "move" one's thoughts to a different place.

Imagery-Changing

As noted earlier, mental images, similar to thoughts, are a product of one's core beliefs and can produce distressing feelings and dysfunctional behaviors. To address disturbing mental images, several techniques have been developed. Using the following scenario, eight imagery-changing techniques are described (J. Beck., 2011).

> Vanessa has a bridge phobia and becomes extremely anxious when driving over a bridge. Even when her husband is driving, she begins to get panicky as they get close to a bridge. As they drive over, she begins to have images of her husband losing control of the car, the car veering off the side of the bridge and plunging into the water. She sees them struggling to get out of the car as it fills with water. Her heart beats frantically as they drive over the bridge, the images deeply embedded in her mind.

> *Following images to completion:* In this technique, the client tells the story about the image to its completion. Generally, one of two things happen: either the client

resolves the story (e.g., Vanessa sees them crashing off the bridge, looks at the therapist, and says, "This is really silly—this will never happen," and begins to challenge the image), or the image is taken to its catastrophic end, which provides important new material the client can work on (e.g., Vanessa sees herself and her husband dying in the crash and worries about what will happen to the children—the underlying concern in the image is worry about ensuring her children's safety).

Jumping ahead in time: In this case, the client jumps ahead in time to "jump over" the distressing image. For instance, while driving over the bridge, Vanessa learns how to image herself safely at the end of the bridge.

Coping in the image. Here we have Vanessa change her image so that she is coping in the image. For instance, as she and her husband near the bridge, she can imagine herself saying to him, "Can I drive? I love going over this bridge." Then, she can imagine herself driving over it.

Changing the image: In this case, the image is changed to one that does not result in distress. This can be done realistically or as a "magical" image. As an example of a magical image, Vanessa might see herself in a fancy convertible going over a golden bridge that has safety nets on the side to catch cars that could fall over. Her hair flows in the wind as she enjoys the ride over the bridge.

Reality-testing the image: Here the therapist uses Socratic questioning to bring the client "back to reality." For instance, the therapist might ask Vanessa, "What is the likelihood of this happening?" "Do you think your anxiety is in line with the probability that this will occur?"

Repeating the image: By describing a distressing image multiple times, the image will often change on its own, sometimes becoming more subdued. For instance, when Vanessa is asked to continually describe the image of the car driving over the bridge, she slowly changes it in her mind's eye to one in which she is still anxious but able to successfully make it over the bridge.

Image-stopping: Similar to thought-stopping, this technique has the client use mechanisms to stop the image in its tracks. For instance, Vanessa might yell out "Stop it!" as she begins to imagine the car veering off the road, or she might snap a rubber band she has placed around her wrist—the snapping being a signal to herself to stop imagining the car veering off the bridge.

Image-distracting: Here the client does something that is incompatible with the anxiety-producing image. So, Vanessa might play Sudoku as her husband drives the car over the bridge. One cannot play Sudoku and be anxious at the same time. Or, she might have a planned phone call to her supervisor to discuss a work situation at the time she knows she will be going over the bridge.

Rational–Emotional Role-Play

Even though clients will come to the realization that their beliefs are dysfunctional, many have difficulty counteracting them due to a strong emotional attachment to the belief (J. Beck, 2011). Rational–emotional role-play allows clients to have a debate between the rational and emotional parts of themselves. Often, the therapist will first debate the client by role-playing the rational part while the client responds with the emotional, dysfunctional part. Then, in order to allow the client to counteract his or her own dysfunctional part, the therapist will switch roles with the client. The following role-play shows the first part of this process, with the therapist playing the rational part and the client playing the emotional, dysfunctional part.

Counselor: "How about we role-play the emotionally dysfunctional and the rational parts of your dilemma around your feelings of being a horrible husband? I'll be the rational part, and you start by being the emotional, dysfunctional part. As that person, tell me how you feel about yourself as a husband."

Client: "I'm a horrible husband, I don't show my wife any respect or listen to her in the least."

Counselor: "I have work to do as a husband, but sometimes I am very romantic with my wife, like when I buy her flowers and take her out for dinner."

Client: "Well, I may be a good husband sometimes, but I know I can just be an idiot and screwball and tend to have little, if any, empathy for her. She'll probably just leave me some day."

Counselor: "I may not be the best husband, but I've been working hard on being better, especially in refence to hearing her and understanding her. I think she sees that."

Client: "I just think that others are better than me."

Counselor: "You know, I've been working hard on being a better husband—being that person I imagine I can be. I think that's a pretty good thing."

Client: "Ahh, I think I see your point. I am really deriding myself, and maybe I'm not the best, but am certainly working on getting better. I need to pat myself on the back for that!"

Counselor: "So, we have a little bit of a different picture here?"

Client: "Well, yes, I guess we do."

In this role-play, notice the various cognitive distortions that make up the client's thinking process (e.g., all or nothing thinking and catastrophizing—see Box 3.2). How can identification of such distortions and associated automatic thoughts help the client? With what core beliefs might this client be struggling? Also, consider what it would be like if the client and therapist switched roles, with the client now being able to be the more rational, functional part of self.

Behavioral and Emotive Techniques

Throughout this chapter I have discussed the connections among beliefs, automatic thoughts, and how one feels and acts. With negative automatic thoughts come negative feelings and dysfunctional behaviors. And it makes sense that if a client is to change his or her automatic thoughts, he or she should also address the emotions and behaviors that have resulted from them. Such a multifaceted approach can help the change process occur more rapidly.

For instance, the husband who insists he is horrible to his wife may want to learn some specific behaviors relative to how to listen to a person (e.g., eye contact, open body posture, etc.). And he may want to monitor his feelings so that when he becomes frustrated with his wife, he walks into another room and begins a relaxation technique. At the same time, he can work on his cognitive distortions and his automatic thoughts. As his thoughts, behaviors, and emotions change, he begins to become who he has always imagined he has wanted to be—a loving, listening, caring husband, with flaws, as we all have.

As another example of a behavioral technique, consider the woman who has a core belief that she is unlovable. From this core belief she has developed a set of behaviors that prevents her from getting close to people. As the person works on addressing her negative core belief, she can also approach her problem behaviorally. For instance, she might set a goal of finding a support group so she can meet others. And, as an emotive technique, once she finds this group, she can have a secondary goal of sharing deeper feelings with some of the people in the group to develop intimacy.

There are literally hundreds of behavioral and emotive techniques that CBT therapists can use in conjunction with their cognitive techniques, and techniques used are only limited by the imagination of the therapist in consultation with the client. To find an appropriate technique, the therapist must have a good sense of the client's underlying cognitive processes (often deduced from a diagnosis and good client history) and then match an appropriate technique.

As the assessment process comes to an end, the therapist should begin to have a picture of the client's life and develop a tentative conceptualization of the client's belief system. Figure 3.4 can be helpful in understanding this process. Therapists will often seek feedback from the client and assess the client's readiness to follow through on a tentative treatment plan. At this time, broad goals can be set (e.g., "alleviation of depression," "getting along better with people at work," etc.).

THE COUNSELING PROCESS

The therapeutic process in CBT can be seen as a series of stages that includes **intake and evaluation, the first session, the second and subsequent sessions,** and **termination.**

Intake and Evaluation

Taking place prior to therapy, intake and evaluation are focused on performing a thorough assessment of the client. This process, which may or may not take place with the client's eventual therapist, helps oriented the client's therapist to the client's problem and focuses on the following broad goals (J. Beck, 2011):

1. Greeting the client and building the therapeutic alliance.
2. Discussing the purpose and process of the session and setting the agenda.
3. Conducting a mood check (e.g., "On a scale of 0 to 100, with 100 being extremely depressed, how depressed do you feel today?").
4. Conducting the assessment.
5. Developing broad initial goals.
6. Eliciting feedback from the client.

A large portion of the intake and evaluation will be focused on the assessment process, which should cover a wide spectrum of the client's life (J. Beck, 2011; Neukrug, 2015). Some of these are highlighted in Box 3.5.

BOX 3.5 CONDUCTING THE ASSESSMENT

The assessment process should have breadth and depth, and some of the areas that should be covered during this evaluation include the following:

1. Client demographics
2. Presenting problems and issues

3. Past and present coping strategies
4. Client and family psychiatric history
5. Family background
6. Social and cultural issues
7. Developmental concerns
8. Substance use and abuse
9. Medical history
10. Family background
11. Educational and vocational history
12. Medical history
13. Mental status (appearance and behavior, emotional state, thinking process, and cognitive functioning)
14. Past and current diagnoses
15. Religious and spiritual background and important values
16. Strengths and coping strategies
17. Administer appropriate assessment instruments (e.g., Beck Depression Inventory II, Beck, Steer, & Brown, 2003)

The First Session

The structure of the first session varies from subsequent sessions because it focuses on building the relationship, instilling hope, and educating and orienting the client to the cognitive model. J. Beck (2011) suggests the following structure for the first session:

1. *Set the agenda:* This part of the session involves the therapist informing the client about what will occur during the first session.
2. *Conduct a mood check:* Here the therapist reevaluates the client with the same assessment instrument given during the intake or some accurate measure that can assess the client's mood (e.g., The Beck Depression Inventory).
3. *Obtain an update.* Near the beginning of the session, clients are asked whether they have any additional concerns, questions, or information to add since their first meeting. To ready the client for change, they are asked about any positive experiences they had since the last meeting. Such experiences can begin to focus them on the change process.
4. *Discuss the diagnosis.* Although identifying a DSM diagnosis is not always necessary with a client, offering a more general diagnosis, such as "You seem pretty depressed," or "You seem to be struggling with a phobia," can be quite helpful. At this point, it

can also be helpful to normalize the clients' experiences by letting them know that others have successfully tackled similar problems, and offering readings or other resources that can help clients begin to understand the cognitive model and what they are struggling with.

5. *Review presenting problem(s) and set goals:* Next, clients begin to review the initial problems identified during the intake interview to ensure that no other issues need to be addressed. At this point, problems can be turned into broad goals. For example, a depressed client who is missing work and feeling lonely might have the broad goals of feeling less depressed, making new friends, and missing less time at work.
6. *Educate the client about the cognitive model:* Here the therapist teaches the client the relationships among thoughts, feelings, and behaviors. Thoughts are broadly defined as what one is thinking about along with images or pictures that pass through one's mind, with the therapist using examples from the client's life to show that situations affect thoughts and that thoughts will often lead to strong feelings and actions. Also, the therapist might use a drawing to highlight this point:

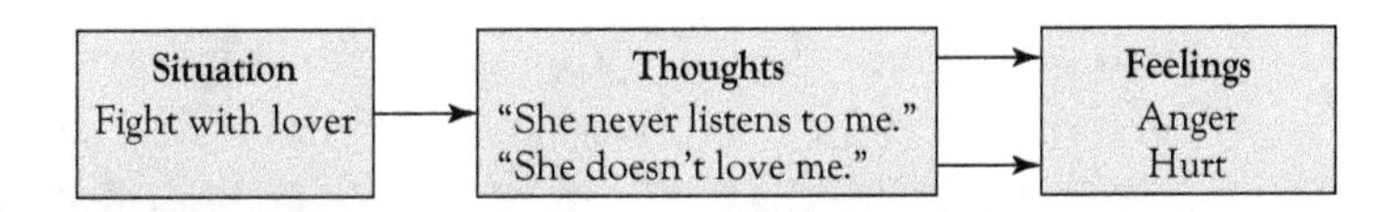

At this point, the focus is on teaching the client how to catch his or her automatic thoughts. Later sessions will focus upon cognitive distortions (and their relationship to automatic thoughts), intermediate thoughts, coping or compensatory strategies, and lastly, core beliefs.

7. *Set expectations for therapy:* Because clients often come to therapy with the idea that the therapist will magically "cure" them, during the first session the therapist demystifies the therapeutic process by describing therapy as a rational and empirical process in which the client examines how he or she can feel better by changing his or her cognitions. Based on the kind of presenting problem, the therapist also offers a realistic estimate on how long this process should take.
8. *Summarize the session and develop homework assignments:* Near the end of this session, the therapist summarizes what was discussed and collaboratively develops tasks that the client can work on at home prior to the next session. Tasks should be achievable, and if the therapist senses the client will not work on one or more specific tasks, he or she should modify the task(s) or come up with others.
9. *Ask for feedback:* Asking for feedback helps to reinforce the collaborative nature of the relationship and assures that the therapist is on target with the direction of therapy.

Feedback can be asked for orally, but Judith Beck (2011) also suggests that the following types of questions can be responded to in writing:

- What did you cover today that's important to you to remember?
- How much did you feel you could trust your therapist today?
- Was there anything that bothered you about therapy today? If so, what was it?
- How much homework had you done for therapy today? How likely are you to do your homework?
- What do you want to make sure to cover at the next session? (p. 77)

Information from the initial intake and the first session allows the therapist to put the pieces of the puzzle together as he or she completes all aspects noted in Figure 3.4. This allows the therapist, and eventually the client, to increasingly understand how the client's history, belief system, coping strategies, and automatic thoughts affect the client's daily life.

Second and Subsequent Sessions

These sessions are focused on strengthening the therapeutic alliance, symptom relief, and obtaining a deeper understanding of the cognitive model. In that light, the therapist hopes to continue to familiarize the client with the CBT model, work collaboratively, help the client solve identified problems, and, as symptom relief is obtained, work toward termination. As sessions continue, this work becomes increasingly focused as the pieces of the puzzle, as highlighted in Figure 3.4, are completed. Judith Beck (1995; 2011) suggests the following structure for the second and subsequent sessions:

1. *Conduct a mood check:* Here the therapist checks in with the client to see how he or she is doing since the last session. In addition to gathering verbal feedback, the therapist asks the client to retake the same instrument that was taken during their last session (e.g., Beck Depression Scale) and/or to conduct a subjective mood check (0–100). In this manner, the therapist can assess progress toward goals.
2. *Set the agenda:* In the earlier sessions, the therapist sets more of the agenda as he or she identifies problems to focus upon and teaches the client about the cognitive model. As the client learns more about the model, along with techniques that can be used to address cognitive distortions, coping strategies, and negative core beliefs, it is the client who increasingly sets the agenda.
3. *Review of homework:* Compliance in doing homework is facilitated by the therapist's review of all homework assignments. When a homework assignment has not been completed, it is important for the therapist to understand the reason why. Not completing a homework assignment due to a family emergency is quite different from ignoring

one because the goals were inappropriate. As sessions continue, the client takes more responsibility for developing his or her own homework assignments.

4. *Shift from automatic thoughts to intermediate and core beliefs.* As sessions continue, the client becomes increasingly familiar with the cognitive model and can begin to understand intermediate and core beliefs and begin the process of disputing them. This process occurs through mental disputations and behavioral changes.
5. *Ask for Feedback:* As in the first session, feedback is critical in every session if the client is to feel as if he or she is a collaborator and if therapy is to be on track (see "The First Session").

Termination

Because it is predicated on the alleviation of identified symptoms, CBT tends to be short-term, and from the very first session, there is an eye to the last session. Although the therapist takes a more directive and educative role early in this process, as the client increasingly learns how to work independently on his or her issues, the therapist takes a lesser role. Figure 3.5 graphically depicts this process.

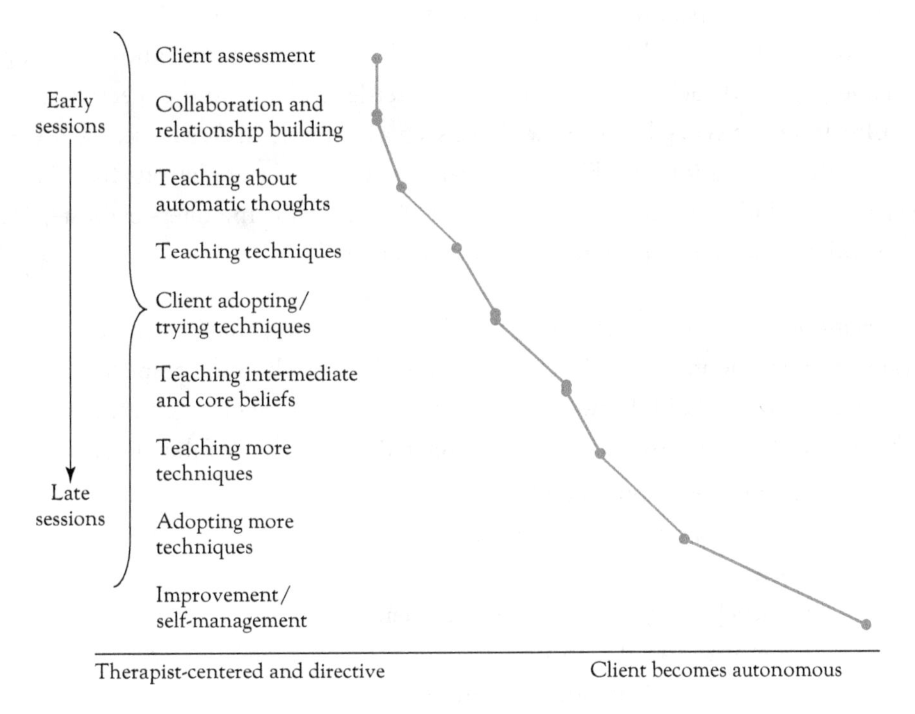

Figure 3.5 Movement of Client toward Termination over Sessions

As therapy continues, the therapist should expect client setbacks as the client struggles to work on his or her problems and as the hypotheses that initially were formed become slightly changed. As the client nears the last session, the therapist should explore his or her thoughts about termination and help the client develop a process in which he or she is conducting self-management sessions (see Box 3.6).

BOX 3.6 JAKE WITH A CBT COUNSELOR

Your instructor might have you view Jake with a counselor who uses an CBT approach to counseling, though he also integrates some other non-CBT techniques. After you view the video, consider how effective the counselor was at doing this.

SOCIAL AND CULTURAL ISSUES

The early days of CBT saw research on its effectiveness mostly conducted on Whites, focused little on cross-cultural issues, and offered little explanation on how to work with diverse clients (Graham et al., 2013; Hays, 2006, 2009). In fact, CBT has been viewed as an approach that has been laden with European American values, focused more on an individual's cognitions as opposed to how the person's cultural context influences cognitions, and as an approach that has largely ignored such cultural aspects as interdependence and collectivism (Hall & Ibaraki, 2016). In recent years, however, we have seen a dramatic shift, as research and articles that focus on the application of CBT with a variety of diverse populations have blossomed (DeAngelis, 2015; Hall & Ibaraki, 2016; Hays, 2009). The following offers **eight steps for providing culturally competent counseling** to diverse clients:

1. *Demonstrate culturally respectful behavior.* One of the ways that the therapist can build rapport with clients from diverse backgrounds is by showing respect. For instance, using the **RESPECTFUL model** (Lewis et al., 2011) can help to eliminate discomfort that is the result of miscommunication related to one of the following influences:

    R – religious/spiritual identity
    E – economic class background
    S – sexual identity
    P – level of psychological development
    E – ethnic/racial identity
    C – chronological/developmental challenges
    T –various forms of trauma and other threats to one's sense of well-being
    F – family background and history
    U – unique physical characteristics
    L – location of residence and language differences (p. 54)

2. *Identify culturally related strengths.* Building the therapeutic alliance is critical in CBT, and focusing on client strengths can facilitate that process. Strengths can include pride in any of the following: cultural identity, religion or spirituality, culturally relevant music, important traditions and celebrations, culturally specific ways of relating, types of food, and more.
3. *Validate a client's feelings of oppression.* Extreme negative feelings may be the result of negative core beliefs, but also may be a function of the environment in which the person works. A client who is working in a racist environment, is dealing with a very real, external problem and cannot expect to have this altered by changing core beliefs. But sometimes such experiences could be heighted by a client's belief system (e.g., "The world is no good"). Validating the client's experience will help build rapport. Focusing on core beliefs that may amplify those feelings can always be discussed later.
4. *Help clients find ways of addressing environmental problems.* When problems are external, clients need to find ways to address them. These could include developing a support system, finding ways to advocate for self, developing effective communication skills to help clients find new ways to interact with others, and increasing self-care activities.
5. *Emphasize collaboration and don't make assumptions about negative beliefs.* Minority clients have often been placed in a "one down" position in society, and when therapists act in an authoritarian manner, or make assumptions about client beliefs and behaviors, clients may "shut down." CBT should be a collaborative process in which clients are invited to discuss their thoughts about a therapist's hypothesis regarding the client's beliefs and behaviors. Therapists should nurture the helping relationship through their body language and by encouraging feedback and discussion about the process.
6. *Avoid challenging core cultural beliefs.* Some therapists might view certain thoughts or behaviors as negative, but, in actuality, they might be an important aspect of a client's culture. For instance, a client who seems by the therapist to be overly "dependent" on a grandparent may come from a culture in which elders are esteemed and viewed to have great wisdom.
7. *Use culturally related strengths and supports to replace unhelpful cognitions with helpful ones.* Internal and interpersonal strengths and support that are culturally meaningful can become mantras for clients. For instance, a Jewish client who is having trouble asserting himself could use the mantra "never again," which is said by many Jews regarding never allowing themselves to again be oppressed. Such a mantra could build strength in a person who feels meek.
8. *Develop homework assignments that are congruent to the client's culture.* Some homework assignments may be viewed indifferently, or even negatively, by clients if they are developed solely from the therapist. Make sure the client is intimately involved with the development of his or her homework and that it matches the client's cultural identity.

One's religious and spiritual focus can greatly impact one's belief system. For instance, where many Unitarians and Reform Jews will find a logical connection between their beliefs and CBT theory, therapists would have to make adjustments with some Asian Americans, evangelical Christians, Orthodox Jews, and Orthodox Muslims by understanding that "other forces" can also be shaping the client's life (Iwamasa et al., 2006; G. McAuliffe, personal communication, March 22, 2020). As with cross-cultural issues, CBT therapists need to understand how the client comes to understand their religion and spirituality and make necessary changes to their approach based on this understanding.

EFFICACY

CBT uses a case conceptualization process in which the therapist assesses the client and then applies a specific treatment plan based on this assessment. In addition, instruments to assess and measure progress in treatment have been developed. Thus, assessing the effectiveness of CBT can seem rather straightforward: Assess, apply your model, and use your instrument to measure change. It is not surprising, therefore, that hundreds of studies to measure the effectiveness of CBT have been conducted over the years (Hofman, et al., 2012; Wampold, 2015). In fact, more than 2,000 research studies have been conducted on CBT, which has shown it has been efficacious with a wide range of disorders (Beck Institute, 2000c; J. Beck, 2011), especially those listed in Box 3.7.

BOX 3.7 CONDITIONS OFTEN TREATED WITH COGNITIVE BEHAVIOR THERAPY

- Anorexia
- Bipolar Disorder
- Bulimia
- Chronic Fatigue Syndrome
- Chronic Pain
- Colitis
- Depression
- Fibromyalgia
- Generalized Anxiety Disorder
- Health Anxiety
- Irritable Bowel Syndrome
- Migraine Headaches
- Obesity
- Obsessive Compulsive Disorder
- Panic Disorder
- Personality Disorders
- Posttraumatic Stress Disorder
- Schizophrenia
- Social Phobia
- Substance Use Disorders

In an attempt to make sense out of all this research, one study examined 269 meta-analyses, most of which were published in recent years (Hofman et al., 2012). The authors found the following:

- High effectiveness for treating cannabis and nicotine dependence, but less helpful with alcohol and opioid dependence.
- Some mixed results in the treatment of depression, dysthymia, and bipolar disorders, though a number of studies did show strong support.
- Strong support for the use of CBT with anxiety disorders and somatoform disorders.
- Some evidence that CBT was effective in stress management compared with other treatments.
- Some preliminary evidence for the use of CBT with distress related to pregnancy complications and female hormonal conditions.
- Strong support for CBT with bulimia and insomnia compared with other treatment modalities.
- Some evidence for the treatment of personality disorders compared with other treatments and for the treatment of anger and aggression.
- Strong support for CBT when working with children who had internalizing disorders (mood and anxiety), but less so for externalizing disorders (e.g., aggressive and antisocial behaviors).
- Some support for the use of CBT with emotional symptoms with older persons.

At first glance, the above results seem pretty impressive. Indeed, it appears that CBT is effective with a wide range of mental health problems—and it is. Yet, there is a "but"—it appears that *all* approaches are pretty much equally effective. Well, at least that is the result of a massive review of the research by Wampold (2015). Reminiscent of Rosenzweig's 1936 research when he said, "All methods of therapy when competently used are equally successful," Wampold finds that his quote stands up to today's rigor and reminds us that Rosenweigh called this the **"dodo bird effect"** (see Box 3.8).

BOX 3.8 THE DODO BIRD EFFECT

The dodo bird was a character in Lewis Carroll's book "Alice in Wonderland" (1918). Issuing a competition to a number of characters who had gotten wet, the dodo bird tells them to run around a lake until they were dry. After doing so, they wanted to know who had won. His response: "EVERYBODY has won, and all must have prizes" (p. 34). And, so it is with approaches to counseling and psychotherapy!

SUMMARY

The cognitive therapy movement began during the 1960s with the development of two parallel theories: Aaron "Tim" Beck's cognitive therapy and Albert Ellis's rational therapy. Later called cognitive behavior therapy and rational emotive behavior therapy, respectively, CBT and REBT are considered the second wave of cognitive behavioral therapies, and the two are known for ushering in the cognitive revolution in psychology. First-wave cognitive behavioral therapy focused almost exlusively on behaviors and included operant conditioning, classical conditioning, and modeling, while third-wave cognitive behavioral therapy took a look at how context impacts the person, and included such therapies as dialectical behavior therapy and acceptance and commitment therapy. This chapter focused on Beck's CBT model.

Beck initially became a psychoanalyst; however, becoming disillusioned with psychoanalysis, and finding that his clients were often aware, or could easily become aware, of "automatic thoughts," he began to develop his own theory that focused on how cognitions mediate how one acts and feels. Over the years, Beck found that different disorders presented with specific features related to the client's cognitive processes. Thus, Beck came up with a logical process that included hypothesizing about the cognitive processes associated with different disorders, developing manuals to assist clinicians in the treatment of various disorders, developing scales to measure the disorder (e.g., depression), and while using the manuals, conducting clinical studies to assess the effectiveness of therapeutic interventions.

Positing a diathesis–stress model of mental disorders, CBT suggests that a combination of genetic predispositions, biological factors, and experiences combine to produce specific core beliefs, some of which may lie dormant and then suddenly appear as the result of stress and other conditions impinging on the person. Cognitive therapy is seen as a rational, pragmatic, educative, empirical, structured, and anti-deterministic approach that proposes that people can manage and effect changes in the way they live in the world in a relatively brief time. This approach has elements of a constructionist perspective when it states that through discourse with others, individuals can change their cognitions and overcome their predispositions.

Cognitive therapists believe that one's core beliefs become the underlying mechanism for the creation of intermediate beliefs that set the attitudes, rules and expectations, and assumptions we live by. These attitudes, rules and expectations, and assumptions can be understood by looking at how situations in life lead to what are called automatic thoughts that result in a set of behaviors, feelings, and physiological responses that end up reinforcing core beliefs. Beck also suggests there are a number of cognitive distortions that tend to be associated with the automatic thoughts we have. Finally, coping or compensatory strategies, usually created early in life, are often developed by individuals to steer themselves away from experiencing their negative core beliefs. But these strategies do not rid persons of their core beliefs, and over time the strategies become maladaptive. Beck and other cognitive therapists believe that through a process called cognitive conceptualization, the therapist can assess the client and begin to make hypotheses about the kinds of automatic thoughts and intermediate and core beliefs that define the person. Then, strategies can be developed to help the individual change his or her beliefs, and ultimately behaviors, feelings, and physiology.

Ten basic principles underlie the practice of CBT and a number of essential and commonly used techniques are implemented in practice. Some of the essential techniques include building a strong therapeutic alliance, educating the client about the cognitive model, Socratic questioning, identifying and challenging automatic thoughts and images, identifying and challenging cognitive distortions, identifying intermediate beliefs, identifying and challenging core beliefs, and doing homework assignments. Some of the commonly used techniques include thought-stopping, imagery-changing, rational–emotional role-play, and behavioral and emotive techniques. In addition, it was noted that hundreds of other specific techniques can be used to help with the change process.

The therapeutic process can be viewed through a series of four stages: (1) intake and evaluation, which includes greeting the client and building the therapeutic alliance, discussing the purpose and process of the session and setting the agenda, conducting a mood check, conducting the assessment, developing broad initial goals, and eliciting feedback from the client; (2) the first session, which includes setting the agenda, conducting a mood check, obtaining an update, discussing the diagnosis, reviewing presenting problems and setting goals, educating the client about the cognitive model, setting expectations for therapy, summarizing the session and developing homework assignments, and asking for feedback; (3) the second and subsequent sessions, which includes conducting a mood check, setting the agenda, reviewing homework, shifting from automatic thoughts to intermediate and core beliefs, and asking for feedback; and (4) termination. The sessions tend to increasingly move toward client self-management as clients learn about the cognitive model and make positive changes in their lives.

Relative to social, cultural, and spiritual issues, it was noted that most of the research on CBT has been conducted on Whites, focused little on cross-cultural issues, and offered little explanation as to how to work with diverse clients. It was also highlighted that European American values, including individualism, have been highlighted in this approach as opposed to a more collectivist orientation. In recent years, however, some have identified ways that the approach could be more adaptable to diverse clients, and eight steps for working with clients from diverse backgrounds were highlighted. Relative to spiritual issues, counselors were warned to understand how to work with those clients who believe that "forces" shape their lives and who believe they have little control over such forces.

When discussing the efficacy of CBT, it was noted that this approach has been widely researched, mostly because it has specific mechanisms for measuring the change process and because Beck has developed manuals that describe how to work with a number of disorders. A number of disorders that have been shown to work well with this approach were listed. Despite its apparent effectiveness with a wide variety of disorders, however, Wampold notes that when compared with other approaches, CBT, generally, is not more effective—they are all effective. This "dodo bird effect" suggests that all methods of therapy are effective when used by competent clinicians.

KEY WORDS AND NAMES

Acceptance and commitment therapy
Active
Adapt one's therapeutic style
Anti-deterministic
Attitudes, rules and expectations, and assumptions,
Automatic thoughts
Automatic thoughts and images
Beck, Aaron
Beck Depression Scale
Beck Institute for Cognitive Behavior Therapy in Philadelphia
Beck, Judith
Behavioral and emotive techniques
Building a strong therapeutic alliance
Cognitive behavioral therapy (CBT)
Cognitive conceptualization
Cognitive distortions
Cognitive model, The
Cognitive revolution in psychology
Cognitive schemas
Cognitive therapy
Collaboration
Commonly used techniques
Compensatory strategies
Constructivist
Continuity hypothesis
Coping or compensatory strategies
Coping or compensatory strategies
Coping strategies
Core beliefs
Dialectical behavior therapy
Diathesis–stress model
Diathesis–stress model of mental disorders
Dodo bird effect
Educating the client about the cognitive model
Educative
Eight steps for providing culturally competence counseling
Ellis, Albert
Empathy, caring, and optimism
Empirical approach
Essential techniques
Frist-wave cognitive behavioral therapy
First session, The
Genetic and evolutionary predisposition toward emotional responses
Homework
Identifying and challenging automatic thoughts and images
Identifying and challenging cognitive distortions
Identifying and challenging core beliefs
Identifying intermediate beliefs
Imagery changing
Intake and evaluation
Intermediate beliefs
Pragmatic
Present-focused approach
Rational
Rational emotive behavior therapy (REBT)
Rational therapy
Rational–emotional role-play
RESPECTFUL model
Second and subsequent sessions, The
Second wave of cognitive behavioral therapies
Socratic questioning
Structured
Ten basic principles
Termination
Third-wave cognitive behavioral therapy
Thought-stopping
Time sensitive

REFERENCES

Bakker, G. (2008). *Practical CBT: Using functional analysis and standardized homework in everyday therapy.* Australian Academic Press.

Beck, A. T. (1964). Thinking and depression: II. Theory and therapy. *Archives of General Psychiatry, 10*, 561–571.

Beck, A. T. (1967). *Depression: Clinical, experimental, and theoretical aspects*. Harper and Row. Republished as *Depression: Causes and treatment*. University of Pennsylvania Press, 1972.

Beck, A. T. (1976). *Cognitive therapy and the emotional disorders*. International Universities Press.

Beck, A. T. (1991). Cognitive therapy: A 30-year retrospective. *American Psychologist, 46*(4), 368–375. https://doi.org/10.1037/0003-066X.46.4.368

Beck, A. T. (2005). The current state of cognitive therapy: A 40-year retrospective. *Archives of General Psychiatry, 62*, 953–959. https://doi.org/10.1001/archpsyc.62.9.953

Beck, A. T., & Haigh, E. A. P. (2014). Advances in cognitive theory and therapy: The generic cognitive model. *Annual Review of Clinical Psychology, 10*, 1–24. https://doi.org/10.1146/annurev-climpsy-032813-153734

Beck, A. T., Rush, A. J., Shaw, B. F., & Emery, G. (1979). *Cognitive therapy of depression*. Guilford Press.

Beck, A. T., Steer, R. A., & Brown, G. K. (2003). *BDI-II manual*. Psychological Corporation.

Beck Institute. (2019a). *Beck Institute 25th anniversary celebration*. https://beckinstitute.org/about-beck/celebration/

Beck Institute. (2019b). *Aaron T. Beck, MD*. https://beckinstitute.org/team/dr-aaron-t-beck/

Beck Institute. (2019c). *What is cognitive behavior therapy (CBT)?* https://www.beckinstitute.org/get-informed/what-is-cognitive-therapy/

Beck, J. S. (1995). *Cognitive therapy: Basics and beyond*. Guilford Press.

Beck, J. S. (2005). *Cognitive therapy for challenging problems*. Guilford Press.

Beck, J. S. (2007). *The Beck diet solution: Train your brain to think like a thin person*. Oxmoor House.

Beck, J. S. (2011). *Cognitive behavior therapy: Basics and beyond* (2nd ed.). Guilford Press.

Beck, J. S., & Busis, D. B. (2015). *The diet trap solution: Train your brain to lose weight and keep it off for good*. HarperCollins.

Carroll, L. (1918). *Alice's adventures in wonderland*. Lee and Shepard.

DeAngelis, T. (2015). In search of cultural competence. *Monitor on Psychology, 46*, 64.

Dobson, K. S. (2012). *Cognitive therapy*. American Psychological Association.

Graham, J. R., Sorenson, S., & Hayes-Skelton, S. A. (2013). Enhancing the cultural sensitivity of cognitive behavioral interventions for anxiety in diverse populations. *Behavior Therapy, 36*(5), 101–108.

Hall, G. C. N., & Ibaraki, A. Y. (2016). Multicultural issues in cognitive-behavioral therapy: Cultural adaptations and goodness of fit. In C. M. Nezu & A. M. Nezu (Eds.), *The Oxford handbook of cognitive and behavioral therapies* (pp. 465–481). Oxford University Press.

Hays, P. A. (2006). Introduction: Developing culturally responsive cognitive-behavioral therapies. In P. A. Hays & G. Y. Iwamasa (Eds.), *Culturally responsive cognitive-behavioral therapy: Assessment, practice, and supervision* (pp. 3–21). American Psychological Association.

Hays, P. A. (2012). Culturally responsive cognitive behavioral therapy in practice. In Neukrug, E. S. & Fawcett, R. C. (2015), *Essentials of testing and assessment: A practical guide for counselors, social workers, and psychologists* (3rd ed). Brooks/Cole.

Hofman, S. G., Asnaani, A., Vonk, I. J. J., Sawyer, M. A., & Fang, A., (2012). The efficacy of cognitive behavioral therapy: A review of meta-analyses. *Cognitive Therapy Research, 36*(5), 427–440. https://doi.org/10.1007/s10608-012-9476-1

Iwamasa, G. Y., Hsia, C., & Hinton, D. (2006). Cognitive-behavioral therapy with Asian Americans. In P. A. Hays & G. Y. Iwamasa (Eds.), *Culturally responsive cognitive-behavioral therapy: Assessment, practice, and supervision* (pp. 117–140). American Psychological Association.

Krapp, K. (Ed.). (2005). Beck, Aaron Temkin. *Psychologists and their theories for students* (Vol. 1, pp. 67–91). Gale Cengage.

Neukrug, E. S. (2018). *Counseling theory and practice* (2nd ed.). Cognella Academic Publishing.

Newman, C. F. (2016). Cognitive restructuring/cognitive therapy. In C. M. Nezu & A. M. Nezu (Eds.), *The Oxford handbook of cognitive and behavioral therapies* (pp. 118–141). Oxford University Press.

O'Connor, K. P. (2015). *A constructionist clinical psychology for cognitive behavior therapy.* Routledge.

Osmo, F., Duran, V., Wenzel, A., de Oliveira, I., Nepomuceno, S., Maderia, M., & Menezes, I. (2018). The Negative Core Beliefs Inventory (NCBI): Development and psychometric properties. *Journal of Cognitive Psychotherapy, 32*(1), 67-84. https://doi.org/10.1891/0889-8391.32.1.67

Padesky, C. A., & Beck, A. T. (2003). Science and philosophy: Comparison of cognitive therapy and rational emotive behavior therapy. *Journal of Cognitive Psychotherapy: An International Quarterly, 17*(3), 211–225. https://doi.org/10.1891/jcop.17.3.211.52536

Rice, R. (2015). Cognitive-behavioral therapy. In E. S. Neukrug (Ed.), *The SAGE encyclopedia of theory in counseling and psychotherapy* (Vol. 1, pp. 194–199). SAGE Publications.

Rosenzweigh, S. (1936). Some implicit common factors in diverse methods of psychotherapy. "At last the Dodo said, 'Everybody has won and all must have prizes.'" *American Journal of Orthopsychiatry,* 6, 412–415.

Scott, J., & Freeman, A. (2010). Beck's cognitive therapy. In N. Kazantzis, M. A. Reinecke, & A. Freeman (Eds.), *Cognitive and behavioral theories in clinical practice* (pp. 28–75). Guilford Press.

The top 10: The most influential therapists of the past quarter-century (2007, March/April). *Psychotherapy Networker.* http://www.psychotherapynetworker.org/index.php/magazine/populartopics/219-the-top-10

Tower, P. (2011). CBT theory. In W. Dryden & R. Branch (Eds.), *The CBT handbook* (pp. 25–44). SAGE Publications.

Weishaar, M. E. (1993). *Aaron T. Beck.* SAGE Publications.

Weishaar, M. E. (2015). Aaron T. Beck. In E. S. Neukrug (Ed.), *The SAGE encyclopedia of theory in counseling and psychotherapy* (Vol. 1, pp. 85–90). SAGE Publications.

CASE STUDY: ANN MEETS WITH A COGNITIVE BEHAVIOR THERAPIST

(Please read about the Millers in Appendix I prior to reading this case study)

Ann sat in the lobby arranging and rearranging the items in her bag. She had completed an intake form and a short questionnaire about her feelings of depression and anxiety, and considered thumbing through one of the parenting magazines on the coffee table as she waited for the counselor Jake had recommended, Carol Allen, to emerge from her office. Ann looked at the family sitting stiffly on the couch directly across from her and offered a weak smile. Carol, a round-faced woman with graying hair and soft wrinkles around her eyes, smiled at Ann and invited her into her office. Ann was already crying before Carol was able to shut the door.

"I don't know where to start, so I'm going to start in the middle, or maybe at the end, I don't know. Two months ago I had my 65th birthday. It has hit me like a ton of bricks. It just got me thinking about my life." Ann paused a moment, reached inside her purse and then, thinking better of it, set her purse aside. "There was a birthday party. My husband, Ted, and my children, Jake and Justine, were there. Jake's wife Angela and my grandchildren, Luke and Celia, were there, too, of course. Evangeline and Dexter, Angela's parents, helped Tom set up the whole thing. A lot of my old friends came, too, and even some of my piano students from way back and then—this is what got me I, think—Justine brought a boyfriend."

"Your daughter, she brought a man with her. What was it about Justine's date that troubled you?" Carol asked.

"Well, Justine moved out of the house last year and into a group home. She had an accident as a child that left her with—I can never quite get this out— she's retarded. I mean, she's intellectually disabled—at least that's what they tell me to say these days. This man she was with, Carl, he lives in the group home, too. He has Down syndrome," Ann explained. "That wasn't what bothered me, though. It was just seeing all my friends and catching up on their lives and watching Jake with his kids and Justine with Carl. I should have been happy for everyone, but to tell the truth, I just felt really cheated. Here I am, 65 years old, and I was robbed of my children's childhood, robbed of a career, and now I'm just left behind. Everyone has their lives, their families and careers, and I—I have nothing to show for my life! Even Justine has a life of her own now, after years and years of having only me." Ann wiped the tears from her cheeks.

"Ann, when you saw your daughter at the party with Carl, can you remember the first thing that popped into your mind?"

"Yes, I thought, 'This is not how it's supposed to be.' I know how selfish that sounds." Ann paused and added, "I have always felt it was unfair that my friends' children grew up without the kinds of troubles that Justine had. And I spent so much time tending to Justine after the accident that my relationship with Jake fell apart. We were so close before, but there's been a distance ever since the accident. Also, I just never could move on with my career. You know,

I had been a piano teacher, and I was hoping to eventually go back to that—my dream had been to start a music school. But Justine just took up so much of my time."

"Have you noticed what kinds of feelings you experience when those thoughts of things not being the way they should be move across your mind?" Carol asked Ann, handing her a box of tissues.

"Sadness, then sometimes anger and regret." Ann wiped her wet cheeks and blew her nose. "I get so depressed that things didn't work out the way that they were supposed to."

"I felt that from you, Ann, a lot of sadness, regret, and anger, and it sounded like there were feelings of being helpless, too, like you were just pushed around by the tide of events and left standing on the shoreline alone." Carol allowed some silence before continuing. "Ann, how often do you think that you have thoughts of how things should have been different?"

"A lot. It was one of the first things I thought about after the doctor told us that Justine had a brain injury and that she wasn't going to recover from it. I remember Ted and I drove home after that consultation with the doctor and the streets were crowded with cars, children in the neighborhood were running around outdoors, and people were playing tennis at the tennis court. It was like nothing had happened. Our world was crumbling, and the rest of the world seemed completely untouched. I remember thinking, this is so unfair." Ann paused a moment. "I find myself thinking about how unfair life is a lot."

"You and Ted and your children have been dealt a rough hand, that's for sure. There is a part of me that agrees with you—what happened in that accident wasn't fair; it was a tragedy. But it seems to have cast a shadow over your whole life. What I would like to do today is talk about how those thoughts you have—I call them your 'automatic thoughts'—affect so much of your life and cause you to feel the way you do. But, before we go on to talk some more about automatic thoughts, I'd like to switch gears for a moment. If it's alright with you, I'd like to take some time going over your intake form and together try to get a sense of where you are right now and hopefully end with some goals for our coming sessions."

After covering more of Ann's history and evaluating her functioning, Carol ended the session by educating Ann about automatic thoughts and their connection to the feelings and behaviors that trouble most people. Carol and Ann explored the feelings Ann experienced when the thoughts of the world being unfair came to mind. Ann agreed to be mindful of the times when these thoughts arise in her mind and to make a note about it. Together, Ann and Carol agreed that in their next session they would work on ways to replace Ann's automatic thoughts with thoughts that are more productive for her and less distressing. Carol also provided Ann with readings about automatic thoughts and thought-stopping strategies.

When Carol and Ann met for their next session, Carol noticed a difference in Ann. "Your eyes look brighter than they did last week, Ann. How did your week go?"

"It was better than the week before; I was busy with some projects at church, so I was distracted. I did my homework, though." Ann reached into her purse and produced a small notebook, which she passed to Carol along with the mood questionnaire form she was asked to fill out as she waited for the session to begin. "I took notes on the reading that you gave me and I kept a little log of my thoughts."

"Oh, this is great, Ann," Carol said as she flipped through the notebook. "And according to your questionnaire, your mood seems to have improved some since last week. It seems that something about our last session was helpful to you. Can you tell me what that was?" Carol asked, creating a bridge between their first session and this one.

"I think it helped a lot to just get some of those feelings out. I just don't think I could say those things to Ted or to any of my friends. But talking about those automatic thoughts was a 'light bulb' moment for me. I have been carrying those thoughts around with me for 30 years, and they really do influence my feelings. When I was writing my log I noticed that when I have those thoughts and then start to feel angry, I really take it out on Ted. I didn't realize how much time I spend criticizing him, but I do," Ann confided. "Other times, I just get depressed."

As the session continued, Carol began to connect Ann's automatic thoughts to a number of cognitive distortions, which she described to Ann, including catastrophisizing, discounting the positive, tunnel vision, and overgeneralization. As the session came to a close Carol offered Ann some homework techniques to use to combat some of her automatic thoughts.

Over the next few sessions, Ann and Carol worked on combating her automatic thoughts. Carol began efforts to teach Ann about the connection between her automatic thoughts, her intermediate thoughts, and her core beliefs. Carol helped Ann chart the relationships among Ann's core beliefs, intermediate beliefs, automatic thoughts, and reactions (see the following).

THE RELATIONSHIPS AMONG ANN'S CORE BELIEFS, INTERMEDIATE BELIEFS, AUTOMATIC THOUGHTS, AND REACTIONS

Core Belief: "I am trapped, a victim, a failure, and powerless."

Intermediate Beliefs Attitude: "Life is unfair." Rule/expectation: "If I try to make things better, I'll just be knocked down again."

Assumption: "No matter what I do to try and change things, my life will still be unfair."

Situation: Birthday party

Some Possible Automatic Thoughts and Images (associated with cognitive distortions):

- "Things did not turn out the way I thought they would."
- "I was cheated."
- "Why did that accident have to happen?"
- "Everyone has moved on and I have nothing."

Images:

- Visualizing the accident.
- Thinking about how Justine was before the accident.
- Thinking about how Jake was before the accident.

Some Possible Reactions:

- Emotional: Sadness, depression, anger, regret, hopelessness
- Physiological: Low energy, lack of attention to health issues
- Behavioral: Staying home, arguments with husband, not making plans for future

"When I came to counseling, Carol, I thought I would be able to come in here, tell you how I was feeling, and you'd give me some good ideas for how to make my life meaningful," Ann said, laughing. "But this is a lot more complicated than I figured it for! Really looking at my thoughts and how they are connected to my core beliefs and then how all that leads to how I act, well that is a lot to consider. I guess this is going to take some time and some discipline?"

"You've already put a lot of work and effort into your counseling work, Ann, and you've made some important strides. I think if you continue as you have been you will reach your goals sooner than you think," Carol replied.

QUESTIONS FOR YOU TO PONDER

1. This therapist spent some time using basic attending skills to listen to Ann. How important do you believe those skills are in cognitive behavior therapy?
2. Although some basic attending skills were used by Carol, she at one point somewhat abruptly shifted gears to make sure the information in the assessment was covered. Do you think this kind of shifting gears is appropriate? How else could Carol have handled this?
3. How easy do you believe it is for most clients to "catch" their automatic thoughts?
4. In this example, some possible cognitive distortions were identified that may be associated with Ann's automatic thoughts. Can you explain how those cognitive distortions feed into Ann's automatic thoughts? Do you believe other cognitive distortions may have also been involved in Ann's thinking processes? If yes, which ones?
5. Ann seems pretty amenable to looking at the cognitive model that Carol is identifying (e.g., automatic thoughts, intermediate thoughts, core beliefs, etc.). Do you think most clients would so readily agree with this process? Why or why not? Do you have any concerns about Ann's willingness to shift attention from the goals she had (exploring her feelings and finding meaning) to Carol's aim to look at the role of her thoughts in her unhappiness?

6. Can you hypothesize about some of the attitudes, rules and expectations, and assumptions (intermediate beliefs) that Ann might have?
7. Using cognitive behavior therapy, how might you address Ann's insight that she takes her anger out on her husband? Do you think you might have suggested creating a goal from this problem? What might this goal look like?
8. Ann was eager to do the homework that Carol assigned. If you were Ann's counselor, how do you think you would work with Ann if she had chosen not to do her homework?
9. How long do you believe it will take Ann to work on changing her core beliefs? Explain.
10. Given endless resources (which often is not a reality!), do you believe that once Ann understands the cognitive behavior therapy process she can do most of the work on her own, or would it be better for her to continue with her therapist for an extended period? Explain.
11. Some of Ann's concerns seemed to have an existential ring. How might an existential therapist work differently with Ann? Which approach would you be more apt to use with Ann? Why?
12. Can you identify any cognitive distortions, intermediate beliefs, or core beliefs of yours that you can work on? How might you go about changing them?

Credits

Fig. 3.1a: Copyright © 2016 Depositphotos/VisualGeneration.

Fig. 3.1b: Copyright © 2019 Depositphotos/AndreyPopov.

Fig. 3.2: J. S. Beck, "Relationships among Core Beliefs, Intermediate Beliefs, and Automatic Thoughts," Cognitive Therapy: *Basics and Beyond*, pp. 36. Copyright © 2011 by Guilford Press.

Fig. 3.4: J. S. Beck, "Relationships among Core Beliefs, Intermediate Beliefs, Coping Strategies, Automatic Thoughts, Behaviors, and Feelings," *Cognitive Therapy for Challenging Problems*, pp. 20. Copyright © 2005 by Guilford Press.

4

Integrative Postmodern Therapy (IPMT)

Using Narrative, Solution-Focused, and Relational Cultural Approaches

Ed Neukrug

LEARNING OUTCOMES

- To understand the roots of integrative postmodern therapy (IPMT) relative to relational cultural therapy, narrative therapy, and solution-focused brief therapy.
- To review the postmodern, social-constructionist view of human nature of IPMT, and based on these philosophies, understand its anti-deterministic, anti-objectivist, non-pathological, positive, strength-based, and largely future-oriented underpinnings.
- To review a number of key concepts of IPMT, including postmodernism; post-structuralism; social constructionism; power; non-pathologizing; thin to thick descriptions; mutually enhancing, empathic, empowering relationships; and re-authoring.
- To explore major techniques of IPMT, including showing mystery, respectful curiosity, and awe; demonstrating acceptance, authenticity, and empathy; scaling; the use of questions; externalizing the problem; analyzing counselor–client power differentials; encouraging discussion about oppression and marginalization; self-reflection exercises; and homework.
- To describe the counseling process of IPMT.
- To examine social and cultural applicability of IPMT.

- To review the efficacy of IPMT.
- To offer a case study that demonstrates the IPMT process.

BRIEF HISTORY OF INTEGRATIVE POSTMODERN THERAPY

The postmodern revolution in counseling blossomed during the 1980s and has greatly changed the manner in which many conduct counseling. Three theories that led this revolution, **relational cultural therapy (RCT)**, **narrative therapy**, and **solution-focused brief therapy (SFBT)**, all adopted groundbreaking ways of working with clients—ways that the traditional mental health system had eschewed. And while each approach used different techniques or ways of being with their clients, they all had the similar theoretical underpinnings of **postmodernism** and **social constructionism**. These philosophical assumptions resulted in approaches that depathologized the counseling relationship, brought the client in as an equal and as a collaborator to the relationship, and challenged traditional views that mental health problems were a result of something intrinsic or embedded within the person.

Relational cultural therapy (RCT) was developed by **Jean Baker Miller** during the 1980s (Backman, 1988; National Library of Medicine, 2015; Sturm, 2015). Highly aware of how traditional therapies tended to pathologize and marginalize women, she established an approach that uplifted women, viewed change as a lifespan process, believed that mutual empathy was the core of a growth-fostering relationship, saw authenticity as critical for mutual empathy, and focused on the importance of relational growth in contrast with focusing on an autonomous self. She saw power differentials among people and societal-sanctioned oppression as the main reasons women felt disconnected from others and from society. Her theory was later expanded to encompass disenfranchised groups and is now used to understand and work with clients who have been historically oppressed.

Narrative therapy, developed by **Michael White** and **David Epstein**, also had its beginnings in the 1980s, and similar to relational cultural therapy, was concerned about how disenfranchised and historically oppressed people were pathologized in the counseling relationship (Neukrug, 2018, Rice, 2015). This approach focused on how **narratives** in a person's family, culture, and society set the stage for the development of a person's understanding of self and the world. Since those in power develop language and laws that are dispersed and adopted throughout society, their perspective tends to be viewed by many as the "correct" way of viewing the world and other perspectives, such as those held by many who have been historically oppressed, are viewed as wrong or anarchistic. Narrative therapy seeks to understand a person's **dominant narratives**, which may be **problem-saturated** and frequently influenced by the dominant narratives in society. In counseling, such narratives are **deconstructed**, in the sense that they are examined from many perspectives, with a particular look at how language was used within the person's social milieu to oppress the individual. Then, new and more positive narratives are brought to the forefront or developed so that the person can **re-author** his or her life. Similar to

RCT, this approach sought to depathologize the client and did not view problems as intrinsic. Also, like RCT, this approach was uplifting and empowering of individuals.

Also developed during the 1980s, solution-focused brief therapy (SFBT), the creation of **Insoo Kim Berg** and **Steven de Shazer**, believed that traditional approaches of counseling focused too much on problems and tended to pathologize clients, and that normalizing the client's experience and finding exceptions and solutions to problems could help clients in a relatively short period (Dewell, 2015; Neukrug, 2018). They demonstrated that respecting and listening to clients and helping them find solutions to their problems was the key to change, as long as the client was ready for such change.

Although the actual practice of these three approaches vary dramatically, they share a number of common elements, which include basic respect for the client, a belief that clients can change relatively quickly, depathologizing and normalizing client concerns, focusing on solutions not problems, that the future can be reconstructed, and empowering clients (Neukrug, 2018). These ideas are anchored in the philosophies of postmodernism and social constructionism, and counselors who are attracted to these philosophies, and the theories associated with them, will often integrate core concepts from RCT, narrative therapy, and SFBT. This chapter will provide an overview of integrative postmodern therapy (IPMT), which brings together some of the most popular concepts and techniques of RCT, narrative therapy, and SFBT.

Want to Meet the Originators of Postmodern Therapies?

Want to hear a brief biography about Jean Baker Miller, Michael White, and Insoo Kim Berg and Steven de Shazer. Go to https://silver.odu.edu/psyadm/ and click on the postmodern and feminist door, and then enter the office of any of these individuals to meet them.

VIEW OF HUMAN NATURE

> In the traditional scientific framework, truth is *discovered*, and in the postmodernist framework, truth is *constructed* (Shapiro, 2015, p. 185).

Integrative postmodern therapy (IPMT) takes a **postmodern** and **social-constructionist** perspective that suggests individuals create their unique realities through interactions or discourses within their social milieu, which includes one's family, culture, community, and society (Combs & Freedman, 2012; Madigan, 2011). From this perspective, **realities are socially constructed, realities are constituted through language, realities are organized and maintained through narrative,** and **there are no essential truths** (Freedman & Combs, 1996).

Realities Are Socially Constructed: IPMT therapists believe that the psychological makeup of the person—that is, beliefs, values, customs, habits, personality style, and so forth—is created from the ongoing interaction and discourse individuals have with their families and the larger cultural "soup" from which they come (e.g., ethnic group, community, society). The dominant culture, subtly but powerfully, pressures all individuals into adopting its truth. When an individual does not fit into the dominant culture's understanding of reality, that person is negatively labeled in some fashion and feels disconnected from society. Thus, those who question the authority or reality of the dominant group are often seen as wrong, bad, evil, stupid, maladaptive, or mentally ill and pressure is placed on them to adopt the dominant reality or face the consequences (e.g., being placed in prison, a psychiatric hospital, being negatively labeled, being stigmatized, and so forth).

Realities Are Constituted through Language: IPMT therapists believe that as individuals become increasingly networked within their social milieu, they develop a particular reality, or point of view, as a function of the language used within that milieu. Examples of how language creates reality are many. For instance, consider how the use of nonsexist language has changed our perceptions of what is real. Today, instead of saying the "nature of man," we say the "view of human nature;" instead of "stewardess" we say "flight attendant, and instead of "men working," we say "people working;" Now consider how the picture in one's mind of a work crew on a highway might change because signs now say "people working" instead of "men working." Since language is closely related to what we come to perceive and to know, one's psychological style is seen as a pliable product of the language used in one's social milieu, not as something inherent within the person. And since context can change, people can have multiple styles or identities depending on the circumstance or settings in which they find themselves. Consequently, the therapeutic environment can offer a new context in which new realities can be potentially created for the client, and for the therapist, as the two dialogue with one another.

Realities Are Organized and Maintained through Narrative: The IPMT therapist views reality as a creation of the individual's discourse with others and a function of the language used in those conversations. The resulting stories people create about themselves then maintain their reality. In addition, the cultural context from which one comes has dominant stories that are often integrated by the person and become a part of the life story of the individual. So, to understand a person, listen to his or her stories. For instance, many Jewish people have heard the words "never again" as part of the story related to the Holocaust and other oppressive experiences over the generations. Certain Jewish holidays acknowledge these experiences, encourage memories of them, and honor the ability of the Jewish people to free themselves from the oppressors while also stating that all peoples should be free. Consider how this dominant narrative may have affected a Jewish person's ways of knowing the world, with vigilance about oppression and mistrust of authority being woven into Jewish culture. IPMT suggests that, much as reading a good novel, one should "read" or listen to the client's stories and join the client in trying to understand his or her dominant stories.

There Are No Essential Truths. Rejecting the notion of an external truth, IPMT therapists believe that our realities are the products of the discourses in our unique, contained world. Although we tend to have **dominant stories** that saturate our lives and define our reality, we also have other stories that play a lesser role in our lives. One can easily recognize the different realities among cultures that are a product of the stories within one's social milieu. For instance, consider the different dominant stories of most Blacks and most Whites regarding policing in the United States. Stories of many Blacks have to do with oppression, police bias, and racist acts being carried out against them, while Whites mostly have stories around the police upholding the law, fighting against injustices, and protecting citizens. As such, is it any wonder many Blacks and Whites view policing in very different ways?

Clients will frequently enter counseling with dominant, **problem-saturated** stories that are the product of the family, cultural, and social milieu in which the client has lived. Such stories can be **deconstructed** and oppressive language that has fed into the problem-saturated stories can be examined. Since we are all **multistoried**, by listening to clients' less frequent or **nondominant stories** and by helping them create new stories, counseling can assist in the emergence of stories that are not problem-saturated for the client. This way of viewing mental disorders contrasts sharply with the traditional view, which assumes there is something permanent and fixed within the person that makes him or her mentally ill (see Box 4.1).

BOX 4.1 IS THE MENTAL HEALTH SYSTEM AN OPPRESSIVE POWER BROKER?

Within today's mental health system, so-called expert objectivists (e.g., therapists) assess clients to determine if they have a mental disorder that aligns with the Diagnostic and Statistical Manual-5 (DSM-5). Mental health professionals have learned how to use DSM-5, and it is firmly integrated into the professional discourse. DSM-5 has become so widely accepted that almost all professionals, and even most laypersons, use it when considering whether a person has a "mental disorder." Although DSM does not, for the most part, suggest etiology, and because DSM's focus is on the symptoms the individual has, it is largely believed by professionals that disorders reside within the individual and is the function of ineffective or abnormal internal structures, which professionals are taught about in their training programs (e.g., core beliefs, id-ego-superego structure, biological impairment, emotional dysregulation system, etc.) in contrast with thoughts, feelings, and behaviors being a process of a malleable trans-relational language process. Thus, mental health training programs and mental health systems (e.g., social service agencies) help to ensure that mental disorders are seen as something within the person, not a result of language and narratives within the client's world, and clients are often blamed and/or pitied for having the mental disorder. IPMT, however, suggests that DSM-5 is reflective of the values of the power brokers who created it, and not reflective of some illusive psychological structures or biological markers that reside within the person. Thus, some say its worth should be questioned.

IPMT assumes people can come to understand their realities that have been created as a function of their social discourse and can **deconstruct** their foundations (i.e., take them apart), and develop or re-author new realities that are empowering (Madigan, 2015). The ability to understand one's realities and re-create new reality means that this approach is **anti-deterministic**. In addition, IPMT is an **anti-objectivist, non-pathological, positive, strength-based**, largely **future-oriented** approach that eschews any therapeutic model that tries to "reduce a person's identity to a solitary, unified pathological definition" (Madigan, 2015, p. 1052; Rice, 2015).

KEY CONCEPTS

Some of the key concepts that underlie IPMT include **post-modernism; post-structuralism; social constructionism; power; non-pathologizing; thin to thick descriptions; mutually enhancing, empathic, empowering relationships**; and **re-authoring**.

Postmodernism

Postmodernism has been defined as the questioning of modernism, particularly the ideas that "truth" could be found through empiricism, analysis, and scientific method (Weinberg, 2008). Although what has been formerly discovered is not necessarily "wrong," postmodernism suggests it is important to question the context in which "truth" became known. For instance, concepts such as Freud's psychosexual stages, or Rogers's concept of the "congruent self," or the existentialist notion of choice, all were seen as holding "truth" within their unique context and time period. Although such models might, at times, offer us helpful ways of understanding self, they are all contingent on a certain way of understanding the world that is bound by the contexts from which they arose.

Postmodernism, as understood through IPMT, suggests that individual truths are reflective of the collective knowledge transmitted through discourse with others, and that individual truths can change as lives move on and context changes (Madigan, 2011). This has great implications for clients as it assumes that each individual's truth is unique, is bound by the context in which the person has lived, and can change within new contexts (e.g., therapeutic relationship). It also means the therapist is not bound by "truths" of any particular theory or way of understanding a person (e.g., DSM-5).

Post-Structuralism

> The basic premise of structuralism is that all things have a structure below the level of meaning, and that this structure constitutes the reality of that thing. The vast majority of psychological practices are based on structuralism. (Madigan, 2011, p. 171)

Considered part of the postmodern movement, **post-structuralism** is a reaction to **structuralism**, which was a concept closely aligned with the scientific revolution and later adopted by the social sciences and other disciplines (Combs & Freedman, 2012). In counseling and psychology, structuralism suggests the existence of inherent structures that affect personality development. The description of these structures is seen through a particular theory's view of human nature. Think of the "structures" that exist in psychoanalysis, or person-centered counseling, or cognitive theory. Each of these theories has a particular belief about the human species' meaning-making system, or ways of understanding the world. These structures are seen as real; that is, they exist within the context in which they are presented. So, beliefs about an id, ego, or superego; an inherent actualizing tendency; or cognitive schemas; are all structures, hypothesized by theorists that individuals end up believing exist. Such beliefs drive how individuals (e.g., a therapist) come to know and operate in the world.

The post-structuralists challenged the revailing structuralist view. They disputed the notion that the psychodynamic theorists, existentialists, cognitive behaviorists, or most other theorists held a monopoly on the truth about the nature of people. And they went a step further: They suggested that beliefs in these truths encourage a myopic way of knowing. Thus, individuals struggling to become less repressed, more self-actualized, or know their cognitive schemas become enveloped by these very processes, and it is these very processes that end up dictating how these individuals come to understand the world. They do not see other ways of knowing as possibilities. In fact, language in society tends to reinforce many "truths" from structural thinking, and those who do not accept these truths are often seen as psychotic, stupid, defensive, immoral, or rebellious. Think of the counseling-related words and phrases that now exist that we take for granted from this structural revolution: unconscious, id, ego, repression, defensiveness, superego, internality, self-esteem, self-actualization, need hierarchy, inner drives, cognitive schemas, and on and on. If you don't believe in the meaning behind these words, you are seen as being outside of the norm—not in the mainstream—a nonbeliever.

A word of warning—post-structuralists are not saying these systems do not exist; they are saying, let's view them as particular knowledge systems, or as ways of understanding the world (Combs & Freedman, 2012). And let's take a look at what believing in any therapeutic system means for the person, his or her family, his or her culture, and society. In the end, the post-structuralists have offered an alternative perspective that has a relativistic outlook—that is, a perspective that suggests there are many ways of knowing, none of which hold absolute truth, and all of which can impact the person in different ways (Marsten et al., 2016).

Social Constructionism

> The realities that each of us take for granted are the realities that our societies have surrounded us with since birth. The realities provide the beliefs, practices, words, and experiences from which we make up our lives, or as we say in post-modernist jargon, "constitute our selves." (Freedman & Combs, 1996, p. 16)

Social constructionism, which became prominent during the 1960s, suggests that knowledge is a function of the historical and social milieu from which the individual comes, and that language and discourse shape mental concepts that become the basis for what is believed to be truth (Gergen, 2015; Richert, 2010; Winslade & Geroski, 2008). Thus, reality is an elusive, constantly changing, concept that only exists among people, not within a person, and so-called "truths" can be empowering for some, but oppressive toward others.

With this in mind, there are many so-called truths relative to Western-based counseling theories that can be challenged, such as "We are the creators of our own fate," "We are individually responsible for what happens to us," and "If we dig deep enough, we can understand why we do certain things." Therefore, the humanist's concept of a self-actualizing tendency, the psychodynamic ideas about making the unconscious conscious, and the cognitive behavioral beliefs about irrational or core beliefs all come into question. These concepts are seen as developed by a powerful elite of mostly White, Western males who promulgated certain ideas within a mostly White mental health profession.

Rather than an "I can pick myself up by the bootstrap" attitude, the social constructionist says that as people interact with one another, they have an ongoing conversation through which meaning is constructed (Combs & Freedman, 2016; Richert, 2010). Thus, identity is constantly in formation and changing as a function of the language used in interaction with others. In fact, from this perspective, one can have a number of "identities" or "selves" depending on the discourses one finds oneself in over time. I am not simply one "Ed." Instead, I have an "Ed" with my partner, a different "Ed" with my colleagues, another Ed ("Dad") with my children, and another Ed ("Eddie") with my siblings; and the Eds, the Dad, and the Eddie change over time. And my sense of self is not embedded within me; it is a changing and evolving self in relation to the various groups within which I find myself. And, to take it one step further, the word "Ed" is not sufficient enough to define all of who "Ed" is.

Power

> Unacknowledged privilege and the subtle or blatant use of power over others inevitably create division, anger, disempowerment, depression, shame and disconnection. (Jordan, 2010, p. 6)

IPMT therapists believe there are certain dominant stories, or so-called truths, promulgated by those in positions of power that tend to maintain the power structure through language and laws and result in the oppression of the historically oppressed (Combs & Freedman, 2012; Guilfoyle, 2014). These dominant stories are internalized by individuals, result in people believing stories that tend to oppress the underclass, and blind clients to other possible stories and opportunities. Thus, stories about how certain historically oppressed groups are "lazy," "stupid," "rebellious," and so on are often subtly, and sometimes blatantly, passed down and become part of the dominant stories of those in power, and are even sometimes internalized and "believed" by the very people whom the stories are about. Since those in power are often unaware of their privileged position that leads to the oppression of others, it can sometimes be helpful for them to examine the stories they have developed and/or promulgated. Helping those in power understand how their language and acts have oppressed nondominant groups, and helping the less powerful see how they have been oppressed by the language and acts of those in power, is an important part of IPMT.

Non-Pathologizing

> ... [W]hen a counselor describes clients in terms of pathological categories, this indicates that he or she has conversed within the context of a professional community, which in turn, has chosen to organize its knowledge accordingly. (Guterman, 2013, p. 26)

IPMT takes a **non-pathologizing** stance because it adheres to the post-structural belief there is not clear evidence there are inherent structures within the individual that lends the client to developing a particular mental disorder. In addition, using language that pathologizes clients results in clients believing the mental health system has jointly come together to endorse the notion there is something inherently wrong with them, and that they are less well than other people (Harrison, 2013). Viewing themselves as damaged goods is discouraging for clients and raises doubt about their ability to live effectively in the world. Instead, IPMT therapists attempt to understand clients' current way of being and offers a positive and optimistic view about clients' ability to change. They suggest there is no one way of acting that is correct, do not try to have their clients meet an elusive societal ideal of how to act, and normalize clients' negative experiences by noting that others have experienced similar feelings, thoughts, and behaviors (Corcoran, 2012; Thomas & Nelson, 2007).

Believing that problems were not inherent in the person, narrative therapists popularized the phrase **"The person is not the problem; the problem is the problem."** This belief **externalizes the problem** (i.e., places the problem outside of the person) and the counselor can help clients understand how the problem might have served a purpose in one's family, community, and society. Redefining the problem in this manner begins to move the client from thin to thick descriptions of the problem and helps the client develop novel solutions to the problem (White & Epston, 1990).

Thin to Thick Descriptions

Encouraging clients to tell their stories is a cornerstone of IMPT because it is believed that a client's life story is the vehicle for understanding the complexity of the client's life (Wong, 2015). When clients initially share their stories, or **narratives**, they often present **thin descriptions** of their stories; that is, they are generally not fully aware of the complexity of their problem-saturated story or that other stories may contradict or deny the problem-saturated story. In addition, early in therapy, much is omitted from clients' initial descriptions due to forgetfulness or feelings of mistrust and embarrassment about sharing intimate details. Thin descriptions of stories often lead clients to thin conclusions about their lives, as they tend to view the world in simple, often dualistic ways (Morgan, 2000). As clients continue to tell their stories, the narrative therapist can help them expand on their problem-saturated stories. This is generally accomplished through the therapist's ability to build a relationship with the client by being respectful, curious, showing empathy, being authentic, and asking questions about their stories. Such therapist qualities tend to invite clients to more fully describe their stories. As stories are more fully understood in their complexity, and as other stories that may contradict or negate problem-saturated stories come to the surface, the client increasingly understands his or her life in more complex ways and develops what are called **thick descriptions** of their life.

Mutually Enhancing, Empathic, Empowering Relationships

The ultimate goal of IPMT is the development of mature, mutually enhancing, empathic relationships in which closeness can be tolerated and individuals feel empowered (Jordan, 2010; Miller, 1976; Sturm, 2015). This occurs with the counselor and, ultimately, with others who can also foster growth-enhancing relationships. IPMT believes that relationships in which empathy and positive affirmations are underscored, and individuals can talk through conflict, result in healthy socio-emotional functioning (Jordan, 2000), whereas abusive, critical, and judgmental relationships lead to a sense of disconnection with others. When disconnection is experienced over time, individuals will behave in ways that inhibit their own abilities to connect with others (Jordan, 2010; Miller, 1976). Called **strategies of disconnection**, these are the unique ways that individuals increase and/or maintain social and emotional distance to avoid pain and hurt. Thus, if historically an individual has experienced abuse when in a close relationship (e.g., parents), that person may develop strategies that paradoxically prevent such closeness in many or even all future relationships, even ones that could be potentially healthy.

For historically oppressed groups, lack of power, privilege, and access can lead to a sense of disconnection from the broader society (Jordan, 2010). Socially sanctioned discrimination and oppression (e.g., racism, sexism, heterosexism, ableism, etc.) can cause an individual to maintain distance from the dominant culture and result in marginalization and isolation from social networks and institutions (Jordan, 2000; Miller & Stiver, 1997). IPMT hopes to help clients understand their sense of being marginalized from society and offers strategies for living in a culture that can be oppressive. IPMT therapists view their role as one of advocate for oppressed groups so they will, at times, work on systemic change to reduce the sense of isolation and disconnection that those from historically oppressed groups can experience.

Re-Authoring

Because clients enter counseling with thin descriptions of their lives based on the social milieu from which they were exposed, they often see their lives and their relationships in dualistic or simple ways. As they increasingly see how the stories in their lives have been influenced by power dynamics and oppressive system, they begin to understand how their problems do not reside in themselves but are a function of the language used in families, communities, cultural groups, and society, and that the rules and laws set up the powerful. Slowly, clients begin to deconstruct their understanding of their problems and reconstruct, or re-author, their lives with new stories and new, empathic, mutually enhancing relationships (Madigan, 2015). As they slowly begin to re-author their stories, they develop a new and reinvigorated sense of self.

TECHNIQUES

The therapist who practices IPMT will integrate a number of techniques from narrative, relational-cultural, solution-focused brief therapy, and other related postmodern approaches. Some of these include **showing mystery, respectful curiosity, and awe**; **demonstrating acceptance, authenticity, and empathy**; **scaling**; **the use of questions**; **externalizing the problem**; **analyzing counselor–client power differentials**; **encouraging discussion about oppression and marginalization**; **self-reflection exercises**; and **homework**.

Showing Mystery, Respectful Curiosity, and Awe

In contrast with therapeutic models in which therapists see themselves as the expert, the IMPT therapist enters the relationship as an **ambassador** to a foreign country might (Murphy, 2015;

Payne, 2006). For instance, an ambassador would be respectful, curious, and show acceptance of people in another culture in his or her attempt to understand the ways of the people. In a similar fashion, the IMPT therapist enters the relationship humbly and is curious about the client's predicament, respectful of the client's ways of being, and accepting of what the client tells him or her. In addition, IMPT therapists demonstrate respect toward their clients by avoiding labels, using non-pathologizing language, and presenting themselves as allies and equal partners (Harrison, 2013; Rice, 2015) They assume that clients have the tools and ability to assist themselves in reducing their own problems and do not fault clients for their situation (Morgan, 2000). This role helps to demystify the relationship and to define it as a discourse between individuals in which both can change.

Demonstrating Acceptance, Authenticity, and Empathy

Key to building a strong therapeutic relationship is the ability to demonstrate acceptance, authenticity, and empathy (Jordan, 2000, 2010; Miller, 1976). IPMT therapists show unconditional love and acceptance to their clients, however clients may present themselves; are able to effectively reflect back both the affect and meaning of the client's experience; and are real with clients, within the limits of the therapeutic relationship. Such realness attempts to lessen what is often perceived as a distance between the counselor and client as the counselor attempts to defuse power differentials within the relationship. Demonstrating acceptance, authenticity, and empathy are particularly important near the beginning of the relationship when clients' talk is often problem-saturated, and they generally want to discuss their problems in detail. Giving clients the opportunity to talk about their problems is respectful and an important aspect to building the relationship and understanding their problems (De Jong & Berg, 2013).

Scaling

Often used near the beginning of a session, **scaling** involves asking clients to subjectively rate themselves between 1 and 10 on an imaginary scale that assesses any of a number of thoughts, feelings, or behaviors from their past, in the present, or what they would like to experience in the future (Figure 4.1).

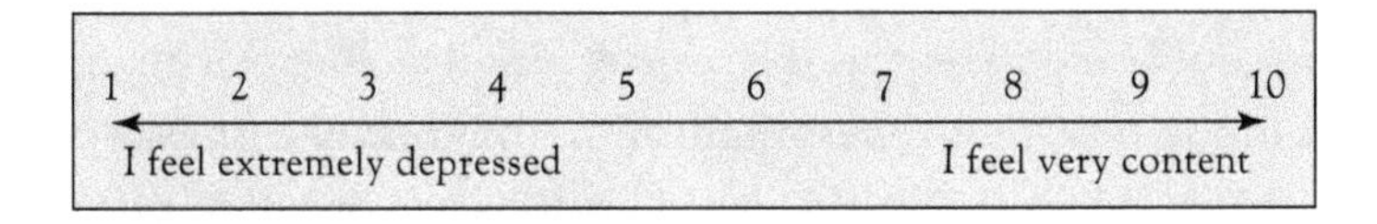

Figure 4.1 Scaling

Scaling helps clients to quickly assess where they have been and whether they have made progress (De Jong & Berg, 2013). For instance, with a fictitious client named Stella, we could ask any of the following scaling questions.

- "With 1 being equal to the worst your depression ever was and 10 being equal to the best you could possibly feel, can you tell me, Stella, where on a scale are you today?"
- "Stella, on the scale of 1 to 10, how effective do you think the journaling has been for you?"
- "Stella, being that today you rated yourself a 3, where do you think you could end up on your imaginary scale of 1 to 10?"
- "I know, Stella, that when you first started counseling you rated yourself at a 3 on our imaginary scale of life satisfaction. Where do you think you are today?"

The Use of Questions

> ... [I]n a therapy of oral tradition, the re-authoring of lives and relationships is achieved primarily, although not exclusively, through a process of questioning. (White & Epston, 1990, p. 17)

Non-threatening, and usually open-ended, questions are widely used in IPMT to help explore a wide range of client issues and to move them from thin to thick descriptions of their lives, begin the re-authoring process, and set the tone for the direction the relationship will take (Combs & Freedman, 2012; Rice, 2015). Questions near the beginning of the relationship will reflect respectful curiosity, mystery, and awe about the client's reason for coming to counseling and serve to encourage the client to discuss his or her problem-saturated story. Other questions may be used to help clients understand their multiple identities. As the relationship continues, questions will focus on externalizing the problem and on mapping its effects. Then, the focus of questions becomes an exploration of coping mechanisms or when there were exceptions to the client's problem-saturated story. As clients are ready to make changes, the therapist may use solution-oriented questions to help the client look at how his or her life could be different in the future. Finally, re-authoring questions are used to help clients examine how their lives might look differently if they were not living out their problem-saturated narrative. Although questions are presented here in a sequential manner (beginning-middle-end), it is not unusual to use any of these questions at any point in counseling if it will help the client move from a thin to a thick description of his or her story and assist the client in moving forward in the change process. The following offers some examples of these different types of questions.

Questions that Demonstrate Respectful Curiosity, Mystery, and Awe

Often used nearer the beginning of the relationship, these questions help the client know that the counselor is focused on the client's situation and is interested in hearing about his or her story. A few typical questions of this type might be:

- "Can you share some of your reasons for coming in today? I'm really interested in hearing about that."
- "I'm wondering if you could tell me more about how this happened to you and how this has affected you?"
- Your story is so interesting, I would love to hear more about it!

Questions That Explore Identity

To fully understand clients' narratives and for them to begin to understand what has impacted their lives, a counselor will ask questions about how family, cultural, and societal messages shaped the client's identities (e.g., gender, ethnicity, disability, etc.). For instance, a counselor could ask some of the following questions:

- "What roles as a wife and a mother have you taken on, and why do you think you took on those roles?"
- "As a [Black person, Hispanic, Asian, White person, etc.], were their times when you were discriminated against? How did that affect you?"
- "What messages did you get at school and in your community about the gender roles [ethnicity, disability, etc.] you should live out?"
- "What roadblocks did you face as a result of your disability?"

Questions That Help to Externalize the Problem

As clients feel increasingly comfortable in counseling, they may be asked questions that can assist in externalizing the problem so they do not feel like there is something inherently wrong with them. Oftentimes, this involves having the client pick a name for the problem—something viewed as external to themselves. For instance, the counselor may ask:

- "If you were to give a name to this problem, what do you think that might be [e.g., 'the black box']?"
- "What would your world look like without ['the black box']?"
- "If you had any means at your disposal, what would you do to rid yourself of ['the black box']?

Coping and Exception-Seeking Questions

These questions focus on times when the individual has coped successfully with the problem or has not had the problem, and are used to identify what was different about the client's life at that point. For example:

- "It's amazing how much of your life was taken up by the problem, yet I think I hear that there were times when that was not the case. Can you tell me about those times?"
- "What was happening in your life during the times when you did not have this problem?"
- "You know, I think I hear that at one point in your life you dealt well with this problem. What were you doing then that was different?"

Solution-Oriented Questions

> Suppose that one night, while you were asleep, there was a miracle and this problem was solved. How would you know? What would be different? (de Shazer, 1988, p. 5)

The above miracle question epitomizes solution-oriented questions that focus on how things would look differently in the future if the problem was solved. Other solution-oriented questions include:

- "If you could change anything in your life so you would feel better, how would things be different?"
- "If there was some deity that could suddenly make your life better, what would your life look like?"

Re-Authoring Questions

These questions help clients examine ways that they can begin to view their lives differently and create a new narrative about how to live their lives:

- "Now that we've identified a series of times when you were free of this problem, any ideas how you can make this happen in the future?"
- "What would your life look like if it were dominated by these other stories rather than [the name of the problem]?"

Externalizing the Problem

One technique IPMT therapists use to reinforce the notion that problem-saturated stories are a manifestation of language used within the client's social milieu, and not something inherently wrong with the client, is to **externalize the problem**; that is, name it as something outside of the person. For instance, John is struggling with depression, and rather than assuming the depression is within him, through some deep-seated psycho-biological process, the therapist suggests that John come up with a name for his depression. John names his depression, "the Big Ugly Box." Then, the problem becomes the box, not something inside of John. Re-naming the problem gives hope to the client as he or she begins to see the origins of the problem differently, and that changing context can help move the client toward a new way of thinking and acting on the problem-saturated story (see Box 4.2).

BOX 4.2 BEATING SNEAKY POO

In a sometimes funny manner, Heins and Ritchie (1988) wrote a short book with comic book–like illustrations that helps children deal with the serious issue of encopresis (fecal soiling). By externalizing the problem, "sneaky poo" becomes the focus of the concern that children, parents, and sometimes medical professionals work together to solve. By focusing on "sneaky poo" rather than the child, children stop experiencing the blame that often comes with encopresis as they separate themselves from the problem. After externalizing the problem, the authors offer hands-on ways that children and their parents can help "sneaky poo" not be a problem any longer.

Analyzing Counselor–Client Power Differentials

> Power exists and has to be taken account for, it cannot be denied. (Miller, 1976, p. 5)

After initial rapport is built, clients are encouraged to analyze power dynamics within the counseling relationship (Jordan, 2001; Miller, 1976). Discussion around the manner in which clients perceive the counselor, and the way the counselor sees the client, can occur in an effort to delimit power and equalize the relationship. Counselors and clients should be aware that with any growth-fostering relationship, including therapeutic ones, a thorough examination of power differentials, real or perceived, should occur. The goal of this examination is to develop a relationship highlighted by equality and a sense of balance for all parties involved. Having an equal relationship with the counselor can be a model for having equal relationships with others.

Encouraging Discussion About Oppression and Marginalization

Traditional counseling approaches have a legacy of viewing problems as something within the person and clients often end up blaming themselves for predicaments that may be partly or fully outside of their control. IPMT believes, however, that oppressive systems, not inherent structures within the person, can lead to a sense of isolation and disengagement from self and others. Thus, one goal of IPMT is "to lessen the experience of isolation, increase the capacity for self-empathy and empathy for others, and develop and appreciate the power of context and limiting cultural/relational images" (Jordan, 2010, p. 35).

Once a strong relational foundation is established, counselors can initiate a dialogue about clients' experiences of oppression and marginalization as it relates to their individual identity statuses (i.e., culture/ethnicity, gender identity, sexual orientation, age) (Butler, 1985; Combs & Freedman, 2012; Crenshaw, 1989; Miller, 1976; MacKinnon, 2013). Such a discourse helps all clients understand how their identity, status, culture, power, and privilege impacts their narratives, understanding of self, and relationships with others. IPMT therapists will often help clients explore how social and political issues have shaped their dominant, problem-saturated stories (White, et al., 1994). Some areas that might be explored by the IPMT therapist include:

- how discrimination and racism have impacted the client's life;
- how gender roles have impacted one's relationships;
- how depression or other symptoms are supported by the broader culture (e.g., women are often "encouraged" to be depressed rather than have a strong voice);
- societal influences that impinge on the individual and feed into his or her dominant, problem-saturated story;
- how medications are used to "quell" the voice of the client;
- ensuring that acts of violence and abuse perpetrated on the client are not seen as something for which he or she is blamed;
- ensuring there is a sense of equality in the therapeutic relationship and that the client feels her or his voice is heard;
- examining how lack of privilege, or privilege, has affected a client's life; and
- examining how "mainstream values" support certain ways of functioning and oppress many minorities.

Self-Reflection Exercises

A number of exercises exist that the IPMT therapist can employ to help clients move from thin to thick descriptions of their stories and provide an opportunity for considering ways of re-authoring their lives. Five such exercises are **re-membering, definitional ceremonies (outsider**

witness groups), telling and retelling stories, re-authoring, and **use of therapeutic documents and other paraphernalia.**

Re-membering

Used by Barbara Myerhoff (1982, 1986) when helping older Jewish people reinvent themselves at a community center, this exercise focuses on helping individuals reconstruct their identities by accenting and expanding on specific positive memories and by limiting problem-saturated memories. Re-membering allows clients to call up powerful positive images from the past, connects clients to something going on in the present, and provides a road map for the future. For instance, a client might have a memory of a time he or she did something heroic. This image can be called on, focused upon, and used as a metaphor for who he or she is now, and how he or she will act in the future. Clients can re-member through many avenues, including journaling, writing stories, meditating or reflecting, viewing videos, and so forth. In addition to re-membering positive memories, clients can delimit memories that have had negative influences on their lives.

Definitional Ceremonies (Outsider Witness Groups)

Also originated by Barbara Myerhoff (1982, 1986), definitional ceremonies, sometimes called outsider witness groups, occur after a client has begun to develop new, thick stories that start to reshape the client's sense of self and involves the retelling and witnessing of the client's new stories. Such a retelling generally occurs with a group of carefully chosen friends, significant people in the client's lives, or individuals who had previously sought consultation for a similar difficulty and have expressed a desire to assist others in the future. Witness should encourage dialogue and discourse about the client's experience, and witnesses should not congratulate, affirm, applaud, or interpret client stories. Such witnessing reinforces and solidifies the client's sense that he or she is moving on (White, 2007).

Reflective Teams

Reflective teams involve carefully selected individuals who observe clients with their therapists and later share their thoughts about their observations with the client and the therapist (Combs & Freedman, 2012). Reflective teams can include significant others, therapists, or individuals who have experienced similar issues in their lives. Sometimes considered a type of definitional ceremony, reflective teams offer clients a mechanism to consider new ways of re-authoring their lives. White (1993, 1995) suggested that the reflective team process be structured in four parts:

1. the reflective team quietly observing the client with the therapist;
2. the therapist and client observing the reflective team discussing the client's dominant narratives and offering potential alternative growth producing stories based on exceptions to the client's problem-saturated stories that were heard;

3. the therapist and client discussing the reflective team responses for potential new realizations and behaviors; and
4. all participants joining together and asking each other why certain ideas were discussed, certain questions asked, and other questions not asked.

As this interview concludes, the client can inform the counselor and reflective teams of those ideas that seem most promising in the development of new narratives.

Telling and Retelling Stories

Telling and retelling stories helps lesser-known stories in a person's life become dominant (Denborough, 2014; Morgan, 2000). By retelling and expanding on these lesser-known stories, new narratives based on past events become predominant. For instance, as a young teenager, a friend described a problem-saturated story of hers that focused on her "promiscuity" (her words). This problem-saturated dominant story resulted in her stating that she was "no good and not worthy of a relationship." Upon encouraging her exploration of other stories when she was a teenager, she focused on times in her life that revolved around her desire to be connected with people and to help people. She realized that a primary goal in her life was to connect with others and help others, and that she only knew how to do this through sex. As she focused on the story of connecting and helping others, this story increasingly became larger and the "promiscuous" part of her former self became a minor part of her narratives. By telling and retelling these new, existing stories, she was able to reinforce her newfound sense of identity of a person who brings people together and helps them with their problems. Telling and retelling can be accomplished through discourse with others; by writing letters or emails to self and others; by writing an autobiography; through creative outlets, such as drawings or sculpting; by making video recordings or computer blogs; by using outside witnesses; by having definitional ceremonies; and so forth.

Use of Therapeutic Documents and Other Paraphernalia

To acknowledge progress and describe change, the use of therapeutic documents and other paraphernalia are often encouraged or provided (Payne, 2006). For instance, clients might journal about how they now view their lives as compared with what their lives were like when the problem dominated everything, or they might write biographies that show the shifting changes in their lives. Therapists can also use documents to show client progress, such as writing letters to clients that affirm their changes, providing medallions that acknowledge shifts in thinking, or giving certificates that acknowledge new ways in which clients now understand themselves (see Box 4.3).

BOX 4.3 WAS THE WIZARD OF OZ AN IPMT THERAPIST?

> ... [A] heart is not judged by how much you love, but by how much you are loved by others—The Wizard. (Langley, et al., 1939, p. 107)

I was always taken by the Wizard of Oz's use of documents and paraphernalia to acknowledge aspects of the Tin Man, Scarecrow, and Lion that they, themselves, did not focus upon. Each of these characters had his own problem-saturated story. The Tin Man saw himself living a heartless life, the Scarecrow thought he was brainless, and the Lion saw himself as a coward. Pointing out to each of the three those times when they were not who they thought they were underscored the notion that they did not have to continue accenting their problem-saturated stories. And to accentuate the importance of their new identities, the Wizard gave each of them something important. To the Tin Man, he gave a large, red, heart-shaped clock that hung from a golden chain; the Scarecrow received a diploma so he would always be reminded that he was smart; and to the Lion, he gave a medal signifying how brave he was.

Homework

From an IPMT perspective, homework means clients have identified areas that they want to change and the therapist is "supportive and persistent" in inquiring about the direction clients wants to go, but not prescriptive about how clients will get there (George et al., 2015; Kim, 2014). Instead, clients may come up with their own ideas about how they want change to look and occur. In a sense, the ball is in the clients' court as they decide how to engage themselves in moving toward their preferred goals.

THE COUNSELING PROCESS

When the counselor first enters the therapeutic relationship, although professional, clients are often disarmed by the friendliness and humility of the IPMT therapist. The therapist will also demonstrate a sense of curiosity about, and mystery and awe toward, the client's situation. The therapist embraces a non-pathological orientation by using nonclinical language and by not diagnosing the client. Many clients will come in with thin descriptions of their lives and offer their own diagnosis of the problem. The goal of the therapist is to deconstruct the diagnosis by using language that avoids the implication that there is something inherently wrong with the client and to help the client develop complex, thick descriptions of his or her life. This will eventually lead to newly developed mutually enhancing, empathic, empowering relationships with others.

Regardless of how the client presents his or her situation, the counselor will demonstrate acceptance and gradually integrate the use of respectful questions, authenticity, and empathic responses. These skills eventually lead to a deepening of the relationship as the client feels more comfortable sharing his or her story. Increasingly, the client's dominant, problem-saturated story (stories) will be expanded upon as the counselor asks more questions about the client's life. Questions about the impact of the client's family, community, career, gender, and times when the client might have felt discriminated against and/or abused are particularly important. Empathic responding and acceptance are used throughout as the counselor listens to the client's responses to questions. At this point, the counselor may ask the client to rank feelings on a scale. This helps the counselor understand the depth of pain experienced and can be used at a later date to indicate improvement in counseling over time. To this end, the scale will be used throughout the relationship to examine gains made.

As the problem-saturated story continues to be uncovered, the counselor may use questions to help the client externalize the problem. This assists the client in seeing the problem is not inherent within him or her, but something that is contextual and can change as the client experiences different contexts (the therapeutic relationship, new people) and develops new stories. Around the same time, the counselor will use questions to uncover periods in the past when the client has been able to cope with similar problems and find instances when there were exceptions to the problems.

As the client increasingly sees the contextual nature of the problem-saturated story that is the result of language and behaviors used in the client's life by family, culture, region, and society, he or she begins to feel empowered to make change. This in when the counselor may use solution-oriented and re-authoring questions to assist in movement toward new narratives and behaviors that become the basis of the client's life. These new narratives and behaviors may be the expansion of old positive stories or new positive ways of living with which the client would like to experiment. Throughout this process, the counselor is checking in with the client to ensure there is not a power relationship between the counselor and the client. The counselor shows acceptance and empathy throughout and as the client experiences change, she or he is better able to demonstrate empathy and acceptance with the counselor and with others. It is not unusual, at this point, for the client to seek new, more empowering and empathic relationships in his or her life.

New client narratives and ways of being are encouraged and reinforced through a number of self-reflection exercises such as re-membering, definitional ceremonies, the use of reflective teams, telling and retelling stories, and the use of therapeutic documents and other paraphernalia. Homework, based on these exercises (e.g., journaling about one's new narratives) may be practiced to reinforce client gains. As clients feel increasingly empowered and better able to show empathy, they build more complex relationships that can work through issues. They also understand how context influences their narratives and seek out situations and systems that are growth producing. At this point, clients are ready to end therapy (see Box 4.4).

BOX 4.4 ANGELA WITH IPMT COUNSELOR

Your instructor might have you view Angela with a counselor who uses an integrative postmodern therapy approach to counseling. After you view the video, consider how effective the counselor was at doing this and reflect on whether you believe it would be better if a counselor practiced a "pure" approach (e.g., strictly narrative, solution-focused behavior therapy, or relational-cultural).

SOCIAL AND CULTURAL ISSUES

> A group that becomes dominant in any society tends to divide people with less power into groups for various historical reasons. These less powerful groups can include divisions by race, class, gender, sexual preference, and the like. The dominant group often gains tremendous power of the less powerful groups in all realms, including economic, social, political, and cultural. (Miller, 2008, p. 147)

More than most other therapies, IPMT takes a close look at how issues of power, racism, and discrimination impacts individuals in negative ways. Thus, IPMT is particularly welcoming of those who have been historically discriminated against. The IPMT therapist, from the beginning, is interested in the kinds of narratives that have been embraced by the client and how those narratives have been fueled by "isms" in society. The IPMT therapist then helps the client understand how dominant narratives, formed by the power elite in society, have overtly and covertly become embedded in the individual's way of seeing the world. One goal of IPMT is to deconstruct these narratives so they have less impact on the individual and so the client can feel empowered and less disengaged from others due to these historically oppressive narratives. Thus, by the end of therapy the IPMT client understands what societal influences have negatively impacted him or her, becomes less reactive to such influences, finds other individuals who empower the client, and becomes an advocate for self and for others in the fight against discrimination and oppression in society.

Although IPMT therapists do not push their values onto their clients, they are not neutral (Combs & Freedman, 2012). In fact, IPMT therapists believe that when therapists are neutral, they subtly support the "isms" of society. This stance lies in the belief that issues of power and subjugation occur in both obvious and subtle ways, are endemic throughout society, and are particularly harmful to clients from diverse backgrounds. Although they will not push their agendas onto clients, they will, in collaboration with the clients, ask questions that might raise issues about oppression, discrimination, and racism (see section on "Encouraging Discussion About Oppression and Marginalization").

IPMT therapists will often include components of intersectionality in their practice. This will include the unpacking of clients' experiences of gender, culture/ethnicity, sexual identity, social class, ability status, religion, spirituality, socioeconomic status, age, and other unique identity factors. IPMT therapists believe it is important to help clients unpack their intersecting identities and examine how their identifies have affected their lived experiences, their mental health, and their perceptions about what they can and cannot do in their lives.

To be an IPMT therapist is to be a social justice activist. If you believe that language creates reality and that language sometimes results in the overt and covert oppression of certain groups, there is no other choice but to advocate for those who are oppressed and to recognize the advantages of those who are privileged (Patrick & Connolly, 2013).

EFFICACY

As you might guess, traditional postmodern approaches to therapy have focused almost exclusively on the subjective experience found in qualitative research (Gergen, 2015). In fact, many postmodern therapists would argue that there is inherent bias in quantitative research, and its so-called "purity" must be called into question when one realizes that every decision a quantitative researcher makes in designing, implementing, analyzing, and interpreting a study is a reflection of the discourses that dominate in his or her world. The subject matter that is chosen, the population to be examined, the kinds of designs that are chosen, even the statistical analysis used, can lead a researcher to certain conclusions—conclusions that the researcher was predestined to find. Thus, qualitative research with its focus on multiple ways of viewing knowledge, and in immersing oneself in a relationship in an attempt to provide possible explanations for the problem being examined, seems more attuned with the postmodern therapist (Heppner, et al., 2016). Unfortunately, although a qualitative research approach seems to be a good fit for postmodern approaches such as IPMT, there is a dearth of good qualitative or quantitative studies that examine postmodern therapies.

Solution-focused brief therapy, however, is somewhat of an exception as a number of studies on this approach have shown some efficacy with a wide range of clients (Kim, 2008; Gingerich & Peterson, 2013). But some researchers question the rigor of past research and suggest more research is needed (Center for Review and Dissemination, 2014; Corcoran & Pillai, 2007). It is also true that although SFBT is philosophically based on postmodernism and social constructionism, its actual implementation seems a bit more hands-on and cognitive-behaviorally oriented, and some may even question whether it can, in its pure form, be placed in this postmodern school.

Some of the few research studies conducted on other postmodern therapies have focused on relational cultural therapy. For instance, relational cultural therapy has specifically been found effective when working with youth of color (Spencer, et al., 2004), working with incarcerated adolescents (Lenz et al., 2012), as an intervention with at-risk mothers of infants (Paris & Dubas, 2005), as a model for mentoring relationships (Beyene et al., 2002; Liang et al., 2002; Spencer, 2006; Spencer & Liang, 2009), in improving relationships between adults and children (Spencer et al., 2004), in assisting couples coping with cancer (Kayser et al., 2007), and in groups for individuals with self-injurious behaviors (Haberstroh & Moyer, 2012). The use of relational cultural therapy was found to reduce the presence of bulimic and depressive symptoms in groups (Tantillo & Sanftner, 2003, 2010) and increase positive relationships in a group of Israeli and Palestinian youth (Morray & Liang, 2005). In addition to these specific presenting concerns, relational cultural therapy has been found useful in diverse settings and is a helpful framework for counselors working with diverse clients (Duffy et al., 2009). Clearly, more research is needed if one is to examine the efficacy of the postmodern therapist, and specifically the efficacy of an integrative approach, such as IPMT.

SUMMARY

One of the more recent schools of psychotherapy, postmodern approaches vary in their delivery of counseling skills, but are based on the same theoretical underpinnings—postmodernism and social constructionism. Three therapies in particular have led the postmodern revolution in counseling: relational cultural therapy, developed by Jean Baker Miller; narrative therapy, developed by Michael White and David Epstein; and solution-focused brief therapy, developed by Insoo Kim Berg and Steven de Shazer. This chapters takes an integrative approach to postmodern therapies and uses ideas from all three of these therapeutic approaches.

Integrative postmodern therapy (IPMT) takes a postmodern and social-constructionist perspective suggesting that individuals create their unique realities through interactions or discourses within their social milieu, which includes one's family, culture, community, and society. From this perspective, realities are socially constructed, realities are constituted through language, realities are organized and maintained through narrative, and there are no essential truths. The ability to understand one's realities and re-create new reality means that IPMT is anti-deterministic. In addition, this approach is anti-objectivist, non-pathological, positive, strength-based, and largely future-oriented.

Key concepts of IPMT that we explored in this chapter included postmodernism; post-structuralism; social constructionism; power; non-pathologizing; thin to thick descriptions; mutually enhancing, empathic, empowering relationships; and re-authoring. Postmodernism questions modernism, and in the counseling realm, many of the theories that came before are questioned, especially in reference to their focus on internal structures being responsible for various types of mental health problems. This post-structural approach, therefore, rejects the notion that there are inherent structures within the person that cause mental illness. Social constructionism suggests that knowledge is a function of the historical and social milieu from which the individual comes, and that language and discourse shape mental concepts that become the basis for what is believed to be truth. Thus, how one develops dominant narratives in life is a function of the language that is used within the client's social milieu.

Since those in power are largely responsible for language and laws that are passed, IPMT therapists focus much on power issues, particularly on how power in counseling relationships and power in society can result in people feeling disengaged and oppressed. Thus, non-pathologizing the counseling relationship and helping clients see how they have been impacted by racism, discrimination, and oppression is a critical aspect of IPMT. As clients increasingly see how they have been influenced by power issues and by their social milieu, they understand their lives in more complex ways and move from thin to thick descriptions of their life stories. They also realize that the "person is not the problem; the problem is the problem." As thick descriptions of their lives are increasingly developed, clients are able to see how their thin descriptions caused disconnection with people and are better able to develop mature, mutually enhancing, empathic relationships in which closeness can be tolerated and individuals feel empowered. Ultimately, through their changed perspective about their problem and with the development of healthier relationships, they are able to reconstruct, or re-author, their lives.

A number of techniques are used in IPMT, including showing mystery, respectful curiosity, and awe; demonstrating acceptance, authenticity, and empathy; scaling; asking about the client's life; the use of questions (e.g., questions that show respectful curiosity, mystery, and awe; help to externalize the problem; focus on coping and exceptions to the problem; focus on solutions, and help clients re-author themselves); externalizing the problem; analyzing counselor–client power differentials; encouraging discussion about oppression and marginalization; self-reflection exercises (re-membering, definitional ceremonies, reflective teams, and telling and retelling stories); and homework. In general, these techniques are used in the order they are presented, and help clients move from thin to thick descriptions of their lives as they increasingly reconstruct or re-author their lives with new stories and develop new, healthier relationships.

The counseling process for IPMT assumes that most clients come to counseling with thin descriptions of their lives and a belief that their problem is inherent, or something deeply held within them. Thus, the goal of the therapist is to deconstruct the client's own diagnosis by using language that avoids the implication that there is something inherently wrong with the client, and to help the client develop complex, thick descriptions of their lives. This will eventually lead to newly developed, mutually enhancing, empathic, empowering relationships with others. To do this, the counselor builds a relationship with the client by showing mystery, respectful curiosity, and awe and by demonstrating acceptance, authenticity, and empathy. They also rely heavily on open-ended questions to explore clients' life stories. For instance, they may ask questions to help clients explore their identity development.

As problem-saturated stories are uncovered, the counselor may use questions to externalize the problem, use other questions to help clients see how they have coped with similar problems, and use exception-seeking questions to help clients see that their life has not always been problem-saturated. As clients increasingly understand that their problem-saturated stories are a result of the context in which they have lived, counselors can help them examine how they can change their problem-saturated stories and develop new narratives. By using solution-focused and re-authoring questions, the counselor assists the client in movement toward new narratives and behaviors that become the basis of the client's life. New client narratives and ways of being are encouraged and reinforced through a number of self-reflection exercises such as re-membering, definitional ceremonies, the use of reflective teams, telling and retelling stories, and the use of therapeutic documents and other paraphernalia. Homework, often based on these exercises (e.g., journaling about one's new narratives), may be practiced to reinforce client gains. As clients feel increasingly empowered and better able to show empathy, they build more complex relationships that can work through issues and increasingly seek out situations and systems that are growth producing. At this point, clients are ready to end therapy.

IPMT takes a very close look at how issues of power, racism, and discrimination impacts individuals in negative ways and how power and oppression is a driving force in the development of problem-saturated stories. Although IPMT therapists do not push their values onto their clients, they are not neutral because they believe that when therapists are neutral, they subtly support the "isms" of society. IPMT therapists will often include components of intersectionality in their practice, including the unpacking of clients' experiences of gender, culture/ethnicity, sexual identity, social class, ability status, religion, spirituality, socioeconomic status, age, and other unique identity factors. Finally, with a focus on power, racism, and discrimination, it is no surprise that IPMT therapists are generally social justice activists.

IPMT therapists lean heavily on qualitative research techniques because they question the validity of quantitative techniques, and believe that understanding the client's experience is particularly important. Although some research on solution-focused brief therapy and relational cultural therapy shows that these approaches have been efficacious with a wide variety of clients, others have questioned the rigor of the research. More research is needed if one is to examine the efficacy of postmodern therapy, and specifically the efficacy of an integrative approach, such as IPMT.

KEY WORDS AND NAMES

Ambassador
Analyzing counselor–client power differentials
Anti-deterministic
Anti-objectivist
Coping and exception-seeking questions
Deconstructed
Definitional ceremonies
Demonstrating acceptance, authenticity, and empathy
de Shazer, Steven
Dominant narratives
Dominant stories
Encouraging discussion about oppression and marginalization
Epstein, David
Externalizing the problem
Future-oriented
Homework
Kim Berg, Insoo

Miller, Jean Baker
Multistoried
Mutually enhancing, empathic, empowering relationships
Narrative therapy
Narratives
Nondominant stories
Non-pathological
Non-pathologizing
Non-pathologizing stance
Outsider witness groups
Positive
Postmodern
Postmodernism
Post-structuralism
Power
Problem-saturated stories
Questions
Questions that demonstrate respectful curiosity, mystery, and awe
Questions that explore identity
Questions that help to externalize the problem
Realities are constituted through language
Realities are organized and maintained through narrative
Realities are socially constructed
Re-author
Re-authoring
Re-authoring questions
Reflective teams
Relational cultural therapy (RCT)
Re-membering
Scaling
Self-reflection exercises
Showing mystery, respectful curiosity, and awe
Social constructionism
Social constructionist
Solution-focused brief therapy (SFBT)
Solution-oriented questions
Strategies of disconnection
Strength-based
Structuralism
Telling and retelling stories
There are no essential truths
Thick descriptions
Thin descriptions
Use of therapeutic documents and other paraphernalia
White, Michael

REFERENCES

Andersen, T. (1987). The reflecting team: Dialogue and meta-dialogue in clinical work. *Family Process, 26*, 415–428. https://doi.org/10.1111/j.1545-5300.1987.00415.x

Backman, M. (1988, July 7). Keeping women in mind. *Profile*. 9–10.

Beyene, T., Anglin, M., Sanchez, W., & Ballou, M. (2002). Mentoring and relational mutuality: Protégés perspectives. *Journal of Humanistic Counseling, 41*, 87–102. https://doi.org/10.1002/j.2164-490X.2002.tb00132.x

Butler, M. (1985). Guidelines for feminist therapy. In Rosewater, L. B., & Walker, L. E. A. (Eds.), *Handbook of feminist therapy: Women's issues in psychotherapy* (32–38). Springer.

Centre for Reviews and Dissemination (2014). *Review of effectiveness of solution-focused brief therapy: A systematic qualitative review of controlled outcome studies*. https://www.ncbi.nlm.nih.gov/pubmedhealth/PMH0056400/

Combs, G., & Freedman, J. (2012). Narrative, poststructuralism, and social justice: Current practice in narrative therapy. *The Counseling Psychologist, 40*, 1033-1060. https://doi.org/10.1177/0011000012460662

Combs, G., & Freedman, J. (2016). Narrative therapy's relational understanding of identity. *Family Process, 55*, 211-224. https://doi.org/10.1111/famp.12216

Crenshaw, K. (1989). Demarginalizing the intersection of race and sex: Black feminist critique of antidiscrimination doctrine, feminist theory and antiracist politics. *University of Chicago Legal Forum*, 139–168.

Corcoran, J. (2012). Review of outcomes with children and adolescents with externalizing behavior problems. In C. Franklin, T. S. Trepper, W. J. Ginerich, & E. McCollum (Eds.), *Solution-focused brief therapy* (pp. 121–129). Oxford University Press.

Denborough, D. (2014). *Retelling the stories of our lives: Everyday narrative therapy to draw inspiration and transform experience.* W. W. Norton.

Dewell, J. (2015). Solution-focused brief family therapy. In E. S. Neukrug (Ed.), *The SAGE encyclopedia of theory in counseling and psychotherapy* (Vol. 2, pp. 943–936). SAGE Publications.

De Jong, P., & Berg, I. K. (2013). *Interviewing for solutions* (4th ed.). Brooks/Cole.

de Shazer, S. (1988). *Clues: Investigating solutions in brief therapy.* W. W. Norton.

Duffy, T., Haberstroh, S., & Trepal, H. (2009). Grounded theory of relational competencies and creativity in counseling: Beginning the dialogue. *Journal of Creativity in Mental Health, 4*, 89–112. https://doi.org/10.1080/15401380902951911

Freedman, J., & Combs, G. (1996). *Narrative therapy: The social construction of preferred realities.* W. W. Norton.

Gergen, K. (2015). *An invitation to social construction* (3rd ed.). SAGE Publications.

George, E., Iveson, C., & Ratner, H. (2015). Solution-focused brief therapy. In E. S. Neukrug (Ed.), *The SAGE encyclopedia of theory in counseling and psychotherapy* (Vol. 2, pp. 946–950). SAGE Publications.

Gingerich, W. J., & Peterson, L. T. (2013). Effectiveness of solution-focused brief therapy: A systematic qualitative review of controlled outcome studies. *Research on Social Work Practice, 23*, 266–283.

Guilfoyle, M. (2104). *The person in narrative therapy: A post-structural, Foucauldian account.* Palgrave Macmillan.

Guterman, J. T. (2013). *Solution-focused counseling* (2nd ed.). American Counseling Association.

Freedman, J., & Combs, G. (1996). *Narrative therapy: The social construction of preferred realities.* W. W. Norton.

Haberstroh, S., & Moyer, M. (2012). Exploring an online self-injury support group: Perspectives from group members. *The Journal for Specialists in Group Work, 73*, 113–132. https://doi.org/10.1080/01933922.2011.646088

Harrison, K. (2013). Counselling psychology and power: Considering therapy and beyond. *Counselling Psychology Review, 28*(2), 107–117.

Heins, T., & Ritchie, K. (1988). *Beating sneaky poo: Ideas for fecal soiling.* http://www.narrativetherapylibrary.com/img/ps/spoo1.pdf

Heppner, P. P., Wampold, B. E., Owen, J., Thompson, M. N., & Wang, K. T. (2016). *Research design in counseling.* Cengage Learning.

Jordan, J. V. (2000). The role of mutual empathy in relational/cultural therapy. *Journal of Clinical Psychology, 56,* 1005–1016. https://doi.org/10.1002/1097-4679(200008)56:8<1005::AID-JCLP2>3.0.CO;2-L

Jordan, J. V. (2010). *Relational-cultural therapy.* American Psychological Association.

Kayser, K., Watson, L. E., & Andrade, J. T. (2007). Cancer as a "we-disease": Examining the process of coping from a relational perspective. *Families, Systems, & Health, 25,* 404–418. http://dx.doi.org/10.1037/1091-7527.25.4.404

Kim, J. S. (2008). Examining the effectiveness of solution-focused brief therapy: A meta-analysis. *Research on Social Work Practice, 18,* 107–116. https://doi.org/10.1177/1049731507307807

Kim, J. S. (2014). *Solution-focused brief therapy: A multicultural approach.* SAGE Publications.

Liang, B., Tracy, A. J., Taylor, C. A., & Williams, L .M. (2002). Mentoring college-age women: A relational approach. *American Journal of Community Psychology, 30,* 271–288. https://doi.org/10.1023/A:1014637112531

Langley, N., Ryerson, F., & Woolf, E. A. (1939). Screenplay of The Wizard of Oz. http://www.sellingyourscreenplay.com/wp-content/uploads/screenplay/scripts/The-Wizard-of-Oz.pdf

Lenz, A. S., Speciale, M., & Aquilar, J. V. (2012). Relational-cultural therapy intervention with incarcerated adolscents: A single-case effectiveness design. *Counseling Outcome Research and Evaluation, 3,* 17–29. https://doi.org/10.1177/2150137811435233

MacKinnon, C. A. (2013). Intersectionality as a method: A note. *Journal of Women in Culture and Society, 38,* 1019–1030. https://doi.org/10.1086/669570

Madigan, S. (2011). *Narrative therapy.* American Psychological Association.

Madigan, S. (2015). Michael White. In E. S. Neukrug (Ed.), *The SAGE encyclopedia of theory in counseling and psychotherapy* (Vol. 2, pp. 1050–1053). SAGE Publications.

Marsten, D., Epston, D., Markham, L. (2016). *Narrative therapy in Wonderland: Connecting with children's imaginative know-how.* W. W. Norton.

Mencher, J. (1997). Intimacy in lesbian relationships: A critical examination of fusion. In J. V. Jordan, (Ed.), *Women's growth in diversity: More writings from the Stone Center* (pp. 311–330). Guilford Press.

Miller, J. B. (1976). *Toward a new psychology of women.* Beacon Press.

Miller, J. B. (2008). Tell the truth about power. *Women & Therapy, 31 (2-4),* 145–161. https://doi.org/10.1080/02703140802146282

Miller, J. B., & Stiver, I. P. (1997). *The healing connection: How women form relationships in therapy and in life.* Beacon Press.

Morgan, A. (2000). *What is narrative therapy? An easy-to-read introduction.* Dulwich Centre.

Morray, E. B., & Liang, B. (2005). Peace talk: A relational approach to group negotiation among Arab and Israeli youth. *International Journal of Group Psychotherapy, 55,* 481–506. https://doi.org/10.1521/ijgp.2005.55.4.481

Murphy, J. J. (2008). *Solution-focused counseling in schools* (2nd ed.). American Counseling Association.

Myerhoff, B. (1982). Life history among the elderly: Performance, visibility, and re-membering. In J. Rub (Ed.), *A crack in the mirror: Reflexive perspectives in anthropology* (pp. 99–120). University of Pennsylvania Press.

Myerhoff, B. (1986). "Life not death in Venice": Its second life. In V. W. Turner & E. M. Bruner (Eds.), *The anthropology of experience* (pp. 261–286). University of Illinois Press.

National Library of Medicine. (2015). *Dr. Jean Baker Miller.* www.nlm.nih.gov/changingthefaceofmedicine/physicians/biography_225.html

Neukrug, E. S. (2018). *Counseling theory and practice* (2nd ed.). Cognella Academic Press.

Paris, R., & Dubas, N. (2005). Staying connected while nurturing an infant: A challenge of new motherhood. *Family Relations, 54,* 72–83. https://doi.org/10.1111/j.0197-6664.2005.00007.x

Patrick, S., & Connolly, C. M. (2013). The privilege project: A narrative approach for teaching social justice and multicultural awareness. *The Journal of Systemic Therapies, 32*(1), 70–86. https://doi.org/10.1521/jsyt.2013.32.1.70

Payne, M. (2006). *Narrative therapy.* SAGE Publications.

Rice, R. (2015). Michael White. In E. S. Neukrug (Ed.), *The SAGE encyclopedia of theory in counseling and psychotherapy* (Vol. 2, pp. 695–701). SAGE Publications.

Richert, A. J. (2010). *Integrating existential and narrative therapy: A theoretical base for eclectic practice.* Duquesne University Press.

Shapiro, J. P. (2015). *Child and adolescent therapy: Science and art* (2nd ed.). John Wiley & Sons.

Spencer, R. (2006). Understanding the mentoring process between adolescents and adults. *Youth and Society, 37,* 287–315.

Spencer, R., Jordan, J. V., & Sazama, J. (2004). Growth-promoting relationships between youth and adults: A focus group study. *Families in Society: The Journal of Contemporary Social Services, 85,* 354–362.

Spencer, R., & Liang, B. (2009). "She gives me a break from the world": Formal youth mentoring relationships between adolescent girls and adult women. *Journal of Primary Prevention, 30,* 109–130. https://doi.org/10.1007/s10935-009-0172-1

Sturm, D. C. (2015). Relational-cultural theory. In E. Neukrug (Ed.), *The SAGE encyclopedia of theory in counseling and psychotherapy* (Vol. 2, pp. 648–640). SAGE Publications.

Tantillo, M., & Sanftner, J. (2003). The relationship between perceived mutuality and bulimic symptoms, depression, and therapeutic change in group. *Eating Behaviors, 3,* 349–364. https://doi.org/10.1016/S1471-0153(02)00077-6

Tantillo, M., & Sanftner, J. (2010). Measuring perceived mutuality in women with eating disorders: The development of the Connection-Disconnection Scale. *Journal of Nursing Measurement, 18,* 100–119. https://doi.org/10.1891/1061-3749.18.2.100

Thomas, F. N., & Nelson, T. S. (2007). Assumptions and practices within the solution-focused brief therapy tradition. In T. S. Nelson & F. N. Thomas (Eds.), *Handbook of solution-focused brief therapy: Clinical applications* (pp. 3–24). Haworth Press.

Weinberg, D. (2008). The philosophical foundations of constructionist research. In J. A. Holstein & J. F. Gubrium (Eds.), *Handbook of constructionist research* (pp. 13–40). Guilford Press.

White, M. (1993). *Narrative therapy using a reflective team.* [Video]. American Counseling Association.

White, M. (1995). *Re-authoring lives: Interviews and essays.* Dulwich Centre.

White, M. (2007). *Maps of narrative practice.* Norton Books.

White, M., & Epston, D. (1990). *Narrative means to therapeutic ends.* Norton.

White, M., Epston, D., & Andrews, J. (1994). *The best of friends: A live interview with Michael White.* [Video]. Master's Works Video Productions.

Winslade, J., & Geroski, A. (2008). A social constructionist view of development. In K. Kraus (Ed.), *Lenses: Applying lifespan development theories in counseling* (pp. 88–113) Lahaska Press.

Wong, Y. J. (2015). *The psychology of encouragement: Theory, research, and applications, 32,* 178–176. https://doi.org/10.1177/0011000014545091

CASE STUDY: MARKUS SEES AN IPMT THERAPIST

(Please read about the Millers in Appendix I prior to reading this case study)

Markus steps into the waiting room of his new therapist, Dr. Gerald Delorio, or "Jerry" as he likes to be called. Markus had called Dr. Delorio a few weeks earlier, and as soon as the therapist reached him, he said, "Please call me Jerry. I know a few things, but the bottom line is we're just two people who are going to talk about a few things you're going through." Markus was a little put off by this response, as he was hoping he could find an expert to tell him what to do, but he figured he'd give him a try anyway.

Markus had seen a therapist before, but his first appointment to Jerry's office was not like anything he had experienced prior. As he sat in the waiting room, there was pleasant music playing, and suddenly Jerry walked out and quickly presented his hand to Markus. Jerry was wearing jeans, sneakers, and a buttoned-down shirt, and Jerry said, "Come in and join me. Would you like a drink—Coke, water, coffee?" "No thanks," said Markus, thinking to himself that it all seemed a bit casual.

As Markus walked into Jerry's office, he saw a couple of odd paintings on the wall, and some relatively older-looking, but comfortable, chairs. "Have a seat," said Jerry. Markus sat in an old, well-used, large and comfortable chair. He felt like he might keep falling in, the chair had so much give to it. Jerry gave a brief overview of his therapeutic approach, which to Markus sounded as if the therapist was simply going to listen to his stories about his life and then offer some ideas on how he might be able to change it. Then, Jerry said, "So, Markus, what brings you here? I really want to hear about *you.*" Markus was taken by how authentic and real Jerry seemed and how the therapist did seem to really want to listen to him.

Markus began talking about his relationship with Rob, and his sister, and his parents. He talked about how depressed he had been in recent months, and maybe a little his whole life.

He shared that he had been adopted and was gay. This is when Jerry really seemed to zone in on what Markus was saying. "So, I bet having the identities of being adopted, Black, and gay, led to some real challenges for you." Markus was a bit surprised that Jerry had focused on these aspects of Markus's life, but also was willing and wanting to talk about them. "Yeah, I've had my challenges. Like, I felt like I was second best—my sister being the 'real' child since she was my parents' biological child. And, being gay, especially being a Black gay person, was very challenging. I got my share of bullying and weird looks in my life. But, maybe it made me a bit stronger too."

"It sounds like being Black and gay, and adopted too, left you feel a bit disengaged from others growing up and not part of the mainstream world," said Jerry. "Yes, exactly," said Markus, acutely aware of how tuned in to him Jerry seemed to be. "I always felt like there was something different about me, and I wonder if this was a cause of some of my depression. Until recently, I thought there was something wrong with me—kind of biologically inferior. I know that sounds weird, but it was how I felt. Then, when gay marriage was legalized, I felt like a weight was lifted off of me." Jerry looked at Markus and with a reassuring tone said, "I wonder how the messages we receive and the laws that are passed can impact our sense of who we are." "Yes, yes," said Markus. "I bet if I lived in a world of adopted, gay, Black people, I would feel pretty normal."

"So, it seems like you have felt a bit isolated and unaccepted, much of your life. And, even though you know better, you still have carried this burden with you. If we were to give that burden a name, what would you call it, Markus?" "Hmm, interesting," replied Markus. "I think I might call it the 'infected me,' because it feels like there's something sick in all of this." "What if we call it the 'illogically ill box,'" said Jerry, "because I think you know there is nothing wrong with you, except that you have been told, by others, that your identities are not normal. A part of you knows you are well. 'The box,' which holds the oppressive stories others told you, is illogically ill—not you. What do you think?" Markus was fascinated by this vision of a box, outside of himself, being a metaphor for all the ills of others and of society. He began to understand what Jerry was getting at—that he was not ill, but others' reactions to him and societal responses to him were oppressive.

Jerry studied Markus for a bit, and asked, "Were there times when the illogically ill box did not impact you so strongly?" Markus thought about it for a moment before answering. "Yes, when I was around other gay men, especially other gay Black men. And, when I met Rob, and I felt loved by him and okay about myself." "So, perhaps a goal for you would be to seek out people who can identify with you and who have positive experiences about who they are," said Jerry.

Markus realized an hour had nearly pasted. He was surprised by what he had talked about during the session. He thought that Jerry would refer him to a psychiatrist for anti-depressant medication and that he would talk about the deep depression he was experiencing. Instead, he ended up talking about his identities as an adopted, gay, Black man—and it felt right.

He began to think about how often he put himself down for who he was and how liberating it always was to be around people who were supportive, caring, and a bit more like him. He began to wonder whether he needed to find more people like that in his life.

"So, how do you think it went today?" asked Jerry. "Pretty good," responded Markus. "I think that maybe I need to make some changes in my life." "You know, therapists like me like to call that 'reconstructing' or 're-authoring' your life." "I think I get that," said Markus. "It's kind of like I have to find new stories and new people to help me define myself and accept myself." "Yes," said Jerry, "you got it. So, if you were to think about how you would like your life to look in the future, what do you see?" Markus paused and thought for a long time, and then said, "Well, there were times in my life when I was not depressed, and usually it was when I was around supportive people. I think to feel like that again, I need to find more people with whom I feel empowered and good around. More people like me." "Interesting," responded Jerry. "Maybe, Markus, you can think this week about ways you can make that happen. Perhaps journal about it. Then, we can talk about that next week." "Sounds like a plan," said Markus.

Markus was a little surprised at how close he felt to Jerry by the end of the session, and when they bid goodbye, they gave each other a big hug. Markus felt as if Jerry had heard him, had encouraged him to look at himself and at how others impact him, and had made some suggestions on how he could begin to make changes in the future. He remembered how cautious he was when he first met Jerry, and how trusting he quickly became of him. He was looking forward to the next session.

QUESTIONS FOR YOU TO PONDER

1. In what ways did Jerry normalize and depathologize the counseling relationship?
2. List ways that Jerry was unconventional and how do you believe these behaviors positively or negatively impact the counseling relationship?
3. Why did you think Jerry did not immediately focus on Markus's depression?
4. How did focusing on Markus's identities nicely fit into the IPMT paradigm related to problem-saturated, dominant narratives?
5. What was the purpose of naming Markus's problems the "illogically ill box"?
6. Do you believe that mental illness and mental health problems are a social construction, inherent, or something in-between? How do your beliefs about mental health issues impact your ability to be an IPMT therapist?
7. How do use of the terms "reconstructing" and "re-authoring" set the tone for making change with Markus and with IPMT therapy in general?
8. How did Jerry use an exception-seeking question to identify positive times in Markus's life?

9. How did Jerry use a solution-oriented question in helping Markus think about the change process?
10. What purpose does journaling serve in the change process in IPMT?
11. Give some examples of how definitional ceremonies could be used with Markus if he were to continue to progress in counseling?
12. If you were to go through IPMT, what problem-saturated narrative(s) would you want to explore. How do you believe your problem-saturated narrative is reflective of messages you received from your social milieu?

5

Dialectical Behavior Therapy (DBT)

Francisca Rivas, Ne'Shaun J. Borden, Johana Rocha, and Kyulee Park

LEARNING OUTCOMES

- To become familiar with Marsha Linehan, the originator of dialectical behavior therapy (DBT).
- To understand the view of human nature of DBT, including its behavioral, existential-humanistic, and Eastern philosophical leanings.
- To examine key concepts related to DBT, including borderline personality disorder, emotional dysregulation and emotional regulation, biosocial theory, dialectical philosophy, behaviorism, Zen Buddhism and mindfulness, and the seven basic assumptions when treating clients using DBT.
- To examine the pretreatment skills of DBT, including assessment, psychoeducation, explanation of the purpose, and a verbal or written agreement.
- To examine skills found in Stages I–IV of individual therapy, including structuring therapy, the diary card, chain analysis, dialectical communication skills, behavioral skills, cognitive skills, and reinforcement of group skills.
- To examine group skills training, specifically the acceptance skills (mindfulness and distress tolerance) and change skills (emotional regulation and interpersonal effectiveness).

- To give a brief explanation of the purpose of consultation team meetings in DBT.
- To offer an understanding of the purpose of phone coaching in DBT.
- To describe the counseling process of DBT.
- To examine social and cultural applicability of DBT.
- To review the efficacy of DBT.
- To offer a case study that demonstrates the DBT process.

BRIEF HISTORY OF DIALECTICAL BEHAVIOR THERAPY

> *The bottom line is that if you are in hell, the only way out is to go through a period of sustained misery. Misery is, of course, much better than hell, but it is painful nonetheless. By refusing to accept the misery that it takes to climb out of hell, you end up falling back into hell repeatedly, only to have to start over and over again. (Linehan, 2015a, p. 461)*

This quote by **Marsha Linehan**, the founder of **dialectical behavior therapy** (DBT), says it all. Those people who struggle with mental illness are in hell, and it takes a lot of effort to get better. And it's going to be slow and hard work as you climb up through purgatory and very slowly move toward a bit of joy in your life. But who is Marsha Linehan?

Born May 5, 1943, in Tulsa, Oklahoma, Marsha M. Linehan is considered the founder of DBT (Carey, 2011). The third child of six, Linehan was a bright student who felt unloved and inadequate compared with her siblings. At 17, while exhibiting symptoms of self-loathing, self-destructiveness, and social withdrawal, a psychiatrist recommended in-patient treatment and diagnosed her as schizophrenic.

Remembered by staff members and fellow patients as frequently attacking herself, burning her wrists with cigarettes, cutting her arms, and banging her head against the wall and floor, at the hospital she was medicated with Thorazine, Librium, and other psychotropic medications and even given electroshock treatments. In a *New York Times* article, Linehan reminisces on those times: "My whole experience of these episodes was that someone else was doing it; it was like 'I know this is coming, I'm out of control, somebody help me; where are you, God?' … I felt totally empty, like the Tin Man; I had no way to communicate what was going on, no way to understand it" (Carey, 2011, para. 14). Later in her life, Linehan would argue that she had been misdiagnosed, treated inappropriately, and believes she had the characteristics of borderline personality disorder, not schizophrenia.

After 26 months of psychiatric treatment, Linehan was released from the hospital. Her discharge summary noted she was one of the most disturbed patients in the history of the hospital, and her doctors doubted her ability to successfully live outside of the hospital.

Vowing to "come back and get others out of here" (Carey, 2011, para. 23), Linehan returned home, but after struggling with suicidal ideation, moved to Chicago in her mid-20s in hopes of starting a new life. Despite having stable employment, she felt lost, confused, and lonely in Chicago. Finding some solace in her Catholic faith, one night while praying she had a transformative realization:

> One night I was kneeling in there, looking up at the cross, and the whole place became gold—and suddenly I felt something coming toward me. It was this shimmering experience, and I just ran back to my room and said, 'I love myself.' It was the first time I remember talking to myself in the first person. I felt transformed. (Carey, 2011, para. 27)

This awareness eventually led Linehan to adopt the paradoxical practice of **radical acceptance** and **commitment to change** that was to become a foundational aspect of DBT. After earning her bachelor's in psychology, and then her master's and doctoral degrees in social and experimental psychology, from Loyola University in Chicago, Linehan pursued a postdoctoral clinical internship at the Suicide Prevention and Crisis Service in Buffalo, New York, and a postdoctoral behavioral therapy program at the State University of New York, Stony Brook. Passionate about working with individuals with suicidal ideation and writing about her ideas for change, over the years she held a number of clinical and faculty positions. Linehan currently serves as professor of psychology and adjunct professor in psychiatry and behavioral sciences at the University of Washington.

From early on, Linehan's research interests included suicidality, parasuicidality, personality disorders, behavior modification, and cognitive behavioral treatment. These areas, along with her interest in radical acceptance, and her work and research with suicidal individuals with borderline personality disorder, led to her theory of DBT and the writing of a number of well-received articles on DBT (Linehan, 1987a, 1987b, 1989).

While finalizing the development of DBT, Linehan decided to take time off from her work to immerse herself in learning radical acceptance. Spending two months at a Buddhist monastery practicing radical acceptance and letting go of desires, under the guidance of a Zen master, her spiritual journey led her to incorporate **mindfulness** as one of the key components of DBT (Gold, 2017; Linehan, 2017a). She continued her spiritual training under Gerald May (American psychiatrist and half-brother of Rollo May), Tilden Edwards (Episcopal priest and founder of Shalem Institute for Spiritual Formation), and Willigis Jager (German Benedictine monk). Linehan herself is a Zen master (Roshi) in the Sanbo-Kyodan School and the Diamond Sangha.

Fearful that speaking openly about her mental illness would undermine her theory and her credibility, for years Linehan was hesitant to talk about her struggles. Then, after one of Linehan's patients said, ". . . . if you were [like us], it would give all of us so much hope" (Carey,

2011, para. 2), Linehan thought it was finally time. It was then that she publicly shared her experiences with mental illness in a talk titled, "Succeeding by Failing, the Personal Story Behind DBT."

Linehan continues to be an active researcher, educator, and advocate of DBT, and has authored more than 100 journal articles, several books, and manuals that have been translated into multiple languages. For her outstanding work, she has received dozens of awards. Some of her more noteworthy awards include: the Louis I. Dublin Award for Lifetime Achievement in the Field of Suicide (1999), Distinguished Scientist Award from the American Psychological Association (APA; 2001), Career Achievement Award from APA (2005), Gold Medal for Lifetime Achievement in the Application of Psychology Award from the American Psychological Foundation (2012), Scientific Research Award from the National Alliance on Mental Illness (2015), Career/Lifetime Achievement Award from the Association of Behavioral and Cognitive Therapies (2016), and the $100,000 Grawemeyer Award in Psychology (2017; Linehan, 2017b).

VIEW OF HUMAN NATURE

DBT's understanding of the person is largely based on the **biosocial model of personality formation**, credited mostly to **Theodore Millon** (1969). Millon suggested that children are born with specific **constitutional factors** related to their physical ability, intellect, drive, energy, and temperament. A childhood's emotional world can be impacted by how these factors are shaped through childhood experiences, such as parenting, peer relationships, and other environmental factors. Childhood experiences that create a **negative** or **invalidating environment** can impact constitutional factors in a manner that lends the child and developing adult toward **emotional volatility** and **dysregulation**, and associated behaviors, and makes them at risk of developing BPD or related mental disorders (Kuo & Fitzpatrick, 2015; Linehan, 2015a).

To treat BPD and related mental disorders, DBT relies on cognitive and behavioral theory while also integrating Eastern philosophy and existential-humanistic concepts (Hayes & Hofmann, 2017; Pederson 2015). Considered a type of **third wave of cognitive behavioral therapy**, DBT and other third-wave approaches view personality formation as a complex interaction between behavior, biology, and context (environment), and focuses on a wide range of techniques to assist clients in accepting and changing their ways of being in the world.

Although DBT relies on several behavioral techniques, it does not solely focus on changing specific behaviors, as did **first-wave cognitive behavioral therapy** (operant conditioning, classical conditioning, and modeling). Also, in contrast with traditional cognitive therapy (**"second-wave cognitive behavioral therapy"**) that tends to zoom in on cognitive distortions and irrational thinking by replacing faulty thinking, DBT focuses on adopting an increasingly flexible and relativistic views of the world so that the person is not embedded in rigid ways of thinking, which tend to exasperate problems. Instead, DBT and related third-wave approaches tend to emphasize "mindfulness, emotions, acceptance, relationships, values, goals, and meta-cognition"

(Hayes & Hofmann, 2017, p. 245), and a number of traditional behavioral techniques and modified cognitive techniques when working with clients

Recognizing that change is slow and difficult, but possible for most clients, DBT suggests the importance of radically accepting clients and encouraging them to accept themselves (Gold, 2017; Linehan, 2017a). With this theme in mind, building the therapeutic alliance by listening, being empathic, and showing radical acceptance is critical and borrows from the humanistic skills of person-centered counseling. Also, other techniques from existential therapy and gestalt therapy are used to encourage clients to examine what is important in their lives and to help them see the polarities within themselves. Understanding the dialectics (polarities) of life, particularly of acceptance and change, is critical to the work of the DBT therapist. In fact, embracing dialectics is so critical that it is viewed as a practice all DBT therapists should actively embrace in their lives. One popular method used to help foster dialectical thinking is the practice of mindfulness, a technique related to the Eastern philosophy of Zen Buddhism. Important for therapists and clients alike in their journey toward accepting themselves, this practice is often viewed as the first step toward change. DBT is an approach grounded in many cognitive behavioral traditions, but clearly integrates existential-humanistic skills, mindfulness, Eastern philosophy, and more as it fosters deeper meaningfulness in clients' lives. It practices radical acceptance, believes that people can change, and uses a wide range of philosophies and techniques to promote such change.

KEY CONCEPTS

Since DBT was developed to treat individuals with **Borderline Personality Disorder** (BPD), this section will start with a short description of BPD. We will then go on to describe some important aspects related to the theoretical underpinnings of DBT, including **biosocial theory, emotional dysregulation and emotional regulation, dialectical philosophy, behaviorism,** and **Zen Buddhism**, and **mindfulness**. We will conclude with the **seven basic assumptions of DBT**.

Borderline Personality Disorder

Through Linehan's early work with suicidal and parasuicidal clients, she realized that many of her clients met some, or all, of the diagnostic criteria for BPD (Linehan, 1993a). Although knowing little about BPD at the time, Linehan (2017a) quickly came up to speed on the emotional, interpersonal, behavioral, and cognitive dysregulation characteristic of BPD. Clients diagnosed with BPD often have a difficult time functioning in relationships, engage in non-suicidal self-injurious behavior, and are at much higher risk of suicidal behaviors. Also, they tend to have a particularly difficult time in counseling, often leaving their practitioners feeling helpless as they struggle to make progress, usually with little success. Kuo & Fitzpatrick (2015) summarize the symptoms needed in DSM-5 for a diagnosis of BPD:

1. frantic efforts to avoid imagined abandonment,
2. instability in interpersonal relationships,
3. identity disturbance,
4. impulsivity,
5. suicidal behaviors,
6. emotional instability,
7. chronic feelings of emptiness,
8. inappropriate or intense anger, and
9. stress-related paranoid ideation or dissociation (p. 294).

Although just 1.4% to 5.9% are diagnosed with BPD, 42.4% of these seek treatment for the disorder (Grant et al., 2009; National Institute of Mental Health, 2017; Lenzenweger et al., 2007). In addition, Ten Have et al. (2016) found that approximately 25% of people have one or two symptoms of BPD and another nearly 4% have three or four symptoms of BPD. Thus, individuals with BPD or related disorders, and individuals who have some of the symptoms of BPD, make up a substantial percentage of those who seek counseling.

With high numbers of individuals with BPD or related symptoms or disorders seeking counseling, Linehan quickly realized the treatment options were not adequate and often resulted in poor outcomes, high dropout rates, and stressed-out practitioners (Linehan, 1993a). She eventually concluded that traditional cognitive behavioral therapies that were often used to treat individuals with BPD focused too much on change and not enough on reducing the ongoing dysregulation, common in clients with BPD. To improve the quality of life for these individuals, Linehan recommended that clinicians go beyond treating the symptoms and recognize, and respond to, the complex cycle of emotional dysregulation some clients endure. Instead of focusing on symptoms, she used a biosocial lens to understand the complexity of their situations and work with them accordingly.

Biosocial Theory

The biosocial model of personality formation, credited mostly to **Theodore Millon's** (1969), suggested that children are born with constitutional factors, such as physical ability, intellectual capacity, drive, energy, and temperament that shapes their view of the world but can be expressed differently as a function of childhood experiences, such as parenting, peer relationships, and other environmental factors. When a mixture of constitutional factors lends a child to being hard-wired for emotional vulnerability, and when that child is brought up in a negative or invalidating environment, he or she is increasingly at risk of developing BPD or other mental disorders (Kuo & Fitzpatrick, 2015; Linehan, 2015a).

Linehan (1993a; Rizvi et al., 2013) suggested that an **invalidating environment** from important caregivers (e.g., parents) can result in heightened emotional responses in some children, difficulty in regulating one's emotional responses, and a slow rate of returning to normality—symptoms typical of individuals with BPD or related disorders. For instance, a caregiver's continued ignoring or discounting of the child's emotional experiences can lead the child to exhibit extreme emotions that are more likely to be attended to. Often, such children then learn to associate those intense emotional expressions with attention.

As these children grow into adulthood, they have an inability to effectively communicate or problem solve when situations become difficult, as they quickly resort to a heightened emotional state in their interactions with others (Crowell, 2009; Rizvi et al., 2013). It also makes it difficult for them to de-escalate their emotions. This constant cycle of emotional volatility makes individuals with BPD, or related mental disorders, have a difficult time understanding polarities in life and that two opposing thoughts can be simultaneously true (e.g., "I'm upset at my partner—I want a divorce," and "My partner brings me a sense of being grounded in life"). Thus, learning how to incorporate a dialectical philosophy is critical for individuals who have symptoms of BPD or related disorders, and a good philosophy for all individuals to embrace.

Emotional Dysregulation and Emotional Regulation

Individuals with BPD, and related disorders, struggle with **emotional dysregulation**, which is the difficulty—or even, inability—to moderate one's emotional experiences (Linehan, 2015a). Such individuals (1) are run by their emotions, (2) have difficulty processing information and cues from others, (3) demonstrate impulsive behaviors, (4) have difficulty in making decisions, and (5) have behaviors that are dictated by cognitive distortions (e.g., all-or-nothing thinking, catastrophizing, overgeneralizing, personalizing, excessive use of "should and must" statements, and more). Pederson (2015) calls such cognitive distortions "stuck thoughts" to minimize stigma associated with the term. In addition, some individuals who cannot regulate their emotions express this problem through overregulation in which they (1) are out of touch and suppress their feelings, (2) experience and show little positive affect, and (3) cannot communicate their feelings effectively with others.

In contrast, **emotional regulation** is marked by an individual's ability to (1) moderate strong emotions so they do not dictate thoughts and behaviors, (2) effectively communicate one's feelings to others, (3) respond to strong emotions in ways that will positively de-escalate a situation, and (4) self-soothe so that strong emotions do not direct one's thinking and acting. Although emotional dysregulation is a hallmark of individuals with BPD, aspects of it are common to many disorders. Therefore, although DBT was originally used solely for individuals with BPD, it has been expanded and used with a wider class of individuals seeking counseling.

Dialectical Philosophy

Dialectical philosophy suggests that "reality is interrelated and connected, made of opposing forces, and always changing" (Rizvi et al., 2013, p. 74). In contrast with other forms of cognitive behavioral treatments that focus on changing symptoms, Linehan suggested a dialectical framework should be the foundational philosophy that grounds the change process (Linehan, 1993). Such a philosophy suggests that reality is grounded in polarities that are always in tension—within the client, within the therapist, and between the client and therapist. For instance, the following show the inability of accepting the polarities of life:

1. A client may see himself or herself as evil and not recognize any goodness within.
2. A therapist believes a client has a borderline personality disorder and, thus, cannot change.
3. A therapist may want the client to be hospitalized, yet the client thinks he or she is well enough to not be hospitalized.

This yin and yang of life suggests that individuals need to increasingly understand opposing forces and simultaneously hold both in consciousness, and that regardless of the polarities with which a person, or persons, is struggling, there needs to be an integration of the opposing forces. For instance, in the first example just given, the client has to also recognize the good in him or her. In the second example, the therapist needs to reconcile the fact that some change is possible for all clients, and in the third example, the therapist and client need to come to a collaborative, satisfactory conclusion that takes into account the therapist's, and client's, differing views on hospitalization.

Acceptance vs. Change: The Overarching Dialectic of DBT

One **dialectic** that is core to the change process in DBT is **acceptance** vs. **change**. For example, depressed clients need to allow themselves to experience their sadness, but also recognize their desire to experience contentment; clients who experience themselves as failures need to envision their successes; and clients who want to use substances need to also see their desire to be clean (Rizvi et al., 2013). Helping clients accept their current state of being, while also helping them recognize the possibilities of change, is the hallmark of the work of the therapist who practices DBT.

Three Common Dialectical Dilemmas of Individuals With BPD

At the core of working with individuals with BPD, or related diagnoses, is understanding three biosocial dialectical dilemmas that clients tend to face as a result of emotional dysregulation: **active passivity** vs. **apparent competence**, **emotional vulnerability** vs. **self-invalidation**, and **unrelenting crisis** vs. **inhibited grieving** (Koemer, 2012). Linehan (1993) suggests that these polarities have a tendency to be more biologically based (in red), in which the person is under-regulated or emotionally out of control; or socially based (in blue), in which the person is overregulated or attempts to overcontrol one's emotions. Neither are good. Individuals with BPD, or related disorders, tend to bounce back and forth between these states of being and have difficulty integrating these two opposite poles (Figure 5.1).

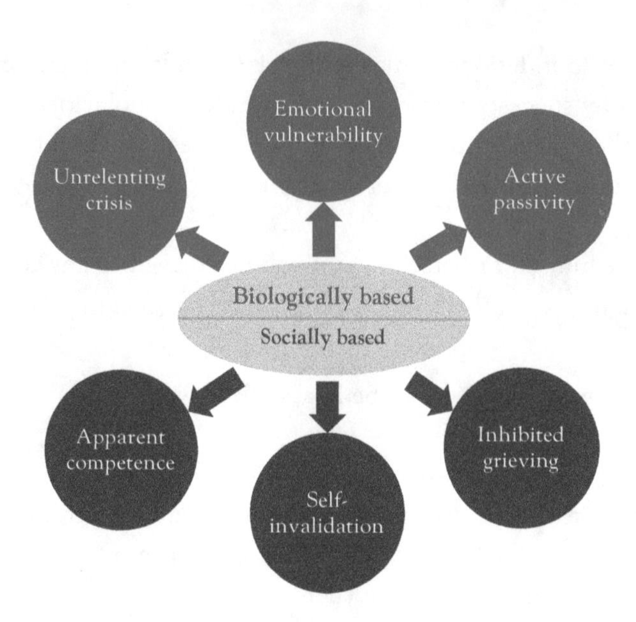

Figure 5.1 Three Common Dialectical Dilemmas

Active Passivity vs. Apparent Competence: Similar to learned helplessness, active passivity allows, and even encourages, others to determine one's fate rather than taking any action oneself. With an emphasis on the word "apparent," apparent competence is the feigning of ability to the point that other people do not know, and cannot read, stressful situations a person may be going through.

Emotional Vulnerability vs. Self-Invalidation: Whereas emotional vulnerability occurs when clients have strong emotional reactions to small situations that lead to excessive worry, overly strong reactions to others, and chaotic interpersonal relationships, self-invalidation is the discounting of one's emotional experience ("I shouldn't feel this way," "I should not be happy," "I should never worry"). Invalidation can sometimes lead to self-injury. Both emotional vulnerability and self-invalidation result in an inability to deal effectively with one's emotions and difficulty in interacting with others in genuine and productive ways.

Unrelenting Crisis vs. Inhibited Grieving: Individuals experiencing unrelenting crisis are in a constant high state of emotional calamity and catastrophe in which they feel some sense of familiarity even though it tends to be destructive to relationships. In contrast, these individuals will sometimes move into an inhibited grieving state in which they avoid or negate their emotions. In either case, constant crises or inability to experience emotions are non-genuine and emotionally draining ways of living in the world, and individuals with BPD have not learned how to integrate these two polarities into their lives.

Healthy individuals achieve balance between active passivity and apparent competence, emotional vulnerability and self-invalidation, and unrelenting crisis and inhibited grieving. For instance, they tend to take responsibility for their lives and do not have a strong need to demonstrate competence to others. They do not overly react to situations or discount their feelings, and they are not in seemingly endless crisis or trying to avoid their emotions. As a result of their biology and social rearing, healthy individuals have found a balance between these polarities that allows them to live relatively genuine lives, with access to their feelings, and the ability to respond to them in measured and reasonable ways.

Behaviorism

When Linehan originally began her work with suicidal and parasuicidal clients, she used standard behavior therapy techniques (Linehan & Wilks, 2015). Such an approach had its origins with traditional behavioral principles, such as classical conditioning, operant conditioning, and modeling paradigms, sometimes called the **first wave of cognitive behavioral therapy**. The advent of the cognitive approaches to therapy, such as Ellis's rational emotive behavior therapy and Beck's cognitive behavioral therapy, added a focus on how thoughts impact problematic behaviors. Known as the **second wave of cognitive behavioral therapy**, these approaches added an important component to behavior therapy—the internal world of the client. Both first- and second-wave cognitive behaviorism, however, focused on problem-solving strategies, and Linehan soon realized this constant focus on changing the problem was frustrating to most clients, with many of them lashing out at their therapists or dropping out of treatment.

Linehan (2016; Linehan & Wilks, 2015) soon recognized that if change were to occur at all, therapists needed to realize the importance of the therapeutic relationship in the change process, be radically accepting of their clients, teach their clients how to accept themselves, help clients understand dialectics, and use a variety of behavioral, cognitive, and other skills to help clients change. Within this context, therapists needed to accept that progress would be slow, that clients would have periodic setbacks and periodic gains, and when working with highly volatile clients, needed to constantly be cognizant of their risk for suicide and self-harm.

Today, most DBT therapists will complete a **functional behavior analysis** of the client's situation, which examines how behaviors are linked to a person's problems. With such an understanding and with the assistance of their therapist and group skills trainer, clients can learn how to accept themselves and also consider change. In the change process, DBT therapists will apply first-wave cognitive behavioral techniques (e.g., operant conditioning, classical conditioning, modeling), help clients examine rigid beliefs (e.g., "I am right and you are wrong") and suggest more flexible ways of thinking, and use a wide range of other techniques to help clients integrate dialectical opposites and become less reactive to the world.

Zen Buddhism and Mindfulness

Linehan's positive experiences with deep prayer and meditation led her to learn about **Zen Buddhism** principles (Swales & Heard, 2009). Zen Buddhist philosophy underscores a number of principles that have been applied to DBT, including the importance of interrelatedness and wholeness, continuous change, and recognizing the polarities of life (Robins, 2002). For instance, DBT asserts that we must help clients see that all things are connected (interrelated) and that addressing, or ignoring, problems will impact all aspects of one's life (the "whole") in complex ways. The idea that change is continuous throughout life suggests that therapists must teach clients to accept themselves in the moment, and learn skills to help them manage their emotions as changes occur. The final principle, recognizing the polarities of life, proposes that opposites exist contemporaneously, which suggests that clients should relinquish their dualistic view of the world (e.g., "I am always a bad parent") and adopt a complex way of thinking that embraces both sides of a polarity ("I am sometimes not a great parent and sometimes a pretty good parent").

Linehan (2015) used these Zen principles to help conceptualize assumptions about clients, develop interventions, and identify treatment targets. In addition, believing that the practice of **mindfulness** embraces many of these Zen concepts, Linehan incorporated mindfulness into DBT by having clients learn it in group skills training, and practice it in individual therapy, during their group sessions, and on their own. It's hoped such practice would help clients be increasingly tuned into the impact their actions have on self and others, be more accepting of themselves, understand that change is part of life, and think in more complex ways.

Seven Basic Assumptions of DBT

Underscoring the dialectic of acceptance and change, and the importance of changing behaviors in all contexts of one's life, are the **seven basic assumptions of DBT** (see Box 5.1).

BOX 5.1 SEVEN BASIC ASSUMPTIONS WHEN TREATING CLIENTS USING DBT

1. *People are doing the best they can.* It is assumed that, at any point in time, people are doing the best they can.
2. *People want to improve.* Any person who is suffering wants to get better. People need to do better, try harder, and be more motivated to change.
3. *Although people are doing the best they can, if they are suffering, they need to try harder and be even more motivated to change.* This dialectic (doing the best one can and needing to try harder) is an important assumption for clients to learn.

4. *People may not have caused all of their own problems, but they have to solve them anyway.* Individuals are ultimately responsible for finding their solutions to their problems, though others (e.g., therapists) can be helpful along the way.
5. *New behavior has to be learned in all relevant contexts.* Any new behaviors that are learned must be generalized to all situations in which they are needed, not just applied to the situation in which they were originally learned.
6. *All behaviors (actions, thoughts, emotions) are caused.* There is a cause, or reason for dysfunctional and toxic behaviors, even if the individual is not aware of the cause.
7. *Figuring out and changing the causes of behavior is a more effective way to change than judging and blaming.* One should not judge or blame oneself, or others. Instead, one should work on finding the causes of behaviors and change them (Linehan, 2015, p. 53; Note: Headings are direct quotes).

TECHNIQUES

DBT's therapeutic process is unique compared with traditional psychotherapies and consists of a pretreatment phase of counseling followed by four modes that occur concurrently: individual counseling, group skills training, consultation team meetings, and between-session phone coaching (see Table 5.1). Treatment typically lasts four to five hours per week, for six months to a year, and employs a variety of techniques within each of the modes (Linehan, 1993-a, -b, 2015a; Peterson, 2015; Van Dijk, 2012).

The following offers an overview of the skills, techniques, and foci of the pretreatment stage of counseling, individual counseling, group skills training, consultation team meeting, and between-session coaching. Keep in mind, however, that DBT requires intensive training, and what is offered here is a smattering of some of the more commonly used skills. If you are interested in more involved training, you can obtain **certification as a DBT therapist**, which involves having a graduate degree in a mental health field, taking didactic training, obtaining clinical experience, taking an exam, and more (www.dbt-lbc.org).

Pretreatment Stage

Usually led by the therapist who will be conducting individual therapy, the **pretreatment stage** involves **orientation and commitment** to the therapeutic process (Linehan, 1993a, 2015a; Pederson, 2015). Usually, a thorough **assessment** of the client's current living situation is conducted, an assessment for suicidality is completed, and a diagnosis is formulated. Then, **psychoeducation** about the diagnosis, the biosocial model, emotional dysregulation, and dialectics is provided. An **explanation of the purpose and process** of individual counseling, group skills training, and between-session coaching is given and the **boundaries of the relationship** are noted. This helps to alleviate any misconceptions about the process that clients may have. Ultimately, if therapy

TABLE 5.1 THE MODES OF DBT TREATMENT

MODE	TIME FRAME	MAJOR GOALS	PROFESSIONALS INVOLVED
Pretreatment	One to three sessions	• Explain purpose and process. • Orient client to therapy and obtain commitment. • Assess client and obtain diagnosis. • Psychoeducation: diagnosis, biosocial model, emotional dysregulation, dialectics, and more. • Explain boundaries. • Obtain verbal and written agreement.	• Usually counselor who is providing individual therapy.
Individual Counseling	One hour per week	• Decrease suicidal and life-threatening behaviors. • Decrease therapy-interfering behaviors. • Increase quality of life behavioral skills. • Reinforce skills learned in group.	• Counselor providing individual therapy.
Group Skills Training	2–2.5 hours per week	• Reduce behaviors very likely to interfere with therapy. • Skills acquisition and skill reinforcement.	• Group skills trainer
Consultation Team Meeting	1–1.5 hours per week	• Keep therapist and skills group trainer motivated. • Consult about treatment and ensure its effectiveness. • Prevent therapist and skills group leader burnout. • Maintain DBT principles in practice via support and accountability.	• Individual counselor, group skills trainer, psychiatrist, others?
Between-Session Coaching	As needed	• Decrease suicidal and life-threatening behaviors. • Increase the generalization of behavioral skills. • Decrease sense of conflict, alienation, and distance from therapist and others.	• Individual counselor

is to progress, the client must agree to attend all individual sessions and group skills training sessions and address suicidal, parasuicidal, and therapy-interfering behaviors as they arise. After the client agrees to the process, a **verbal or written agreement** is obtained, usually based on a six-month to one-year therapeutic renewable plan. This helps to reinforce accountability to the treatment process.

Stages I–IV of Individual Therapy

Individual therapy in DBT can be seen through a prism of four stages: **Stages I-IV of individual therapy**, which involve the following:

Stage I: A focus on safety and stabilization, in the following order: behaviors that are life threatening, behaviors that interfere with therapy, and behaviors that decrease the quality of life.

Stage II: A focus on behaviors that cause misery and "quiet desperation," often due to past trauma and invalidation.

Stage III: A focus on behaviors that cause problems in everyday living so that clients can live a life of relative contentment, with its ups and downs.

Stage IV: A focus on finding deeper meaning, spiritual fulfillment, and ongoing capacity for success and joy.

When conducting individual therapy, techniques are a function of the stage in which the client is presenting at the time of treatment. Since those clients who are in Stage 1 are dealing with issues that are life-threatening, interfere with therapy, or decrease the quality of life, these concerns should be addressed first. Although there is generally linear movement in DBT, stages can sometimes overlap and clients can, at times, fall back to earlier stages. The following delineates some of the guidelines and techniques used in the various stages.

Structuring Therapy

Regardless of the stage of treatment, **structuring therapy** is important and often looks like the following (Pedersen, 2015; Van Dijk, 2012):

- Greet the client warmly; ensure maintenance of the therapeutic alliance.
- Address the affective state of the client.
- Conduct mindfulness to ground client and counselor.
- Inquire about other aspects of treatment (e.g., group skills training).
- Inquire about homework assignments.

- Review diary card.
- Conduct work of the session based on acquired knowledge just obtained.
- Set goals and assign homework when appropriate.
- Conduct a final mindfulness exercise.
- Say goodbye and give an appointment reminder.

Diary Card

Most counselors who practice DBT have clients complete a daily **diary card** that is submitted weekly. The diary card helps clients focus on their emotions during the week, and if the client is experiencing suicidal or parasuicidal ideation, phone coaching is required. There are numerous versions of the diary card (Brodsky & Stanley, 2013), and a shortened version of one, for one day of the week, is shown in Table 5.2.

TABLE 5.2 MODIFIED EXAMPLE OF A DIARY CARD

DAY OF WEEK: MONDAY	DIARY CARD				
List Strong Emotions → Note Strength → (Low = 1; High = 5)	Depression (4)	Hopelessness (4)	Apathy (3)	Other:	Other:
Urges: → Note Strength → (Low = 1; High = 5)	Suicide (2)	Cutting (5)	Other:	Other:	Other:
Behaviors: →	Cutting	Other:	Other:	Other:	Other:

More involved diary cards may track a wide range of issues, such as levels of suicidal ideation, self-injurious behaviors, treatment-interfering behaviors (TIB), levels of strong feelings (e.g., depression, anxiety, and anger), medications used, sleep, energy level, substance use, self-care skills, and more (Pederson, 2015). If a diary card is not completed during a week, a chain analysis is conducted with the client and will take the place of an individual therapy session, thus reinforcing the importance of completing the diary card.

Chain Analysis

This involves a detailed examination of a problematic behavior that needs to be addressed. Such an analysis generally examines the following items (Van Dijk, 2012):

- the problem behavior (often identified in the diary card),
- how the environment is linked to the prompting event,
- links in the chain of events between the prompting event and the problem behavior,
- negative and positive consequences of the problem behavior,
- ways to decrease one's vulnerability to the problem behavior,
- ways to prevent the prompting event from occurring again,
- ways to decrease the chain of events that led to the problem, and
- ways to correct or repair the harm—or make amends—related to the problem behavior (see Box 5.2).

BOX 5.2 CHAIN ANALYSIS

Name of Client: Jeremiah Bully Picker
Problem Behavior: Skin picking (excoriation disorder)
Environmental Vulnerability: Work-related stress due to project deadline and lack of sleep.
Prompting Event: Argument with partner.
Links in the Chain: "I came home from work and started talking with my wife about the day. She told me that I was being nasty to her in my tone. I said I was not. She said I was not able to hear myself, and I got angry. I angrily told her she was wrong, and she said she was not. I got even more angry and got close to yelling at her that she was driving me crazy. She told me there was something wrong with me and to go away. I felt like hitting her, but smartly went upstairs to my bedroom and watched TV. At this point, I started picking at my skin. I had a few scabs on my hand and arm, and I picked them so badly they were bleeding. I looked at the bleeding scabs and felt embarrassed by what I had done and, for a moment, felt like life was not worth living. I got some Band-Aids to stop the bleeding so I could no longer pick them. My wife came upstairs, saw what I had done and told me she felt badly about the whole incident. She rubbed my back and told me she loved me. I told her I loved her too, and then I took a long nap."
Negative Consequences: 1. Resulted in argument and emotional distance from wife. 2. Damaged my body and felt badly about myself.
Positive Consequences: 1. Wife apologized and took care of me. 2. Took a nap, which made me feel better later.

Ways to Decrease Vulnerability in the Future:
1. Find a stress reliever (e.g., meditation, mindfulness exercises, working out) before coming home. 2. Seek doctor for temporary pills to help me sleep. 3. Seek antidepressant that also has anti-compulsive behavior effects.
Ways to Prevent Prompting Event:
1. Don't go directly home after a very stressful day at work. Instead, practice a stress-reducing behavior (exercise, meditation, mindfulness, etc.). 2. If I see an argument beginning, defuse it or walk away and do something else.
Ways to Decrease the Chain of Events:
1. When I feel really stressed, I should recognize it and do something to alleviate it (e.g., mediation, exercise, etc.). 2. If I feel really stressed, I should practice my communication skills with my wife and let her know that I am not in a good place. 3. When I see myself escalating an argument through anger, I should remove myself from the situation. 4. When I see myself escalating an argument through anger, I should be humble and explain that my anger is not a good thing to my wife. 5. When I get the urge to pick at my skin, I should immediately put Band-Aids on any scabs I have, take a tranquilizer, and/or take a brisk walk.
Ways to Correct, Repair, or Make Amends:
1. I should apologize to my wife for my anger. 2. I should explain to my wife that I am emotional roller-coaster, that I am sorry for that, and I am working on it in therapy so that we could have a better marriage. 3. I should tell myself that although I picked at my skin, I need to forgive myself and that I am working on lessening my symptoms while accepting that I have this problem.

Dialectical Communication Skills

A variety of communication skills are used in DBT that support the dialectical strategy of acceptance and change, assist people in seeing situations in a more complex manner, and help clients consider other points of view (Pederson, 2015; Van Dijk, 2012). Some of the more frequently used skills include radical acceptance, reciprocal communication, irreverent communication, playing the devil's advocate, using metaphors, making lemonade out of lemons, the exception rule, wise mind, role reversal, and understanding the three dialectics. Using the chain analysis example in Box 1.2, let's look at some examples of these.

Radical acceptance: In the tradition of some existential-humanists, this means hearing the client fully, showing empathy, and offering unconditional positive regard to the client. Here the counselor accepts that the client is doing everything he or she is capable of doing within his or her current understanding of the world.

- *Counselor:* "Sounds like this whole thing was a very painful experience for you. On the one hand, you felt justified getting angry with your wife. On the other hand, you were upset at how things ended up with her and how you started to pick at your scabs."

Reciprocal communication: This involves a give and take conversation with the client in which the counselor is genuine, warm, egalitarian, a good listener, empathic, respectful, understanding of the client's predicament, and self-disclosing in appropriate ways. These responses are crucial to the development of the therapeutic alliance, validates the client, and can be reinforcing of change.

- *Counselor:* "I'm hearing that you had a really good experience with your partner *after* the argument. It shows me you have really worked on defusing upsetting situations. I know, from my own life, how good that must feel. What are your thoughts?"
- *Client:* "I did feel good after we had talked things through and was more hopeful about working on my problems. Maybe we can look at my goals again."
- Counselor: "Yes, that sounds great."

Irreverent communication: Whereas radical acceptance and reciprocal communication is the "yin," irreverent communication is the "yang" in that it is provocative, confrontational, and direct. It includes responses that clients might not want to hear with its purpose being to help the client see the world differently, push them off-balance so they can get rebalanced, and shift their affective focus.

- *Counselor:* "I thought we agreed to abide by your contract for therapy, yet this past week when you got angry at your partner you ended up picking the scabs on your arm. That certainly was not in the contract."

Playing the devil's advocate: Here the counselor suggests a different perspective than what the client is suggesting. This allows the client to reexamine what he or she is doing. It reminds the client that "an ideal brain is the devil's workshop."

- *Counselor:* "Well, you're telling me you don't want your anger to take over when you are with your partner, but I think I'm hearing that when you get into it with her, there are some secondary gains that are reinforcing. For instance, sounds like you like the feeling of being in control and proving yourself right."

Using metaphors: A metaphor offers an alternative mechanism for clients to understand their problem and is processed by the brain in a different manner than a traditional counselor response. It thus offers an opportunity for clients to understand their situation in a new way.

- *Counselor:* "Good job eventually removing yourself from that toxic situation. As soon as you realized it was not healthy, you left like lightning."

Making lemonade out of lemons. This technique takes a problem situation and turns it into a potentially positive experience.

- *Counselor:* "The argument with your wife, and the eventual picking, really gave you an opportunity to practice those skills that you learned!"

The exception rule: Borrowed from solution-focused brief therapy (SFBT), this technique has clients consider times when problematic behaviors were not in a person's life so that they can identify the context in which it was occurring and try to replicate it.

- *Counselor:* "So we talked about times when you did not feel inflicted with the need to pick at your skin. Can you tell me what was going on in your life then that was different than now?"

The wise mind: This is when the counselor asks an emotionally activated client to consider a situation from his or her wise mind. The wise mind is the place between the logical mind and emotional mind. It is accessed when the client is able to obtain a deeply meditative or aware state that allows him or her to contact a personal place where one can recognize feelings and respond to them rationally.

- *Counselor:* "Right now, you are really upset and convinced that your partner wants to constantly irritate you. But, let's try accessing your wise mind for a moment. Breathe in and out, focus on your body, and consider the situation. Let yourself be in your body for a moment. Go deep inside yourself, as if you are observing your emotions and the situation. Now, using your wise mind, reflect on the situation and consider whether you think your partner wants to constantly irritate you?"

Role reversal: This is asking the client to take on the role of a person with whom there are ongoing problems so that the client can see a different perspective on the problems.

- *Counselor:* "Can you talk to me like you are your wife. From her perspective, what would she tell me about the fight you had?"

Understanding the three common dialectics: As noted earlier, clients in DBT are often struggling with one or more of the polarities of active passivity/apparent competence, emotional vulnerability/self-invalidation, and unrelenting crisis/inhibited grieving. Stuck on one side of the polarity, or bouncing back and forth between the polarity, they maintain a type of rigidness in their approach to the world. Through psychoeducation and encouragement, therapists can help clients understand the polarity they are struggling with and move them toward integration of the two sides.

- *Counselor:* "So, as we have talked before Jeremiah, one of your fallback positions is emotional vulnerability, which quickly turns into self-invalidation. Look at how you quickly get upset at your wife and then want to discount your feelings and yourself. You even say maybe 'life isn't worth living.' And then you want to ignore your emotions, and you start to self-pick. Can you think of other ways you could have handled that situation without reacting so strongly followed by self-injury?"

Behavioral Skills

Core to change in DBT is its focus on behavioral techniques. Thus, any DBT counselor should be familiar with the basics of operant conditioning, classical conditioning, and modeling, or first-wave behavioral techniques. DBT therapists often perform a **functional behavior analysis** of behaviors to identify the contingencies involved when a behavior is reinforced. A **chain analysis**, discussed earlier, is a type of functional analysis of behaviors. For instance, if we were to look at Jeremiah's chain analysis in Box 5.2, we can begin to see the reinforcement contingencies involved in some of his behaviors:

1. *Stress related to project deadline and lack of sleep*: Better time management and intentional sleep-inducing behaviors can be positively reinforcing as Jeremiah experiences less stress and is positively reinforced for his work habits.

2. *Negative tone of wife (perceived by husband) and wife telling him there is something wrong with him*: Attempts at punishment by wife that eventually leads to a decrease in the behavior (husband leaves the situation).
3. *Picking at skin*: Skin-picking behavior releases endorphins, which are addicting and reinforces the behavior. The compulsive behavior then becomes classically conditioned as it is associated with a decrease in anxiety and anger.
4. *Placing Band-Aids on bleeding scabs*: Extinction technique of response block.
5. *Wife rubbing his back and telling him she loved him*: Positive reinforcement of chains can potentially reinforce similar behaviors in the future.

This functional analysis of Jeremiah's behaviors offers several opportunities for behavioral interventions. For instance, by encouraging better time management, in the future Jeremiah can space out his work project and be positively reinforced for his work habits. Intentional sleep-inducing habits can also reduce stress, which will result in better work habits and increase positive reinforcement. In addition, mindfulness, or many of the other skills learned in group skills training, can be used to lessen his stress when he comes home. Such skills lessen the likelihood of his wife punishing him for his behaviors. Jeremiah can also learn to identify possible negative consequences of his interaction with his wife and take preemptive measures when he returns home. He could practice, with his wife, new interpersonal skills he has learned in group skills training and can avoid certain interactions with her (take a nap immediately when he gets home, read a book, or watch TV). Preemptively placing Band-Aids on scabs can lessen the likelihood of picking and the immediate reinforcement he obtains from the release of endorphins. Can you think of other behavioral interventions that can be done in any of the links just cited (see Box 5.3)?

BOX 5.3 BEHAVIORAL RESPONSES TO JEREMIAH

Take a look at the links identified in Jeremiah's chain analysis and come up with three behavioral interventions that will lessen the likelihood he will get into an argument with his wife and/or skin pick. Share with others.

1. ______________________________.
2. ______________________________.
3. ______________________________.

Behavioral techniques are powerful ways of changing behaviors and can be used in many ways in DBT. For instance, the counselor can model effective behaviors, reinforce positive behaviors of the client, teach the client how to use self-management techniques to reinforce positive behaviors, teach other people in the client's life to reinforce positive behaviors, and more.

Cognitive Skills

Whereas traditional cognitive therapies view thoughts as something that need to be replaced or disputed, in DBT thoughts are one additional mechanism to focus upon to increase cognitive complexity and consider other points of view (Pederson, 2015). But first, and critical to the DBT process, the therapist must validate and accept the client's current cognitive perspective as it is assumed that it makes sense within the client's current contextual framework (e.g. his or her biological, behavioral, and cognitive makeup). It is also important to not attempt to expand a client's perspective when he or she is emotionally dysregulated, as emotionally unregulated people tend to be locked into their cognitive distortions.

Pedersen (2015) identifies 14 cognitive distortions that individuals sometimes embrace and suggests the dialectical shift they can be encouraged to take. They include:

- *Black and White Thinking:* Believing things are always one way.
  Dialectical Shift: Consider other or opposite points of view.
- *Regret Orientation:* Having ongoing remorse about the past.
  Dialectical Shift: Focus on current change one can make.
- *Mind reading:* Assuming you know what others are thinking.
  Dialectical Shift: Checking out assumptions with others.
- *Minimization/Magnification:* Making a large concern very small or small concern very large.
  Dialectical Shift: Examine a concern carefully and fully before responding as a check on its accuracy.
- *Catastrophizing:* Making a situation much worse than it actually is.
  Dialectical Shift: Focus squarely on a situation and work it while remembering most situations do not end in catastrophe.
- *Fortune-telling:* Predicting the future negatively.
  Dialectical Shift: Focus on current problem-solving techniques.
- *Overgeneralizing:* Generalizing too broadly.
  Dialectical Shift: Get facts and check out assumptions for all situations.
- *Selective information gathering:* Filtering information so it reinforces current thinking.
  Dialectical Shift: Gather information from alternative points of view.

- *Labeling:* Making a person or situation a label (e.g., "You're a borderline personality").
  Dialectical Shift: Describe behaviors or the context of situation in nuanced ways.
- *Personalization:* Always making situations about you.
  Dialectical Shift: Deciphering what is, and what is not, about you and not taking situations too personally.
- *Emotion Mind Reasoning:* Not using reason; always infiltrating thoughts with emotions.
  Dialectical Shift: Use mindfulness and other skills to access one's wise and rational mind.
- *Should Statements:* Judging the situations and assuming they will unfold in a certain way.
  Dialectical Shift: Allowing situations to unfold naturally and examining what is, not what should be.
- *Discounting Positives:* Focusing on negatives and downplaying positives.
  Dialectical Shift: Embrace the positives.
- *Blaming:* Assuming others are responsible for our actions and problems.
  Dialectical Shift: Taking responsibility for one's own actions and problems.

Reinforcing Group Skills Training

In the next section on group training skills, you will learn about a number of acceptance and change skills techniques that clients learn in their group skills training sessions. These skills are particularly important if clients are to develop healthy interpersonal relationships, and it is critical that they are constantly reinforced both in the group and individual sessions. Therefore, near the beginning of each individual therapy session the counselor will inquire what the client has learned during his or her group sessions and if the client had followed through on practicing new skills during the week. During the individual sessions, and particularly during phone coaching, counselors can help clients remember the skills they have learned and how to apply them, and positively reinforce those clients who have practiced their skills during the week. In this case, practice makes perfect and **reinforcement of group skills training** by the therapist, and others in the client's life, can help ensure that the skills become a natural aspect of the client's way of being.

Group Skills Training

Group skills training consists of four modules—**mindfulness, distress tolerance, emotional regulation**, and **interpersonal effectiveness**—and has a curriculum that spans 24 weeks, which is often duplicated to create a yearlong program (Linehan, 2015a). Stressing the dialectic, mindfulness, and distress tolerance skills are types of **acceptance skills,** while emotional regulation and interpersonal effectiveness skills are types of **change skills** (see Figure 5.2).

The four group skills training modules are taught in order and divided into four sections: "(1) a beginning ritual, (2) review of homework practice since the last session, (3) presentation of new material, and (4) a closing 'wind-down'" (p 54). For instance, a session could begin with a mindfulness exercise, followed by the group members sharing their attempts at working on their homework, followed by the skills trainer presenting a new behavioral skill, and ending with a wind-down discussion in which each participant shares what he or she observed during the session. Group members are strongly encouraged to stay on topic and not talk about issues unrelated to the skills being taught. If they do deviate from the topic, group leaders will redirect them to the skills being addressed.

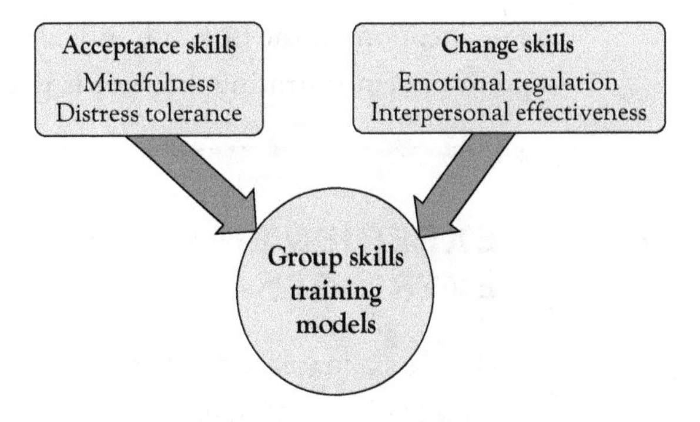

Figure 5.2 Acceptance and Change Skills

In addition to the four sections, Linehan (1993b, 2015a) created three hierarchical goals, or priorities, that are worked toward in skills training: 1) stopping behaviors that very likely will destroy therapy, 2) acquisition, strengthening, and globalization of skills, and 3) reducing behaviors that interfere with therapy. Most of the skills are taught in a specific order. If a client misses one module, he or she can make it up; however, skills training requires participation in all modules and ongoing practice of these skills. The following is a brief overview of the four modules of mindfulness, distress tolerance, emotional regulation, and interpersonal effectiveness techniques.

Mindfulness (Acceptance Skill)

> Mindfulness is not a place we get to. Mindfulness is a place we are (Linehan, 2015a, p. 152).

Drawing from her experiences with deep prayer and Zen Buddhism, Linehan incorporated **mindfulness** into DBT (Linehan, 1993a; 1993b; 2015a). Mindfulness helps clients be present to their experience, listen nonjudgmentally to themselves, and become a neutral observer of what is happening internally and externally. Whereas meditation can be a type of mindfulness, mindfulness does not have to be meditative. Mindfulness is a way of living that occurs on an ongoing basis. It allows a person to become one with the moment as he or she observes oneself experiencing life.

Linehan (2015a) describes the "What" and "How" skills of mindfulness. **What skills** involve *observing* events, emotions, and behavioral responses without labeling or terminating them—even when they are unpleasant, *describing* observed physical and environmental events by applying verbal labels to them, and *participating* in activities fully, without self-consciousness. **How skills** describe the process of observing, describing, and participating in mindfulness. This involves being *nonjudgmental* in one's evaluation of self; being *one-mindful,* or focusing one's attention on the task at hand; and being *effective*, which is letting go of a need to prove a point or demonstrating that one is right or one is wrong (Experiential Exercise 5.1).

EXPERIENTIAL EXERCISE 5.1: MINDFULNESS EXERCISES

Here are a few very quick mindfulness exercises you can practice. Remember, mindfulness allows one to have acute awareness while being nonjudgmental and accepting of whatever comes into consciousness. While doing this exercise, you should observe, describe, participate fully, be nonjudgmental, be one-mindful (focused on task), and be effective (don't try to prove a point).

Observe a flower or a leaf: Hold a flower or leaf in your hand and look at it. Describe the leaf to yourself as if you are observing it for the first time.

Observe your thoughts: Sit comfortably and close your eyes. Let your thoughts wander and observe where they are. Do not judge or critique them, just observe them.

Observe your feelings: Sit comfortably and close your eyes. Allow yourself to experience any emotions you are having without your thoughts about them getting in the way.

Mindful eating: While having a meal, observe and describe to yourself what you are eating and how you are eating. Allow yourself to fully engage in eating without evaluating the food or yourself and focus on the process of eating.

Mindful listening: Sit with a person and listen acutely to what he or she has to say. Do not judge. Do not jump in and give advice. Do not critique the person to yourself. Just allow yourself to hear the other person fully. Periodically, paraphrase back what the person has said to you so that he or she can continue to speak.

When you have finished one or more of the exercises, talk with others about what you may have learned through the mindfulness exercises. How was it different, if at all, from how you usually experience yourself or others? Consider how mindfulness can be helpful in accepting or changing symptoms?

Mindfulness can help clients experience where they are in the moment and make decisions about where they want to go. Pederson (2015) suggests that individuals who are struggling in life but not in deep pain may use mindfulness to understand their current state of being, eventually deciding to accept their situation or set goals to change. On the other hand, those in deep pain may decide that rather than focusing on their pain, to instead shift their attention to something else such as a task, a deep-breathing exercise, or something positive in their lives.

Distress Tolerance Skills (Acceptance Skills)

DBT theory believes it is important to be able to tolerate a crisis, endure pain skillfully, accept and find meaning in distressing events, and not act impulsively during a crisis (Linehan, 1993a). To achieve these goals, DBT teaches a multitude of distress tolerance techniques which are identified as crisis survival skills or reality accepting skills.

Crisis Survival Skills: These are short-term solutions used to help tolerate painful situations and lessen the likelihood of a client acting impulsively (Linehan, 2015a). The six survival strategies:

1. *STOP Skills.* This stands for Stop, Take a step back, Observe, and Proceed mindfully.
2. *Pros and Cons:* Here clients consider the positive or negative consequences of acting, or not acting, on their impulses.
3. *TIP Skills:* These exercises are used to change body chemistry to lessen emotional arousal. TIP stands for Temperature, Intense exercise, Paced breathing, and Paired muscle relaxation.
4. *Distracting with Wise Mind ACCEPTS*: These distracting methods reduce contact with emotional stimuli. ACCEPTS is defined as "Activities (discordant to the negative emotion), Contributing, Comparisons, Emotions (opposite to the current negative emotion), Pushing away from the situation, Thoughts, and Sensations." (Linehan, 2015a, p. 417).
5. *Self-sooth.* This involves using activities that help soothe the senses of vision, hearing, smell, taste, and touch.
6. *IMPROVE the Moment.* This involves focusing on the following items to improve the quality of life: "Imagery, Meaning, Prayer, Relaxing actions, One thing in the moment, Vacation, and Encouragement" (Linehan, 2015a, p 417).

Reality Accepting Skills: To reduce the suffering that is associated with crisis and increase freedom for individuals when painful situations cannot be changed, Linehan (2015a) has developed **reality accepting skills**, which include:

1. *Radical Acceptance*: This is the complete and total acceptance of the facts of reality.
2. *Turning the Mind*: The first step toward acceptance, it involves "turning the mind" toward acceptance. A skill that takes time to develop, it must be practiced over and over again.
3. *Willingness*: This is the surrendering to, and immersing oneself in, the process of life. It is contrasted with willfulness, which is trying to direct life.

4. *Half-smiling and Willing Hands*: These exercises assume that our muscles reflect, or reject, acceptance. Half-smiling is the practice of relaxing facial muscles and turning the lips slightly upward, while willing hands is the practice of unclenching hands and keeping palms and fingers relaxed.
5. *Mindful of Current Thoughts*: This skill is aimed at having clients practice observing their thoughts as a brain function that involves neural firings, not necessarily thoughts that hold truth or are absolute facts about one's life. This helps to make client's thoughts less reactive.

Emotional Regulation Techniques (Change Skills)

Dysfunctional emotion regulation can lead to a wide range of serious behavioral problems, such as substance abuse, self-harming practices, overeating, overcontrol, and emotional suppression (Linehan, 2015a). Thus, emotional regulation techniques are used to proactively decrease emotional dysregulation and develop positive emotions. To work on emotional regulation, Linehan suggests it is important for clients to understand and name emotions, change unwanted emotions, reduce vulnerability to the emotional mind, and manage extreme emotions.

Understanding and Naming Emotions: Emotions help us communicate with others about our state of being, alert us to something that is happening ("I'm scared!"), and are signals to how we might want to control and influence behaviors. If we are to respond realistically to our emotions, **understanding and naming emotions** becomes critical and is easier to do if we can "observe and describe (1) the event prompting the emotion; (2) the interpretations of the event that prompted the emotion; (3) the history prior to the prompting event that increases sensitivity to the event and vulnerability to responding emotionally; (4) the phenomenological experience, including the physical sensation, of the emotion; (5) the expressive behaviors associated with the emotion; and (6) the aftereffects of the emotion on other types of functioning" (Linehan, 2015a, p. 319).

Changing Unwanted Emotions: Once we are clear on what emotions we are struggling with, we can begin the process of changing them, which can happen in numerous ways. For example, one can use mindfulness to experience the primary emotion. This prevents secondary emotions, which exaggerate the dysfunctional emotional state (e.g., guilt about the emotion), from being exhibited and results in an uncomfortable, but tolerable, situation. Also, a person can practice opposing an emotion, and try to exhibit a different, less toxic emotion. Changes in facial expressions and posture can also help elicit different emotions from a person. One other technique would be to purposely set out to increase pleasurable experiences in one's life that would lead to more positive emotions.

Reducing Vulnerability to the Emotional Mind: In this block of skills training, a client learns to manage emotions by acquiring positive emotions, taking care of his or her physical body, building skill mastery, and learning how to cope prior to difficult situations. Positive emotions can be built in multiple ways. For instance, individuals can surround themselves with more pleasurable experiences or valued events that result in increased daily positive experiences and create a life worth living. Increasing positive emotions increases resiliency, thus making it easier to handle negative experiences. Also, a number of basic activities can help an individual feel better and reduce emotional dysregulation. For example, eating healthy, getting enough sleep, getting exercise, dealing effectively with illnesses, not using illicit drugs, and acquiring other healthy habits can all help to build skill mastery, are preventative measures for difficult situations that may arise, and increase self-efficacy.

Managing Extreme Emotions: Extreme emotions can occur in any person's life but are more frequent with those who have BPD or related disorders. One method of lessening an extreme emotion is by mindfully attending to one's current emotions without judgment, inhibitions, or distractions. This results in the lessening, or extinguishing, of secondary emotions (e.g., shame, guilt), which leads to the ability to attend to the primary emotion. At this point, one is more likely to find the primary emotion to still be extremely annoying, but tolerable.

Interpersonal Effectiveness Skills

Linehan (1993b; 2015a) believes most people have reasonably effective interpersonal skills but lack the ability to employ them effectively. Thus, through group skills training, a client learns how to strengthen and use interpersonal skills. Three kinds of interpersonal effectiveness techniques are: 1) obtaining objectives while maintaining relationships and self-respect, 2) building relationships and ending destructive ones, and 3) walking the middle path.

Obtaining Objectives While Maintaining Relationships and Self-Respect: These skills teach individuals how to get what one needs, how to say no, and how to effectively manage interpersonal conflicts. Linehan (2015a) has outlined nine specific skills training modules that work toward this core skill.

Modules 1 through 4: Here, the focus of skills training is on identifying factors that are interfering with one's interpersonal effectiveness.

Module 5: This focuses on how to obtain one's wants through the mnemonic DEAR MAN: Describe, Express feelings, Assert wishes, Reinforce, (stay) Mindful, Appear confident, and Negotiate.

Module 6: This focuses on relationship effectiveness skills that are taught with the mnemonic GIVE: (be) Gentle, (act) Interested, Validate, (use an) Easy manner.

Module 7: For this module, group members learn skills to keep one's self-respect and use the mnemonic FAST: (be) Fair, (no) Apologies, Stick to values, (be) Truthful.

Module 8: Here, the group works on the intensity one uses when asking for what he or she wants and learning what intensity to use when saying no.

Module 9: This module focuses on trouble shooting, or looking at where the client fails in his or her interpersonal effectiveness skills and why.

Building Relationships and Ending Destructive Ones: The second section of interpersonal effectiveness techniques focuses on developing and maintaining relationships and on ending relationships that may be damaging or destructive. Here, Linehan (2015a) outlines three modules:

Module 1: Finding Potential Friends: The first set of skills focus on individuals becoming active participants in finding others who might become friends.

Module 2: Mindfulness of Others: Here, group members learn how to be sensitive and nonjudgmental of others and how to describe their own thoughts, feelings, and reactions without being blaming or critical of others. Using mindfulness techniques can help a person respond in such ways.

Module 3: How to End Relationships: Now that the trainer has taught the skills needed to actively find friends and being mindful of others, the group moves to learning how to effectively end destructive and damaging relationships. Linehan believes that staying in damaging relationships for too long is just as impactful as not having any relationships.

Walking the Middle Path: Originally developed for work with adolescents and their caregivers, these skills have been found to also be critical for adults (Linehan, 2015a). They include teaching dialects, validation, and strategies for changing behavior.

Module 1: Dialectics: Here, clients are taught how behavior is in the moment and also how it impacts the broader system; how reality is made up of polarities (e.g., change and acceptance); how rigid, dualistic thinking prevents individuals from changing; and that change is continuous throughout life.

Module 2: Validation: Group members in this module learn how to overcome invalidation, how to validate themselves, and the importance of validation in interpersonal relationships.

Module 3: Strategies for Changing Behavior: This is where several behavioral skills are taught, including a wide variety of operant conditioning techniques and how behaviors are contingent on one another. These are the same kinds of skills that counselors use when assisting in behavioral change processes (see Box 5.2 and p. 165).

Consultation Team Meetings

The third mode of dialectical behavior therapy is the **consultation team meeting**. This is a weekly meeting, lasting, on average, one hour to 90 minutes and consisting of two to eight professionals (Linehan, 2015a). For example, a consultation team might be composed of a licensed psychiatrist, licensed therapist, and group skills trainer.

Linehan describes the job of the consultation team as "therapy for the therapist by the therapist" (Linehan, 2015b, minute 47:30). Therapy for the therapist is important as working with clients with BPD, or a related disorder, can be extremely taxing. Consultation team meetings allow all those involved in treatment to coordinate with one another about the treatment plan and helps to ensure that all involved are on the same page. In addition, skills learned in group can be reinforced in individual therapy, and vice versa, and these skills can be discussed in the consultation team meeting. Similar to clients, treatment team members commit to consultation team meetings, and if they miss meetings the team tries to address the consultation-interfering behavior. If they continue to miss, the provider should no longer state he or she is a DBT therapist (Swales & Heard, 2009).

Between-Session Coaching

In dialectical behavior therapy, **between-session coaching**, usually by phone, is an ongoing treatment mode incorporated into the therapeutic process. **Phone coaching**, which is focused mostly on skills training and reinforcement of newly learned skills, is time-limited and has specified rules that are set when the counselor–client contract is developed. Clients are also told that they *must* call to obtain assistance in practicing the skills they learned prior to any self-harm they are considering. Linehan (1993a, 2015a) suggests that in addition to reinforcing skills training, phone coaching can help build the therapeutic alliance, offer an additional venue in supporting clients when they are in distress, reinforce new behaviors, and offer more immediate help when a client is struggling with an interpersonal conflict.

Linehan (2015b) states that she added this component to DBT because she found it unfair that the counselor had so much control over the client's time. Although available, phone coaching is not a 24/7 access line for the client, but an added form of communication, which has limits set at the discretion of the therapist. This can be done by setting rules on availability, such as taking phone calls Monday, Wednesday, and Fridays from noon to 4 p.m. Other boundaries may also be set. For instance, if a client does not uphold proper phone etiquette (e.g., hangs up on the therapist), then he or she is not allowed to phone the therapist for a week.

Summation of Techniques Section

Dialectical behavior therapy contains five components: the pretreatment change, and the four stages of individual therapy, group skills training, consultation team meetings, and between session coaching which often takes the form of phone coaching. These components work hand in hand, as the client moves from a more crisis-oriented, emotionally dysregulated state marked by destructive behaviors and cognitive rigidity to an ability to moderate his or her emotions and think in more complex and relativistic ways. Along this path, while in group skills training, the client learns a number of specific techniques and ways of living in the world that are reinforced in individual therapy, and vice versa. Phone coaching is available for clients who need emotional support between sessions and also offers clients an opportunity to connect with their therapist during the week and fine-tune some of their newly learned skills. Consultation team meetings occur weekly so that the treatment team members can consult with one another about the treatment plan and provide support regarding their work with clients. Table 5.3 summarizes some of the skills taught and goals achieved in the various modes of DBT.

TABLE 5.3 SKILLS ACHIEVED AND GOALS ATTAINED IN DBT MODES

Pretreatment Stage	• Orientation and commitment • Assessment • Psychoeducation • Explanation of the purpose and process • Boundaries of the relationship • Verbal or written agreement
Individual therapy (Stages I–IV)	• *Structuring Therapy*: In every session, the therapist builds an alliance, addresses affect state, conducts mindfulness, inquires about treatment (e.g., group skills), inquires about homework, reviews diary card, conducts session, sets goals and homework, says goodbye.
	• *Diary Card:* Focus on emotions, suicidal ideation, self-injurious behaviors, strong feelings—and, sometimes, medications, sleep, energy level, substance use, self-care, and more.
	• *Chain Analysis:* Identifies problem behavior, environmental vulnerability, prompting event, links in chain, negative and positive consequences, ways to decrease vulnerability, ways to decrease chain, and ways to correct, repair, or make amends.
	• *Dialectical Communication Skills*: Radical acceptance, reciprocal communication, irreverent communication, playing the devil's advocate, using metaphors, making lemonade out of lemons, the exception rule, wise mind, role reversal, and understanding the three dialectics.
	• *Behavioral Skills:* Functional analysis, chain analysis, operant conditioning, classical conditioning, modeling (first-wave behavioral techniques).

	• *Cognitive Skills:* Making dialectical shifts from one's cognitive distortions (see 14 types of cognitive distortions listed).			
	• *Reinforcing Group Skills Training:* Practicing and reinforcing skills learned in group.			
Group Skills Training	*Acceptance Skills*	Mindfulness	What Skills: Observing, describing, participating	
			How skills: Being nonjudgmental, one-mindful, and effective	
		Distress Tolerance	Crisis Survival Skills	1. STOP Skills, 2. Pros and Cons, 3. TIP Skills, 4. Distracting with Wise Mind ACCEPTS, 5. Self-Sooth, 6. Improving the Moment
			Reality Acceptance Skills	1. Radical Acceptance, 2. Turning the Mind, 3. Willingness, 4. Half-smiling and Willing Hands, 5. Mindful of Current Thoughts
	Change Skills	Emotional Regulation Techniques	• Understanding and naming emotions • Changing unwanted emotions • Reducing vulnerability to the emotional world • Managing extreme emotions	
		Interpersonal Effectiveness Techniques	• Modules 1–4: Factors interfering with interpersonal effectiveness • Module 5: How to obtain wants: "DEAR MAN" • Module 6: Effective skills: "GIVE" • Module 7: Self-respect: "FAST" • Module 8: Working on intensity of communication • Module 9: Trouble shooting—failures in communication	
Consultation Team Meetings	• Consists of therapist, group skills trainer, psychiatrist, others? • "Therapy for the therapist" • Coordination of treatment and skills			
Between-Session Coaching	• Helps build therapeutic alliance • Helpful in stopping suicidal or self-harming behaviors • Helpful in reinforcing skills learned • Helpful in offering immediate help when a conflict arises			

THE COUNSELING PROCESS

> The first thing with getting behavior under control is keeping them [clients] alive because I guarantee you, therapy does not work for dead people. (Linehan, 2015b, minute 24:54)

DBT was originally developed for individuals with borderline personality disorder, but in recent years has been expanded to related disorders and even to other problem behaviors. Clients who initially see a DBT therapist first participate in a pretreatment stage in which the therapist and client jointly agree whether this type of therapy is the best approach for the client. During the pretreatment stage the therapist will explain the purpose and process of DBT and orient the client to DBT. Early on in this stage, the therapist will conduct an assessment and come up with a diagnosis. Psychoeducation about the client's diagnosis, the biosocial model, emotional dysregulation, dialectics, the therapeutic process of DBT, and more are explained. The client then decides whether he or she is ready to commit to the rigorous DBT process.

If the client agrees to undergo DBT, he or she will be committing to six months to one year, or more, of treatment, which involves a combination of individual counseling, group skills training, and periodic between-session coaching. After assessing and dealing with any self-harm or therapy-interfering behaviors, each individual counseling session will be structured in a similar manner. Here, clients will do mindfulness, talk about progress in group skills training, discuss any homework assigned, review their diary cards to address how they are doing in their lives, set goals and obtain homework (based, at least in part, on the diary card), conduct a final mindfulness exercise, and set a time for the next appointment.

In addition to individual therapy, clients during the week will undergo group skills training. Here, they will learn various acceptance techniques (e.g., mindfulness and a variety of distress tolerance techniques) and a number of change techniques (e.g., emotional regulation and interpersonal effectiveness skills). These skills are practiced in group and reinforced in individual counseling.

During the week the client will have an opportunity to contact the therapist, usually via phone, to discuss any problematic behaviors or to fine-tune newly learned skills. Meanwhile, the therapist will meet with the group-skills trainer, and probably a psychiatrist or other treatment team members, to discuss progress and any issues that might interfere with their ability to work with the client, and to offer support to one another.

Over the course of therapy, clients learn new behaviors, develop more flexible ways of thinking, and apply a variety of acceptance and change techniques that help to moderate their emotional dysregulation and live a life that is a less chaotic, emotionally moderated, and more joyful.

SOCIAL AND CULTURAL ISSUES

Relative to cross-cultural counseling, DBT has been shown to be applicable across the lifespan with efficacy demonstrated with children as young as 7 years and with older adults (Behavioral Tech, 2017). Suitable for individuals from any sexual orientation, gender, race, ethnicity, and from most cultures, DBT has been implemented globally in more than 25 countries for a wide range of diagnoses.

Despite being used worldwide, in many countries health care is limited and finding a therapist—no less, a treatment team—would be difficult (World Health Organization, 2019). Also, in economically disadvantaged countries, paying for, or having government funding of, a whole treatment team would be burdensome. Although adaptations can be made, one has to wonder whether such changes would detract from the effectiveness of DBT.

Linehan's incorporation of Zen Buddhist practices, dialectics, and Western practices (e.g., behaviorism) represents a challenge for individuals from many cultures. How individuals come to understand self, and others, vary (Kessel et al., 2014), and some individuals may come from a culture that eschews traditional Western practices, while others may feel similarly about Eastern practices of Zen Buddhism and its related technique of mindfulness. Thus, when working with all clients, an understanding of their ethno-psychological makeup is crucial, and appropriate cultural adaptations need to be made (Bernal et al., 2009; Ramaiya et al., 2017).

To address these cross-cultural challenges, researchers have created adaptations of DBT when working with a variety of individuals from different cultural backgrounds. Adaptations have included using a model that does not rely on a large treatment team, ensuring communication is accurate when there are language and communication differences, addressing concerns with the DBT model if a person comes from a collectivist culture, and adjusting how DBT is delivered based on religious and spiritual values of the client (Cheng & Merrick, 2017; Mercado & Hinojosa, 2017). Such cultural adaptations make DBT more accessible to a larger group of diverse clients; however, they may have a negative impact on the outcomes of DBT (Ramaiya et al., 2017). Although DBT is a relatively new approach to therapy, it already has a wide body of knowledge showing its efficacy. Cross-cultural efficacy is still in question, however, and as more studies are completed, whether DBT works with a wide variety of clients will be assessed.

EFFICACY

The goal of DBT is to teach clients skills they can use to regulate their emotions and eliminate maladaptive behavior. Therefore, it's not surprising that DBT has been shown to be efficacious with managing suicidal ideation and behavior, self-injury, depression, anger, emotional dysregulation, and anxiety (Behavioral Tech, 2017). As one might expect, DBT is one the most effective approaches in treating individuals with BPD, since that is what it was originally developed for (Koons et al., 2001; Kröger et al., 2013; Panos, et al., 2014).

Evidence has also demonstrated that DBT is often more effective and less costly than treatment-as-usual (TAU), which may include psychotherapy, medication, or a fusion of both

(Behavioral Tech, 2016). DBT has also been shown to be effective in treating individuals with dual diagnoses (Behavioral Tech, 2016, 2017; Harned et al., 2012, 2014).

DBT is a relatively new treatment mode, yet in a short period it has developed a fairly substantial research base and continues to be widely researched. For instance, Behavioral Tech (2018), a Linehan Institute Training Company, notes that there have been "an average of 8 published and peer-reviewed DBT articles per year from 1993 to 2000, 41 publications per year from 2001 to 2010, and 78 per year since 2011" (para. 1). Behavioral Tech (2017) also identifies those disorders in which there have been one or more randomized controlled studies (RCT) that have shown efficacy (other, non-RCT studies show promise for the use of DBT with additional disorders). They report efficacy for the following disorders:

- Borderline personality disorder, including those with co-occurring:
  - Suicidal and self-harming behavior
  - Substance use disorder
  - Posttraumatic stress disorder
  - High irritability
- Cluster B personality disorders
- Self-harming individuals with personality disorder
- Attention deficit hyperactivity disorder (ADHD)
- Posttraumatic stress disorder related to childhood sexual abuse
- Major depression, including:
  - Treatment of resistant major depression
  - Older adults with chronic depression and one or more personality disorders
- Bipolar disorder
- Transdiagnostic emotion dysregulation
- Suicidal and self-harming adolescents
- Preadolescent children with severe emotional and behavioral dysregulation
- Binge-eating disorder
- Bulimia nervosa ("For what conditions is DBT effective?")

SUMMARY

This chapter began by describing the development of DBT by its originator, Marsha Linehan. Struggling with self-loathing and self-harming behaviors, at 17 Linehan was diagnosed with schizophrenia and hospitalized for 26 months (she believes she had BPD). Due to the treatment she received, which included heavy psychotropic medication and shock treatment, she was determined to help others after she was discharged from the hospital. Eventually, she obtained her doctorate in psychology, and became enamored with Zen Buddhism, mindfulness, and behaviorism early in her career. Her interest in mindfulness led to the belief that radical acceptance of one's condition is a prerequisite for change, and this philosophy, mixed with her interest in behaviorism, eventually resulted in the development of DBT, which she used to treat clients with suicidal and parasuicidal tendencies and diagnosed with borderline personality disorder.

The chapter next examined DBT's view of human nature. Although a behavioral approach, DBT evolves from the more recent tradition of third-wave cognitive behavioral therapy, which views personality formation as a complex interaction between behavior, biology, and context (environment), and focuses on a wide range of techniques to assist clients in accepting and changing their ways of being in the world. This approach borrows from traditional behavioral work in helping clients understand their behavioral consequences and in helping them change their behaviors, looks at how cognitions can be modified so that individuals can see the world in less rigid and more complex ways, and instead of stressing changing symptoms, it focuses on the dialectic of acceptance and change; that is, one must be able to hold both in consciousness and move forward, accordingly. Teaching mindfulness is one method clients can use to learn acceptance. This approach also stresses the importance of building a therapeutic alliance, and we thus see several person-centered and existential techniques being used, such as listening, empathy, and showing radical acceptance. In addition, other humanistic techniques are used to encourage clients to examine what is important in their lives and help them understand the polarities within which they live.

After exploring DBT's view of human nature, we examined a number of key concepts. First, we described borderline personality disorder (BPD), identified several symptoms found in making such a diagnosis, and noted that DBT was designed for individuals with BPD and related disorders. We then described the biosocial theory of personality formation, which suggests that children are born with a certain temperament that can be shaped by childhood experiences. When children are biologically hard-wired for emotional vulnerability and are brought up in invalidating environments, they are more likely to struggle with BPD or a related disorder. Such individuals, we noted, have emotional dysregulation. As a result, they tend to be run by their emotions, have difficulty processing information and cues from others, demonstrate impulsive behaviors, have difficulty making decisions, and have behaviors that are dictated by cognitive distortions, called "stuck thoughts." These individuals need help through therapy to function in the world.

We went on to note that dialectical philosophy is a cornerstone of DBT and that it suggests that reality is composed of interrelated opposing forces and is constantly changing. This philosophy supports the notion that individuals need to understand polarities of life, such as the dialectic of acceptance of self and the need to change. We noted the three common dialectics found in individuals with BPD and related disorders: active passivity vs. apparent competence, emotional vulnerability vs. self-invalidation, and unrelenting crisis vs. inhibited grieving.

The next key concept we examined was behaviorism, and we again highlighted the difference between first-, second-, and third-wave cognitive behavioral therapy. We noted that DBT draws heavily from third-wave philosophy. Using this backdrop, we noted that in the change process DBT therapists will apply first-wave cognitive behavioral techniques (e.g., operant conditioning, classical conditioning, modeling), help clients complete a functional behavior analysis of their problem situations, help clients examine rigid beliefs (e.g., "I am right and you are wrong") and suggest more flexible ways of thinking, and use a wide range of other techniques to help clients integrate dialectical opposites and become less reactive to the world.

Highlighting Zen Buddhism and its relationship to mindfulness was the next key concept, and we unscored the notion that mindfulness helps clients see the interconnectedness of life and the polarities within which we all live. Mindfulness practice helps clients see the impact they have on self and others and helps them be more accepting of themselves while understanding that change is a part of life. The last key concept we noted were the seven basic assumptions of DBT: people are doing the best they can; people want to improve; although people are doing the best they can, if they are suffering they need to try harder and be even more motivated to change; people may not have caused all of their own problems but will have to solve them anyway; new behavior has to be learned in all relevant contexts; all behaviors (actions, thoughts, emotions) are caused; and figuring out and changing the causes of behavior is a more effective way to change than judging and blaming.

A good portion of the chapter focused on the techniques used in DBT. DBT's therapeutic process consists of a pretreatment phase of counseling followed by four modes of therapy, which occur concurrently: individual counseling, group skills training, consultation team meetings, and between-session coaching, often phone coaching. Treatment typically lasts for four to five hours per week, for six months to a year, and employs a variety of techniques within each of the modes. A summary table (Table 5.3) is provided in the chapter that identifies the major techniques and goals of all of the phases and modes of DBT.

These four modes of DBT work hand in hand, as the client moves from a more crisis-oriented, emotionally dysregulated state marked by destructive behaviors and cognitive rigidity to an ability to moderate his or her emotions and think in more complex and relativistic ways. Along this path, while in group skills training, the client learns a number of specific techniques and ways of living in the world that are reinforced in individual therapy, and vice versa. Between-session, often phone coaching is available for clients who need emotional support between sessions, which also offers clients an opportunity to connect with their therapist during the week and fine-tune some of their newly learned skills. Consultation team meetings occur weekly so that the treatment team can consult with one another about the treatment plan and support one another regarding their work with clients.

As the chapter neared its conclusion, we examined several social and cultural issues related to DBT. We noted that DBT is used in 25 countries and is suitable for children and adults and individuals from any sexual orientation, gender, race, ethnicity, and from most cultures.

We noted that DBT may at times need to adapt the approach if a client is wary of Eastern philosophy techniques (e.g., mindfulness) or of Western techniques (e.g., classical behaviorism). Knowing the ethno-psychological makeup of the client is crucial and some adaptations of DBT to other cultures have been successful. We also talked about the importance of adapting DBT if a client is from a collectivist culture.

Within the final part of the chapter we noted that DBT is particularly efficacious with treating suicidal ideation and behavior, self-injury, depression, anger, emotional dysregulation, and anxiety. As one might expect, it also shows particular efficacy with individuals with BPD or related disorders. DBT has been shown to be cost-effective and is often better than treatment as usual (TAU) (e.g., psychotherapy with or without medication). Although a relatively recent addition to psychotherapeutic theories, DBT has quickly amassed a large body of respectable research, much of which uses randomized controlled studies (RCT). Near the end of this section we delineated a number of disorders for which at least one RCT study had been conducted and for which DBT showed promise as a treatment modality.

KEY WORDS AND NAMES

Acceptance skills
Active passivity vs. apparent competence
Biosocial model of personality formation
Biosocial theory
Behaviorism
Behavioral skills
Between-session coaching
Borderline personality disorder
Certification as a DBT therapist
Chain analysis
Change skills
Cognitive skills
Commitment to change
Constitutional factors
Consultation team meetings
Crisis survival skills
Dialectical communication skills
Dialectical philosophy
Dialectic
Diary card
Distress tolerance skills
Emotional dysregulation
Emotional regulation
Emotional regulation skills
Emotional volatility and dysregulation
Emotional vulnerability vs. self-invalidation
First, second, and third waves of cognitive behavioral therapy
Functional behavior analysis
Group skills training
How skills
Interpersonal effectiveness skills
Invalidating environment
Linehan, Marsha
Millon, Theodore
Mindfulness
Phone coaching
Pretreatment stage
Radical Acceptance
Reality accepting skills
Reinforcement of group skills training
Seven basic assumptions of DBT
Stages I–IV of individual therapy
Structuring therapy
Unrelenting crisis vs. inhibited grieving
What skills
Zen Buddhism

REFERENCES

Behavioral Tech. (2016). *Peer-reviewed & published randomized controlled/comparative trials.* https://behavioraltech.org/wp-content/uploads/2018/04/RCT4ModesResearchDatatoDate2016.06.28-new-logo.pdf

Behavioral Tech. (2017). *How DBT helps.* https://behavioraltech.org/research/how-dbt-

Behavioral Tech. (2018). *DBT research updates.* https://behavioraltech.org/research/evidence/

Bernal, G., Jiménez-Chafey, M., & Domenech Rodríguez, M. (2009). Cultural adaptation of treatments: A resource for considering culture in evidence-based practice. *Professional Psychology: Research and Practice, 40*(4), 361–368. https://doi.org/10.1037/a001640

Brodksy, B. S., & Stanley, B. (2013). *The dialectical behavior therapy primer: How DBT can inform clinical practice.* John Wiley and Sons.

Carey, B. (2011, June 23). Expert on mental illness reveals her own fight. *The New York Times.* http://archive.nytimes.com/www.nytimes.com/2011/06/23/health/23lives.html

Crowell, S. E., Beauchaine, T. P., & Linehan, M. M. (2009). A biosocial developmental model of borderline personality: Elaborating and extending Linehan's theory. *Psychological Bulletin, 135*(3), 495. https://doi.org/10.1037/a0015616

Cheng, P., & Merrick, E. (2017). Cultural adaptation of dialectical behavior therapy for a Chinese international student with eating disorder and depression. *Clinical Case Studies, 16*(1), 42–57. https://doi.org/10.1177/1534650116668269

Gold, S. S. (2017). *Marsha Linehan, PhD, ABPP.* https://behavioraltech.org/about-us/trainers-consultants/marsha-linehan-phd-abpp/

Harned, M., Korslund, K., & Linehan, M. (2014). A pilot randomized controlled trial of dialectical behavior therapy with and without the dialectical behavior therapy prolonged exposure protocol for suicidal and self-injuring women with borderline personality disorder and PTSD. *Behaviour Research and Therapy, 55,* 7–17. http://dx.doi.org/10.1016/j.brat.2014.01.008

Harned, M., Korslund, K., Foa, E., & Linehan, M. (2012). Treating PTSD in suicidal and self-injuring women with borderline personality disorder: Development and preliminary evaluation of a dialectical behavior therapy prolonged exposure protocol. *Behaviour Research and Therapy, 50*(6), 381–386. https://doi.org/10.1016/j.brat.2012.02.01

Hayes, S. C., & Hofman, S. G. (2017). The third wave of cognitive behavioral therapy and the rise of process-based care. *World Psychiatry, 16*(3), 245–246. https://doi.org/10.1002/wps.20442

Kessel, F., Cole, P., & Johnson, D. (Eds.). (2014). *Self and consciousness: Multiple perspectives.* Psychology Press.

Koemer, D. (2012). *Doing dialectical behavior therapy: A practical guide.* Guilford Press.

Koons, C. R., Robins, C. J., Tweed, J. L., Lynch, T. R., Gonzalez, A. M., Morse, J. Q., … Bastian, L. A. (2001). Efficacy of dialectical behavior therapy in women veterans with borderline personality disorder. *Behavior Therapy, 32*(2), 371–390. https://doi.org/10.1016/S0005-7894(01)80009-5

Kröger, C., Harbeck, S., Armbrust, M., & Kliem, S. (2013). Effectiveness, response, and dropout of dialectical behavior therapy for borderline personality disorder in an inpatient setting. *Behaviour Research and Therapy, 51*(8), 411–416. https://doi.org/10.1016/j.brat.2013.04.008

Kuo, J. R., & Fitzpatrick, S. (2015). Dialectical behavior therapy. In E. Neukrug (Ed.), *The SAGE encyclopedia of theories in counseling and psychotherapy* (Vol. 1, pp. 292–297). SAGE Publications.

Lenzenweger, M. F., Lane, M., Lorganger, A. W., & Kessler, R. C. (2007). DSM–IV personality disorders in the national comorbidity survey replication. *Biological Psychiatry, 62*, 553–564. https://doi.org/10.1016/j.biopsych.2006.09.019

Linehan, M. M. (1987a). Dialectical behavior therapy: A cognitive behavioral approach to parasuicide. *Journal of Personality Disorders, 1*(4), 328–333. https://doi.org/10.1521/pedi.1987.1.4.328

Linehan, M. M. (1987b). Dialectical behavior therapy for borderline personality disorder: Theory and method. *Bulletin of the Menninger Clinic, 51*(3), 261–276.

Linehan, M. M. (1989). Dialectical behavior therapy: A treatment for borderline personality disorder. Translated into German as: Dialektische Verhaltenstherapie bei Borderline-Personlichkeitsstorungen. *Praxis der klinischen Verhaltensmedizin und Rehabilitation*, 8, 220–227.

Linehan, M. M. (1993a). *Cognitive behavioral therapy of borderline personality disorder.* Guilford Press.

Linehan, M. M. (1993b). *Skills training manual for treating borderline personality disorder.* Guilford Press.

Linehan, M. M. (2015a). *DBT skills training manual* (2nd ed.). Guilford Press.

Linehan, M. M. (2015b, Nov 17). *Marsha Linehan, Ph.D., ABPP—balancing acceptance and change: DBT and the future of skills training* [Video File]. https://www.youtube.com/watch?v=JMUk0TBWASc&t=1861s

Linehan, M. M. (2016). Behavior therapy: Where we were, where we are and where we need to be going. *Cognitive and Behavioral Practice, 23*(4), 451–453. https://doi.org/10.1016/j.cbpra.2015.12.002

Linehan, M. M. (2017a, April 14). *Marasha Linehan discusses: How she learned radical acceptance* [Video file]. https://www.youtube.com/watch?reload=9&v=OTG7YEWkJFI

Linehan, M. M. (2017b). *Curriculum vitae.* https://depts.washington.edu/uwbrtc/wp-content/uploads/Linehan-CV-Aug-2017.pdf

Linehan, M. M., & Wilks, C. R. (2015). The course and evolution of dialectical behavior therapy. *American Journal of Psychotherapy, 69*(2), 97–110. https://doi.org/10.1176/appi.psychotherapy.2015.69.2.97

Mercado, A., & Hinojosa, Y. (2017). Culturally adapted dialectical behavior therapy in an underserved community mental health setting: A Latina adult case study. *Practice Innovations,2*(2), 80–93. https://doi.org/10.1037/pri0000045

Millon, T. (1969). *Modern psychopathology: A biosocial approach to maladaptive learning and functioning.* W. B. Saunders.

National Institute of Mental Health. (2017). *Personality disorders.* https://www.nimh.nih.gov/health/statistics/personality-disorders.shtml

Panos, P. T, Jackson, J. W, Hasan, O., & Panos, A. (2014). Meta-analysis and systematic review assessing the efficacy of dialectical behavior therapy (DBT). *Research on Social Work Practice, 24*(2), 213–223. https://doi.org/10.1177/1049731513503047

Pederson, L. (2015). *Dialectical behavior therapy: A contemporary guide for practitioners.* John Wiley & Sons.

Ramaiya, M., Fiorillo, D., Regmi, U., Robins, C., & Kohrt, B. (2017). A cultural adaptation of dialectical behavior therapy in Nepal. *Cognitive and Behavioral Practice, 24*(4), 428–444. https://doi.org/10.1016/j.cbpra.2016.12.005

Rizvi, S. L., Steffel, L. M., & Carson-Wong, A. (2013). An overview of dialectical behavior therapy for professional psychologists. *Professional Psychology: Research and Practice, 44*(2), 73–80. https://doi.org/10.1037/a0029808

Robins, C. J. (2002). Zen principles and mindfulness practice in dialectical behavior therapy. *Cognitive and Behavioral practice*, 9(1), 50–57. https://doi.org/10.1016/S1077-7229(02)80040-2

Swales, M. A., & Heard, H. L. (2009). *Dialectical behavior therapy.* Routledge.

Ten Have, M., Verheul, R., Kaasenbrood, A., van Dorsselaer, S., Tuithof, M., Kleinjan, M., & de Graaf, R. (2016). Prevalence rates of borderline personality disorder symptoms: A study based on the Netherlands Mental Health Survey Incidence Study. *BMC Psychiatry, 16,* 1–10. https://doi.org/10.1186/s12888-016-0939-x

Van Dijk, S. (2012). *DBT made simple: A step-by-step guide to dialectical behavior therapy.* New Harbinger.

World Health Organization. (2019). *Global health workforce, finances remain low for mental health.* https://www.who.int/mediacentre/news/notes/2015/finances-mental-health/en/

CASE STUDY: JAKE'S EXPERIENCE WITH A DBT THERAPIST

(Please read about the Millers in Appendix I prior to reading this case study)

Jake is seeing Dr. Duhamel, a DBT therapist for three weeks now. Initially, Dr. Duhamel did a thorough assessment of Jake's situation and came up with a diagnosis of generalized anxiety disorder and a secondary diagnosis of panic disorder. It was also clear that Jake has struggled with related symptoms since childhood. Although he has had periodic respites from the symptoms, they often reoccur—and when they do, he experiences little control over them and becomes particularly reactive. After conducting the assessment and explaining the biosocial model to Jake, Jake agreed to give DBT six months. Jake meets with Dr. Duhamel weekly and also meets for 2–2.5 hours weekly with a group skills trainer and five other clients who are also in DBT therapy. Here, they learn a number of skills they can use to accept themselves, regulate their emotions, and change. Also, phone coaching to practice and reinforce skills is available at designated times during the week, should Jake need it. We pick up at Jake's third session with Dr. Duhamel.

Jake arrives to his individual counseling session looking frazzled and exhausted. Dr. Duhamel notices Jake's wrinkled shirt along with his unkempt hair and beard and greets him warmly. As Jake sits, he apologizes. "I am so sorry for being late. I'm not sure what happened. I set three alarms because I didn't want to be late again. I'm so sorry—I'm just a loser." Dr. Duhamel replied with a smile, "It sounds like you had quite the morning. I'm glad you made it to counseling today. Can you tell me a little more about what is going on?"

"I'm just not myself anymore, and I don't know why," replied Jake. "I don't know who I'm becoming. I've rarely been late to work since I've been at my job, but I'm now constantly late to my meetings, to my counseling sessions, to everything. I'm barely sleeping and I'm losing it. There, I said it. I'm losing it and I'm disappointing others—even you." Dr. Duhamel patiently nods and assures him, "You've been through a lot in the past and particularly recently. This can be a difficult curve ball to manage. And, as you know, the skills that you are learning in group, and being reinforced here, are critical if you are to gain a sense that your life is moving forward." Jake nods in agreement.

Dr. Duhamel then switches gears, and says, "Before we do anything else, let's do a quick mindful breathing exercise, Jake." Jake replies with an "Okay," and with the therapist's guidance, the two men practice mindful breathing. When they finish, Jake slowly opens his eyes and says, with brief laughter, "I've been trying to practice mindful breathing at home like I've learned in group and practiced here. It always seems easier when I have a guide." "You know, Jake, I appreciate that you've been trying at home," said Dr. Duhamel. "That shows a lot of commitment and hope, and I understand when you're under stress, it can be difficult to do. Remember, when you practice mindfulness to observe yourself and the actions around you without judgment—almost as if you are watching yourself in a movie. Don't forget, it's important not to judge yourself or others. You know, there's an app you can use that can help guide you. I can give that to you later. That might help when you feel like you're getting out of control." "Okay, sure—that might be helpful," says Jake.

Dr. Duhamel then suggests to Jake that they review his diary card, which Jake dutifully filled out every day and brought in for his individual session. As they review it together, Dr. Duhamel notes how almost every day Jake's frustration level is very high (a "5" out of 5), and his anger is usually associated with it (usually a "4"). He also notes periodic moments of panic, which are always rated a "5." Jake also records on this diary card that he is sleeping very poorly. "Well, first I notice that your depression and sense of hopelessness is not particularly high," says Dr. Duhamel. "That's great. However, your frustration, anger, and panic are pretty high, and I'm concerned about your lack of sleep. I think you've pretty much struggled with many of these symptoms, on and off, most of your life." "Yeah, no kidding," says Jake. Continues Dr. Duhamel: "And, I understand how things have gotten worse since the incident with your kids rolling the car into the street. That certainly was a trigger for you and brought out those old memories of Justine becoming seriously injured." "Yeah," says Jake. "I think that I've always been an 'on edge' type of person but that accident with Justine just set me off. And, ever since then, and especially lately, it's been much worse."

"So, Jake, this way of living is kind of who you are. Not always, but a fair amount of the time you feel vigilante about making sure everything is safe, and it is associated with a lot of anxiety, frustration, and periodic panic. And when it gets worse, it gets really worse. I'm actually impressed with how much you've done with your life despite all of the strong feelings you have. I wonder if there are certain ways of thinking that you buy into, that feed into your strong feelings?" Jake asks, "What do you mean, 'ways of thinking'?" "Well, let me show you what we call 'cognitive distortions' that some people adopt, or believe, and see if you relate to any of them," answers Dr. Duhamel, who takes out a plastic tablet that has 14 cognitive distortions listed. "These are called distortions because they tend to lock a person into viewing the world in one way, which is not really the way the world is. Can you relate to any of them?" Jake looks them over, and says, "Well, yeah, I certainly catastrophize. I always think things will go bad. And, I do some fortune-telling, in that I'm always predicting that something bad will happen if things don't go my way. I guess I personalize and make should statements a lot also, and I know I blame others when things don't go my way."

"That's a great start, Jake," says Dr. Duhamel. "You know, when you view the world in that way, it makes it very difficult to make changes. It's kind of like you're always sure things are going to happen in a certain way and you're always asking people to do it your way. And, when they don't, it's their fault. Does that make sense?" "Well, yeah," says Jake. "I know I can be overwhelming with Angela and the kids." Dr. Duhamel then offers a suggestion. "Well, how about we try a few things this next week that can begin to loosen up that tight thinking you have?" "Sure, I'm willing to try anything," says Jake.

Dr. Duhamel talks about counteracting some of the rigid thinking that takes place with cognitive distortions and suggests that when Jake "catches" himself thinking that way, he take a few deep breaths, and consider letting go of those thoughts. He reminds him of the acronym "STOP Skills" that Jake recently learned in group, which stands for Stop, Take a step back, Observe, and Proceed mindfully. Dr. Duhamel suggests that Jake use that acronym when he sees himself wrapped up in one or more of his cognitive distortions.

"Okay, Jake. This is a great start. You are just beginning your journey into accepting who you are and making change. Remember, we talked about the dialectics—the opposites in life. And the importance of acceptance and change." "Yes, I think I get that—I think," says Jake. "So, you know *how* you have been living, but you also see that there are some steps you can begin to take to make your life a bit better," says Dr. Duhamel. "First, you're going to practice your mindfulness, which will help you not get so caught up in your feelings. And, you're going to reflect on your cognitive distortions, and begin to loosen up some of that tight thinking of yours. And, you'll use the STOP Skills acronym to help you reflect on those cognitive distortions. I'd also like you to continue with your weekly diary, and, of course, if you need some phone coaching, you can call in at the designated times. And Jake, can you do one more thing for me?' "Sure, what is it?" asks Jake. "This next week, if you have a situation with your wife or kids that seems out of control, write it down in detail. I'd like to do what's called a chain analysis with you. This will help us understand the triggers that make you upset and find ways of combating them in the future. That sound okay?" "Sure," Jake answers. "I think that's a great idea."

"So, one more time—practice mindful breathing, consider alternative ways of thinking that do not lock you into cognitive distortions, practice your STOP Skills, do your diary, and make a note of any particularly difficult situation you have with your kids or wife. Okay?" "Sure thing," says Jake. "That sounds great." "Oh yeah, and one more thing before you leave today," Dr. Duhamel says. "Let me show you that app."

Jake is at the beginning of his journey with Dr. Duhamel and the DBT process. As he continues, he'll learn more skills he can practice to help monitor and manage his emotions and develop richer and more meaningful relationships in his life. As he continues to accept himself, and work toward change, his life should become a bit calmer and more meaningful. But, it's going to take time, acceptance, and work.

QUESTIONS FOR YOU TO PONDER

1. Describe Jake's emotional dysregulation. How do you think he developed this style of being in the world and what hope, if any, do you think he has to change it?
2. Can you identify the secondary emotion of guilt that Jake experiences due to his emotional dysregulation?
3. Does Dr. Duhamel exhibit radical acceptance? If yes, how? Is there more he can do to show radical acceptance?
4. Describe how mindful breathing can assist Jake in monitoring and managing his emotional dysregulation.
5. Describe how Dr. Duhamel practices both acceptance and change with Jake.
6. In what ways can the STOP Skills acronym be useful for Jake and his family?
7. Do you believe there are additional cognitive distortions Jake did not identify with that may have him struggling?
8. What is the purpose of the chain analysis?
9. Do you believe Jake will always struggle with strong emotions?
10. Explain what the purpose of phone coaching is and why do you think Jake may be reticent to use it? How can we encourage Jake to use it responsibly?
11. If Jake were to follow the treatment procedures properly, what do you think his life would look like after six months?
12. What cognitive distortions can you identify for yourself?

Credit

6

Acceptance and Commitment Therapy (ACT)

John C. Wren, Robert R. Armbruster, and Abie Tremblay

LEARNING OUTCOMES

- To gain a historical understanding of ACT and learn about its originator, Steven C. Hayes.
- To examine ACT's view of human nature relative to it being a third-wave cognitive behavioral approach.
- To examine key concepts of ACT, including relational frame theory (RFT), the theoretical foundation for ACT; how human suffering is caused by the nature of language; the six processes of psychological inflexibility, which are cognitive fusion, experiential avoidance, being stuck in the past or the future, attachment to a conceptualized self, lack of clarity of values, and unworkable action; and the six processes of psychological flexibility, which are defusion, acceptance, contact with the present moment, self-as-context, values, and committed action.
- To review a number of key techniques important to the practice of ACT, including compassion, acceptance, respect, and empathy; promoting a collaborative and egalitarian relationship; taking a history; obtaining informed consent and goal setting; psychoeducation; using analogies, metaphors, stories, paradoxes, and mindfulness; and exercises related to psychological flexibility.
- To describe the counseling process of ACT.

- To examine social and cultural applicability of ACT.
- To review the efficacy of ACT.
- To offer a case study that demonstrates the ACT process.

BRIEF HISTORY OF ACCEPTANCE AND COMMITMENT THERAPY

Acceptance and commitment therapy (ACT, pronounced like the word "act") is a **third-wave cognitive behavioral therapy** (Hayes, 2004; Hayes et al., 2012). The first wave, pure behavior therapy such as that proposed by **B. F. Skinner** (1957), was characterized by a rejection of the unobservable constructs of psychoanalytic theory (e.g., id, ego, superego) and a focus on applying evidence-based behavioral principles to correct problematic behaviors and emotions (Hayes, 2004; Hayes et al., 2006). Stimuli were believed to evoke behavioral responses and change was produced by eradicating old responses and conditioning new responses.

The mechanistic and strict behavioral focus of behavioral therapy, however, omitted consideration of cognitions, and new theories soon arose that suggested cognitive processes and symbolic memory played a critical role in the development of behaviors (Bandura, 1977). With little evidence that Skinner's approach was on target, and on the heels of Bandura (1977) suggesting that behavior could be a response to thoughts, **Aaron Beck**, **Albert Ellis**, and others began **second-wave cognitive behavioral therapies**, which focused on how cognitions mediated behaviors, feelings, and physiological responses (Hayes, 2004; Hayes et al., 2006).

Although the popularity of these new cognitive therapies flourished (increasingly termed cognitive behavioral in deference to the first wave), the practice of directly changing the content of thoughts and beliefs began to be challenged (Hayes, 2004; Hayes et al., 2006; Hayes et al., 2004a). It became evident that attention to simply changing out behaviors, or cognitions, did not adequately address mechanisms of change (Hayes et al., 2006).

With questions regarding the nature of change of first- and second-wave cognitive behavioral approaches, the third wave of cognitive behavioral therapies were born and included dialectical behavior therapy (DBT; Linehan, 1993), functional analytic psychotherapy (FAP; Kohlenberg & Tsai, 1991), integrative behavioral couples therapy (IBCT; Christensen et al., 2015), mindfulness-based cognitive therapy (MBCT; Segal et al., 2013), and ACT. While remaining committed to an empirical, principle-based approach, these new therapies incorporated constructs generally considered less empirical such as spirituality, values, and mindfulness (Hayes et al., 2004a, 2006). Rather than attempting to change thoughts, most third-wave therapies attempt to change the context (Cloud, 2006). ACT itself is characterized by a return to a fundamentally behavioral approach, but one in which cognitions are treated from a behavior analytic point of view within a contextual focus (Hayes, 2004; Hayes et al., 2006).

Steven C. Hayes is credited as the founder of ACT. Currently a Foundation Professor at the University of Nevada, Reno, "Hayes was listed by the Institute for Scientific Information as the 30th highest impact psychologist in the world from 1986 to 1990" (Podina & David, 2017, p. 178). Growing up in southern California in the 1960s, Hayes wanted to study something that would combine his interest in the humanities with his passion for science—and although he knew little about the subject, he chose psychology. Although raised Catholic, by the time he attended Loyola Marymount University, a Jesuit university in Los Angeles, he no longer considered himself Catholic (Hayes, 2008). While there, he was inspired both by Skinner's work and also by **Irving Kessler**, a recent addition to the faculty who demonstrated the connection between behaviorist theory and clinical practice. He also took part in the counterculture movement prominent at the time, and became enamored with Eastern philosophies, particularly the writings of **D. T. Suzuki** and **Alan Watts.** After graduation, Hayes continued this interest by spending time in an Eastern religious commune run by **Swami Kriyananda.** In 1972, Hayes married his high school sweetheart, **Angel Butcher**, three years after the birth of their daughter.

Hayes went to West Virginia University (WVU) for his doctoral training, becoming immersed in the behavior analysis work for which WVU was, and remains, renowned. After an internship at Brown University, where he was heavily influenced by **David Barlow's** treatment of anxiety disorders, he joined the faculty of the University of North Carolina at Greensboro in 1977. His nine years there would prove tumultuous. The Psychology Department became divided between the behavioral faculty and the cognitive faculty, and the conflict was intense (Hayes, 2008). During one department meeting in 1978, as tensions rose, Hayes found himself unable to speak, and he thought he might be having a heart attack. This was his first panic attack, and they became more frequent over the next two years (Cloud, 2006). Adding to the stress during this period, he and Angel divorced (Hayes, 2004). By 1980, his anxiety made it almost impossible for him to lecture, and he avoided public spaces such as restaurants or movie theaters almost entirely (Cloud, 2006). In part, his attempts over the next three years to overcome his anxiety disorder, which by now made life unlivable, led him to the development of ACT (Hayes, 2008). He realized that the standard ways of coping, such as tranquilizers or trying to process a panic attack cognitively and thus control it, only led to focusing on the panic and making the condition worse (Hayes, 2016).

Hayes, with his first doctoral student **Robert D. Zettle**, began to investigate how clinical issues (e.g., anxiety disorders) were impacted by language, verbal behavior, and rule-governed behavior (rigid thinking based on rules given to us by others) (Zettle, 2011). In particular, they were attempting to apply, from a radical perspective, Beck's practice of having clients distance themselves from their thoughts and beliefs, or as Hayes (2016) said, "It's being able to look at your thoughts, not just [coming] from your thoughts" (11:48). This early therapeutic form was named **comprehensive distancing** to demonstrate that it went far beyond Beck's "distancing." Over the following years it was to grow into ACT (Hayes, 2008; Zettle, 2011).

Over the same period of time, Hayes was beginning to develop **relational frame theory (RFT)**, a behavioral and contextual approach to language and which informs the practice of act, though some suggest the link between RFT and Act is tenuous (Barnes-Homes et al., 2016; Blackledge & Drake, 2013; Hayes et al., 2001). The first detailed account of RFT was presented at the 1985 Association for Behavior Analysis (ABA) convention (Hayes & Brownstein, 1985). Hayes has written 46 books, 650 articles, and has been president of several professional societies. He has received many awards, including the Lifetime Achievement Award from the Association for Behavioral and Cognitive Therapy. Google scholars lists him as one of the most cited scholars globally ("Steven C. Hayes Ph.D.," 2020).

VIEW OF HUMAN NATURE

Similar to other third-wave cognitive behavioral therapies, ACT focuses more on the context of an individual's thoughts and emotions than the content. Whereas **first- and second-wave cognitive behavioral approaches** (e.g., behavioral therapy, CBT) assumed that behaviors or cognitions are maladaptive and need to replaced, third-wave approaches suggest that "no thought, feeling or memory is inherently problematic, dysfunctional, or pathological: rather, it all depends on the context." (Harris, 2009, p. 34). ACT is a type of **functional contextual theory** because it examines the current and past biological, social, physical, and cultural context (or environment) in which **private events**, sometimes called **psychological events** (things people do, think, or feel), are formed (Fox, 2004–2020). Thus, rather than replacing behaviors or cognitions, acceptance and adjusting their context, is the key to living a more meaningful life.

ACT is based on relational frame theory (RFT), which is a behavioral description of how human language and cognition are developed and how individuals create webs **of relational frames** that mediate the things they do, think, and feel (their private events). Relational frames can lead to painful emotions and dysfunctional behaviors when they result in rigid thinking and experiential avoidance that prevent individuals from seeking values important to their lives; however, by helping clients build **psychological flexibility**, which includes using mindfulness, acceptance, and what is called cognitive defusion (not being rigidly attached to our thoughts), individuals can change the context of their negative thoughts, feelings, and memories and lessen their impact. Individuals do this by Accepting and being present with their painful thoughts, feelings, and memories; Choosing a valued direction in life; and Taking action so they can live a more meaningful and less symptomatic life. This contrasts greatly with theories that view thoughts, feelings, memories, and related behaviors as part of a "faulty machine" that needs to have parts replaced (Harris, 2009; see Box 6.1).

You can see that ACT is rooted in behaviorism, as RFT is based on how stimuli become reinforced into a web of relational frames; has Eastern influences as it uses mindfulness, meditation, and related philosophies to develop psychological flexibility; and has some humanistic tendencies in its belief that people can move forward in life. But it is clearly its own theory, and a part of the third-wave cognitive behavioral movement, along with **dialectical behavior therapy, mindfulness-based therapies**, and others.

BOX 6.1 FOCUS OF FUNCTIONAL CONTEXTUALISTS COMPARED WITH OTHER PSYCHOLOGICAL THEORIES

- *Psychodynamic therapists:* Focus on changing faulty ego development.
- *Existential-humanistic therapists:* Focus on changing feelings and related incongruent behaviors, generally attributed to low self-esteem.
- *Cognitive therapist:* Focus on changing faulty, irrational, or negative beliefs.
- *Narrative therapists:* Focus on changing the person's problem-saturated narratives.

In Contrast:

- *Functional contextualists*: Changing the context in which thoughts, feelings, and behaviors occur so that their function (e.g., being painful) no longer holds the same power. (In ACT, the development of psychological flexibility can assist with changing the context.)

KEY CONCEPTS

This section begins with an overview of relational frame theory (RFT), a complex theory that underlies the basis for the practice of ACT, though most counselors are more involved with the application of ACT rather than its underlying theory. Here, we will offer a very condensed version of RFT in somewhat down-to-earth terms, so that when you practice ACT, you understand why you do what you do. The section then transitions to a discussion about how RFT is related to language development and how the mind can foster psychological inflexibility and human suffering. The six processes of psychological inflexibility we discuss are cognitive fusion, experiential avoidance, being stuck in the past or the future, attachment to a conceptualized self, lack of clarity of values, and unworkable action. The section concludes with the six processes of psychological flexibility to which ACT therapists help clients strive. These are defusion (watch what you're thinking), acceptance (open up), contact with the present moment (be here now), self-as-context (pure awareness), values (know what matters), and committed action (do what it takes).

Relational Frame Theory

> Relational frame theory (Hayes et al., 2001) is a comprehensive functional contextual program of basic behavioral research on human language and cognition. (Hayes et al., 2004b, p. 21)

Relational frame theory (RFT) explains how what we do, think, and feel (our private events), and the language that we use, are related to the manner in which stimuli were reinforced and subsequently associated with one another into a matrix of **relational frames** (ways that we come to see the world) that are unique for each person (Fox, 2004–2020). We cannot undo this matrix, but we can add to it and modify it.

RFT posits that as increasing numbers of stimuli become associated with one another, each of us creates a unique web of relational frames from which we view the world (Hayes et al., 2012a). For example, a child might be reinforced for a **derived stimulus relationship** between the word *cat* and the warm, furry animal the child sees (Figure 6.1, Arrow 1). Thus, *cat* is equal to the warm, furry animal and because of the way the human mind works, a warm, furry animal is equal to a *cat*. Then, a child is taught that the word *rabbit* is a warm, fury animal (Arrow 2). So, cats are warm, furry animals and rabbits are warm, furry animals, and because of how the human mind works, a relationship is formed between a rabbit and a cat, since both are warm, furry animals (Arrow 3). In addition, a derived stimulus relationship is formed between the warm, furry animal *cat* and the word *rabbit* (Arrow 4), and between the warm, furry animal *rabbit* and the word *cat* (Arrow 5). Thus, cats are related to rabbits and rabbits are related to cats. At some point, a child may be scratched by a cat (Arrow 6), and then when someone says the word *cat* the child will get upset (Arrow 5). So, *cats* and *warm, furry animals* can scratch. And since cats are related to rabbits, rabbits have now been secondarily associated with getting scratched (Arrow 8). And one can readily see how this can become generalized to other warm, furry animals. Low and behold, a phobia has been formed! We can also see how someone can develop a series of relational frames that lead to such thoughts as being at home with no animals is better than being with warm, furry animals—that scratch. Here, we see an **arbitrary** relationship has been formed between warm,

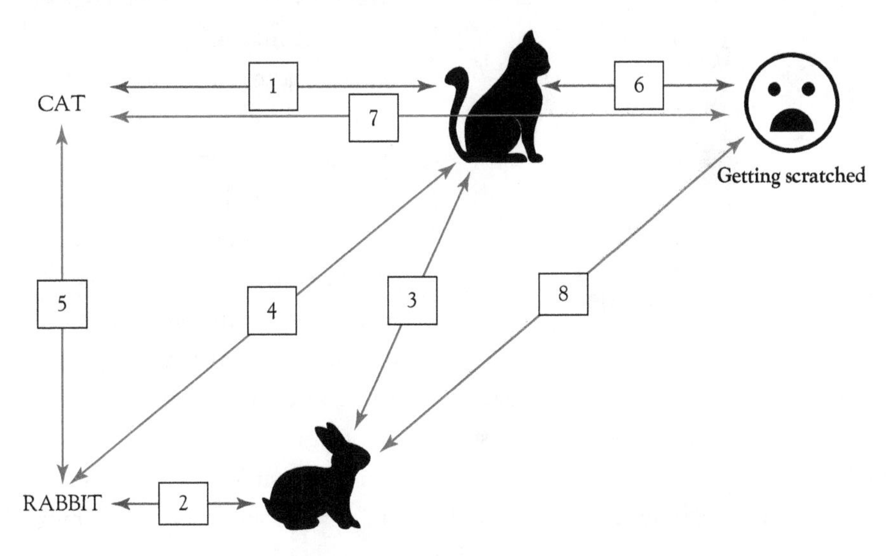

Figure 6.1 Relational Networks

furry animals and being scratched. It's arbitrary, because it is unique to this individual's situation and not a "given" in life.

You can see how our relational frames are the basis for a person's private events, which can be helpful and also unhelpful (unhelpful: all warm, furry animals scratch). When two or more stimuli become related to one another, it is called **combinatorial entailment** (they *combine*). So, imagine the infinite number of relational frames humans develop as many stimuli become associated in arbitrary ways with many other stimuli. These relational frames are "the patterns of relational responding that occur within different contexts for which each person gets reinforced" (Gross & Fox, 2009, p. 91) and are the basis for our cognition and our language development. Because it is a web of relationships, it is complicated, involved, and not easy to change. You cannot take it apart, but you can accept it as it is and create new webs of relationships that can change how the original web functioned.

HUMAN SUFFERING IS CAUSED BY THE NATURE OF LANGUAGE

> ACT highlights the ways that language traps clients into attempts to wage war against their internal lives. (Dewane, 2008, para. 9)

ACT assumes that humans suffer as a result of the complexity of the relational frames they have developed and the associated language that is used, which can include **private language** or **public language** (Harris, 2006). Private language includes "thinking, imagining, daydreaming, planning, visualizing and so on" (p. 4), often called **cognition** (e.g., a person thinking: "Those warm, fury animals are going to scratch me! I'm scared of them"). Public language includes "speaking, talking, miming, gesturing, writing, painting, singing, dancing, and so on" (p. 4) (e.g., a person announcing, "Let's ban all warm, furry, animals!"). The word **mind** is symbolic of the different kinds of language we have developed (Figure 6.2).

Figure 6.2 Private and Public Language

Although language can be used to help us understand one another and the world, to find solutions to major problems (e.g., invention, scientific revelations, etc.), to show empathy, and to advocate for important causes, language can also increase suffering. For instance, public language can be used to lie, bully, respond in sexist and discriminatory ways, and more. Private language can cause us to judge and feel bad about ourselves, imagine negative things from the past that cause us pain or imagine things about the future that might cause us anxiety, and develop rules about how we should live our lives that can constrict our behaviors. Thus, language can result in painful **private experiences** (emotions, memories, thoughts, sensations, and other internal experiences) and the making of poor choices. For instance, the person who has the thought while working out that "I could have a heart attack like my dad had" thereby avoids working out in the future. Or, the individual who constantly thinks his or her spouse *should* act differently becomes verbally abusive and the relationship deteriorates. Or, the person who has the mantra "life will be good when I retire" lives a depressive life as he waits for his retirement. Here's where language wreaks havoc on the person. Thus, the primary reason why our mind is not our friend is because we developed the kinds of language usage that results in **psychological inflexibility**.

PSYCHOLOGICAL INFLEXIBILITY

Psychological inflexibility describes six interrelated processes that result in an inability to act in a manner consistent with one's values (Hayes, 2009; Törneke, et al., 2008). They are interrelated because they tend to impact one another in various ways. The six processes are cognitive fusion, experiential avoidance, being stuck in the past or the future, attachment to a conceptualized self, lack of clarity of values, and unworkable action (Harris, 2009). These six processes can be contrasted with the six parallel processes of psychological flexibility: defusion (aka "cognitive defusion"), acceptance, contact with the present moment, self-as-context, values, and committed action. Psychological flexibility will be discussed in the next section.

Psychological inflexibility that causes a mental health problem is readily reinforced due to its short-term benefits, despite the fact that it has long-term detrimental effects. For instance, a person with a social phobia is fearful of being judged and rejected in social situations and, thus, avoids such situations. Avoiding social situations does result in short-term relief as the individual does not have to experience the anxiety or panic of being in social situations; however, this results in a life inconsistent with one's desire of wanting to be with others. The following describes the six processes of psychological inflexibility.

Cognitive Fusion

Cognitive fusion occurs when one becomes caught up in thoughts that cause serious distress, yet one continually thinks about such thoughts despite the fact that ruminating causes more distress. Cognitive fusion is evident when one is rigidly attached to thoughts that tend to be rule-bound, judgmental, leave little room for change, and involve black and white thinking (Hayes, 2004; Harris, 2009). Often, such thoughts

- seem as absolute truth,
- seem that they must be followed,
- dominate one's understanding of self,

- seem that they have to be eliminated immediately,
- are about the past or about the future and cause constant worry, and/or
- seem impossible to let go of despite the fact they negatively impact one's life.

Such thinking is often fused with painful memories from major caretakers and results in disappointment, rejection, failure, abuse, and feelings of low self-worth. Such experiences result in self-statements such as "I am no good," I can't ever succeed," "I am not worthy," "Why try, it won't work out," and so forth (Harris 2009). In ACT, clients are encouraged to recognize these thoughts, and not try to stop them but not get hooked into believing them. It's as if the "self" is on a bus and the riders are the individual's thoughts. Here, the self can observe the thoughts but not get caught up in them. Or, imagine a deck of cards, one by one being thrown at you. Now, imagine the cards are thoughts. Instead of trying to catch the cards ("thoughts"), the individual learns how to just look at them as they pass by. The opposite of cognitive fusion is defusion, which will be examined in the next section on psychological flexibility.

Experiential Avoidance

> For us humans, private events readily acquire aversive stimulus functions through relational framing, and thereby also become objects of avoidance. (Törneke et al., 2008, p. 149)

From an evolutionary perspective, human beings have developed problem-solving mechanisms to address external problems that could threaten their survival (Harris, 2006). For instance, after discovering that bears can kill and realizing that throwing rocks at them can only go so far, humans developed more complex strategies to avoid bears. Although avoidance strategies may work well when dealing with external threats, such as bears that stalk, they have not been so helpful when applied to symptoms, which can include difficult feelings, memories, sensations, and thoughts. In fact, trying to avoid difficult feelings, memories, and thoughts actually increases difficult feelings, memories, or thoughts.

For instance, the individual who is depressed naturally wants to fight off or avoid his or her sad feelings. Attempts at avoiding one's depression, however, generally result in a person becoming more depressed, such as when a person refuses to discuss painful depressive feelings, never deals with the pain, and lives with unresolved painful feelings. Or the person who purposefully avoids social contact due to a fear of being anxious around people and then becomes depressed and anxious because he or she has no friends or acquaintances. Experiential avoidance is often fueled by cognitive fusion. For instance, the anxious person who is avoiding interacting with others is often obsessed with thoughts such as "I'm not good enough to be around others" (thinking probably fused with early painful memories from caretakers—"You're not good enough"). Thus, this individual does not live out his or her values of wanting to be with people, which would enrichen his or her life. The opposite of experiential avoidance is acceptance of self, which will be discussed in the next section.

Being Stuck in the Past or Future

Instead of living in the present, these individuals obsess about the past or ruminate about the future. They think about how things would have been "if only ... " or worry about how things might be in the future. It is the individual who is always thinking about his or her abuse from the past and how it negatively impacted him or her, or it is the individual who refuses to find a partner because he or she is worried that the relationship will fail. The opposite of being stuck in the past or future is being able to have contact with the present moment, which will be addressed in the next section.

Attachment to a Conceptualized Self

Our conceptualized self is the self we have come to know based on our life story, and often includes such things as our name, cultural background, age, gender, marital status, occupation, degrees we hold, activities we embrace, avocational activities, labels we adhere to, and so forth. We all have a conceptualized self, but when we rigidly adhere to one or more aspects of it, we *become* our self-description as opposed to *having* a description of self. For instance, the psychiatrist who is fused with his or her perceptions of what it is to be a psychiatrist is not able to consider alternative mechanisms of treating clients, and believes he or she must always play the role of "psychiatrist"—even with friends and those with whom he or she is close. The opposite of attachment to a conceptualized self is having a flexible understanding of self within one's context, which will examined in the next section.

Lack of Clarity of Values

This is when one's cognitive fusion, experiential avoidance, being stuck in the past or future, or a rigid conceptualized self prevents a person from having clarity about one's values and from acting in a manner that embraces such values. For instance, the depressed individual unhappy and unsatisfied in his or her current career is obsessed with thoughts of not being capable on the job (cognitive fusion), avoids finding a new job (experiential avoidance) because he or she is anxious about what the future might hold (being stuck in the future), and strictly adheres to the career roles he or she has taken on (rigid conceptualized self). The opposite of lack of clarity of values is having clarity about one's values, which will examined in the next section.

Unworkable Action

These are feelings, thoughts, and behaviors that are antithetical to purposeful, intentional, and mindful actions that prevent one from moving toward chosen values. They include actions that are impulsive, reactive, and automatic—not thought through. It is the abusive spouse, the substance abuser who automatically takes drugs, the individual who refuses to consider finding a partner despite the fact he or she is lonely, the person dissatisfied at his or her job who complains but does not look for other work, and so forth. The opposite of unworkable action is committed action, which will be discussed in the next section.

Since the goal of ACT is to "create a rich and meaningful life while accepting the pain that inevitably goes with it" (Harris, 2006, p. 2), one needs to learn how to disengage from psychological inflexibility and adopt a new way of living that embraces psychological flexibility.

PSYCHOLOGICAL FLEXIBILITY

The antithesis of psychological inflexibility, **psychological flexibility**, refers to the ability of an individual to live in the present moment, accept one's current state of being, and to act in accordance with his or her chosen values (Hayes, et al., 2012b). Psychological flexibility is composed of six core interrelated dimensions or processes: **defusion (watch what you're thinking), acceptance (open up), contact with the present moment (be here now), self-as-context (pure awareness), values (know what matters)**, and **committed action (do what it takes)** (Harris, 2009; Hayes et al., 2012a, 2012b). Visually, this can be seen in the Hexaflex model (Figure 6.3). Notice

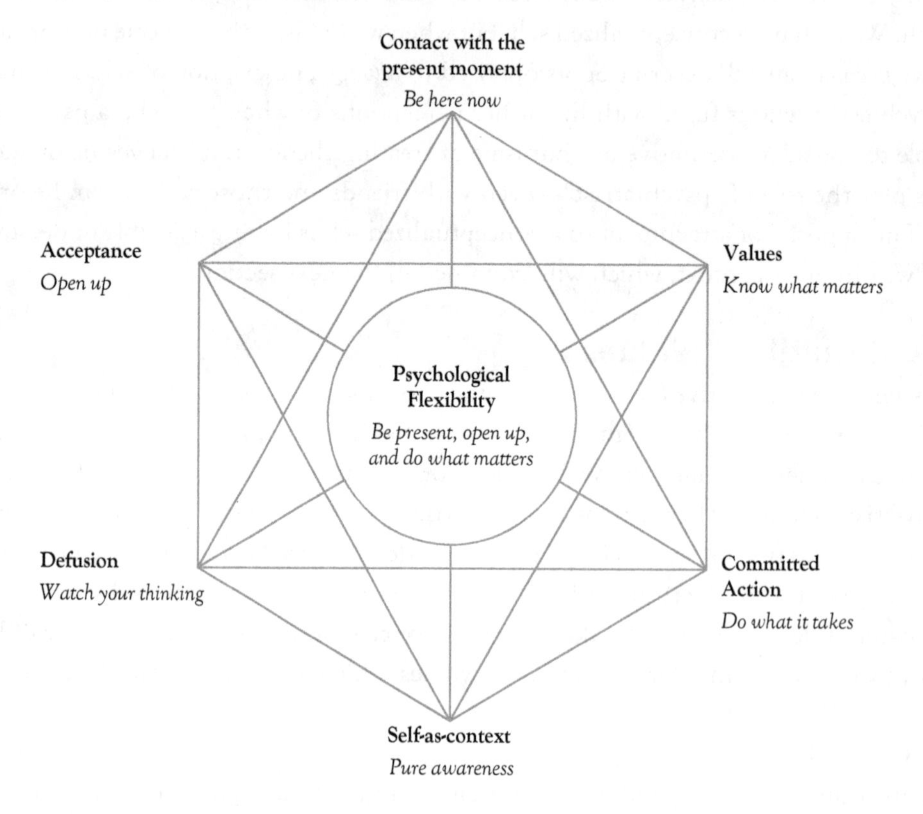

Figure 6.3 The Hexaflex Model

how lines connect the various processes, indicating how they are interrelated or impact one another, and together develop psychological flexibility. Examples of how these processes are used in counseling will be given in the techniques section that follows this section. Meanwhile, let's take a look at each of these processes.

Defusion (Watch What You're Thinking)

Whereas cognitive fusion is being attached to one's thoughts, defusion (aka "cognitive defusion") is letting go of one's thoughts and understanding that one is not dictated by one's thoughts. Harris (2009) notes that a defused state is one in which a thought:

- may or may not be true
- is definitely not a command you have to obey or a rule you have to follow
- is definitely not a threat to you
- is not something happening in the physical world: it is merely words or pictures inside your head
- may or may not be important—you have a choice as to how much attention you pay it
- can be allowed to come and go of its own accord without any need for you to hold on to or push it away (p. 21)

People who are cognitively defused are able to take a step back from their thoughts and watch what they are thinking, imagining, or remembering. They have the ability to not get too attached or caught up in their thoughts. For instance, this could be an individual who has been an abusive spouse, who has learned to take a moment to stop and think about his or her thoughts, and has learned mindfulness exercises to separate and watch—but not necessarily respond to—his or her thoughts. This enables the person to take a new purposeful action that is loving toward his or her spouse.

Acceptance (Open Up)

Acceptance is allowing oneself to experience (open up to) difficult private experiences (emotions, memories, thoughts, sensations, and other internal experiences) so that the individual can make powerful choices that are more congruent with one's values (Batten & Ciarrochi, 2015; Harris, 2009; Neale-McFall, 2015). For instance, a person who values being in relationships, but has been hurt by them in the past, is depressed and may avoid future relationships for fear of being hurt again. Acceptance would be the act of allowing oneself to experience the hurt in the moment, not participate in experiential avoidance, and choose, despite one's pain, to take actions that would result in being in a loving relationship again.

Contact With the Present Moment (Be Here Now)

Flexible attention to the present moment is the process of coming in contact with the here and now (Neale-McFall, 2015). This occurs when one experiences the moment, suspends judgment, lets go of expectations, and gives complete, purposeful attention to one's psychological or physical world. It is the ability to move from narrow, focused attention to broad, diffuse attention, and also opens up a person to moving from things that have happened in the past, or things that might happen in the future, to what is happening in the now. This can be of great value as anxiety and worry are often a function of focusing solely on what has occurred or what will occur. For instance, the person who had been abused as a child and constantly obsesses about the abuse can use mindfulness exercises to help him or her focus upon, and feel grounded in, the present. This lessens rumination about the past and allows the individual to think about healthy choices for the future.

Self-as-Context (Pure Awareness)

Consider this:

Are you the thoughts in your head?

or,

Are you your awareness of your thoughts in your head?

As children are raised, they develop certain narratives that becomes their *I*, or the way that they view themselves. For instance, they might think of themselves as bright, athletic, less than ... , better than ... , pretty, a worrier, and so forth. They view their self in relationship to the content that describes them, sometimes called **self-as-content**. This necessary simplification is a useful shorthand way to think about and describe who and what one is (Törneke, 2010); however, as we grow older, it can dominate thoughts, influence behaviors, and become a rigid way of viewing self. In contrast, self-as-context is the ability to detach from these narratives and the content of our thoughts, our feelings, and our experiences associated with them. It is considered by some to be a transcendent state, or meta-awareness of self, in which one defuses or separates self from one's content. This concept is similar to a state achieved during meditation (Hayes et al., 2012a). This is the individual who is a psychiatrist but not rigidly wed to this role. This person is open to alternative ways of treating individuals and does not need to maintain the role of "psychiatrist" when with friends or with his or her partner (see Box 6.2).

BOX 6.2 WHO AM I?

I remember spending five days at a values clarification workshop where I was asked not to state what I did for work, what degrees I held, or even what I had studied in school. I was suddenly devoid of my "self-as-content." This became a struggle for me, as I realized I was attached to my degrees and my profession—they defined who I was. But slowly, through meditative, mindfulness, and related experiences, I began to get in touch with a new me—a me that no longer constantly needed to be the content of who I was and was able to be different "Me's" depending on the context in which I found myself.—Ed Neukrug

Values (Know What Matters)

> Life is what happens while you are busy making other plans. (John Lennon, 1980, min. 2:18)

In ACT, values are those activities that bring joy and meaning to a person's life, and they are reflective of a person's larger purpose (Harris, 2009, 2015). ACT therapists suggest it is important to distinguish between a **goal-focused life** and a **value-focused life**, with the former being focused on attainment of the goal and the latter being focused on the process, or journey, taken in living one's values. In the latter, the individual gains a sense of fulfillment, purpose, and meaning even when goals are not achieved. A goal-focused life results in disappointments, feelings of being a failure, and a sense of emptiness if goals are not reached. Although a goal-focused life brings small moments of joy and happiness when goals are obtained, happiness is fleeting, whereas a value-focused life brings enjoyment from the journey, and attainment of a specific goal becomes one moment of joy within the context of the larger journey.

Some common values of the value-focused life revolve around becoming a better parent, maintaining health, having satisfactory family relationships, developing deeper intimacy in relationships, having satisfactory employment, developing ourselves personally, enjoying avocations, becoming involved in community and environmental issues, deepening one's spirituality or religion, and building social relationships (Harris, 2009). A wide variety of values clarification exercises can be used to help individuals determine what values are most salient so they can make the best choices for themselves in their lives. One particular exercise is similar to the miracle question asked in solution-focused brief therapy:

> If you could wave a magic wand so that all these problematic thoughts and feelings no longer had any impact on you, what would you start doing, or do more of? What would you stop doing, or do less of? How would you behave differently toward your friends, partner, children, parents, relatives, work colleagues, and so on? How would you act different at home, at work, and at play? (Harris, 209, p. 56)

Committed Action (Do What It Takes)

Committed action requires "taking effective action, guided by our values" (Harris, 2009, p. 11) in situations that elicit both positive and negative emotional experiences. The long-term purpose of committed action is for the client to determine and work toward goals that are helpful in maintaining harmony with stated values. Harris (2009) lists the steps of committed action as:

1. Choose a domain of life that is a high priority for change.
2. Choose the values to pursue in this domain.
3. Develop goals guided by those values.
4. Take action mindfully. (p. 209)

Doing what it takes could require the professional counselor to teach traditional behavioral interventions—e.g., goal setting, skills training, exposure therapy, negotiation, time management, assertiveness training—so the client will be able to tolerate the emotions arising during committed action. It is always important, however, to remember that the focus should be on development of a value-focused, not goal-focused, life. As one example, it is the lonely, depressed individual who has been fearful of seeking a partner for fear of being hurt again who can now accept the pain from past hurts, not ruminate about future concerns, and be willing to take deliberate and purposeful actions toward finding a new partner.

TECHNIQUES

There are a wide range of techniques that ACT therapists use, many of which relate to the development of psychological flexibility. Here, we will examine the techniques of **compassion, acceptance, respect, and empathy**; **promoting a collaborative and egalitarian relationship**; **taking a history**; **obtaining informed consent and goal setting**; **psychoeducation**; **using analogies, metaphors, stories, paradoxes, and mindfulness**; and **exercises highlighting the six core processes of the Hexaflex model**.

Compassion, Acceptance, Respect, and Empathy

Developing a working alliance in ACT is critical, and often accomplished by the ACT therapist using a variety of common skills that have been shown to be related to positive outcomes in counseling (Wampold & Imel, 2015). Thus, the ACT therapist brings himself or herself into the relationship through having compassion for the client's predicament, being accepting of where the client is currently at, showing respect for the client, and developing an empathic relationship that demonstrates to the client he or she is being heard (Harris, 2006).

Promoting a Collaborative and Egalitarian Relationship

ACT therapists understand that we all have life struggles with which we wrestle and that increased psychological flexibility may be helpful to the client in his or her path through life, just as it's been helpful to the therapist in his or her struggles in life. Thus, counselors do not approach counseling from a perspective of an expert; instead, the counselor is **collaborative**, develops an **egalitarian relationship**, and shares tools that he or she has used to develop increased psychological flexibility.

> I don't want you to think I've got my life completely in order. It's more as if you're climbing your mountain over there and I'm climbing my mountain over here. It's not as if I've reached the top and I'm having a rest. It's just that from where I am on my mountain, I can see obstacles on your mountain that you can't see. So I can point those out to you, and maybe show you some alternative routes around them. (Harris, 2006, p. 8)

Taking a History

Within the first couple of sessions, ACT counselors will obtain a history regarding the client's current symptoms and ways of being in the world (Harris, 2009). The work of ACT therapists will vary depending upon their theoretical leaning; however, they tend to assess for the following when taking a history:

1. *The Presenting Complaint*: An examination of the presenting complaint including a review of experiential avoidance activities that make the client feel worse.
2. *Initial Values Assessment*: An examination of the client's values, such as those things that bring purpose to the client's life, activities that would bring joy, ways the person would like to grow and change, meaningful relationships, and more.
3. *Life Context/History*: A review of family and social history that includes such things as medical issues, counseling history, family and other important relationships, vocational concerns, financial history, and so forth.
4. *Psychological Inflexibility*: Examining issues such as constant worry about past or future, attachment to rigid rules and beliefs, marked experiential avoidance, attachment to a rigid identity, difficulty identifying thoughts and feelings, and more.
5. *Motivational Factors*: Identifying dreams and desires the client has and how external factors (e.g., the economy) and internal factors (e.g., rigid thinking) prevent a person from being motivated?
6. *Psychological Flexibility and Client Strengths*: Discovering areas in which the client is flexible as per the Hexaflex model and identfiying positive strengths the client has (e.g., affability).

Obtaining Informed Consent and Goal Setting

Following a thorough assessment, the client is informed about what is involved in the ACT process and the fact that there will be a number of experiential and skills exercises in which to participate. The client is also informed that there could be some adverse effects of counseling, such as allowing oneself to experience one's pains and hurts. After being informed about the general process of ACT, treatment goals are developed and an agreement on the number of sessions is decided. Generally, those with less psychological flexibility will entail a longer treatment protocol (e.g., perhaps a year in therapy) (Harris, 2009). Goals are fairly straightforward, focused on managing, not changing, difficult feelings and thoughts, and emphasizing new behaviors that can help a person move toward important values in his or her life.

Psychoeducation

Explaining the Hexaflex model to clients is an important aspect of ACT as the techniques used are directly related to the six processes found on the model (Harris, 2009). After a history has been developed and areas of psychological inflexibility determined, therapists can work with clients on those areas with which they seem to be most struggling. As the therapist addresses these areas, he or she can identify them for the client, explain what purpose they serve, and suggest exercises and homework they can use to become psychologically more flexible.

Using Analogies, Metaphors, Stories, Paradoxes, and Mindfulness

ACT is known for its wealth of exercises, many of which are creative and playful, and most of which address the six areas of psychological flexibility. A number of these use analogies, metaphors, stories, paradoxes, and mindfulness (Ciarrochi & Bailey, 2008; Stewart, et al., 2001; Törneke, 2010). All of these techniques use symbolic language, which tends to be embedded in different neural channels than more traditional talk therapy and can result in significant long-term changes (Riddell, 2016). Here, we define these common approaches to working with clients in ACT. Some of these techniques will also be used in the next section to demonstrate how the six core processes of psychological flexibility are developed.

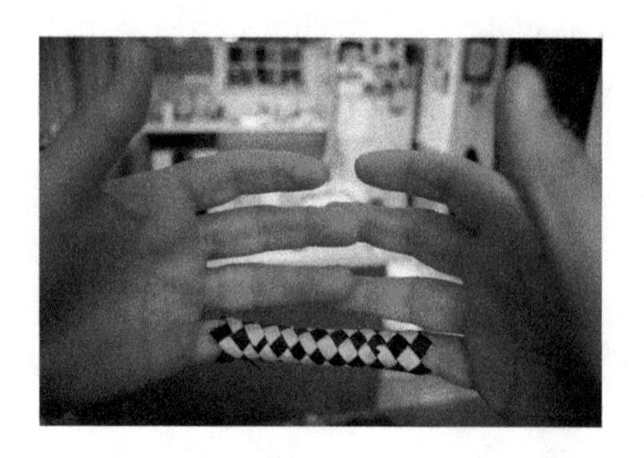

Analogies

An analogy is a direct comparison between two or more things, which on the surface are often unlike one another but relay an important message to the person. For instance, to a client who is fused with the idea that his spouse must change, one might say, "Trying to get your wife to change is like trying to pull your fingers apart in the Chinese finger trap. The more you try to change her, the less likely you will see any results."

Metaphors

A metaphor is applied when comparing an abstract or symbolic thought or image to a situation in an attempt to get a person to understand a concept in new ways. For instance, a counselor might say to a person who has been struggling with anxiety, "Sounds like you're in quicksand." This may help a client become aware of how the struggles with anxiety have been dragging the client deeper into the anxiety (Ciarrochi & Bailey, 2008).

Stories

Stories allow individuals to detach themselves from the direct experience of what they are going through. Such detachment allows a client to understand his or her situation in a new way. For instance, a counselor who is working with a reactive client who has difficulty controlling his emotions may tell a story about a person who could find no peace in his life and decided to become a cloistered monk who chanted most of the day. After spending a few years doing this, he came back to his former life and found that he was able to use what he learned from being cloistered to moderate his reaction to people.

Paradoxes

Since the paradox of ACT is that one should attempt to accept difficult private experiences rather than avoid them, therapists often suggest that clients experience difficult emotions and thoughts rather than evade them. For example, a client who views herself as a victim and harbors resentment toward other people with whom she works may constantly try to act nice toward them to avoid any conflict. This has the result of maintaining the symptoms (feelings of constant resentment and irritability). Her therapist suggests that she "own her resentment" and role-play a conversation with one or two of these individuals. During the role-plays, she allows herself to become angry and resentful, and she suddenly realizes that much of her resentment has to do with her jealousy of these people for what they had accomplished, not a function of how they were treating her.

Mindfulness

Although not meditation, mindfulness is based on the contemplative traditions (e.g., Buddhism) and is a here-and-now practice that allows a person to experience negative emotions without being dominated by them, detach oneself from one's thoughts, and let go of rigid adherence to dogmatic beliefs. In other words, accept self, observe self, and move toward cognitive defusion (Hayes et al., 2012a: Kabat-Zinn, 2003; Ong et al., 2012). For those who have difficulty with the word *mindfulness*, alternative ways of introducing a mindfulness exercise can be used, such as, "Let's do an exercise to help you accept and understand some of the negative feelings you experience." A typical mindfulness exercise might start out in the following manner:

Sit in a comfortable seat.

Close your eyes and take some deep breaths, listening to your breath.

Breathe in, then let it go.

Focus on your breath and become one with it.

As you increasingly feel relaxed, watch your thoughts as they go.

Remember that they are only thoughts, and you are simply observing them.

Exercises Highlighting the Six Core Processes of the Hexaflex Model

The following provides one, short exercise for each of the six processes that go into the development of psychological flexibility. ACT has dozens of exercise one can use in developing defusion, acceptance, contact with the present moment, self-as-context, values, and committed action. It is important to remember that the processes, and the exercises, are interrelated and may reflect more than one of the six processes. As you read about these exercises, consider if any of them are a type of analogy, metaphor, story, paradox, or mindful exercise.

Defusion Exercise

The purpose of defusion exercises are to help clients recognize their thoughts and help them detach from them. Such exercises help clients understand that thoughts need not be an unconscious process, but something one can notice, watch, and/or act upon. Defusion exercises can be traced back to 1916 when English psychologist **Edward Titchener** developed the "milk, milk, milk" exercise (Snyder et al., 2011). After saying the word "milk" for about 45 seconds, Titchener realized that the word became a sound and lost its cognitive association with the physical experience of drinking a cool, white, creamy-tasting liquid. The following exercise can help a person move from a cognitively fused to cognitively defused state:

Counselor: "I know you sometimes have thoughts that are critical and demeaning of your spouse and these thoughts are followed by verbally abusive language. Close your eyes and imagine those thoughts are on a train and you are on a station platform, watching the train and thoughts go by. Can you see those thoughts? As you watch them, realize that those thoughts are separate from you—are something that does not dictate who you are and what you will do."

Exercises such as the one above can be practiced in the office and at home. And when the client begins to have similar thoughts when his or her spouse is present, he or she can practice the exercise in an effort to detach self from the thoughts and lessen the possibility of a verbally abusive reaction to his or her spouse.

Acceptance Exercise

If you remember, acceptance is about being at peace, and accepting one's thoughts, feelings, memories, and experiences in the moment. It is not, however, about resignation. Paradoxically, it is often the first step toward change. Box 6.3 shows a mindfulness exercise that helps a client accept his or her pain and consider movement toward a new life space.

BOX 6.3 MINDFULNESS EXERCISE FOCUSED ON ACCEPTANCE

Counselor: "Close your eyes and let yourself sit comfortably in the chair. Listen to everything that you can hear, everything you can smell, and watch your thoughts go by. Now, let yourself feel all of what you can feel. Breathe in deeply and allow yourself to experience all of your feelings. Don't try to push them away—experience them. As the feelings arise, observe them and know that they are an important message to yourself. Think about what the feeling is telling you and let yourself experience your feelings and what those feelings might mean. As you allow yourself to experience the feelings, remember, that these feelings are an important message to you in your life. Now, in your mind's eye, write down those feelings on a pad of paper. Those feelings can be used at a later point to help you make some choices about what you want to do with your life. Now, slowly relax and think about a pleasant space in your life. Take in some deep breaths, and when you feel ready, open your eyes." (The client might then be given a pad to actually write down those feelings.)

A second example of an acceptance exercise shows a client who had a pet cat named Boots that died a year ago and learns how to accept the pain associated with her death. The client has been avoiding feelings of grief (experiential avoidance). In this example, the counselor hears the client quickly mention Boots, but then change the subject:

Counselor: "When you just mentioned Boots, I think I saw grief in your body for a moment there. Where did you notice it?"

Client: "In my throat and behind my eyes. I just don't want to feel all those feelings when I think about her."

Counselor: "It feels like the feelings are the problem and not the solution."

Client: "They are so intense. Like they will last forever and never go away. I'm afraid to open the flood gates."

Counselor: "Our feelings feel real and permanent, but they are temporary and will ebb and flow within us; we can just observe them when they occur."

Client: [sits quietly, then becomes tearful and cries].

Counselor: [Gives space for client to feel these feelings]

Counselor: "As you experience your feelings, what do you notice in this moment? Where do you feel it in this moment? What name would you give this sensation?"

Acceptance of the grief allows the individual to examine the situation and take appropriate action, if wanted, so that the client can move on with his or her life. Appropriate action will vary based on one's values.

Contact with the Present Moment Exercise

Contact with the present moment has to do with learning how to focus on the moment, not rigidly focus on one's past or future, and learning how to zoom in and zoom out from a narrow to a broad focus. It can be particularly helpful in stopping a client from becoming distracted by upsetting thoughts. The following mindfulness exercise is an example of a counselor who is working with a very distraught client because she is concerned that her partner is going to leave her. Her mind is filled with thoughts of what can or may happen and her distress is palpable. The exercise is intended to help distract her from her thoughts and be in the moment with her body. It helps her stop thinking about the past or future and focus on the present.

Counselor: ". … Your mind's pulling you all over the place. You're being tossed around in a storm of thoughts and feelings and while that's going on, you can't think effectively or act effectively. There's one thing you need to do before anything else: you need to drop an anchor."

Client: "What do you mean?"

Counselor: "Okay. Push your feet hard into the floor. Feel the ground beneath you. Now sit up in your chair and notice how you're sitting. And look around the room and notice what you can see. Notice what you can hear. Notice what you're doing right now—notice that you and I are in this room, talking to each other. Now take a few deep breaths and see if you can breathe down into your feet. And keep them firmly pressed into the floor. And notice how your mind keeps trying to pull you somewhere else and see if you can stay present. Notice the room around you. Notice what we're doing here, right now." (Harris, 2009, p. 167)

Self-As-Context Exercise

Instead of getting caught up in the content of what we do, ACT therapists try to find ways to help clients look at the context of who they are. Here is a story that could be shared with clients who are rigidly attached to certain life roles.

> While working on his farm, a farmer noticed that his old horse was sick. Rather than keeping him, he let the horse go free into the mountains. His neighbors came by and said, "We're so sorry that your horse is gone, you must be very sad," at which point the farmer said, "Perhaps."
>
> A few days later, the horse came back, well again, and brought with him a number of healthy young horses. His neighbors again came by and told him what good fortune he had. His reply was, "Perhaps."
>
> The next day the farmer asked his son to train the new horses, and while doing this, a horse threw him, and the son had a very serious broken leg that resulted in difficulty working. The villagers again bemoaned the farmer's misfortunate, but the farmer again replied, "Perhaps."
>
> A few months later war broke out, but due to his son's difficulty walking, he was deferred from the draft. The villagers told the farmer he and his son must be relieved, at which point the farmer said, "Perhaps."
>
> After the war, the villagers told the farmer he must be concerned that his son could not work as hard as the other young men, due to his difficulty walking. The famer responded, "Perhaps."
>
> As the men returned from war, many of them had mental health issues and PTSD. The villagers told the farmer that he must be happy that his son was not inflicted with these concerns and despite his disability, could still work. The farmer responded," Perhaps."

Values

Learning what one cherishes and those qualities that give meaning to a person's life is critical if a person is to move toward living a life that best match his or her values. But values should not be rule-based; once they become something we *have* to seek, they become burdensome and lose their meaning. The Bull's Eye in Box 6.4, adapted from Dahl and Lundgren (2006), helps people examine how they are living their lives and if they are living out values that are important to them.

BOX 6.4 BULL'S EYE VALUES EXERCISE

Relative to each of the following five domains, write a short statement regarding the type of person you would like to be and how you might develop yourself as you live out your life.

1. *Work/Education* (career, education, place of employment)
2. *Relationships* (partner, children, friends, coworkers, relatives)
3. *Personal Growth* (counseling, spirituality, religion, creativity)
4. *Physical Health* (exercise, diet, mind-body exercises, addressing disease)
5. *Leisure* (avocations, recreation, relaxation, play)

In the following bull's eye, put an X in each area to reflect where you are today, with the bull's eye representing you fully living out your values and the outer circle representing extreme incongruence between how you are living and the values you want to embrace.

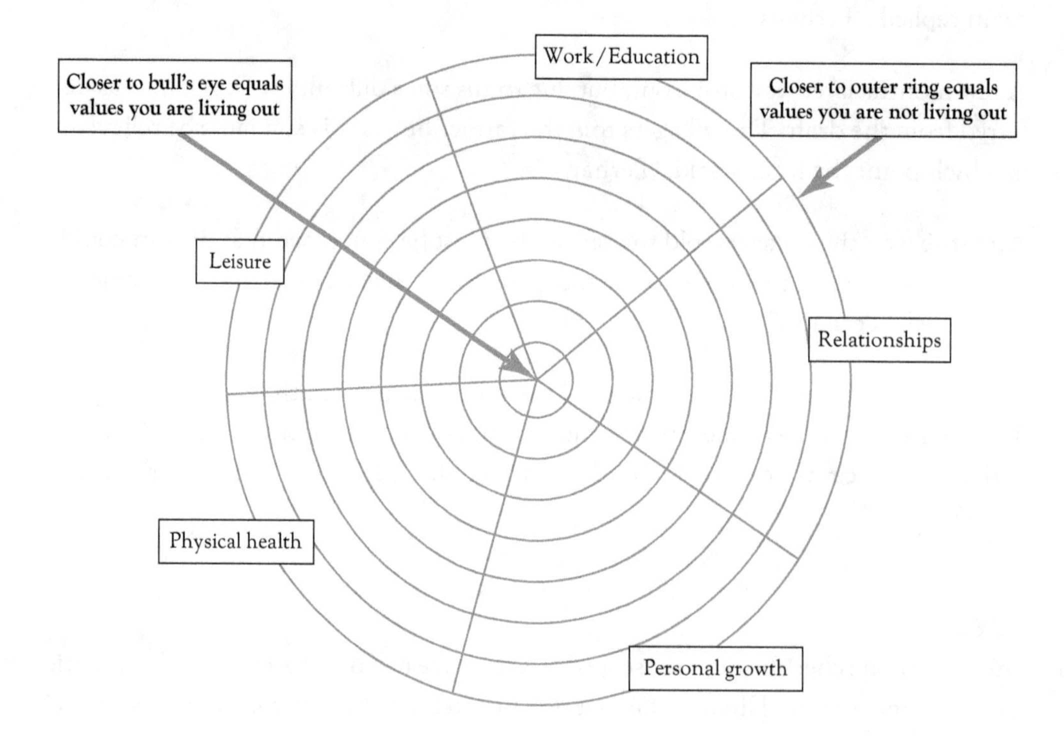

Committed Action

Identifying important values is the first step toward committing oneself toward living those values. Using Box 6.4, here is an exercise that moves one toward living one's values:

1. Identify one or two of the five domains in which you would like to take action.
2. Identify specific values to live out more fully within the chosen domain(s).
3. Develop goals for living out those values.
4. Develop strategies to use in reaching those goals.
5. Take action mindfully.
6. Use "SMART goals" when committing oneself to action:
   a. *Specific:* Identify specific actions to take, such as when and where to take them and what exactly will be occurring.
   b. *Meaningful:* Make sure goals are guided by the individual's values, are meaningful to the person, and not fulfilling someone else's desires.
   c. *Adaptive:* Ensure goals will improve the individual's life in meaningful ways, can help move the person in the direction he or she wants to go, and can be modified if needed.
   d. *Realistic:* Make sure goals are doable, that the individual has the skills to achieve them, and that the amount of time needed to achieve goals are considered.
   e. *Time-framed:* Set dates and times, if possible, to work on achieving goals.

THE COUNSELING PROCESS

The basic therapeutic process of ACT is to work through the six core processes of the Hexaflex model, which allows the client to develop greater psychological flexibility and includes establishing goals toward committed action based on chosen values. The following eight steps describe a general direction of therapy, though movement back and forward between steps can easily be done, based on the client's needs in the moment.

1. *Building the Working Alliance*: Initially, the therapist develops a working alliance with the client by demonstrating compassion, acceptance, respect, and empathy.
2. *Developing a Collaborative and Egalitarian Relationship*: Although the therapist has some specific skills to guide the client along his or her path toward great psychological flexibility, he or she does not have an air of being the "expert." Instead, the therapist develops a collaborative and egalitarian relationship with the client, suggesting certain techniques but being willing to back off if the client seems not ready or opposed to any specific technique.

3. *Taking A History*: Early in the relationship, the therapist takes a history from the client to help understand his or her current level of psychological flexibility and those values deemed important to the client. This includes gathering information about the presenting complaint, doing a values assessment, conducting a life context/history, examining psychological inflexibility, identifying motivational factors, and examining client psychological flexibility and strengths.
4. *Obtaining Informed Consent and Setting Broad Goals*: Here, the therapist obtains informed consent and sets broad goals based on the history that was taken. Goals are straightforward and focused on managing, not changing, difficult feelings and thoughts. They also begin to emphasize new behaviors that can help a person move toward identified values.
5. *Psychoeducation Regarding Psychological Flexibility*: At this point, the therapist explains the Hexaflex model to the client and, in conjunction with the client, identifies areas to address and homework that can be worked upon.
6. *Implementing Exercises to Develop Psychological Flexibility*: Here, exercises that address acceptance, defusion, being in the moment, and self-as-context can be implemented so that the client can begin to develop psychological flexibility.
7. *Clarifying Values and Embracing A Value-Focused Life*: Concurrently, or soon after implementing exercises to develop psychological flexibility, the client can increasingly clarify important values to embrace and work on committed action toward living a value-focused life and maintain psychological flexibility.
8. *Living A Value-Focused Life*: As clients increasingly gain increased psychological flexibility, they are better able to live in the world without being haunted by private experiences that cause distress. They are also better able to accept their life circumstances while making moves toward developing values in sync with their identities. And, they are more adept at living in the world without the aid of counseling.

SOCIAL AND CULTURAL ISSUES

As a context-based theory, ACT allows clients to freely choose their own values, derived from the cultural habits and ways of thinking that are most precious in the client's life. This client-chosen context is, therefore, the aspect of ACT that can enable it to succeed in diverse cultures. As Hayes et al. (2012a) note, "Values work done well is inherently culturally adapted since the client sets the agenda and is the final expert" (p. 325).

ACT can challenge counselors to grow in their own psychological flexibility when the client's values differ vastly from those of the therapist. In these cases, therapists need to adapt their skills and techniques to make them cross-culturally appropriate (e.g., use culturally relevant metaphors and mindfulness techniques). Because counselors themselves are practicing acceptance, defusion, being present, and understanding differing values, they can more effectively work with distressing clients who are different from them (Hayes et al., 2012a).

While ACT has been used cross-culturally, it's applicability with different cultures has rarely been examined. One exception is a study by Woidneck et al. (2012) who conducted a literature search for controlled trials of ACT that reported race or ethnicity of the subjects. Unfortunately, they found that the cultural composition of the subjects was reported in only a small proportion of the studies. Of those that did report cultural composition, ACT was found to be effective, but there was no analysis of differential effects of race or ethnicity on outcomes.

There is strong correspondence between ACT and the central tenets of Buddhism, and it has demonstrated good results when used in a Buddhist Cambodian community in Toronto (Fung, 2014); however, clients who reject Eastern philosophies, such as mindfulness, may have difficulty adopting ACT principles. This is why it is sometimes important to describe techniques in ways that sit comfortably with clients. Instead of using the word *mindfulness*, some might be more comfortable with "Here's a focusing exercise," or "Here's a breathing exercise that you might find helpful."

EFFICACY

Despite being a relatively recent addition to the catalog of psychotherapeutic methods, ACT has been extensively evaluated in a substantial number of controlled studies (Powers et al., 2009), including at least seven meta-analyses (A-Tjak et al., 2015; Bluett et al., 2014; Hacker et al., 2016; Krafft, et al., 2018; Öst, 2014; Powers et al., 2009; Ruiz, 2012). ACT has been found to be more effective than waitlist or treatment-as-usual (TAU) for depression and anxiety (Twohig & Levin, 2017), addiction (Luom et al., 2012), chronic pain (Cosio & Schafer, 2015), obsessive-compulsive disorder (Bluett et al., 2014; Twohig et al., 2010), panic disorder (Meuret et al., trichotillomania (Woods et al., 2006), symptom reduction in borderline personality disorder (Morton et al., 2012), psychosis (Bach et al., 2012; Gaudiano & Herbert, 2006), and a transdiagnostic psychiatric inpatient population (Pinto et al., 2017). ACT has also shown effectiveness in improving the mental health of patients with medical conditions including cancer (Hulbert-Williams et al., 2015; Rost et al., 2012), epilepsy (Lundgren et al., 2006), and tinnitus (Hesser et al., 2012).

In addition to traditional individual and group methods of treatment, ACT has demonstrated effectiveness in abbreviated format (e.g., Bach et al., 2012; Ivanova et al., 2015; Kohtala, et al., 2017), through Internet-based delivery (Fiorillo et al., , 2017; Hesser et al., 2012; Lappalainen et al., 2014), delivered within a workshop (Stewart et al., 2016), and through bibliotherapy (Jeffcoat & Hayes, 2012; Muto et al., 2011).

Although meta-analyses have generally shown a significant improvement in outcomes with ACT when compared with waitlist, psychological placebo, or TAU (A-Tjak et al., 2015; Bluett et al., 2014; Hacker et al., 2016; Öst, 2017; Powers et al., 2009), when compared with an active control condition, such as cognitive-behavioral therapy (CBT), the results become less clear. Most studies have found negligible differences in effectiveness between ACT and other therapies (A-Tjak et al., 2015; Bluett et al., 2014; Hacker et al., 2016; Öst, 2014; Powers et al.,

2009). But Krafft et al. (2018) found improved outcomes with ACT compared with educational interventions in reducing stigma toward mental illness. Ruiz (2012) also found superior results with ACT compared with CBT, and that the improvements tend to be directly related to the theoretical processes found in ACT (e.g., more cognitive defusion and less experiential avoidance) while CBT did not show improvement based on its theoretical processes (e.g., reduction in automatic thoughts).

SUMMARY

ACT is considered a third-wave cognitive behavioral therapy, which rejects the mechanistic approach of first-wave behaviorism and second-wave cognitive behavioral approaches. Whereas first- and second-wave approaches assume the client has adopted maladaptive behaviors and/or thoughts that need to be replaced, third-wave approaches suggest that thoughts, feelings, and memories are not inherently problematic and that context defines how they are experienced. This new approach incorporates several Eastern approaches, such as spirituality and mindfulness, in helping an individual accept who they are and change the context of their experiences.

ACT was developed by Steven C. Hayes, who was inspired by B. F. Skinner and influenced by Irving Kessler, both of whom modeled how behaviorism could be incorporated into clinical practice. Hayes was also influenced by individuals who were involved in the counterculture movement and who practiced Eastern philosophies, such as D. T. Suzuki, Alan Watts, and Swami Kriyananda. After experiencing panic attacks, Hayes realized that trying to control the attacks cognitively just led him to focus on them more and made the condition worse. Thus, he and his doctoral student, Rober D. Zettle, began to examine how language, verbal behavior, and rule-governed behavior impacts clinical issues. In particular, he began to look at how one can distance oneself from one's thoughts and beliefs. Slowly, Hayes began to develop relational frame theory (RFT), which took a behavioral and contextual approach to understanding language and cognition, and the place that relational frames have in developing psychological inflexibility and preventing people from psychological flexibility and symptom relief.

RFT suggests that private events, sometimes called psychological events (the unique things people do, think, or feel), are developed through derived stimulus relationships. As increasing numbers of stimuli become associated with one another, through a process called combinatorial entailment, RFT hypothesizes that individuals create unique webs of relational frames from which they experience the world.

Unique relational frames are the basis for each person's private language, which includes how one thinks, daydreams, and visualizes, collectively called cognition, and one's public language, which includes speaking talking, writing, miming, and so forth. Since language is based on unique relational frames that are reinforced in arbitrary ways, language can be helpful or harmful. For instance, private language can help us understand others and the world, and public language can be used to show empathy and advocate for important causes.

Private and public language, however, can also cause pain, such as when public language is used to lie, bully, respond in sexist and discriminatory ways, and when private language is used to judge ourselves, imagine negative things from the past, think about things in the future that might cause anxiety, or used to develop rules about how we should live our lives that constrict behaviors. Because language can be harmful, our mind is not always our friend and we sometimes develop language usage that results in psychological inflexibility, which was described as six processes: cognitive fusion, experiential avoidance, being stuck in the past or the future, attachment to a conceptualized self, lack of clarity of values, and unworkable action.

It was noted that one of the main purposes of ACT was to develop psychological flexibility as symbolized by the Hexaflex model, which involves defusion (watch what you're thinking), acceptance (open up), contact with the present moment (be here now), self-as-context (pure awareness), values (know what matters), and committed action (do what it takes). Psychological flexibility helps individuals learn how to Accept and be present with their painful thoughts, feelings, and memories; Choose a valued direction in life; and Take action so they can live a more meaningful and less symptomatic life.

ACT uses a number of techniques to develop psychological flexibility and work toward committed action, including compassion, acceptance, respect, and empathy, all important to building a working alliance; the importance of promoting a collaborative and egalitarian relationship; taking a history; obtaining informed consent and goal setting; psychoeducation; using analogies, metaphors, stories, paradoxes, and mindfulness; and any of a variety of exercises highlighting the six core processes of the Hexaflex mode.

The therapeutic process of ACT can be seen through eight steps: (1) building the working alliance, (2) developing a collaborative and egalitarian relationship, (3) taking a history, (4) obtaining informed consent and setting broad goals, (5) psychoeducation regarding the Hexaflex model, (6) implementing exercises to develop psychological flexibility, (7) clarifying values and embracing a value-focused life, and (8) living a value-focused life.

Since ACT allows clients to freely choose their own values, which are derived from the cultural habits and ways of thinking that are most important in the client's life, ACT can be used with diverse cultures. ACT therapists need to adapt their skills and techniques to ensure that they are culturally appropriate, as not all the techniques would be readily accepted by all clients (e.g., mindfulness). ACT has had little cross-cultural research, and more is needed to show its efficacy with different groups.

Despite its relatively young age, ACT has shown efficacy treating a wide range of conditions. It has also shown efficacy in both individual and group formats, in abbreviated form, through Internet-based delivery, and through bibliotherapy. Although meta-analyses have shown a significant improvement in outcomes when compared with waitlist, psychological placebo, or treatment-as-usual (TAU), when compared with an active control condition such as cognitive-behavioral therapy (CBT), the results become less clear.

KEY WORDS AND NAMES

Acceptance (open up)
Analogies
Arbitrary stimuli
Attachment to a conceptualized self
Beck, A.
Being stuck in the past or future
Butcher, A.
Cognition
Cognitive fusion
Collaborative and egalitarian relationship
Combinatorial entailment
Committed action (do what it takes)
Compassion, acceptance, respect, and empathy
Comprehensive distancing
Contact with the present moment (be here now)
Defusion (watch what you're thinking)
Derived stimulus relationship
Dialectical behavior therapy
Ellis, A.
Exercises highlighting the six core processes of the Hexaflex model
Experiential avoidance
First- and second-wave cognitive behavioral approaches
Flexible attention to the present moment
Functional contextual theory
Goal-focused life
Hayes, S. C.
Hexaflex model
Kessler, I.
Kriyananda, Swami
Lack of clarity of values
Metaphors
Mind
Mindfulness
Mindfulness-based therapies
Obtaining informed consent and goal setting
Paradoexes
Private events
Private experiences
Private language
Psychoeducation
Psychological events
Psychological flexibility
Psychological inflexibility
Public language
Relational frame
Relational frame theory (RFT)
Second wave of behavioral therapies
Self-as-context (pure awareness)
Skinner, B. F.
Stories
Suzuki, D. T.
Taking a history
Third-wave cognitive behavioral therapy
Titchener, E.
Unworkable action
Value-focused life
Values (know what matters)
Watts, A.
Zettle, R. D.

REFERENCES

A-Tjak, J. G. L., Davis, M. L., Morina, N., Powers, M. B., Smits, J. A. J., & Emmelkamp, P. M. G. (2015). A meta-analysis of the efficacy of acceptance and commitment therapy for clinically relevant mental and physical health problems. *Psychotherapy and Psychosomatics, 84*(1), 30–36. https://doi.org/10.1159/000365764

Bach, P., Hayes, S., & Gallop, R. (2012). Long-term effects of brief acceptance and commitment therapy for psychosis. *Behavior Modification, 36*(2), 165–181. https://doi.org/10.1177/0145445511427193

Bandura, A. (1977). Self-efficacy: Toward a unifying theory of behavioral change. *Psychological review, 84*(2), 191–215. https://doi.org/10.1037/0033-295X.84.2.191

Barnes-Holmes, Y., Hussey, I., McEnteggart, C., Barnes-Holmes, D., & Foody, M. (2016). Scientific ambition: The relationship between relational frame theory and middle-level terms in acceptance and commitment therapy. In R. D. Zettle, S. C. Hayes, D. Barnes-Holmes, & A. Biglan (Eds.), *The Wiley handbook of contextual behavioral science* (pp. 365–382). John Wiley & Sons.

Batten, S. V., & Ciarrochi, J. V. (2015). *Acceptance and commitment therapy.* In E. Neukrug (Ed.), *The SAGE encyclopedia of theory in counseling and psychotherapy* (Vol. 1, pp. 7–10). SAGE Publications.

Blackledge, J. T., & Drake, C. E. (2013). Acceptance and commitment therapy: Empirical and theoretical considerations. In S. Dymond & B. Roche (Eds.), *Advances in relational frame theory: Research & application* (pp. 219–252). New Harbinger.

Bluett, E. J., Homan, K. J., Morrison, K. L., Levin, M. E., & Twohig, M. P. (2014). Acceptance and commitment therapy for anxiety and OCD spectrum disorders: An empirical review. *Journal of Anxiety Disorders, 28*(6), 612–624. https://doi.org/10.1016/j.janxdis.2014.06.008

Christensen, A., Dimidjian, S., & Martell, C. R. (2015). Integrative behavioral couple therapy. In A. S. Gurman, J. L. Lebow, & D. K. Snyder (Eds.), *Clinical handbook of couple therapy* (5th ed., pp. 61–94). Guilford Press.

Ciarrochi, J. V., & Bailey, A. (2008). *A CBT practitioner's guide to ACT: How to bridge the gap between cognitive behavioral therapy & acceptance & commitment therapy.* New Harbinger.

Cloud, J. (2006). Happiness isn't normal. *Time, 167*, 58–67.

Cosio, D., & Schafer, T. (2015). Implementing an acceptance and commitment therapy group protocol with veterans using VA's stepped care model of pain management. *Journal of Behavioral Medicine, 38*(6), 984–997. https://doi.org/10.1007/s10865-015-9647-0

Dahl, J., & Lundgren, T. (2006). *Living beyond your pain: Using acceptance and commitment therapy to ease chronic pain.* New Harbinger.

Dewane, C. J. (2008). The ABCs of ACT: Acceptance and commitment therapy. *Social Work Today, 8.* https://www.socialworktoday.com/archive/090208p36.shtml

Fiorillo, D., McLean, C., Pistorello, J., Hayes, S. C., & Follette, V. M. (2017). Evaluation of a web-based acceptance and commitment therapy program for women with trauma-related problems: A pilot study. *Journal of Contextual Behavioral Science, 6*(1), 104–113. http://dx.doi.org/10.1016/j.jcbs.2016.11.003

Fox, E. (2004–2020). An introduction to relational frame theory. https://foxylearning.com/tutorials/rft

Fung, K. (2014). Acceptance and commitment therapy: Western adoption of Buddhist tenets? *Transcultural Psychiatry, 52*(4), 561–576. https://doi.org/10.1177/136346151453754

Gaudiano, B. A., & Herbert, J. D. (2006). Acute treatment of inpatients with psychotic symptoms using acceptance and commitment therapy: Pilot results. *Behaviour Research and Therapy, 44*(3), 415–437. http://dx.doi.org/10.1016/j.brat.2005.02.007

Gross, A. C., & Fox, E. J. (2009). Relational frame theory: An overview of the controversy. *The Analysis of Verbal Behavior, 25*(1), 87–98. https://doi.org/10.1007/BF03393073

Hacker, T., Stone, P., & MacBeth, A. (2016). Acceptance and commitment therapy—Do we know enough? Cumulative and sequential meta-analyses of randomized controlled trials. *Journal of Affective Disorders, 190*, 551–565. https://doi.org/10.1016/j.jad.2015.10.053

Harris, R. (2006). Embracing your demons: An overview of acceptance and commitment therapy. *Psychotherapy in Australia*, 12(4), 2–8.

Harris, R. (2009). *ACT made simple: An easy-to-read primer on acceptance and commitment therapy.* New Harbinger.

Harris, R. (2015). *Values vs. goals.* https://www.youtube.com/watch?v=T-lRbuy4XtA

Hayes, S. C. (2004). Acceptance and commitment therapy, relational frame theory, and the third wave of behavioral and cognitive therapies. *Behavior Therapy, 35*(4), 639–665. https://doi.org/10.1016/S0005-7894(04)80013-3

Hayes, S. C. (2008). *Career influences and a brief intellectual autobiography.* http://www.stevenchayes.com/about/career-influences-and-a-brief-intellectual-autobiography/

Hayes, S. C. (2016, January 23). *Psychological flexibility: How love turns pain into purpose.* https://youtu.be/o79_gmO5ppg

Hayes, S. C., & Brownstein, A. J. (1985). *Verbal behavior, equivalence classes, and rules: New definitions, data, and directions.* Paper presented at the Annual meeting of the Association for Behavior Analysis, Columbus, OH. https://contextualscience.org/publications/hayes_brownstein_1985

Hayes, S. C., Strosahl, K. D., & Wilson, K. G. (2012a). *Acceptance and commitment therapy: The process and practice of mindful change* (2nd ed.). Guilford Press.

Hayes, S. C., Pistorello, J., & Levin, M. E. (2012b). Acceptance and commitment therapy as a unified model of behavior change. *The Counseling Psychologist, 40*(7), 976–1002. https://doi.org/10.1177/0011000012460836

Hayes, S. C., Barnes-Holmes, D., & Roche, B. (2001). Relational frame theory: A précis. In S. C. Hayes, D. Barnes-Holmes, & B. Roche (Eds.), *Relational frame theory: A post-Skinnerian account of human language and cognition* (pp. 141–154). Springer.

Hayes, S. C., Wilson, K. G., Gifford, E. V., Follette, V. M., & Strosahl, K. (1996). Experiential avoidance and behavioral disorders: A functional dimensional approach to diagnosis and treatment. *Journal of Consulting and Clinical Psychology, 64*(6), 1152–1168. http://dx.doi.org/10.1037/0022-006X.64.6.115

Hayes, S. C., Masuda, A., Bissett, R., Luoma, J., & Guerrero, L. F. (2004a). DBT, FAP, and ACT: How empirically oriented are the new behavior therapy technologies? *Behavior Therapy, 35*(1), 35–54. https://doi.org/10.1016/S0005-7894(04)80003-0

Hayes, S. C., Stroshal, K. D., Buntinh, K., Twohig, M., & Wilson, K. (2004b). What is acceptance and commitment therapy. In S. C. Hayes & K. D. Strosahl (Eds.), *A practical guide to acceptance and commitment therapy* (pp. 1–30). Springer.

Hayes, S. C., Luoma, J. B., Bond, F. W., Masuda, A., & Lillis, J. (2006). Acceptance and commitment therapy: Model, processes and outcomes. *Behaviour Research and Therapy, 44*(1), 1–25. https://doi.org/10.1016/j.brat.2005.06.006

Hesser, H., Gustafsson, T., Lundén, C., Henrikson, O., Fattahi, K., Johnsson, E., … Kaldo, V. (2012). A randomized controlled trial of internet-delivered cognitive behavior therapy and acceptance and commitment therapy in the treatment of tinnitus. *Journal of Consulting and Clinical Psychology, 80*(4), 649–661. https://doi.org/10.1037/a0027021

Hulbert-Williams, N. J., Storey, L., & Wilson, K. G. (2015). Psychological interventions for patients with cancer: Psychological flexibility and the potential utility of acceptance and commitment therapy. *European Journal of Cancer Care, 24*(1), 15–27. https://doi.org/10.1111/ecc.12223

Ivanova, E., Jensen, D., Cassoff, J., Gu, F., & Knäuper, B. (2015). Acceptance and commitment therapy improves exercise tolerance in sedentary women. *Medicine & Science in Sports & Exercise, 47*(6), 1251–1258. http://dx.doi.org/10.1249/MSS.0000000000000536

Jeffcoat, T., & Hayes, S. C. (2012). A randomized trial of ACT bibliotherapy on the mental health of K–12 teachers and staff. *Behaviour Research and Therapy, 50*(9), 571–579. http://dx.doi.org/10.1016/j.brat.2012.05.008

Kabat-Zinn, J. (2003). Mindfulness-based interventions in context: Past, present, and future. *Clinical Psychology: Science and Practice, 10*(2), 144–156. https://doi.org/10.1093/clipsy/bpg016

Kohlenberg, R. J., & Tsai, M. (1991). *Functional analytic psychotherapy: Creating intense and curative therapeutic relationships.* Plenum.

Kohtala, A., Muotka, J., & Lappalainen, R. (2017). What happens after five years?: The long-term effects of a four-session acceptance and commitment therapy delivered by student therapists for depressive symptoms. *Journal of Contextual Behavioral Science,* 6(2), 230–238. http://dx.doi.org/10.1016/j.jcbs.2017.03.003

Krafft, J., Ferrell, J., Levin, M. E., & Twohig, M. P. (2018). Psychological inflexibility and stigma: A meta-analytic review. *Journal of Contextual Behavioral Science, 7,* 15–28. https://doi.org/10.1016/j.jcbs.2017.11.002

Lappalainen, P., Granlund, A., Siltanen, S., Ahonen, S., Vitikainen, M., Tolvanen, A., & Lappalainen, R. (2014). ACT internet-based vs. face-to-face? A randomized controlled trial of two ways to deliver acceptance and commitment therapy for depressive symptoms: An 18-month follow-up. *Behaviour Research and Therapy, 61,* 43–54. http://doi.org/10.1016/j.brat.2014.07.006

Lennon, J. (1980). *Beautiful boy.* https://www.youtube.com/watch?v=Lt3IOdDE5iA

Linehan, M. (1993). *Cognitive-behavioral treatment of borderline personality disorder.* Guilford press.

Lundgren, T., Dahl, J., Melin, L., & Kies, B. (2006). Evaluation of acceptance and commitment therapy for drug refractory epilepsy: A randomized controlled trial in South Africa—a pilot study. *Epilepsia,* 47(12), 2173–2179. https://doi.org/10.1111/j.1528-1167.2006.00892.x

Luoma, J. B., Kohlenberg, B. S., Hayes, S. C., & Fletcher, L. (2012). Slow and steady wins the race: A randomized clinical trial of acceptance and commitment therapy targeting shame in substance use disorders. *Journal of Consulting and Clinical Psychology, 80*(1), 43–53. http://dx.doi.org/10.1037/a0026070

Meuret, A. E., Twohig, M. P., Rosenfield, D., Hayes, S. C., & Craske, M. G. (2012). Brief acceptance and commitment therapy and exposure for panic disorder: A pilot study. *Cognitive and Behavioral Practice, 19*(4), 606–618. https://doi.org/10.1016/j.cbpra.2012.05.004

Morton, J., Snowdon, S., Gopold, M., & Guymer, E. (2012). Acceptance and commitment therapy group treatment for symptoms of borderline personality disorder: A public sector pilot study. *Cognitive and Behavioral Practice, 19*(4), 527–544. https://doi.org/10.1016/j.cbpra.2012.03.005

Muto, T., Hayes, S. C., & Jeffcoat, T. (2011). The effectiveness of acceptance and commitment therapy bibliotherapy for enhancing the psychological health of Japanese college students living abroad. *Behavior Therapy, 42*(2), 323–335. https://doi.org/10.1016/j.beth.2010.08.009

Neal-McFall, C. W. (2015). Acceptance and commitment group therapy. In E. Neukrug (Ed.), *The SAGE encyclopedia of theory in counseling and psychotherapy* (Vol. 1, pp. 5–7). SAGE Publications.

Ong, J. C., Ulmer, C. S., & Manber, R. (2012). Improving sleep with mindfulness and acceptance: A metacognitive model of insomnia. *Behaviour Research and Therapy, 50*(11), 651–660. https://doi.org/10.1016/j.brat.2012.08.001

Öst, L.-G. (2014). The efficacy of acceptance and commitment therapy: An updated systematic review and meta-analysis. *Behaviour Research and Therapy, 61,* 105–121. https://doi.org/10.1016/j.brat.2014.07.018

Öst, L.-G. (2017). Rebuttal of Atkins et al. (2017). Critique of the Öst (2014) meta-analysis of ACT. *Behaviour Research and Therapy, 97,* 273–281. https://doi.org/10.1016/j.brat.2017.08.008

Pinto, R. A., Kienhuis, M., Slevison, M., Chester, A., Sloss, A., & Yap, K. (2017). The effectiveness of an outpatient acceptance and commitment therapy group programme for a transdiagnostic population. *Clinical Psychologist, 21*(1), 33–43. https://doi.org/10.1111/cp.12057

Podina, I. R., & David, D. (2017). Acceptance and commitment therapy. In A. Vernon & K. A. Doyle (Eds.), *Cognitive behavior therapies: A guidebook for practitioners* (pp. 177–208). American Counseling Association.

Powers, M. B., Zum Vörde Sive Vörding, M. B., & Emmelkamp, P. M. G. (2009). Acceptance and commitment therapy: A meta-analytic review. *Psychotherapy and Psychosomatics, 78*(2), 73–80. https://doi.org/10.1159/000190790

Riddell, P. (2016). Metaphor, simile, analogy and the brain. *Changing English: Studies in culture and education, 23*(4), 363–374. https://doi.org/10.1080/1358684X.2016.1228443

Rost, A. D., Wilson, K., Buchanan, E., Hildebrandt, M. J., & Mutch, D. (2012). Improving psychological adjustment among late-stage ovarian cancer patients: Examining the role of avoidance in treatment. *Cognitive and Behavioral Practice, 19*(4), 508–517. https://doi.org/10.1016/j.cbpra.2012.01.003

Ruiz, F. J. (2012). Acceptance and commitment therapy versus traditional cognitive behavioral therapy: A systematic review and meta-analysis of current empirical evidence. *International Journal of Psychology and Psychological Therapy, 12*(3), 333–358.

Segal, Z. V., Williams, J. M. G., & Teasdale, J. D. (2013). *Mindfulness-based cognitive therapy for depression* (2nd ed.). Guilford Press.

Skinner, B. F. (1957). *Verbal behavior.* Appleton-Century-Crofts.

Snyder, K., Lambert, J., & Twohig, M. P. (2011). Defusion: A behavior-analytic strategy for addressing private events. *Behavior Analysis in Practice, 4*(2), 4–13. https://doi.org/10.1007/BF0339177

Steven C. Hayes Ph.D. (2020). *Psychology Today.* https://www.psychologytoday.com/us/experts/steven-c-hayes-phd

Stewart, C., G. White, R., Ebert, B., Mays, I., Nardozzi, J., & Bockarie, H. (2016). A preliminary evaluation of acceptance and commitment therapy (ACT) training in Sierra Leone. *Journal of Contextual Behavioral Science, 5*(1), 16–22. https://doi.org/10.1016/j.jcbs.2016.01.001

Stewart, I., Barnes-Holmes, D., Hayes, S. C., & Lipkens, R. (2001). Relations among relations: Analogies, metaphors, and stories. In S. C. Hayes, D. Barnes-Holmes, & B. Roche (Eds.), *Relational frame theory: A post-Skinnerian account of human language and cognition* (pp. 73–86). Springer.

Törneke, N. (2010). *Learning RFT: An introduction to relational frame theory and its clinical application.* Context Press.

Törneke, N., Luciano, C., & Salas, S. V. (2008). Rule-governed behavior and psychological problems. *International Journal of Psychology and Psychological Therapy, 8*(2), 141–156.

Twohig, M. P., Hayes, S. C., Plumb, J. C., Pruitt, L. D., Collins, A. B., Hazlett-Stevens, H., & Woidneck, M. R. (2010). A randomized clinical trial of acceptance and commitment therapy versus progressive relaxation training for obsessive-compulsive disorder. *Journal of Consulting and Clinical Psychology, 78*(5), 705–716. http://dx.doi.org/10.1037/a002050

Twohig, M. P., & Levin, M. E. (2017). Acceptance and commitment therapy as a treatment for anxiety and depression: A review. *Psychiatric Clinics of North America, 40*(4), 751–770. doi:10.1016/j.psc.2017.08.009

Wampold, B. E., & Imel, Z. E. (2015). *The great psychotherapy debate: The evidence for what makes psychotherapy work* (2nd ed.). Routledge.

Woidneck, M. R., Pratt, K. M., Gundy, J. M., Nelson, C. R., & Twohig, M. P. (2012). Exploring cultural competence in acceptance and commitment therapy outcomes. *Professional Psychology: Research and Practice, 43,* 227–233. https://doi.org/10.1037/a0026235

Woods, D. W., Wetterneck, C. T., & Flessner, C. A. (2006). A controlled evaluation of acceptance and commitment therapy plus habit reversal for trichotillomania. *Behaviour Research and Therapy, 44*(5), 639–656. https://doi.org/10.1016/j.brat.2005.05.006

Zettle, R. D. (2011). The evolution of a contextual approach to therapy: From comprehensive distancing to ACT. *International Journal of Behavioral Consultation and Therapy, 7*(1), 76–82. http://dx.doi.org/10.1037/h0100929

CASE STUDY: JAKE'S ENCOUNTER WITH AN ACCEPTANCE AND COMMITMENT THERAPIST

(Please read about the Millers in Appendix I prior to reading this case study)

As Jake pulled into the parking lot of Waterside Psychotherapy, he began wondering whether making an appointment to see yet another therapist was wise or not. He had seen a couple of therapists over the last year or so and had some temporary relief from his anxiety; however, he still suffered from intense periods of anxiety related to his family and their safety. Because he was concerned about traffic, Jake arrived 45 minutes early for his appointment, but did not want to sit in the waiting room that long. As he waited in his car, he sized up the building. Right off, it was obvious it used to be someone's home because it was situated on the main road into a residential neighborhood and had what appeared to be homes on either side of it. He began to wonder what type of therapist would work in a repurposed house, which only intensified his debate about the wisdom of seeing yet another therapist.

After what seemed like hours, Jake finally climbed out of his car and entered the building. The reception area was on the small side, neatly decorated with a couple cushioned couches, some armchairs, and one of those decorative indoor waterfalls. After completing the initial paperwork, Jake tried to settle in to wait for his therapist, Mildred Jones, to appear, but he had a difficult time sitting still. After what seemed like another hour, a diminutive older woman entered the waiting room, approached him, and said, "Mr. Miller, my name is Ms. Mildred Jones, please feel free to call me Mildred, or Ms. Jones, whatever you feel comfortable with." Now he really wasn't sure whether this had been a good idea; he wondered how this tiny, kind-looking older woman could possibly relate to what he was going through.

As Jake settled into another cushioned couch inside of Mildred's office, he took in the rest of the office. It was small, with a recliner in one corner, the couch against one wall, Mildred's cluttered desk in another corner near the only window in the room, and a large overstuffed bookcase opposite the couch. As Mildred spun her desk chair around to face Jake, she asked, "What brings you in today, Jake?"

Jake's response was almost robot-like as he suddenly couldn't help reciting everything he had been through. "Well, I'm just anxious and angry all of the time lately. It all started about a year ago when Luke, my son, and Celia, my daughter, were playing in my car and it accidentally rolled into the street. You see, I had a similar incident with my sister, Justine, when I was about my son's age and it resulted in her having serious cognitive impairment. Well, it's kind of like I'm stressed and angry all the time now. It's affecting everything I do. I am constantly on edge, always worried about making sure my kids are safe, having flashbacks about the accident with my sister, and not getting along with my wife, Angela. I'm up half the night worrying about things and making sure the doors are locked and the kids are safe at sleep. I even think it's impacted my performance at work. I've taken some Xanax and seen a couple of counselors, but it hasn't seemed to help much. Honestly, I think if only the kids would listen to me more and Angela would homeschool the kids, everything would be alright." Jake continued to talk, sometimes almost rambling, as Mildred listened, showed compassion and respect, and was empathic.

After Jake spoke for nearly 30 minutes, Mildred took a deep breath, a breath that was almost reassuring to Jake—as if she was encouraging Jake to "slow down." Jake settled in his chair, and Mildred looked at him, and said, "You know, Jake, this is a pretty complicated and involved story you're telling me, and I'd like to understand it fully. I hope that we can jointly work on solving some of this so you and your family can feel better. To help us both understand exactly what's going on, what about I get some information from you. Does that seem okay with you?" Jake was already feeling comfortable with Mildred, despite his early doubts, and said, "Sure."

At this point Mildred began collecting a lot of information so she could understand the breadth and depth of Jake's situation. It included such things as the full nature of the presenting problem, values that are important in Jake's life, when and how symptoms arise, how motivated Jake seemed to work in therapy, and questions that sought to understand Jake's strengths and his level of psychological flexibility.

At the end of the session, Mildred said, "You know, here's my take on your situation. First, I hear how much you love your wife and children, and how important it is for you to have a loving family that communicates well with one another. I can see how your history has brought you to the point that it is very difficult for you to do anything but what you are currently doing to make the situation better. This includes becoming very anxious and upset when your children and your wife don't listen to you about safety issues. It seems to me that you are very motivated to do something in therapy, but you are just a bit lost about what to do. I think you are pretty wed to trying to take control of your anxiety and trying to enforce certain behaviors on your family. However, I'm hoping that after we talk for a while, you'll see that what you're doing is not working."

Jake listened intensely, thinking that she was right on target with everything she was saying. "You know, our session today is about over, but I think I have some ideas about how I might be able to work with you. How about we talk about some of these things next week. But, perhaps, between this week and next week, if you feel comfortable, you can try something for me. You know the old saying, 'a rolling stone gathers no moss,' I think you're kind of a rolling stone right now, rolling over everything in your life. I'm wondering if you can slow down a bit and instead of reacting as strongly as you are, make a few notes about your reactions when you feel strongly. So, when you're about to have a strong reaction to the kids or to Angela, make some notes about your thoughts rather than just reacting to your thoughts, kind of like you're observing yourself. Do you think you can do this?" Jake thought about it for a moment and then agreed he could do that. "Okay, it's a deal," said Mildred. "Do that for a week, and the next time we meet we will talk about how that went, and then I'm going to introduce some other ideas I have for you."

A week later, Jake came back to see Mildred. She warmly invited him into her office, and asked, "How'd things go last week?" "You know," Jake replied, "I think a little better. Believe it or not, thinking about what's going on and writing down my thoughts seemed to reduce some of my anxiety and frustration a tiny bit."

"That's great, and it leads into what I want to talk about with you. You see, I practice what is called acceptance and commitment therapy, or ACT. With ACT, we believe that people often get caught up in a certain way of thinking, talking, and responding that is just not so helpful for them. We believe it's kind of a style people develop over years of living a certain way. Sometimes, it's important for a person to take a step back and begin to practice some new ways of responding—or even new ways of not responding. And, perhaps most importantly, I hope these new ways will help you gain what you really want—a loving family that can communicate well with one another. But before we move any further, does this make sense to you?"

Jake said it did make sense, and Mildred continued. "You're an engineer, and I would guess you like to understand models or theories of how things work, so I'm going to show you something called the Hexaflex model and explain how we use this in therapy." Mildred explained the model, and after she finished, asked, "What do you think?" "Well," said Jake, "It's a little bit out there, but also interesting. I think I'm willing to try some of it."

"You know," said Mildred, "you already did when I asked to observe your thoughts. That was a type of cognitive defusion. And, if I must say, I think it did help a bit. I have a bunch of other things we can do—around acceptance, living in the present, how you identify who you are, and reaching your goals based on your values that you already identified as important to you. What do you think?" "Let's go for it," Jake answered. At that point, Mildred obtained informed consent about the process of therapy and the real work began.

Over the next few months, Jake worked on addressing his anxiety, frustration, and anger in a number of ways. He became more accepting of his anxiety, frustration, and anger. Lived more in the present (thought less about the situation with Justine and worried less about the future). He began to observe his thoughts when he would begin to become frustrated, which allowed him to be less reactive in his life, and he learned how his role as father and engineer sometimes locked him into feeling as if he had to respond in a controlling, all-knowing way. As he became more accepting of himself, less reactive, and less caught up in acting in a role, things began to settle down in his home and many of his symptoms lessened. Soon, Mildred encouraged Jake to be a bit more playful with the kids and romantic with Angela, which Jake quickly embraced since this was what he had wanted all along.

The work took time, and Jake was not always perfect in the way he responded. But clearly over time he became a better father, a more loving husband, a more focused engineer who enjoyed his work more, and a more hopeful human being.

QUESTIONS FOR YOU TO PONDER

1. During the first session Mildred spent a fair amount of time gathering information from Jake. How does this inform ACT therapy? Would you feel comfortable doing an intake such as this?
2. How does Mildred show that she is collaborative and wants to build a relationship with Jake?
3. How did Mildred use psychoeducation with Jake and what purpose did it serve?
4. Can you explain how experiential avoidance has actually made Jake's symptoms worse?
5. Early on, Mildred uses a metaphor, "A rolling stone gathers no moss," to address Jake's psychological inflexibility. How comfortable would you be in using metaphors, analogies, and similar techniques? Do you think that using a metaphor was helpful?
6. What signs of cognitive fusion can you identify that apply to Jake?
7. What signs of "self-as-content" can you identify that apply to Jake?
8. A large part of what Jake will be doing is accepting himself and the anxiety and frustration he feels. How can this help Jake move to a new way of being that is more in line with his values?
9. What other techniques do you believe could be employed with Jake that are in line with the ACT process of therapy?
10. What do you think is Jake's prognosis?
11. How effective do you believe ACT would be with Jake's children? How about with Angela?
12. Can you identify aspects of your life in which you exhibit psychological inflexibility related to cognitive fusion, experiential avoidance, being stuck in the past or the future, attachment to a conceptualized self, lack of clarity of values, or unworkable action? Is there anything you can do to move toward more psychological flexibility?

Credits

7

Motivational Interviewing (MI)

Tony Dice, Betsy Zimmerman, and Rawn Boulden

LEARNING OUTCOMES

- To learn about the creators of motivational interviewing (MI), William Miller and Stephen Rollnick, and the history of its development.
- To review the existential-humanistic, postmodern, and cognitive behavioral underpinnings of MI and the non-theoretical alignment MI has with other theories.
- To learn key concepts of motivational interviewing, including motivation, the MI Spirit (compassion, collaboration, acceptance, and evocation), ambivalence, change talk, avoiding confrontation, and FRAMES (Feedback, Responsibility, Advice, Menu of options, Empathy, and Self-efficacy).
- To become familiar with techniques often used in MI, including assessing importance, confidence, and readiness for change; empathy; OARS (open-ended questions, affirmations, reflecting, and summarizing); developing discrepancy; eliciting change talk; listening to sustain talk (rolling with resistance); information and advice giving; and goal setting.
- To describe the counseling process of MI.
- To examine social and cultural applicability of MI.
- To review the efficacy of MI.
- To offer a case study that demonstrates the MI process.

BRIEF HISTORY OF MOTIVATIONAL INTERVIEWING

> Motivational interviewing is "[t]he ability to trust the wisdom of someone to know what is best for them and to structure a supportive and purposeful activity, in the case of motivational interviewing, a conversation, so that they work it out for themselves." (Rollnick, 2013, minute 2:30)

Originally developed during the 1980s for the treatment of substance abuse, the application of MI quickly expanded to gambling problems, eating disorders, anxiety disorders, chronic disease management, health-related disorders, and more recently to a wide range of mental health problems (Arkowitz et al., 2017a; Dean 2015). Let's take a look at the origins of MI and see how it has developed over time.

Although both **William Richard Miller** and **Stephen Rollnick** have been credited as the founders of motivational interviewing, due in large part to their 1993 seminal text, *Motivational Interviewing: Helping People Change*, the origins of MI actually took place 10 years earlier. This is that story.

Born June 27, 1947, William Richard Miller was the older of two children raised by a poor, religious family in the small Appalachian coal-mining town of Shamokin, PA ("Conversation With," 2009). Miller's father worked for the railroad while his mother worked in a local factory. When he was 13, Miller's 8-year-old sister, Frances, died from complications of diabetes. This resulted in an emotionally difficult time and a crisis of faith for Miller. Eventually wanting to attend the seminary, Miller began his undergraduate studies at Lycoming College in Williamsport, Pennsylvania, where he majored in psychology. His college experience opened him up to new ways of viewing the world and challenged him to reflect on difficult life questions. With his crisis of faith continuing, and a newfound interest in the scientific method, Miller eventually turned to agnosticism, decided not to attend the seminary, and applied to graduate schools in psychology.

In 1969, Miller began graduate school at the University of Wisconsin. The Vietnam War was raging, and after one semester he was drafted. Filing as a conscientious objector, he was assigned to work as a psychiatric aid at Mendota State Hospital in Madison, Wisconsin (Moyers, 2004). Following in the footsteps of **Carl Rogers**, who had previously worked at Mendota State with schizophrenic clients, Miller found himself immersed in **person-centered counseling** principals developed by Rogers. His experiences led him to again apply to graduate school, this time at the University of Oregon's psychology program. Describing himself as a long-haired, leftist, hippie, to help pay for his studies Miller worked in a Veterans Affairs (VA) clinic treating alcoholics.

Using his Rogerian training, Miller was captivated by the stories shared by those in treatment and a sense of empathy grew for this struggling population (Moyers, 2004). Completing his master's in neurobiology in 1973, his newfound interest in addictions coupled with his love of university living and a budding new relationship with Kathy, whom he would later marry, prompted him to stay at the University of Oregon to pursue his PhD in clinical psychology ("Conversation With," 2009). As Miller navigated studies, he could not shake the notion there was a progressive nature to alcoholism and other addictions. This led him to believe that earlier interventions might lead to more positive results. Thus, for his dissertation, Miller studied problem drinking with individuals who had not yet developed a severe disorder. After gaining his PhD. in 1976, Miller obtained a position as assistant professor of psychology at the University of New Mexico, which had just opened a new alcohol treatment program. William and Kathy assimilated well into their new life, and he conducted research mostly on alcoholism.

During a sabbatical, Miller was invited to lecture at the Hjellestad Clinic in Norway, an alcoholism treatment center where his expertise in behavioral therapies was sought (Miller & Rollnick, 2013; Moyers, 2004). The staff psychologists asked Miller to meet with them every other week for an open discussion about current treatment issues. At one of these meetings, Miller was asked to role-play a therapist counseling one of their more difficult clients who was being role-played by another therapist (Moyers, 2004). Unbeknownst to Miller, it was common practice for European trained psychologists to interrupt these exercises with a bombardment of questions with the intent of understanding interventions. At first, Miller struggled with the constant interruptions, when the clinical team would ask questions such as: "What are you thinking right now?," "Why did you do what you just did?," "You just made this empathic statement, why didn't you make these other empathic statements?," and "Why did you ask that specific question?" The action of verbalizing his decision-making process gave Miller a conscious awareness of his underlying set of decision parameters that he had been using at a near unconscious level. It was then that Miller realized he was using targeted reflections, specific lines of questioning, and other intentional interventions to get clients to initiate arguments for change. Over the remainder of his sabbatical, he chronicled these decision parameters as they emerged, and by the end of his visit to Norway he produced a rough draft of a paper he called "Motivational Interviewing" ("Conversation With," 2009).

To illicit feedback, Miller shared this work with several of his colleagues and, to his surprise, heard from the editor of *Behavioral Psychotherapy* that he wished to publish his work (Moyers, 2004). Although Miller told the editor he had no data to support his ideas, the editor insisted the paper was strong enough, and it was published in 1983 (Miller, 1983). Miller then returned to New Mexico to further develop his theory and conduct research ("Conversation With," 2009).

Initially, Miller conceptualized MI as a method to nudge potential patients into accepting help (Moyers, 2004). To this end, Miller began a robust literature review of existing work related to brief intervention treatments. He distilled his findings down to the interventions he found to be most successful and combined them with his MI technique. This approach was then delivered to patients in a single session known as **The Drinker's Check-Up** (Miller,

1983; Miller & Sovereign, 1989). A study was conducted to test the efficacy of this approach with the expectation there would be a substantial increase in patients entering treatment upon realizing, as a result of the session, that they needed more intensive therapy. To Miller's surprise, hardly any of the patients entered treatment! But the patients who did complete this single session of MI reported positive outcomes without entering traditional treatment ("Conversation With," 2009). These findings, along with data collected from subsequent replications of the study, led Miller to view MI as a stand-alone treatment modality. Miller captured this in his publication of "Motivational Interviewing with Problem Drinkers: II. The Drinker's Check-up as a Prevention Intervention" in the *Journal of Behavioral Psychotherapy* (Miller et al., 1988). While MI had not yet gained a footing in the United States, that was all about to change.

In 1990, while on sabbatical at the University of New South Whales, in Sydney, Australia, Miller met South African Stephen Rollnick (Miller & Rollnick, 2004). Rollnick recognized Miller's name from both his 1983 article and also the popularity MI had gained in United Kingdom and elsewhere (Moyers, 2004). Rollnick, who had become a self-taught MI instructor, could not believe he was meeting the well-known Miller and pleaded with him to write more on the topic ("Conversation With," 2009). The following year, Miller and Rollnick coauthored *Motivational Interviewing: Helping People Change*, the definitive text on MI (Moyers, 2004). Since then, this text has been translated into 16 languages and is in its third edition. With each subsequent edition, the text has broadened its application well beyond the treatment of addictions and is now commonly used throughout psychotherapy, corrections, health care, and more (Arkowitz, et al., 2017a).

When asked in an interview conducted by the journal, *Addiction*, why he thought MI was so successful, Miller spoke to its "trialability," meaning that it can be used in small amounts and produce almost immediate change or progress. ("Conversation With," 2009). In addition, Miller thought its rapid adoption by the field was a function of there being a lot of frustrated practitioners who have encountered patients lacking in motivation. MI provides them with a tool to assist in moving these patients forward. Miller also spoke to its universality in that its basic skills can be used in conjunction with other approaches. "It is fairly compatible with other things that practitioners do, such as 12-Step approaches and behavior therapy, so you do not have to be converted to MI and forsake everything you have done before ("Conversation With," 2009, p. 890). This compatibility can be seen in its frequent use with cognitive behavioral therapy and in 12-step recovery approaches. Miller points out that MI does not require changing the practitioner's entire theoretical perspective and allows for continued use of other modalities already in place. Miller describes MI's approach as one that becomes almost intuitive; one that appears to make sense to the practitioners that use it (Arkowitz et al., 2017a).

An emeritus distinguished professor of psychology and psychiatry at the University of New Mexico, Miller has published 40 books, more than 400 articles, and has collaborated with prestigious organizations worldwide (Arkowitz et al., 2017a; Miller & Rose, 2009). He has received the Innovator Combating Substance Abuse award from the Robert Wood Johnson Foundation, two career achievement awards from the American Psychological Association, the international Jellinek Memorial Award, and the American Society of Addiction Medicine's Brinkley Smithers Distinguished Scientist Award. Miller lives with his wife, Kathy, in Albuquerque, New Mexico, and although his prodigious rate of productivity has slowed, he is still highly active with the **Motivational Interviewing Network of Trainers (MINT)**, an organization that he started with Steve Rollnick in 1997.

VIEW OF HUMAN NATURE

Defined as "a person-centered counseling style for addressing the common problem of ambivalence about change" (Miller & Rollnick, 2013, p. 21), the goal of MI is to increase clients' motivation for change and have them commit to the change process. In MI, motivation is seen as the key to change, caused by many external and internal factors, fluctuating in all of us, and influenced by the clinician.

Steeped in **existential-humanistic philosophy** and **phenomenology**, MI employs empathy and acceptance to understand the worldview of the client. It encourages the building of an **equal and egalitarian relationship**, thus suggesting the importance of a shared journey in the counseling relationship, in contrast to the objectivistic notions of many psychodynamic and cognitive behavioral approaches.

Although MI has a directive component that suggests offering advice concerning useful ideas for change can be helpful, it mostly employs a nondirective approach that assumes that the client has the resources to examine his or her own ambivalence about the change process, and, with the counselor, can jointly come up with strategies for change. The approach also trusts that clients have intrinsic motivation for change, though they sometimes can become caught up in their own ambivalence in the change process. In addition, the egalitarian, **non-pathological** stance of MI and its focus on client **empowerment** has a **postmodern** flavor that rejects the objectivist and deterministic view of many theories of the past and does not assume there is an inherent "correct" model of therapy that must be used with all clients.

As a stand-alone-approach, it is considered a brief approach to counseling steeped in existential-humanistic philosophy, postmodernism, with a touch of directiveness and goal setting reminiscent of cognitive behavioral therapies. Motivational interviewing, however, is often seen as **trans-theoretical** because it can be employed with many different theoretical perspectives (Arkowitz et al., 2017a; "Motivational Interviewing," 2019). This is largely due to the fact that it favors building a working alliance, which is critical to all counseling theories, and its basic process of focusing on ambivalence in the change process can be adapted to other theoretical approaches. Once a client commits to the change process, any theoretical perspective that might be useful in tackling a particular client's problems could be helpful.

KEY CONCEPTS

Of course, one of the most important concepts in MI is **motivation**, and a number of key assumptions related to motivation are discussed in this section. Also, in this section is a description of the **MI Spirit**, which include the elements of compassion, collaboration, acceptance, and evocation. Other key concepts we will explore include **ambivalence**, **change talk**, **avoiding confrontation**, and **FRAMES**, which is an acronym for Feedback, Responsibility, Advice, Menu of options, Empathy, and Self-efficacy.

Motivation

> MI is based not on standing in front of a student [or client] and pulling him or her toward change, or on standing behind him or her and pushing, but on coming alongside. (Rollnick et al., 2016, p. 13)

A central component of change in MI, motivation is viewed as coming from the client, not the counselor (Rosengren, 2009). Instead of pushing the client, the counselor comes from a place of curiosity—a place that strives to know more about the client and the client's circumstances. This process allows the counselor to assist the client in unearthing his or her sometimes hidden motivation. A number of assumptions about motivation that drive MI theory have been identified (Miller, 1999):

- *Motivation is a key to change:* Motivation is a complex construct that includes a number of factors, all of which can be important to the change process. Some include the individual's sense of self, biological factors, social factors, developmental issues, etc.
- *Motivation is multidimensional:* Motivation includes internal urges, external pressures and goals, perceptions of risks and benefits, and cognitive assessment of the situation.
- *Motivation is dynamic and fluctuating:* Motivation can vary over time and can vacillate in intensity.
- *Motivation is influenced by social interactions:* Internal factors are critical for change, but external factors help create conditions for change.
- *Motivation can be modified:* A wide variety of elements can modify a person's motivation, and a skilled clinician can assist in helping set up those conditions.
- *Motivation is influenced by the clinician's style:* The ability of the counselor to build a therapeutic relationship is probably as important, or more so, than the specific skills the clinician uses.
- *The clinician's task is to elicit and enhance motivation:* Clinicians should have a wide range of techniques to assist the client in the change process.

To a large degree, the unmotivated client is seen as a myth in MI. Instead, the client is viewed as an individual who waxes and wanes in his or her motivation, and one who can become motivated under the right circumstances. MI theorists argue that creating the right circumstances is done partly by the clinician having an attitude that is solicitous of the client. Such an attitude is encompassed by four attributes that represent what is called the MI Spirit.

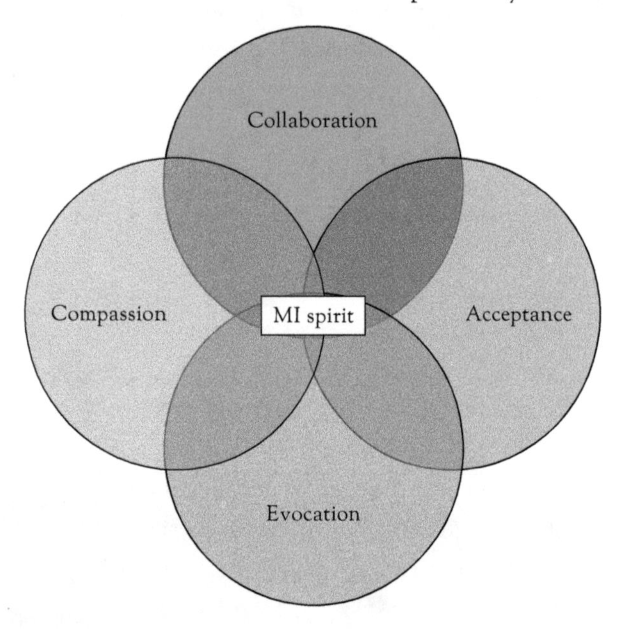

Figure 7.1 The MI Spirit

The MI Spirit

In contrast with theoretical orientation, MI is grounded in what is called a "spirit," which is embraced by the counselor and involves **compassion, collaboration, acceptance**, and **evocation** (Miller & Rollnick, 2013; Figure 7.1). The presence of these factors increases the effectiveness of MI and the likelihood of positive client outcomes. Whereas the top three elements are focused on the development of the relationship, the last element has to do with evoking—or drawing out from the client—why change is important for him or her. Let's examine each of these elements.

Compassion

Compassion involves the counselor consistently having the safety, well-being, and best interest of the client at the forefront (Miller & Rollnick, 2013). It means the counselor's heart is in the right place and involves the counselor having a client-centered, not counselor-centered, approach and ensures that clients are not being exploited (Cialdini, 2007). This approach suggests that the counselor is nonjudgmental, able to show understanding of a wide range of feelings and experiences, and that the counselor respects the client regardless of the path he or she has taken in life.

Collaboration

Instead of employing a hierarchical, expert-like approach, the client views the counselor as a collaborator who strives to foster a space that supports growth without demanding it. Here the counselor is respectfully curious about the client and works to understand and accept the client's goals, which may contrast from the counselor's intuitions. A collaborative therapeutic relationship takes time to nurture, so the collaborative counselor does not compare his or her client's level of comfort with another client, nor should he or she expect a linear progression toward a strong therapeutic alliance (Rollnick et al., 2016). Often viewed as a partnership, this relationship entails being nonjudgmental, believing the client is the expert on his or her own experiences, listening, periodically asking questions, seeing the world through the client's eyes, and helping the client unfold his or her own experiences so he or she can make better choices in life.

Acceptance

MI suggests that acceptance has four components: **absolute worth**, **accurate empathy**, **autonomy support**, and **affirmation**. Here are short descriptions of each of these qualities:

Absolute worth: Miller & Rollnick (2013) state that "acceptance involves prizing the inherent worth and potential of every human being" (p. 17). This speaks to MI's roots in person-centered counseling principles, especially that of **unconditional positive regard (UPR)**. Rogers suggested it is common for individuals to have **conditions of worth** placed on them that result in people living incongruently as they live their lives as they believe others would want them to. In contrast, when individuals are afforded UPR, or absolute worth, there is total acceptance of them, which allows them to feel heard and become open to expressing who they are—their true selves, and thus free to change. In the counseling relationship, absence of absolute worth breeds judgment, which hinders the therapeutic alliance. On the other hand, UPR allows clients to truly be themselves and fosters positive client outcomes.

Accurate empathy: Another concept rooted in person-centered counseling, accurate empathy is the ability to hear the content of what a person is describing and his or her feelings accurately—as if the listener is that person, without losing that "as if" quality (Neukrug, 2017; Rogers, 1957, 1962). It's getting inside the world of another and understanding the individual in deep ways. From a phenomenological perspective, it's as though you can understand the direct, subjective experience of the client. Accurate empathy is not showing sympathy, which occurs when one feels pity or feels sorry for another. It is also not identifying with a person, which is thinking you understand an individual's situation because you went through something similar. But it is having deep understanding of the person—an understanding that can only be validated when the client says, verbally or nonverbally, "Yes, that's right—that's what I'm feeling."

Autonomy support: A counselor who employs autonomy support does not tell clients what to do; instead, he or she creates the environment that allows choices to naturally bubble up into the client's consciousness (Miller & Rollnick, 2013). Such an environment reduces defensiveness and helps engender a positive climate that fosters "free will" regarding the change process and further develops the therapeutic relationship. Autonomy support is a natural outgrowth of showing absolute worth, affirming clients, and demonstrating accurate empathy. But it is also verbally reinforced by counselors through positive change statements, such as, "I support whatever you think is best, and I'm here to help you."

Affirmation. Lastly, affirmation involves positively acknowledging a client's strengths and supporting a client's movement toward change (Miller & Rollnick, 2013). Hearing positive affirmations can help clients recognize areas where they have made strides, which can act as a self-fulfilling prophecy and promote continued growth. The antithesis of affirmation involves identifying client weaknesses and being directive regarding how the client should address them. An approach such as this encourages dependency, reduces autonomy, and potentially raise the client's defenses.

Evocation

Many early approaches to counseling employed a medical model in which the therapist was the "expert," objectified the client based on his or her diagnosis, and prescribed treatment based on the theoretical orientation the therapist practiced (Schumacher & Madson, 2015). In contrast, the role of the MI counselor is to elicit information from the client in order to evoke, or unveil, the client's natural tendency toward change (Miller & Rollnick, 2013). This process assumes that all clients, sometimes unknowingly, are motivated by a desire for change and hope for the future. The evocation process is collaborative and person-centered and involves inquiring about clients' understanding of their issues, exploring reasons why clients might want to change or want to not change, gently asking clients how they might change, exploring deeply held values and beliefs that may help guide their change process, discussing reasons that prevent change, and examining current behaviors that inhibit change (Herman et al., 2014). MI aims to help clients understand what prevents change and evoke a dialogue, often called **change talk**, that situates clients toward the change process.

Ambivalence

> A common pattern is to think of a reason for changing, then think of a reason not to change, then stop thinking about it. The path out of ambivalence is to choose a direction and follow it, to keep moving in the chosen direction. (Miller & Rollnick, 2013, p. 7)

Although many individuals desire change, they are hesitant to do so (Miller & Rollnick, 2013). Such ambivalence is tricky as individuals can become stuck in "ambivalence-land" for years. They may spend significant amounts of time going back and forth between possibilities and sometimes, when they move forward, the path back seems more appealing. A number of reasons for ambivalence exist, including:

- *Understanding the reasons for—and against—change:*
  Example: "If I leave my partner, I'll have less tension in my life. If I leave my partner, I'll be lonely."
- *Playing down the importance of change:*
  Example: "I could stop drinking, but my drinking really doesn't impact anybody that negatively."
- *Being defeated by failed attempts at change:*
  Example: "I know I'm depressed, but nothing has worked in the past."
- *Creating disequilibrium through the change process:*
  Example: "I started to communicate more with people, but every time I tried, I would get really anxious. I just wasn't used to being a communicator."

The human condition of wanting change, yet struggling with it or avoiding it outright, is common, and experienced by all individuals at some points in their lifetime. MI, however, sees hope in ambivalence. Instead of viewing ambivalence as a negative state of being, it is seen as a sign of the desire for change. After all, one cannot experience ambivalence unless the individual recognizes, on some level, that change is an option. Thus, MI views the mere presence of ambivalence as progression toward change, as one internally struggles between maintaining the status quo and moving forward in the change process. With this in mind, MI counselors work with clients to increase the amount of **change talk** and decrease the amount of **sustain talk** (Schumacher & Madson, 2015).

Change Talk

> To say that one must, can, wants, or has good reasons to change is not to say that one will. (Miller and Rollnick, 2013, p. 162)

One of the most important processes in MI is to help clients see their own natural desire to change. Miller and Rollnick (2013) suggest there are two types of change talk, preparatory and mobilizing. Together, these types of change talk are known by the acronym **DARN CATS**.

The "DARN" involves **preparatory change talk**. Desire involves the client discussing his or her awareness about, and longing to, make change (e.g., "I want to quit smoking"). Ability focuses on the client's confidence in his or her capacity to make change (e.g., "I know that I can quit smoking if I work hard at it."). Reason identifies the positive impact that change can have (e.g., "If I quit smoking I would have more energy, and I'm less likely to get a smoking related disease"), and Need identifies the urgency of the presenting problem (e.g., "I really should quit smoking because I've been doing it for a while, and I've seen other people my age with smoking-related illnesses"). By exploring "DARN," clients can begin to identity the disadvantages of the status quo (Miller & Rollnick, 2013).

The "CATS" represents **mobilizing change talk**, is more action-oriented and demonstratew an increased desire to implement change. For instance, Commitment is when a client says "I promise to quit smoking," Activation, is the client acknowledging "I am ready to quit smoking starting within the week," and Taking Steps, might be when the client throws away his or her cigarettes, gets medication to help quit, and practices relaxation when he or she is stressed. Later in this chapter, under techniques, we will examine some ways that counselors can elicit change talk.

Avoiding Confrontation

As you might suspect, collaboration, not confrontation, is the creed of MI (Dean, 2015). Building an egalitarian and collaborative relationship in MI is critical if the counselor is going to evoke the change process. Whereas confrontation can lead to defensiveness, result in clients avoiding important topics in the counseling relationship, and lead to clients dropping out of counseling, an egalitarian and collaborative relationship will encourage client openness, honesty, thoughtfulness, and insightfulness, and help them take a careful look at those aspects of themselves that need to be challenged and changed. Thus, MI therapists are encouraged to avoid confrontation, sidestep power struggles, and listen to sustain talk (formerly called **rolling with resistance**) while also being careful to not convey approval or reinforcement of problematic behaviors.

Frames

Similar to many brief approaches to counseling, MI employs a number of standard interventions that can come under the general heading of **FRAMES**, which is an acronym for Feedback, Responsibility, Advice, Menu of options, Empathy, and Self-efficacy (Miller, 1996; Miller & Rose, 2009). Below are brief definitions of each of these.

Feedback: Based on the presenting problem, offer feedback to the client regarding the negative consequences of the problem and listen to how the client reacts to your feedback.

Responsibility: Underscore the fact that the client, alone, is responsible for making his or her own decision regarding what to do about his or her problematic behavior.

Advice: Offer, when reasonable and receptive to the client, advice on ways to modify the problematic behavior.

Menu of options: Offer a variety of options, goals, and strategies that the client can select from when addressing problematic behaviors.

Empathy: Listen, be empathic, and be nonjudgmental.

Self-efficacy: Be optimistic about the client's ability to make changes in his or her life and feel good about himself or herself.

TECHNIQUES

Keeping in mind the MI Spirit discussed earlier (compassion, collaboration, acceptance, and evocation), the importance of not confronting the client, and the FRAMES acronym as a general direction in counseling, there are some specific techniques that counselors tend to use when practicing motivational interviewing. These include **assessing importance, competence, and readiness to change; listening and empathy; OARS (open-ended questions, affirmations, reflecting, and summarizing); developing discrepancy; eliciting change talk; listening to sustain talk (rolling with resistance); information and advice giving;** and **goal setting** (Miller & Rollnick, 2013). Although Miller and Rollnick (2009) suggest that these are general techniques used in MI, they also note they should not be considered structured guidelines for clinicians to use in all sessions.

Assessing Importance, Confidence, and Readiness to Change

When a client initially comes to counseling wanting to discuss one or more problematic behaviors, it is critical to address how important change is for the client and how confident the client feels about implementing the change. To assess this, MI counselors will often use a scale, called a **Ruler,** to determine importance and confidence (Miller & Rollnick, 2013).

0	1	2	3	4	5	6	7	8	9	10
Not at all important										Extremely important

0	1	2	3	4	5	6	7	8	9	10
Not at all confident										Extremely confident

Miller and Rollnick (2013) suggest that clients generally fit under one of four profiles after they are assessed on the two scales (see Box 7.1). For Groups 2, 3, and 4 there is work to be done early in counseling because clients either see their problem behaviors as low in importance (Groups 2 and 4), do not have the confidence of being able to tackle their problem(s) successfully (low self-efficacy: Groups 3 and 4), or believe their problems are of importance and see themselves as having low confidence (Group 3). Clients in Group 1, in contrast, should be able to work well and fast in counseling.

BOX 7.1 PROFILES OF CLIENTS

		Importance: High	Importance: Low
Confidence	High	1	2
	Low	3	4

OARS

Focused on during the early part of counseling to develop the therapeutic alliance and assess readiness for change, but important throughout the counseling process, are a number of basic counseling skills known by the acronym OARS (Miller & Rollnick, 2013). These skills call for the use of **Open-ended questions, Affirmations, Reflecting, and Summarizing.**

Open-Ended Questions

One way to ensure clients are in the driver's seat is to use open-ended questions. Such questions allow clients the freedom to respond in a variety of ways and create an environment in which the client directs the focus of the session (Neukrug, 2019). Open-ended questions are seen as more client-centered than closed questions, which tend to ask for dichotomous or limited responses and, thus, cut-off discussion. For instance, a closed question that could limit discussion might be: "Do you think your mom or dad was more emotionally labile in your family? In contrast, open-ended questions invite discussion, such as the counselor who asks, "Can you tell me about your relationship with your parents?" In MI, questions are often focused on the problematic behavior and invite the client to consider the change process. For instance, an open-ended question that invites a client to consider the benefits of stopping his or her drinking behavior might be: "What types of benefits would you experience from quitting?" In general, Miller and Rollnick (2013) suggest that the counselor mix open-ended questions with reflections, with open-ended questions taking a back seat to reflections—perhaps two reflections to each open-ended question.

Affirmations

The use of affirmations go far in developing a positive working alliance and in building client self-esteem (Neukrug, 2019). Affirmations, and their close cousins encouragement and support, are all important skills that can be used to maintain focus on the client and their experience (Miller, 1983; Miller & Rollnick, 2013). Affirmation can range from short statements such as

"Good job" to "You really worked hard on accomplishing your goals, and it seems like you did a lot." These positive responses are less about praising the client and more about making a positive statement concerning something the client has accomplished. Whereas praise tends to foster a dependent relationship between the counselor and the client, affirmation is less likely to do so. Thus, one is less likely to praise the client by saying, "I'm really proud of you for getting to those AA meetings," and more likely to affirm the client by noting, "You really went all out to get to those AA meetings" (Miller & Rollnick, 2013).

Reflecting

Much as open-ended questions and affirmation, reflecting what a person has said is important in building the therapeutic alliance and particularly critical near the beginning of the counseling relationship (Neukrug, 2019; Wampold & Imel, 2015). Reflecting, sometimes called, **reflective listening**, is often described as a short statement, or paraphrase, that demonstrates the counselor has accurately heard the client and is taking an active part in his or her journey.

Some have suggested using three types of reflecting skills in MI: **simple reflection**, **amplified reflection**, and **double-sided reflection** (Dean, 2015). Simple reflection is echoing what the client said, such as when the counselor paraphrases a client's frustration about drinking: "Sounds like you're really frustrated about your continued alcohol use." Amplified reflection paraphrases and intensifies what the client said and thus focuses a bit more on the change process, as it tends to highlight the discrepancy between what the client is doing and what the client wants: "Your frustration about your continued drinking is really getting to you." Finally, double-sided reflection reflects back what the client has said, and more boldly states the discrepancy between what the client is experiencing and what he or she wants: "So, I know how your continued drinking has been really frustrating for you as I also know how much you want to stop drinking." Although reflective listening is important in all counseling approaches, this type of reflecting is a bit more focused on the change process. Thus, on one hand the client feels as though he or she is being heard and supported, while on the other hand the client is being gently encouraged, through the reflective process, to change.

Summarizing

Miller and Rollnick (2013) suggest that summaries are essential in pulling together what a client has said and identify three types of summaries. First, **collecting summaries** occur when a counselor pulls together a number of interrelated themes, often the result of clients exploring their identified problems. After employing this summary, the counselor can end with an open-ended question that will invite the client to continue his or her discovery process in session. For example:

> *Counselor:* "I'm hearing a few different things today. For instance, you are not happy in your relationship and would like it to feel more intimate. Also, you have some

concerns about your career goals and whether you are moving in the right direction vocationally. Finally, you seem to be wary about the amount you have been, as you stated, 'numbing yourself,' through your drinking. Any other concerns that you have? Is there anything I missed here?"

The second type of summary, **linking summaries**, is used to connect two or more previously discussed ideas. For instance, a linking summary might be:

Counselor: "Seems like you've been working hard to alleviate some of the stress in your life and you're feeling better. I remember you saying that you've used some of these same skills in the past to relieve stress and they were also successful then."

Sometimes, linking summaries can be used in reflecting back ambivalence about change (Miller & Rollnick, 2002, 2013). For example, here we see a counselor summarizing reasons a client has expressed for both maintaining and changing current behavior:

Counselor: "So, I hear how your use of marijuana is concerning to you. Because you're smoking every day, you sometimes think that you are not fully taking control of your life—that pot makes you a bit more lackadaisical and not focused on some of the things you need to do for your family and at work. On the other hand, I also hear you saying that your life, particularly your work life, is very stressful and smoking pot is relaxing for you and gets you away from some of the worries you have in your life. Want to talk about all of that some more?"

Third, **transitional summaries** are helpful when the counselor and client are shifting from one transition to another, such as when a session is about to end and the counselor is considering what's going to happen during the next session. These responses tend to be a bit more involved than collecting and linking summaries as they are pulling together a wide range of information. Miller and Rollnick (2013) recommend including a beginning statement that introduces the transitional summary to the client. Example:

Counselor: "So, we need to end our session today and think about the next time we're getting together. So first let me review some of the major issues we have discussed thus far. You first talked about the fact that your doctor was concerned about the amount you were drinking. Although you first dismissed her concerns, you then said you began thinking about it and even worrying about it some. You also said it's not just the alcohol, but the anti-anxiety pills you use with the alcohol. All in all, you were worried that you might be addicted to one or both. When we talked about what you can do about the drinking and the anxiety pills, you at first said you needed them because your life would be just too awful if you didn't have something to calm you down and make you feel good. However, then you began to wonder if the drugs and alcohol might be deleteriously affecting your marriage and even your parenting. So, we ended with you wondering if you should do something about the drinking and the pills. Does that accurately pull tougher all of what you talked about?"

Listening and Empathy

As MI is grounded in many person-centered counseling principles, it's not surprising that good **listening** skills and **empathy** are critical tools to use in the counseling relationship (Cole, 2012). Neukrug (2019) describes good listening as an active process that involves:

1. Talking minimally
2. Concentrating on what is being said
3. Not interrupting
4. Not giving advice
5. Not expecting to get something from the relationship
6. Hearing the client's content
7. Hearing the client's affect
8. Using good nonverbal behaviors to show you are hearing the client, such as having good and appropriate eye contact, using head nods, saying "uh-huh," and so forth
9. Asking clarifying questions such as "I didn't hear all of that, can you say it again" or "Can you explain that in another way so I'm sure I understand you?"
10. Not asking questions (other than clarifying questions) (p. 49)

Empathy takes listening one step further and involves the counselor placing himself or herself in the shoes of the client to better understand the client's worldview and cognitions (Bayne & Neukrug, 2017). Although critical at the beginning of any therapeutic relationship (Neukrug, 2019), empathy can be used seamlessly throughout the therapeutic process and can also be relied upon to heal ruptures in the counseling relationship. To be empathic also means that the counselor refrains from judging, chastising, or accusing the client. It is only through this nonjudgmental stance that counselors can hear clients fully, which allows them to feel accepted and validated. Clients who feel understood and validated are more likely to feel comfortable opening up in sessions (Cole, 2012).

The basic ingredients to a good empathic response is to reflect back the client's feelings and the content of what the client has said accurately (Neukrug, 2019). Miller and Rollnick (2013) describe a 5-point scale, similar to the original Carkhuff scale that operationalized empathy as defined by Carl Rogers (Neukrug, 2019). In short, they stated that counselors can show little or deep empathy, as defined in the following scale:

1. Clinician has no apparent interest in client's point of view. Gives little or no attention to the client's perspective.
2. Clinician makes sporadic efforts to explore the client's perspective. Clinician's understanding may be inaccurate or may detract from the client's true meaning.
3. Clinician is actively trying to understand the client's perspective, with modest success.
4. Clinician shows evidence of accurate understanding of client's worldview. Makes active and repeated efforts to understand client's point of view. Understanding mostly limited to explicit content.
5. Clinician shows evidence of deep understanding of client's point of view, not just for what has been explicitly stated but also what the client means and has not said. (Miller & Rollnick, 2013, pp. 392-393).

Volumes have been written on how to make good empathic responses and varying ways to bring depth and meaning into the responses (Neukrug, 2017). Suffice to say, empathy is a critical tool in MI and should be used wisely and throughout the counseling relationship.

Developing Discrepancy

> The idea of developing discrepancy has been part of MI since the very beginning … this important motivational factor is a discrepancy between present and desired states, the distance between a personal goal and the status quo (Rollnick & Miller, 2013, p. 243).

A process as opposed to any specific technique, developing discrepancy points out the inconsistencies between the client's current maladaptive or problematic behaviors and the client's desired attainment of goals based on personal values (e.g., drinking too much and becoming verbally aggressive vs. wanting to be a role model for one's children) (Miller & Rollnick, 2013). This process involves the counselor building a strong therapeutic alliance, assisting the client in identifying maladaptive or troubling behaviors in his or her life, eliciting values and goals important to the client, and using a variety of skills to demonstrate discrepancies between current behaviors and the values and goals identified by the client. By revealing the discrepancy, this process raises clients' awareness regarding their ambivalence toward change ("I want to be … , but I actually am … ") and ultimately helps them decide whether they want to initiate the change process.

MI diverts from its client-centered underpinnings when it prompts, or directs, clients to compare their maladaptive behaviors with desired values and goals (Miller & Rollnick, 2013). Seasoned counselors create a delicate balance of support and challenge that guides their clients toward greater recognition of discrepancies. Support is accomplished through the use of client-centered techniques and affirmations, while challenge occurs when the counselor uses directive techniques, such as double-sided listening and change talk.

Individuals receiving counseling usually have a sense of the incongruity in their lives between where they are and where they want to be. The counselor's role is to illuminate this incongruity while avoiding the pitfall of trying to change the client to match what someone else thinks the client should act like (the counselor, a partner, a friend). Ultimately, the counselor must aim for the *client* to articulate why and how he or she should change. When clients observe their current behavior as impeding salient individual goals based on expressed values, the likelihood of the client's own motivation to change increases, clients assume responsibility for change, and clients feel empowered to develop strategies for change. There are many ways to illuminate client incongruities, some of which we already discussed, including the use of open-ended questions, the various forms of reflection, the different types of summarizing, and empathy. One often used method is by eliciting change talk, which includes a number of strategies. Let's take a look.

Eliciting Change Talk

Eliciting change talk is one of the primary goals of MI (Miller & Rollnick, 2002, 2013). Change talk is seen as a collaborative process whereby the counselor uses a series of questions and statements that encourage, but do not push, clients to reflect on what change, if any, might be important in their lives (Miller & Rollnick, 2013). Change talk uses support and challenge and helps clients explore the possibility of change, and encourages them to begin to identify plans to implement these changes.

Counselors employing motivational interviewing look for the smallest of client talk that hints at motivation or wanting to change (Cole, 2012). Once identified, the counselor magnifies the change talk and spends time allowing the client to explore these newfound thoughts. Increased change talk often leads to an increased likelihood to change. Miller and Rollnick (2002, 2013) identify a number of ways of eliciting change talk, which we will briefly describe here.

Asking Evocative Questions

This involves simply asking open-ended questions about the client's situation that may evoke change talk. If the client responds positively, the counselor can then reply with reflections and empathy. Miller and Rollnick (2013) suggest using the "DARN" from the DARN CATs acronym discussed earlier (<u>D</u>esire, <u>A</u>bility, <u>R</u>eason, <u>N</u>eed) when formulating questions. Here are some examples:

Desire: "How do you wish your life would look in the future?"
Ability: "What aspect of your life do you think you can change?"
Reason: "How do you think your life would be better if things were changed?"
Need: "What part of your life needs to be changed?"

Using the Importance Ruler

Here, the counselor simply asks questions related to the client's score on the importance ruler with the goal being to have him or her talk about how important change might be.

Counselor: "So, I see you rated yourself a 6 on importance and not a 0. Seems like you have some desire to change. Can you tell me about that?"

Note that asking the client why he or she is higher than a 0 (a "6" in this case) enables the counselor to talk with the client about the fact that he or she sees change as important. Asking "Why is it not 10?" could make the client feel defensive, think that he or she hasn't tried enough, is not capable of change, or that change is too difficult. Here's another example that uses the ruler to elicit thoughts about moving forward in the change process:

Counselor: "Any ideas about how we can get you to go from a 6 to an 8?"

Here again, we're not focusing on why the client is not at an "8," but on thoughts he or she might have about how to get to an "8." This approach has a much more positive spin to it and is more likely to induce change talk and movement toward one's goals.

Exploring the Decisional Balance

Sometimes, a counselor can employ a decision balance sheet to help clients look at both sides of their behavior. This can lead to helping clients focus clearly on the aspect of their lives that are causing problems (see Box 7.2).

In this process, counselors can use open-ended questions that help to explore the different polarities of a behavior. For instance, the client who is struggling with anger issues might be initially asked:

Counselor: "So, what are the positive aspects of your anger?"

Then, at a later point the counselor might ask:

Counselor: "So, we discussed some of the positive sides of your anger, how about we look at the downside of your anger?"

BOX 7.2 DECISIONAL BALANCE SHEET

Continue Expressing Anger		Begin to Limit Expression of Anger	
Benefits	**Costs**	**Benefits**	**Costs**
People hear to me.	I turn people off.	I will be more liked by people.	I won't be myself.
I communicate what I want.	I don't hear what others want.	I won't explode at people.	I will feel like I'm never me.
I'm not controlled by others.	I'm controlling of others and they don't like me.	I'll have more loving relationships.	I might feel smothered.
I let go of my feelings.	I sometimes feel guilty after.	I won't feel guilty about my behavior.	I won't be able to let go of my feelings.
My children will listen to me.	My children won't respect me.	I'll be a better role model for my children.	

Similarly, the counselor can ask open-ended questions to help the client look at the positive and negative aspects of limiting anger. The client, or the counselor, can write the various responses on a sheet of paper and explore the various benefits and costs of one's anger during the session or at a later point.

Elaborating

Sometimes, simply asking a client to elaborate on a problem can help elicit change talk. Let's take a look at a dialogue and see how this might occur.

Client: "You know, sometimes I get pretty angry at my kids and my wife."

Counselor: "Tell me more about this. What happens?"

Client: "Well, I've gotten so angry at them, that my wife starts to cry and my kids go into their room, and I see them cowering."

Counselor: "That sounds like that must be pretty hard on you."

Client: "Well, yes, I hate to make my wife cry, and I really don't want to see my kids like that. I feel evil."

Counselor: "Any other ways you see this affect you and your family?"

Client: "Yes, I think it just puts distance between all of us."

You can see how just elaborating on a problem can bring insight about the issues at hand. As clients more fully see the problem, they often take more responsibility for it and want to embrace the change process.

Querying Extremes

Asking clients to describe the extremes of concerns they have about their problematic behaviors can lead them to see the need to take some action. Here's an example of a client who is having issues with anger:

Counselor: "What concerns you most about your anger?"

Client: "Well, you know, I've never said this to anyone, but I'm worried that if I get really angry, I might hit someone or hurt someone."

Counselor: "I'm sure that must be disconcerting for you. Any thoughts about what could be the best results for you if you were to be able to handle your anger better?"

Client: "Well, for sure, I'd be calmer and not be fearful of hurting someone. And, probably, I'd just be a better person all around."

When querying extremes, it can also be useful to explore positive consequences of making a change:

Counselor: "So what do you think would happen if you did something different with your anger?"

Client: "I think if I were less angry, my wife and kids would be more loving to me."

Counselor: "Anything else?"

Client: "I'd probably feel better about myself. I really don't like myself when I feel angry."

Looking Back

Sometimes, when clients look back at times when they did not have the problem, they can explore what was different then and also remember times that were better. This can motivate them to change.

> *Counselor:* "So, tell me. Was there a time in your life when you did not have this problem?"
>
> *Client:* "Yes, there was. I felt much different then ... and much better."
>
> *Counselor:* "So, what was different in your life then?"
>
> *Client:* "Well, I had less stress, fewer responsibilities, and more friends. Those things really made a difference."

You can see how the above conversation could lead to specific goals the client might decide to strive toward, including stress reduction, letting go of some responsibilities in life, and developing a stronger network of friends.

Looking Forward

Helping clients look ahead in their lives and envisioning a time when things are better, can elicit change talk. A classic example developed by solution-focused brief therapists is the **miracle question**:

> Suppose that one night, while you were asleep, there was a miracle and this problem was solved. How would you know? What would be different? (de Shazer, 1988, p. 5)

Exploring Goals and Values

Doing exercises to examine clients' goals and values can often jump-start a clients' motivation toward change as they realize they are not living out the lives they really want to live. Simple values clarification exercises can be enlightening to clients (Kirschenbaum, 2013). Even just asking clients to identify important areas related to their interpersonal lives, intrapersonal self, career path, avocations, spiritual self, and physical health can be enlightening to individuals (see Box 7.3). Specific values clarification exercises are abundant and can help clients decipher what is important in their lives and whether they are moving in the direction to live a more meaningful and fulfilled life.

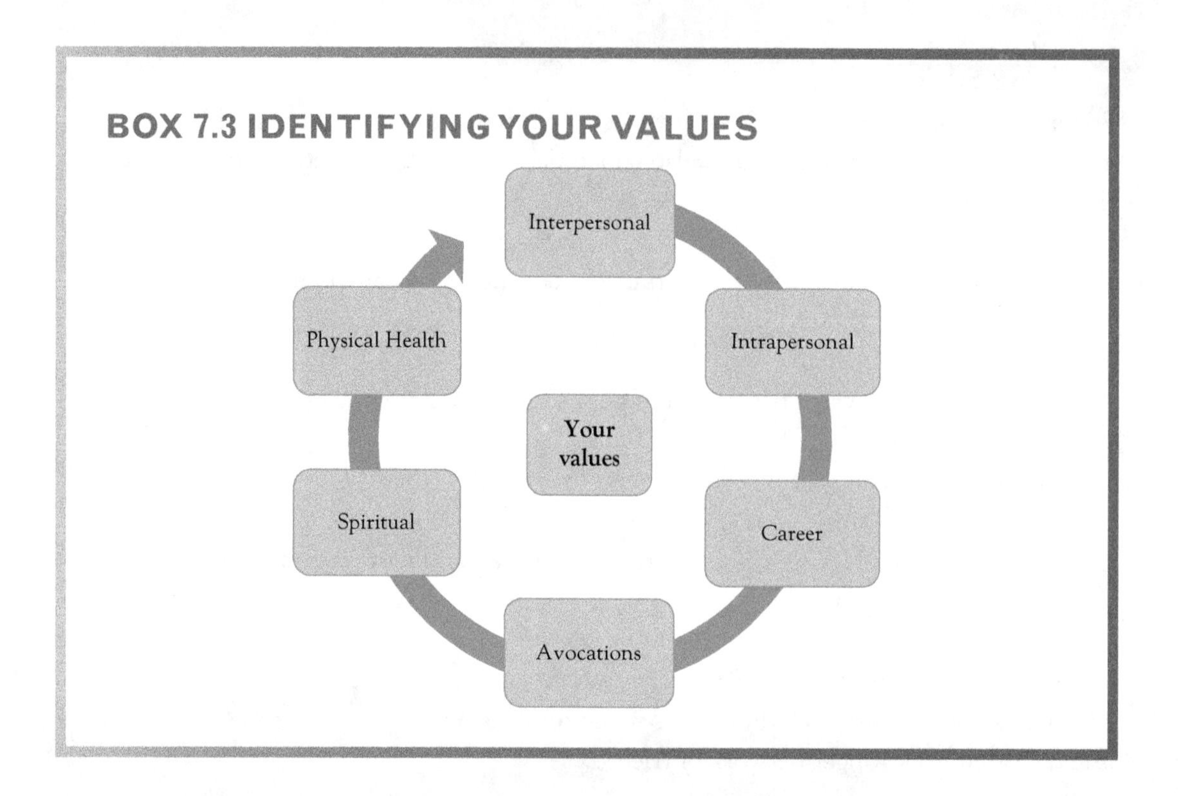

Listening to Sustain Talk (Rolling With Resistance)

The term **rolling with resistance** became popularized and highlighted the notion that counselors should "go with the flow" when clients seem reticent to change (Miller & Rollnick, 2002). In more recent years, however, Miller and Rollnick (2013) have used the term **sustain talk**, instead of "resistance." Sustain talk suggests that "the client's own motivations and verbalizations [are] favoring the status quo" (p. 197). This term, they believe, is less likely to pathologize the client as the word "resistance" is viewed by some as a problem that is inherent within the person. Whether you call it rolling with resistance or **listening to sustain talk**, it epitomizes the notion that clients are, in the moment, not wanting to change. Rollnick and Miller (2002, 2013) suggest that in staying true to the spirit of MI, it is important to listen to the sustain talk (roll with resistance) and remember that it is the counselor's job to raise clients' consciousness about discrepancies and resistance to change, not challenge where the client is at. In fact, MI counselors normalize sustain talk as a common and comprehensible element of growth, accept clients where they are, respect and even embrace client resistance, avoid attempting to give the client the "secret recipe" to success, and offer opportunities for clients to develop a dialogue of change.

Counselors listen attentively to sustain talk, avoid **discord** in the relationship, and do not embark on the **righting reflex**, which occurs when clients are criticized, given advice when not asked for it, and blamed, shamed, or asked to move toward change when they are not ready (Cole, 2012). Instead of creating discord, counselors should maintain the basic assumption that the client is competent, knows his or her unique needs, and can develop solutions to confront the concerning behavior. Continued client resistance can also be viewed as a sign that the counselor should reflect on how he or she is responding to the client and consider shifting his or her approach.

Oftentimes, listening to sustain talk involves using simple reflections, empathy, and being nonjudgmental as the counselor allows the client to express his or her resistance. Here's a snapshot of listening to sustain talk in which a counselor uses simple reflection and empathy when working with a teenager who appears unmotivated to attend school every day.

> *Client:* "Yeah ... I just don't see how it's a big deal. I hate getting up at 5 a.m. and I'm never really able to focus because I'm so tired. Honestly, going to school seems pointless."
>
> *Counselor:* "I can see how getting up early can be difficult; I know it must be tough, and I can understand how your fatigue impacts your concentration."
>
> *Client:* "Exactly, but my parents and teachers don't seem to understand."
>
> *Counselor:* "That's rough when they don't get it. They don't seem to understand what's causing you to miss school, right?"
>
> *Client:* "Right."

Counselors who listen to sustain talk will sometimes respond with a statement that allows the client to contemplate change. For instance, in the preceding scenario, the counselor could follow up with:

> *Counselor:* "You know, I see how hard it is for you to get up at such an ungodly hour, and I also know that you want to do well in school."

This reflection of the client's discrepancy allows the client to continue to think about both parts of the dilemma—hating to get up early and wanting to do well.

Another way that counselors can help clients consider the change process is by utilizing a **reframe** of the client's sustain talk. For instance, a client who knows his or her drinking is problematic states, "I simply am not capable of stopping. I've been trying for the past six months to no avail." The counselor could say, "Seems like you realize drinking is not good for you, but how to stop has not been easy and you've been thinking hard about it for the past six months. Can you share some of the many thoughts you've had?" Such a reframe acknowledges the problematic behavior but also affirms the client's efforts and allows the client to continue to contemplate about ways to deal with the problem. Consider how different a response this is compared with a counselor who might say, "Seems like you realize drinking is not good for you and you don't want to do anything about it at this point." This second response feeds into the resistance to change and would most likely fuel client's defensiveness. Whether using simple reflections, empathy, reframing, or subtle change talk, it is critical that counselors listen to their client's sustain talk (roll with resistance) if they are to support clients and build the therapeutic alliance.

Information and Advice Giving

Clients who are ambivalent to change are at times not aware of the impact of the current behavior or situation. For example, a client who presents with alcohol-related issues may not be aware of the physical effects of alcohol abuse. Here, the counselor can educate his or her client on the effects of alcohol and how the current behavior may be impacting desired goals (Miller, 1983). Although useful at times, information and advice giving is not a primary focus of MI. In fact, the pitfalls of information and advice giving are well known, and include fostering a dependent client–counselor relationship, seeing the counselor as all-knowing and giving up one's power to find solutions on one's own, and not providing information or advice that is helpful (Neukrug, 2019). But sometimes providing information and advice to clients can assist the counselor in developing discrepancy and further promote change talk.

Goal Setting

After clients have made some commitment to change and know the general direction they would like to move toward, goals can be developed in collaboration with the counselor. Here, counselor expertise and advice may come into play, as specific techniques from other therapeutic approaches, particularly cognitive behavioral techniques, can be employed. Since MI is trans-theoretical, various techniques from different counseling theories can be applied, based on the approach practiced by the counselor.

THE COUNSELING PROCESS

Although MI is often applied alongside other theoretical approaches, there is a general flow to the MI process, which will be described here. First, the MI therapist enters the therapeutic partnership embracing the MI Spirit, which calls for a sense of compassion, collaboration, and acceptance toward the client. Compassion, in the sense that the counselor is concerned about the client and his or her well-being; collaboration, because the relationship is seen as a joint partnership as opposed to a counselor being an expert telling the client what to do; and acceptance, meaning that the client is viewed as someone with inherent self-worth who should be afforded unconditional positive regard for the manner in which he or she lives in the world. In addition, the counselor views his or her role as one in which confrontation is limited and change talk through evocation is encouraged. The counselor also uses the FRAMES model to provide a perspective on how to work with clients. This includes giving **feedback** to clients about their presenting problem and listening to how clients respond to the feedback, remembering that clients are ultimately **responsible** for the decisions they make about their lives, giving **advice** if clients are receptive to it, offering a **menu** of options regarding goals, showing **empathy** throughout the process, and viewing clients as having **self-efficacy** in that they have the ability to make changes in their lives.

With the MI Spirit and the FRAMES model in the "back pocket" of the counselor, there is generally a flow throughout the therapeutic process that involves four processes: engaging, focusing, evoking, and planning (Miller & Rollnick, 2013). Miller and Rollnick see this process as "sequential and recursive" (p. 26) as though it's a staircase that one can walk up yet move back down if necessary (see Box 7.4). Let's take a brief look at these four processes.

BOX 7.4 FOUR PROCESSES IN MI

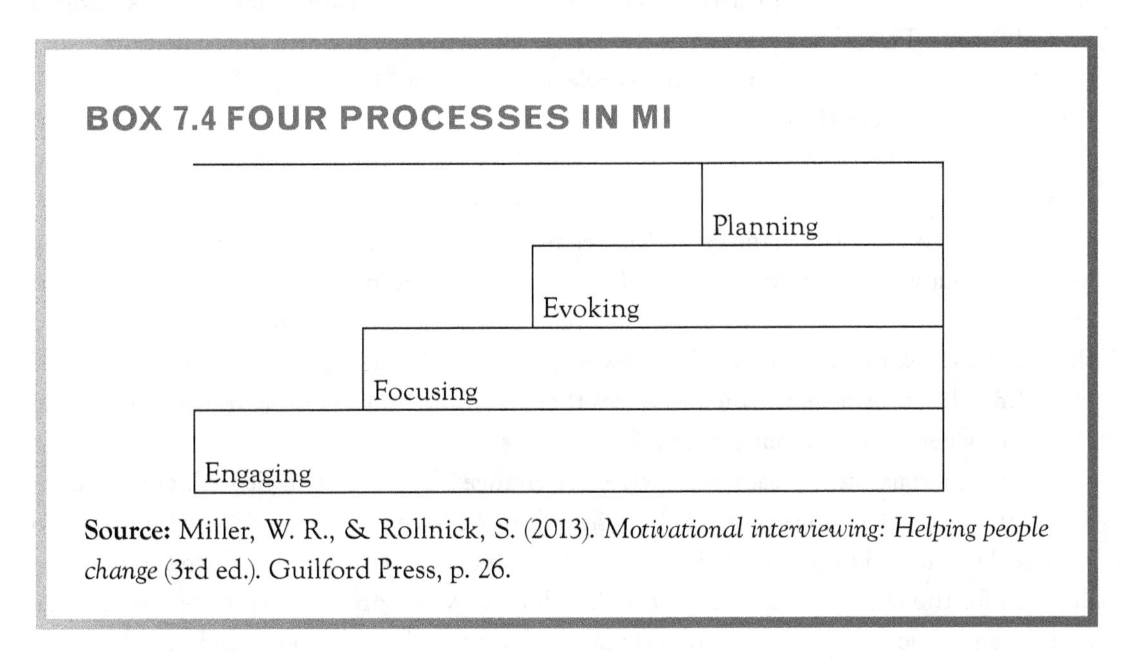

Source: Miller, W. R., & Rollnick, S. (2013). *Motivational interviewing: Helping people change* (3rd ed.). Guilford Press, p. 26.

Engaging

When clients initially start working with a counselor it is critical that the counselor builds a working alliance that is engaging to the client. Done well, this initial process is predictive of positive client outcomes and it is generally best if the counselor embraces the MI spirit of compassion, collaboration, and acceptance, and listens well, demonstrates empathy, and is affirming of the client.

Focusing

As the relationship builds, the counselor and client become increasingly focused on the direction in which the client wants to move. Miller and Rollnick (2013) suggest that this involves the counselor's ability to "develop and maintain a specific direction in the conversation about change" (p. 27). Here, counselors may inquire about the presenting problem and assesses the client's willingness, importance, and readiness toward change. Although open-ended questions, good listening, and empathy are used throughout the relationship, they are especially important during this early part of the therapeutic partnership as the counselor and client collaborate with each other, continue to build the therapeutic alliance, and focus on specific topics to address in counseling. Effective reflective listening is also used to focus the session on the client and the client's goals, and empathy and affirmations can be used to help solidify the counseling relationship and are important for highlighting client self-efficacy.

Evoking

In this third process, the counselor uses his or her skills to elicit the client's own motivations toward change. This is the antithesis of the expert–client model, in which the counselor pushes the client toward change. Evoking an attitude toward change is accomplished by developing discrepancies between the client's current circumstances or behaviors and the client's desired circumstances or behaviors and may be facilitated by educating the client about the problem, using specific OARS skills that highlight discrepancies, or by using specific change talk skills, which also highlight discrepancies. As discrepancies are highlighted, clients realize they have a choice about where they want to take their lives. At this point, specific values clarification exercises and the exploration of goals can begin as the client increasingly knows that he or she wants to look forward and explore new ways of being in the world. Although empathy is used throughout, using empathic responses that reinforce stated goals can help solidify the client's new perspective about change.

Oftentimes, as clients ready themselves for change, they also struggle with ambivalence and fear about the change process. This should not be seen as a client's unwillingness to change, but instead as a sign of the expected ambivalence associated with the impending decision for the client to make, or not make, change. Managing the client's fear of change and the ambivalence of how this change might impact the client, however, can be a daunting task. Here, the counselor's role in the therapeutic collaboration is to normalize the presence of ambivalence and reframe it as part of the change process and support the client's belief, or self-efficacy, in his or her ability to make this change. In addition, it is here that counselors will listen to sustain talk, as clients will sometimes be reticent to move forward. Counselors should always approach their clients aware that the clients are in the driver's seat, and that they choose whether to change. As ambivalence lessens, clients who choose to change can return to their focus on goals that align with their values.

Planning

As client's increasingly become ready to change, they begin to develop a fairly strong sense of the direction they want to move in and how they want to get there. Since counselors have a wealth of knowledge about techniques to achieve specific goals, they can share their ideas with their clients. In collaboration with their clients, techniques should be chosen based on the client's problems, temperament, view of the world, and cultural background, and what works best for specific treatment issues. Increasingly, in this process, clients become committed toward change and a specific plan of action.

SOCIAL AND CULTURAL ISSUES

MI emphasizes the importance of acceptance, respect, and curiosity while stressing collaboration and the use of empathy, all while honoring the subjective worldview of the client. These core attitudes and skills can be applied with a wide range of clients (Arkowitz et al., 2017a). Additionally, showing humility, showing respect, and adopting a "client is the expert" posture when working with diverse populations inherently allows for a deep respect for social, cultural, and spiritual differences and acceptance that the client's worldview may be different from the therapist's (McMaster & Griva, 2015; Miller & Rollnick, 2013). With this as the backdrop, it's interesting that some U.S. studies have indicated that MI has more efficacy with clients from diverse backgrounds than with White clients (Hettema et al., 2005; Miller & Arkowitz, 2017). With positive client outcomes with diverse clients, and with MI counselors taking a nonjudgmental stance with clients and being amenable to understanding perspectives form multiple realities, it has found appeal and is used extensively outside of Western countries.

Despite its appeal internationally and nonpathological and accepting stance, concerns about MI's effectiveness within specific cultures have been voiced (Lee, Tavares et al., 2015; McMaster & Griva, 2015). Specifically, the use of MI might be questionable when a client's internal locus of control is superseded by his or her culture's religious beliefs, morality, social values, or parental decisions. In these cases, MI's focus on the individual might be too discordant with the collectivist nature of the client's culture. In these instances, external forces may produce strong belief systems that downplay the importance of self in relation to the group or look askance at autonomy or the honoring of the clients own decision-making process (Miller, & Rollnick, 2013). Additionally, because MI relies heavily on empathy as a means to access feelings, cultures that refrain from the expression of feelings may find themselves in a state of disequilibrium or discomfort that could harm the therapeutic relationship. Finally, fidelity to MI treatment; that is, the ability to provide MI treatment adequately to different cultures may be challenging, especially in light of how empathy and complex reflective listening skills are interpreted in other cultures (Lee et al., 2015). Despite these potential cross-cultural problems, the future of MI with diverse clients from the United States and internationally, seems promising though adaptations for cross-cultural counseling using MI will need to be made (McMaster & Griva, 2015).

EFFICACY

Despite being a relatively new approach to counseling, within the past three decades there have been more than 200 randomized clinical trials published associated with MI and MI-related interventions (Miller & Arkowitz, 2017). This ever-growing pool of data has produced varying results. In the majority of these studies, some of which were meta-analyses, patients receiving MI were compared with those receiving a different type of treatment or no treatment at all. The early studies on MI found positive change in a variety of concerns, with particular efficacy when working with those with substance abuse, problem drinking, and health care issues (Britt et al., 2004; Heckman et al., 2010; Hettema et al., 2005; Lundahl et al., 2010; Lundahl et al., 2013; Rubak et al., 2005).

As more studies were conducted, efficacy with anxiety, depression, gambling, and eating disorders were shown (Arkowitz et al., 2008). More recently, Arkowitz et al. (2017a), in a review of research, found that MI has been used with some success in the treatment of emotional disorders, obsessive-compulsive disorders, anxiety, post-traumatic stress disorder, comorbid substance use disorders, depression, suicidal ideation, addictions, gambling, smoking cessation, intimate partner violence, and eating disorders. In addition, there also seems to be some success in the treatment of phobias, sex offenders, sleep problems, and with parents dealing with young adults with schizophrenia (Arkowitz et al., 2017b).

Interestingly, when MI was combined with other treatment modalities, specific effects and adherence to treatment were extended over time; that is, MI was shown to have an enhancing effect when combined with other forms of treatment (Hettema et al., 2005). Additionally, some studies indicated that MI had greater effectiveness when used with patients with severe problems (Handmaker et al., 1999; Westra et al., 2009). When comparing MI with other therapeutic approaches, similar treatment outcomes were found, with the exception that MI required fewer sessions (Babor & Del Boca, 2003; Hodgins et al., 2001).

Probably one of the most important research questions is MI's efficacy as a stand-alone approach versus an approach to be combined with other theoretical orientations (Arkowitz et al., 2017c). The simple answer is that it is probably efficacious with both. If combined with other approaches, however, Arkowitz et al. (2017c) suggest the four processes of engaging, focusing, evoking, and planning need to be present, providers should be adequately trained in MI, and the treatment should be conducted in a manner that allows for comparisons with other treatment approaches. Research on MI has evolved quickly, and many studies show positive results. As MI continues to be used, refined, and combined with other therapeutic modalities, the usefulness of MI as a major therapeutic intervention will become clearer.

SUMMARY

Motivational interviewing (MI) was developed by William Miller after his work at an alcoholism treatment center where he found that a combination of person-centered counseling skills and brief intervention skills increased client acceptance of help and positive therapeutic outcomes. In 1990, Miller met Stephen Rollnick, and upon Rollnick's encouragement, they expanded the theory and wrote *Motivational Interviewing: Helping People Change.*

MI is steeped in existential-humanism and phenomenology and borrows heavily form person-centered counseling, though it also has a directive component. In addition, MI shows some postmodern influence related to empowering clients, being nonpathological, and developing equal and egalitarian relationships. It is also often seen as trans-theoretical, as the basis of MI can be used with any client and the actual techniques and process of change—after a client has decided to make change—can be used with most theoretical approaches.

MI is based on a theory of motivation, which suggests that motivation is key to change, and is multidimensional, dynamic and fluctuating, influenced by social interactions, can be modified, is influenced by the clinician's style, and should be elicited by the clinician. The overarching model of MI is the MI Spirit, which suggest how a counselor should bring himself or herself into the counseling relationship. This model comprises the elements of compassion, collaboration, acceptance (absolute worth, accurate empathy, autonomy support, and affirmation), and evocation, which is related to using change talk to encourage clients to look at the change process. Other key concepts include understanding that clients will face ambivalence about change; developing change talk, which facilitates the change process with clients and can be done in numerous ways; and avoiding confrontation, which involves listening to sustain talk, sometimes called rolling with resistance. Miller and Rollnick suggest two categories of change talk: preparatory change talk and mobilizing change talk, known by the acronym DARN CATS: Desire, Ability, Reason, Need, Commitment, Activation, and Taking Steps. A final key concept, known by its acronym FRAMES, has to do with the general manner in which the counselor conducts therapy, and stands for Feedback, Responsibility, Advice, Menu of options, Empathy, and Self-efficacy.

Keeping in mind the MI Spirit, remembering to avoid confrontation, and remembering the FRAMES acronym as a general direction for conducting counseling, there are some specific techniques that counselors use when practicing motivational interviewing. These include using a "ruler" to assess willingness, importance, and readiness to change; using OARS (Open-ended questions; Affirmations; simple, amplified, and double-sided Reflective listening; and collecting, linking, and transitional Summaries); showing empathy; developing discrepancy; eliciting change talk (evocative questions, importance ruler, exploring the decisional balance, elaborating, querying extremes, looking back, looking forward including the miracle question, and exploring goals and values); listening to sustain talk (rolling with resistance), which looks at avoiding discord and not doing the righting reflex; information and advice giving; and goal setting. With the MI spirit and the FRAMES acronym in the "back pocket" of the counselor, the above skills are used within the four processes of counseling: engaging, focusing, evoking, and planning.

MI employs a number of techniques and ways of being with clients that make it particularly amenable to working with a wide range of diverse cultures. Some of these include being accepting, empathic, respectful, nonjudgmental, curious, and not coming on as the expert. This egalitarian, collaborative, and nonpathologizing relationship shows deep respect of cultural differences, and studies have shown positive outcomes with diverse cultures. The approach is used internationally, though some cultures that are more collectivist in nature may have problems with the development of an internal locus of control, which MI tends to encourage.

Despite being a recent theory, MI has developed a sizable amount of research that shows fairly good efficacy across a variety of client populations. When combined with other treatment modalities, MI has been shown to have an enhancing effect. It also seems to show good efficacy with severe problems. Although some confusion exists over whether MI is best used as a stand-alone theory or an approach to be combined with other theories, research seems to indicate that both approaches show some efficacy. MI is a relatively new therapy that has shown efficacy with many populations and is continuing to develop. Although its popularity has soared in recent years, its future as a mainstay of a therapeutic regime seems bright but still somewhat unknown.

KEY WORDS AND TERMS

Absolute worth
Acceptance
Affirmations
Ambivalence
Amplified reflection
Assessing importance, competence, and readiness for change
Autonomy support
Avoiding confrontation
Change talk
Collaboration
Collecting summaries
Compassion
Conditions of worth
Confidence to change
DARN CATS
Developing discrepancy
Discord
Double-sided reflection
Eliciting change talk
Empathy
Empowerment
Engaging
Equal and egalitarian relationship
Evocation
Evoking
Existential humanistic philosophy
Focusing
FRAMES
Information and advice giving
Linking summaries
Listening
Listening to sustain talk
MI Spirit
Miller, William Richard
Mobilizing change talk
Motivation
Motivational Interviewing Network of Trainers (MINT)
Nondirective
Nonpathological stance
OARS
Open-ended questions
Person-centered counseling
Phenomenological perspective
Phenomenology
Planning
Postmodern
Preparatory change talk
Readiness to change
Reflecting
Reflective listening
Reframe
Righting reflex
Rogers, Carl
Rolling with resistance
Rollnick, Stephen
Ruler
Seven types of change talk
Simple reflection
Summarizing
Sustain talk
The Drinker's Check-Up
Transitional summaries
Trans-theoretical
Willingness to change

REFERENCES

Arkowitz, H., & Miller, W. R. (2008). Learning, applying, and extending motivational interviewing. In H. Arkowitz, H. A. Westra, W. R. Miller, & S. Rollnick (Eds.), *Motivational interviewing in the treatment of psychological problems* (pp. 1–25). Guilford Press.

Arkowitz, H., Miller, W. R., & Rollnick, S. (Eds.) (2017a). *Motivational interviewing in the treatment of psychological problems* (2nd ed.). Guilford Press.

Arkowitz, H., Miller, W. R., & Rollnick, S. (2017b). Preface. In H. Arkowitz, W. R. Miller, & S. Rollnick (Eds.), *Motivational interviewing in the treatment of psychological problems* (2nd ed., pp. vi–viii). Guilford Press.

Arkowitz, H., Miller, W. R., & Rollnick, S. (2017c). Conclusions and future directions. In H. Arkowitz, W. R. Miller, & S. Rollnick (Eds.), *Motivational interviewing in the treatment of psychological problems* (2nd ed., pp. 365–387). Guilford Press.

Arkowitz, H., Westra, H. A., Miller, W. R., & Rollnick, S. (Eds.) (2008). *Motivational interviewing in the treatment of psychological problems.* Guilford Press.

Babor, T. F., & Boca, F. K. (2003). *Treatment matching in alcoholism.* Cambridge University Press.

Bayne, H., & Neukrug, E. (2017). Metaphors for empathy: Getting into character. In S. E. Stewart-Spencer & C. J. Dean, C. J. (Eds.), *Metaphors and therapy: Enhancing clinical supervision and education* (pp. 80–88). Independent Therapy.

Britt, E., Hudson, S. M., & Blampied, N. M. (2004). Motivational interviewing in health settings: A review. *Patient Education and Counselling, 53,* 147–155. https://doi.org/10.1016/S0738-3991(03)00141-1

Cialdini, R. B. (2007). *Influence: The psychology of persuasion.* Collins Business.

Cole, C. (2012). *Core concepts of motivational interviewing.* Psychotherapy.net.

Conversation with William R. Miller. (2009). *Addiction, 104,* 883–893. https://doi.org/10.1111/j.1360-0443.2009.02544.x

Dean, L. M. (2015). Motivational interviewing. In E. Neukrug (Ed.), *The SAGE encyclopedia of theory in counseling and psychotherapy* (Vol. 2, pp. 668–672). SAGE Publications.

De Shazer, S. (1988). *Clues: Investigating solutions in brief therapy.* W. W. Norton.

Handmaker, N. S., Miller, W. R., & Manicke, M. (1999). Findings of a pilot study of motivational interviewing with pregnant drinkers. *Journal of Studies in Alcohol,* 60(2), 285–287. https://doi.org/10.15288/jsa.1999.60.285

Heckman, C. J., Egleston, B. L., & Hofmann, M. T. (201). Efficacy of motivational interviewing for smoking cessation. A systematic review and meta-analysis. *Tobacco Control, 19,* 410–416. http://dx.doi.org/10.1136/tc.2009.033175

Herman, K. C., Reinke, W. M., Frey, A. J., & Shepard, S. A. (2014). *Motivational interviewing in schools: Strategies for engaging parents, teachers, and students.* Springer.

Hodgins, D. C., Currie, S. R., el-Guebaly, N. (2001). Motivational enhancement and self-help treatments for problem gambling. *Journal of Clinical Psychology, 69*(1), 50–57. https://doi.org/10.1037/0022-006X.69.1.50

Hettema, J., Steele, J., & Miller, W. R. (2005). Motivational interviewing. *Annual Review of Clinical Psychology, 1*, 91–111. https://doi.org/10.1146/annurev.clinpsy.1.102803.143833

Kirschenbaum, H. 2013. *Values clarification in counseling and psychotherapy: Practical strategies for individual and group settings*. Oxford University Press.

Lee, C., Tavares, T., Popat-Jain, A., & Naab, P. (2015). Assessing treatment fidelity in a cultural adaptation of motivational interviewing. *Journal of Ethnicity in Substance Abuse, 14*, 208–219. https://doi.org/10.1080/15332640.2014.973628

Lundahl, B., Kunz, C., Brownell, C., Tollefson, D., & Burke, B. L. (2010). A meta-analysis of motivational interviewing: Twenty-five years of empirical studies. *Research on Social Work Practice, 20*(2), 137–160. https://doi.org/10.1177/1049731509347850

Lundahl, B., Moleni, T., Burke, B. L., Butters, R., Tollefson, D., Butler, C., & Rollnick, S. (2013). Motivational interviewing in medical care settings: A systemic review and meta-analysis of randomized controlled trials. *Patient Education and Counseling, 93*(2), 157–168. https://doi.org/10.1016/j.pec.2013.07.012

McMaster, F., & Griva, K. (2015). Motivational interviewing across cultures: Training notes. *The European Health Psychologist, 17*(3), 122–128.

Miller, W. R. (1983). Motivational interviewing with problem drinkers. *Behavioural Psychotherapy, 11*, 147–172. https://doi.org/10.1017/S0141347300006583

Miller, W. R. (1996). Motivational interviewing: Research, practice, and puzzles. *Addictive Behaviors*, 6, 835–842. https://doi.org/10.1016/0306-4603(96)00044-5

Miller, W. R, & Arkowitz, H. (2017). Learning, applying, and extending motivational interviewing. In H. Arkowitz and W. R. Miller (Eds.), *Motivational interviewing in the treatment of psychological problems* (2nd ed., pp. 1–32). Guilford Press.

Miller, W. R., & Rollnick, S. (2002). *Motivational interviewing: Preparing people for change* (2nd ed.). Guilford Press.

Miller, W. R., & Rollnick, S. (2004). Talking oneself into change: Motivational interviewing, stages of change, and therapeutic process. *Journal of Cognitive Psychotherapy, 18*, 299–308. https://doi.org/10.1891/jcop.18.4.299.64003

Miller, W. R., & Rollnick, S. (2009). Ten things that motivational interviewing is not. *Behavioural and Cognitive Psychotherapy, 37*, 129–140. https://doi.org/10.1017/S1352465809005128

Miller, W. R., & Rollnick, S. (2013). *Motivational interviewing: Helping people change* (3rd ed.). Guilford Press.

Miller, W. R., & Rose, G. S. (2009). Toward a theory of motivational interviewing. *American Psychologist, 64*, 527–537. https://doi.org/10.1037/a0016830

Miller, W. R., & Sovereign, R. G. (1989). The check-up: A model for early intervention in addictive behaviors. In T. Løberg, W. R. Miller, P. E. Nathan, & G. A. Marlatt (Eds.), *Addictive behaviors: Prevention and early intervention* (pp. 219–231). Swets & Zeitlinger.

Miller, W. R., Sovereign, R. G., & Krege, B. (1988). Motivational interviewing with problem drinkers: II. The drinker's check-up as a preventive intervention. *Behavioural Psychotherapy, 16*, 251–268. https://doi.org/10.1017/S0141347300014129

Motivational Interviewing. (2019). *Psychology Today*. https://www.psychologytoday.com/us/therapy-types/motivational-interviewing

Moyers, T. (2004). History and happenstance: How motivational interviewing got its start. *Behavioural and Cognitive Psychotherapy, 18*, 291–298. https://doi.org/10.1891/jcop.18.4.291.6399

Neukrug, E. (2017, February 2). Creative and novel approaches to empathy. *Counseling Today*. http://ct.counseling.org/2017/02/creative-novel-approaches-empathy/

Neukrug, E. (2019). *Counseling and helping skills: Critical techniques to becoming a counselor*. Cognella Academic Publishing.

Rollnick, S. (2015). *Motivational interviewing with the guru, Stephen Rollnick*. https://www.youtube.com/watch?v=lF1i32ucPvE

Rogers, C. R. (1957). The necessary and sufficient conditions of therapeutic personality change. *Journal of Consulting Psychology, 21*, 95–103. https://doi.org/10.1037/h0045357

Rogers, C. R. (1962). The nature of man. In S. Doniger (Ed.), *The nature of man in theological and psychological perspective* (pp. 91–96). Harper & Brothers.

Rollnick, S., Kaplan, S., & Rutschman, R. (2016). *Motivational interviewing in schools: Conversations to improve behavior and learning*. Guilford Press.

Rollnick, S., & Miller, W. R. (1995). What is motivational interviewing? *Behavioural and Cognitive Psychotherapy, 23*, 325–334. https://doi.org/10.1017/S135246580001643X

Rosengren, D. (2009). *Building motivational interviewing skills: A practitioner workbook*. Guilford Press.

Rubak, S., Sandbaek, A., Lauritzen, T., & Christensen, B. (2005). Motivational interviewing: A systematic review and meta-analysis. *British Journal of General Practice, 55*, 305–312.

Schumacher, J., & Madson, M. (2015). *Foundations of motivational interviewing: Tips and strategies for addressing common clinical challenges*. Oxford University Press.

Wampold, B. E., & Imel, Z. E. (2015). *The great psychotherapy debate: The evidence for what makes psychotherapy work* (2nd ed.). Routledge.

Westra, H. A., Arkowitz, H., & Dozois, D. J. A. (2009). Adding a motivational interviewing pretreatment to cognitive behavioral therapy for generalized anxiety disorder: A preliminary randomized controlled trial. *Journal of Anxiety Disorders, 23*, 1106–1117. https://doi.org/10.1016/j.janxdis.2009.07.014

CASE STUDY: ROB SEES A MOTIVATIONAL INTERVIEWING THERAPIST

(Please read about the Millers in Appendix I prior to reading this case study)

Markus's partner, Rob, was nervous about seeing a counselor and asked Markus if he would go with him. As they sat in the waiting room, holding hands yet staring into space, Rob worried about his drinking. Dr. Al Nickabee emerged and said, "Mr. Johnson, why don't you come in." Rob looked at Dr. Nickabee and said, "Do you mind if Markus comes in with me—well, at least initially." "Of course not—why don't you both come in," said Dr. Nickabee. Marcus and Rob walked in and sat in two comfortable chairs next to each other. Dr. Nickabee sat across from the two and said, "So what brings you in today?" Rob looked at Markus, and said, "You tell him," at which point Markus answered. "Well, Rob was away for a number of months on government business—I missed him terribly, but when he got back, I suddenly realized that he has this problem—this drinking problem. I realized that we used to go through at least a bottle of wine a night, and suddenly, while he was gone, I went through like a bottle a week. Rob was just drinking too much, and I'm also wondering if his drinking negatively impacts our relationship." Rob sat in silence but nodded his head as if to say "yes."

Dr. Nickabee looked at the two men, and said, "So, the two of you are in kind of agreement that Rob's drinking could be a bit out of control, and maybe it's also not so good on the relationship." "Yeah, that's it," said Rob softly. Continued Dr. Nickabee: "Well, you know, Rob, I think that's something we can work on together, if you want to." "Well, kind of," responded Rob. "Well, 'kind of,' is good enough for me," said Dr. Nickabee.

For the remainder of the session, Dr. Nickabee took a history and obtained more information about Rob's and Markus's relationship. The session ended, and Rob said, "You know, I think I'm ready to come back alone next week."

The next week Rob showed up at the session by himself, and Dr. Nickabee invited him in. "I'm so glad to see you today. How'd the week go?" "So-so," replied Rob. "Can you tell me the good and bad aspects of the week?" the therapist asked. "Well, I definitely was thinking more about my drinking, and I wish I wasn't drinking so much. But I also think that my drinking calms me down in some ways. You know, I have a pretty stressful job for the government. They're always sending me some place, and I know Markus isn't happy with that. And, you know, my sleep—it sucks. I'm up half the night thinking about things, so I'll often take a drink in the middle of night just to calm me down." "Ah, I see," said Dr. Nickabee. "You're seeing that the drinking may not be so good on your relationship but may offer some other benefits."

Dr. Nickabee studied Rob, and said, "Let me ask you something. If your life was just as you would want it, what would it look like—especially in relationship to your drinking and your relationship?" Rob sat still for a minute to ponder the question. Then he blurted out, "Well, I definitely would be drinking less, be spending more time with Marcus, and feeling less stress about work and life in general." "Well, that's a great start, Rob," said Dr. Nickabee. "If I'm hearing you right, you really want to have more time and more intimacy with Markus, and want to have a calmer life with less alcohol—oh yeah, and better sleep." "Yes, that's exactly right," said Rob.

"So, Rob, have you thought about ways you can change your life so that it fits your vision of what you want a bit more?" asked Dr. Nickabee. "Well, I have, but it just seems like a lot of work." Dr. Nickabee thought for a moment, and said, "Well, I think I'm hearing you—on one hand you want this other life, but on the other hand, it's just seems like it will be a royal pain getting there." "Yes, you hit it on the nose, Dr. Nickabee."

"Rob, I just want to check something out with you. I know you said that you drink at night sometimes to help you sleep. Just want to know if you're aware that drinking actually hinders sleep?" "Okay, okay … I've heard that," said Rob. "I guess in the moment it helps, but in the long run it doesn't." "Okay Rob, just want to be on the same page," said Dr. Nickabee.

"So, Rob, I sometimes use the acronym DARN CATS to help me, and whoever I'm working with, look at the change process. It standards for **D**esire to change, **A**bility to change, **R**eason to change, **N**eed to change, and then **C**ommitment, **A**ctivation, and **T**aking **S**teps to change. How would you feel like discussing those steps?" "I'm okay with it," Rob answers. "Let's see where it takes me."

"Okay, Rob, how about on a scale of 1 to 10, with 10 being very important and 1 being least important, how much do you want to change? And, let's do the same for willingness to change." "Well, Dr. Nickabee, I know I want to change my drinking. It's really important to me. I know it negatively affects my relationship and probably my sleep. Maybe that's a 9. On willingness, however, I may only be a 6. It's going to be damn hard." "So, you really think it's important but not sure you can embrace it totally right now?" asked Dr. Nickabee. "Yeah, that's right," said Rob. "What about 'Ability' to change?" "Well, I think I can do it if I really want to," answered Rob. "I know what steps I would need to take." "Oh, really," said Dr. Nickabee. "What would that be?" "Well, I think I would start going to some AA meetings—that would help motivate me." "Great, Rob, but I notice that you only focused on the drinking. What about your stress, sleep, and relationship with Markus?" "Well, honestly, Dr. Nickabee, all is important, very important, but a bit overwhelming. Can we take one thing at a time?" Dr. Nickabee again studied his client. "You know, Rob, what I really want for you is to feel good about yourself and focus on what you need to focus on, and you're telling me all is important, but you want to, for now, focus more on your drinking. That makes sense to me." Rob physically relaxes and sits back in his chair, as if to say, "Yes, it's just a bit overwhelming, thanks for hearing me."

"Let's keep looking at that acronym," said Dr. Nickabee. "As for 'Reason,' I think I can answer that for you. You know drinking is not good for you, and even know it probably isn't good for your sleep or your relationship." "Yeah, that's dead on," said Rob "And what about 'Need,' or urgency of the problem?" asked Dr. Nickabee. "Well, I need to do this eventually," answered Rob. "I know I could put it off but might as well do it now."

"Okay, Rob, this seems pretty clear to me. You think this is all important, you think there's a need and probably shouldn't put it off. You see some issues in a number of areas in your life, but pretty much just want to focus on the drinking right now. You also see that your drinking may impact other parts of your life, such as work, sleep, and your relationship with Markus. So, we've pretty much identified the problem, but the commitment, action, and steps are a bit unclear. Maybe we can focus on that." Rob nodded in agreement.

"So, Rob, I got all these things rolling through my head of things that you can do." "Like what?" asked Rob." "Well, you can go to AA meetings, take better care of your health—maybe work out, not drink at night, spend more time with Markus, do some relaxation exercises, and more." "Whoa, hold on, that's a bit much," Rob said in protest. "Oh, sorry—yeah, I guess I got ahead of myself," replied Dr. Nickabee. "You clearly said that drinking was the focus you wanted. I just see you as so capable, I think I got ahead of myself—and certainly ahead of you. My bad! Let's see what YOU want to do." "Well, you know Dr. Nickaee, I actually want to do all that stuff, but I question my ability."

"You are quite something, Rob. You're insightful, wanting a good relationship, know what to do, and willing to make some moves. I'm impressed! But as you said, let's take it slow. If you were to pick one thing to do between this week and next week, what might that be?"

"Hmm. All those things you mentioned sound good, but I think the most tangible would be to go to an AA meeting," answered Rob. "That sounds great," said Dr Nickabee. "Let's make that our goal for next week." "Okay," said Rob. "You know, I might join a gym too, but I'm not making promises on that one." "I think all of this is a great start," said Dr. Nickabee. "You came in here last week with Markus a bit wary of what this was all about. You and Markus identified some things that are troubling both of you. You clearly seemed motivated and came back today. You focused on a number of things that you want to change in your life, but also clearly noted that you want to take things one step at a time. You pretty much identified that the drinking would be your focus, and you decided to go to at least one AA meeting this week. You also said you might go to the gym—but I have no expectations about that as you clearly told me 'maybe.' I've got to say, two sessions and I'm rather impressed with where you are. I look forward to seeing you next week and see what you've done."

"Dr. Nickabee, thanks so much. On one hand, these things seem pretty obvious to me, but you did help me set up my priorities and you kind of seem like a coach for me—in my corner cheering me on. It makes me more motivated to do something. I'm actually kind of excited. See you next week."

"Great, I'm looking forward to it. Oh yeah, one more thing before you leave. I have a list of AA meetings in the area, can I give you that?" "Yes, absolutely," Rob replied, taking the list. The therapist shakes his client's hand, and, with a smile, says, "Looking forward to next week."

QUESTIONS FOR YOU TO PONDER

1. How does Dr. Nickabee embody the MI Spirit relative to compassion, collaboration, and acceptance? Give some examples.
2. How does Dr. Nickabee roll with resistance with Rob? Provide a couple examples.
3. What examples, if any, of simple reflection, amplified reflection, and double-sided reflection does Dr. Nickabee use?
4. How does Dr. Nickabee incorporate information and advice going into his work with Rob?
5. What kind of summaries does Dr. Nickabee incorporate in his work with Rob?
6. Give examples of how Rob manifests ambivalence about changing.
7. How does Dr. Nickabee work with Rob's discrepancies about change?
8. Dr. Nickabee uses a number of mechanisms to develop discrepancies. Describe the types he uses. Would you have used any he did not use?
9. What do you think of Dr. Nickabee's use of the DARN CATS acronym?
10. Give examples of how Dr. Nickabee uses listening to address sustain talk (rolling with resistance).
11. Discuss how you think Dr. Nicabee handled pushing Rob to do too much. Do you believe he did the right thing by backing off? Might you have handled it differently?
12. Provide examples of some areas of your life where you have discrepancies. Do you believe this approach might work with you?

Credits

Fig. 7.1: Source: https://coping.us/motivationalinterviewing/overviewofmi.html.

Img. 7.2: W. R. Miller and S. Rollnick, "Profiles of Clients," *Motivational Interviewing: Helping People Change*, pp. 213. Copyright © 2013 by Guilford Press.

8

Positive Counseling

Kira Mari Candelieri Marcari, Kathleen Brown, and Clara Adkins

LEARNING OUTCOMES

- To understand the history of positive counseling and learn about Martin Seligman and other major theorists involved in its development.
- To examine the view of human nature of positive counseling, including identifying strengths and positive qualities, logical positivism, anti-determinism, intentionality, and the build-what's-strong approach.
- To identify select key concepts of positive counseling, including sustaining psychological well-being, the human default toward negativity, strengths theory, the broaden and build theory of positive emotions, and the PERMA model.
- To identity often used techniques of positive counseling, such as assessing well-being (e.g., Ryff's Six Dimensions of Psychological Well-Being, the Quality of Life Inventory, and the Five Paths of Happiness), identifying things done well, increasing one's positivity ratio, mindfulness, strength-based exercises, gratitude exercises, hope and optimism exercises, and other positive psychotherapy interventions.
- To describe the counseling process of CPT.
- To examine social and cultural applicability of CPT.
- To review the efficacy of CPT.
- To offer a case study that demonstrates the CPT process.

BRIEF HISTORY OF POSITIVE COUNSELING

> One evening, an old Cherokee Indian told his grandson about a battle that goes on inside people. He said, "My son, the battle is between two 'wolves' inside us all. One is Evil. It is anger, envy, jealousy, sorrow, regret, greed, arrogance, self-pity, guilt, resentment, inferiority, lies, false pride, superiority, and ego. The other is Good. It is joy, peace, love, hope, serenity, humility, kindness, benevolence, empathy, generosity, truth, compassion, and faith." The grandson thought about it for a minute and then asked his grandfather, "Which wolf wins?" The old Cherokee simply replied, "The one you feed." (author unknown, cited in Martin, 2013, p. 57)

Similar to this indigenous folklore, many in the helping professions now believe it is more beneficial for clients to focus on the positive aspects of self than spend months or years focusing on problems. In fact, the study of happiness and positivity dates back thousands of years. For instance, Democritus (~ 460 BCE–370 BCE) believed that "a happy life is not exclusively the product of a favorable fate or external circumstances but rather of a man's cast of mind" (Kesebir & Diener, 2009, p. 60). Over the centuries, others also dabbled in the study of happiness, though a focus on the negative or pathological side of the individual often took precedence over a positive focus.

In the United Sates during the 20th century, the treatment of mental health problems was mostly focused on pathology and how to fix people who were deemed ill (Frisch, 2015; Neukrug, 2016). This focus on what was wrong with people was reflected in the counseling theories that dealt mostly with problems, the American Psychiatric Association's Diagnostic and Statistical Manual that focused on mental disorders, the training obtained in graduate and medical schools, and the development of clinics and centers around the country to house what were called the mentally ill and psychiatrically depraved. There were, however, inklings of a positive psychology focus throughout this period (Froh, 2004; Rich, 2001, Neukrug, 2018). For instance, even some of the early psychodynamic theorists, such as Carl Jung and Alfred Adler, talked about the importance of enhancing individuals' strengths and helping people prosper through the goals of positive psychology. Many early humanists focused on enhancing human potential, and **Abraham Maslow** even had a chapter in one of his books called "Positive Psychology." In addition, individuals such as **Thomas Szasz** and **William Glasser** questioned the emphasis on mental illness within mental health professionals. Glasser, in particular, stressed the importance of using positive language. So, within the mental health system that was largely focused on symptoms and pathology, there were a burgeoning group of people who were questioning this emphasis and looking more toward the positive aspects of people. Then, in the latter part of the 20th century, we began to see an increased amount of research and writing on such topics as happiness and subjective well-being, by **Ed Diener**; flow, meaning, and optimal experiences, by **Mihaly Csikszentmihalyi**; positive emotions, by **Barbara Fredrickson**; hope, by **Charles "Rick" Snyder;** and well-being and resilience, by **Carol Ryff.**

In 1998, **Martin Seligman**, the president of the American Psychological Association, decided it was time to launch the **positive psychology** movement (Frisch, 2015). Seligman encouraged research and articles in the field and developed a section on positive psychology in the counseling psychology division of APA (Seligman & Csikszentmihalyi, 2000). Seligman had been known for his experiments on **learned helplessness** (Seligman, 1972; Seligman & Maier, 1967), in which he showed that dogs that received electric shocks in a situation they could not avoid would subsequently not avoid a similar situation when escape *was* possible. They had learned to be helpless. Subsequent research on humans showed that certain types of cognitive styles tend to lead to learned helplessness in people. After years of research on learned helplessness, Seligman shifted perspectives and realized that individuals can modify their thinking and actions and learn how to be positive! He called this **learned optimism** (Seligman, 1990). Seligman's change of focus from learned helplessness to learned optimism coincided with an experience he had with his 5-year-old daughter (see Box 8.1).

BOX 8.1 EXCERPT FROM MARTIN SELIGMAN

The notion of a positive psychology movement began at a moment in time a few months after I had been elected president of the American Psychological Association. It took place in my garden while I was weeding with my 5-year-old daughter, Nikki. I have to confess that even though I write books about children, I'm really not all that good with them. I am goal-oriented and time-urgent, and when I am weeding in the garden, I am actually trying to get the weeding done. Nikki, however, was throwing weeds into the air and dancing around. I yelled at her. She walked away, came back, and said, "Daddy, I want to talk to you." "Yes, Nikki?" "Daddy, do you remember before my fifth birthday? From the time I was three to the time I was five, I was a whiner. I whined every day. When I turned five, I decided not to whine anymore. That was the hardest thing I've ever done. And if I can stop whining, you can stop being such a grouch." This was for me an epiphany, nothing less. I learned something about Nikki, something about raising kids, something about myself, and a great deal about my profession. First, I realized that raising Nikki was not about correcting whining. Nikki did that herself. Rather, I realized that raising Nikki was about taking this marvelous skill—I call it "seeing into the soul"—and amplifying it, nurturing it, helping her to lead her life around it to buffer against her weaknesses and the storms of life. Raising children, I realized, is more than fixing what is wrong with them. It is about identifying and nurturing their strongest qualities, what they own and are best at, and helping them find niches in which they can best live out these positive qualities. ... " (Seligman & Csikszentmihalyi, 2014, p.3).

Seligman's conversation with his daughter, Nikki, reminded him of the importance of focusing on individual competencies and skills as opposed to the negative aspects of life. Professionally, he realized that the mental health field would have focused on correcting Nikki's whining, rather than nurturing her positive aspects of self and her strengths. To Seligman, psychotherapy had stepped away from trying to increase the quality of life and fostering natural aptitude, to attempting to fix the negative ailments of an individual. He decided to use his presidency to advocate for a shift within the mental health field. The field of positive psychology thrived throughout his 7-year term, seeing the creation of organizations such as the Positive Psychology Steering Committee and the Positive Psychology Network, conferences such as the Positive Psychology Summit, and a variety of publications. These developments furthered the establishment of the positive psychology movement and, subsequently, positive counseling or therapy (Lopez, 2009; Schulman, 2009; Snyder & Lopez, 2002).

Although Seligman popularized positive psychology, the movement did not pop out of nowhere. For instance, its beginning can be traced back to the writings the humanistic psychologists who, like the positive psychology movement, was strength-based (Joseph & Linley, 2006; Linley, 2009). However, the humanists were wed to many existential concepts and believed that people were inherently good; whereas, those who embrace positive psychology believe that people are inherently capable of good and bad feelings and actions, and that our actual behaviors are the result of a multitude of factors, including upbringing, the system in which one lives, culture, genes, and perhaps a little bit of mystery. So, if we're capable of being bad or good, the positive psychology movement suggests we make efforts to focus on the strengths and positive feelings of the person. The current wave of those involved in positive psychology has emphasized the importance of having people focus on the more positive emotions, the study of positive traits, and mechanisms for establishing institutions that emphasize the positive (Peterson, 2006). The **Positive Psychology Center** (2019) at the University of Pennsylvania suggests that the goals of positive psychology include building a science that supports:

- Families and schools that allow children to flourish
- Workplaces that foster satisfaction and high productivity
- Communities that encourage civic engagement
- Therapists who identify and nurture their patients' strengths
- The teaching of positive psychology
- Dissemination of positive psychology interventions in organizations and communities (para. 4)

Although many of the ideas of positive psychology are critical to positive counseling, there are differences between the two movements (Rashid, 2009). Whereas positive psychology represents a broad-based approach that can be applied to many settings, positive counseling is specifically focused on how to use many of the ideas proposed by the positive psychology movement in counseling and psychotherapy. Today, there are a number of therapies that "are consistent with the ambition of positive psychology to facilitate well-being and not simply to alleviate distress and dysfunction" (Joseph & Linley, 2009, p. 758) and other therapies integrate many of the ideas from the positive psychology movement into their existing approaches (McAuliffe, 2019). However, are few approaches that fully integrate positive psychology precepts into their approach. Thus, this chapter will focus on the underlying view of human nature of positive counseling, examine some of the key concepts to positive counseling, provide some typical techniques that might be used when practicing positive counseling, and examine how theory and techniques may be applied to positive counseling as an adjunct to traditional therapies and as a stand-alone approach.

VIEW OF HUMAN NATURE

Although the positive psychology and resulting positive counseling movements evolved out of earlier epistemologies, especially those of humanistic psychology, there are strong distinctions between the views of human nature of positive psychology and humanistic psychology:

> The theorists, researchers, and practitioners advancing these perspectives hold different understandings about the nature of being human; differ widely in those aspects of psychological functioning they find most interesting; and, when seeking grounding or inspiration for their work in philosophy, look for it in very different schools of philosophic thought. (Waterman, 2013, p. 131)

Waterman (2013) argues that the basic philosophical underpinnings of each of the approaches are vastly different, though their goals are similar and include "promoting the potentials and well-being of their clients" (p. 131). How they get there, however, is very different. For instance, as just noted humanistic psychologists believe people are born inherently good, whereas positive psychologists view people as being capable of being good and bad. The humanistic psychology movement tends to rely on an examination of a number of basic **existential tenets**, and thus focuses on how one makes meaning in life and how the choices one has made results in his or her **phenomenological perspective**, or unique way of viewing the world. Allow a person to truly see themselves and make choices that are meaningful to their natural state of being, and they will make choices that actualizes their inherent goodness. Positive psychology and positive counseling, however, focus on assisting the person in **identifying strengths and positive qualities** and helping an individual strengthen identified areas to live a more fruitful, fulfilling, and positive life. Instead, it believes that individuals can better their lives through **logical positivism**, which means that they can make their lives better through a logical analysis of their situation. Thus, if people can embody both strengths and weaknesses, positive counseling suggests that counselors should help clients recognize and build upon their strengths.

Positive counseling, sometimes called positive psychotherapy, assumes that mental disorders; negative thoughts, feelings, and behaviors; and psychopathology occur when "growth, fulfillment, and happiness is thwarted" (Rashid, 2009, p. 749). Thus, symptoms are not seen as interminably embedded in the person, but rather as qualities any of us might exhibit under certain circumstances, and qualities that individuals can transcend if taught how to do so. In fact, positive counseling believes that human strengths are as inherent and present as human weaknesses:

> ... Mother Theresa's compassion for the poor, Gandhi's and Martin Luther King Jr's struggle for civil rights, Eleanor Roosevelt's altruism, Aung San Suu Kyi and Shareen Abadi's political and social courage are considered as authentic and valuable in their own right ... (Rashid, p. 2009, p. 749)

Positive counselors believe clients have been conditioned to talk about their negative qualities in therapy but, with a little direction, can be led to a discussion about the attainment of happiness, contentment, and joy. This is viewed as a **build-what's-strong approach** in contrast with a "fix-what's-wrong" approach (Duckworth et al., 2005, p. 631). Although problems and negative aspects of a person can also be discussed in counseling, it is important that there is a balance. In fact, Frederickson suggests that, in general, clients should have a 3:1 positive to negative ratio in their lives, and thus it makes sense there would be more of a positive focus in positive counseling than a negative one.

Positive counseling is an **intentional practice** that is **anti-deterministic**. It assumes people can change and develop a more positive outlook on life as they choose to embrace contentment, happiness, and joy in their lives. Although pains and hurts can be discussed, with intentionality, loving kindness and positive emotions can be vastly increased.

KEY CONCEPTS

Positive counseling is a relatively new addition to the 300 or so theories that are used today (Neukrug, 2015). Influenced largely by the positive psychology movement, positive counseling is shaped by its view of human nature; however, there is no "one theory" of positive counseling (Joseph & Linley, 2009; McAuliffe, 2019). Thus, we present here a number of key concepts that some practitioners who practice positive counseling would most likely embrace. They include **sustaining psychological well-being, the human default toward negativity, strengths theory, the broaden and build theory of positive emotions**, and the **PERMA model**.

Sustaining Psychological Well-Being

McAuliffe (2019) highlights three factors that impact one's sense of well-being. First, he suggests there is a **genetic set-point** for temperament, which means that certain aspects of our personality are largely determined by our genes. Thus, if one has a tendency for depression, there is a range, or variability, for that depression, but it is limited to some degree by one's set-point. Although one's set-point does sound somewhat deterministic, McAuliffe suggests "factors can determine whether, at any given time, an individual is in the upper or lower continuum of her or his range" (p. 6). Thus, changing **circumstances** can impact one's set-point in ways that result in the person being in the lower or the upper range. For instance, if one grows up in poverty with little resources, such circumstances would very likely prod that person toward the lower end of his or her set-point, while access to resources and loving, positive parents would push a person toward the high end of his or her set-point. Finally, **intentional activities**, such as practicing positive behaviors and thoughts and setting goals that lend oneself to positive outcomes, can push a person to the higher end of his or her set-point. Clearly, it is this last piece that counselors can mostly impact, though advocacy work can also positively impact one's circumstances.

The Human Default Toward Negativity

When you received grades in school, did you focus more on the lower or higher grades you received? And, when you were given an evaluation of your performance at work or in an activity (e.g., sports), did the critical or complimentary feedback stand out? Humans have a natural tendency to focus on the negative, and McAuliffe (2019) suggests the **positive is customary**, in the sense that we hardly notice it when it occurs. So, when a person receives positive recognition, it's accepted but rarely stands out to any great degree. But negative critiques will often stand out, and sometimes even hit us like a brick. Or, feeling good is taken for granted; however, when we feel badly, we take notice. Thus, the counselor's role is to counteract this default toward the negative. In fact, one of the most important things a counselor can do is attend to the positive aspects in a person's life, such as strengths, positive feelings, and positive attributes.

Strengths Theory

Strengths theory suggests it is more important to focus on a person's strengths and manage, not repair, a person's weak areas (Magyar-Moe, 2009). In fact, most people, including most therapists, first focus on wanting to repair or fix a weak area. Most counselors, for instance, initially assess what is "wrong" with a person and then spend lots of time trying to fix it. Strengths theory proponents suggest that focusing on human deficits is the result of the following four errors in thinking:

1. *Fixing a weakness makes a person stronger and remarkable.*
    - The reality is that fixing a weakness may make one average, but not make one great. Stopping drinking is a remarkable achievement for an alcoholic of which he or she should be very proud, but does not make one remarkable.

2. *Strengths will develop naturally.*
   - Although we might like to believe if one is born with certain strengths, he or she will naturally become an Olympic gold medalist or Nobel prize winner, the reality is that to optimize strengths, one needs to focus upon them and nurture them.
3. *Strengths and weaknesses are opposites.*
   - In truth, there is not a direct relationship between strengths and weaknesses and focusing on one does not necessarily impact the other in dramatic ways. For instance, we cannot make a person empathic by focusing on how he or she is not empathic.
4. *A person can do anything he or she focuses on.*
   - We all are good at some things and not so good at other things, and focusing on trying to be expert at something in which one has little talent can actually develop a failure identity. This does not mean we shouldn't try to be more successful in areas we deem important (even areas we have little talent in), but we need not expect that we will be perfectly good in everything.

The Broaden and Build Theory of Positive Emotions

Magyar-Moe (2009) summarize five hypotheses that underscore the importance of positive emotions, collectively called the broaden and build theory of positive emotions. They include the broaden, build, undoing, resilience, and flour hypotheses.

1. The **broaden hypothesis** suggests that increased positive emotions can broaden one's **thought-action responses**, which means that one has an increased ability to think about the consequences of behaviors before taking action. This results in a greater number of potential positive options from which to choose. In contrast, negative emotions tend to narrow one's repertoire of responses.
2. The **build hypothesis** suggests that positive emotions assist individuals in building their personal resources in the areas of "physical resources (i.e., coordination, cardiovascular health, and muscle strength), social resources (i.e., friendships, social skills, and support), intellectual resources (i.e., knowledge and problem-solving), and psychological resources (i.e., creativity, optimism, and resilience)" (Magyar-Moe, 2009, p. 8). These newly built resources tend to stay, even if a person is not experiencing positive emotions in a period of their lives.
3. The addition of positive emotions when struggling with negative emotions is the basis of the **undoing hypothesis**, which suggests that positive emotions can reduce the hold that negative emotions have on one's cognitive and physical well-being.
4. The **resilience hypothesis** suggests that positive emotions build on other positive emotions in that one has an upward spiral of positivity. Such positivity helps in building

resilience and enables individuals to have an easier time when struggling with difficult situations, and a faster time in bouncing back from difficult situations.

5. The **flourish hypothesis** suggests it is important to have an optimal level of positive to negative emotions, with Fredrickson (2009) suggesting a 3:1 ratio as being ideal. It is important to recognize that negative feelings are important, because one cannot experience the positive unless there is a contradictory feeling with which to compare it.

The PERMA Model

The PERMA model, developed by Seligman (2002, 2011, 2012), outlines five of the major attributes critical to experiencing a sense of well-being: **P**ositive emotions, **E**ngagement, **R**elationships, **M**eaning, and **A**chievement (**PERMA**) (Figure 8.1). Assessing whether these attributes are being addressed in counseling, education, business, or other settings is important to understanding whether individuals are experiencing a sense of life satisfaction—or well-being. Let's examine each of these important attributes.

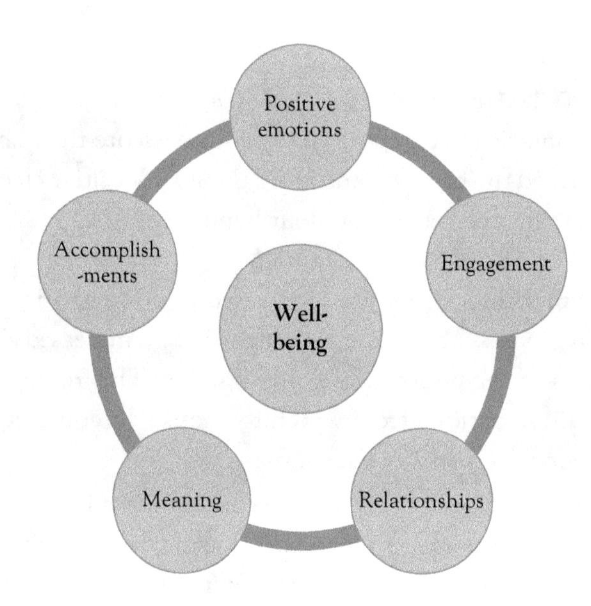

Figure 8.1 Seligman's PERMA Model of Well-Being

Positive Emotions

If a client can find the ability to harness and appreciate his or her **positive emotions**, then a ripple effect of positivity will follow in the client's relationships and daily actions. Positive emotions can be examined from the past, present, and future (Seligman, 2002). Figure 8.2 is a graphic of the different kinds of positive emotions one might experience at varying points throughout one's life.

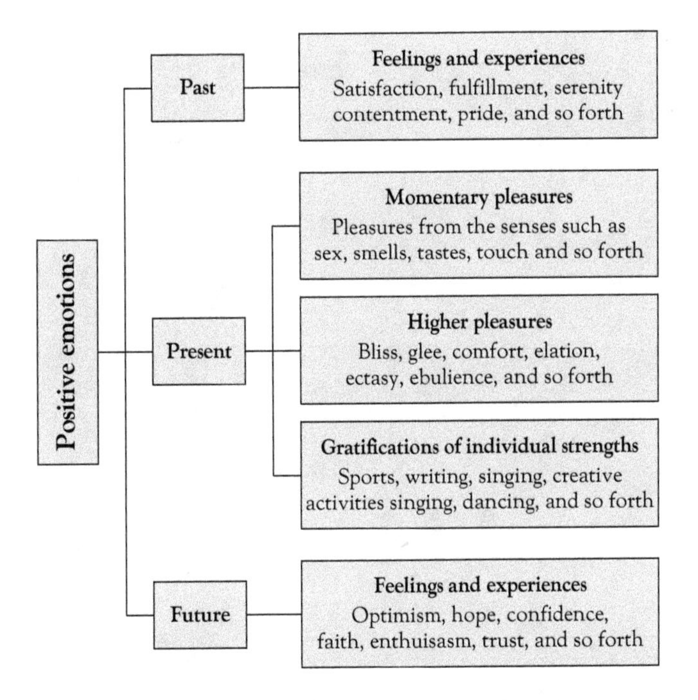

Figure 8.2 Varying Types of Positive Emotions

Engagement

Having a sense of **engagement**, in which one may lose track of time and become completely absorbed, is an important piece of well-being. This could be something as simple as becoming active in a sport (e.g., running), playing music (e.g., playing piano), participating in a hobby (e.g., woodworking), or any activity in which one becomes fully engaged. Engagement is closely related to the concept of **flow**, which is the process of being immersed in and surrendering to an activity perceived as important (Csikszentmilhalyi, 1997, 2009). Related to the creative process, when one experiences flow, concentration is heightened, loss of track of time is experienced, a reduction or elimination of negative thoughts occurs, and there is an absence of the fear of failure. Flow is more likely to be achieved when an individual's perception of the skill level, and the perception of the challenge of the task level, are high (see *upper right* quadrant of Figure 8.3). Other feeling states will be experienced based on the perceived challenge and skill levels. For instance, high perceived skill level and low perceived challenge level will result in a relaxed state (see *lower right* quadrant of Figure 8.3), whereas high perceived challenge level and low perceived skill level results in anxiety (see *upper left* quadrant of Figure 8.3).

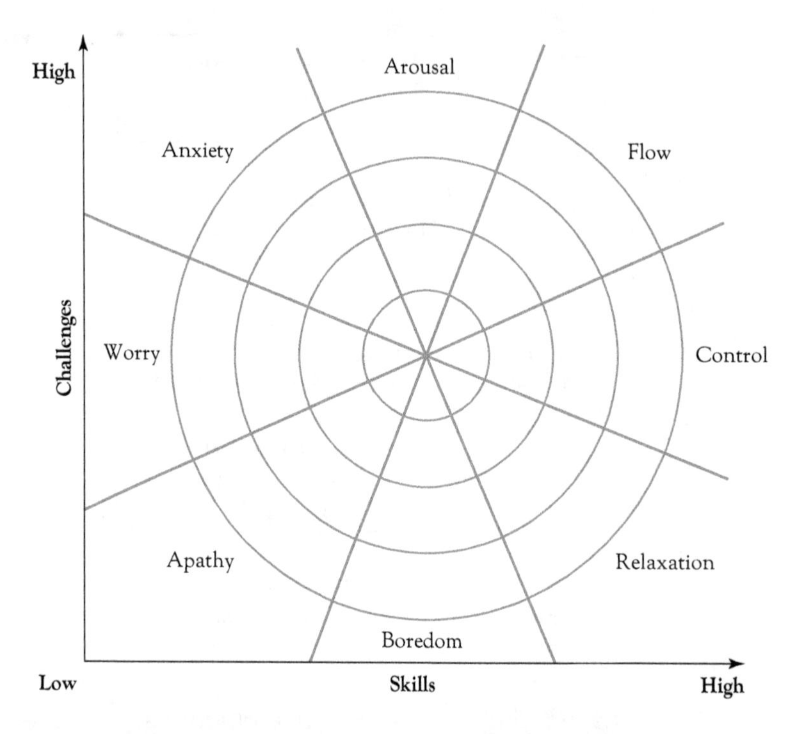

Figure 8.3 State of Flow

Relationships

Humans are social creatures, and we rely on connections with others to flourish. Having deep, meaningful **positive relationships** is vital to our well-being. Such relationships are based on some or all of the following attributes: love, emotional connections, physical interactions, and intimacy. Having connections with others helps an individual feel a sense of being grounded and safe, which is critical if one is going to feel positive emotions, such as joy and love, when connecting with others. Such connections also help to develop a sense of meaning in life.

Meaning

In contrast to the existential therapies that spend the bulk of the time focusing on existential dilemmas deeply rooted in the client's lack of understanding of his or her purpose and meaning in life, positive counseling is much more intentional in identifying and practicing those behaviors that will bring a sense of meaning and purpose for the person. Thus, understanding what is important to a person is focused upon and choices are made to increase those behaviors. This results in increased positive feelings toward self and others.

Accomplishment

We all thrive when we are succeeding, achieving our goals, and bettering ourselves, especially when our goals are in alignment with our development of meaning and purpose in life. Developing and realizing our **accomplishments** aids in the development and experience of feelings of pride and worth. Accomplishing something in life seems critically related to self-discipline and grit, much more so than IQ (Csikszentmihalyi, 2014; Duckworth, 2016; see Box 8.2).

BOX 8.2 YOUR PERMA: MEASURING YOUR LEVEL OF FLOURISHING

Seligman (2019) has developed a number of instruments to assess happiness. If you would like to assess your PERMA, go to the link that follows, then click "login" and register. Next, click on the "Questionnaires" link and choose the questionnaire that reads "PERMA." Of course, feel free to take any of the many questionnaires listed on the site.

URL: https://www.authentichappiness.sas.upenn.edu/

TECHNIQUES

Positive counseling can be used as a stand-alone approach or in combination with other treatment modalities. The decision to use positive counseling on its own or in conjunction with another theory can be complex, and the therapist, in consultation with the client, should consider the efficacy of each approach. Often, when clients are struggling with more severe pathology and will be in counseling for longer periods, more traditional approaches to address problems are used; however, these are also good opportunities to include positive counseling techniques as a "value added" option for clients. Combining positive counseling with a more traditional approach can help ameliorate presenting problems while enhancing positive emotions in clients' lives. When clients come in with less severe symptoms, however, the use of positive counseling techniques, on their own, may be enough to help a person increase his or her sense of well-being, with the general target being a 3:1 ratio of positive to negative emotions. Today, there are many techniques with a positive focus that can help increase a person's sense of well-being. The following represent a few of the more commonly used ones: **assessing areas of well-being, identifying things done well, increasing one's positivity ratio, mindfulness, strength-based exercises, gratitude exercises, hope and optimism exercises,** and **other positive psychotherapy interventions.**

Assessing Well-Being

Although there are many ways to assess one's well-being, or lack thereof, instruments often used are Ryff's Six Dimensions of Psychological Well-Being and the Quality of Life Inventory.

Ryff's Six Dimensions of Psychological Well-Being

To help clients identify optimal levels of well-being, Ryff's (1989) **Six Dimensions of Psychological Well-Being** was modified so clients could assess their levels of well-being in six areas:

autonomy, personal growth, environmental mastery, purpose in life, positive relations, and self-acceptance (Fava & Ruini, 2003; Ruini, 2014; see Table 8.1).

TABLE 8.1 MODIFICATION OF THE SIX DIMENSIONS OF PSYCHOLOGICAL WELL-BEING ACCORDING TO RYFF'S MODEL

DIMENSIONS	IMPAIRED LEVEL	OPTIMAL LEVEL
Environmental mastery	The subject has or feels difficulties in managing everyday affairs; feels unable to change or improve surrounding context; is unaware of surrounding opportunities; lacks sense of control over external world.	The subject has a sense of mastery and competence in managing the environment; controls external activities; makes effective use of surrounding opportunities; is able to create or choose contexts suitable to personal needs and values.
Personal growth	The subject has a sense of personal stagnation; lacks sense of improvement or expansion over time; feels bored and uninterested with life; feels unable to develop new attitudes or behaviors.	The subject has a feeling of continued development; sees self as growing and expanding; is open to new experiences; has sense of realizing own potential; sees improvement in self and behavior over time.
Purpose in life	The subject lacks a sense of meaning in life; has few goals or aims, lacks sense of direction, does not see purpose in past life; has no outlooks or beliefs that give life meaning.	The subject has goals in life and a sense of directedness; feels there is meaning to present and past life; holds beliefs that give life purpose; has aims and objectives for living.
Autonomy	The subject is overconcerned with the expectations and evaluation of others; relies on judgment of others to make important decisions; conforms to social pressures to think or act in certain ways.	The subject is self-determining and independent; able to resist social pressures; regulates behavior from within; evaluates self by personal standards.
Self-acceptance	The subject feels dissatisfied with self; is disappointed with what has occurred in past life; is troubled about certain personal qualities; wishes to be different than what he or she is.	The subject has a positive attitude toward the self; accepts his or her good and bad qualities; feels positive about past life.

DIMENSIONS	IMPAIRED LEVEL	OPTIMAL LEVEL
Positive relations with others	The subject has few close, trusting relationships with others; finds it difficult to be open and is isolated and frustrated in interpersonal relationships; is not willing to make compromises to sustain important ties with others.	The subject has warm and trusting relationships with others; is concerned about the welfare of others; is capable of strong empathy, affection, and intimacy; understands give-and-take of human relationships.

Source: Fava, G. A., & Ruini, C. (2003). Development and characteristics of a well-being enhancing psychotherapeutic strategy: Well-being therapy. *Journal of Behavior Therapy and Experimental Psychiatry, 34, 51.*

Ruini & Fava (2009) suggest that clients should refer to Table 8.1, while using a diary, to identify those times when they have, and have not, experienced a sense of well-being. They can then become their own experts on identifying those thoughts that prevent them from continuing to experience a sense of well-being. Counselors can challenge clients' negative thoughts and suggest pleasurable activities to help them focus on positivity. In a relatively short amount of time, clients can "feed" themselves with positive thoughts and activities, which result in good feelings and a positive sense of well-being. Although Ryff's Six Dimensions of Psychological Well-Being can be used with many approaches that employ positive counseling techniques, **Giovanni Fava** developed one approach, called **well-being therapy**, that specifically used this scale (Fava, 2009; Fava & Ruini, 2003; Ruini & Fava, 2009; Ruini et al., 2015).

The Quality of Life Inventory

Frisch's (2006, 2015) **Quality of Life Inventory** assesses 16 areas of life to obtain an individual's overall satisfaction with life score. Frisch assumes that happiness is derived from having an individual's needs, wants, and goals fulfilled within these 16 areas. After taking the questionnaire, the individual obtains an overall quality of life score, which can range from very low, to low, to average, to high. In addition, each of the 16 areas is given a score that ranges from – 6 (dissatisfaction) to + 6 (satisfaction), with any score below a 0 indicating an area of concern. Frisch stresses that after a client identifies dissatisfaction areas, only those areas that are deemed important by the client are areas that will be targeted. The 16 areas are shown in Table 8.2.

TABLE 8.2 16 AREAS OF QUALITY OF LIFE THERAPY

1. *Health* is being physically fit, not sick, and without pain or disability.
2. *Self-Esteem* means liking and respecting yourself in light of your strengths and weaknesses, successes and failures, and ability to handle problems.
3. *Goals-and-Values* (or Philosophy of Life) are your beliefs about what matters most in life and how you should live, both now and in the future. This includes your goals in life, what you think is right or wrong, and the purpose or meaning of life as you see it. It may or may not include spiritual beliefs.
4. *Money* (or Standard of Living) is made of three things. It is the money you earn, the things you own (like a car or furniture) and believing that you will have the money and things that you need in the future.
5. *Work* means your career or how you spend most of your time. You may work at a job, at home taking care of your family, or at school as a student. WORK includes your duties on the job, the money you earn (if any), and the people you work with.
6. *Play* (or Recreation) means what you do in your free time to relax, have fun, or improve yourself. This could include watching movies, visiting friends, or pursuing a hobby like sports or gardening.
7. *Learning* means gaining new skills or information about things that interest you. LEARNING can come from reading books or taking classes on subjects like history, car repair, or using a computer.
8. *Creativity* is using your imagination to come up with new and clever ways to solve everyday problems or to pursue a hobby like painting, photography, or needlework. This can include decorating your home, playing the guitar, or finding a new way to solve a problem at work.
9. *Helping* (Social Service and Civic Action) means helping others in need or helping to make your community a better place to live. HELPING can be done on your own or in a group like a church, a neighborhood association, or a political party. HELPING can include doing volunteer work at a school or giving money to a good cause. HELPING means helping people who are not your friends or relatives.
10. *Love* (or Love Relationship) is a very close romantic relationship with another person. LOVE usually includes sexual feelings and feeling loved, cared for, and understood.
11. *Friends* (or Friendships) are people (not relatives) you know well and care about who have interests and opinions like yours. FRIENDS have fun together, talk about personal problems, and help each other out.
12. *Children* means how you get along with your child (or children). Think of how you get along as you care for, visit, or play with your child.

13. *Relatives* means how you get along with your parents, grandparents, brothers, sisters, aunts, uncles, and in-laws. Think about how you get along when you are doing things together like visiting, talking on the telephone, or helping out.
14. *Home* is where you live. It is your house or apartment and the yard around it. Think about how nice it looks, how big it is, and your rent or house payment.
15. *Neighborhood* is the area around your home. Think about how nice it looks, the amount of crime in the area, and how well you like the people.
16. *Community* is the whole city, town, or rural area where you live (it is not just your neighborhood). Community includes how nice the area looks, the amount of crime, and how well you like the people. It also includes places to go for fun like parks, concerts, sporting events, and restaurants. You may also consider the cost of things you need to buy, the availability of jobs, the government, schools, taxes, and pollution.

Source: Frisch, M. B. (2006). *Quality of life therapy: Applying a life satisfaction approach to positive psychology and cognitive therapy*. John Wiley & Sons, p. 23.

Once an area has been identified as rated low on the Quality of Life Inventory, the **five paths of happiness**, or **CASIO TECHNIQUE**, can be used to help the client increase satisfaction in that area. CASIO is an acronym for Circumstance, Attitude, Standards, Important, and Other, and Frisch notes that this is done in the following ways:

a. changing their *circumstances* or situation by asking themselves, "What do I want?" and "How can I get it?" or "How can I change my behavior or the situation to make it better?";
b. changing their *attitude* by getting all the facts, finding a better way to look at the problem, and seeing themselves survive and thrive eventually, even if the worst happens;
c. setting more realistic but challenging goals and *standards* for being satisfied in the area of concern;
d. emphasizing what is most *important* and controllable in the area; and
e. boosting satisfaction in *other* areas of life that they care about even though they are not areas of concern (Frisch, 2015, p. 786).

Identifying Things Done Well

Research indicates that if clients, for one week, "write down three things that went well today and why they went well" (Seligman, 2012, 9:51) they are more likely to experience a sense of well-being than clients who do not perform this task. In addition, he suggests that this simple exercise is addictive as people enjoy the process of writing down the things they do well. The exercise is simple and straightforward (Vilhauer, 2019):

1. Next to your bed, keep a pad of paper and before you go to sleep briefly write down three things that went well today, and why they went well.
2. In the morning when you awaken, read your list.
3. Every night add three additional things.
4. Do this for one week, or longer.

Increasing Positive Emotions

Positive emotions lengthens one's thought to action responses. In other words, one is less reactive. Thus, working on increasing positive emotions with clients is a technique useful for improving mental health and well-being (Kobau et al, 2011). Fostering the growth of positive emotions is particularly helpful in treating problems rooted in negative emotions, such as anxiety, depression, and aggression (Fredrickson, 2001). Counselors can cultivate positive emotions by emphasizing enjoyable activities and helping clients find positive meaning in their lives.

Using a 3:1 **positivity ratio** of positive to negative emotions, there will be an increase in happiness and psychological growth, a longer life, increased intuition and creativity, more resilience to adversity, and a decrease in health problems (Fredrickson, 2001, 2009; Fredrickson & Losada, 2005). By going to the website in Box 8.3, an individual can determine his or her positive ratio. After identifying one's positivity ratio, the individual can decide whether he or she should make an intentional effort at increasing positive emotions. Many of the techniques suggested within this section of the chapter can be used in an intentional effort at increasing positive emotions.

BOX 8.3 POSITIVITY RATIO

Fredrickson suggests that our positivity to negativity ratio should be approximately 3:1. If you would like to determine your positivity ratio, go to the following URL and take the test: www.positivityratio.com/single.php

Mindfulness

Mindfulness is a present-focused awareness of one's feelings, sensations, and environment through a nurturing and accepting lens with which we pay attention to ourselves (McAuliffe, 2015; Snyder & Lopez, 2007). The practice of mindfulness gives the client the ability to be consciously aware of many aspects of self and can help in promoting overall well-being. Practicing mindfulness allows the client to be open and connected to more positive states and may aid in building a client's positive character strengths, which is a core component of positive counseling (Niemiec, 2013). By being present through mindfulness, one lets go of past or future worries, focuses on thoughts and feelings without judgment and with compassion, and develops greater flexibility in responding to difficult situations over time (Hammond, 2015). There are numerous ways to practice mindfulness, and Box 8.4 offers one method through the **five senses orientation exercise.**

BOX 8.4 FIVE SENSES ORIENTATION EXERCISE

1. Place yourself in a comfortable seated position. Ensure that your feet are planted flat on the ground, your posture is comfortably erect, and your hands are placed on top of your thighs.
2. Take a moment to bring consciousness to your breathing. Pay close attention to the inhale and exhale and the space between breaths.
3. One at a time, bring attention to each of your five senses. Allow your awareness to focus on each sense for a minute at a time. Sometimes it is helpful to close your eyes as you work through each sense.
   a *Hearing*: Notice all the sounds around you. Perhaps the hum of an air conditioner or the hiss of a heater? Maybe some of the sounds are occurring within you, such as the gurgle of your stomach or the gulp as you swallow.
   b *Smell*: Shift your awareness to the smells of the environment surrounding you. Maybe you smell the fabric softener on your shirt, or the soap you used earlier in the day. If outside, perhaps you smell the sweet fragrance of flowers in bloom or maybe you smell the smoke from a neighbor's grill.
   c *Taste*: Take a moment to inhale and swallow. Run your tongue along the inside of your teeth or the roof of your mouth. Your mouth may taste minty fresh, or it may taste like the cup of coffee you drank with breakfast. Let yourself experience the taste in your mouth.
   d *Touch*: Bring awareness to all that your body is touching. Give notice to the sensation of your body in the chair and the clothes on your skin. Maybe your hands are cool to the touch or maybe you are feeling warm.
   e *Sight*: Take a moment to open your eyes if they have been closed. Take in all of the colors, shapes, and textures around you. Scan your space slowly and perhaps you may notice something you had not seen before.

When you have finished all five senses, take a moment to pause and think about all that you have taken in over the last five minutes or so. Are you feeling any differently now than you were before the exercise?

Strength-Based Exercises

> A strength is a pre-existing capacity for a particular way of behaving, thinking, or feeling, that is authentic and energizing to the user, and enables optimal functioning, development and performance. (Linley, 2008, p. 9)

The focus of **strength-based exercises** is to identify individual strengths and develop them to achieve identified goals (Frisch, 2015; Lopez, 2009). Strengths are something that people enjoy doing, are good at, and, once identified, will want to do it more frequently. There are many kinds of strength-based exercises, and here we identify three types: **strength-spotting**, **using exception-seeking questions**, and **using surveys and inventories to identify strengths.**

Strength-Spotting: To help identify strengths, counselors can use structured interviews employing strength spotting, which identifies patterns of success, energy toward the strength, appetite toward the strength, and other things (Carter & Page, 2009). Also, a client can conduct a self-assessment of his or her strengths. Such assessments often take a little time, as the client goes through a three-step process of capturing the strength, by noting when one feels good, powerful, confident—and not tired, frustrated, or upset; clarifying the strength, by asking oneself when the strength applies and when it does not; and confirming the strength, which examines what one is doing, how one is doing it, how one feels about it, and the success one has in doing it.

Exception-seeking Questions. Because some people tend not to see the positive ways they have coped in life, counselors can ask **exception-seeking questions** that focus on ways in which clients were able to handle difficult times. Here, the counselor is assisting the client in "making lemonade out of lemons." For instance, for the client who suggests she is always depressed and never hungry, the counselor can ask, "With your depression, how was it that you were able to get out of bed and go to work? What resources did you use to accomplish that?" The counselor might go on to say, "I know you haven't been hungry, yet you managed to eat. What enabled you to do so and what foods did you like?" The counselor might also ask: "So, I know you were depressed last week, but can you share some moments when you laughed or felt a bit uplifted? What was different about those moments?" Or, "You know, you've mentioned that you were able to get through similar times in the past. What was different about those times? What did you do to get through those times?"

Strength Surveys and Inventories: Strength inventories and surveys are an additional way of identifying and developing strengths. For instance, Seligman's (2011) **24 Survey of Character Strength Test** can be used to identify an individual's top virtues (Figure 8.4). After an individual takes the questionnaire, he or she should review his or her top virtues and look for any surprises. Then, using the top five strengths of the various virtues, the individual should reflect on whether he or she agrees with those top five. Seligman then suggests that at an appropriate time the person should "exercise" his or her top strengths. For instance, if one's top strength is kindness and generosity (under the virtue "Humanity and Love"), the individual could develop something he or she can do, perhaps a couple hours a week, to practice this strength (e.g., volunteering at a homeless shelter). Seligman (2019) offers several happiness scales and inventories one can take at the Authentic Happiness website (www.authentichappiness.sas.upenn.edu/). Using the various scales and *based* on what a client wants to focus upon (e.g., happiness, optimism, life satisfaction), a client can discuss the results with his or her counselor, who can then help guide the client toward behaviors that can increase one's happiness in life.

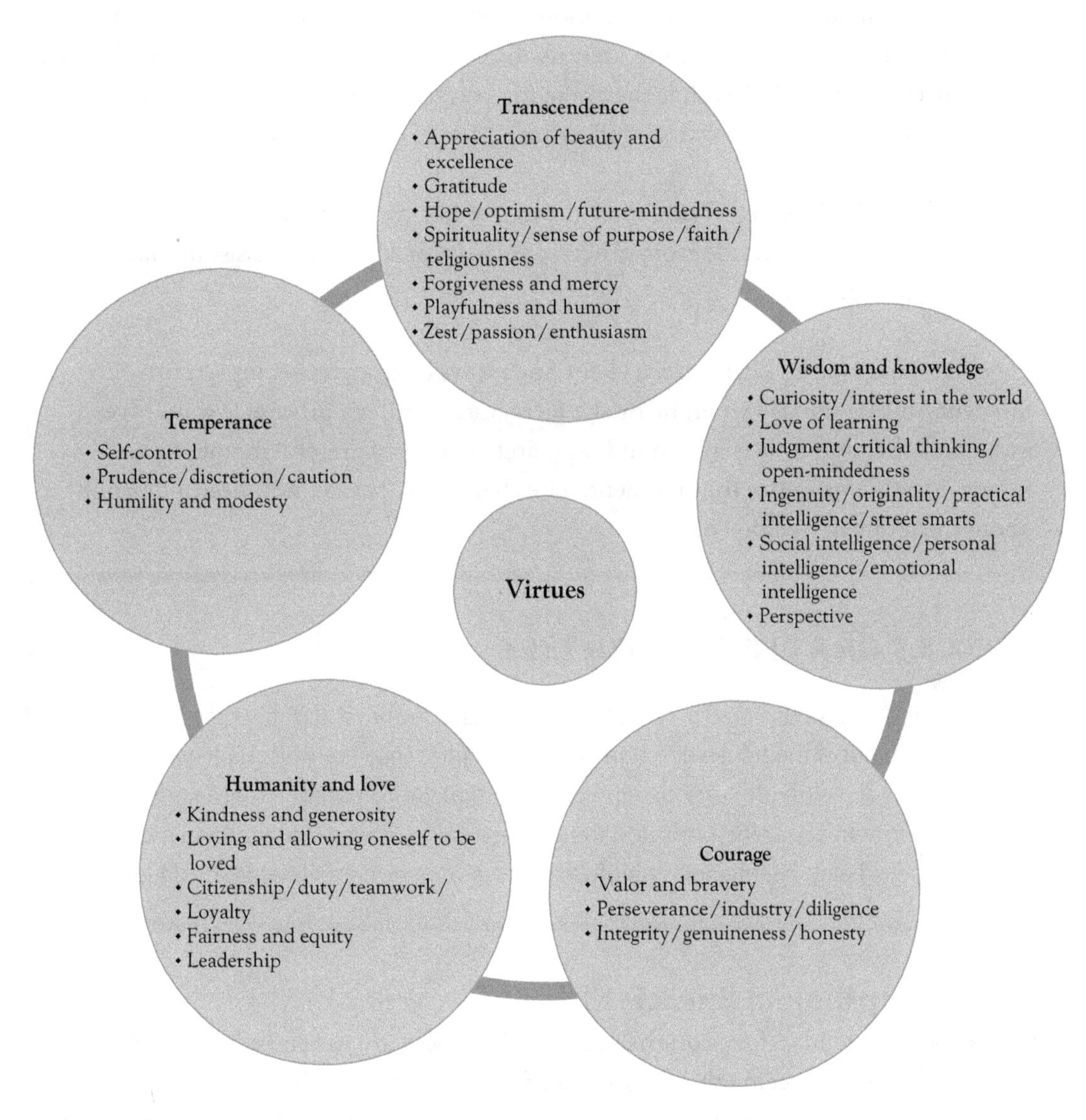

Figure 8.4 24 Strengths in Five Virtue Clusters

Gratitude Exercises

Gratitude is "the tendency to see all life as a gift" and has been "conceptualized as an emotion, an attitude, a moral virtue, a habit, a personality trait, and a coping response" (Emmons, 2009, p. 442). Gratitude appears to be related to well-being, as happy people tend to be grateful people. One of the most common emotions experienced by people, gratitude seems to also be related to resilience—people who can experience gratitude are more resilient and better able to cope with life's difficulties; however, gratitude often does not come easily to people and needs to be cultivated and nurtured. McAuliffe (2019) notes that gratitude comes in many forms, including appreciating self, appreciation of others, being thankful for life and nature, and more. Gratitude exercises help to identify, highlight, and show appreciation for those positive aspects of clients' lives that they take for granted. Several gratitude exercises have been identified over the years, and the following represents a couple of those:

> *Keeping A Gratitude Journal:* The simple process of noting down times when one experiences a sense of gratitude from others, to others, or to life, can assist in increasing positive emotions.
>
> *Expressing Gratitude for Life:* Here, a client finds ways of recognizing important moments during the day when he or she feels gratitude. This process first involves awareness that gratitude is all around us, being mindful of grateful moments, and letting oneself experience that moment. The client may, or may not, keep a journal about the moment (see Box 8.5).

BOX 8.5 GRATITUDE FOR LIFE

Every spring two mourning doves lay eggs in a nest they have built over my front door. Often, I rush out of the house and don't even recognize they are there. But when I slow down and become mindful, I notice the birds. At that very moment, I feel a sense of joy and wonderment about the birds and the process of life. Those birds remind me of the importance of being intentionally mindful about the wonderment of nature (Ed Neukrug).

Hope and Optimism Exercises

Whereas optimists tend to focus on the positive, those who are pessimists naturally focus on the negative. Similar to seeing the glass as half full or half empty, those who are more pessimistic view negative events as something that is a function of inherent personality characteristics and are ongoing (Magyar-Moe, 2009). Optimists, however, believe a negative event is a function of external factors that are specific to the situation at hand. For instance, if a person were fired from a job, a pessimist might say, "I am just a failure at this, and I don't know what I'm doing [internal, not external attribution]. I'll never be any good at anything [generalizing to other settings]." In contrast, an optimist might say, "I got fired because my supervisor was not informed in my theory of counseling and didn't understand how well I implemented it [external, not internal attribution]. This will not very likely occur in my next job [specific to this job only].

Counselors who help clients focus on hope and optimism will have them examine past, present, and potentially future positive aspects of their lives, note exceptions to negative events in their lives, help clients learn how to shift their attention to the positive, and assist them in projecting a positive future. One exercise, developed by Rashid (2008) to help people focus more on the optimistic side of their personalities, suggests doing the following:

1. Identify three times when an important door was closed on you.
2. Identify what doors were opened as a result of each door that was closed.
3. After the door was closed, how long did it take you to figure out what doors were opened?
4. What prevented you from seeing what doors were opened?
5. In the future, what can you do to help you see the opened doors more quickly?

This exercise helps individuals begin to find alternative—and more optimistic—ways of viewing the world, thus slowly developing a more positive outlook on life.

Other Positive Psychotherapy Interventions

There are many other activities that could be used to draw out positive aspects of the person (Magyar-Moe, 2009; McAuliffe, 2019). In addition, creating positive techniques are only limited by the imagination of the counselor. Once a counselor embraces a positive focus, activities to help clients become more positive are endless.

Although all counselors and therapists could integrate positive psychotherapy techniques into their approach, it is clearly more amenable to some therapies. For instance, it would be more difficult to integrate positive psychology into psychodynamic approaches, which focus on problems, assumes there are inherent structurers within the person that cause struggle and strife, and look mostly at the past. However, some of the more humanistic, CBT, and postmodern approaches can easily integrate these strategies.

THE COUNSELING PROCESS

As already noted, positive counseling can be used as a stand-alone approach, or in combination with other therapeutic modalities. Here, we will present the process that typically occurs when a client undergoes **well-being therapy** by **Giovana Fava** (Fava, 2009; Fava & Ruini, 2003; Ruini & Fava, 2009; Ruini et al., 2015). Well-being therapy is a positive counseling approach that integrates some cognitive behavioral techniques into its work with clients. This will give you a sense of how traditional therapeutic models can be used within a positive counseling approach. Then, we will offer a path a client may take when undergoing a stand-alone approach to positive counseling.

Well-Being Therapy

A short-term approach to therapy, well-being therapy usually lasts for eight sessions and "emphasizes self-observation, with the use of a structured diary, and is directive and problem-oriented, based on an educational model" (Ruini & Fava, 2009, p. 512). The therapy integrates some traditional cognitive behavioral techniques as a client passes through its three phases:

> *Initial sessions:* During these sessions, clients are asked to identify times when they have experienced a sense of well-being. Using a structured diary that can be completed at home, they are asked to record those episodes and rate them on a scale of 0 to 100 (100 = the most intense well-being that the individual could experience).
>
> *Intermediate sessions:* Lasting two or three sessions, in this phase, clients are asked to examine how their moments of well-being had been interrupted prematurely and are taught how to observe their thoughts, especially those irrational or automatic thoughts that prevented them from continuing to experience a sense of well-being. This phase helps the therapist distinguish which aspects of Ryff's dimensions (see Table 8.1, pp. 278–279) are being hindered by irrational and automatic thoughts. At this point, the counselor might challenge the client's irrational or automatic thoughts; however, the main focus for the client is on learning how to observe his or her sense of well-being. It is here that the client begins to learn how to "feed" his or her good feelings and positive sense of well-being. Finally, in this phase, the therapist might begin to suggest pleasurable activities to encourage a continued sense of well-being.
>
> *Final sessions:* Ryff's six psychological dimensions are increasingly explained to the client, and the therapist tries to zero in on those dimensions that are compromising a sense of well-being (e.g., a person who is being dominated by another individual

in his or her life may be experiencing a low sense of well-being on the autonomy dimension) (see Table 8.1, pp. 278–279). Cognitive behavioral techniques are used to confront negative thoughts and to work on developing new behaviors. Then, and most important, the client is asked to continue to observe and "feed" his or her sense of well-being by keeping a journal, reflecting on moments of well-being, expanding his or her problem-solving skills, and partaking in activities that lead to an increased sense of well-being. Although just one approach to positive counseling, well-being therapy is an important contribution to working with clients, and preliminary research seems to bear out its efficacy (Ruini et al., 2015).

Positive Counseling as a Stand-Alone Approach

There are dozens of positive counseling techniques a counselor can use to help clients build a more optimistic perspective on life and help clients thrive (Gander et al., 2013; Lyubomirsky & Layous, 2013; Park & Peterson, 2006; Park et al., 2004; McAuliffe, 2019). Below are eight typical steps a counselor would take when implementing positive counseling with a client as a stand-alone approach:

1. Client comes to counseling and presents with non–life-threatening, nonpathological, counseling concerns.
2. Through a professional disclosure statement, the counselor informs the client of the approach to be used.
3. The counselor uses psychoeducation to teach the client that positive counseling is a strengths-based approach.
4. The counselor assesses the client's strengths through an interview or use of a survey or questionnaire and identifies which areas the client might want to build upon.
5. Based on the client assessment, and in consultation with the client, the counselor chooses those techniques best suited to help the client. For example, a client showing mild depression and a desire to expand upon his or her transcendent virtues of gratitude and playfulness Figure 8.4, p. 285) may choose specific gratitude and playfulness interventions.
6. The counselor teaches the client about positive counseling interventions, instructs the client on how to use them in session, and encourages the client to continue practicing them outside of the session.
7. During regular scheduled sessions, the counselor regularly checks in with the client to ensure the client is utilizing positive counseling techniques, assesses his or her effectiveness, and makes adjustments or additions as needed.
8. As the client increasingly integrates a more positive outlook into his or her life, the client is seen less frequently, and the counselor weans the client out of counseling.

SOCIAL AND CULTURAL ISSUES

Positive counseling has been criticized as being embedded in Western values and potentially difficult to use with non-Western populations. In fact, Kubokawa and Ottawa (2009) suggest that "Western ideologies and assumptions underlie the entire foundation of positive psychology, which make research and practice almost impossible to transcend to non-Western cultures" (p. 6). More specifically, they suggest that such values as individualism, the promotion of an independent self, the importance of happiness, and the need to embrace positive emotions are all important values of a Western society, and not necessarily shared by other cultures. As an example, they suggest that the concept of "duty and obedience" to elders and parents would be eschewed in Western culture, but embraced by many cultures, such as East Asian countries. In addition, they note that striving for happiness, so revered in Western cultures, is not a universal cultural value. In fact, they point out that in some cultures, pessimism is more pervasive, though depressive symptoms are not. These cultures would not embrace the idea that it is important to be optimistic.

Christopher and Hickinbottom (2008) are equally critical of positive psychology's Western-oriented nature. They question the methodologies used to assess for positive psychology's efficacy, and even go so far to say that when positive psychology is applied locally, it perpetuates the status quo, and "When it is applied across cultures, it is culturally disrespectful, often resulting in psychological imperialism, or what cross cultural psychologists refer to as an imposed etic ... "(p. 581).

Recognizing some of the inherent problems with positive counseling and psychology relative to cross-cultural sensitivity, Lomas (2015) suggests that it is time to "forge a bridge between positive psychology and cross-cultural psychology" and name it **"positive cross-cultural psychology"** (p. 60). Lomas suggests that we embrace **universalism** by examining common factors, within all cultures, that impact well-being cross-culturally, such as homelessness, adequate nutrition, satisfying employment, and health. Lomas also suggests that we practice **relativism** when employing positive psychology methods; that is, we recognize that cultures will define well-being differently and that it's important to apply their definitions rather than use a Western perspective of what is well-being. As one example, Lomas shows how **universal relativism can be embraced by a positive cross-cultural psychology** (Figure 8.5).

Although positive psychology and positive counseling have been slow to embrace a cross-cultural perspective, there are some exceptions. For example, the **Penn Resilience Program (PRP)** is a school program designed to help adolescent students enhance their ability to handle daily stressful situations. The PRP has been found to be cross-culturally effective for adolescents in several countries and communities and adolescents who have diverse racial and ethnic backgrounds (Seligman et al., 2009). In addition, certain positive counseling interventions, such as expressing gratitude and initiating acts of kindness, could be beneficial for clients from collectivist cultures because they focus on the community and socializing with others (Sin & Lyubomirsky, 2009).

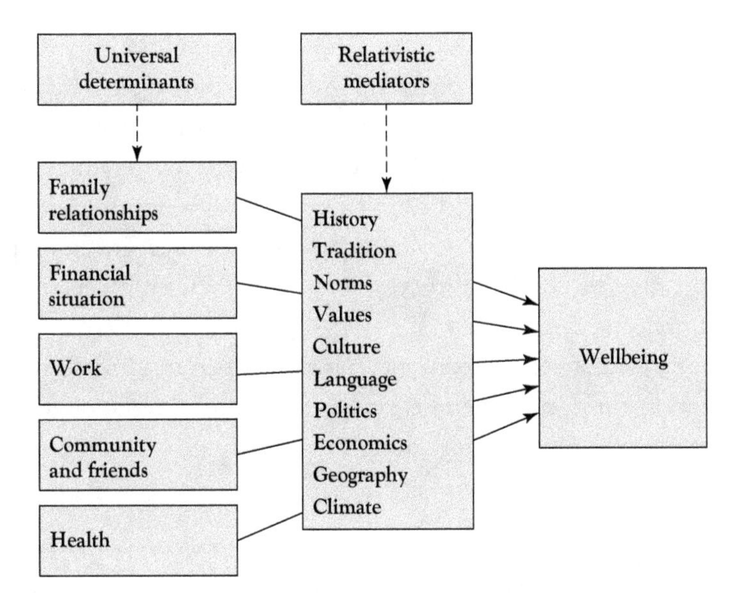

Figure 8.5 Universal Factors and Relativistic Mediators of Well-Being

EFFICACY

On the heels of the development of positive psychology, Danner et al. (2001) examined the autobiographies of 180 Catholic nuns when they were in their early 20s for positive emotions and correlated positive emotional content with longevity six decades later. They found "positive emotional content in early-life autobiographies was strongly associated with longevity … " (p. 804). So, you might say, if you want to live longer, you better start embracing your positive emotions. Although an interesting study, in point of fact research on the effects of positivity and positive counseling is relatively new and still in its early stages. Nevertheless, with the purpose of these interventions being to increase positive feelings, positive thoughts or positive actions as opposed to reduction of symptoms, problems, or disorders (Bolier et al., 2013), some preliminary results are promising.

Some studies have examined the efficacy of specific techniques used in positive counseling. For instance, incorporating mindfulness techniques within counseling has shown to help promote well-being by increasing positive affect and decreasing negative affect (Seear & Vella-Brodrick, 2013). Similarly, using strength-based exercises and a gratitude exercise increased happiness and decreased depression (Seligman et al., 2005). Finally, Seligman et al. (2006) suggest that "treatments for depression may usefully be supplemented by exercises that explicitly increase positive emotion, engagement, and meaning" (p. 774). And, they also showed that such exercises can be delivered on the Internet.

In some cases, positive counseling may be as, or more, effective than traditional psychotherapy. For instance, in comparing a positive-oriented psychotherapy group to a cognitive behavior therapy group, the positive-oriented group was found to be more effective at increasing happiness for clients suffering from major depression (Asgharipoor et al., 2012). A 2016 study by Marrero et al. suggests that positive psychology interventions increased happiness, self-acceptance, positive relations with others, optimism, and self-esteem for college students.

A couple of meta-analyses have bolstered the probability that positive psychology interventions are efficacious. For instance, Sin and Lyubomirsky (2009) examined 51 studies and concluded that positive psychology interventions enhanced well-being and decreased depressive symptoms. A second, more recent meta-analysis by Bolier et al. (2016) examined 39 studies and suggests that positive psychology interventions were somewhat effective in increasing well-being and in decreasing depression.

Although a young field, it seems apparent that positive counseling techniques on their own, or in combination with other therapeutic interventions, have shown some success in increasing the sense of well-being for individuals in counseling.

SUMMARY

This chapter began with a brief overview of the history of positive counseling. We noted that over the 20th century, mental health counseling was mostly focused on pathology and how to fix problems. With influence from the positive aspects of some counseling theories, however, there was an increased focus on well-being and positivity. Meanwhile, well-being, in many forms, began to be studied. For instance, Ed Diener studied happiness and subjective well-being; Mihaly Csikszentmihalyi studied flow, meaning, and optimal experiences; Barbara Fredrickson examined positive emotions; Charles "Rick" Snyder looked at hope; and Carol Ryff researched well-being and resilience. Then, in 1998, Martin Seligman, who was president of the American Psychological Association, launched the positive psychology movement. Seligman had studied learned helplessness, but decided he wanted to take a more positive look at the person and began to study learned optimism. Through several of his initiatives, the positive psychology movement, and along with it, positive counseling, was born.

The view of human nature of positive psychology, and the resulting positive counseling movement, borrowed from earlier epistemologies such as humanistic psychology. The ideas of positive counseling are different, however, than those from whence it came. Positive psychology and positive counseling focus on assisting people in identifying strengths and positive qualities and helping people live a more fruitful and positive life. It does not focus on the existential dilemmas and concerns of a person, such as humanistic psychology does. Instead, it believes that individuals can better their lives through logical positivism, which means that people can make their lives better through a logical analysis of their situation. Positive counseling assumes that mental disorders; negative thoughts, feelings, and behaviors; and psychopathology occur when growth, fulfillment, and happiness are thwarted. Thus, symptoms are not seen as interminably embedded in the person. Therefore, positive psychology researchers have focused on how people can make a shift from negative to positive emotions, thoughts, and behaviors. This is viewed as a "build-what's-strong" approach in contrast with a "fix-what's-wrong" approach. Finally, positive counseling is an intentional practice that is anti-deterministic.

Positive counseling is still in its formative stage; however, some key concepts that many individuals tend to adhere to were discussed in this chapter. For instance, in sustaining psychological well-being, we noted that there probably is a genetic set-point for temperament, that circumstances can impact the set-point to a certain degree, and that intentional activities, such as practicing positive behaviors, can help a client have outcomes nearer to the higher end of his or her set-point. We also noted that there is a human default toward negativity and that the "positive is customary" in the sense that it is not unusual to hardly notice the positive aspects of life. Thus, one needs an intentional effort to notice and sustain positivity. We also highlighted strengths theory, which suggests it is important to focus on a person's strengths, not repair a person's weaknesses. Related to this, we noted four errors in thinking that people often make: fixing a weakness makes a person stronger, strengths will develop naturally, strengths and weaknesses are opposites, and a person can do anything he or she focuses on.

Another key concept, the broaden and build theory of positive emotions, underscored five hypotheses of positive emotions. The broaden hypothesis suggests that increased positive emotions can broaden the possible thought-action responses, which means we are more in touch with how our thoughts impact the types of actions we make. The build hypothesis suggests that positive emotions assist individuals in building their personal resources in the areas of physical, social, intellectual, and psychological resources. The undoing hypothesis suggests that positive emotions can reduce the hold that negative emotions have on one's cognitive and physical well-being. The resilience hypothesis suggests that positive emotions build on positive emotions in that one has an upward spiral of positivity. Finally, the flourish hypothesis suggests it is important to have an optimal level of positive to negative emotions, which was suggested as a 3:1 ratio. The next key concept we highlighted was the PERMA model. This model outlines five of the major attributes critical to experiencing a sense of well-being: **P**ositive emotions, **E**ngagement, **R**elationships, **M**eaning, and **A**chievement (**PERMA**).

Positive counseling can be a stand-alone approach to counseling or a "value added" approach when used in combination with traditional forms of counseling. In either case, we identified a number of important techniques often used in positive counseling, including assessing well-being through an instrument such as Ryff's Six Dimensions of Psychological Well-Being or the Quality of Life Inventory, identifying things done well, increasing one's positivity ratio, mindfulness, strength-based exercises, gratitude exercises, hope and optimism exercises, and other positive psychotherapy interventions.

We noted the therapeutic process might vary in positive counseling, depending on whether it is a stand-alone approach or an approach that is combined with another therapeutic modality. We gave an example of well-being therapy, which combines cognitive behavioral techniques with the use of Ryff's six psychological dimensions. Next, we identified eights steps a client and counselor usually pass through when positive counseling is used as a stand-alone approach.

Some have criticized positive counseling as being too embedded in Western values, such as individualism and the promotion of an independent self. Others have noted that some cultures are naturally more pessimistic; however, less depressed. These cultures would not embrace the idea that it is important to be optimistic. Some have suggested that applied across cultures, positive counseling is a type of imperialism. But others suggest it is possible for positive counseling to develop a bridge between itself and cross-cultural issues. They name this "positive cross-cultural psychology," and suggest it is important to embrace universalism and relativism in this approach. One program, the Penn Resilience Program (PRP), has embraced a cross-cultural perspective, which has been found to be effective for adolescents in several countries and communities, and with adolescents who have diverse racial and ethnic backgrounds. In addition, it was noted that certain positive counseling interventions, such as expressing gratitude and initiating acts of kindness, could be beneficial for clients from collectivist cultures.

Although a relatively new approach, some studies have shown positive outcomes from the use of positive counseling. One study of nuns showed that those who had a more positive outlook on life lived longer. Other studies have shown that positive counseling has been effective in the treatment of depression and promotes positive affect and decreases negative affect. In at least one case, positive group counseling was shown to be more effective than cognitive behavior group therapy in the treatment of depression. Two meta-analyses suggest that positive counseling increases well-being and decreases depression.

KEY WORDS AND NAMES

Accomplishments
Anti-deterministic
Broaden hypothesis
Build hypothesis
Build-what's-strong approach
CASIO technique
Circumstance
Csikszentmihalyi, Mihaly
Diener, Ed
Engagement
Exception-seeking questions
Existential tenet
Fava, Giovanna
Five paths of happiness
Flourish hypothesis
Fredrickson, Barbara
Genetic set-point
Glasser, William
Gratitude exercises
Hope and optimism exercises
Identifying things done well
Identifying strengths and positive qualities
Increasing one's positivity ratio
Intentional activities
Intentional practice
Learned helplessness
Learned optimism
Logical positivism
Meaning
Mindfulness
Other positive psychotherapy interventions
Penn Resilience Program (PRP)
PERMA
Phenomenological perspective
Positive cross-cultural psychology
Positive emotions
Positive is customary
Positive psychology
Positive Psychology Center
Positive relationships
Positivity ratio
Purpose
Quality of Life Inventory
Relativism
Resilience hypothesis
Ryff, Carol
Ryff's six dimensions of psychological well-being
Self-acceptance
Seligman, Martin

Snyder, Charles "Rick"
Strength-based exercises
Strength-spotting
Survey of Character Strength Test
Sustaining psychological well-being
Szasz, Thomas
Though-action responses
Undoing hypothesis
Universal relativism can be embraced by a positive cross-cultural psychology
Universalism
Using exception-seeking questions
Using surveys and inventories to identify strengths
Well-being therapy

REFERENCES

Asgharipoor, N., Aliasghar, A. F., Hamidreza, A., & Sahebi, A. (2012). A comparative study on the effectiveness of positive psychotherapy and group cognitive-behavioral therapy for patients suffering from major depressive disorder. *Iran Journal of Psychiatry and Behavioral Sciences, 2*(2), 33–41.

Bolier, L., Haverman, M., Westerhof, G., Riper, H., Smit, F., & Bohlmeijer, E. (2013, February 8). Positive psychology interventions: A meta analysis of randomized controlled studies. *PMC Public Health*, 13–119. https://bmcpublichealth.biomedcentral.com/articles/10.1186/1471-2458-13-119

CAPP (n.d.). *Be your best self with STRENGTHS.* https://www.strengthsprofile.com/en-gb/about/aboutus

Carter, D., & Page, N. (2009). Strengths coaching. In S. J. Lopez (2009), *The encyclopedia of positive psychology* (Vol. 2, pp. 949–957). Oxford University Press.

Christopher, J. C., & Hickinbottom, S. (2008). Positive psychology, ethnocentrism, and the disguised ideology of individualism. *Theory & psychology, 18*(5), 563–589. https://doi.org/10.1177/0959354308093396

Csikszentmihalyi, M. (1997). *Finding flow: The psychology of engagement with everyday life.* Basic Books.

Csikszentmihalyi, M. (2009). Flow. In Lopez, S. J. (Ed.), *The encyclopedia of positive psychology* (Vol. 1, pp. 394–400). Wiley Blackwell.

Csikszentmihalyi, M. (2014). *Flow and the foundations of positive psychology: The collected works of Mihaly Csikszentmihalyi.* Springer.

Danner, D. D., Snowdon, D. A., & Friesen, W. V. (2001). Positive emotions in early life and longevity: Findings from the nun study. *Journal of Personality and Social Psychology, 80,* 804–813. https://doi.org/10.1037/0022-3514.80.5.80

Duckworth, A. (2016). *Grit: The power of passion and perseverance.* Simon & Schuster.

Duckworth, A. L., Steen, T. A., & Seligman, M. E. P. (2005). Positive psychology in clinical practice. *Annual Review of Clinical Psychology, 1,* 639–651. https://doi.org/10.1146/annurev.clinpsy.1.102803.144154

Fava, G. A. (2009, June 19). *Well-being therapy.* Workshop presented at the First World Congress on Positive Psychology. Philadelphia, PA.

Fava, G. A., & Ruini, C. (2003). Development and characteristics of a well-being enhancing psychotherapeutic strategy: Well-being therapy. *Journal of Behavior Therapy and Experimental Psychiatry, 34,* 45–63. http://dx.doi.org/10.1016/ S0005-7916(03)00019-3

Fredrickson, B. L. (2001). The role of positive emotions in positive psychology: The broaden-and-build theory of positive emotions. *American Psychologist, 56*, 218–226. https://doi.org/10.1037/0003-066X.56.3.218

Fredrickson, B. (2009, June 19). *Positivity: The path to flourishing.* Workshop presented at the First World Congress on Positive Psychology. Philadelphia, PA.

Fredrickson, B. L., & Losada, M. F. (2005). Positive affect and the complex dynamics of human flourishing. *American Psychologist, 60*, 678–686. https://doi.org/10.1037/0003-066X.60.7.678

Frisch, M. B. (2006). *Quality of life therapy: Applying a life satisfaction approach to positive psychology and cognitive therapy.* John Wiley & Sons.

Frisch, M. B. (2015). Positive psychology. In E. Neukrug (Ed.), *The SAGE encyclopedia of theories of counseling and psychotherapy* (Vol. 2, pp. 783–787). SAGE Publications.

Froh, J. J. (2004). The history of positive psychology: Truth be told. *The Psychologist, 16*(3), 18–20.

Gander, F., Proyer, R. T., Ruch, W., & Wyss, T. (2013). Strength-based positive interventions: Further evidence for their potential in enhancing well-being and alleviating depression. *Journal of Happiness Studies, 14*(4), 1241–1259. https://doi.org/10.1007/s10902-012-9380-0

Hammond, C. F. (2015). Mindfulness techniques. In E. Neukrug (Ed.), *The SAGE encyclopedia of theories of counseling and psychotherapy* (Vol. 2, pp. 653–656). SAGE Publications.

Joseph, S., & Linley, P. A. (2009). Positive therapy. In S. J. Lopez (2009), *The encyclopedia of positive psychology* (Vol. 2, 758–759). Oxford University Press.

Kesebir, P., & Diener, E. (2009). *In pursuit of happiness: Empirical answers to philosophical questions. The science of well-being: The collected works of Ed Diener.* Social Indicators Research Series, 37, 59–74. https://doi.org/10.1007/978-90-481-2350-6

Kobau, R., Seligman, M. E., Peterson, C., Diener, E., Zack, M. M., Chapman, D., & Thompson, W. (2011). Mental health promotion in public health: Perspectives and strategies from positive psychology. *American Journal of Public Health*, 101(8), e1–e9. doi:10.2105/AJPH.2010.300083

Kubokawa, A., & Ottaway, A. (2009). Positive psychology and cultural sensitivity: A review of the literature. *Graduate Journal of Counseling Psychology, 1*(2). https://epublications.marquette.edu/cgi/viewcontent.cgi?article=1029&context=gjcp

Linley, A. (2008). *Average to A+: Realising strengths in yourself and others.* CAPP Press.

Linley, A. (2009). Positive psychology. (History). In S. J. Lopez (Ed.), *The encyclopedia of positive psychology* (Vol. 2, pp. 742–745). Wiley Blackwell.

Lomas, T. (2015). Positive cross-cultural psychology: Exploring similarity and difference in constructions and experiences of wellbeing. *International Journal of Wellbeing, 5*(4), 60–77. https://doi.org/10.5502/ijw.v5i4.437

Lopez, S. J. (2009). The future of positive psychology: Pursuing three big goals. In S. J. Lopez, & D. R. Snyder (Eds.), *The Oxford handbook of positive psychology* (2nd ed., pp. 689–694) Oxford University Press.

Lyubomirsky, S., & Layous, K. (2013). How do simple positive activities increase well-being? *Current Directions in Psychological Science, 22*(1), 57–62. https://doi.org/10.1177/096372141246980

Magyar-Moe, J. L. (2009). *Therapist's guide to positive psychological interventions.* Elsevier.

Martin, A. (Ed.). (2013). *The Phoenix chronicles: Oath of the Phoenix.* Xlibris.

McAuliffe, G. J. (2019). *Positive counseling: A guide to assessing and enhancing client strength and growth.* Cognella Academic Press.

Neukrug, E. (20015). *The SAGE encyclopedia of theory in counseling and psychotherapy.* SAGE Publications.

Neukrug, E. (2016). *The world of the counselor* (5th ed.). Cengage Learning.

Neukrug, E. (2018). *Counseling theory and practice* (2nd ed.). Cognella Academic Press.

Niemiec, R. M. (2013, June 24). Top 12 Reasons you should combine mindfulness and strength. *Psychology Today.* www.psychologytoday.com/us/blog/what-matters-most/201306/top-12-reasons-you-should-combine-mindfulness-and-strength

Park, N., & Peterson, C. (2006). Moral competence and character strengths among adolescents: The development and validation of the Values in Action Inventory of Strengths for Youth. *Journal of Adolescence, 29,* 891–905.

Park, N., Peterson, C., & Seligman, M. E. P. (2004). Strengths of character and well-being. *Journal of Social and Clinical Psychology, 23*(5), 603–619. https://doi.org/10.1521/jscp.23.5.603.50748

Peterson, C. (2006). *A primer in positive psychology.* Oxford University Press.

Positive Psychology Center. (2019). *Our mission.* http://ppc.sas.upenn.edu/our-mission

Rashid, T. (2008). Positive psychotherapy. In S. J. Lopez (Ed.), *Praeger perspectives. Positive psychology: Exploring the best in people, Vol. 4. Pursuing human flourishing* (pp. 188–217). Praeger.

Rashid, T. (2009). Positive psychotherapy. In S. J. Lopez (Ed.), *The encyclopedia of positive psychology* (Vol. 2, pp. 749–752). Wiley-Blackwell.

Rich, G. J. (2001). Positive psychology: An introduction. *Journal of Humanistic Psychology,* 41, 8–12.

Ruini, C. (2014). The use of well-being therapy in clinical settings. *The Journal of Happiness & Well-Being,* 2(1), 75–84.

Ruini, C., & Fava, G. A. (2009). Well-being therapy for generalized anxiety disorder. *Journal of Clinical Psychology, 65,* 510–519. https://doi.org/10.1002/jclp.20592

Ruini, C., Albieri, E. & Vescovelli, F (2015). *Journal of Contemporary Psychotherapy, 45,* 129. https://doi.org/10.1007/s10879-014-9290-z

Ryff, C. D. (1989). Happiness is everything, or is it? Explorations on the meaning of psychological well-being. *Journal of Personality and Social Psychology,* 6, 1069–1081. doi:1037/0022-3514.57.6.1069

Schulman, P. (2009). Positive psychology network. In S. J. Lopez (Ed.), *The encyclopedia of positive psychology* (Vol. 2, pp. 746–748). Wiley Blackwell.

Seear, K. H., & Vella-Brodrick, D. A. (2013). *Efficacy of positive psychology interventions to increase well-being: Examining the role of dispositional-mindfulness.* Social Indicators Research, 114, 1125–1141.

Seligman, M. E. (1972). Learned helplessness. *Annual Review of Medicine, 23,* 407–412. https://doi.org/10.1146/annurev.me.23.020172.002203

Seligman, M. E. (1990). *Learned optimism.* Random House.

Seligman, M. E. (2002). *Authentic happiness. Using the new positive psychology to release your potential for lasting fulfillment.* Free Press.

Seligman, M. E. (2011). *Flourish.* Simon & Schuster.

Seligman, M. E. (2012). *Professor Martin Seligman discusses his formula for wellbeing: PERMA.* https://www.youtube.com/watch?v=iK6K_N2qe9Y&t=410s

Seligman, M. E. (2019). *Authentic happiness.* https://www.authentichappiness.sas.upenn.edu/

Seligman, M. E., & Csikszentmihalyi, M. (2000). Positive psychology: An introduction. *American Psychologist, 55*(1), 5–14. https://doi.org/10.1037/0003-066X.55.1.5

Seligman, M. E., & Maier, S. F. (1967) Failure to escape traumatic shock. *Journal of Experimental Psychology, 74*(1), 1–9. https://doi.org/10.1037/h0024514

Seligman, M. E., Rashid, T., Parks, A. C. (2006). Positive psychotherapy. *American Psychologist, 61,* 774–788. https://doi.org/10.1037/0003-066X.61.8.774.

Seligman, M. E. P., Steen, T. A., Park, N., & Peterson, C. (2005). Positive psychology progress: Empirical validation of interventions. *American Psychologist, 60,* 410–421. http://dx.doi.org/10.1037/0003-066X.60.5.410

Seligman, M. E., Ernst, R. M., Gillham, J., Reivich, K., & Linkins, M. (2009). Positive education: Positive psychology and classroom interventions. *Oxford Review of Education, 35*(3), 293–311. https://doi.org/10.1080/03054980902934563

Sin, N. L., & Lyubomirsky, S. (2009). Enhancing well-being and alleviating depressive symptoms with positive psychology interventions: A practice-friendly meta-analysis. *Journal of Clinical Psychology, 65*(5), 467–487. https://doi.org/10.1002/jclp.20593

Snyder, C. R., & Lopez, S. J. (2002). The future of positive psychology. In C. R. Snyder & S. J. Lopez (Eds.), *The handbook of positive psychology* (pp. 751–767). Oxford University Press.

Snyder, C. R., & Lopez, S. J. (2007). *Positive psychology: The scientific and practical explorations of human strengths.* SAGE Publications.

Vilhauer, J. (2019). *One exercise sure to make you feel about yourself: With a minimum of effort, change the way you see your world.* https://www.psychologytoday.com/us/blog/living-forward/201501/one-exercise-sure-make-you-feel-better-about-yourself

CASE STUDY: ANN'S EXPERIENCE IN POSITIVE COUNSELING

(Please read about the Millers in Appendix I prior to reading this case study)

Jake and Angela's positive experiences in counseling helped them realize the pain and suffering that Jake's mother, Ann, has gone through since the car accident with Justine. Although Jake's counselor did not believe it was wise that *he* see Jake's mother, he did have a referral to

Dr. Barbara Federoni, or "Dr. B.," as many call her. Dr. B. practices a form of positive counseling, and Jake's counselor thought this might be a particularly good fit for Ann.

Jake and Angela accompanied Ann to her first session with Dr. B. Ann was reluctant to go, but with their prodding, she relented. Sitting in Dr. B.'s waiting room, Ann was impressed with how cozy it was and the bright colors that filled the room. After a few minutes, a woman in her 60s walked out. Wearing a flowing and colorful dress, and with a bright smile, the woman looked directly at Ann and said, "Hi there, I assume you're Ann. So happy to meet you. And, is this Jake and Angela?" Both nod "Yes." "So, Ann, would you like to come in by yourself, or do you want Jake and Angela to accompany you?" Ann looks at Dr. B. and says, "Well, I've come this far, I might as well take the leap and do this on my own." "Good decision," Dr. B. says.

Ann walks into Dr. B.'s office, which is about as bright and cozy as the waiting room. She looks around at all the knickknacks, and nonverbally shows her approval to Dr. B. "Yeah, I know I have a lot of stuff in here. Someday, I'll have to sort it all out and get rid of some of it," says Dr. B. "So, I kind of know a bit about you from the referral paperwork. You are married, have two children and two grandchildren. And one of your children, Justine, was involved in a very serious accident a while back that resulted in some severe cognitive impairment. Is that right?" "Well, yeah," says Ann. "You want to tell me a bit more about your family and why you think you're here today?"

Ann goes on to talk about Jake, Justine, and the accident. She tells Dr. B. that since the accident, about 32 years ago, she was never the same. "I'm always in a cloud, always worried about Justine and how she is doing, never go to church any longer, and my relationship with my husband—well, that's kind of nonexistent now. I guess I'm the classic depressive." After a moment, she continues: "You know, since that accident, I think I lost my heart." Dr. B. sighs, and says, "It certainly seems that things have changed a lot since that day—that your marriage, your relationship with your children, and the very core of who you were changed on that day." "Yes, that's exactly it," says Ann.

The two talk more about Ann's life, and as the session nears its ending, Dr. B. begins to describe the type of counseling she does. She notes that many people have a positive to negative emotion ratio that is less than 3:1, and she suspects that since the accident, Ann's is pretty low. Ann nods her head as if to agree. After an explanation of positive counseling, Dr. B. says, "You know, I think that I might be able to help you a bit—well, at least help you begin to see the world in a different way so that you can enjoy your life a bit more. Any thoughts?" Ann looks down, almost in tears, and says, "Yeah, I think I would like that." Before Ann leaves, Dr. B. suggests that when Ann gets home, she take the positivity scale, which is online, and report back to her during the next session as to what her score is. Ann agrees, and says, "You know, this is the first time in a long time that I have any hope." "That's great," Dr. B. says. "Can't wait to see you next week."

The next week Ann comes in for her appointment, and Dr. B. immediately asks, "Were you able to take the positivity ratio scale?" "Yes," answers Ann, "and I only got a 1:2. Pretty bad, huh?" "Well, I've seen lower," Dr. B. says, "but it does indicate that you're living in the world with a lot of negative emotions. Maybe we can work together to help you see the world in a more positive light—kind of like seeing the glass as half full rather than half empty." "That would be great," says Ann.

Ann sees Dr. B. weekly for a few weeks. At first, Dr. B. uses much empathy and listening, and Ann shares her sadness about the "loss" of her child. As the weeks pass, Dr. B. begins to integrate a number of positive counseling techniques into the sessions. One of the first things she does is to ask Ann to take the Survey of Character Strength Test. Ann identifies her five highest strengths in the following order: gratitude, religiousness, forgiveness, kindness and generosity, and citizenship. Ann decides she only wants to work on the top four for now, and Dr. B., in consultation with Ann, begins to set some goals, including the following:

1. List things you are grateful for relative to your daughter and son.
2. Start going back to church and get involved with events at church.
3. Write a letter to your son, which you don't have to send, that says you forgive him for the accident.
4. Find a charity that you might want to become involved in.

As the sessions continue, Dr. B. begins to integrate some cognitive behavioral techniques. She teaches Ann about the A-B-C's, with the "B" being the irrational belief. She shows Ann how her irrational belief that "Life should always be fair and just" has impacted how she feels since the accident. She teaches Ann that the Accident (the "A"—antecedent event) did not lead to the Consequences (the "C"—depression). Instead, she teaches her that it was her *belief* about the accident, that life should always be fair and just, that led to the depression. She helps Ann see that she has carried this irrational belief, and related ones, since the accident and it has helped to create the "clouds" in her life and depressive feelings. Meanwhile, Ann is slowly taught how to dispute some of her irrational beliefs, and as she does this, she works on the four goals that were set in consultation with Dr. B.

Over the next few months, Ann begins to realize how grateful she is that Justine has a full life and is happy most of the time. She also realizes that is she grateful for Jake, Angela, and the grandchildren. She writes a letter to Jake, forgiving him for the accident, and then follows this up with a conversation with him—telling Jake she loves him and is so grateful for Angela and the children that he brought into her life. She begins to return to church and gets involved with mission work the church is sponsoring. Slowly, she is building on the four strengths she identified: gratitude, religiousness, forgiveness, and kindness and generosity. Even her relationship with her husband seems to be better these days.

After about nine months of counseling, Dr. B. says, "Hey, you've been doing so great, Ann, how about you take that the positivity scale again." "Definitely," Ann replies. The next week Ann quickly announces: "I got a 2.5:.1.6, that's a real turn-around for me. I guess it reflects that I feel much more hopeful and positive about life. I see what you mean when I first came in here, and you talked about seeing the glass half empty rather than half full. I think I'm seeing it half full now—maybe even more than half." Dr. B. replies that "You've done great work here, and in your life, and it looks like it will be sustainable. What do you think—is it time for you to stop coming here?" Ann looks down and says, "Well, you know, I have been thinking about that. How about a few more weeks to get settled into not coming—you know, to let me get used to the thought, and then we'll see how I do." "Sounds good to me," says Dr. B. After a few more sessions, Ann terminates counseling and thanks Dr. B., who reminds her that she can always return for a "refresher," but that much of what she has learned in counseling will stay with her. "Yeah, I think I know that," says Ann. "Thanks so much for all your help!"

QUESTIONS FOR YOU TO PONDER

1. Jake's counselor thinks that Ann would do well in positive counseling. Why do you think he came to that conclusion? Do you agree?
2. Dr. B. uses a lot of empathy and listening at first. Why do you think she does that? Do you believe that is in line with positive counseling?
3. How does Dr. B. incorporate psychoeducation into her practice with Ann?
4. Do you believe using the positivity scale is important in counseling? Why or why not?
5. What was the purpose of Ann taking the Survey of Character Strength Test? How does it fit into a positive counseling framework?
6. Based on Ann's strengths, Dr. B., in consultation with Ann, came up with a number of goals for Ann. What did you think of those goals? Were there some others you may have come up with?
7. What was the purpose of integrating cognitive behavioral techniques in the sessions? Do you believe Ann would have made such progress if these techniques were not used?
8. If you were doing positive counseling, would you do it as a stand-alone approach or integrate it with another theory? What theory would you integrate it with?
9. Do you believe changes made in positive counseling are sustainable—that they build on themselves and that one is unlikely to go back toward one's former way of living?
10. What is your positivity ratio? What does it say about you?
11. After reviewing the Survey of Character Strengths Test, what do you think are your top five strengths?
12. Based on items 11 and 12, what goals would you make for yourself?

Credits

Fig. 8.3: Mihaly Csikszentmihaly, "State of Flow," *Finding Flow*. Copyright © 1997 by Perseus Books Group.

Table 8.1: Giovanni A. Fava and Chiara Ruini, Modification of the Six Dimensions of Psychological Well-Being According to Ryff's model, from "Development and Characteristics of a Well-Being Enhancing Psychotherapeutic Strategy: Well-Being Therapy," *Journal of Behavior Therapy and Experimental Psychiatry*, vol. 34, no. 1, pp. 51. Copyright © 2003 by Elsevier B.V. Reprinted with permission.

Table 8.2: Michael B. Frisch, "Sixteen Areas of Quality of Life Therapy," *Quality of Life Therapy: Applying a Life Satisfaction Approach to Positive Psychology and Cognitive Therapy*. Copyright © 2006 by John Wiley & Sons, Inc. Reprinted with permission.

Img. 8.1: Copyright © 2013 Depositphotos/chones.

9

Neurocounseling

Carlos Zalaquett and Lauren Parker

LEARNING OUTCOMES

- To become familiar with the history of neurocounseling.
- To examine the wellness, strength-based, developmental, and structural biological nature of neurocounseling.
- To learn about key concepts of neurocounseling, including neuroplasticity; neurogenesis; attention, arousal, and focus; the limbic system and emotions; changes in brain functioning over the lifespan; empathy and mirror neurons; microskills relationship to neural networks; brainwaves; wellness, positivity, and neuroplasticity; and self-regulation.
- To review major techniques used in neurocounseling, including neuroeducation, assessing lifestyle, biofeedback and self-regulation skills (diaphragmatic breathing, mindfulness, and technological approaches to biofeedback), neurofeedback, and neuroscience-informed therapies such as prolonged exposure therapy (PE) and eye movement desensitization and reprocessing (EMDR).
- To describe the counseling process of neurocounseling.
- To examine social and cultural applicability of neurocounseling.
- To review the efficacy of neurocounseling.
- To offer a case study that demonstrates the neurocounseling process.

BRIEF HISTORY OF NEUROCOUNSELING

> [P]sychological science in the 21st century can and should become not only the science of overt behavior, not only the science of the mind, but the science of brain function. (Cacioppo & Decety, 2009, p. 17)

Neurocounseling is an emerging and complex modality increasingly being integrated into the counseling process (Field et al., 2017). Its history, however, can be traced back to the beginnings of counseling theory development. In fact, in the late 1800s Freud, who was trained as a neurologist, at first believed that there was an intimate connection between neural processing and psychological states and that manipulation of structures in the brain would lead to answers of most psychological problems (Miller & Katz, 1989; Northoff, 2012). But "modern day" manipulation of physiology in mental health treatment occurred a bit later (Chatters et al., 2017). For instance, during the 1930 **Edmund Jacobson** (1938) described progressive muscle relaxation to assist in the treatment of psychosomatic disorders. During the 1960s **biofeedback** was born when instruments, such as thermometers and electrocardiograms, were used to help clients track and ultimately change physiological responses so that people could achieve deep relaxation, better sleep, and control over other body functions to increase wellness (Tart, 1969). Since that time, biofeedback has been used to "teach self-regulation of physiological processes" (Myers & Young, 2012, p. 21) and has progressed to include achievement of peak performances in athletes, meditators, and others (Field et al., 2017).

By the end of the 1960s, **Joe Kamiya's** (1969) studies on consciousness demonstrated that by using a simple reward system, people could learn to alter their brain wave patterns, offering the first electroencephalogram (EEG) **neurofeedback (NFB) training**. For instance, this allowed individuals to distinguish **alpha waves** from other brainwaves and ultimately enter an alpha state that is more associated with relaxation and stress relief. This type of training progressed to the treatment of many behavioral and biological processes that helped to focus attention and concentration and relieve anxiety and post-traumatic stress disorders.

Whereas biofeedback utilizes feedback from body activity, neurofeedback employs feedback from brain activity (Crockett et al., 2017). Thus, **neurofeedback**, "... sometimes called biofeedback for the brain" (Russell-Chapin, 2016, p. 94) or **EEG biofeedback**, is a more specific form of biofeedback (Association for Applied Psychophysiology and Biofeedback [AAPB], 2011; Neurofeedback Alliance, n.d.). The goal of biofeedback and neurofeedback is to enable a person to take a more active role in self-mastery of behaviors and emotions and in recovering and maintaining health. Using instruments and techniques, clients can track and change physiological responses, a process called **self-regulation**, to promote wellness and enhance functioning (AAPB, 2011). Self-regulation involves the ability to consciously focus attention, become aware of environmental factors and our physical and emotional reactions, bring memories of previous successful adaptations to bear in the present situation, and regain an emotional state and sense of well-being useful to resolve current distress or challenges (Ford & Blaustein, 2013). Neurofeedback procedures can provide a mechanism for self-regulation by helping individuals regulate what were previously thought of as nonvolitional neural functions (Thibault et al., 2015).

Continuing advances in **positron emission tomography (PET)** scans, **functional magnetic resonance imaging (fMRI)**, and the modern use of an **electroencephalogram (EEG)** have created a paradigm shift for counseling and psychology as they can demonstrate the intimate relationship between our brainwaves and our biomechanics (Ivey & Zalaquett, 2011; Ivey et al., 2018). In fact, today, we can measure changes in the brain during normal conversation, or during individual counseling. We can also show how skills, such as listening, empathy, and strength building, and also behavioral, cognitive, and interpersonal therapy, can lead to positive feelings and corrective behaviors and the development of new neural pathways (Grawe, 2007; Montes, 2013). Research also demonstrates that social conditions, such as trauma, poverty, abuse, or harassment, can measurably harm the development of the brain (Clearfield & Niman, 2012; Likhtik et al., 2008; Zalaquett & Ivey, 2014; Zalaquett et al., 2018).

Affirming the importance of neuroscience and psychotherapy, at the 100th anniversary of the New York State Psychiatric Institute of Columbia University, **Eric Kandel** (1998) noted that new learning alters the expression of genes, which results in structural changes in the brain, and postulated that psychotherapy would also produce such changes:

> Insofar as psychotherapy or counseling is effective and produces long-term changes in behavior, it presumably does so through learning, by producing changes in gene expression that alter the strength of synaptic connections and structural changes that alter the anatomical pattern of interconnections between nerve cells of the brain (p. 460).

One of the fist appearances of the word "neurocounseling" was in a 2013 edition of *Counseling Today*, in which it was defined as the integration of counseling and neuroscience to provide specific interventions to mental health concerns (Montes, 2013). Within this article, one of the leaders in the neurocounseling field, **Lori Russell-Chapin**, stated, "I'd been saying to graduate students for years, once we know more about the brain, it's going to change how we do therapy … I really do think the brain is the final frontier … " (p. 33). She goes on to note that neuroscience represents the "physiological underpinnings of many of our mental health concerns. Helping clients better understand that our brains and bodies are constantly working together to create healthy living or dysregulated living is a must" (Russell-Chapin, 2016, p. 93). Sometimes called the **newest force in counseling**, this approach tends to be client-centered and supports a strength-based wellness model (Crockett et al., 2017).

Pioneering the integration of neuroscience in counseling and therapy, **Allen Ivey**, **Mary Bradford Ivey**, and **Carlos Zalaquett** began integrating relevant neuroscientific evidence into their textbooks and publishing articles describing how neuroscience was confirming the effectiveness of counseling and therapy practices, and its importance for social justice work (Ivey & Zalaquett, 2011; Zalaquett & Ivey, 2014). At a keynote address at the American Counseling Association's (ACA) national conference, in 2013, Allen Ivey described how the integration of neuroscience findings was essential for the future of the discipline. For example, negative stress leads to neuronal damage, which manifests as symptoms of mental health concerns whereas a positive therapeutic relationship helps establish new neural pathways and improve mental health (Montes, 2013). **Chad Luke**, another expert on neuroscience in counseling, has also written and talked extensively on the subject.

Neuroscience has the potential of changing how we view and diagnose mental health issues. Recently, the National Institute of Mental Health developed a Research Domain Criteria (RDoC) initiative that offers a potentially new direction to traditional diagnosis procedures that are based on the *Diagnostic and Statistical Manual* (DSM-5) (American Psychiatric Association, 2013; Kozak & Cuthbert, 2016; Insel, 2013). By examining the relationship between psychopathology to psychology and biology, such as genetics and neuroscience, it is hoped there could be a new classification system that is based on observable behaviors and neurobiological measures.

Today, there is increased interest in neurocounseling among all the helping professions, and we are beginning to see neuroscience information infused in counseling theory and skills textbooks (e.g., Ivey et al., 2017; Luke, 2016; Zalaquett et al., 2018). In addition, neuroscience offers specific modalities that focus on brain-based counseling, such as biofeedback, neurofeedback, self-regulation, eye movement desensitization and reprocessing (EMDR), and prolonged exposure (PE) therapy. It also provides a potential foundation for new theoretical models based on observable behaviors and neurobiological measures (Insel, 2013). As we move into the 21st century, we will very likely see increased integration of neuroscience into counseling and the development of theoretical models based on such integration.

VIEW OF HUMAN NATURE

Neurocounseling is a **wellness** and **strength-based approach** that integrates **neuroeducation**, a form of psychoeducation regarding how activities and environment affect general health and the **structural biology** of the brain. Optimizing health and lifestyle increases wellness and reduces stress and stimulates **neuroplasticity**, a condition required for successful neural change (Davidson & McEwen, 2012; Miller, 2016). Although some stress can be helpful and necessary for optimal development, when stress becomes overwhelming it begins to damage neural networks (Ivey et al., 2018). In contrast, living a healthy lifestyle in multiple dimensions equates to greater well-being and self-regulation, reduces stress, and lessens the potential for damage to neural networks.

Specific lifestyles can positively or negatively impact one's neuroplasticity. For instance, **physical exercise** has been found to encourage neuroplasticity and improve mental functioning (Rock et al., 2012; Russell-Chapin, 2017b). Exercise releases **brain-derived neurotrophic factors**

(BDNF), which helps neurons grow, mature, and maintain themselves, and is a major factor in neuroplasticity (Bliss et al., 2010; Cooke, 2011; Jones, 2017a). Regarding nutrition, research into the **gut-microbiome-brain connection** is exploring implications for anxiety and depression, and a diet high in processed foods appears to contribute to **brain dysregulation** (Russell-Chapin, 2017b). **Sleep hygiene** (e.g., adequate sleep) plays a critical role in the consolidation of memories, emotional control, and even creativity (Rock et al., 2012). Additionally, during sleep, **glial cells** become active and play a key role in removing brain waste via the **glymphatic pathway**; however, when sleep is insufficient, toxins accumulate and brain function is compromised (Benveniste et al., 2017; Russell-Chapin, 2017b).

In addition, **lifestyle habits** can also impact neuroplasticity. For instance, Ivey et al. (2014) assess several areas of a person's lifestyle, and through psychoeducation help clients focus on areas where functioning is low. These areas include exercise, nutrition, sleep, social relations, intimacy, cognitive challenge, cultural health and cultural identify, meditation, drug and alcohol use, medication and supplement use, positive thinking, spirituality, nature, smoking, screen time, relaxation and having fun, education, money and privilege, helping others, joy and humor, and art, music, and dance. By understanding how lifestyle affects brain health, the **neurocounselor** can help clients focus on those areas that need improvement and provide them with the motivation to make real, concrete, changes toward better neural functioning (Miller, 2016).

Neurocounseling has a **developmental focus** and neurocounselors must have knowledge of neurobiological changes in the brain that occur throughout life, and associated emotional and behavioral responses, if they are to offer informed, effective interventions (Codrington, 2010; Lorelle & Michel, 2017). Brain development begins in the womb and occurs throughout the lifetime, and early detrimental influences to brain development, such as toxins, disease, and abuse, can impact a person over his or her lifetime (Knokel, 2018; National Research Council and Institute of Medicine, 2000). Although major changes in the brain occur to the age of 24 (Arain et al., 2013), the brain continues to change over one's lifetime and despite some decline in ability after the age of 40, some neuroplasticity continues throughout one's lifespan. This is why knowledge of developmental brain changes, and their consequential challenges, must be incorporated into neuro-informed counseling (Luders, 2014; Singh-Manoux et al., 2012).

Critics of neurocounseling suggest it offers a reductionist view of human behavior that disregards the experiential nature of counseling, offers a objectivist medical model of intervention, and is antithetical to the humanistic foundations of counseling (Hansen et al., 2014; Wilkinson, 2018). Wilkinson (2017) argues that neuroeducation is simply a specialized form of psychoeducation and biofeedback, rooted in behaviorism. Russell-Chapin (2017), in contrast, asserts that because the tools of neurocounseling provide physiological self-regulation, it is, in fact, a strength-based theory.

Some have offered methods for integrating neuroscience into the counseling practice without losing the integrity of the counseling relationship. For instance, Luke et al. (2019) suggest that neuro-informed counseling can help counselors understand the human experience and help clients understand and normalize their experiences. Although this may seem counterintuitive for those who view neurocounseling as reductionistic and formulated from the medical model, understanding physiological factors can be empowering for clients, and offering information regarding ways of eliminating toxins can encourage neuroplasticity and enhance motivation for change. The integration of neuroscience and counseling presents a person-first model of counseling in which neuroscience is utilized as another tool to support clients in achieving their therapeutic goals (Bergstrom et al., 2014; Sullivan et al., 2018).

KEY CONCEPTS

This section examines central concepts of neurocounseling that include **neuroplasticity; neurogenesis; attention, arousal, and focus; the limbic system and emotions; changes in brain functioning over the lifespan; empathy and mirror neurons; microskills relationship to neural networks; brainwaves; wellness, positivity, and neuroplasticity; and self-regulation**.

Neuroplasticity

Neuroplasticity is "the ability of the brain to alter its structure and function in response to external or internal changes in the environment, including development, learning, memory, brain injury, and disease" (Field et al., 2017, p. 261). In other words, the brain can undergo structural changes as a result of events such as injury, illness, and stress; wellness activities and stress reduction; and through learned experiences (Davidson & McEwen, 2012; Tardif et al., 2016). If exposed to healthy stimuli, throughout the lifespan new connections and new neural networks can be developed and the brain can rewire itself, as connections between neurons, and the relative strength of these connections, become stronger (Schwartz & Begley, 2003).

The counseling process engages the brain to build new neural networks by guiding clients in visualizing new realities, exploring unique beliefs, and practicing alternative behaviors (Ivey et al., 2018). The result is new neural pathways that become stronger through the repeated, guided practice that the counseling process provides (Lillard & Erisir, 2011; Ratey, 2008). Mental health disorders, including depression, bipolar disorder, autism, schizophrenia, and drug addiction, inhibit neuroplasticity (Collingridge et al., 2010). Effective counseling can, however, permanently change neural networks and how people feel, think, and behave.

Neurogenesis

Neurogenesis can be described as the brain's ability to regrow damaged or lost neurons from stem cells, which are undifferentiated cells that can morph into any of a number of different types of cells, including neurons. This process contributes to positive neuroplasticity (Ivey et al., 2018; Jones, 2017a). Although neurogenesis occurs throughout one's lifetime, it decreases as one ages (Alvarez-Buylla & Lim, 2004); however, healthy activities can ensure the optimal level of neurogenesis as a function of one's age and genetics.

Attention, Arousal, and Focus

Attention is essential to acquire, update, and correct learning and understanding, and can be assessed through brain imaging (Lodge & Harrison, 2019). When a client and counselor attend to each other, the brains of each become focused and changes in brain chemistry and structure, over time, can be seen. Attention involves two processes: **arousal** and **focus**. Arousal, in contrast with sleep, involves the turning on of a network of neurons in the brain stem called the **reticular activating system**. Once aroused, the executive functions of the **frontal cortex** can determine the direction of attention (Ivey et al., 2018). The ability to focus one's attention in certain activities, such as counseling, can positively affect brain development and how one thinks, acts, and feels. For instance, focused relaxation and meditation "can actually alter gene activity—the way that genes express themselves and thus influence the body" (Benson & Proctor, 2010, p. xii). Thus, learning how to control one's arousal and focus can lead to well-being.

The Limbic System and Emotions

The **limbic system**, which consists of the **hypothalamus**, **hippocampus**, **amygdala**, and other areas of the brain, is often called the **seat of human emotions**. It lies below the **cerebrum,** which contains the **cerebral cortex** (gray matter) that controls **executive functioning** (see Figure 9.1).

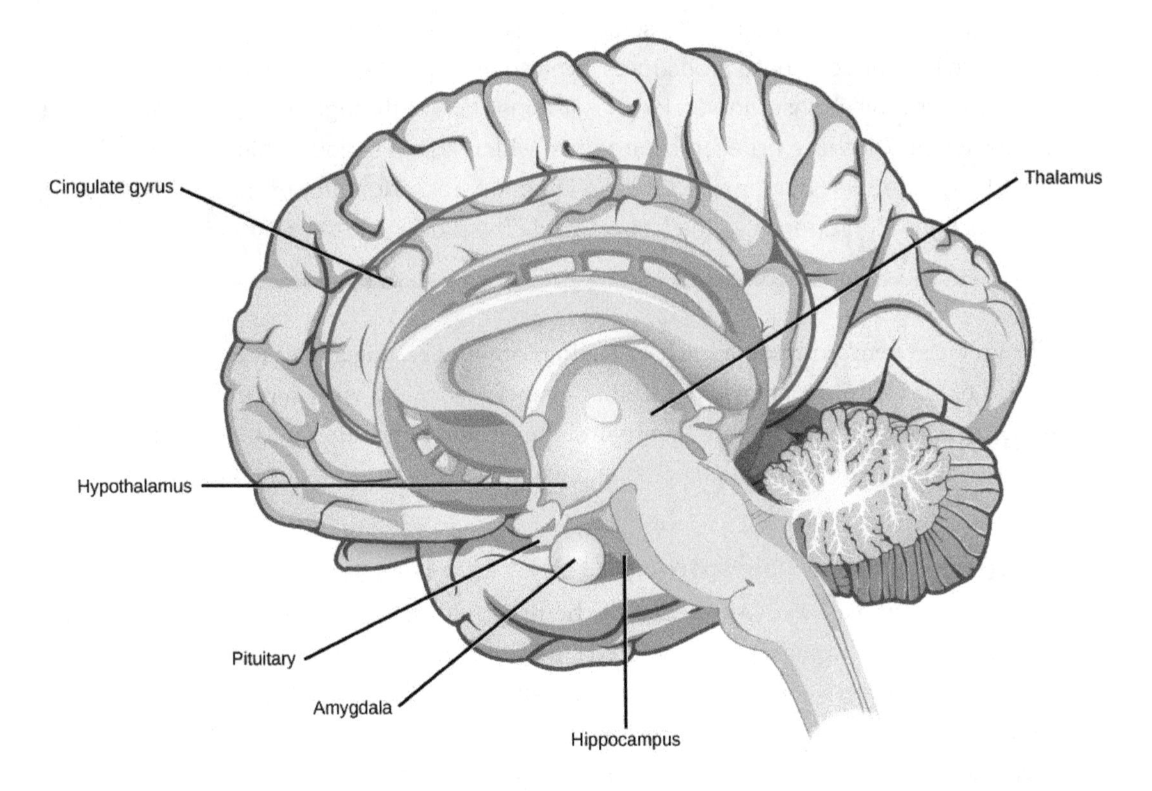

Figure 9.1 The Limbic System

The fact that the limbic system lies below the **cerebral cortex** is metaphorically interesting as it is the cerebral cortex that can put breaks on the emotions of the limbic system. Sometimes in severe stress or emotional overload, however, the limbic system can overwhelm the control held by the cerebral cortex. In fact, starting in the 1930s and until the 1980s, **prefrontal lobotomies**, a surgical procedure to sever the connection between the limbic system and the prefontal cortex, were conducted on thousands of individuals, almost always leaving the person affectless, passive, and lacking motivation (see Box 9.1).

BOX 9.1 LOBOTOMIES IN AMERICA

> As those who watched the procedure described it, a patient would be rendered unconscious by electroshock. Freeman would then take a sharp ice pick-like instrument, insert it above the patient's eyeball through the orbit of the eye, into the frontal lobes of the brain, moving the instrument back and forth. Then he would do the same thing on the other side of the face (National Public Radio, 2005, para. 8).

During the 1930s through the 1950s, between 40,000 and 50,000 lobotomies were performed, mostly on individuals with schizophrenia and severe depression, in an effort to reduce their affect. These procedures involved drilling holes in the patient's skulls to access their brain or inserting an ice pick-like instrument through the eyeball into the frontal lobes. For these gruesome surgeries, which would seriously blunt a person's affect, change their personality, or even kill them, the originator of the procedure, Antonoi Egas Moniz, received the Nobel Prize! (Tartakovsky, 2019)

The limbic system's amygdala is where feelings of sadness, anger, pleasure, and fear reside, and it also helps to store memories so similar events associated with certain feelings can be remembered. Along with the hypothalamus and the pituitary and adrenal glands, the amygdala functions as an important coping mechanism when faced with stress and danger.

Changes in Brain Functioning Over the Lifespan

Neurocounselors must have knowledge of the neurobiological changes in the brain that occur throughout the lifespan and associated emotional and behavioral responses if they are to incorporate informed, effective interventions with their clients (Codrington, 2010; Lorelle & Michel, 2017). Brain development begins during pregnancy and occurs throughout the lifetime, though early detrimental influences, such as diseases (e.g., rubella), prenatal alcohol consumption, nutrition deficiencies, stress, and toxins (e.g., lead paint) can impact a person over his or her lifetime (Knokel, 2018; National Research Council and Institute of Medicine, 2000).

Lifespan changes can be significant and observable in sessions with children or adolescent clients. The prefrontal cortex, heavily involved in executive functioning, rewires itself from puberty to 24 years old (Arain et al., 2013) and serves a crucial role in the theory of the mind and in rational decision making. These changes interact with the limbic system to produce more emotionally driven or volatile behavior, especially during adolescents (Siegel, 2013), explaining why adolescent thoughts and behaviors may appear disorganized, selfish, incomplete, or irrational to a counselor (Lorelle & Michel, 2017; Xi et al., 2011). This is one of the reasons why play therapy is particularly helpful for young children, but not as useful for adolescents (Jones, 2017b).

As humans age past their mid-20s, the myelin sheath surrounding neurons begins to degrade, which results in the slowdown of brain receptors. Every decade after the age of 40, the human brain decreases in volume and weight by approximately 5% and there is a continual decline in ability to recall memories, learn new information, or utilize reasoning skills (Luders, 2014; Singh-Manoux et al., 2012); however, some neuroplasticity continues throughout one's lifespan and knowledge of developmental brain changes, and their consequential challenges, must be incorporated into neuro-informed counseling.

From a neurocounseling perspective, treatment and intervention is informed as much by developmental stage as by presenting symptoms, disease, injury, or trauma. The brain continues to develop and change throughout the lifespan, and this understanding helps a clinician form richer and fuller case conceptualizations and treatment plans for their clients (Jones, 2017b).

Empathy and Mirror Neurons

Behaviors of others can be unconsciously taken in by an observer and mimicked. For instance, when one is around someone who is depressed, that person may unconsciously show those same expressions of sadness, thus reinforcing a cycle of sadness. In contrast, when one listens with energy and interest, others may pick up this positive affect.

> Expressions can … transmit emotions to others—the sight of a person showing intense disgust turns on in the observer's brain areas that are associated with the feeling of disgust. Similarly, if you smile, the world does indeed smile with you (up to a point). Experiments in which tiny sensors were attached to the "smile" muscles of people looking at faces show the sight of another person smiling triggers automatic mimicry—albeit so slight that it may not be visible. … the brain concludes that something good is happening out there and creates a feeling of pleasure. (Carter 1999, p. 87)

The imitation of emotional expression is mediated by **mirror neurons**, which are parallel neurons in the observer that fire when that person watches another individual behave.

In other words, mirror neurons allow one to mimic the experience of others and understand the basis of the other person's experience.

The ability to imitate the behaviors of others suggests that "The basic building blocks [of empathy] are hardwired into the brain and await development through interaction with others ..." (Decety & Jackson, 2004, p. 71). When a counselor is empathic, he or she is able to experience the world of the client due to mirror neurons, and the client's mirror neurons can be awakened as the counselor demonstrates empathy. In other words, the counselor is demonstrating empathy and the client is learning about empathy as he or she experiences the counselor's empathy. Thus, "Being empathic with patients may be more than just something that helps them 'feel better'; it may create a new state of neural activation with a coherence in the moment that improves the capacity for self-regulation" (Siegel, 2006, p. 255).

Decety and Jackson (2006) point out that those with an antisocial, criminal personality have a reduced ability to appreciate the emotions of others. Not only is there less firing of mirror neurons, but there also appears to be a dysfunction of the energizing amygdala and hippocampus (long-term memory). It is possible that training in empathy, and related microskills, may increase the effectiveness of our mirror neurons and diminish other nonempathic responses (Ivey et al., 2018).

Microskills Relationship to Neural Networks

Recognizing the dynamic interaction between our environment and our neural networks, traditional therapeutic interventions and **microskills** have been found to change neural networks. Microskills are the basic foundational skills involved in effectively helping relationships (Ivey et al., 2018), and new technological developments in neural imaging have allowed clinicians to see that microskills affect neural networks in areas of the brain responsible for positive client outcomes (Ivey et al., 2017, 2018; Kawamishi et al., 2015). Neuroplasticity is the process that allows for the rewiring of the brain that can result in emotional, behavioral, and cognitive improvements for the client (Ivey et al., 2017).

Brainwaves

Brainwaves, produced by synchronized, or repetitive, electrical pulses from neurons communicating with one another in our brain, are the foundation of all our thoughts, emotions, and behaviors. Brainwaves change according to what you are doing and feeling. Slow-frequency brainwaves predominate when we are resting, sleepy, or tired. Fast-frequency waves predominate when we are focused, very alert, or wired.

There are five types of brain waves, each measured by the frequency at which they register on the electroencephalogram (EEG). Brainwaves are measured in hertz (cycles per second). The EEG is an instrument that detects electrical activity in the brain using small metal discs (electrodes) attached to the scalp (Mayo Clinic, 2018a). Individual brainwave presentations correlate to specific client concerns and through neurofeedback and other practices, clients can work to change and regulate these patterns, thus resulting in more positive feelings, thoughts, and behaviors (Russell-Chapin, 2016). Counselors can use brainwaves to diagnose, monitor, treat, and assess outcomes of interventions (see Picture 9.1).

Picture 9.1 Individual with Electrodes Attached to Scalp.

Field, Jones, & Russell-Chapin (2017) outline the five categories of brain waves and their potential functions, which are listed based on the frequency of hertz (Hz), which is a measurement of cycles per second (Ehlers & Kupfer, 1999).

1. *Delta waves* (1–3 Hz): The slowest of brainwaves, delta waves are generated during deep relaxation, meditation, and dreamless sleep. They seem to be most related to empathy, healing, and regeneration. On average, women seem to have more delta wave activity.
2. *Theta waves* (4–7 Hz): This twilight state occurs when one is falling in and out of sleep, or daydreaming, and can be readily achieved in meditative states. This state is deeply relaxing and is often considered the gateway to creativity, learning, memory, and intuition.
3. *Alpha waves* (8–15 Hz): Sometimes called the resting state of the brain, alpha waves are related to relaxed consciousness, calmness, decreased stress, and mind/body integration.
4. *Beta waves* (16–31 Hz): These brainwaves dominate one's waking state and are related to alertness, being attentive, problem solving, focused mental activity, decision making, and unease, anxiety, depression, and fight and flight.
5. *Gamma waves* (32–100Hz): Gamma waves oscillate quickly and are often associated with conscious awareness, perception, innovation, and "bursts of insight" (Field et al., 2017, p. 144). Some evidence suggests there is a relationship between gamma waves with schizophrenia and autism (Hirano et al., 2015; Rojas & Wilson, 2014).

Wellness, Positivity, and Neuroplasticity

Raising a client's consciousness regarding the mind/body interaction is key to neurocounseling. For instance, it is important to help clients know there is a connection between chronic stress and depression, anxiety, bipolar disorder, schizophrenia, and post-traumatic stress disorder

(Douthit & Russotti, 2017), and that too much stress can inhibit neuroplasticity while a reduction in stress can enhance it (Davidson & McEwen, 2012; Tardif et al., 2016). After clients gain this knowledge, **focusing on wellness and the positives** can lead to them making choices that will strengthen the ability of the brain to make new neural networks. For example, the neurotransmitter dopamine is released when situations are pleasant and positive, preparing the brain for new learning and the development of new neural networks. In contrast, extreme toxins, abuse, trauma, making poor lifestyle choices, and negative thinking can result in the loss of neural connections (Kahneman, 2011).

Counselors and psychotherapists who focus primarily on negative issues and problems build a self-reinforcing circularity between the demons of the amygdala and the frontal cortex. In contrast, wellness activities such as exercise, positive reframing of old stories, enhancing interpersonal relationships, meditation, leisure activities, and developing lifelong positive habits all facilitate one's ability to control and modify negative thinking and feeling. As the client discovers how to make lifestyle changes, there is a rewiring of the brain that reduces negative symptoms and improves wellness (Russell-Chapin, 2017b).

Self-Regulation

Self-regulation is the individual's ability to gain, or regain, a sense of control over one's physiology, behavior, cognition, and emotions in an effort to seek a more satisfying life. In fact, the goal of most counseling approaches is to learn how to regulate oneself. As one example, a primary goal of dialectical behavior therapy (DBT) is to assist with emotional regulation by learning how to moderate one's feelings, de-escalate emotional situations, and self-soothe (Koemer, 2012). In addition to therapy, specific types of biofeedback and neurofeedback can also be part of the self-regulation process. By obtaining feedback about your body and mind states, one can learn how to move toward states of relaxation, emotional stability, and the development of new neural networks based on positive states of being.

TECHNIQUES

This section will review major techniques used in neurocounseling, including **neuroeducation**, **assessing lifestyle**, **biofeedback and self-regulation skills (diaphragmatic breathing, mindfulness, and technological approaches to biofeedback)**, **neurofeedback**, and **neuroscience-informed therapies** such as **prolonged exposure therapy (PE)** and **eye movement desensitization and reprocessing** (EMDR).

Neuroeducation

> Neuroeducation is a didactic or experiential-based intervention that aims to reduce client distress and improve client outcome by helping clients understand the neurological processes underlying mental functioning. (Miller, 2016, p. 105)

By understanding the neurological basis for their symptoms, clients begin to believe that change is possible. Understanding that change is achieved through practice and repetition, and that it does not happen quickly, also helps them cope with the unsteady pace of success and setbacks in counseling (Miller, 2016). Thus, the neurocounselor provides education regarding basic structures and functions of the brain to highlight the necessary interactions between the brain and behavior.

One simple way to help clients understand how brain structures influence emotional responses, and to learn techniques to mediate such responses, is the **hand model of the brain** (Jones, 2017a; Siegel, 2017). The lower part of the brain is represented by the wrist and thumb and reflects the spinal cord, brain stem, and limbic system, including the hippocampus and the amygdala (Figure 9.2). This is the **emotional center of the brain**, which also mediates the **flight or fight response**. The upper part of the brain, **the cortex**, is represented by the four remaining fingers, with the area around the tips of the fingers being the **prefontal cortex** and the area around the joints of the fingers being the **cerebral cortex**. The cortex allows one to think and use logic and moral reasoning. Sometimes, when individuals are too tired or are in situations that could trigger emotional dysregulation, the lower part of the brain can take over and **"flip one's lid,"** as is represented on the left side of Figure 9.2. But individuals can again gain control over the lower part of their brain. This is represented on the right side of Figure 9.2 where we see the prefontal cortex wrapping itself over the lower part of the brain and communicating with the cerebral cortex in an effort to control the lower part of the brain.

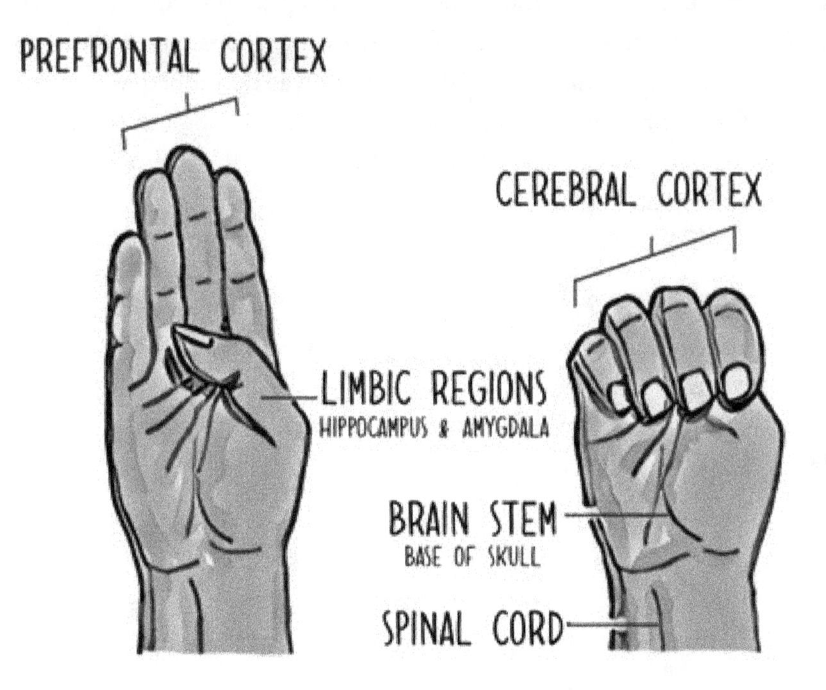

Figure 9.2 Hand model of the Brain

This model is an analogy for how individuals can learn specific techniques that encourage the upper part of the brain to fire (e.g., the use of specific cognitive techniques) and reduce responses from the lower part of the brain. This process is called using **neuroscience-informed interventions**.

As clients learn the neurological basis for their symptoms, through **neuroeduction**, they tend to experience an increase in compassion and empathy for self and others and a reduction in the shame they feel about their past behaviors (Miller, 2016). They also lower the likelihood of blaming others for their problems as they realize their part in destructive relationships and that they can have some control of changing themselves.

Assessing Lifestyle

As clients increasingly understand the mind/body connection and have clarity about how behaviors affect their brain development and their thinking, feelings, and behaving, they are ready to assess those areas of their lives in which they may have undue stress or behaviors that can sabotage neural plasticity. One activity in which clients can obtain a self-assessment is through Ivey and others' (2018) **Therapeutic Lifestyle** Changes Inventory. This instrument assesses 20 dimensions of life, and clients can rank order those areas they most want to work on (see Table 9.1).

Similar to Therapeutic Lifestyle Changes Inventory, Myers & Sweeney (2004) developed the **indivisible self model**, an evidence-based model of wellness that examines multiple aspects of one's life experience, including the creative, coping, social, essential, and physical self, and demonstrates the interrelated effects the dimensions have on the overall well-being of the individual. Finally, the **healthy mind platter** was developed as a model that provides a framework for optimal brain functioning facilitated through daily engagement in seven mental activities to enhance brain matter and well-being (Rock et al., 2012; Siegel, 2019) (see Figure 9.3, then Box 9.2).

TABLE 9.1 THERAPEUTIC LIFESTYLE CHANGES INVENTORY

HOW HEALTHY IS YOUR LIFESTYLE? Allen Ivey, Mary Bradford Ivey, and Carlos Zalaquett © 2014

Name____________________ Gender______ Age______

Race/Ethnicity____________________ Date________________

Circle your response

ALIOSTRESS/EUSTRESS/STRESS LEVELS: What is your level of stress?											
	1 Eustress, life is generally calm and interesting, few major or minor stressors, recover from stress fairly quickly. Pleasant, happy life.	**2** Manageable, stressors can be troublesome, but recover. Some tough stressors time to time. Life is good.	**3** Often feel stressed, some times for days, loose some sleep, old stressful events often with me. However, generally life is good.	**4** Constant feeling of stress, pressure, sleep problems, old events still with me. Can blow up, but manage. Life is OK, but . . .	**5** Chronic stress, tired, angry, sleep difficulties, feel sad, easy to blowup, fall apart, out of control. Need to change my life.		1	2	3	4	5
1. Exercise: How frequently do you exercise (walk, swim, bike, garden, run, rock climb)?											
	1	**2**	**3**	**4**	**5**		**1**	**2**	**3**	**4**	**5**
	5-7 days weekly	4-5 days weekly	2-3 times weekly	Occasional	Couch potato						
2. Nutrition: What is your typical diet?											
	1	**2**	**3**	**4**	**5**		**1**	**2**	**3**	**4**	**5**
	Vegan, vegetarian, fish	Low fat, lean meat, fruit, vegetables	Mediterranean, Paleo	Stn. Amer. Diet	Fast food, fries, sugar						
3. Sleep: How many hours nightly, including how restful is your sleep?											
	1	**2**	**3**	**4**	**5**		**1**	**2**	**3**	**4**	**5**
	7-9 hours	7 hours	Sleep challenges	Many meds	Serious difficulty						
4. Social relations: How connected are you to others—close relationships, family, friends, groups?											
	1	**2**	**3**	**4**	**5**		**1**	**2**	**3**	**4**	**5**
	Well-connected	Connected	Friends, some groups	Somewhat social	Alone, angry, sad						
4a. Intimacy, Sex Life: How satisfied are you with your sex life?											
	1	**2**	**3**	**4**	**5**		**1**	**2**	**3**	**4**	**5**
	Highly	Moderately	Somewhat	Dissatisfied	Do not care						

(Continued)

TABLE 9.1 (CONTINUED)

5. Cognitive Challenge: How actively do you involve yourself in mind-expanding cognitive challenges?											
	1	**2**	**3**	**4**	**5**		**1**	**2**	**3**	**4**	**5**
	Joy in constantly learning, searching for the New	Involved, active	Moderately interested, reads some books, puzzles	Some, no more than 3 hours	None						
6. Cultural Health and Cultural Identity: Awareness of cultural issues influencing, you, including sense of cultural identity.											
	1	**2**	**3**	**4**	**5**		**1**	**2**	**3**	**4**	**5**
	Empathy for self & others. Sees self-in-relation, race/ ethnicity, etc. awareness, life vision	At least two of the preceding plus life vision	One of the preceding, some life vision	Slightly aware of issues	Oppressive, no real life vision						
7. Meditation, Yoga, etc.: How often you engage in this practice?											
	1	**2**	**3**	**4**	**5**		**1**	**2**	**3**	**4**	**5**
	Daily	3-4 weekly	Aware, occasional	Absent	Hyper, cannot do						
8. Drugs, Alcohol: Use of alcohol or other drugs?											
	1	**2**	**3**	**4**	**5**		**1**	**2**	**3**	**4**	**5**
	None	Moderate	Has become part of life	Becomes a focus	Addicted						
9. Medication and Supplements: How aware are you of possible issues plus appropriate contact with physicians?											
	1	**2**	**3**	**4**	**5**		**1**	**2**	**3**	**4**	**5**
	Regular contact with physician, follows directions	Frequent contact	Occasional, some difficulty following directions	Seldom	Never						
10. Positive thinking/optimism/ happiness: Do you have resilient positive attitudes and a good level of happiness?											
	1	**2**	**3**	**4**	**5**		**1**	**2**	**3**	**4**	**5**
	Resilient, positive, optimistic	Most of the time	Usually, not always	Seldom	Infrequent						
11. Belief, Values: How engaged are you with living a meaningful life?											
	1	**2**	**3**	**4**	**5**		**1**	**2**	**3**	**4**	**5**
	A life center	Involved	Occasional involvement	Never	Not interested						

11a. Spirituality, Religiosity: Do you participate in spiritual or religious activities?											
	1	**2**	**3**	**4**	**5**		**1**	**2**	**3**	**4**	**5**
	Daily	Between 2–4 days	Once a week	Holidays only	Do not believe						
12. Nature/Green/Garden: How often you engage in outside/nature activities?											
	1	**2**	**3**	**4**	**5**		**1**	**2**	**3**	**4**	**5**
	Gets outdoors often	Frequent	Sometimes	Seldom	Almost never						
13. Smoking: Do you smoke? If yes, how much?											
	1	**2**	**3**	**4**	**5**		**1**	**2**	**3**	**4**	**5**
	Never	Never, but exposed to secondary	Stopped smoking	Tries to stop	Still smoking						
14. Screen time (TV, Cell, iPad, Computer): Amount of time in front of a screen?											
	1	**2**	**3**	**4**	**5**		**1**	**2**	**3**	**4**	**5**
	None	2 hours or less daily	4 hours	6 or more	Never off-line						
15. Relaxation and Having Fun: How frequently you involved in leisure or relaxation activities?											
	1	**2**	**3**	**4**	**5**		**1**	**2**	**3**	**4**	**5**
	Something every day	5-6 hours weekly	3-4 hours	Limited & stressed	Workaholic and/ stressed out						
16. Education: What level of education have you completed?											
	1	**2**	**3**	**4**	**5**		**1**	**2**	**3**	**4**	**5**
	College, serious hobby	College	Comm. College	High school/GED	Drop out						
17. Money and Privilege: What is your financial situation? Do you benefit from privilege because of race or other factor?											
	1	**2**	**3**	**4**	**5**		**1**	**2**	**3**	**4**	**5**
	Have it all, privileged	Comfortable	Making it	On edge, but Ok	Poor, oppressed						
18. Helping others/community involvement/social justice action: How frequently you help others or your community?											
	1	**2**	**3**	**4**	**5**		**1**	**2**	**3**	**4**	**5**
	Daily action	Weekly action	Often involved	No time	Destructive						
19. Art, Music, Dance, Literature: How frequently you release your artistic abilities?											
	1	**2**	**3**	**4**	**5**		**1**	**2**	**3**	**4**	**5**
	Daily	Several times weekly	Moderate/frequent	Occasional	None						

(Continued)

TABLE 9.1 (CONTINUED)

20. Joy, Humor, Zest for Living, Keeping it Simple, Not Overdoing: How happy or how much fun do you have?											
	1	**2**	**3**	**4**	**5**		**1**	**2**	**3**	**4**	**5**
	Life is a blast	Fun most of the time	Moderately happy	Now and then	Never						
SELF-EVALUATION OF GENERAL LIFESTYLE											
Work: What is the level of your work or retirement activities?											
	1	**2**	**3**	**4**	**5**		**1**	**2**	**3**	**4**	**5**
	Fully employed. Retired, never bored	Partial Employment. Retired and active	Temporary Work. OK, but sometimes bored	Jobless. Bored, less happy	Given up work Inactive, depressed						
In Control: How much in control of your life are you?											
	1	**2**	**3**	**4**	**5**		**1**	**2**	**3**	**4**	**5**
	In full control of my life	Mostly in control	Somewhat in con-trol	Low control	Out of control						
Health: How healthy are you?											
	1	**2**	**3**	**4**	**5**		**1**	**2**	**3**	**4**	**5**
	Very healthy	Occasional issues	Good, but could be better	Major issue	Very poor						
Stability: How stable is your life currently?											
	1	**2**	**3**	**4**	**5**		**1**	**2**	**3**	**4**	**5**
	Highly stable	Moderately	Some ups and downs	Unstable	Chaotic						
Resilience: Your ability to bounce back from life challenges											
	1	**2**	**3**	**4**	**5**		**1**	**2**	**3**	**4**	**5**
	Back "at it" soon	Temporarily troubled	Worry a fair amount	Difficult, but do it	Overwhelmed						
Satisfaction: How satisfied are you with your current lifestyle?											
	1	**2**	**3**	**4**	**5**		**1**	**2**	**3**	**4**	**5**
	Highly	Moderately	Somewhat	Dissatisfied	Helpless						
Action: How ready are you to make changes to increase your wellbeing?											
	1	**2**	**3**	**4**	**5**		**1**	**2**	**3**	**4**	**5**
	Ready to change	Want to change	Thinking about it	Some interest	Not interestedv						

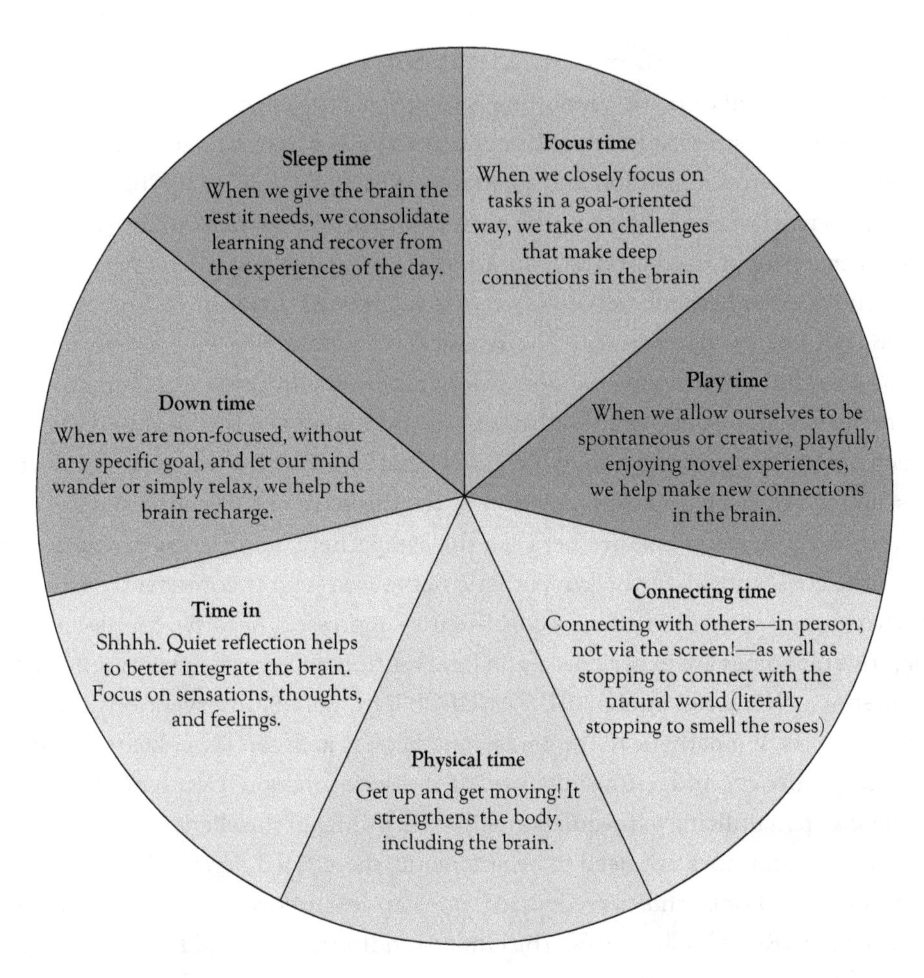

Figure 9.3 The Healthy Mind Platter

BOX 9.2 FOCUSING ON LIFESTYLE CHANGE

Using the Therapeutic Lifestyle Changes Inventory in Table 9.1, identify those areas where you received a score of three or higher. Then, using the seven mental activities of the healthy mind platter in Box 9.2, rank order those areas from highest to lowest based on how much you tend to focus on that mental activity during your day. Then, using both lists, identify areas you need to work on to decrease stress and increase life satisfaction. As noted in the chapter, working on decreasing stress and focusing on positive change can increase neuroplasticity and make long-term changes in how one thinks, acts, and feels.

Biofeedback and Self-Regulation Skills

Because a primary goal of neurocounseling is to provide the client concrete ways to regulate physical responses to stress, it is helpful for clients to have a basic understanding of the physiology involved in stress activation and suppression (Russell-Chapin, 2017b). In simple terms, stress is experienced when the **sympathetic nervous system** is activated and the **parasympathetic nervous system** is suppressed, and is reduced when the parasympathetic nervous system is activated and the sympathetic nervous system is suppressed (Douthit & Russotti, 2017; Ivey et al., 2018). All stress is not harmful. For instance, sympathetic nervous system activation is a necessary condition for attention, motivation, processing information, immune function, and performance (Jones et al., 2017). Intense or prolonged levels of sympathetic nervous system activation, however, can lead to increased heart rate, blood pressure, and anxiety along with disruptions in sleep and dysregulation of the digestive and immune systems (Douthit & Russotti, 2017). Thus, a balance between the sympathetic and parasympathetic nervous systems is the goal, and when the sympathetic nervous system is consistently activated and the parasympathetic nervous system is consistently suppressed, negative emotional, physical, and cognitive outcomes are experienced and intervention becomes necessary (Crockett et al., 2017; Ivey et al., 2018; Jones et al., 2017; Russell-Chapin, 2017b). Interventions that shift the activation from the sympathetic to the parasympathetic system can lower heart rate and blood pressure, reduce anxiety, and restore immune and digestive function (Douthit & Russotti, 2017).

The first step in utilizing **self-regulation skills** is instilling in the client a realization that the response to a stressor does not need to be automatic; there is a difference between a reaction and a response, and once this is recognized, one can learn how to physiologically respond in a different way (Russell-Chapin, 2017b). Understanding that the **fight or flight** sympathetic reactions of the limbic system and the amygdala, for example, can be regulated through self-regulation techniques provides clients a framework from which to view such skills (Russell-Chapin, 2017b). Although many techniques can be used to assist in self-regulation, three popular approaches are **diaphragmatic breathing**, **mindfulness**, and **technological approaches to biofeedback**.

Diaphragmatic Breathing

An imbalance between the parasympathetic and sympathetic systems often involves slow, irregular, and shallow breaths, which are associated with distress, including anxiety, depression, and trauma (Crockett et al., 2017). Diaphragmatic breathing, by engaging the diaphragm in full, deep breathes, increases the absorption rate of glucose and oxygen, improving overall well-being and reducing anxiety, as the brain mechanisms involved in calming and relaxing begin to engage (Crockett et al., 2017; Russell-Chapin, 2017b). In sessions, once the client understands the basic associated neurobiology of healthy breathing, neurocounselors can lead guided breath awareness exercises to help clients notice and address irregularities within their own breathing, including "pace, depth, use of nose versus mouth, location of movement, volume, inhale/ exhale ratio, texture, comfortability, ease, and difficulty" (Crockett et al., 2017, p.171).

Mindfulness

Mindfulness is another technique that can be used to teach clients self-regulation skills (Russell-Chapin, 2017b). An introduction to mindfulness often involves focusing on how all the senses perceive a given experience, such as eating a favorite food or spending time with a loved one, and noticing the characteristics of the experience without judgment (Crockett et al., 2017; Russell-Chapin, 2017b). As clients understand the application of mindfulness by using simple, concrete examples, they become more adept at focusing on the present while withholding judgment. It is then that they can comprehend the connection between external stimuli and their internal reactions and begin to develop an ability to change their reactions through attention and focus (Crockett et al., 2017) (see Box 9.3).

BOX 9.3 MINDFULNESS EXERCISES

The Mayo Clinic (2018b) has several easy suggestions for practicing mindfulness exercises. After you examine the following exercises, pick one or two and practice it for the next week. See how it may positively affect your stress and anxiety level, and if conducted over long periods, can positively impact your neuroplasticity:

- **Pay attention.** It's hard to slow down and notice things in a busy world. Try to take the time to experience your environment with all of your senses—touch, sound, sight, smell, and taste. For example, when you eat a favorite food, take the time to smell, taste, and truly enjoy it.
- **Live in the moment.** Try to intentionally bring an open, accepting, and discerning attention to everything you do. Find joy in simple pleasures.
- **Accept yourself.** Treat yourself the way you would treat a good friend.
- **Focus on your breathing.** When you have negative thoughts, try to sit down, take a deep breath and close your eyes. Focus on your breath as it moves in and out of your body. Sitting and breathing for even just a minute can help.

You can also try more structured mindfulness exercises, such as:

- **Body scan meditation.** Lie on your back with your legs extended and arms at your sides, palms facing up. Focus your attention slowly and deliberately on each part of your body, in order, from toes to head or head to toes. Be aware of any sensations, emotions, or thoughts associated with each part of your body.

- **Sitting meditation.** Sit comfortably with your back straight, feet flat on the floor and hands on your lap. Breathing through your nose, focus on your breath moving in and out of your body. If physical sensations or thoughts interrupt your meditation, note the experience and then return your focus to your breath.
- **Walking meditation.** Find a quiet place 10 to 20 feet in length and begin to walk slowly. Focus on the experience of walking, being aware of the sensations of standing and the subtle movements that keep your balance. When you reach the end of your path, turn and continue walking, maintaining awareness of your sensations. (Mayo Clinic, 2018b, Section "What are some examples of … ")

Technological Approaches to Biofeedback

Various technological approaches to biofeedback are available to teach self-regulation skills that focus on decreasing muscle tension, decreasing skin conductance, maintaining body temperature, lowering respiration and heart rates, and lessening heart rate variability (HRV), all of which require specific training and equipment (Crockett et al., 2017; Russell-Chapin, 2017b). Neurocounselors may wish to receive comprehensive or specialized training (Crockett et al., 2017), or refer to trained clinicians when appropriate. Similar to the non-technological self-regulation strategies previously described, technological approaches teach a client how to engage in self-regulation by providing biofeedback that will result in decreased stress, improved performance, increased resiliency, and improved health. Eventually, the client learns how to engage in such self-regulation outside of sessions and without technology-provided biofeedback (Crockett et al., 2017; Russell-Chapin, 2017b) (see Box 9.4).

BOX 9.4 USING BIOFEEDBACK TO REDUCE STRESS

Next time you are in a state of stress, take your pulse. Then, practice one or two of the mindfulness exercises in Box 9.3 for about 10 minutes. Then, take your pulse again. Has it gone down? If yes, this non-technological approach is one indicator of how you can control your bodily states. With the use of technology, feedback can involve monitoring biological states you cannot normally monitor on your own and ultimately change your neural networks.

Neurofeedback (NFB)

> Neurofeedback as a clinical approach to the resolution of psychological and behavioral problems has its origins in the study of the brain's electrical activity and behavioral psychology. The development of the human electroencephalogram (EEG) combined with the application of principles of learning, knowledge of the brain's neuroplasticity, and principles of biofeedback and self-regulation, have made it possible to detect, monitor, and change the brain's electrical activity related to many emotional and physiological disorders. (Chapin & Russell-Chapin, 2014, p. 87)

Neurofeedback (NFB) is administered by a trained clinician and involves measuring and training brain waves and increasing connectivity among neural networks (Chapin & Russell-Chapin, 2014). A noninvasive treatment, electrodes are attached to the scalp to read the electrical activity of the brain, which is displayed and analyzed through computer software programs (Collura, 2013). Relying on the principles of operant and classical condition, NFB depends on reinforcers and inhibitors to teach a client how to self-regulate the electrical activity of his or her brain (Chapin & Russell-Chapin, 2014; Collura, 2013). Electrical activity is measured in terms of brain waves, and the amplitude of specific brainwaves correlate with mental states. Changes to the brain wave patterns work to address psychological symptoms or behaviors. Changing brain wave activity can occur through simple operant conditioning techniques. For instance, after the counselor solicits favored puzzles, games, music, or movies from the client, when desired brain waves are produced, the reward of the chosen activity is produced (the music will play, the puzzle unfold, etc.), and when the brain waves remain dysregulated, the reward is withheld (the music stops, the puzzle freezes, etc.). As part of a thorough client assessment, NFB can be used to determine irregularities in brainwaves, and coupled with the information gained through a comprehensive biopsychosocial evaluation, protocols to address these brain wave irregularities can be selected as part of the treatment plan. As the client learns to achieve the desired brain wave patterns through regular sessions, NFB works as another tool to develop self-regulation abilities that clients can learn to utilize in daily life (Russell-Chapin, 2016).

Neuroscience-Informed Therapies

Although there are a number of therapies that have been informed by neuroscience, two in particular have been popular in the past few years: **prolonged exposure (PE) therapy** and **eye movement desensitization response**. Here, we offer a very brief explanation of both.

Prolonged Exposure Therapy (PE)

Prolonged Exposure (PE) is "an empirically supported efficacious treatment for post-traumatic stress disorder" and is commonly used in treatment with combat veterans (McNally, 2007; Stojek et al., 2018, p. 1). Stojek and collaborators assert that traumatic events disrupt the networks of interconnected regions in the brain. PE increases the connectivity within and between the disrupted regions and reestablishes functional coherence between the ventromedial prefrontal cortex (vmPFC), amygdala, and the hippocampus. These processes increase the regulation of emotional responses in stressful situations. In other words, PE rearranges the fear circuitry in the brain—amygdala, hippocampus, and prefrontal cortex.

PE therapy is performed in nine to 12 sessions of about 90 minutes of duration. When beginning PE, the goal of the counselor is to gather as much information as possible from the individual regarding the stress he or she is experiencing, while also providing psychoeducation to the client. The client is also provided with a "toolbox" of relaxation techniques in these earlier sessions. After rapport has been sufficiently built and the client has been provided with ways to relieve agitation and stress that may arise from the process of PE therapy, the counselor will begin introducing exposure to traumatic events during the client's remaining sessions (Mackinson & Young, 2012).

Eye Movement Desensitization and Reprocessing (EMDR)

EMDR is a therapy that was originally designed to treat trauma victims, such as those that were experiencing post-traumatic stress disorder (PTSD). Memories from the trauma were thought to not be integrated into the total memory system and specific triggers would often bring back the original trauma. From a neuroprocessing perspective, **eye movement desensitization and reprocessing (EMDR)** is explained by the **adaptive information processing (AIP)** model, which suggests that neural pathways in the amygdala and hippocampus store traumatic memories that become trapped and not integrated within the wider adaptive memory network (EMDR Institute, 2019a; Shapiro & Solomon, 2015). When a situation triggers this trapped memory, the memory becomes present, as if it is occurring in the present with all of the physical, emotional, and perceptual experiences it originally had. These stored memories are targeted, and through the use of bilateral dual attention stimulation, such as eye movement or the use of taps or tones, the targeted memory becomes integrated within the general memory network and becomes part of the client's total life experience.

Why EMDR works is not totally clear, though it may have to do with how memory gets stored during rapid eye movement sleep (which this process seems to mimic), or due to the stimulation of an automatic relaxation response that becomes increased through the process, or due to a decrease in the vividness of the disturbed memory as a byproduct of the process. In addition, some posit that past traumas can become embedded in our psyche and that catharsis of embedded memories can lead to healing. Others have suggested that core beliefs maintain negative experiences, and that new cognitions and behaviors, one goal of EMDR, helps a person adopt new ways of being in the world. In either case, EMDR treatment involves eight phases that sometimes can be completed within a few sessions, but often take longer (EMDR Institute, 2019b; Shapiro & Solomon, 2015).

Phase 1: Client History and Treatment Planning: In this phase, an in-depth history of the client is taken and a treatment plan is formed. In particular, the therapist focuses on what the problem is along with the symptoms of the problem, situations from the past that caused the problem, current issues that continue distress, and those behaviors and skills needed in the future to alleviate the problem. In-depth discussion of the problem is not necessary; however, the client does need to identify what the problem is. Usually, this phase takes one to two sessions.

Phase 2: Preparation: Generally lasting one to two sessions, but sometimes longer (depending on the issue), this phase involves building a trusting relationship through the use of empathy and related skills, and the start of teaching the client a range of relaxation and coping techniques. Although EMDR is known for the use of eye movements, the therapeutic relationship should not be underestimated, as it is critical that the client "buy into" the process if it is to be successful (Dworkin, 2005). In addition, teaching a variety of cognitive behavioral relaxation techniques and coping skills helps clients begin the process of self-managing their anxiety.

Phase 3: Assessment: Using the problem situation identified in Phase 1, the client in this phase isolates negative beliefs associated with the event. Such negative self-statements or core beliefs could be "I am not lovable," "I am worthless," or "I am not capable." After picking one or more negative beliefs, the client identifies positive beliefs that contradict the negative ones. Using the subjective units of disturbance (SUD) scale, the client rates his or her level of discomfort from 0 to 10, with 0 being the most relaxed within the context of the problem and a 10 being the most upset. The client can relay his or her rating when thinking about the negative event, negative self-statements, or the newly identified positive self-statement.

Phase 4: Desensitization: During Phase 4, the therapist has the client focus on upsetting images, negative beliefs, emotions, and physical sensations related to a traumatic or upsetting event. At the same time, the therapist directs the client in a series of eye movements or related stimulations (e.g., tapping, listening to rhythmic tones). Then, the therapist tells the client to "blank it out" (or "let it go") and take a deep breath, and then asks, "What do you get now?" (Shapiro, 2002b, p. 38). At this point, the therapist will continue with treatment based on the type of response the client gives. If the client is still bothered by the initial upsetting image and related symptoms, desensitization will be repeated; however, clients will often leave the initial image and move on to another image related to the traumatic event. A decision to move on is made if a there is a SUD level of 0, 1, or 2.

Phase 5: Installation: As clients' level of upset decreases, there is a natural increase in the positive cognitive beliefs they identified in Phase 3. Thus, the purpose of this phase is to strengthen those positive beliefs. Using what is called the Validity of Cognition (VoC) scale, which runs from a 1 (completely false) to a 7 (completely true), the goal is to have clients reach the high end of the scale in reference to their newly chosen positive cognitive beliefs. In this phase, the therapist encourages the pairing of the positive cognition with the traumatic event. So, a person who was verbally abused as a child and always told he was "stupid" will pair the image of being told he was stupid with a statement such as, "I am capable and smart." Other activities might also be used at this time to reinforce the positive self-statement, such as the client deciding to confront a parent directly about the statements made in early life. This confrontation, if done correctly, could help to anchor the positive belief.

Phase 6: Body Scan: Because the body will sometimes continue to hold the tension from traumatic or upsetting events beyond what our minds are consciously saying, clients are asked to scan their bodies while remembering the target event. If tension is still present, additional processing is done (Phases 4 and 5).

Phase 7: Closure: The closure phase ensures that the client finishes each session feeling better than when the session began and helps clients focus on ongoing feelings of "psychological stability." Thus, at the end of each session, clients are encouraged to practice the self-management techniques learned in Phase 2. In addition, clients are encouraged to keep an ongoing journal to record their progress, to practice the self-management techniques at home, and to use relaxation recordings at home to maintain their stability.

Phase 8: Reevaluation: At the beginning of each EMDR session, the therapist reviews the client's journal with the client and talks with the client about any additional targets (problems) that need to be addressed. As processing continues, new issues will arise and the focus of treatment will change. As new issues emerge, clients will recycle through Phase 3 to Phase 8. And as new targets are dealt with, client anxiety, over time, will lessen and psychological stability will be maintained without further treatments being necessary.

EMDR's success in treating a number of disorders and problems is promising, and this approach will very likely expand its research base to clearly define why it has been so efficacious (EMDR Institute, 2019c; Shapiro & Solomon, 2015).

THE COUNSELING PROCESS

A neuroscience-informed approach will often start with a general clinical assessment of the client's problem. This assessment might include a traditional intake interview as well as a variety of qualitative and quantitative assessments focused on client wellness. Included in this assessment might be the Therapeutic Lifestyle Changes Inventory, the indivisible self model, or the healthy mind platter, discussed earlier. In addition, a **quantitative electroencephalogram (qEEG)** may be administered to capture brain wave presentations, which may be interpreted to correlate to possible behaviors or symptoms. Along with knowledge of developmental changes (Jones, 2017b), this assessment helps the neurocounselor perform a neuroscientific conceptualization of behaviors, emotions, thoughts, and feelings necessary to conduct intentional work with a client by focusing on a treatment plan and selecting appropriate interventions (Russell-Chapin, 2017a). The treatment plan will strengthen existing neural networks and identify, develop, and reinforce weak neural pathways.

Neurocounseling can stand on its own if the counselor is trained in structural biology, brain changes as a function of age, and the processes of neurofeedback. For instance, here a neuro-informed approach can focus on how modulating one's own brain waves can positively impact lifestyle and how lifestyle can positively impact changes in brain waves. Most counselors, however, are trained solely in a theoretical approach to counseling. Through workshops and courses on neurofeedback, counselors can begin to integrate neuro-informed treatments into their existing theoretical approach. Here, counselors can share with clients the process by which chosen interventions will change neural networks, and how such changes will translate into psychological and emotional improvement, increasing a client's agency in the change process (Miller, 2016).

SOCIAL AND CULTURAL ISSUES

The effect of stress on well-being and emotional health has been highlighted as a central concept to neurocounseling. As such, an understanding of how various sources of stress, including that suffered by victims of social injustice and oppression and members of marginalized groups, is fundamental to the successful implementation of counseling interventions (Ivey et al., 2018). For the neurocounselor, this understanding highlights not only the necessity of appropriate interventions through the course of counseling, but also the importance of advocating for social justice issues in order to alleviate significant sources of stress for diverse populations (Douthit & Russotti, 2017; Zalaquett & Ivey, 2018). Key social justice issues, such as poverty, abuse, bullying, racism, sexism, heterosexism, discrimination, and other forms of oppression, are all stressful. Stressful events can curtail normal brain development in newborns and youngsters, and negatively affect brain neurogenesis and plasticity in adults. Thus, these social justice issues are detrimental to the psychological, physical, and social well-being of individuals (Zalaquett & Ivey, 2014, 2018).

Neurocounselors must exercise cultural competence in their work with clients as they build upon an existing theoretical framework to incorporate neuro-informed elements, ensuring they are attending to cultural sensitivities, intersecting identities, and various physical needs (Douthit & Russotti, 2017). Advocacy for minorities who are most likely to be the victims of social injustice is thus critical for neurocounselors. In general, more research is needed to demonstrate the efficacy of neurocounseling, but in particular, research is needed to explore applications with diverse populations.

EFFICACY

As neurocounseling is still a relatively new approach, its efficacy with different populations is still being determined (Field et al., 2017). A number of populations, however, have been identified as possibly benefiting from a neuro-informed approach to counseling, including people affected by trauma, substance use disorders, attention deficit/hyperactivity disorder, anxiety, depression, and other concerns.

Trauma

Counselors working with people affected by trauma should consider using neuroscience-informed interventions appropriate to the altered neural response patterns typical of this population (Jones et al., 2017; Navalta et al., 2018). For example, intense or constant stress endured by a developing brain exposed to adverse childhood experiences often results in physical and mental illness (Griffith, 2018). One meta-analysis found decreased hippocampal volume in adults who had experienced childhood maltreatment-related PTSD, but not in children with maltreatment-related PTSD (Woon & Hedges, 2008), suggesting the hippocampal volume is affected over time, and early interventions may have the potential to address this change. In a random control treatment (RCT) pilot study, NFB produced significant reductions in PTSD symptoms, improved affect regulation, and had an effect size comparable to other evidence-based PTSD treatments (Gapen et al., 2016). In addition, a review of five studies examining the effect of NFB on PTSD suggested that NFB is probably efficacious for PTSD treatment (Reiter et al., 2016).

Substance Use Disorders

Understanding the full range of neural representations of substance use disorders (SUD) and appropriate neuro-informed interventions offer promising results (Hall & Walker, 2017). For instance, when transcendental meditation (TM) was compared with treatment-as-usual involving an in-patient population with alcohol use disorder, there were no significant differences between the treatment groups. Individuals who practiced TM twice-daily, however, experienced lower levels of relapse, and regular TM practice was correlated with reduced stress, reduced craving, and less frequent alcohol use at follow-up (Gryczynski et al., 2018).

Peniston & Kulkosky (1989) provided brain wave training (BWT) protocol that included alpha/theta brain wave training, skin temperature biofeedback relaxation, and alcohol refusal imagery to people with alcohol addiction and found that compared with controls, the BWT group had reductions in self-reported depression symptoms, physiological indicators of stress, and abstinence throughout 13 months of follow-up. This protocol was clinically evaluated with positive results in several studies (Sokhadze, 2016).

The Peniston BWT protocol was modified to treat psychostimulant disorders, known as the Scott-Kaiser modification (Sokhadze et al., 2014). In a study with 121 participants from a residential treatment program, the majority of whom were poly-drug users, NFB in addition to treatment-as-usual (TAU) was compared with TAU alone, and participants in the NFB + TAU group stayed in treatment significantly longer, had greater abstinence rates at one year, and demonstrated significantly greater improvements on impulsivity and attention variables than those in the control group (Scott et al., 2005). In a review of the research of NFB for the treatment of SUD, Sokhadze et al., (2008) determined that NFB combined with residential treatment for alcohol use disorder, stimulant use disorders, and mixed substance use disorders is probably efficacious. Given the additive success of NFB in the treatment of a variety of SUDs, Sokhadze et al. (2014) recommended future NFB treatment for SUD be formally integrated with established behavioral interventions, such as CBT, motivational enhancement therapy, and maintenance medication.

Attention Deficit/Hyperactivity Disorder

In a review of the efficacy literature on NFB and attention deficit/hyperactivity disorder (ADHD), Chapin & Russell-Chapin (2014) concluded that the strongest critics of NFB for ADHD treatment rated the intervention as "probably efficacious," while the strongest proponents found it "efficacious and specific" to ADHD. Van Doren et al. (2018) conducted a meta-analysis of 10 RTC studies among children with ADHD and found that within-group NFB effects on inattention were of medium effect size post-treatment, but large effect size at follow-up.

Anxiety and Depression

In efficacy literature reviews for anxiety and depression, Chapin & Russell-Chapin (2014) reported that NFB for anxiety can be considered "probably efficacious" to "efficacious," and that NFB for depression can be considered "possibly efficacious." In a study targeting amygdala functioning in people with major depressive disorder, Young et al. (2014) found that participants who had undergone NFB training, combined with positive autobiographical memory recall, were able to regulate amygdala function and experienced improved mood. Similarly, a small study of Korean college students with depressive symptoms found NFB, combined with meditation, resulted in significant improvements after treatment and at four-month follow-up in both psychosocial flourishing and affect (Hwang et al., 2017). In their systematic review,

Thabrew et al. (2018) identified nine studies, four of which were RTCs, that used different kinds of biofeedback including heart rate variability (HRV), biofeedback assisted relaxation therapy, and electroencephalography. This combination was effective in lessening anxiety and HRV excercises reduced depression in two studies. Finally, in a multiphase mixed-methods pilot study examining use and perceptions of neuro-informed CBT (n-CBT), Field et al. (2016) found the majority of counselors in the study believed n-CBT to be most effective in working with people with a range of anxiety and depressive disorders and reductions in both anxiety and depression symptoms were reported.

Other Concerns

Neuro-informed counseling has been proposed for group counseling (Luke & Diambra, 2017), career counseling (Luke & Field, 2017), and working with athletes (Chapin, 2017). Biofeedback has been found to be effective in managing stress among individuals who must perform under stress for occupational success (Kennedy & Parker, 2018). From a wellness perspective, the incorporation of biofeedback and neurofeedback techniques may eventually show efficacy of a wide range of counseling approaches.

As the preceding review indicates, neurocounseling is a theory in the making, and thus requires thoughtful development and rigorous evaluation. Continued research into the effectiveness of neuro-informed techniques is paramount.

SUMMARY

This chapter examined neurocounseling and began with its relatively brief history. It was noted that neurofeedback is a type of manipulation of physiology to increase mental health, such as progressive relaxation, started by Edmund Jacobson in the 1930s or biofeedback in the 1960s. Neurofeedback itself first became popular in the 1960s by Joe Kamiya, who examined the kinds of training needed for a person to change brain wave activity.

Over the years, with advances in PET and MRI scans and the use of the EEG, there was an increased focus on measuring changes in the brain. Then, in 1998, Eric Kandel noted that counseling could change gene expression and alter neural networks. In the counseling profession, some of the early pioneers of neurocounseling included Lori Russell-Chapin, Allen Ivey, Mary Bradford Ivey, Carlos Zalaquett, and Chad Luke. Soon called one of the newest forces in counseling, this approach has taken on increased popularity in recent years as an an approach that can be integrated into one's existing theoretical framework and as a stand-alone method.

The view of human nature for neurocounseling includes a wellness and strength-based approach that integrates neuroeducation. It is based on the fact that positive changes in one's environment and health can impact the structural biology of the brain through a process that stimulates neuroplasticity. Although many factors can positively change neural networks, some that were highlighted included physical exercise, sleep hygiene, gut-microbiomes, and lifestyle habits. It was also noted that significant brain changes occur over time. Thus, neurocounseling has a developmental focus because it is important for counselors to know potential changes in neural networks as people age.

A number of key concepts were discussed. For instance, we touched on the concept of neuroplasticity, which is the ability of the brain to alter its structure and function; neurogenesis, which is the ability of the brain to regrow damaged or lost neurons; and attention, arousal, and focus, which is related to how the brain changes as a function of one's ability to focus one's attention, such as when one is in counseling. We also delineated the parts of the limbic system, which is often called the seat of emotions and lies beneath the cerebral cortex. We highlighted the notion that there are major changes in brain functioning over one's lifespan; that mirror neurons are the mechanisms for a person to mimic the behaviors of others; that empathy can be observed by a client from a counselor and be learned, neurologically, by mirror neurons; and that microskills have been found to change neural networks. Finally, this part of the chapter reviewed the function of different brainwaves (delta, theta, alpha, beta, and gamma waves); how focusing on wellness and being positive can increase neuroplasticity; and that different types of therapy (e.g., DBT), and specific types of biofeedback and neurofeedback, can lead to self-regulation, which is important in relaxation, emotional stability, and an increase in neuroplasticity.

There are many neurocounseling techniques we explored in this chapter. For instance, we examined neuroeducation, which is teaching clients through didactic or experiential-based interventions the neurological basis for change (e.g., learning the hand model of the brain); the importance of assessing lifestyle by using self-assessments such as the Therapeutic Lifestyle Changes Inventory, the indivisible self model, and the healthy mind platter; learning about self-regulation skills through biofeedback, especially how it relates to the sympathetic and parasympathetic systems (e.g., using diaphragmatic breathing, mindfulness, and technological approaches to biofeedback such as heart rate variability (HRV) and lowering respiration rates); neurofeedback, which involves attaching electrodes to the scalp and measuring and training clients how to alter brainwaves; and using neuroscience-informed therapies such as prolonged exposure therapy (PE) and eye desensitization movement reprocessing (EMDR).

A neuroscience-informed approach to counseling, it was noted, often starts with a general clinical assessment. This might include a traditional intake interview; use of assessments such as the Therapeutic Lifestyle Changes Inventory, the indivisible self model, or the healthy mind platter; assessing brainwaves through an EEG; and applying appropriate developmental knowledge to the treatment plan. Neurocounseling can stand on its own if the counselor is trained in structural biology or, if the counselor obtains training through workshops and courses, it can be integrated into the counselor's existing approach.

Since the major focus of neurocounseling is identifying areas of stress within a person, it was noted that social justice issues, such as poverty, abuse, bullying, racism, sexism, heterosexism, discrimination, and other forms of oppression, can all negatively impact neural networks. Advocacy for minorities who are most likely to be the victims of social injustice is thus critical for neurocounselors.

Relative to the efficacy of neurocounseling, we noted it has shown some benefit for the following populations: people affected by trauma, substance use disorders, attention deficit/hyperactivity disorder, anxiety, and depression. We also noted it has been proposed for other types of counseling such as group work, career counseling, and working with athletes. We concluded that neurocounseling is a theory in the making, and thus requires thoughtful development and rigorous evaluation. Continued research into the effectiveness of neuro-informed techniques is paramount.

KEY WORDS AND NAMES

Adaptive information processing (AIP)
Alpha waves
Amygdala
Assessing lifestyle
Arousal
Attention
Biofeedback
Biofeedback and self-regulation skills
Brain dysregulation
Brain-derived neurotrophic factors (BDNF)
Brainwaves
Cerebral cortex
Cerebrum
Chapin, Lori-Russell
Developmental focus
Diaphragmatic breathing
EEG biofeedback
Electroencephalogram (EEG)
Emotional center of the brain
Empathy and mirror neurons
Executive functioning
Eye movement desensitization and reprocess (EMDR)
Fight or flight
Fight-fight response
Flip one's lid
Focus
Focusing on wellness and the positives
Functional magnetic resonance imaging (fMRI)
Glial cells
Glymphatic pathway
Gut-microbiome-brain connection
Hand model of the brain
Hippocampus
Hypothalamus
Indivisible self model
Ivey, Allen
Ivey, Mary Bradford
Jacobson, Edmund
Kamiya, Joe
Kandel, Eric
Lifestyle habits
Luke, Chad
Microskills
Microskills relationship to neural networks
Mindfulness
Mirror neurons which
Neurocounseling
Neurocounselor
Neuroeducation
Neurofeedback
Neurofeedback training
Neurogenesis
Neuroplasticity
Neuroscience-informed therapies
Neuroscience-informed interventions
Newest force in counseling
Parasympathetic nervous system
Phase 1: Client History and Treatment Planning
Phase 2: Preparation
Phase 3: Assessment
Phase 4: Desensitization
Phase 5: Installation
Phase 6: Body Scan
Phase 7: Closure
Phase 8: Reevaluation
Physical exercise

Positron emission tomography (PET)
Prefrontal lobotomies
Prefontal cortex
Prolonged exposure therapy (PE)
Psychological stability
Quantitative electroencephalogram (qEEG)
Seat of human emotions
Self-regulation.
Self-regulation skills
Sleep hygiene
Strength-based approach
Structural biology
Subjective units of disturbance (SUD) scale
Sympathetic nervous system
Technological approaches to biofeedback
The healthy mind platter
The limbic system and emotions
Therapeutic Lifestyle Changes Inventory
Validity of Cognition scale (VoC)
Wellness
Wellness positivity and neuroplasticity
Zalaquett, Carlos

REFERENCES

Alvarez-Buylla, A., & Lim, D. A. (2004). For the long run: Maintaining germinal niches in the adult brain, *Neuron, 42,* 683–686. http://dx.doi.org/10.1016/S0896-6273(04)00111-4

Arain, M., Haque, M., Johal, L., Mathur, P., Nel, W., Rais, A., ... Sharma, S. (2013). Maturation of the adolescent brain. *Neuropsychiatric Disease and Treatment, 9,* 449–460. doi:10.2147/NDT.S39776

Association for Applied Psychophysiology and Biofeedback (2011). *Biofeedback, mind-body medicine, and the higher limits of human nature.* https://www.aapb.org/i4a/pages/index.cfm?pageID=3383

Benson, H., & Proctor, W. (2010). *Relaxation revolution.* Scribner.

Bergstrom I., Seinfeld S., Arroyo-Palacios J., Slater M., & Sanchez-Vives M. V. (2014). Using music as a signal for biofeedback. *International Journal of Psychophysiology, 93,* 140–149. https://doi.org/10.1016/j.ijpsycho.2013.04.01

Benveniste, H., Lee, H., & Volkow, N. D. (2017). The glymphatic pathway: Waste removal from the CNS via cerebrospinal fluid transport. *The Neuroscientist, 23*(5), 454–465. http://doi.org/10.1177/1073858417691030

Bliss, T. V. P., & Cooke, S. F. (2011). Long-term potentiation and long-term depression: A clinical perspective. *Clinics,* 66(S1), 3–17. http://doi.org/10.1590/S1807-59322011001300002

Cacioppo, J., & Decety, J. (2009). What are the brain mechanisms on which psychological processes are based? *Perspectives on Psychological Science, 4,* 10–18.

Carter, R. (1999). *Mapping the mind.* Universtity of California Press.

Chapin, T. J. (2017). Wellness and optimal performance. In T. A. Field, L. K. Jones, & L. A. Russell-Chapin (Eds.), *Neurocounseling: Brain-based clinical approaches* (pp. 133–146). American Counseling Association. http://doi.org/10.1002/9781119375487.ch8

Chapin, T. J., & Russell-Chapin, L. A. (2014). *Neurotherapy and neurofeedback: Brain-based treatment for psychological and behavioral problems.* Routledge.

Chatters, S., Zalaquett, C. P., & Ivey, A. E. (2017). Neuroscience-informed counseling theory. In T. A. Field, L. K. Jones, & L. A. Russell-Chapin (Eds.), *Neurocounseling: Brain-based clinical approaches* (pp. 101–114). American Counseling Association. http://doi.org/10.1002/9781119375487.ch6

Clearfield, M. W., & Niman, L. C. (2012). SES affects infant cognitive flexibility. *Infant Behavior & Development, 35*, 29–35. https://doi.org/10.1016/j.infbeh.2011.09.007

Codrington, R. (2010). A family therapist's look into interpersonal neurobiology and the adolescent brain: An interview with Dr. Daniel Siegel. *Australian and New Zealand Journal of Family Therapy*, 31, 285–299. https://doi.org/10.1375/anft.31.3.28

Collingridge, G. L., Peineau, S., Howland, J. G., & Wang, Y. T. (2010). Long-term depression in the CNS. *Nature Reviews Neuroscience, 11*(459–473). http://doi.org/10.1038/nrn2867

Collura, T. F. (2013). *Technical foundations of neurofeedback*. Routledge.

Crockett, J. E., Gill, D. L., Cashwell, T. H., & Myers, J. E. (2017). Integrating non-technological and technological peripheral biofeedback in counseling. *Journal of Mental Health Counseling, 39*(2), 163–179. http://doi.org/10.17744/mehc.39.2.06

Davidson, R. J., & McEwen, B. S. (2012). Social influences on neuroplasticity: Stress and interventions to promote well-being. *Nature Neuroscience, 15*(5), 689–695. http://doi.org/10.1038/nn.3093

Decety, J., & Jackson, P. L. (2004). The functional architecture of human empathy. *Behavioral and Cognitive Neuroscience Reviews 3*, 71–100. https://doi.org/10.1177/1534582304267187

Decety, J., & Jackson, P. L. (2006). A social-neuroscience perspective on empathy. *Current Directions in Psychological Science, 15*, 54– 58. https://doi.org/10.1111/j.09637214.2006.00406.x

Douthit, K. Z., & Russotti, J. (2017). Biology of marginality: A neurophysiological exploration of the social and cultural foundations of psychological health. In T. A. Field, L. K. Jones, & L. A. Russell-Chapin (Eds.), *Neurocounseling: Brain-based clinical approaches* (pp. 45–60). American Counseling Association. http://doi.org/10.1002/9781119375487.ch3

Dworkin, M. (2005). *EMDR and the relational imperative: The therapeutic relationship in EMDR treatment*. Routledge.

Ehlers, C. L., & Kupfer, D. J. (1997). Slow way sleep: Do young adult men and women age differently? *Journal of Sleep Research*, 6(3): 211–15. https://doi.org/10.1046/j.1365-2869.1997.00041.x

EMDR Institute. (2019a). *Frequent questions?* http://www.emdr.com/frequent-questions/

EMDR Institute. (2019b). *What is EMDR?* http://www.emdr.com/what-is-emdr/

EMDR Institute. (2019c). *The efficacy of EMDR*. http://www.emdr.com/efficacy/

Field, T. A. (2014). Integrating left-brain and right-brain: The neuroscience of effective counseling. *The Professional Counselor*, 4(1), 19–27. http://doi.org/10.15241/taf.4.1.19

Field, T. A., Beeson, E. T., & Jones, L. K. (2016). Neuroscience-informed cognitive-behavior therapy in clinical practice: A preliminary study. *Journal of Mental Health Counseling, 38*(2), 139–154. http://doi.org/10.17744/mehc.38.2.05

Field, T. A., Jones, L. K., & Russell-Chapin, L. A. (Eds.). (2017). *Neurocounseling: Brain-based clinical approaches*. American Counseling Association. http://doi.org/10.1002/9781119375487

Ford, J. D., & Blaustein, M. E. (2013). Systemic self-regulation: A framework for trauma-informed services in residential juvenile justice programs. *Journal of Family Violence, 28*, 665–677. http://doi.10.1007/s10896-013-9538-5

Gapen, M., van der Kolk, B. A., Hamlin, E., Hirshberg, L., Suvak, M., & Spinazzola, J. (2016). A pilot study of neurofeedback for chronic PTSD. *Applied Psychophysiology and Biofeedback, 41*(3), 251–261. http://doi.org/10.1007/s10484-015-9326-5

Grawe, K. (2007). *Neuropsychotherapy: How the neurosciences inform effective psychotherapy*. Psychology Press.

Griffith, S. (2018). *The relationship between childhood adversity and adult relationship health for economically marginalized, racially and ethnically diverse individuals* (Doctoral dissertation, Old Dominion University, Norfolk, VA.).

Gryczynski, J., Schwartz, R. P., Fishman, M. J., Nordeck, C. D., Grant, J., Nidich, S., ... O'Grady, K. E. (2018). Integration of Transcendental Meditation into alcohol use disorder (AUD) treatment. *Journal of Substance Abuse Treatment, 87*, 23–30. http://doi.org/10.1016/j.jsat.2018.01.009

Hall, S. B., & Walker, K. D. (2017). Clinical nseuroscience of substance use disorders. In T. A. Field, L. K. Jones, & L. A. Russell-Chapin (Eds.), *Neurocounseling: Brain-Based Clinical Approaches* (pp. 147–164). American Counseling Association. http://doi.org/10.1002/9781119375487.ch9

Hansen, J., Speciale, M., & Lemberger, M. E. (2014). Humanism: The foundation and future of professional counseling. *The Journal of Humanistic Counseling, 53*, 170–190. https://doi.org/10.1002/j.2161-1939.2014.00055.

Hirano, Y., Oribe, N., Kanba, S., Onitsuka, T., Nestor, P. G., & Spencer, K. M. (2015). Spontaneous gamma activitiy in schizophrenia. *JAMA Psychiatry, 72*(8), 813–821. doi: http://dx.doi. org/10.1001/jamapsychiatry.2014.2642

Hwang, K., Kwon, A., & Hong, C. (2017). A preliminary study of new positive psychology interventions: Neurofeedback-aided meditation therapy and modified positive psychotherapy. *Current Psychology, 36*(3), 683–695. http://doi.org/10.1007/s12144-016-9538-8

Insel, T (2013, April 29). *Transforming diagnosis*. National Institute of Mental Health. http://www.nimh.nih.gov/about/director/2013/transforming-diagnosis.shtml

Ivey, A. E., Daniels, T., Zalaquett, C. P., & Ivey, M. B. (2017). Neuroscience of attention: Empathy and counseling skills. In T. A. Field, L. K. Jones, & L. A. Russell-Chapin (Eds.), *Neurocounseling: Brain-based clinical approaches* (pp. 81–100). American Counseling Association. http://doi.org/10.1002/9781119375487.ch5

Ivey, A. E., & Zalaquett, C. (2011). Neuroscience and counseling: Central Issue for social justice leaders. *Journal for Social Action in Counseling and Psychology, 3*(1)–11, 103–116. https://openjournals.bsu.edu/jsacp/article/view/341

Ivey, A. E., Ivey, M. B., & Zalaquett, C. P. (2014). *Therapeutic Lifestyle Changes Inventory*. © Ivey, A. E., Ivey, M. B., & Zalaquett, C. P.

Ivey, A. E., Ivey, M. B., & Zalaquett, C. P. (2018). *Intentional interviewing and counseling: Facilitating client development in a multicultural society* (9th ed.). Cengage Learning.

Jacobson, E. (1938). *Progressive relaxation.* University of Chicago Press.

Jones, L. K. (2017a). Anatomy and brain development. In T. A. Field, L. K. Jones, & L. A. Russell-Chapin (Eds.), *Neurocounseling: Brain-based clinical approaches* (pp. 1–26). American Counseling Association. http://doi.org/10.1002/9781119375487.ch1

Jones, L. K. (2017b). Neurophysiological development across the life span. In T. A. Field, L. K. Jones, & L. A. Russell-Chapin (Eds.), *Neurocounseling: Brain-based clinical approaches* (pp. 27–44). American Counseling Association. http://doi.org/10.1002/9781119375487.ch2

Jones, L. K., Rybak, C., & Russell-Chapin, L. A. (2017). Neurophysiology of traumatic stress. In T. A. Field, L. K. Jones, & L. A. Russell-Chapin (Eds.), *Neurocounseling: Brain-based clinical approaches* (pp. 61–80). American Counseling Association. http://doi.org/10.1002/9781119375487.ch4

Kamiya, J. (1969). Operant control of the EEG alpha rhythm and some of its reported effects on consciousness. In C. Tart (Ed.), *Altered states of consciousness* (pp. 489–501). Wiley.

Kandel, E. R. (1998). A new intellectual framework for psychiatry. *The American Journal of Psychiatry,* (April), 457–469. https://doi.org/10.1176/ajp.155.4.457

Kahneman, D. (2011). *Thinking, fast and slow.* Farrar, Straus, and Giroux.

Kawamichi, H., Yoshihara, K., Sasaki, A. T., Sugawara, S. K., Tanabe, H. C., Shinohara, R., … Sadato, N. (2015). Perceiving active listening activates the reward system and improves the impression of relevant experiences. *Social Neuroscience, 10,* 16–26. https://doi.org/10.1080/17470919.2014.954732

Kennedy, L., & Parker, S. H. (2018). Biofeedback as a stress management tool: A systematic review. *Cognition, Technology & Work.* http://doi.org/10.1007/s10111-018-0487-x

Koemer, D. (2012). *Doing dialectical behavior therapy: A practical guide.* Guilford Press.

Konkel L. (2018). The brain before birth: Using fMRI to explore the secrets of fetal neurodevelopment. *Environmental Health Perspectives, 126*(11), 112001. https://doi.org/10.1289/EHP2268

Kozak, M. J., & Cuthbert, B. N. (2016). The NIMH research domain criteria initative: Background, issues, and pragmatics. *Psychophysiology, 53,* 286–297. https://doi.org/10.1111/psyp.12518

Lillard, A. S., & Erisir, A. (2011). Old dogs learning new tricks : Neuroplasticity beyond the juvenile period. *Developmental Review, 31*(4), 207–239. http://doi.org/10.1016/j.dr.2011.07.008

Likhtik E, Popa D, Apergis-Schoute J, Fidacaro, G.A., & Paré, D. (2008). Amygdala intercalated neurons are required for expression of fear extinction. *Nature, 31,* 642–645. https://doi.org/10.1038/nature0716

Lodge, J. M., & Harrison, W. J. (2019). The role of attention in learning in the digital age. *The Yale Journal of Biology and Medicine,* 92, 21–28. https://doi.org/10.1038/nature07167

Lorelle, S., & Michel, R. (2017). Neurocounseling: Promoting human growth and development throughout the life span. *Adultspan Journal, 16*(2), 106–119. http://doi.org/10.1002/adsp.12039

Luders, E. (2014). Exploring age-related brain degeneration in meditation practitioners. *Annals of the New York Academy of Sciences, 13071*(1), 82–88. https://doi.org/10.1111/nyas.12217

Luke, C. (2016). *Neuroscience for counselors and therapists: Integrating the sciences of mind and brain.* SAGE Publications.

Luke, C., & Diambra, J. F. (2017). Neuro-informed group work. In T. A. Field, L. K. Jones, & L. A. Russell-Chapin (Eds.), *Neurocounseling: Brain-based clinical approaches* (pp. 179–194). American Counseling Association. http://doi.org/10.1002/9781119375487.ch11

Luke, C., & Field, T. A. (2017). Neuro-informed career-focused counseling. In T. A. Field, L. K. Jones, & L. A. Russell-Chapin (Eds.), *Neurocounseling: Brain-based clinical approaches* (pp. 195–210). American Counseling Association. http://doi.org/10.1002/9781119375487.ch12

Luke, C., Miller, R., & McAuliffe, G. (2019) Neuro-informed mental health counseling: A person-first perspective. *Journal of Mental Health Counseling, 41*, 65–79. https://doi.org/10.17744/mehc.41.1.06

Mackinson, R. A., & Young, J. S. (2012). Cognitive behavioraltherapy and the treatment of posttraumatic stress disorder: Where counseling and neuroscience meet. *Journal of Counseling & Development, 90*, 131–140. http://dx.doi.org/10.1111/j.1556-6676.2012.00017.x

Mayo Clinic (2018a). *EEG (electroencephalogram).* https://www.mayoclinic.org/tests-procedures/eeg/about/pac-20393875

Mayo Clinic. (2018). *Healthy lifestyle consumer health: Mindfulness exercises.* https://www.mayoclinic.org/healthy-lifestyle/consumer-health/in-depth/mindfulness-exercises/art-20046356

McNally, R. J. (2007). Mechanisms of exposure therapy: How neuroscience can improve psychological treatments for anxiety disorders. *Clinical Psychology Review, 27*, 750–759. https://doi.org/10.1016/j.cpr.2007.01.003

Miller, R. (2016). Neuroeducation: Integrating brain-based psychoeducation into clinical practice. *Journal of Mental Health Counseling, 38*, 103–115. http://doi.org/10. 17744/mehc.38.2.02

Miller, N. S., & Katz, J. L. (1989). The neurological legacy of psychoanalysis. *Comprehensive Psychiatry, 30*(2), 123–134. https://doi.org/10.1016/0010-440X(89)90064-3

Montes, S. (2013, November). The birth of the neuro-counselor? *Counseling Today, 56*(6), 32–40.

Myers, J. E., & Sweeney, T. J. (2004). The indivisible self: An evidence-based model of wellness. *Journal of Individual Psychology, 60*(3), 234–245. http://doi.org/http://dx.doi.org/10.1007/s10658-014-0538-y

Myers, J., & Young, J. (2012). Brain wave biofeedback: Benefits of integrating neurofeedback in counseling. *Journal of Counseling and Development, 90*(1), 20–29. http://doi.org/10.1111/j.1556-6676.2012.00003.x

National Public Radio. (2005). *My lobotomy: Howard Dully's journey.* https://www.npr.org/2005/11/16/5014080/my-lobotomy-howard-dullys-journey

National Research Council and Institute of Medicine. Committee on Integrating the Science of Early Childhood Development (2000). In J. P. Shonkoff & D. A. Phillips (Eds), *From neurons to neighborhoods: The science of early childhood development* (pp. 182–219). National Academies Press.

Navalta, C. P., McGee, L., & Underwood, J. (2018). Adverse childhood experiences, brain development, and mental health: A call for neurocounseling. *Journal of Mental Health Counseling, 40*(3), 266–278. http://doi.org/10.17744/mehc.40.3.07

Northoff, G. (2012, April 2) Psychoanalysis and the brain—why did Freud abandon neuroscience? *Frontiers in Psychology, 3*. https://doi.org/10.3389/fpsyg.2012.00071

Peniston, E. G., & Kulkosky, P. J. (1989). Alpha-theta brainwave training and beta-endorphin levels in alcoholics. *Alcoholism: Clinical and Experimental Research, 13*(2), 271–279. http://doi.org/10.1111/j.1530-0277.1989.tb00325.x

Ratey, J. (2008). *Neuroscience and the brain: Implications for counseling and therapy* [DVD]. https://www-academicvideostore-com.proxy.lib.odu.edu/microtraining

Reiter, K., Andersen, S. B., & Carlsson, J. (2016). Neurofeedback treatment and posttraumatic stress disorder. *The Journal of Nervous and Mental Disease, 204*(2), 69–77. http://doi.org/10.1097/NMD.0000000000000418

Rock, D., Siegal, D. J., Poelmans, S. A. Y., & Payne, J. (2012). The healthy mind platter. *NeuroLeadership Journal*, (4), 1–23.

Rojas, D. C., & Wilson, L. B. (2014). γ-band abnormalities as markers of autism spectrum disorders. *Biomarkers in medicine*, 8(3), 353–368. https://doi.org/10.2217/bmm.14.15

Russell-Chapin, L. A. (2016). Integrating neurocounseling into the counseling profession: An introduction. *Journal of Mental Health Counseling, 38*(2), 93–102. http://doi.org/10.17744/mehc.38.2.01

Russell-Chapin, L. A. (2017a). Neurocounseling assessment. In T. A. Field, L. K. Jones, & L. A. Russell-Chapin (Eds.), *Neurocounseling: Brain-based clinical approaches* (pp. 115–132). American Counseling Association. http://doi.org/10.1002/9781119375487.ch7

Russell-Chapin, L. A. (2017b). The power of neurocounseling and self-regulation skills. In J. K. Edwards, A. Young, & H. J. Nikels (Eds.), *Handbook of strengths-based clinical practices: Finding common factors* (pp. 151–163). Routledge.

Schwartz, J., & Begley, S. (2002). *The mind and the brain: Neuroplasticity and the power of mental force*. Harper Collins.

Scott, W. C., Kaiser, D., Othmer, S., & Sideroff, S. I. (2005). Effects of an EEG biofeedback protocol on a mixed substance abusing population. *The American Journal of Drug and Alcohol Abuse, 31*(3), 455–469. http://doi.org/10.1081/ADA-200056807

Shapiro, F. (2002a). (Ed.). *EMDR as an integrative psychotherapy approach: Experts of diverse orientations explore the paradigm prism*. American Psychological Association.

Shapiro, F. (2002b). EMDR treatment: Overview and integration. In F. Shapiro (Ed.), *EMDR as an integrative psychotherapy approach: Experts of diverse orientations explore the paradigm prism* (pp. 27–56). American Psychological Association.

Shapiro, R. (2005). (Ed.). *EMDR solutions: Pathways to healing*. W. W. Norton.

Shapiro, R. (2009). (Ed.). *EMDR solutions II: For depression, eating disorders, performance, and more.* W. W. Norton.

Shapiro, F., & Forrest, M. S. (1997). *EMDR: The breakthrough "eye movement" therapy for overcoming anxiety, stress, and trauma.* Perseus Books.

Shonkof, J. P., & Phillips, D. A. (2000). (Eds.). *From neurons to neighborhoods: The science of early childhood development.* National Academies.

Siegel, D. J. (2006). An interpersonal neurobiology approach to psychotherapy. *Psychiatric Annals, 34*(6), 248–256.

Siegel, D. J. (2013). *Brainstorm: The power and purpose of the teenage brain.* Penguin.

Siegel, D. (2019). *The healthy mind platter.* https://www.drdansiegel.com/resources/healthy_mind_platter/

Siegel, D. J. (2017). Interpersonal connection, compassion, and well-being: The science and art of healing relationship. In J. Loizzo, M. Neale, & E. J. Wolf (Eds.), *Advances in contemplative psychotherapy: Accelerating healing and transformation* (pp. 118–130). Routledge.

Singh-Manoux, A., Kivimaki, M., Glymour, M., Elbaz, A., Berr, C., Ebmeier, K., … Dugravot, A. (2012). Timing of onset of cognitive decline: Results from Whitehall II prospective cohort study. *BMJ, 344*(7840), D7622. doi: https://doi.org/10.1136/bmj.d7622

Sokhadze, E. T. (2016). Lessons learned from Peniston's brainwave training protocol. In A. Martins-Mourao & C. Kerson (Eds.), *Alpha theta training in the 21st century: A handbook for clinicians and practitioners* (pp. 105–132). Foundation for Neurofeedback and Neuromodulation Research.

Sokhadze, E. M., Cannon, R. L., & Trudeau, D. L. (2008). EEG biofeedback as a treatment for substance use disorders: Review, rating of efficacy, and recommendations for further research. *Applied Psychophysiology and Biofeedback, 33,* 1–28. http://doi.org/10.1007/s10484-007-9047-5

Sokhadze, E. M., Trudeau, D. L., & Cannon, R. L. (2014). Treating addiction disorders. In D. S. Cantor & J. R. Evans (Eds.), *Clinical Neurotherapy: Application of techniques for treatment* (pp. 265–299). http://doi.org/10.1016/B978-0-12-396988-0.00011-8

Stojek, M. M., McSweeney, L. B., & Rauch, S. (2018). Neuroscience informed prolonged exposure practice: Increasing efficiency and efficacy through mechanisms. *Frontiers in Behavioral Neuroscience, 12,* 281. https://doi.org/10.3389/fnbeh.2018.00281

Sullivan, M. B., Erb, M., Schmalzl, L., Moonaz, S., Noggle Taylor, J., & Porges, S. W. (2018). Yoga therapy and polyvagal theory: The convergence of traditional wisdom and contemporary neuroscience for self-regulation and resilience. *Frontiers in Human Neuroscience, 12,* 67. https://doi.org/10.3389/fnhum.2018.00067

Tardif, C. L., Gauthier, C. J., Steele, C. J., Bazin, P.-L., Schäfer, A., Schaefer, A., … Villringer, A. (2016). Advanced MRI techniques to improve our understanding of experience-induced neuroplasticity. *NeuroImage, 131,* 55–72. http://doi.org/10.1016/j.neuroimage.2015.08.047

Tart, C. T. (1969). *Altered states of consciousness: A book of readings.* Wiley.

Tartakovsky, M. (2019, Nov. 10). *The surprising history of the lobotomy.* https://psychcentral.com/blog/the-surprising-history-of-the-lobotomy/

Thabrew, H., Ruppeldt, P., & Sollers, J. J. (2018). Systematic review of biofeedback interventions for addressing anxiety and depression in children and adolescents with long-term physical conditions. *Applied Psychophysiology and Biofeedback, 43*(3), 179–192. http://doi.org/10.1007/s10484-018-9399-z

Thibault, R. T., Lifshitz, M., Birbaumer, N., & Raz, A. (2015). Neurofeedback, self-regulation, and brain imaging: Clinical Science and fad in the service of mental disorders. *Psychotherapy and Psychosomatics, 84*, 193–207. http://doi:10.1159/000371714

Van Doren, J., Arns, M., Heinrich, H., Vollebregt, M. A., Strehl, U., & K. Loo, S. (2018). Sustained effects of neurofeedback in ADHD: A systematic review and meta-analysis. *European Child & Adolescent Psychiatry, 28*(3), 293–305. http://doi.org/10.1007/s00787-018-1121-4

Wilkinson, B. D. (2018). The limits of neuroscience in counseling: A humanistic perspective and proposed model. *The Journal of Humanistic Counseling, 57*, 70–78. http://doi.org/10.1002/johc.12067

Woon, F. L., & Hedges, D. W. (2008). Hippocampal and amygdala volumes in children and adults with childhood maltreatment-related posttraumatic stress disorder: A meta-analysis. *Hippocampus, 18*, 729–736. http://doi.org/10.1002/hipo.20437

Xi, Zhu, Niu, Zhu, Lee, Tian, & Wang. (2011). Contributions of subregions of the prefrontal cortex to the theory of mind and decision making. *Behavioural Brain Research, 22*, 587–593. 10.1016/j.bbr.2010.09.031

Young, K. D., Zotev, V., Phillips, R., Misaki, M., Yuan, H., Drevets, W. C., & Bodurka, J. (2014). Real-time fMRI neurofeedback training of amygdala activity in patients with major depressive disorder. *PLoS ONE, 9*(2), 1–13. http://doi.org/10.1371/journal.pone.0088785

Zalaquett, C. P., & Ivey, A. E. (2014). Neuroscience and psychology: Central issues for social justice leaders. In H. Friedman & C. Johnson, *The Praeger handbook of social justice and psychology* (Vol. II, pp 173–192). Praeger.

Zalaquett, C. P., & Ivey, A. (2018). The role of neuroscience in advancing social justice counseling. In C. Lee (Ed.), *Counseling for Social Justice* (pp. 191–204). American Counseling Association.

Zalaquett, C., P., Ivey, A., & Ivey, M. B. (2018). *Essential theories of counseling and psychotherapy: Everyday practice in our diverse world.* Cognella Academic Press.

CASE STUDY: JAKE'S EXPERIENCE IN NEUROCOUNSELING

(Please read about the Millers in Appendix I prior to reading this case study)

Ever since Jake's children accidentally pushed his car out of park and it moved down the driveway, Jake has been filled with anxiety and trying to control everything his family does, sometimes through angry outbursts. He also has difficulty sleeping and has nightmares about the accident he had with his sister, Justine, years ago. In addition, every day upon returning home from work and parking his car in the driveway, he has a panic attack. Jake has been struggling with anxiety his entire life, and despite having seen many therapists, it has not gotten any better. This time Jake decides to see a cognitive behavioral therapist who integrates neuroscience into his work with clients.

Jake enters the office of Dr. Jim Oliver. The office looks very modern and is sparkling clean. Jake takes a seat in the waiting room, and before long, a tall man in a suit comes out. He extends his hand to Jake, and says, "I'm Dr. Oliver, glad to meet you. Why don't you come into my office." His office is as clean and sparkling as the waiting room, and there are some unusual machines placed around the room. Dr. Oliver explains how he integrates neuroscience into his cognitive behavioral therapy approach to counseling and describes the basic tenets of each approach. He goes on to note that he takes a wellness perspective with people and likes to obtain a good history from them so he can assess those areas where they are stressed, as stress lessens the ability for neuroplasticity and change.

Dr. Oliver's first session is longer than the usual intake and lasts up to three hours. He first conducts a traditional intake with Jake, getting a thorough history, family background, and mental status. He then asks Jake to take the Therapeutic Lifestyle Change Inventory to assess those areas in his life where he is stressed and not attending to his own wellness. Next, he takes Jake on a visual journey while he's hooked to an electroencephalogram (EEG). Here, he attaches small electrodes (flat metal discs) to his scalp. The electrodes, which are attached to the EEG, measure brain wave signals. At first, he simply gets a baseline, and finds that Jake is in the high alpha, low beta wave region. He then asks Jake to close his eyes and begin to visualize himself driving home and up his driveway. Quickly, Dr. Oliver sees that Jake's brainwaves switch into the high beta wave area, indicating anxiety and a fight and flight response. It is quickly clear that Jake's response to his visualization is reflective of his anxiety and is probably related to PTSD or a phobia.

Jake's anxiety, angry outbursts, nightmares, combined with insomnia and intrusive thoughts and images, are most likely the result of his direct involvement with an acute traumatic event (the accident with Justine). These symptoms appear to be the result of the client's negative core beliefs of helplessness regarding his inability to save his sister from injury during the accident. This negative core belief is serving as a foundation for his intermediate beliefs and resulting in cognitive distortions, which are manifesting themselves as the symptoms he is experiencing. The client's cognitive distortions include catastrophizing, *should* statements (Angela and the children "should" act in a certain way to avoid a problem), and overgeneralization about the possibility of something else horrible happening as a result of the car incident. Based on the constellation of symptoms, the time the client has been experiencing these symptoms, the fact that they began immediately following direct exposure to the original traumatic event, and the lack of any other evidence supporting an alternate diagnosis, this client's preliminary diagnosis of post-traumatic stress disorder and possible generalized anxiety disorder are possible.

During Jake's second session, Dr. Oliver says, "Well, based on my assessment of what you're going through, there are a number of areas I think we can work on. We can hopefully get you a bit of relief from all of the anxiety you have been struggling with." "Boy, I hope so," answers Jake. "Honestly, my life has been hell lately." "Let me tell you what I'm thinking," Dr. Oliver says. "Based on your history, it seems like you have some residual PTSD from the original accident with Justine, or at least a bit of a phobic reaction to certain situations, like when you come home from work and drive up your driveway. I also can tell that based on the responses to the Therapeutic Lifestyle Change Inventory, there are several areas that you are not attending to that are probably increasing stress in your life. And, as we talked about during our last session, stress is the worst thing for making new neural connections and changing behaviors and feelings. So, here's my proposal."

Dr. Oliver goes on to say that he would like to do the following:

1. Using CBT, focus on Jake's automatic thoughts and images and cognitive distortions, and eventually, his core beliefs.
2. Based on the Therapeutic Lifestyle Change Inventory, focus on three of his lowest scores: lack of positive thinking, lack of joy, and being too stressed (rarely feeling relaxed).
3. Teach neuroeducation and self-regulation techniques to help Jake learn to self-regulate his sympathetic and brain's stress reactions.
4. Conduct Prolonged Exposure (PE) for his phobic reaction to driving up his driveway.
5. Use the EEG to assess changes in his phobic reaction and his overall state of being.

Dr. Oliver starts with CBT, and Jake quickly catches on. "It's amazing all of these 'automatic thoughts' I have that I never caught before," says Jake. "And, I see how they're related to those cognitive distortions. I particularly catastrophize." Over time, Dr. Oliver hopes Jake will move toward understanding his intermediate beliefs and his core belief of helplessness, but for now, he seems to be making good progress and has been able to catch some of his negative automatic thoughts and images, and even replace them with positive thoughts.

After consulting with Jake, based on the Therapeutic Lifestyle Change Inventory, Dr. Oliver and Jake jointly decide that Jake will take his kids out and do more playful things, such as going to the local putt-putt mini golf, movies, and bowling. He also has begun an exercise regime to help reduce some of his stress.

Using newly learned neuroscience-based information and skills to self-regulate his physiological reaction, Jake and Dr. Oliver are ready to start PE. Here, Dr. Oliver has Jake make a hierarchical list of how anxious he feels at different points from his driveway. He is most anxious at the very top of his driveway and least anxious a block away. He then designs a system in which Jake will start with the lowest part of the anxiety (a block away) and sit there, in his car, for 30 minutes, twice a day. When he no longer feels anxiety (this might take a few days), he will go up to the next item on his hierarchy (e.g., a half block away). He will continue moving up the hierarchy until he is at the top of the driveway. This will very likely take several days, or perhaps even a few weeks. It is hoped that over time Jake's conditioned response to anxiety will be extinguished.

To assess changes over time, Dr. Oliver also has Jake hooked to the EEG every two or three weeks. There, he has him visualize the driveway and monitors his brainwaves. It is hoped that after a few weeks his brainwaves will remain in the low alpha wave range, indicating little anxiety.

After a few weeks pass, Jake is feeling a lot better. "I can't believe how much progress I've made in a short time," says Jake. "This process took a while to develop," says Dr. Oliver, "and for you to fully recover, it will take some time."

Over the next few weeks, Dr. Oliver and Jake examine his intermediate and core beliefs, tackle more of the distressing areas identified on the Therapeutic Lifestyle Change Inventory, continue to practice self-regulation skills and PE, and assess his brainwaves through the EEG. Over time, Dr. Oliver hopes to show Jake how to move into theta and delta waves, indicating relaxation and deep meditation. He also hopes Jake will continue to practice behaviors that bring him more joy, positivity, and love in his life. Finally, Dr. Oliver hopes that Jake can turn his core belief of helplessness into a belief that he can help himself and others.

QUESTIONS FOR YOU TO PONDER

1. Do you believe a CBT approach is helpful with Jake?
2. Would you feel comfortable conducting a three-hour intake interview? Why or why not?
3. Do you believe integrating neuroscience into Dr. Oliver's approach is worthwhile?
4. In what ways is neuroscience integrated into Dr. Oliver's approach?
5. In what ways is Dr. Oliver's approach wellness and strength-based?
6. Dr. you believe determining a diagnosis is congruent with a wellness approach to counseling?
7. Can you come up with any other cognitive distortions with which Jake might be struggling?
8. How would you feel using prolonged exposure therapy (PE)? How ethical is PE since it causes Jake to initially feel more anxious?
9. How does using the Therapeutic Lifestyle Change Inventory, PE, and CBT relate to a neuroscience approach and neural pathway changes?
10. If you were working with Jake, what theoretical orientation do you believe would work best with him?
11. Would you consider integrating neuroscience techniques into your theoretical approach (from Item 9)?

12. If you were in counseling, would you want neuroscience integrated into the approach that your counselor used? What techniques would you want him or her to use?

Credits

Fig. 9.1: Copyright © by CNX OpenStax (cc by 4.0) at https://commons.wikimedia.org/wiki/File:Figure_35_03_06.jpg.

Img. 9.1: Copyright © by Alexhvl15 (cc by-sa 4.0) at https://commons.wikimedia.org/wiki/File:EEG.png.

Fig. 9.2: Source: https://lucymarymulholland.wordpress.com/2018/10/10/dr-daniel-siegels-hand-model-of-the-brain/.

Table 9.1: Carlos Zalaquett, Allen Ivey, and Mary Bradford Ivey, "Therapeutic Lifestyle Changes," *Essential Theories of Counseling and Psychotherapy: Everyday Practice in Our Diverse World*, pp. 46–50. Copyright © 2019 by Cognella, Inc. Reprinted with permission.

10

Complementary, Alternative, and Integrative Modalities (CAM)

Kevin C. Snow and Christine Ciecierski Berger

LEARNING OUTCOMES

- To define and provide a brief history of non- complementary, alternative, and integrative approaches to counseling and psychotherapy.
- To explain the holistic, wellness, and mind-body view of human nature of complementary, alternative, and integrative approaches.
- To understand the key concepts of CAM, including the holistic care approach; complementary, alternative, and integrative health; complementary practices of natural products, mind and body practices, and other complementary health approaches; popular complementary, alternative, and integrative health approaches; and ethical concerns and best practices of CAM use.
- Briefly examine a few of the many techniques of CAM, including the natural products of herbs (aka botanicals), vitamins, minerals, and probiotics; the mind-body practices of yoga, chiropractic and osteopathic manipulation, meditation and mindfulness, acupuncture, relaxation techniques, tai chi and qigong, hypnotherapy, and other mind-body practices; and other complementary health approaches, such as Ayurvedic medicine, traditional Chinese medicine, homeopathy, and naturopathy.
- To examine the different ways that the counseling process can be delivered when practicing CAM.

- To review social and cultural issues related to CAM.
- To examine the efficacy of select CAM approaches.
- To provide a case example of how CAM might be integrated into, or used in, a complementary fashion with counseling.

BRIEF HISTORY OF COMPLEMENTARY, ALTERNATIVE, AND INTEGRATIVE APPROACHES

This chapter takes a broad look at some non-mainstream practices used in counseling and psychotherapy generally known as **complementary** and **alternative medicine** and/or **modalities** (**CAM**), and sometimes called **complementary, alternative, and integrative approaches**. The CAM umbrella is wide, encompassing diverse approaches many people recognize immediately, such as mindfulness and meditation, breathing techniques, and prayer; to less familiar approaches that involve energy work, such as emotional freedom techniques (EFT, or "tapping"); to hands-on approaches such as Reiki, or healing touch. Some of these non-mainstream methods are conducted alongside or within more traditional psychotherapy and counseling while others are done in place of traditional, Western psychotherapeutic practices (Berger, 2015). Today, we may be in the midst of a paradigm shift as complementary, alternative, and integrative therapeutic approaches become ever more popular; however, many of these practices actually have deep roots in ancient cultures and have been practiced for thousands of years, making them far from new practices (Berger, 2015; Kraus, 2015). There are hundreds of CAM approaches, but we will concentrate on some of the more popular ones that can be categorized under three areas: natural products, mind body practices, and other complementary health approaches.

Do you take a multivitamin every morning? Have you ever been to a chiropractor for a stiff neck? When was the last time you engaged in deep breathing exercises, yoga, or meditation? Have you ever relied on a specialty herbal tea, such as chamomile, or taken supplements such as Valerian root, to help you reduce stress or sleep? Have you applied or taken CBD oil to treat an ailment? If you have engaged in any of these practices, and many more, than you have participated in a CAM approach to health or healing. Such approaches to the healing/helping arts have been on the rise dramatically in the United States over the past two decades. In fact, according to the 2012 National Health Interview Survey (NHIS), which is the most recent comprehensive national survey of CAM practices, 34% of adults in the United States reported using CAM methods (Clarke et al., 2015). An additional 11.6% of children and youth also used CAM practices, demonstrating the broad age range of individuals using a CAM approach in their health care (Black et al., 2015).

Americans became more acquainted with Eastern health-care approaches during the 1960s and 1970s. It was then that diplomatic relations with China were resumed and increasing numbers of Americans ventured to Eastern countries, such as China and India, and became aware of such Eastern health and spiritual traditions as acupuncture, mindfulness, and Ayurveda (Harrington, 2007). At that time, many Western-trained health professionals became curious about the potential benefits of Eastern health perspectives and techniques. For example, **Daniel Goleman** and **Richard Davidson**, pioneers of the mindfulness movement in the United States, were Harvard University students who traveled to India in the 1970s and became intrigued with the contemplative practices they found there (Gates et al., 2009). Goleman and Davidson connected with **Jon Kabat-Zinn** while he was designing the clinical and research program Mindfulness-Based Stress Reduction (MBSR). These individuals were part of a larger group of mental health professionals who introduced mindfulness to the United States as an important wellness tool. This group launched most of the mindfulness programs and research. Another pioneer in this area was psychiatrist **James Lake** who began to write articles and books on how to use multiple CAM approaches to treat specific mental disorders. Two of his key books, *Integrative Mental Health: A Therapist's Handbook* (2015) and *An Integrative Paradigm for Mental Health Care: Ideas and Methods Shaping the Future* (2019), provide a map to conceptualize and treat mental disorders using an evidence-based holistic CAM approach.

It is important to understand that what the United States and other Western cultures deem CAM practices have been considered common holistic health and spiritual practices in Eastern cultures for thousands of years (Cooper, 2007; Fennell et al., 2009). For instance, certain CAM practices, such as yoga and meditation, have roots in such ancient religions as Hinduism or Buddhism, thus making it difficult to trace or pinpoint exactly by who, when, and where they were created (Barnett & Shale, 2012). Early Eastern medicine traditions, such as **traditional Chinese medicine (TCM)**, include herbal medicine, acupuncture, and the practices of qigong and tai chi, all of which are designed to balance *chi* (or life force energy). The Indian system of Ayurveda, along with commonly known practices such as meditation, yoga, and deep breathing techniques, have been in use for several thousand years in their countries of origin, and are practiced extensively today in non-Western countries, particularly India, China, Japan, Tibet, and Korea; in diverse countries within Africa, and Central and South America; and in Pacific Island nations (Berger, 2015; Kraus, 2015).

Although the roots of many non-mainstream approaches are hundreds, or even thousands, of years old, these approaches within the confines of traditional Western psychotherapy, counseling, and medicine are frequently seen as emerging as they increase in popularity and gain wider use (Barnett & Shale, 2012; Berger, 2015; Ventola, 2010). For example, chiropractic care, a bodywork approach many might be familiar with for the treatment of neck and back pain, was frequently ostracized since its development in 1895, but this practice has become mainstream and is now accepted by numerous insurance companies through the more than 70,000 licensed practitioners in the United States today (American Chiropractic Association, 2019). Chiropractic care can be traced back more than 120 years, yet many other CAM approaches have a much longer history, are currently "emerging" in the Western or conventional health paradigm, and are increasingly accepted by clinicians trained in Western helping practices (Barrett et al., 2003; Mamtani & Cimino, 2002).

In recent years, people in general, and mental health professionals in particular, have sought CAM practices for such reasons as valuing wellness promotion and illness prevention (Upchurch & Rainisch, 2015); frustration with actual or perceived limits of Western medicine, often due to chronic health conditions with inconclusive treatments; and potential philosophical or spiritual values or interest (Berger & Johnson, 2017; White et al., 2008). With the increasing use of complementary health approaches in the United States, in 1991 the federal government allotted funds to the National Institutes of Health (NIH) to research CAM practices (Barnett & Shale, 2012). The **Office of Alternative Medicine** was thus created in 1992 to explore this new area of research and eventually developed into the **National Center for Complementary and Alternative Medicine** (**NCCAM**) in 1999 (Pearson & Chesney, 2007).

Today, NCCAM is known as the **National Center for Complementary and Integrative Health** (**NCCIH**, 2017a). This name change reflected a move away from these approaches being used almost exclusively in a complementary and/or alternative manner to them being increasingly used in an integrative fashion. NCCIH's mission is "to define, through rigorous scientific investigation, the usefulness and safety of complementary and integrative health interventions and their roles in improving health and health care" (NCCIH, 2017b, "Our Mission"). According to the National Health Survey, adults in the United States spend more than $30 billion on the many CAM procedures (NCCIH, 2017c). Although the most cited reasons for using complementary health is for back pain, other chronic pain, and psychosomatic problems, a wide number of complementary health approaches are practiced today for various health-related reasons, including for the treatment of mental health issues. It is important to note that CAM is a "big tent" area of health. As such, there are many practices and terms. The initial descriptor and the one still most widely used is CAM but other terms include **integrative medicine, integrative health, functional medicine,** and **complementary** and **integrative health**.

Many of these practices can be explored by interested individuals as stand-alone treatments or through specialty practitioners (e.g., **homeopathic physicians, shamans** or **curanderos, Reiki** practitioners, and other **healers**), with these practitioners obtaining training in each modality. An increasing number of counselors and other mental health professionals, however, have begun to include them in their Western, or conventional, counseling and psychotherapy practices (Berger et al., 2017). Illustrating this point, many articles in *Counseling Today* and in *Psychology Today* explored how professional counselors and psychologists have integrated CAM practices within their counseling work. For example, Fisher (2015) discussed her use of Reiki, an ancient Japanese energy technique formalized into a modern practice in 1922, for clients with depression. Marks-Stopforth (2009) discussed the use of yoga, meditation, and relaxation techniques with groups of adolescent boys, while Meyers (2019a) discussed how some helpers use relaxation, meditation, deep breathing, and progressive muscle relaxation with trauma clients. Still other helpers have recommended acupuncture for the treatment of women experiencing menopause (Meyers, 2019b), shared the benefits of healing touch with children and adults in counseling (Moffat, 2016), and explored nutritional and dietary therapies for individuals with

ADHD and autism spectrum disorders (Harrell, 2016). Berger noted that some CAM practices have become so pervasive within the counseling profession that CAM has become part of her and other counselors' identities (as cited in Irving-Johnson, 2019).

VIEW OF HUMAN NATURE

CAM approaches take a **holistic** perspective toward healing, which means that they focus on the needs of the whole person as opposed to utilizing narrowly focused assessments and treatments common to Western medicine (Berger, 2015; Weil, 2013). In addition, CAM looks at a client's overall **wellness** while being cognizant of, and attending to, the client's cultural background and beliefs.

Most of Western health traditions follow specific, localized, and targeted assessment and treatment protocols that grew out of surgical and pharmacological advances and the use of vaccines. These were indeed remarkable; however, specialization soon became equated with treatment and limits began to arise, such as when people experience chronic pain and other chronic health conditions that do not respond to such focused treatments. As some people struggled with these limits, they sought Eastern approaches, and what they found was a wholly different paradigm of self, life, and health.

Western approaches tend to be linear and material: what you can see is what you can treat. Eastern approaches developed before modern Western medicine, and through trial and error, proposed that the mind and body are not separate and that an intervention in one sphere of the self would very likely influence other spheres (Chan et al., 2002; Harrington, 2007; Larson-Presswalla, 1994). Another Eastern health assumption is that the **mind, body, and spirit work in harmony** and that health promotive behaviors, such as CAM, prevent health problems and maintain balance (Furnham, 2002; Schuster et al., 2004). Finally, within traditional Chinese medicine (TCM) there is an assumption that humanity is not separate from nature at large. Therefore, TCM practitioners consider natural elements such as the seasons, woods, metals, and animals when assessing and treating individuals (Jagirdar, 1989).

Ultimately, these "new" theories and approaches offer a different framework for conceptualizing client issues, and developing treatment plans as the sources of client problems can be viewed from very "old" thinking and practices for healing/health. A significant feature of many CAM approaches is an emphasis on the **inherent mind/body connection** within each person and seeking to connect or **integrate the mental, physical, and spiritual** aspects of the self to bring about improved health (Barnett & Shale, 2012; Lake, 2009). For instance, when working with a client who is depressed, rather than focusing solely on the symptoms of depression, a counselor might focus on an individual's total wellness, which Myers & Sweeney (2008) suggest, in their **indivisible self model,** includes one's **creative self** (e.g., thinking, emotions, control or personal mastery, work, positive humor), **coping self** (e.g., leisure, stress management, self-worth, realistic beliefs), **social self** (e.g., friendship, love), **essential self** (e.g., spirituality, gender identity, cultural identity, self-care), and **physical self** (e.g., nutrition, exercise; see Box 10.1).

BOX 10.1 ASSESSING YOUR WELLNESS

Score yourself, from 1 to 5, on each of the following five factors, with 5 indicating the area you most need to work on. Then, find the average for all five factors (creative self, coping self, etc.). Next, write down the ways you can better yourself in any of the factors for which your scores seem problematic (most likely, scores between a 3 and 5). You might also want to consider how your scores may change as a function of the context in which you find yourself.

Factors

Creative Self: This is related to our uniqueness in our interpersonal relationships and how we come to make sense of our place in the world. It is highlighted by our ability to be mentally sharp and open-minded (thinking), being in touch with our feelings (emotions), being intentional and planful and knowing how to express our needs (control), being effective at work and using our skills successfully (work), and having the capacity to deal with life as it comes at us (positive humor).

Coping Self: This is related to our ability to deal with life's events and to effectively cope with negative situations. It is composed of developing leisure activities (leisure), successfully coping with stress (stress management), valuing ourselves and having good self-esteem despite problems (self-worth), and having the capacity to be imperfect while recognizing it is unrealistic to think we can be loved by all (realistic beliefs).

Social Self: The social self is related to how we are connected to others through our friendships, intimate relationships, and through familial bonds. It is composed of the ability to connect with others in supportive, emotional, and sometimes sexual ways (friendship and intimacy). Additionally, it is the part of us that can share deeply with others and be mutually respectful and appreciative (love).

Essential Self: This has to do with how we make meaning in our relationships with ourselves and others. It is recognizing the part of us that is beyond our mind and body (spirituality), feeling comfortable in the way we identify with our gender (gender identity) and with our culture (cultural identity), and being able to care for ourselves through self-care and by minimizing harm in our environment (self-care).

Physical Self: This part of ourselves is reflected through our biological and physical self and is related to ensuring that we have adequate physical activity in our lives (exercise) and eat well, have a good diet, and avoid being overweight or underweight (nutrition).

Context

Context has to do with systems in which we live, such as family, community, social and political systems, work environment, and global system. When assessing yourself on the five factors, consider how your sense of self changes based on the context in which you find yourself.

CAM approaches underscore the notion that no one method or model is all-encompassing. Physicians, energy healers, or shamans do not have all the answers, but then again neither do professional counselors and psychotherapists. With this in mind, it behooves mental health practitioners to be aware of this movement, educate themselves about these approaches, and consider using such techniques, when appropriate, in their own practices to better respond to client needs (Barnett & Shale, 2012). In general, we recommend one of two ways of working with CAM: becoming trained in specific practices and integrating them directly into counseling practice, or becoming informed about your local CAM network to make effective and ethical CAM referrals for clients in a team treatment approach.

One way of further informing yourself of these approaches and their worldviews is to consult information from NCCIH, which continues to fund and publish studies on CAM approaches (see NCCIH, 2019a). Notable books on CAM approaches include:

- *Complementary and Integrative Treatments in Psychiatric Practice* (Gerbard et al., 2017)
- *Energy Medicine* (Eden & Feinstein, 2008)
- *Full Catastrophe Living: Using the Wisdom of Your Body and Mind to Face Stress, Pain, and Illness* (Kabat-Zinn, 2013)
- *Fundamentals of Complementary and Alternative Medicine* (Micozzi, 2015).
- *Integrative Mental Health Care: A Therapist's Handbook* (Lake, 2015)
- *Integrative Psychiatry* (Monti & Beitman, 2009)
- *Meditation Interventions to Rewire the Brain* (Tarrant, 2017)
- *Nutrition Essentials for Mental Health: A Complete Guide to the Food-Mood Connection* (Korn, 2016)
- *The Science Behind Tapping* (Stapleton, 2019)
- *Yoga Skills for Therapists* (Weintraub, 2012)

Other ways to become informed of the CAM view of human nature and its various key concepts and techniques include joining and attending meetings of professional associations supportive of CAM practices. Some associations that offer conferences and publications related to alternative, complementary, and integrative health include **Alternative Therapies in Health and Medicine** (www.alternative-therapies.com), the **Association for Humanistic Psychology** (www.ahpweb.org), the **Association for Comprehensive Energy Psychology** (www.energypsych.org), the **American Holistic Health Association** (www.ahha.org), the **Institute of Noetic Sciences** (www.noetic.org), and the **Association for Creativity in Counseling** (www.creativecounselor.org).

KEY CONCEPTS

Five important areas of CAM involve 1) having a **holistic care** approach; 2) understanding the difference between **complementary, alternative, and integrative health**; 3) having knowledge of the complementary practices of **natural products, mind and body practices, and other complementary health approaches**; 4) knowing some **popular complementary, alternative, and integrative health approaches**; and 5) understanding **ethical concerns and best practices** of CAM use.

Holistic Care

One foundational concept in understanding CAM is its connection to holistic care (Berger, 2015; Weil, 2013). Holistic care practices embrace **holism**, which is the notion of treating mind and body problems as intimately and intricately linked, as opposed to the traditional, Western medicine approach of separating mind and body problems as in the disease model so prevalent in U.S. medical care. This Western model often treats problems of the body and mind in isolation from each other. For example, mental health treatment is generally seen as distinct from treatments for medical conditions, such that mental health professionals are trained, licensed, and practice independently of medical practitioners, such as neurosurgeons or cardiologists.

To illustrate further, an overweight person with high blood pressure who goes to his or her family physician to seek help for anxiety or depression will most likely be referred to various health-care practitioners to address each medical and psychological issue separately. They might be referred to a dietician for the weight issue, a professional counselor for mental health symptoms, a cardiologist for the elevated blood pressure, and continue routine checkups with the family physician. Other issues underlying the depression or anxiety, such as spiritual or relational struggles, may be ignored entirely. In contrast, a holistic perspective views issues as linked, and the person is treated from a conjoined mind/body perspective (Berger, 2015; Weil, 2013). Thus, a holistic approach takes into account bodily, medical, mental, spiritual, emotional, relational, and other areas of the person from an interconnected perspective with the belief that deficits in one area impacts other areas in complex and mysterious ways, with treatment aimed at restoring and maintaining overall client well-being.

Complementary, Alternative, and Integrative Health

Mental health professionals should be familiar with three broad areas of non-mainstream approaches to wellness if they are to consider using them in their practice: (a) **complementary health**, which is the term used when a practice or a product is considered non-mainstream and is used in addition to a conventional approach; (b) **alternative health**, the term used when non-mainstream approaches are used in place of conventional medicine; and (c) **integrative health**, the term used when non-mainstream approaches are integrated into mainstream health (NCCIH, 2018a).

For our purposes, it is assumed that most practitioners will typically practice using an integrative approach to their traditional psychotherapy. Examples of using non-mainstream practices in an integrative manner include mindfulness techniques, meditation, or deep breathing practices that a clinician could safely and ethically incorporate within a clinical session. For instance, it is common for mental health clinicians to make use of deep breathing exercises and mindfulness meditation practices to assist clients struggling with anxiety or recovering from crisis and trauma situations (Marks-Stopforth, 2009). A clinician could smoothly integrate these practices into his or her existing psychotherapeutic practice, regardless of one's therapeutic theory of choice (e.g., REBT, person-centered, individual psychology) because they are mainly used as relaxation or stress management tools.

Although many will use an integrative approach, a fair number of clinicians may also use a complementary approach, such as when a counselor refers a client to an outside expert who practices a technique that could be helpful for the client (e.g., a client is referred to a transcendental meditation group run by a trained leader to reduce anxiety and gain inner calmness).

Natural Products, Mind and Body Practices, and Other Complementary Health Approaches

The NCCIH divides complementary health approaches into three subgroups: **natural products, mind and body practices**, and **other complementary health approaches** (NCCIH, 2018a). The following offers brief explanations of these practices.

Natural Products

This group of products includes herbs (aka botanicals), vitamins and minerals, natural supplements/nutraceuticals, and probiotics. Some examples: valerian root, melatonin, herbal teas, fish oil, CBD oil, B vitamins, etc. This category of products is generally consumed orally in food, teas, or as dietary supplements, or applied topically to the body in creams, lotions, or ointments. These can be purchased over the counter, but the best way to work with them is through a Chinese herbalist, a naturopathic doctor, or another integrative medicine practitioner who is competent in working with these natural products.

Mind and Body Practices

This group includes a number of procedures or techniques administered by a trained practitioner or healer designed to integrate or connect the mind/body experience to health/mental health issues. This category includes such practices as yoga, chiropractic and osteopathic manipulation, meditation, massage therapy, acupuncture, relaxation techniques, tai chi, qigong, healing touch, hypnotherapy, movement therapies, Reiki, emotional freedom techniques (EFT, or tapping), and other approaches. While most of these modalities require specific training, some also require licensure, such as acupuncture, massage, and chiropractic/osteopathy, or certification, such as yoga.

Other Complementary Health Approaches

This last group embraces approaches not covered in the above two categories, including those approaches practiced by traditional healers, such as shamans and curanderos, and/or practices that include combinations of specific regimens of diet, exercise, supplements, and lifestyle choices. Some of these include Ayurvedic medicine, traditional Chinese medicine (TCM), homeopathy, and naturopathy.

Popular Complementary, Alternative, and Integrative Health Approaches

Berger (C. Berger, personal communication, January 5, 2020) identifies a number of popular practices of complementary, alternative, and integrative health that are conducted complementarily, or as alternatives, to counseling and psychotherapy (see Table 10.1). This list covers many popular CAM therapies, but it does not include all of the many diverse approaches in practice today that fit under the CAM umbrella. In fact, the NCCIH website includes a comprehensive "A to Z" listing of more than 400 CAM-related health topics for interested readers (NCCIH, 2019b).

TABLE 10.1 SOME PROMINENT COMPLEMENTARY AND ALTERNATIVE APPROACHES TO COUNSELING AND PSYCHOTHERAPY

Acupuncture	Massage
Advanced Integrative Therapy	Meditation
Alexander Technique	Mindfulness
Aromatherapy	Naturopathy
Ayurveda	Prayers and Affirmations
Contemplative Psychotherapy	Rebirthing and Breathwork
Ecotherapy	Reiki
Emotional Freedom Techniques (EFT)	Somatic Experiencing
Energy Psychology	Sound Healing
Healing Touch	Therapeutic Touch
Heartmath	Traditional Healing
Herbal Medicine	Traditional Chinese Medicine
Homeopathy	Visualization and Guided Imagery
Integrative Nutrition	Yoga

Ethical Concerns and Best Practices

For clinicians interested in integrating CAM techniques into their practice, it is necessary to obtain appropriate training specific to CAM practices, and to explore government certification, licensure, or other regulations if they exist. If a clinician fails to do so, he or she may be acting unethically and could face potential liability problems.

Although it is assumed many licensed mental health clinicians will be practicing CAM from an integrative perspective, this may not always be the case. Practitioners who are appropriately trained and/or credentialed may also move between traditional and nontraditional practices to address a client's healing. For example, someone who is both a licensed therapist (e.g., counselor, social worker, psychologist) and also a Reiki master may hold separate counseling sessions and Reiki sessions for the same client, or may integrate these within the same session as illustrated earlier with meditation and deep breathing (Fisher, 2015). Still other mental health professionals will practice a strict adherence to a counseling approach but recommend a client to a CAM practitioner via a referral process.

When choosing to integrate a CAM approach into a counseling session, it is very important that the clinician outline his or her training and scope of competence. Licensed therapists have very specific ethical parameters regarding appropriate training in new and emerging modalities:

> Counselors practice in specialty areas new to them only after appropriate education, training, and supervised experience. While developing skills in new specialty areas, counselors take steps to ensure the competence of their work and protect others from possible harm (American Counseling Association [ACA], 2014, Section C.2.b., New Specialty Areas of Practice),

and

> Psychologists planning to provide services, teach, or conduct research involving populations, areas, techniques, or technologies new to them undertake relevant education, training, supervised experience, consultation, or study (American Psychological Association [APA], 2017, Section 2e: Competence).

In addition, whatever approach is used, ethically it should be shown that there is some evidence to support its efficacy:

> When providing services, counselors use techniques/procedures/modalities that are grounded in theory and/or have an empirical or scientific foundation (ACA, 2014, Section C.7.a., Scientific Basis for Treatment),

and psychologists should ensure they are:

"[E]valuating and using research evidence in both basic and applied psychological science" (APA, 2019, Section e).

Finally, some best practices to consider, if one is to integrate or refer to CAM practices, include those listed in Box 10.2 (Feinstein, 2011; Murphy, 2015).

BOX 10.2 BEST PRACTICES WHEN USING CAM APPROACHES

1. Have a clear-cut rationale why you are integrating or referring to CAM practices.
2. Ensure that the practice is evidence-based or evidence-supported.
3. Obtain appropriate training and credentials in the CAM practice if you are to integrate it into your counseling approach.
4. Explore whether there is a professional association for the modality with its own ethics code that can guide you.
5. If you are integrating the CAM practice into your counseling approach, obtain adequate supervision for your CAM modality.
6. Ensure that CAM practitioners, to whom you might refer, are appropriately trained and/or credentialed in the CAM practice they are using.
7. Carefully collaborate with your client about the use of any CAM modality.
8. Carefully consider the CAM modality and whether it is appropriate for your client's presenting problem(s).
9. Consider what cautions, contraindications, or safety issues might be involved.
10. Obtain informed consent about why you are using these CAM technique(s) with your client to accomplish treatment goals.
11. Have an attorney review your documentation.

TECHNIQUES

CAM contains such breadth and depth that it is difficult to know where to begin when exploring techniques. And with more than 400 CAM approaches, it seems inevitable that almost any list will be incomplete (NCCIH, 2019b). Additionally, with some CAM approaches, it is difficult to distinguish a technique from a theory. Looking at the list in Table 10.1, you will see several diverse CAM approaches listed such as Reiki, meditation, aromatherapy, and therapeutic touch. Are these theories, approaches, practices, or techniques? For our purposes here, we will approach these as potential techniques, though others may argue that some of these approaches could be viewed as a theory. Using NCCIH's three categories of **natural**

products, mind and body practices, and **other complementary health approaches**, clinicians should be familiar with certain popular techniques that follow but be aware that this is only an overview of a few select CAM techniques.

Natural Products

This category includes the use of herbs, vitamins, minerals, probiotics, and other products often known as dietary supplements (NCCIH, 2018a). Most of these substances are consumed orally in teas, pills, supplements, or powders mixed into other beverages, or applied topically in the form of creams, tinctures, oils, or other applications.

Herbs (aka botanicals). The NCCIH offers a partial list of more than 50 herbs used for CAM (NCCIH, 2019c), but in reality there are many more available to consumers of varying quality, as many of the products are not regulated in the same way medicine is in the United States (U.S. Food and Drug Administration, 2018). Many of these herbs, or botanicals, are common household products one can find in the kitchen spice drawer, at the grocery store, or at pharmacy aisles, yet others are somewhat more exotic and available through specialized natural food stores, Chinese medicine practitioners, or other outlets. These herbs include familiar products such as garlic, tea tree oil, chamomile, aloe vera, gingko biloba, CBD oil, lavender, and cinnamon, and less familiar products such as milk thistle, bitter orange, yohimbe, feverfew, chasteberry, valerian root, and noni.

Vitamins and minerals. Many individuals regularly take vitamins and minerals without realizing that their usage is an aspect of CAM. According to the NCCIH (2018b):

> Vitamins and minerals are essential substances that our bodies need to develop and function normally. The known vitamins include A, C, D, E, and K, and the B Vitamins: thiamin (B1), riboflavin (B2), niacin (B3), pantothenic acid (B5), pyridoxal (B6), cobalamin (B12), biotin, and folate/folic acid. (para. 1)

In addition to these vitamins, many other minerals important to proper health used as CAM treatments include " … calcium, phosphorus, potassium, sodium, chloride, magnesium, iron, zinc, iodine, sulfur, cobalt, copper, fluoride, manganese, and selenium" (NIH, 2018b, para. 1). Although healthy diets usually include the bulk of the essential **vitamins and minerals**, many individuals take them as additional supplements on their own or as part of multivitamin or multi-mineral supplements.

Probiotics. According to NCCIH: "probiotics are live microorganisms (in most cases, bacteria) that are similar to beneficial microorganisms found in the human gut. They are also called 'friendly bacteria' or 'good bacteria.' Probiotics are available to consumers mainly in the form of dietary supplements and foods" (NCCIH, 2017d, para. 1). Some very familiar foods, such as yogurt, are classified as **probiotics** and can also be found in dietary supplements and other products for oral consumption or topical application. There is some evidence that using probiotics to regulate gut health can have a positive impact on mental health in general and depression specifically (Bested et al., 2013; Huang et al., 2016).

In the natural products category, it is important for counselors to present this information to clients as education and not in a prescriptive fashion. One can recommend websites, local practitioners, or books such as *The Psychobiotic Revolution* (Anderson et al., 2017) to inform clients about the potential mental health impact of natural products. It is critical that mental health professionals refrain from suggesting specific items or creating a treatment plan made up of natural products as most of this information is beyond the scope of their practices.

Mind and Body Practices

This category includes many approaches, some quite familiar, for the integration of mind/body health, often involving specially trained, certified, or licensed practitioners. Here, we will look at yoga, chiropractic and osteopathic manipulation, meditation, acupuncture, relaxation techniques, tai chi and qigong, hypnotherapy, emotional freedom techniques (EFT), Reiki and other biofield therapies, and other mind and body practices.

Yoga

Originally rooted in ancient Indian religion and philosophy, but now often utilized independently of these traditions, **yoga** has become a popular approach that uses various types of body positioning, breathing exercises, and relaxation or meditation techniques for mind/body healing (NCCIH, 2018c). There are several types of yoga, which can be found at both nontraditional and traditional places, such as yoga and hot yoga studios, retreat centers, or your local workout location. Yoga has been found to assist with trauma treatment (Emerson et al., 2009; Macy et al., 2018), to decrease anxiety (Hofmann et al., 2016), and to decrease depression (Uebelacker & Broughton, 2016). Yoga has grown in popularity with both clients and mental health professionals, and as such, the research base for yoga as a complementary or integrative modality has grown. To become a registered yoga teacher requires a specific number of hours, so counselors might seek this training to use yoga in sessions, or they might refer clients to yoga classes in the local community.

Chiropractic and Osteopathic Manipulation

Often called "spinal manipulation" or "spinal and manipulative therapy," **chiropractic and osteopathic manipulation** have become fairly mainstream in society (NCCIH, 2017e). Trained practitioners, such as chiropractors, physicians (e.g., osteopathic doctors, naturopathic physicians), physical therapists, and athletic trainers, engage in spinal and other limb manipulation by generally using force from their hands to alleviate pain and correct various bodily issues.

Meditation and Mindfulness

Meditation, similar to yoga, also has traditional roots in a wide range of spiritual and religious philosophies (NCCIH, 2017f), specifically those of India, Japan, Tibet, and China. Many kinds of meditation and related mindfulness-based activities are designed to calm and center the mind and invite the user to increase awareness of both internal and external states, and become more cognizant of life around and within the user. Meditation is often taught by a trained teacher and sometimes practiced in groups, but individuals can easily learn meditation practices and implement them on their own. Counselors can readily incorporate meditation and **mindfulness** practices into their sessions as most of these practices do not require specific credentialing.

There are many types of meditation, but three of the most often used types in counseling are Vipassana or insight meditation, transcendental meditation (TM), and guided imagery or visualization. Vipassana meditation is a type of Buddhist mindfulness meditation that invites the user to sit quietly and follow his or her breath, while observing thoughts, feelings, and sensations. The goal is to clear extraneous thoughts and to develop awareness or insight within. TM is taught as a specific proprietary system and focuses the mind on a mantra, or word. Guided imagery can be helpful for beginner meditators because these meditations have structure and have more internal boundaries. In addition, there are easy to use smartphone apps that have improved the likelihood that clients will practice meditation. Some of these include Calm, Headspace, and Insight Timer.

Although some types of mindfulness or meditation can be helpful for clients, some are contraindicated. For example, for people with active psychosis or traumatic dissociation, it is not recommended to have clients sit and follow their breath. This type of meditation is too unstructured with few internal boundaries and can lead to increased agitation or physiological arousal (Compson, 2014).

Acupuncture

Primarily stemming from traditional Chinese medicine (TCM) but used widely in many Asian countries and the United States, **acupuncture** involves the "stimulation of points on the body using a variety of techniques" by "penetrating the skin with thin, solid, metallic needles that are manipulated by the hands or by electrical stimulation" of a trained practitioner (NCCIH, 2017g, para. 1). Acupuncture works on chi, or the subtle energy system that runs on meridians through the body. This energy is not visible to the naked eye, but manipulation of the energy through acupuncture produces desired effects. The needles are very thin, about the width of a hair, and are barely felt upon insertion. Licensure is required for acupuncture in all but six states and is most often considered an alternative therapy. Currently, it is often covered by many forms of health insurance. One form of acupuncture, ear acupuncture, is used in more than 2,500 addiction treatment centers since it's been shown to help manage cravings during withdrawal from alcohol, opiate, and cocaine dependence (Smith et al., 2010). Acupuncture is used to treat a variety of issues, often involving chronic pain, and has even been used for surgery, including open heart surgery (Litscher et al., 2015; Zhou et al., 2011). While acupuncture is mostly used to treat physical health issues, it has been shown to be effective with addiction, as stated earlier, and there is some evidence it may be helpful for anxiety, though the research rigor is limited (Pilkington et al., 2007; see Box 10.3).

BOX 10.3 ACUPUNCTURE ANESTHESIA

In 1971, a Japanese newspaper article on acupuncture anesthesia in China reported that low frequency electrical acupuncture (LFEA) was being used for anesthesia in abdominal operations such as appendicitis, and that the consciousness of the patients remained clear during the operations. This report accelerated fundamental study on acupuncture anesthesia and analgesia, and acupuncture treatment was used for analgesia in the treatment of pain in Japan. The first examination of acupuncture anesthesia was done in China in about 1960. In Japan, Masayoshi Hyodo pioneered 30 cases of acupuncture anesthesia, in 1972, at Osaka Medical College, and became one of the more experienced persons using acupuncture anesthesia. Acupuncture anesthesia has some benefits: (i) it is simple and easy without complicated tools; (ii) there are no side effects; (iii) non-painful areas are induced without the involvement of innervations of the areas stimulated by acupuncture; (iv) the anesthetic effects last after acupuncture anesthesia; and (v) the wound heals more quickly (Taguchi, 2008, p. 153).

Tai Chi and Qigong

These two related practices are part of traditional Chinese medicine, and similar to acupuncture and other CAM practices, have roots in ancient Chinese and other Asian cultures. These practices utilize various body movements and postures, usually done slowly and methodically, to improve "mental focus, breathing, and relaxation" (NCCIH, 2019e, para. 4). **Tai chi and qigong** are designed to move chi in specific ways to balance the mind and body. Although similar to martial arts, especially in the case of tai chi, these practices are used to improve movement, balance, stability, and improve quality of life and mood elevation, and even reduce chronic pain and anxiety.

Hypnotherapy

Also referred to as hypnosis, or self-hypnosis when practiced solo, **hypnotherapy** involves an induced, deep trance or state of deep concentration used for the treatment of diverse conditions such as anxiety, chronic pain, and for smoking cessation, and for other conditions such as irritable bowel syndrome (NCCIH, 2017h). There is some limited evidence that hypnosis can be helpful as a treatment for depression and as a complementary therapy for PTSD in veterans (Alladin, 2012; Abramowitz et al., 2007).

Emotional Freedom Techniques (EFT)

Emotional freedom techniques (EFT), also known as "tapping," is a self-acupressure technique that works on the meridians of the subtle energy body, very similar to acupuncture, but one uses sequences of tapping instead of needles to stimulate energy points. It was created by **Gary Craig** in the 1990s and is an outgrowth of another therapy called thought field therapy, created by **Roger Callahan** in the 1980s. EFT combines tapping with some cognitive techniques to address a multitude of issues. On one level it appears to decrease physiological arousal, which helps clients feel calm, but on a deeper level it seems to change clients' habitual emotional reactions to stressful events. EFT has been shown to reduce food cravings (Stapleton et al.,2016), trauma (Church et al., 2013; Sebastian & Nelms, 2017), depression (Nelms & Castel, 2016), and anxiety (Clond, 2016), among many other disorders.

Reiki and Other Biofield Therapies

Reiki is the most popular of a category of healing therapies called biofield therapies. In contrast with the meridian energy-based approaches, such as acupuncture and EFT, biofield therapies address the human subtle energy biofield, which is also part of the Eastern subtle energy system and considered to be a field of energy that encompasses and extends about eight feet out from the body. These therapies also include **chakras**, which are the third part of the subtle energy system. Seven of the most often discussed chakras are spinning wheels of subtle energy that follow a central column of the body, from the perineum up to the top of the head and beyond. Biofield therapies such as Reiki, therapeutic touch, and healing touch, work with the biofield and the chakras. Some of these therapies are more spiritual than others, but all of them aim to clean, clear, and balance energy for optimum wellness in mind, body, and spirit. Many biofield approaches have options for hands-on or hands-off techniques. Reiki is the most popular modality and is now offered in at least 64 hospitals in the United States for reasons ranging from stress management, speeding up wound and surgical healing, pain management, and addressing other mental health concerns related to physical health conditions. Reiki has been shown to reduce burnout in mental health professionals (Rosada et al., 2015), and depression, pain, and anxiety in older adults (Richeson et al., 2010), among many other issues. Healing touch, another biofield therapy, has been shown to assist with grief counseling (Berger et al., 2017) and PTSD in returning active duty military (Jain et al., 2012), and has helped in other select problems.

Other Mind and Body Practices

There are many other mind and body practices that could be listed here, such as movement therapies, including the Feldenkrais method, Alexander technique, and Pilates; or touch therapies such as deep connective tissue massage, Rolfing, and more (NCCIH, 2018a). True for all CAM categories, there are many mind and body practices, too many to list here.

Other Complementary Health Approaches

This category includes treatments and approaches not addressed by the other two categories of natural products and mind and body practices. It includes such diverse approaches as those conducted by shamans, curanderos, or other spiritual, religious, indigenous, or traditional healers, and other practices that do not clearly fit into the first two categories. A few of these practices we will examine include ayurvedic medicine, traditional Chinese medicine, homeopathy, and naturopathy.

Ayurvedic Medicine

According to the NCCIH, Ayurveda or Ayurvedic medicine is an "ancient Indian medical system ... based on ancient writings that rely on a 'natural' or holistic approach to physical and mental health" (NCCIH, 2019f, para. 4). Still very popular in India, this ancient medical approach utilizes mostly plant-based products, and a specific regimen of exercise, lifestyle behaviors, and diet to achieve health and wellness. The foundation of Ayurveda suggests that individuals have one of three types of energy combinations: kapha, pitta, and vata. Once one's type is recognized, then a holistic health plan is created to optimize health and wellness.

Traditional Chinese Medicine

Traditional Chinese medicine (TCM) is another ancient holistic health practice that uses a combination of methods already discussed, such as acupuncture and tai chi, along with various traditional Chinese herbal products for overall health regulation and the treatment of a variety of health and mental health issues (NCCIH, 2019g). Practitioners of TCM are often acupuncturists or Chinese herbalists.

Homeopathy

Homeopathy, or **homeopathic medicine**, is a 200-year-old medical approach originating in Germany based on two core notions: (a) "'like cures like,'—the notion that a disease can be cured by a substance that produces similar symptoms in healthy people"; and (b) the "'law of minimum dose'—the notion that the *lower* the dose of the medication, the *greater* its effectiveness" (NCCIH, 2018b, para. 5). Homeopathic remedies are generally highly individualized, vary for different people with the same conditions, and involve the use of minerals, plants, and animal products that are consumed or applied topically. Due to the law of minimum dose, some homeopathic products contain so few traces of the original healing substance as to be undetectable.

Naturopathy

Sometimes called naturopathic medicine, **naturopathy** finds its roots from a combination of early 19th century European medical practices and much older traditional healing approaches, and includes many approaches already discussed, such as the use of herbs, minerals, and dietary supplements; dietary and lifestyle guidelines; and homeopathy; along with the use of stress reduction, exercise, and even Western counseling and psychotherapy (NCCIH, 2017i). In some cases, licensed health-care specialists, such as chiropractors and osteopathic physicians, provide naturopathic medicine alongside their health practice, and in other cases trained naturopathic physicians are licensed for independent practice in some states. Other traditional healers, sometimes called **naturopaths**, administer this type of health care following training, though there tends to not be certification by a government organization.

Final Thoughts

The list of key concepts in the use of CAM health-care practices discussed here is a good place to start for interested counselors and psychotherapists if they are to begin to familiarize themselves with the broad area of complementary and alternative approaches. To explore further, mental health clinicians are encouraged to examine the additional resources and research available through the National Center for Complementary and Integrative Health (NCCIH, 2019a) and other resources cited in the reference list for this chapter.

THE COUNSELING PROCESS

Because the variance in CAM practices is so great, it is nearly impossible to indicate what a therapeutic process looks like. Some of these non-mainstream approaches would be directly integrated into the counseling relationship while other approaches may be suggested as an adjunct to counseling. Still others may be utilized in an "add-on" fashion, perhaps at the end of a session, and in some cases, a method might be recommended instead of counseling. Regardless of how you are using CAM, one should always reflect on the best practices listed in Box 10.2 earlier in this chapter. In addition, whether you are integrating, complementing, or using a non-mainstream approach as an alternative to counseling, some of the questions that you want to consider include the following:

- What is its modality?
- What is it used for?
- What is it effective with?
- What are the cautions or contraindications?
- What training is required?
- Is there a credentialing process involved?

- How will you integrate it into the therapeutic process?
- What is the ethical use of the modality?
- What is the research on the approach?

Integrating Non-Mainstream Practices

Figuring out how to incorporate some non-mainstream techniques into existing counseling is the probable path of most mental health clinicians, so we will briefly address the therapeutic process from this integrative perspective. After reflecting on the ethical concerns of CAM practice and the best practices noted earlier, in Box 10.2, a counselor might then integrate a specific practice into his or her counseling approach. For instance, progressive muscle relaxation is one example of how a non-mainstream approach could be used to help relieve anxiety. As most anxiety disorders have somatic origins or components, engaging the body directly using the muscles can be very helpful in regulating anxious feelings (Olatunji, et al., 2006). This approach is similar to a guided meditation but utilizes muscle contraction and deep breathing to elicit relaxation, calm, and peace of mind for an individual. A typical progressive muscle relaxation intervention could take 10 to 20 minutes or more to conduct and, once taught, clients can learn to use this technique on their own. Take a look at Box 10.4 and consider if you could integrate this approach into your counseling sessions.

BOX 10.4 PROGRESSIVE MUSCLE RELAXATION

What follows is a dialogue between a client experiencing significant stress and his counselor guiding him through the progressive muscle relaxation technique.

Client: "As I've been telling you, my stress levels have been off the charts! Work, home, family, friends ... lately everything in my life seems to be making me feel crazy. Some days, I feel like a heart attack is just around the corner. Today was particularly bad. I just don't know how to let all this go."

Counselor: "You know, as I sat here and listened to you share just now, I could see, feel, and hear how stressed out you are right now. I'm wondering if you'd try something with me? A way for you to relax, in the moment, before we explore the effect of all this stress in your life."

Client: "A way to relax? I need that. I'll try it!"

Counselor: "Okay. This is called progressive muscle relaxation. Please, get comfortable in your chair: Put your hands in your lap or by your side, close your eyes if you're willing to, or stare at a spot on the ground or ceiling, and feel yourself settle into the chair. Next, I'd like you to start taking deep breaths, slowly in and out. Breathe from your diaphragm ... watch as your belly button rises and falls slowly as you breathe in and out. Breathe with me. Breathe in and hold to the count of four: one ... two ... three ... four. Hold. Now breathe out to the count of eight: one ... two ... three ... four ... five ... six ... seven ... eight. Hold. And repeat: breathe in ... one ... two ... three ... four. Hold. Out, one ... two ... three ... four ... five ... six ... seven ... eight. Hold [this continues for a minute or two, holding the breath for a few seconds before breathing in and then out each time]."

Counselor: "Now, I want you to start at your toes and scrunch them up as tightly as you can, and hold that position for 10 seconds, then let go [counts to 10]. Next, I want you to arch your feet, and hold that for 10 seconds ... then relax. Now, we are going to move up to your calf muscles. Tighten your calves and hold them for 10 seconds. Then release. Next we will move to your thigh muscles. Tighten them as hard as you can, without hurting yourself, and again hold that position for 10 seconds and release. One ... two ... [this continues through various muscle groups up the body, through the hips, the abdomen, the chest, the arms, and even the neck, head, and facial muscles until all muscle groups have been tensed, held to the count of 10, and then relaxed]. Now that we've finished the relaxation exercise, how do you feel?"

Client: "Wow. Um ... I feel really calm. At peace even. It feels like the stress I walked in here with has washed out of the room."

Counselor: "Washed out of the room. That's a great visual image we can use to symbolize the stress flowing away from you and the calm of relaxation coming back in, in a wave of peace. This is an exercise you can repeat almost anywhere you can sit or lie calmly in quiet: at work, in a parked car, at home. You can even use some soothing or other calming sounds, such as trickling water to help enhance the relaxation. I'd like us to try this each week, before we start our counseling sessions, and I'd also like you to experiment with using this technique in your life outside of counseling and report back on its effectiveness."

Client: "Alright. It felt silly at first, but I feel so good now. Yes. I'll give it a try!"

There are multiple ways to integrate relaxation techniques and other non-mainstream techniques into one's practice, so explore the research, online tutorials, and training opportunities that abound today to learn about these methods. Some non-mainstream methods require significant, specialized training and others are more easily learned and used, such as deep breathing exercises or meditation.

Complementary Treatment of Non-Mainstream Practices

Some approaches, that fall under the category of complementary treatments, can be used by counselors in a team treatment approach. These are likely to be modalities such as nutrition or acupuncture, that require extensive education and credentialing, and counselors are not very likely to be fully trained in them. In these cases, we recommend that counselors become acquainted with competent and ethical CAM practitioners in their local communities so they can make good referrals and consultation for team treatment. As always, consider the ethical guidelines noted earlier and the best practices delineated in Box 10.2 when referring to a CAM practitioner.

Alternative Treatment of Non-Mainstream Practices

There are some instances when a counselor may want to consider the use of an alternative approach *instead of* counseling. For instance, for a person who has severe back pain which is causing the client to be depressed, a counselor might work with the client while referring the client for acupuncture. Some clients have such success with acupuncture for back treatments, that the counselor might realize there is little reason for the client to continue to see him or her, and have the client just continue with the acupuncturists. These are important considerations because as it is important for some people to be in counseling, it is also important to know when to refer to other specialists instead of starting or continuing counseling. In fact, both the ACA and APA note that it is important to refer a client when it is clear that they no longer need services (ACA, 2014; APA, 2017).

SOCIAL AND CULTURAL ISSUES

Based on the earlier discussion of the nature and history of many CAM approaches, you are probably not surprised that some CAM techniques can have great utility when working with diverse clients. For instance, when working with immigrants from China or India, relying on traditional Chinese medicine or Ayurveda—practices with which these individuals may be familiar—could be used (Kraus, 2015). In this sense, developing an understanding of various CAM approaches can be an effective way for counselors to enhance cultural competence.

CAM approaches seem to be popular with diverse groups of people. For example, a 2007 National Health Interview Survey (NHIS) examined the ethnic breakdown of individuals in the United States most likely to use CAM approaches. It found that "American Indian or Alaska Native adults (50.3%) and White adults (43.1%) were more likely to use CAM than Asian adults (39.9%) or Black adults (25.5%)." Despite these ethnic differences, it is clear that a relatively large proportion of all ethnic groups are interested in using CAM practices (Barnes & Bloom, 2008). Interestingly, CAM use was shown to be decreasing for some diverse groups between 2002 and 2015, with roughly two percentage point drops in use among Hispanic and African American individuals yet rising about the same 2% among White adults in America (Clarke et al., 2015). Cost of CAM products may influence its use. For instance, CAM use was most common among adults with higher levels of education, women between the ages of 30 to 69, adults living in Western countries, and recovering smokers who were recently hospitalized (Barnes & Bloom, 2008)—largely individuals who are most likely to have higher incomes or more disposable funds.

Research has demonstrated that other diverse groups implement CAM practices at relatively high rates. For example, Tsai (2007) found that 50% of Chinese American women have used herbal/homeopathic remedies for health issues, 30% of Native American women, and similarly high rates of White, Hispanic, and African American women (29%, 26%, and 21%, respectively). In a study that examined cancer survivors, Campesino and Koithan (2010) found that 49% of their African American and Hispanic patients used CAM as a component of their treatment, and Ahn et al. (2006) found significant CAM usage among Chinese and Vietnamese Americans. Mehta et al. (2007) found higher rates of mind/body approaches among Indian individuals (31%) than Filipinos (22%) and Chinese (21%), and higher herbal medicine usage among Chinese (32%) than Filipino (26%) and Indian (19%) individuals.

Today, many clinicians have been responding to the interest in CAM among clients by incorporating these practices into their work (Barnett & Shale, 2013); however, professional counselors and psychotherapists should never presume that individuals from a diverse group will automatically be interested, knowledgeable, or willing to use CAM approaches. As with any clinical treatment, it is important to keep in mind that all clients are unique, whether they share cultural traits or not, and that the individual or the people (e.g., the family unit, couple, parent and child) one works with and their interest in CAM will differ based on the relevance, or **salience**, of the treatment to that individual or unit (McAuliffe, 2020). A good counselor keeps in mind salience and explores ideas and practices openly with clients.

EFFICACY

CAM approaches to counseling and psychotherapy are growing increasingly popular in clinical work, but are CAM practices effective? Since the breadth and depth of CAM approaches are significant, it is impossible to examine all of the research on the many different approaches. The federal government, however, through NCCIH, believes that CAM is important enough to invest significant resources into studying the "usefulness and safety" (NCCIH, 2017b, par. 2) of complementary, alternative, and integrative practices. Although there has been much research, over the past 20 years, many of the more controversial CAM approaches, such as homeopathy, energy healing, or some herbal remedies, have not been explored sufficiently using controlled research studies. Here are a few examples of some of the research conducted on CAM practices:

- A recent experimental study examined the effectiveness of mindfulness-oriented recovery enhancement (MORE) for opioid use disorders and chronic pain in individuals receiving methadone management treatment. MORE is "an integrative behavioral group therapy that involves training in mindfulness, reappraisal, and savoring skills showed promise" (NCCIH, 2019h, para. 1). Participants reported decreased cravings, reduction in overall stress, and less pain than those not receiving this treatment. In a related pain study, researchers found people with higher "innate mindfulness reported less pain" (NCCIH, 2018g, para. 4). The results demonstrated a need to develop " ... better nonpharmacologic approaches to pain management, such as biofeedback, mindfulness meditation, or behavioral therapies, that specifically target increases in mindfulness and reductions ... " (NCCIH, 2018g, para. 5).

- A study of individuals suffering from fibromyalgia compared the benefits of aerobic exercise (a standard treatment) with tai chi (C. Wang et al., 2018). The results indicated that tai chi was as or more beneficial than aerobic exercise and that participants who participated in tai chi sessions were more committed and gained more benefit over time.
- A recent study examined the benefits of drugs derived from grape juice and grape seeds to treat depression (J. Wang et al., 2018). This study demonstrated how substances, derived from the grape, can be developed into bioactive dietary polyphenol preparation (BDPP), a natural product that has been shown to enhance resilience and stress coping in mice. The authors saw promise of further developing these natural products into effective drugs used alongside other psychiatric drugs to treat depression and related disorders.

In addition to these studies, the NIH (2018) summarized a number of other CAM efficacy studies:

- The herb ginkgo biloba was ineffective in reducing dementia and Alzheimer's disease.
- Spinal manipulation is somewhat effective in reducing lower back pain.
- By examining the brain through imaging technology, it appears as if the mind can block certain pain signals.
- Acupuncture seems to reduce pain related to osteoarthritis of the knee, offer relief for nausea from chemotherapy, reduce lower back pain, and decrease tension headaches.
- Glucosamine alone or in combination with chondroitin (alone or in combination) seems to show some efficacy for arthritis of the knee.
- Tai chi seems somewhat effective for those with fibromyalgia and in improving sleep, mood, and quality of life.
- Natural therapies (e.g., dietary supplements) can sometimes be detrimental, such as when the herb kava, used for anxiety, stress, and anxiety, was linked to liver damage;

when St. John's wort, used for depression, interacted with other drugs to make it less effective; and when Ayurvedic medicine products purchased on the Internet were found, one-fifth of the time, to contain mercury or arsenic.

Through these examples and other research cited earlier in the chapter, it can be seen that many different kinds of CAM approaches are being investigated and have demonstrated usefulness for clients of health-care professionals, including mental health practitioners. Yet there is still significant room for caution in other untested areas of CAM, particularly some herbal and dietary supplements that are not regulated by the U.S. Food and Drug Administration. As studies increasingly discriminate those CAM practices that work from those that may be doubtful, counselors will be able to increasingly integrate, complement, or refer to CAM practices.

SUMMARY

This chapter examined several complementary, alternative, and/or medicine (CAM) approaches, sometimes called complementary, alternative, and integrative methods. We noted that the CAM umbrella is wide, encompassing hundreds of approaches and that they are increasingly becoming more popular. Many of the approaches have deep roots in ancient cultures, and in this chapter we focused on some of the more popular ones in three areas: natural products, mind body practices, and other complimentary health approaches. CAM approaches vary dramatically, so it is difficult to classify them under one theory or technique. Most are also relatively new to the Western world and are still emerging as types of health-care treatment. In fact, the Office of Alternative Medicine wasn't created until 1992, eventually morphed into the National Center for Complementary and Alternative Medicine (NCCAM) in 1999, and then the National Center for Complementary and Integrative Health (NCCIH), as it's known today, with its purpose being to scientifically study usefulness and safety of CAM. Today, approximately one in four individuals use CAM products and, as a country, the United States spends $30 billion a year on such products.

Complementary health approaches take a holistic approach to healing, which considers the needs of the whole person, compared with just looking at one aspect of the person, as Western medicine tends to do. It also is based on a wellness approach that looks at an inherent mind-body connection and at integrating the mental, physical, and spiritual aspects of the person in healing. One model of wellness discussed was Myer's and Sweeney's indivisible self model, which includes understanding one's creative self, coping self, social self, essential self, and physical self. Several books and associations were highlighted that inform CAM approaches to counseling.

In exploring key concepts of CAM, it was noted that CAM has a holistic care approach, which takes the notion of treating mind and body problems as intimately and intricately interlinked or interdependent, contrasted with the traditional, Western medicine approach of separating mind and body problems, as in the disease model so prevalent in U.S. medical care. We highlighted the differences between complementary health, alternative health, and integrative health, noting that complementary health is the term used when a practice or a product is considered non-mainstream and is used in addition to a conventional approach; alternative health is the term used when non-mainstream approaches are used instead of conventional medicine; and integrative health is the term used when non-mainstream approaches are integrated into mainstream health. We also noted the differences between, and identified several, natural products, mind and body practices, and other complementary health approaches. The chapter next identified some popular complementary, alternative, and integrative health approaches. Finally, in this section we identified several ethical concerns, including ensuring that clinicians have the proper training and credentials to practice non-mainstream approaches and to make sure that whatever approach they do practice, they are evidence-based or evidence-supported. Eleven best practices when using non-mainstream approaches were also noted.

Noting there are well in excess of 400 CAM techniques, the chapter broke them down into three categories. Natural products include the use of herbs, vitamins, minerals, probiotics, and other products often known as dietary supplements. Mind and body practices include many approaches for the integration of mind/body health, often involving specially trained, certified, or licensed practitioners. Here, we briefly looked at yoga, chiropractic and osteopathic manipulation, meditation, acupuncture, relaxation techniques, tai chi and qigong, hypnotherapy, and other mind and body practices. Some of the other complementary health approaches examined included Ayurvedic medicine, traditional Chinese medicine, homeopathy, and naturopathy.

Examining the counseling process using CAM techniques is not easy, as CAM approaches can be integrated into counseling, used at the beginning or end of a session, sometimes used as an adjunct to counseling, and even sometimes used as an alternative to counseling. We suggested that a counselor ask the following questions when considering the use of CAM techniques: What is its modality?, What is it used for?, What is it effective with?, What are the cautions or contraindications?, What training is required? Is there a credentialing process involved?, How will you integrate it into the therapeutic process?, What is the ethical use of the modality?, and What is the research on the approach? We gave one example on how a counselor could integrate a progressive muscle relaxation mind and body technique into a session, but noted that other CAM techniques are not so easily integrated and may be better at the end of a session or as an adjunct to counseling. We also noted that sometimes, it is best to refer to an alternative method rather than start or continue with counseling, such as when one is thriving in the alternative method and no longer benefitting from counseling.

Relative to social and cultural issues, it was noted that CAM products often have utility when working with diverse clients and some figures were provided highlighting how people of all ethnic groups tend to use CAM products. It was also mentioned that those who use CAM products might use them because the individuals are of higher income, therefore making such products more accessible to them. We also delineated some diverse groups that are more likely to utilize specific CAM products. Finally, we noted that salience, or the awareness that all clients are unique even if they share cultural traits, is critical when working with CAM approaches, pointing out that a good counselor keeps in mind salience and explores ideas and practices openly with clients.

When discussing efficacy, it was noted that the NCCIH was created, in part, to examine the usefulness and safety of CAM products. With so many products, it was hard to identify all the research that has been conducted. Some that were highlighted included the positive usefulness of mindfulness-oriented recovery enhancement (MORE), the positive effects of tai chi on some ailments, and the potential use of a derivative from grapes in treating depression. We also noted that the NIH summarized a number of CAM studies showing that ginkgo biloba was ineffective in reducing dementia and Alzheimer's disease; spinal manipulation is somewhat effective in reducing lower back pain; the mind can block pain signals; acupuncture is effective in a variety of diseases; glucosamine may help for arthritis of the knee; tai chi seems to help with fibromyalgia, sleep, mood, and quality of life; and a number of dietary supplements have been shown to be detrimental (e.g., cause liver damage, make other drugs less effective, and contain mercury or arsenic).

KEY WORDS AND NAMES

Acupuncture
Alternative health
Alternative therapies in health and medicine
American Holistic Health Association
Association for Comprehensive Energy Psychology
Association for Creativity in Counseling
Association for Humanistic Psychology
Ayurvedic medicine
CAM
Chakras
Chi
Chiropractic and osteopathic manipulation
Complementary and alternative medicine and/or modalities (CAM)
Complementary health
Complementary alternative and integrative approaches
Complementary and integrative health
Coping self
Callahan, Roger
Craig, Gary
Creative self
Curanderos
Davidson, Richardson
Emotional freedom techniques (EFT)
Essential self
Ethical concerns and best practices
Functional medicine
Goleman, Daniel
Healers
Herbs
Holism
Holistic care
Homeopathic
Homeopathic medicine
Homeopathic physicians
Homeopathy
Hypnotherapy
Indivisible self model
Inherent mind/body connection
Institute of Noetic Sciences
Integrate the mental, physical, and spiritual
Integrative or holistic care
Integrative health

Integrative medicine
Lake, James
Meditation
Mind and body practices
Mind, body, and spirit work in harmony
Mindfulness
National Center for Complementary and Alternative Medicine (NCCAM)
National Center for Complementary and Integrative Health (NCCOH)
Natural products
Naturopaths
Naturopathy
NCCAM
NCCIH
Office of Alternative Medicine
Other complementary health approaches
Other mind and body practices
Physical self
Physicians
Popular complementary, alternative, and integrative health approaches
Probiotics
Progressive muscle relaxation
Reiki
Relaxation techniques
Salience
Shamans
Social self
Tai chi and qigong
Traditional Chinese medicine (TCM)
Vitamins and minerals
Wellness
Yoga
Kabat-Zinn, Jon

REFERENCES

Abramowitz, E. G., Barak, Y., Ben-Avi, I., & Knobler, H. Y. (2008). Hypnotherapy in the treatment of chronic combat-related PTSD patients suffering from insomnia: A randomized, zolpidem-controlled clinical trial. *Intl. Journal of Clinical and Experimental Hypnosis, 56*(3), 270–280. https://doi.org/10.1080/00207140802039672

Ahn, C.A, Ngo-Metzger, Q., Legdeza, A. T. R., Massagli, M. P., Clarridge, B. R., & Philips, R. S. (2006). Complementary and alternative medical therapy use among Chinese and Vietnamese Americans: Prevalence, associated factors, and effects of patient-clinician communication. *American Journal of Public Health, 96*(2). 647–653. https://doi.org/10.2105/AJPH.2004.048496

Alladin, A. (2012). Cognitive hypnotherapy for major depressive disorder. *American Journal of Clinical Hypnosis, 54*(4), 275–293. https://doi.org/10.1080/00029157.2012.654527

American Chiropractic Association (2019). *Origins and history of chiropractic care.* https://www.acatoday.org/About/History-of-Chiropractic

American Counseling Association. (2014). *Code of ethics.* http://www. counseling.org/docs/ethics/2014-aca-code-of-ethics.pdf?sfvrsn=4

American Psychological Association. (2017). *Ethical principles of psychologists and code of conduct.* https://www.apa.org/ethics/code/

American Psychological Association. (2019). *Policy statement on evidence-based practice in psychology.* https://www.apa.org/practice/guidelines/evidence-based-statement

Anderson, S. C., & Cryan, J. F., & Dinan, T. (2017). *The psychobiotic revolution: Mood, food, and the new science of the gut-brain connection..* National Geographic Partners.

Barnes, P. M., & Bloom, B. (2008). Complementary and alternative medicine use among adults and children: United States, 2007. *National Health Statistics Reports, 12*, 1–24.

Barrett, B., Marchand, L., Scheder, J., Plane, M. B., Maberry, R., Appelbaum, D., ... & Rabago, D. (2003). Themes of holism, empowerment, access, and legitimacy define complementary, alternative, and integrative medicine in relation to conventional biomedicine. *The Journal of Alternative & Complementary Medicine, 9*(6), 937–947. https://doi.org/10.1089/107555303771952271

Barnett, J. E., & Shale, A. J. (2012). The integration of complementary and alternative medicine (CAM) into the practice of psychology: A vision for the future. *Professional Psychology: Research and Practice, 43*(6), 576–585. https://doi.org/10.1037/a002891

Barnett, J. E., & Shale, A. J. (2013). Alternative techniques. *Monitor on Psychology*, 44(4), 48.

Berger, C. (2015). Complementary and alternative approaches: Overview. In E. S. Neukrug (Ed.), *The SAGE encyclopedia of theory in counseling and psychotherapy* (Vol. 1, pp. 208–213). SAGE Publications.

Berger, C. C., Cheston, S., & Stewart-Sicking, J. (2017). Experiences of healing touch and counseling on a bereaved population: A grounded theory. *Journal of Creativity in Mental Health, 12*(2), 166–179. https://doi.org/10.1080/15401383.2016.1201032

Berger, C. C., & Johnson, K. F. (2017). Complementary and integrative health assessment for practitioners scale: Initial development and validation. *Journal of Mental Health Counseling, 39*(4), 305–319. https://doi.org/10.17744/mehc.39.4.03

Bested, A. C., Logan, A. C., & Selhub, E. M. (2013). Intestinal microbiota, probiotics and mental health: From Metchnikoff to modern advances: Part II—contemporary contextual research. *Gut Pathogens, 5*(1), 3. https://doi.org/10.1186/1757-4749-5-3

Black, L. I., Clarke, T. C., Barnes, P. M., Stussman, B. J., & Nahin, R. L. (2015, February 10). *National health statistics reports: Use of complementary health approaches among children aged 4–17 years in the United* States: National Health Interview Survey, 2007–2012. https://www.cdc.gov/nchs/data/nhsr/nhsr078.pdf

Campesino, M., & Koithan, M. (2010). Complementary therapy use among racial/ethnic groups. *The Journals for Nurse Practitioners*, 6(8), 647–648. https://doi.org/10.1016/j.nurpra.2010.05.001

Chan, C., Ying Ho, P. S., & Chow, E. (2002). A body-mind-spirit model in health: An Eastern approach. *Social Work in Health Care, 34*(3-4), 261–282. https://doi.org/10.1300/J010v34n03_02

Church, D., Hawk, C., Brooks, A. J., Toukolehto, O., Wren, M., Dinter, I., & Stein, P. (2013). Psychological trauma symptom improvement in veterans using emotional freedom techniques: A randomized controlled trial. *The Journal of Nervous and Mental Disease, 201*(2), 153–160. https://doi.org/10.1097/nmd.0b013e31827f6351

Clark, T. C., Black, L. I., Stussman, B. J., Barnes, P. M., & Nahin, R. L. (2015). *Trends in the usage of complementary health approaches among adults: United States, 2002–2012*. http://www.cdc.gov/nchs/data/nhsr/nhsr079.pdf

Clond, M. (2016). Emotional freedom techniques for anxiety: A systematic review with meta-analysis. *The Journal of Nervous and Mental Disease, 204*(5), 388–395. https://doi.org/10.1097/NMD.0000000000000483

Compson, J. (2014). Meditation, trauma and suffering in silence: Raising questions about how meditation is taught and practiced in Western contexts in the light of a contemporary trauma resiliency model. *Contemporary Buddhism, 15*(2), 274–297. https://doi.org/10.1080/14639947.2014.935264

Cooper, E. L. (2007). Is there room for paradox in CAM? *Evidence-Based Complementary and Alternative Medicine, 4*(2), 135–137. https://doi.org/10.1093/ecam/nem053

Eden, D., & Feinstein, D. (2008). *Energy medicine: Balancing your body's energies for optimal health, joy, and vitality* (updated and expanded ed.). Penguin Group.

Emerson, D., Sharma, R., Chaudhry, S., & Turner, J. (2009). Trauma-sensitive yoga: Principles, practice, and research. *International Journal of Yoga Therapy, 19*(1), 123–128.

Feinstein, D. (2011). *Ethics handbook for energy healing practitioners: A guide for the professional practice of energy medicine and energy psychology.* Energy Psychology Press.

Fennell, D., Liberato, A. S., & Zsembik, B. (2009). Definitions and patterns of CAM use by the lay public. *Complementary Therapies in Medicine, 17*(2), 71–77. https://doi.org/10.1016/j.ctim.2008.09.002

Fisher, C. (2015). Reiki and psychotherapy. *Counseling Today.* https://ct.counseling.org/2015/04/reiki-and-psychotherapy/

Furnham, A. (2002). Complementary and alternative medicine. *The Psychologist, 15*(5), 228–231.

Gates, B., Cullen, M., & Nisker, W. (2009). Interview with Richard Davidson, Daniel Goleman & Jon Kabat-Zinn: Friends in mind, friends at heart. *Inquiring Mind,* 25, 2. https://www.inquiringmind.com/article/2504_davidson-goleman_kabatzinn/

Gerbard, P. L., Muskin, P. R., & Brown, R. P. (2017). *Complementary and integrative treatments in psychiatric practice.* American Psychiatric Association.

Harrington, A. (2007). *The cure within: A history of mind-body medicine.* Norton.

Harrell, M. (2016, February 8). Gut health and healthy brain function in children with ADHD and ASD. *Counseling Today.* https://ct.counseling.org/2016/02/gut-health-and-healthy-brain-function-in-children-with-adhd-and-asd/

Huang, R., Wang, K., & Hu, J. (2016). Effect of probiotics on depression: A systematic review and meta-analysis of randomized controlled trials. *Nutrients,* 8(8), 483. https://doi.org/doi: 10.3390/nu8080483.

Irving-Johnson, D. (2019, September). Recognizing a role for complementary and alternative therapies in counseling. *Counseling Today, 62*(3), 14-16.

Jagirdar, P. C. (1989). The theory of five elements in acupuncture. *The American Journal of Chinese Medicine, 17*(03n04), 135–138. https://doi.org/10.1142/S0192415X89000218

Jain, S., McMahon, G. F., Hasen, P., Kozub, M. P., Porter, V., King, R., & Guarneri, E. M. (2012). Healing touch with guided imagery for PTSD in returning active duty military: A randomized controlled trial. *Military Medicine, 177*(9), 1015–1021. https://doi.org/10.7205/MILMED-D-11-00290

Kabat-Zinn (2013), *Full catastrophe living: Using the wisdom of your body and mind to face stress, pain, and illness.* Bantam Books.

Korn, L. (2016). *Nutrition essentials for mental health: A complete guide to the food-mood connection.* Norton.

Kraus, K. L. (2015). Non-Western approaches. In E. S. Neukrug (Ed.), *The SAGE encyclopedia of theory in counseling and psychotherapy* (Vol. 1, pp. 208–213). SAGE Publications.

Lake, J. (2019). *An integrative paradigm for mental health care: Ideas and methods shaping the future.* Springer.

Lake, J. (2015). *Integrative mental health care: A therapist's handbook.* Norton.

Larson-Presswalla, J. (1994). Insights into Eastern health care: Some transcultural nursing perspectives. *Journal of Transcultural Nursing, 5*(2), 21–24. https://doi.org/10.1177/104365969400500204

Litscher, G., Simonis, H., & Kröll, W. (2015). Anesthesia and acupuncture. *World Journal of Anesthesiology, 4*(1), 1–4. doi:10.5313/wja.v4.i1.1

Macy, R. J., Jones, E., Graham, L. N., & Roach, L. (2018). Yoga for trauma and related mental health problems: A meta-review with clinical and service recommendations. *Trauma, Violence, & Abuse, 19*(1), 35–57. https://doi.org/10.1177/1524838015620834

Mamtani, R., & Cimino, A. (2002). A primer of complementary and alternative medicine and its relevance in the treatment of mental health problems. *Psychiatric Quarterly, 73*(4), 367–381. https://doi.org/10.1023/A:1020472218839

Marks-Stopforth, C. (2009, September 14). Getting adolescent boys to buy in to yoga, meditation, and relaxation. *Counseling Today.* https://ct.counseling.org/2009/09/reader-viewpoint-getting-adolescent-boys-to-buy-in-to-yoga-meditation-and-relaxation/

McAuliffe, G. (2020). Culture: Clarifications and complications. In G. McAuliffe (Ed.), *Culturally alert counseling: A comprehensive introduction* (3rd ed., Chap. 2). SAGE Publications.

Mehta, D. H., Phillips, R. S., Davis, R. B., & McCarthy, E. P. (2007). Use of complementary and alternative therapies by Asian Americans. Results from the National Health Interview Survey. *Journal of General Internal Medicine, 22*(6) 762–767. https://doi.org/doi:10.1007/s11606-007-0166-8

Meyers, L. (2019a, February 22). Touched by trauma. *Counseling Today.* https://ct.counseling.org/2019/02/touched-by-trauma/

Meyers, L. (2019b, January 7). Talking about menopause. *Counseling Today.* https://ct.counseling.org/2019/01/talking-about-menopause/

Micozzi, M. S. (2015). *Fundamentals of complementary and alternative medicine* (5th ed.). Elsevier.

Moffat, G. K. (2017, March 7). The healing language of touch. *Counseling Today.* https://ct.counseling.org/2017/03/healing-language-appropriate-touch/

Monti, D. A., & Beitman, B. D. (2010). *Integrative psychiatry.* Oxford University Press.

Murphy, M. (2015). *Practicing energy healing in integrity: The joy of offering your gifts legally and ethically.* Territorial.

Myers, J. E., & Sweeney, T. J. (2008). Wellness counseling: The evidence base for practice. *Journal of Counseling and Development, 86*, 482–493. https://doi.org/10.1002/j.1556-6678.2008.tb00536.x

National Center for Complementary and Integrative Health. (2017a). *About NCCIH.* https://nccih.nih.gov/about

National Center for Complementary and Integrative Health. (2017b). *NCCIH facts-at-a-glance and mission.* https://nccih.nih.gov/about/ataglance

National Center for Complementary and Integrative Health. (2017c). *Use of complementary health approaches in the U.S.: National health interview survey (NHIS).* https://nccih.nih.gov/research/statistics/NHIS/2012/key-findings

National Center for Complementary and Integrative Health. (2017d). *Probiotics.* https://nccih.nih.gov/health/probiotics

National Center for Complementary and Integrative Health. (2017e). *Spinal manipulation.* https://nccih.nih.gov/health/spinalmanipulation

National Center for Complementary and Integrative Health. (2017f). *Spinal manipulation.* https://nccih.nih.gov/health/spinalmanipulation

National Center for Complementary and Integrative Health. (2017g). *Acupuncture.* https://nccih.nih.gov/health/acupuncture

National Center for Complementary and Integrative Health. (2017h). *Hypnosis.* https://nccih.nih.gov/health/hypnosis

National Center for Complementary and Integrative Health. (2017i). *Naturopathy.* https://nccih.nih.gov/health/naturopathy

National Center for Complementary and Integrative Health. (2018a). *Complementary, alternative, or integrative health: What's in a name?* https://nccih.nih.gov/health/integrative-health#term

National Center for Complementary and Integrative Health. (2018b). *Vitamins and minerals.* https://nccih.nih.gov/health/vitamins

National Center for Complementary and Integrative Health. (2018c). *Yoga.* https://nccih.nih.gov/health/yoga

National Center for Complementary and Integrative Health. (2018f). *Homeopathy.* https://nccih.nih.gov/health/homeopathy

National Center of Complementary and Integrative Health. (2018g). *New study links mindfulness, brain changes, and pain sensitivity.* https://nccih.nih.gov/research/results/spotlight/mindfulness-brain-changes-and-pain-sensitivity

National Center of Complementary and Integrative Health. (2019a). *Home page.* https://nccih.nih.gov/

National Center of Complementary and Integrative Health. (2019b). *Health topics A–Z.* https://nccih.nih.gov/health/atoz.htm

National Center of Complementary and Integrative Health. (2019c). *Herbs at a glance.* https://nccih.nih.gov/health/herbsataglance.htm

National Center of Complementary and Integrative Health. (2019d). *Relaxation techniques for health.* https://nccih.nih.gov/health/stress/relaxation.htm

National Center of Complementary and Integrative Health. (2019e). *Tai chi and qi gong: In depth.* https://nccih.nih.gov/health/taichi/introduction.htm

National Center of Complementary and Integrative Health. (2019f). *Ayurvedic medicine: In depth.* https://nccih.nih.gov/health/ayurveda/introduction.htm

National Center of Complementary and Integrative Health. (2019g). *Traditional Chinese medicine: What you need to know.* https://nccih.nih.gov/health/whatiscam/chinesemed.htm

National Center of Complementary and Integrative Health. (2019h). *Mindfulness-oriented recovery enhancement (MORE) may reduce opioid cravings and chronic pain.* https://nccih.nih.gov/research/results/spotlight/more-may-reduce-opioid-cravings-and-chronic-pain

National Institute of Health. (2018). *Research portfolio online reporting tools: Complementary and alternative medicine.* https://report.nih.gov/NIHfactsheets/ViewFactSheet.aspx?csid=85

Nelms, J. A., & Castel, L. (2016). A systematic review and meta-analysis of randomized and nonrandomized trials of clinical emotional freedom techniques (EFT) for the treatment of depression. *Explore, 12*(6), 416–426. https://doi.org/doi:10.1016/j.explore.2016.08.001

Noetic Sciences. (2017). *About IONS: History.* http://www.noetic.org/about/history.cfm

Pearson, N. J., & Chesney, M. A. (2007). The CAM education program of the national center for complementary and alternative medicine: An overview. *Academic Medicine, 82*(10), 921–926. https://doi.org/doi:10.1097/ACM.0b013e31814a5014

Pilkington, K., Kirkwood, G., Rampes, H., Cummings, M., & Richardson, J. (2007). Acupuncture for anxiety and anxiety disorders—a systematic literature review. *Acupuncture in Medicine, 25*(1–2), 1–10. https://doi.org/10.1136/aim.25.1-2.1

Richeson, N. E., Spross, J. A., Lutz, K., & Peng, C. (2010). Effects of Reiki on anxiety, depression, pain, and physiological factors in community-dwelling older adults. *Research in Gerontological Nursing, 3*(3), 187–199. https://doi.org/10.3928/19404921-20100601-01

Rosada, R. M., Rubik, B., Mainguy, B., Plummer, J., & Mehl-Madrona, L. (2015). Reiki reduces burnout among community mental health clinicians. *The Journal of Alternative and Complementary Medicine, 21*(8), 489–495. https://doi.org/10.1089/acm.2014.0403

Schuster, T. L., Dobson, M., Jauregui, M., & Blanks, R. H. (2004). Wellness lifestyles I: A theoretical framework linking wellness, health lifestyles, and complementary and alternative medicine. *The Journal of Alternative & Complementary Medicine, 10*(2), 349–356. https://doi.org/10.1089/107555304323062347

Sebastian, B., & Nelms, J. (2017). The effectiveness of emotional freedom techniques in the treatment of posttraumatic stress disorder: A meta-analysis. *Explore, 13*(1), 16–25. https://doi.org/10.1016/j.explore.2016.10.001

Smith, M. O., Carter, K. O., Landgren, K., & Stuyt, E. B. (2010). Ear acupuncture in addiction treatment. In *Addiction Medicine* (pp. 1237–1261). Springer.

Stapleton, P., (2019). *The science behind tapping: A proven stress management technique for the mind and body.* Hay House.

Stapleton, P., Bannatyne, A. J., Urzi, K. C., Porter, B., & Sheldon, T. (2016). Food for thought: A randomized controlled trial of emotional freedom techniques and cognitive behavioural therapy in the treatment of food cravings. *Applied Psychology: Health and Well-Being*, 8(2), 232–257. https://doi.org/10.1111/aphw.12070

Taguchi R. (2008). Acupuncture anesthesia and analgesia for clinical acute pain in Japan. *Evidence-based complementary and alternative medicine*, 5(2), 153–158. https://doi.org/10.1093/ecam/nem056

Tarrant, J. (2017). *Meditation interventions to rewire the brain: Integrating neuroscience strategies for ADHD, anxiety, depression & PTSD.* PESI.

Tsai, P. (2007). *Use of complementary and alternative medicine by Chinese American women: Herbs and health care resources* (Order No. 3294645). Available from ProQuest Dissertations & Theses Global (304728553).

Uebelacker, L. A., & Broughton, M. K. (2016). Yoga for depression and anxiety: A review of published research and implications for healthcare providers. *Rhode Island Medical Journal*, 99(3), 20.

Upchurch, D. M., & Rainisch, B. W. (2015). The importance of wellness among users of complementary and alternative medicine: Findings from the 2007 National Health Interview Survey. *BMC Complementary and Alternative Medicine*, 15(1), 362.

U.S. Food and Drug Administration. (2019). *Dietary supplements.* https://www.fda.gov/food/dietary-supplements/

Ventola, C. L. (2010). Current issues regarding complementary and alternative medicine (CAM) in the United States, Part 1: The widespread use of CAM and the need for better-informed health care professionals to provide patient counseling. *Pharmacy and Therapeutics*, 35(8), 461–468.

Wang, C., Schmid, C. H., Fielding, R. A., Harvey, W. F., Reid, K. F., Price, L. L., … McAlindon, T. (2018). Effect of tai chi versus aerobic exercise for fibromyalgia: Comparative effectiveness randomized control trial. *BMJ*, *360*(k85). doi: https://doi.org/10.1136/bmj.k851

Wang, J., Hodes, G. E., Zhang, H., Zhang, S., Zhao, W., Golden, S.A., … Pasinetti, G. M. (2018). Epigenetic modulation of inflammation and synaptic plasticity promotes resilience against stress in mice. *Nature Communications*, 9. https://doi.org/10.1038/s41467-017-02794-5

Weil, A. (2013). *Spontaneous happiness: A new path to emotional well-being.* Hodder & Stoughton.

Weintraub, A. (2012). *Yoga skills for therapist: Effective practices for mood management.* Norton.

White, M. A., Verhoef, M. J., Davison, B. J., Gunn, H., & Cooke, K. (2008). Seeking mind, body and spirit healing—Why some men with prostate cancer choose CAM (complementary and alternative medicine) over conventional cancer treatments. *Integrative Medicine Insights*, *3*, IMI-S377.

Zhou, J., Chi, H., Cheng, T. O., Chen, T. Y., Wu, Y. Y., Zhou, W. X., … Yuan, L. (2011). Acupuncture anesthesia for open heart surgery in contemporary China. *International Journal of Cardiology*, *150*(1), 12–16. https://doi.org/10.1016/j.ijcard.2011.04.00

CASE STUDY: CAM WITH LILLIAN

(Please read about the Millers in Appendix I prior to reading this case study)

Feeling depressed and overwhelmed due to some recent changes in her family, Lillian has been struggling for a few weeks. Her husband, James, has been experiencing depression over a recent diagnosis of prostate cancer. He is concerned how upcoming surgery will impact his relationship with his wife, especially their sexual relationship. Although Lillian is concerned about the surgery, she is not worried about their sex life. In addition, she is a social worker with a full case load, and between her job, her husband's worry, and her usual care of their two children, she is feeling increasingly depressed and anxious. And while close to her older sister, Angela, some resentment has arisen over Lillian feeling her sister is constantly treating her as if she were still a child. Angela took care of Lillian when they were children, as Lillian was born with a hip deformity and needed constant care until her teenage years.

Lillian grew up learning about shamanism and natural forms of healing during her summers in Nigeria, so when a friend recommended Dr. Denitra Jackson for counseling, she made an appointment. Lillian's family used herbs and other techniques to heal family members and have done so for as long as she can remember, and healing in its many forms tends to appeal to her. Dr. Jackson is a licensed therapist who integrates complementary or alternative modalities (CAM) into her work with clients, specifically mindfulness and emotional freedom techniques (EFT). She is also a registered yoga teacher (RYT) and introduces simple yoga poses to her clients as well.

The office in which Dr. Jackson works is on the second floor of an old Victorian home. When Lillian entered the waiting room, she immediately sensed the warmth and coziness, the "good vibes," and the soft smell of lavender coming from an essential oil diffuser. Lillian also heard soft, ambient music in the waiting room. The overall feeling was of relaxation and calm. Dr. Jackson greeted Lillian with an outstretched hand, in a friendly gesture. They shook hands and Dr. Jackson invited Lillian into the office. The space was arranged differently from most other counselor offices that Lillian had been in. It was large and colorful, with a variety of wall hangings, some inspirational and some with depictions of scenes from global cultures, including symbols from India and China. There was a couch and a chair, but there was also a table and a large open space with two yoga mats spread out at the far end of the room.

The session began with Dr. Jackson explaining that she has been trained in traditional counseling methods, mainly CBT, person-centered, and some types of psychodynamic therapies, but that she shifted her practice to a more integrative CAM model after she attended a training on mindfulness for her annual continuing education credits. "I was taken with the underlying philosophy of mindfulness, which emphasizes that people are inherently whole in mind and body," Dr. Jackson said. "American culture has taught us to feel constantly stressed and disconnected. Mindfulness and meditation can help you develop awareness of yourself and cultivate an attitude toward self and others that is nonjudgmental and curious about your experiences." Dr. Jackson added that she learned more about Eastern health approaches, specifically subtle energy, known as chi, and received training in emotional freedom techniques (EFT). Later, she said, she studied to become a registered yoga teacher.

"Our bodies and minds have an incredible ability to heal and return to balance if we only learn to manage them and our energy system," she said, "and I can show you how." She paused for Lillian's acknowledgement and continued: "One key way is to recognize stress and imbalance before they become overwhelming, and these tools can help you monitor and release stress and tension each day. Using these mind-body tools can help you get in touch with your inner wisdom and inherent peace and calm, which should help guide you as you make challenging life decisions from a more authentic place."

Before the session began, Dr. Jackson had asked Lillian to complete a conventional biopsychosocial intake assessment, but she included some additional sections on nutrition, exercise/movement, meditation or prayer, spirituality, creative endeavors, and self-care/wellness practices or problems. Lillian was surprised that Dr. Jackson wanted to know about her diet. She asked about it after the initial introductions, and Dr. Jackson explained, saying, "Food can have a definite impact on mental health, for the positive or for the negative." In the informed consent forms and process, Dr. Jackson included information about her training and credentials, and also the multiple modalities she practices: conventional talk therapy with a CBT focus, simple yoga poses, aromatherapy using essential oils, and EFT.

Dr. Jackson began the session by using some basic listening skills and building the relationship. She then began to spend some time talking about Lillian's cognitions, especially some beliefs she has about not being "good enough." The two decided to work on these beliefs in future sessions so that Lillian could focus on how her negative core beliefs impact her relationships with others. While talking about her negative core beliefs and the concerns she had about her husband and sister, Dr. Jackson noticed that Lillian's breathing became shallow, her shoulders tensed, and her facial expression showed her anguish as she began speaking more rapidly. Noticing these changes in Lillian, Dr. Jackson asked her if she would like to do some things to calm down and focus a bit, and Lillian agreed. First, they practiced diaphragmatic breathing with longer exhalations through the nose to stimulate the activity of the parasympathetic nervous system, or calming system of the body.

Next, Dr. Jackson explained there were yoga poses that could also help Lillian and invited her to walk to the yoga mats so she could demonstrate one pose. Lillian immediately expressed concern about the difficulty with her one leg, but Dr. Jackson assured her that the poses could be adapted. Together, they practiced the pond pose (*tadagasana*), lying on the floor to stretch and relax the diaphragm, and then the upward-facing dog (*urdhva mukhas svanasana*) pose to help Lillian open her throat and also expand her ability to communicate clearly in her own voice.

Finally, Dr. Jackson stood and demonstrated arm swings to Lillian, who mirrored them, flexing and stretching her shoulders. Dr. Jackson explained that this movement could be a way to also loosen and release the burdens Lillian was bearing regarding herself and her family,

Lillian replied: "It was kind of strange to use my body in here, because I thought it was just going to be talking! But the breathing and yoga DID help me feel calmer and more grounded in my body, and my feelings became less overwhelming."

With that insight, Lillian continued, saying, "I feel emotionally disconnected from my husband. I know he is very stressed out and experiencing a lot of anxiety, but I don't know how to help him because he won't talk to me about his feelings about the upcoming prostate surgery. It's starting to affect my kids and I feel like my family might be spiraling out of control." She also said she's been feeling increasingly depressed, and that she spends a lot more time at work to avoid being with her husband and kids. She revealed that she feels very guilty, admitting all of this to Dr. Jackson. "But it's the truth!" she exclaimed.

As Lillian spoke, Dr. Jackson asked whether any of the thoughts and feelings she just described were related to other concerns she has had—currently or in the past. Lillian began to talk about her mixed feelings regarding her sister. "I love Angela so much, but sometimes I also resent her. She took such good care of me when I was a child, and we're very close. But sometimes she just treats me like I'm a little kid. I get a bit angry with her sometimes. And I then feel guilty about my anger!"

In the last 5–10 minutes of the session, Dr. Jackson summarized what she believed were important aspects of Lillian's story. The two discussed how the activities presented in the session impacted Lillian, and Dr. Jackson asked whether Lillian would be willing to practice the breathing and yoga poses on her own between sessions. Lillian hesitated, saying she wasn't sure if she'd remember how to do them, so the two practiced the techniques once more and Dr. Jackson gave Lillian handouts with information and resources that Lillian could read between sessions.

"One of the modalities I often use with clients," Dr. Jackson explained, "is EFT tapping. We don't have time today to demonstrate it, so I'm going to also give you a handout to take a look at before our next meeting. It's quite a different way of dealing with problems and concerns, but there's research that supports how effective it can be and you can read a little before we dive into how to use it next time. How does that sound?" Dr. Jackson also reminded Lillian that during the next session they will continue to talk about her negative core belief of not believing she is good enough.

Dr. Jackson concluded the session by leading Lillian through a guided imagery meditation to reinforce the techniques they had practiced, and also highlighting feelings of focus, contentment, and peace. In the visualization exercise, Dr. Jackson asked Lillian to put any lingering concerns in any secure container she could imagine. She also encouraged Lillian to exercise, journal, pray, or meditate as ways to manage her anxiety until her next session. Along with the handouts, she gave Lillian a referral for an integrative nutritionist who could help her plan a diet to manage anxiety and depression, and who could potentially recommend herbal supplements to help lift her mood using natural means.

When asked what the most memorable part of the session was, Lillian replied, "How calm I felt after we did that breathing exercise and the yoga poses. I haven't felt THAT calm in weeks!"

QUESTIONS FOR YOU TO PONDER

1. How is this counseling session different from more conventional counseling sessions?
2. Why do you think that Dr. Jackson began with basic listening and examining core beliefs?
3. Why do you think Dr. Jackson used breathing exercises early in the session?
4. How does the invitation to engage her body help Lillian in this counseling session? What concerns might you have about Dr. Jackson using diaphragmatic breathing and yoga poses with Lillian?
5. What are some ethical concerns that you might have about Dr. Jackson's training and qualifications?
6. How do these CAM techniques impact Lillian's physiology? How do those changes impact her mood?
7. Lillian felt a change in her body and mind in that she became more peaceful, calm, and grounded after using these CAM tools. What do you believe would be the positives and negatives of subsequently talking about Lillian's life after she has become more peaceful and grounded?
8. Why did Dr. Jackson conclude the session with a guided imagery meditation, and for what purpose does it serve?
9. What types of clients do you believe would appreciate CAM techniques in counseling and why? What types of clients do you believe would not appreciate this approach and why?
10. How effective would the offering of CAM practices as homework be?
11. Would you feel comfortable introducing other CAM practices into a session? Why or why not?
12. If you were a client, are there any CAM practices you would like to integrate or do as an adjunct to counseling? Why would the practices that you chose appeal to you?

Appendix I

Introduction to the Millers

Jake and Angela Miller recently celebrated their 15th anniversary with their friends, parents, and children. Jake's father and mother, Ted and Ann, were there and brought Jake's sister, Justine. Ted and Ann met in Atlanta and have been married 42 years. Ted earned a law degree and has worked in corporate law ever since, while Ann worked as a piano teacher until her twins, Jake and Justine, were born. The twins are now 41.

Angela's parents, Dexter and Evangeline, celebrated with the family. Dexter and Evangeline met at college in California 41 years ago. Dexter, whose parents were from Nigeria, is an English professor at a mid-size private university. Evangeline worked as a social worker facilitating adoptions. Due in part to her work, Evangeline and Dexter eventually adopted two African American children when Angela was 5; Lillian was an infant and Markus was 2 years old. Angela is their only biological child and is now 40 years old. Lillian, a social worker, is married and has two children. Markus just left his job as a high school English teacher to pursue his PhD in literature. Markus is partnered with Rob.

Jake and Angela met in graduate school, and today Jake works as a structural engineer and Angela is an art teacher at an elementary school. They have two children, Luke, 10, and Cecile (Celia), 7. Although the family and extended family have had few mental health concerns, Jake recently has had some bouts with anxiety, which have begun to affect his relationship with his wife and children. The situation has become so difficult that it has placed a strain on Jake's and Angela's relationship. In addition, their growing tensions might be contributing to problems their children recently began to experience at school.

In the chapters in the text you will see Jake, Angela, Lillian, Markus, Rob, and Ann go through the various therapies in the book. The following provides some descriptions of these six members of the Miller family to help you understand their background when reading about the therapy they are going through. This is followed by a genogram of the entire family to give you broader context of these family members.

Jake

Until the age of 10, Jake remembers having a happy childhood. From what he could tell, his parents got along well with each other. He describes his childhood as such: "I don't really remember anything *bad* happening when I was a kid. It seemed like my parents had a lot of fun together, got along well, sometimes teased each other, and were affectionate. What stands out for me is how much fun my twin sister Justine and I had when we were kids. We were into everything—climbing on the roof of the house or digging holes under the shed until the floor caved in, that kind of thing. There was nothing that Justine wouldn't try, she was funny, really quick, you know, and so brave. Nothing scared her. That was before the accident."

In describing the accident, Jake says, "One day, my twin sister Justine got it in her head that we would take Dad's car out of the garage and park it on the other side of the wooded area across the interstate. It was a joke for April Fools' Day. We were only 10, and of course I was scared, but Justine was sure it would be a good trick. Before I knew it we were in the car, and I was driving! Justine was laughing. I remember that she had her bare feet curled up under her and, as always, no seat belt. I guess I didn't look or something 'cause right after I pulled the car out onto the interstate, a semi hit the car and Justine went through the windshield. She was never the same. She was out for a long time, and when she finally came out of her coma, she had a serious brain injury. She had to learn to talk again and all that. When she did talk ... well, she wasn't Justine anymore."

Jake notes that today Justine is cared for by her parents and is able to maintain a job at a local fast-food restaurant, but she continues to have serious cognitive impairment. Although Jake tends to get along with her, he periodically quips at her, telling her he thinks she can do better than she's been doing.

After the accident, Jake began to have problems with anxiety. He had a hard time sleeping and had nightmares. He notes: "Things changed a lot at our house. It seemed like no one ever laughed anymore, and we didn't *do anything.* Before the accident, my parents would come up with something spontaneous and fun and we would get up and go! But after Justine changed, things at the house got real quiet, and I always felt that something bad was going to happen. I was afraid to leave the house sometimes."

Jake's parents took Jake to a psychiatrist briefly to address the nightmares and anxiety, but they did not talk about his feelings together as a family and rarely referred to the accident. As the years passed, Jake's anxiety lessened, and he was only occasionally disturbed by anxiety or nightmares.

Although Jake sounds proud when describing his wife and children, in recent months he has been struggling with a number of issues. "We've been having problems with Luke," Jake says. "He's fearless, like Justine was—and always into something! He's not bad, just mischievous, but lately he's been getting into trouble at school. A couple of months ago, Luke and Celia were playing in the car and Luke knocked the car out of park. I was mowing the lawn and came around the corner just in time to see the car roll into the street. I felt my chest tighten. I couldn't breathe. I thought I was having a heart attack! Since the incident with the car I am anxious all the time. I can't sleep and when I do, I have nightmares. I've been afraid for Angela to take the car and ... I guess I've been difficult to deal with."

Jake is constantly checking all of the locks, making sure the car is in "park," and always "checking" on the children. He has even asked Angela to homeschool the children to make sure they are safe. He also is aware his relationship with Angela is different: "Angela and I just seem kind of disconnected lately." Jake also reports having anxiety that has caused him to miss work lately, and he is very concerned he will get a poor performance evaluation.

Angela

When Angela was growing up, she spent the fall and spring on a university campus where her father taught and spent summers in Nigeria with her father's family. Angela reflects on her time growing up, saying, "I enjoyed spending time with my grandparents, but somehow I always felt out of place. When I was in Nigeria, my cousins treated me differently because as far as they were concerned, I was 'White' and an American, but when I was back in America I was 'Black.' But I really didn't feel 'Black' either. In fact, most of the time I felt more like a Nigerian kid than an American. You'd never catch me talking to my parents or teachers the way the kids at school talked to adults!"

"No matter where we were there was always one constant—my role as caretaker. Lillian, my adopted sister, was born with a congenital hip deformity that made walking difficult. It was my job to see to Lillian and make sure she had what she needed. I was never free to just go out and play with the other kids. I always had to stay near Lillian. I felt so trapped when I watched the other children on their bikes or playing chase. That's how I feel now, with Jake's demands. I feel trapped watching everyone else live their lives and still, after all these years, not really knowing who I am."

Today, Angela is feeling at a loss. In fact, she even confided in her children's school counselor, noting: "I really don't know what is happening to our family. Jake has just gotten so anxious that it is a full-time job keeping up with all his fears. He gets so angry with me for insisting Celia go to school, and Luke just won't listen to him at all. I feel like I'm a character in one of those really bad movie-of-the-week things. Sometimes I go into the bathroom, turn on the water in the tub, and cry. I don't want to live my life this way."

Markus

Markus is Angela's younger adopted brother. African American and gay, Markus always felt a bit different from everyone else. Growing up, he had a particularly close relationship with his sister Angela, who was his babysitter, caretaker, and generally looked out for him. As he grew older, he increasingly began to feel stronger about his gay and Black identities, but always felt he needed someone to take care of him—to be dependent upon. When he met Rob, he fell in love, but also developed somewhat of a codependent relationship with him. He always felt he needed Rob's love, and when Rob would leave for periods of time, Markus missed him so much that it was hard for him to work. He would worry that Rob would leave or reject him. Currently, Rob is wondering about the intersectionality of his identities, being male, Black, gay, and adopted. Rob was an English teacher and is currently working on his PhD in literature.

Rob

Rob is Markus's partner, and is a Type A personality. He works hard and plays hard and is always on the go. His job with the government takes him away for weeks, and sometimes for months at a time. He loves Markus, but sometimes feels a bit overwhelmed by Markus's need to be with him all the time. He sometimes feels secretly happy that his job is taking him away for a while. Over the years, Rob has developed a drinking problem. His Type A personality sets him up for stress on the job, and the stress continues into the night. He takes a few drinks at night, and then drinks to help him sleep. Rob is insightful, recognizes the patterns he has developed in his relationship with Markus, and has some awareness that drinking has become a problem.

Ann

Ann is Jake and Justine's mother and Angela's mother-in-law. Up until the accident with the car, when Justine was seriously injured and had severe cognitive impairment, Ann described her life and family as "just fine and normal." Ann had been a piano teacher and had hoped to start a music school, but after the accident, her life "fell apart." It was then that she spent most of her time caring for Justine and falling into a depression that would last most of her life. Ann always felt that her life did not turn out as she had expected. Currently, she continues to feel depressed, believes that Justine's life has been ruined, and can feel little enjoyment with Jake's children—her grandchildren. She simply feels that life has been unfair to her.

Lillian

Lillian, the younger adopted sister of Angela, was born with a hip deformity and despite a number of surgeries, still walks with a cane. Her medical difficulties, however, made her particularly sensitive to the disabilities of others, and she eventually obtained her MSW and works with a variety of clients in private practice, though her specialty is individuals with disabilities. Angela spent a large amount of time caring for Lillian when she was a child. The two sisters are very close, though Lillian feels that sometimes Angela still treats her as a kid, and some resentment has built up around that. In addition, Lillian's husband has been feeling increasingly depressed since a recent diagnosis of prostate cancer. He will need surgery and is concerned about how the surgery will impact his life, especially the level of sexual intimacy with Lillian. Lillian is feeling a bit overwhelmed by her job, the demands of her children, and the depression of her husband.

GENOGRAM AND HIGHLIGHTS OF NUCLEAR FAMILY

A genogram of the Miller family and a brief listing of some of the major issues facing each family member follow.

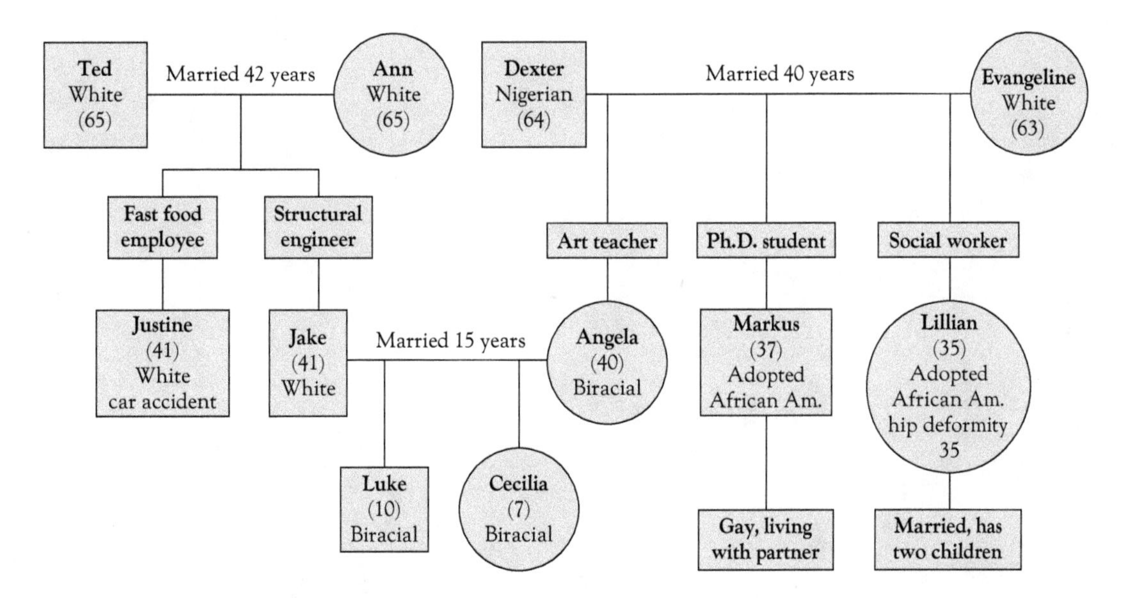

Index

D

Q

R

About the Editor

Born and raised in New York City, Dr. Ed Neukrug obtained his B.A. in psychology from SUNY Binghamton, his M.S. in counseling from Miami University of Ohio, and his doctorate in counselor education from the University of Cincinnati.

After teaching and directing a graduate program in counseling at Notre Dame College in New Hampshire, he accepted a position at Old Dominion University in Norfolk, Virginia, where he currently is a professor and chair of the Department of Counseling and Human Services. In addition to teaching, Dr. Neukrug has worked as a counselor at a crisis center, an outpatient therapist at a mental health center, an associate school psychologist, a school counselor, and as a private practice psychologist and licensed professional counselor.

Dr. Neukrug has held a variety of positions in local, regional, and national professional associations in counseling and human services. In addition, he has published numerous articles and has received a number of grants and contracts with school systems and professional associations. He is the recipient of numerous awards, including the prestigious President's Award (twice) from the National Organization of Human Services and the Fellows Award from the American Counseling Association. Dr. Neukrug has written dozens of articles and chapters in books and has written or edited 12 books, including:

1. *Counseling Theory and Practice* (2nd Edition)
2. *Contemporary Theories in Counseling and Psychotherapy*
3. *A Brief Orientation to Counseling: Professional Identity, History, and Standards* (2nd Edition)
4. *Skills and Techniques for Human Service Professionals: Counseling Environment, Helping Skills, Treatment Issues* (2nd Edition)
5. *The World of the Counselor: An Introduction to the Counseling Profession* (5th Edition)
6. *Experiencing the World of the Counselor: A Workbook for Counselor Educators and Students* (4th Edition)

7. *Theory, Practice and Trends in Human Services: An Introduction* (6th Edition)
8. *Essentials of Testing and Assessment: A Practical Guide for Counselors, Social Workers, and Psychologists* (3rd Edition)
9. *Skills and Tools for Today's Counselors and Psychotherapists: From Natural Helping to Professional Counseling*
10. *Counseling and Helping Skills: Critical Techniques to Becoming a Counselor*
11. *The SAGE Encyclopedia of Theory in Counseling and Psychotherapy*
12. *Dictionary of Counseling and Human Service: An Essential Resource for Students and Professional Helpers*

In addition to the above books, he is currently working on an introduction to clinical mental health counseling book. Look for its release in early 2021 from Cognella Academic Publishing. Dr. Neukrug has also developed a number of helping and counseling videos, as well as open access content. Information about all of his books, videos, and other counseling materials can be found at www.counselingbooksetc.com and at www.odu.edu/~eneukrug.

About the Contributors

Clara Adkins, doctoral candidate in the Counselor Education and Supervision program at Old Dominion University, has experience supervising graduate counseling students, teaching counseling and human services courses, and providing clinical services to college students. She has written chapters in books, published articles, presented at conferences, and has a particular interest in counselor self-care, which she has presented and written about.

Robert R. Armbruster was born in New Zealand and educated in England, graduating from Cambridge University before coming to the U.S. He served 24 years in the U.S. Navy as a submarine officer, retired, and worked for eight years as a contractor supporting the Navy. He is now pursuing a degree in mental health counseling.

Christine Ciecierski Berger is an Assistant Professor of Counseling at Old Dominion University. She specializes in the study and practice of integrating complementary and alternative medicine (CAM) into the field of mental health counseling. She has published articles and book chapters on meditation, healing touch, emotional freedom techniques, and the impact of CAM on counselor wellness.

Ne'Shaun J. Borden is an assistant professor in the Department of Counseling at Idaho State University. Ne'Shaun is also a licensed mental health counselor (LMHC) in Florida and a nationally certified counselor (NCC). Ne'Shaun's research interests include group counseling with adolescents, school-based mental health services, and best practices in mental health service provision with justice-involved youth.

Rawn Boulden is an Assistant Professor of School Counseling within the Department of Counseling, Rehabilitation Counseling, and Counseling Psychology at West Virginia University in Morgantown, WV. He has years of professional experience as a lecturer, researcher, and licensed school counselor. His scholarly pursuits generally include school counseling, school climate, exceptional education, and psychometric research.

Kathleen Brown is experienced working with a wide range of clients and specializes in crisis counseling and acute mental healthcare within integrated care settings. Having finished her PhD in counselor education and currently in residency for her LPC, she is an active advocate for social justice and human rights issues. Her research interests include self-care through mindfulness and authenticity, psychosomatic connections on mental health, marginalized communities and access to mental health resources, and the transgenerational impact of trauma.

Kira Candelieri-Marcari is a Licensed Professional Counselor (LPC), Nationally Certified Counselor (NCC), and a Certified Clinical Mental Health Counselor (CCMHC). A practicing clinician, she works to provide therapeutic services to low-income individuals with emotional and/or behavioral disabilities. Her research interests include children, adolescents and teens with emotional and behavioral disabilities; alternative education systems; and positive behavioral interventions and supports in therapeutic settings.

Tony Dice is a doctoral candidate in counseling at Old Dominion University and professional substance abuse group practitioner. Tony's experience as a therapist, paramedic, firefighter, Navy SEAL, and drug addict have allowed for a unique understanding of the human condition. His growing number of publications and workshops in the field of addiction have led to numerous presentations at the international, national, and regional levels.

Kyulee Park is an assistant professor in the Department of Family & Community Medicine at Eastern Virginia Medical School and a licensed professional counselor (LPC) in Virginia. Kyulee's research interests include integrated behavioral and primary healthcare, interprofessional education, access to healthcare, and social justice and advocacy issues in counseling.

Lauren Parker, M.Ed., NCC, CRC, has worked in crisis intervention and substance use disorder prevention as a supervisor and administrator for ten years and as a mental health and rehabilitation counselor. She is currently completing her doctoral degree in the Counselor Education Program at Pennsylvania State University.

Amber Pope is clinical field coordinator and instructor in the Counseling & Human Services Department at Old Dominion University. She has worked as a counselor and counselor educator for 10 years, specializing in couples counseling, gender and sexuality development, and LGBTQ-related counseling. She utilizes emotionally focused therapy and dialectical behavior therapy as her primary theoretical approaches, integrating solution-focused, mindfulness, and interpersonal process techniques and interventions.

Francisca "Frankie" Rivas has been working in the mental health field for four years, working with a variety of clientele and specializing in addictions counseling. Frankie is a nationally certified counselor and working on her licensed professional counselor hours in the state of Virginia. Frankie is passionate about her research in substance use disorders, student training and development, and the mental health needs of individuals from historically marginalized backgrounds.

Johana Rocha is an assistant professor in the Department of Educational Psychology and Special Services at The University of Texas at El Paso. Johana is a resident in counseling and a nationally certified counselor. Johana's research interests involve clinical supervision with a focus on supervisee and supervisor preparation as well as supervisees' best practices in supervision.

Kevin C. Snow, PhD, assistant professor of counselor education at Marywood University, has over 20 years of diverse experience in community and clinical mental health and has been teaching, publishing, and leading in the field of counselor education and human services since 2012. He has many articles, book chapters, and one book in print and is an active conference presenter.

Abie Tremblay is a Licensed Professional Counselor in Virginia. She has found Acceptance and Commitment Therapy one of the best tools when working with incarcerated clientele. She is a retired naval officer, mother of four, and has hosted 15 foreign exchange students. She lives in Virginia with her partner and her therapy poodle.

John C. Wren, master's degree in mental health counseling candidate at Old Dominion University, has worked for the federal government for 36 years. Through life experiences and his own experiences with counseling, he decided to change the direction of his career and pursue a second career in Counseling.

Carlos Zalaquett, professor in the Department of Educational Psychology, Counseling, and Special Education at Penn State University, serves as president of the Pennsylvania Mental Health Counselors Association and the Interamerican Society of Psychology. He is an internationally recognized author and expert on mental health, diversity and social justice, and education. He is the director of the neuroscience-based research laboratory.

Betsy Zimmerman has worked in the mental health field for eight years, primarily serving as an outpatient clinician. Betsy is a nationally certified counselor (NCC) and is continuing to work toward her licensed professional counselor credential in Virginia. Her research and professional interests include substance abuse counseling, college counseling, college student adjustment, and working with special populations within college counseling.

Printed in the USA
CPSIA information can be obtained
at www.ICGtesting.com
LVHW082304181023
761494LV00015B/31

9 781516 581283